William Harvey's natural philosophy was a view of the world that he had put together during his education in Cambridge and Padua. It contained ways of structuring knowledge, formulating questions and arriving at answers that directed the programme of work in which he discovered the circulation of the blood. Harvey addressed himself to people with related philosophies, and it is necessary to be aware of seventeenth-century modes of exposition and evaluation of knowledge if we are to understand how Harvey's contemporaries reacted to his work.

This book, the most extensive discussion of Harvey to be published for over twenty-five years, reports extensively on the views of those who wrote for and against him. It is a study of a major change in natural philosophy and of the forces which acted for and, equally important, against change. In a period traditionally central to historians of science, it is argued here that natural philosophy and particularly Harvey's specialty within it – anatomy – was theocentric. Harvey's contribution was experiment; and the revolution which occurred in the seventeenth century was concerned not with science but with experiment and the status of natural knowledge.

# William Harvey's natural philosophy

# William Harvey's natural philosophy

Roger French

*Lecturer in the History of Medicine and Director
of the Wellcome Unit for the History of Medicine,
University of Cambridge*

CAMBRIDGE
UNIVERSITY PRESS

Published by the Press Syndicate of the University of Cambridge
The Pitt Building, Trumpington Street, Cambridge CB2 1RP
40 West 20th Street, New York, NY 10011–4211, USA
10 Stamford Road, Oakleigh, Melbourne 3166, Australia

First published 1994

Printed in Great Britain at the University Press, Cambridge

*A catalogue record for this book is available from the British Library*

*Library of Congress cataloguing in publication data*
French, R. K. (Roger Kenneth)
William Harvey's natural philosophy/Roger French.
    p.    cm.
Includes index.
ISBN 0 521 45535 9
1. Harvey, William, 1578–1657. 2. Blood – Circulation – Research –
History. 3. Human anatomy – Research – History. I. Title.
QP26.H3F74 1994
611 – dc20 93–36181 CIP

ISBN 0 521 45535 9 hardback

WD

For Anne

# Contents

# Figures

# Acknowledgments

I am very grateful to Andrew Wear, who read the manuscript of this book at an early and a later stage and made a number of suggestions which greatly improved it. I am also indebted to Don Bates, who generously gave his time to reading the book in a pre-publication stage and whose comments have also been useful. To these Harvey scholars I should add a third, my colleague in Cambridge, Andrew Cunningham, with whom I have had many useful discussions on the history of natural philosophy.

# Introduction

This is the story of Harvey's natural philosophy, how he acquired it, what it was and how while practising it he discovered that the blood circulates around the body. It is also the story of how that discovery and its natural philosophy were met and understood by people with different philosophies and how as a result they accepted or dismissed Harvey's doctrines.

Before Harvey's doctrine changed natural philosophy and medicine as a whole – that is, before it was 'accepted' – some sort of consensus had to exist. Unless there was widespread agreement that the blood circulated, it would have remained a minority view, and to most people a false one. Without some kind of consensus the natural philosophy of the time would not have changed (and historians are agreed that it changed so rapidly that it amounted to a revolution in what used to be called 'science'). This story accordingly includes considerations about mechanisms which contributed to or discouraged the formation of a consensus. Such mechanisms include formal structures of argument and expression, developed and used in the universities and common to most educated men. Such structures had a role in Harvey's natural philosophy before he discovered the circulation, in his announcement of its discovery and in other people's reaction to that discovery.

Another factor that made a consensus possible was the structure and arrangement of groups of people, whether in medical faculties, professional colleges or wider national and religious groups. Some attention has been paid to these groups therefore, and an attempt has been made to show how membership of a group might incline a man to accept or reject a novelty. This book accordingly examines important authors in their setting, in an approximate chronological order, across Europe.

In such a story the reasons why and the materials with which some people resisted Harvey's doctrine are as important as the arguments of those who agreed with him. (In addition to his followers and opponents, there was also a large number of people who misunderstood Harvey.) Clearly, in seeking to understand mechanisms of change within natural philosophy we must know why some people resisted change, sought to refine the traditional picture or promoted different novelties. It is for these reasons that this book reports fairly

1

extensively on the natural philosophies of those of Harvey's contemporaries who left records of their views on the Harvey affair. No major figure who published for or against Harvey during his lifetime has, I think, been omitted. These figures have been known to historians who have worked on Harvey, but I do not know of any systematic or detailed account of what most of them had to say, and I have attempted to remedy that here. It is generally agreed that when Harvey died the battle for the circulation had been won, which makes for a convenient *terminus ad quem* for this account. By then too the 'revolution' in natural philosophy was in full swing, and the natural philosophy of the schools was under fierce attack. I have made some suggestions about the roles played by Harvey's natural philosophy, by the devices of the schools and by groupings of people in this 'revolution'.

I have also tried to understand the priorities in the minds of people who knew about Harvey's work. To most people who had the leisure to think about it in the seventeenth century, the unresolved problems about the motion of the heart and blood stemming from Harvey's publication were secondary – very secondary – to bigger problems about personal salvation, the correct interpretation of God's will, the coming millennium or the current wars. It is only with hindsight that we see Harvey's discovery as fundamental to a later 'biomedical science'. To the men of the mid-seventeenth century it was a question of whether they could, or felt they had a need to, fit Harvey's doctrines in with the more important things in their minds. I have therefore tried to suggest that what was in their minds, whether or not it may fit into categories of the religious, the rational or the philosophical, determined whether they could or wanted to accommodate what Harvey had said.

It will accordingly be clear that this account of change does not depend on the truth-value of Harvey's doctrines, on seeing him as a modern or on interesting intellectual configurations of the seventeenth century. These have been the features of much Harvey scholarship in the past, and I have been less concerned to show that the circulation was accepted because it was true than to show that it came to be seen as true because it was accepted. Harvey, his followers and his opponents could not see the motion of blood as one could see an eclipse or the height of mercury in a glass tube and a whole network of things lay between the uncommitted and his acceptance or rejection of the circulation: arguments, observation, rhetoric, social and intellectual groupings, his age, nationality, religion, training and occupation.

# 1    Natural philosophy and anatomy

When Harvey raised his scalpel to begin the Lumleian anatomy lectures at the College of Physicians, he was embarking on an exercise in which he was to discover the circulation of the blood. To understand that discovery we need to understand what Harvey was doing when he made it. What kind of enterprise was his anatomy teaching? Why was Harvey doing it?

The answers to these two questions are not as straightforward as they might seem. Certainly anatomy was a medical business, Harvey was a physician and the college a place where medical education might properly proceed. But Harvey's own account of the nature of anatomy makes us aware of the care with which we must use modern categories of such kinds. Harvey opened his anatomy lectures with a general statement on the nature of anatomy, that is, a kind of introduction, or more strictly, an *accessus*, to anatomy.[1] Here he gave five headings to which 'anatomy' could be reduced: the description, *historia*, of the major organs; 'action, function and purpose of the parts'; observation of rarities and morbid conditions; solving problems in the authors; and skill in dissection. This description largely agrees with his subsequent account of the kinds of anatomy, the different ways in which it can be practised.[2] The first was public, teaching anatomy, concerned with *historia* of the major organs in the 'three venters' (abdomen, thorax, head) of the body. The second was philosophical anatomy, concerned with the purposes of the organs (the 'action, function and purpose' of his anatomical *accessus*) and the relationship of the body, the microcosm, with the world at large, the macrocosm. In third place

---

[1] An *accessus* was the device used by a teacher to introduce his class to a new text or topic. It located the matter at hand within the rest of 'philosophy' and asked a rote of questions of the text which helped to explain it to the pupils, such as, what was the intention of the author? How is the text divided up? Originally a device of early Aristotelian scholarship (it asked, why did Aristotle make his work so difficult?) it came to be applied to the other subjects like medicine. See R. K. French, 'A note on the anatomical accessus of the middle ages', *Medical History*, 23 (1979), 461–8.

[2] G. Whitteridge, ed., *The Anatomical Lectures of William Harvey. Prelectiones Anatomie Universalis De Musculis*, Edinburgh and London, 1964, p. 5.

3

was medical anatomy, which dealt with the organ systems and morbid states ('rarities and morbid conditions'). Last was 'mechanical' anatomy, the physical process of cutting.

Two things are notable about these ways of characterising anatomy. The first is that among his contemporaries and predecessors Harvey was unusual in not giving a religious purpose to anatomy. It was common for anatomists to place at the top of their lists of the parts or the functions of anatomy the purpose of knowing oneself in order to revere the Creator. The second is that medical anatomy is low – third – on Harvey's list. Here Harvey agrees with other anatomists, for whom the medical use of anatomy was always subsidiary to the philosophical, descriptive and religious.[3]

So Harvey's view of anatomy was by no means the same as our own. We like to see anatomy as having primarily a medical use. We would even like to identify with the early seventeenth-century physician and with Galen in the second century AD in maintaining that anatomy should be the basis of *rational* medicine (see below for the 'rationality' of Galen's medicine). But even here there is something that has to be explained. It was Harvey the physician who was teaching anatomy, as physicians had taught anatomy for 300 years. Surgeons, to whose *practice* anatomy was much more essential, do not have anything like the same share in the history of anatomy as physicians.[4] The reason for the dominance of the physicians over the surgeons has to do with the institutional history of the two trades, and we shall see below that this, too, contributed to what it was that Harvey was doing when lecturing on anatomy.

Although Harvey announced that the lectures were to be *anatomia popularis*, public or teaching anatomy, yet his interest throughout is philosophical. Of the philosophy taught in the schools, Harvey is using a form of *natural* philosophy. We hear nothing of the other two philosophies, moral and rational. In what follows in this book we shall be looking at Harvey as a natural philosopher, and at his natural philosophy, his medicine and his anatomy.

---

[3] See for example C. Bauhin, *Theatrum anatomicum*, Frankfurt, 1605, in which these sentiments are made clear in the address to the Landgrave of Hesse. Bauhin seems to depend heavily on the earlier textbook of du Laurens: A. Laurentius, *Historia anatomica humani corporis et singularum eius partium multis controversijs et observationibus novis illustrata*, Frankfurt, n.d., but the *Ad lectorem* dated 1599. Harvey made extensive use of both authors. See also C. Varolius, *Anatomiae, sive de resolutione corporis humani*, Frankfurt, 1591: dedication, p. 2.

[4] There are of course exceptions, such as Berengario da Carpi and others in Italy. But here the surgeons were educated alongside the physicians and most of those who wrote anatomies did so in a philosophising way, not topographically and surgically. See R. K. French, 'Berengario da Carpi and the use of commentary in anatomical teaching', in A. Wear, R. K. French and I. Lonie, *The Medical Renaissance of the Sixteenth Century*, Cambridge University Press, 1985, pp. 42–74.

## Physicians and rational medicine

To understand why the Lumleian lectures were given by a rationalist physician, philosophising to the extent that he discovered the circulation, and not by a surgeon teaching the structure and disposition of bones, blood vessels and nerves, we have to jump briefly back to the origins of Western medicine. Hippocratic medicine, dating from the fourth and fifth centuries BC and regarded since the Western Middle Ages as the foundation of medicine, was not based on anatomy. Nor was that of China or India. But Galen, revered in the later West as the 'Prince of physicians second only to Hippocrates', thought of himself as a Hippocratic yet spent much of his medical education seeking out anatomy teachers. Combining this anatomical knowledge with an early and extensive philosophical education, Galen rationalised Hippocratic medical practice on an anatomical basis.

He had good reason to do so. As a provincial Greek doctor in Rome, Galen was in a dangerously competitive situation. He arrived, moreover, with two considerable disadvantages. His medical system contained two techniques which he had derived from the Hippocratic writings. One of them, letting blood from a vein, was painful and unsightly. The other, prognosis, came close to augury and could be politically dangerous. Yet by means of his anatomy and philosophy, Galen turned these two disadvantages so much in his favour that he became physician to the emperor. His success lay in being able to tell his patient a convincing story about the treatment he was getting. Galen could relate therapeutic techniques like the letting of blood to the structure of the body, to its functioning, and from here by a microcosmic–macrocosmic parallel to the fundamentals of the world picture. His early successes were among Aristotelians, and it was largely with Aristotle's philosophy that Galen had put Hippocratic precepts and practice into a rationalised understanding of the natural world. From Galen the worried patient not only got reassurance that his doctor knew by experience about the kind of disease he was suffering from, but that he understood the *causes*; and hence also, by rational prognosis, the outcome. This was not available from doctors of other sects in Rome.[5]

Part of Galen's scheme of microcosm and macrocosm was 'nature', partly the deified nature of Pliny and the Stoics (among whom was Marcus Aurelius, Galen's emperor), partly the Platonic demiurge (the creative principle in the *Timaeus*) and partly Aristotle's nature-of-a-thing. The theme of Galen's great natural-philosophical work *On the Use of the Parts of the Body* is how nature, working with materials of limited scope, has put together the body in the best

---

[5] For Galen's career in Rome see for example P. Brain, *Galen on Bloodletting*, Cambridge University Press, 1986; also V. Nutton, *Galen on Prognosis. Edition, Translation and Commentary*, Berlin (Corpus Medicorum Graecorum), 1979.

possible way.[6] Each part, each kind of material, has its own natural actions, which nature has selected as appropriate for the overall function of the complex parts and the body as a whole. That the body was created by a higher agency, which created with wisdom and foresight, made Galen's doctrines acceptable in the Christian West.

The essentially commercial reasons that made Galen's rationalism – his 'good story' – a success, were also present in the later history of Western medicine. The medieval doctor who diagnosed an unseen patient from a sample of his urine was demonstrating his grasp of natural processes. The astrological doctor who diagnosed the nature of unseen urine had a whole new theoretical field of which to show his mastery. In both cases too prognosis impressed the patient in a similar way.[7]

Rational medicine – the 'theory' of medicine – was also extremely useful when medical men wanted to demonstrate that their subject was a true *scientia* or part of philosophy and so justified as a university discipline. By the time Galen's *On the Use of the Parts of the Body* was available in the West, Mondino had – just – begun to teach anatomy by human dissection (his *Anathomia* is thought to have been completed in 1316). To consider anatomy as fundamental to medicine was essentially part of the rationalist position that argued from structure to function to malfunction to treatment. Only the rational, learned physician was in a position to make that argument. The public ceremony of human dissection was partly a teaching device, but it was also very much a public statement that a certain kind of doctor, the learned and rational, was doing something that characterised him and his special knowledge (see figs. 1–3).[8] In contrast, however much they needed anatomy, surgeons were outside this group and did not rely on a rationalist medicine. They did not dissect[9] because they were not able to call attention to the

---

[6] Galen, *On the Usefulness of the Parts of the Body*, trans. M. T. May, 2 vols., Cornell University Press, 1968, especially book 17, Galen's 'epode'.

[7] See my chapter in *Medicine from Salerno to the Black Death*, ed. L. Garcia Ballester, R. K. French, J. Arrizabalaga and A. R. Cunningham, Cambridge University Press, forthcoming 1993/4.

[8] From the first, Mondino conducted his anatomies in accordance with an anatomical *accessus* (of six routine observables: position, substance, size, number, figure and connections) that derived from Aristotelian scholarship by way of John of Alexandria's commentary on Galen's *De sectis*. See Mondino's text in Berengario's edn of 1521, p. 42v. Only later did Mondino or his pupil add a seventh, observation of morbidity, which corresponded to a 'medical' use of anatomy. See French, 'Accessus'. On anatomy as a rationalist display, see my chapter in the forthcoming (Routledge) encyclopaedia of medical history. It is evident from the words of the anatomists that anatomy was the kind of knowledge that could be used as a criterion to weed out the quacks and empirics. See the dedication of Andrés de Laguna, *Anatomica methodus, seu de sectione humani corporis contemplatio*, translated by J. R. Lind, in his *Pre-Vesalian Anatomy*, Philadelphia, 1975, p. 263.

[9] In Italy the more learned surgeons did dissect. The emphasis here is on the contrast between the physicians and surgeons in the north, where Harvey was lecturing.

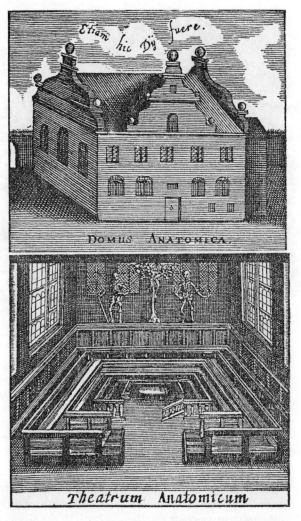

Fig. 1. The 'anatomy house' and its contained theatre, from Thomas Bartholin, *Vasa lymphatica*, a tercentenary edition by V. Maar (1916). The words floating above the anatomy house remind the reader that here too are gods: the anatomists normally gave priority to a religious purpose in explaining the nature of and reasons for anatomy. The phrase is probably designed to recall the story of Heraclitus at the stove, calling in fellow philosophers hesitating at the door: 'There are gods here too.'

Fig. 2. Dissections as display: the anatomy theatre at Leiden in 1610. The human skeletons carry placards reminding the reader of his mortality and the need to know himself. The skeletons of the larger animals, the stuffed bodies of the smaller and the display of instruments of dissection add up to a powerful visual image of an important aspect of the medicine of the learned, rational and university-educated physician. The presence of fashionable visitors underlines the message.

anatomical component of a 'good story'. This went hand in hand with the different story of the surgeons' institutionalising and educating themselves, and it would be too simple to conclude that the surgeons did not dissect because they were less successful than the physicians in their incorporation and education. So it was not a surgeon giving the Lumleian anatomy lectures,[10]

[10] It is true that the barber-surgeons dissected in Harvey's time, but even there, in Surgeons Hall, the lectures were delivered by a physician and the College of Physicians took good care to maintain their control over the surgeons. The college could summon, fine and imprison surgeons, and in 1627 they defeated the surgeons' attempt to claim the right of giving internal medicine. See Sir Geoffrey Keynes, *The Life of William Harvey*, Oxford, 1966, pp. 49, 69, and P. Allen, 'Medical education in seventeenth century England', *Journal of the History of Medicine* 1 (1946), 115–43; 139.

Fig. 3. John Banister lectures on anatomy to the London barbers and surgeons in 1581. The text however is that of a learned and rational physician, Realdo Colombo, and is philosophical and vivisectional rather than topographical and surgical. Above the text, the words commemorating the importance of the occasion praise anatomy as an approach to God.

despite the fact that they had been intended as surgical lectures.[11] And it was no accident, bearing in mind the physicians' corporate need to hold anatomies, that natural philosophy came high on their list of reasons for doing so. Natural philosophy had been taken into the theory of medicine as part of the 'good story', and its use in anatomy helped to mark off its boundary with empirical surgery. The same may be said about the practice of anatomists in very generally giving a religious reason at the top of their lists. The natural world that formed the subject-matter of natural philosophy and of rationalist medicine was a created world. Part of the very rationality of the natural world was that it had been put together in a reasoned way by God; and that rational man could, albeit incompletely, understand God's reasons. It was not piety or expedience that prompted the anatomists' first reason for doing anatomy. Rather, because their readers shared their world picture, the anatomists were adding to the rationality of their anatomy, indeed, they were adding the ultimate or necessary rationality.

## Natural philosophy, anatomy and medicine

Having seen why it was Harvey the physician giving the lectures, and having seen some reasons why the anatomy should have been philosophical, we must look in more detail at what natural philosophy was.

'Natural philosophy' in this book means something quite specific. It is that subject which was put together almost exactly 400 years before Harvey's anatomy lectures and subsequently taught and modified within the universities on the basis of statutory texts, masters' commentaries and disputed questions.[12] It was constructed from Aristotle's 'nature books', the *libri naturales*. The basic text was the *Physics*, which laid down the principles of natural motion which were then demonstrated in action in a range of examples in texts that deal with the motions involved in generation and corruption, in the heavens and earth, in meteorology and in living things. Above all, medieval natural philosophy came to be embodied in a *textbook*.[13] By the middle of the thirteenth century, first the English Nation of the University of Paris and then the Parisian Arts Faculty as a whole drew up statutes that specified which of the nature books of Aristotle were to be read in order to proceed to the degrees of bachelor and master of arts.[14] The statutes gave rise to an industry of copying the texts to provide students with the statutory books with plenty of room for notes.[15] Many European universities adopted the Parisian statutes,[16]

---

[12] It is hoped that a full discussion of natural philosophy in this sense will be published in a book by the author and A. R. Cunningham.

[13] We may take as characteristic of the collection the contents of the British Library MSS. Royal 12 G II (which belonged to Rochester Abbey and was postilled by Henry of Rainham), 12 G III and 12 G V: the *Physics, De celo et mundo, De generatione et corruptione, De memoria et reminiscentia, De anima, De morte et vita, De differentiis spiritus et anime, De somno et vigilia* and the *De sensu et sensato*. The textbook of natural philosophy has been recognised in a sense, that is, as part of another process, the diffusion of Aristotelianism: see G. Lacombe, A. Birkenmajer, M. Dulong and A. Franceschini, *Aristoteles Latinus*, Rome, 1939. It will be evident that in the tradition of scholarship from Lacombe to Schmitt the principal interest has been the *fortuna* of the works of Aristotle and their 'diffusion', and in this tradition the texts we are presently considering are called the *corpus vetustius* (and the latter texts, the *corpus recentius*).

[14] For example *In isto libro habentur omnes libri parvorum naturalium ad gradum magisterii* (in a fourteenth-century hand in a 'recent collection' in the ducal library at Gotha, q.v. in Lacombe, Birkenmajer, Dulong and Franceschini, *Aristoteles Latinus*.

[15] The Royal 12 G series of MSS. contains about four times as much space for notes as for the text.

[16] Most universities followed Paris closely in their arts education. See J. Hale and J. Highfield, *Europe in the Late Middle Ages*, London, 1965, p. 28.

and volumes containing the nature books (and most often nothing else), probably copied in Paris, found their way all over Europe.[17] This was the textbook of natural philosophy, generally addressed as in Paris to the intending master.[18]

But it is not enough to know that medieval natural philosophy was the teaching of Aristotle's nature books. If we want to know the nature of natural philosophy we need to go beyond the texts. Why should any knowledge of nature be necessary in the medieval university? Why choose Aristotle's? The answers to these questions do not lie in the texts but in the purposes for which the texts were used. The university of Paris (whose institutional arrangements were widely copied)[19] began as a consortium[20] of masters who had decided that their common purposes could be better achieved by co-operation rather than competition. The consortium had some of the features of a religious confraternity[21] and by uniting the masters achieved some political weight in the economic field with the city and the king and in religious affairs when dealing with the bishop and the pope.

In the period before the universities, the duty of controlling the cathedral schools had been the job of the bishop's chancellor, and the original purpose of the schools had been to educate the clergy. Recognition of the consortium of masters by the pope was a legal precondition of the existence of the university, but it meant that the masters had to accept that the chancellor had the right to grant the licence to teach to the master's students. What the chancellor wanted was good churchmen, sound in doctrine and behaviour, and he gave

[17] For example British Library MS. Royal 12 G II is one of a family of MSS. annotated in Oxford. For the teaching of arts in Oxford see J. M. Fletcher, 'The Faculty of Arts', in *The History of the University of Oxford*, ed. T. H. Aston, vol. I: *The Early Oxford Schools*, ed. J. I. Catto, pp. 309–99; 275, 389. Also A. A. Callus, 'Introduction of Aristotelian learning to Oxford', *Proceedings of the British Academy* (1943), 229–81; 272.

[18] See note 14 above. Compare the printed works: *In hoc opere continentur totius philosophia naturalis* (Paris, 1510); *Libri octo physicorum . . . totum negotium physicum et universalia philosophie principia* (Leipzig, 1503, 1512; Cracow, *c.* 1503; Liptz, 1506). The natural-philosophy textbook was matched by similar volumes containing the dialectical and moral works of the earlier part of the arts course. The ethical works of Aristotle, like the natural, emphasise the search for Good, here that which characterises the proper behaviour of the individual, the family and the city-state. Proper behaviour was of course exactly what the church, controlling knowledge in the universities, wanted. We shall see in later chapters that this social role of knowledge was always important.

[19] See Hale and Highfield, *Europe*, p. 28.

[20] The source for the records of Paris in this period is H. Denifle, *Chartularium Universitatis Parisiensis*, Paris, 1889, vol. I.

[21] H. Rashdall, *The Universities of Europe in the Middle Ages*, ed. F. M. Powicke and A. B. Emden, 3 vols., Oxford University Press, 1936; vol. I, p. 299. The term *consortium* is used frequently by the masters in the middle of the thirteenth century, referring back to the early years of the century. By the middle of the century at least it is clear that one of the political weapons wielded by the group was to threaten a cessation of lectures. Denifle, *Chartularium*, I, p. 242.

the licence accordingly. But the masters could and did argue that the chancellor was not part of their consortium, which as a legal body controlled who entered it. Entering it was to become a master: they called it inception. Most of the masters taught the arts, which were in great demand by the students. To incept (we should say to take the degree) as a Master of Arts therefore was to agree to obey the rules of the masters' consortium. One of these rules was that the bachelor, before incepting as a master, should read natural philosophy.

The ambitious and well-placed master of arts could go on to read theology or law or medicine. We have already touched on the topic of the medical men constructing the theory of their subject on the basis of natural philosophy, and in a similar way the arts served as a basis for higher studies in theology. Indeed it can be argued (although this is not the place to do so at any length) that natural philosophy was a necessary preliminary to theology. In Paris as elsewhere the teaching of theology had been seized by the friars, much to the anger of ambitious artists (the statutes[22] of whom were part of their political fight with the friars). But the friars were not teaching simply the traditional sacred-page theology of the monastic schools, but a vigorous dialectical theology, partly directed against heresy and embodying a great deal of Aristotle's work on natural topics. The Dominicans indeed came to set up their own schools devoted to Aristotelian natural studies[23] (shortly after the promulgation of the Parisian statutes for natural philosophy) and as the agents of the papacy in the control of orthodoxy they had considerable influence in what was taught elsewhere also.[24]

There were a number of reasons why Aristotle's works should have found favour in the universities. There is a high degree of internal coherence not only throughout the works on the natural world, but between them and the dialectical and ethical works. Secondly, the two latter groups of subjects were also represented in the universities by textbooks, and they were subjects which taught how to argue and how to behave. The church, through the licensing by the chancellor, had an interest in ensuring that all educated men acted as they should. It had no direct interest in natural philosophy for the important thing was He who had made the world, not the particular form in which He had

---

[22] *Chartularium*, I, pp. 240ff.

[23] M. W. Sheehan, 'The religious orders 1220–1370', in *The History of the University of Oxford*, vol. I. Rashdall, *Universities*, vol. II, p. 371.

[24] An important ally of the Dominicans of the earlier thirteenth century was William of Auvergne, who was an Inquisitor and who for related reasons wrote a book on the natural world as Creation, explicitly against the heretics and full of Aristotle's physical doctrines. He was also Bishop of Paris and Chancellor of its university and he ensured, if not always deliberately, that this part of Aristotle's works formed a part of the teaching of that university. His *Opera omnia* were printed in Rouen in 1674.

chosen to make it. But knowledge of the natural world was part of an educated man's knowledge and it connected to his knowledge of ethics and reason. It could be used to extend biblical knowledge of the creation, and in general, if there was to be knowledge in thirteenth-century Europe, it had to be knowledge that was at least tolerated by the church.[25]

This is shown by the later history of natural philosophy. In 1277 a large number of propositions, developed out of the material of the arts course by Averroists like Siger of Brabant, were condemned in Paris.[26] These propositions, considered together, read like a theologian's nightmare of what an arts course might turn into if not kept firmly under control. It was kept firmly under control. God's omnipotent power was restated ('nature' had been offered in propositions within the arts faculty as an autonomous source of natural activity) and almost certainly teaching in the arts underwent a change. Certainly the statutory 'old collection' of Aristotle's nature books was at about this time replaced by the 'new collection', which included a wider range of Aristotelian texts (many of which are now recognised as spurious). In other words a natural philosophy that stepped out of line could not be allowed as knowledge in the thirteenth century. It is in this sense that school natural philosophy in this book is said to be religious, part of the apparatus that centred on God and his Creation. Anatomists until Harvey's time had good reason to begin with the relationship between man's body and its Creator.

The promulgation of the new collection was an attempt to widen the Aristotelian coverage of the natural world. But other changes were also taking place in teaching. The first notes made by students are interlinear glosses and, in the ample margins of the old collection, larger notes and glosses (called 'postils' because they were placed 'after the words' of the text – *post illa verba*) designed to emend where necessary and to explain the text. The postils add up to brief commentaries. But later the notes are much briefer and are uncon- cerned with the accuracy of Aristotle's text. They often incorporate signs or numbers that more loosely link the topic of that part of the text to discussions – probably now disputed questions rather than commentaries – that must have been written elsewhere. In other words, the words of Aristotle are now more

---

[25] The story of the banning of Aristotle's physical works in Paris in 1210 and 1215 is compara- tively well known. The ban was effective until in re-organising education in Paris in 1231 Gregory IX set up a commission to discover whether Aristotle's physical works were more dangerous than useful. Denifle, *Chartularium*, I, p. 143; F. van Steenberghen, *Aristotle in the West. The Origins of Latin Aristotelianism*, Louvain, 1955, p. 84. The outcome is not entirely clear. Traditionally the first figure to teach the *libri naturales* in Paris was Roger Bacon in about 1245, perhaps in an Oxford manner familiar to him. The condemnation of 1270 also shows the church's concern with what constituted knowledge.

[26] On Siger, see F. van Steenberghen, *Maître Siger de Brabant*, Louvain/Paris, 1977. See also J. F. Wippel, 'The condemnations of 1270 and 1277 at Paris', *The Journal of Medieval and Renaissance Studies*, 7, no. 2 (1977), 169–201.

simply places from which to jump to bigger, separate disputations.[27] We shall see below the importance of these scholastic techniques.

## Demonstration: the techniques of natural philosophy

Natural philosophy was not only a body of opinion or a corpus of knowledge, set out by statute and modified by teachers. It was also a set of techniques that in some sense *demonstrated* that knowledge. This ranged from formal Aristotelian demonstrative proof (that a thing cannot be otherwise) to simple teaching (that this knowledge exists). Indeed, techniques of this kind were of the essence to natural philosophy as a subject of the schools. There was a parallel in 'theology'. Monastic knowledge of God was the result of the monk's contemplation upon a passage of the sacred page. But when theology came to be taught systematically in the schools of the late twelfth and early thirteenth centuries it was taught by means of devices of pedagogy that were independent of the subject-matter and could be applied to the teaching of other disciplines. In the first instance this was Aristotelian dialectic, part of Aristotle's 'universal arts' that had no subject matter of their own and could be applied to any *scientia*. Already by the twelfth century Aristotle was known in the schools as the fencing master, who supplied the weapons for disputation and who supplied also the rules of the contest.[28]

So when in the thirteenth century natural philosophy came to be taught as a *scientia*, it was taught – established – dialectically. Aristotle himself characteristically began his examination of a topic by rejecting on logical grounds the views of others, so strengthening his own view. The medieval regent master developed these rejections. His first job in beginning to teach a new text to his students was to locate them in Aristotle's philosophy as a whole. If they had read the *Physics* and were about to embark on *De celo et mundo*, he would remind them in a little *accessus* that Aristotle had set out the principles of mobility in abstract and was now turning to concrete examples. If they had reached *De anima*, the master would almost certainly want to add to Aristotle's rejection of the ideas of Anaxagoras, Alcmaeon and others, by reference to the Fathers of the Church, or to Plato, who had been *the* philosopher to the Western church before the thirteenth century.

---

[27] Some such change is also suggested by the incorporation of non-Aristotelian material in these volumes. Sometimes material from Platonic sources is found in a commentary. Occasionally the notes stop entirely and the space is taken up with a work like Peckham's *Optics*. What may be behind these departures from the *libri naturales* is the activity of the Franciscans. It is hoped that a separate discussion of the Franciscans' natural philosophy will appear elsewhere.

[28] Godfrey of St Victor, *The Fountain of Philosophy: A Translation of the Twelfth Century Fons Philosophiae of Godfrey of St Victor*, trans. E. A. Synan, Toronto (Pontifical Institute), 1972, pp. 21, 23.

There were a number of techniques the master had to help him explain and enlarge on Aristotle's text. There was the gloss, generally inserted between the lines of Aristotle's text (which had been written widely spaced by the scribe so that it could receive glosses). The gloss explained an obscure word or expanded a terse phrase. The postil was a marginal note, connected by a symbol to a word of the text, and serving to expand the meaning and very often to refer to other authors on the same point. Most often, perhaps, the master would refer here to the views of Averroes, the Commentator on the physical works. On other occasions the commentary of recent scholars like Alfred of Shareshill would be cited. A third device used by the commentator when he wished to refine, or disagree with, the text was *distinctio*. This was a technique derived from the scholarship of the sacred page, where, for example, to illuminate the meaning of a word like 'grace', a number of examples of its usage in different parts of the Bible would be compared. The dialectical *distinctio* in contrast consisted of a logical examination of a term to draw out hidden meanings. (This might be aided, of course, by a comparison with the use of the word in the commentators.) One form of the *distinctio* surviving in common speech is to *distinguish* when an author is speaking 'strictly' and when 'broadly'.[29]

By the early fourteenth century, a commentary was a complex affair. The commentator began with an elaborate *accessus* in which he related the topic under discussion to the rest of philosophy, gave the author's reasons for writing and often analysed the book in question in terms of Aristotle's four causes. He then divided the text into short sections, choosing places where the author's argument seemed to reach a new stage. He explained to the reader what the author was doing at each of these stages, which he identified by means of the initial phrase. This stage of the commentary was the *expositio* in which the commentator (he often preferred to be called an 'expositor') demonstrated the logical morphology of the text. He then analysed each of these sections, perhaps a sentence or two long. At this stage the commentator could use *distinctiones* and quote other authors. He could also raise *dubia* and *quaestiones* himself. If either technique threw up differences of meaning, then the commentator had to resolve them one by one and so achieve a *determinatio*. If he were an anatomist or a medical man he could at this stage refer to his own observations, which were treated like quotations from other commentators and resolved in the same way.[30]

---

[29] This discussion is based mainly on a group of manuscripts that once belonged to Rochester Abbey and were glossed and postilled in Oxford. They are now in the British Library: MSS. Royal 12 G II, Royal 12 G III and Royal 12 G V.

[30] An example of such a commentary is that by Gentile da Foligno on the *Canon* of Avicenna. It was published during the Renaissance. See R. K. French, 'Gentile da Foligno and the *via medicorum*', in J. D. North and J. J. Roche, *The Light of Nature. Essays in the History and Philosophy of Science presented to A. C. Crombie*, Dordrecht, 1985, pp. 21–34.

The form of the disputation is rather better known. In general, the proponent selected a thesis – a short proposition, perhaps a traditional disputed question set out so as to expect a positive answer – and defended it against his opponent. The opponent attacked the logical form of the thesis and the arguments in its favour, drew *distinctiones* from the terms of the proposition in the hope of drawing out a meaning inconsistent with the thesis and cited authors with contrary views but with some authority. If it was a disputation between students, a master would be in charge to make sure the rules were obeyed, to help when necessary and to provide a *determinatio* at the end.

A 'disputed question' is a term that can be applied to a number of scholastic devices. It might originally simply have meant an informal question that a perplexed pupil raised during a master's lesson. The master found that explaining the matter was a useful way of teaching. It seems for example that the teaching of Aristotle in Oxford moved away from the commentary to disputed questions.[31] Secondly, the *dubia* and *quaestiones* raised by a commentator were often listed separately, no doubt for the convenience of those undertaking disputations. Thirdly, an author when not engaged in a commentary might maintain his view by systematically raising and solving all possible objections before restating his thesis as if it were 'proved'.

These scholastic techniques remained part of school natural philosophy up to Harvey's time at least. Often they are somewhat below the surface to the eyes of the modern reader, but they were clear enough to Harvey and those who read his book. They must be in our mind too if we are to understand what made such people agree or disagree with Harvey.[32]

## Consensus

Part of the purpose of this book is to examine how natural philosophy changed, particularly as a result of Harvey's activities. Indeed, within the subject known as 'history of science' there could scarcely be a bigger question than how change takes place, and traditionally historians of science have seen the seventeenth century and its 'revolution' as central to their concerns. But however radical or profound new ideas might be, natural philosophy can hardly be said to have changed until there was some sort of agreement about the truth of those ideas among educated people.

---

[31] Callus, 'Aristotelian learning'.

[32] It would be a mistake to assume that the Renaissance swept away the scholasticism of the thirteenth century. Although Renaissance commentaries sometimes ignore the rigid syllogistic form of some of the older commentaries and concentrate on the ancient authors, yet many scholastic features often remained. The nature of the Renaissance commentary remains largely unexplored; see N. Siraisi, *Avicenna in Renaissance Italy. The* Canon *and Medical Teaching in Italian Universities after 1500*, Princeton University Press, 1987, p. 178.

There are many reasons why a consensus might be reached – economic, religious, political – and among them those concerned with education are accessible to the historian. Natural philosophy as part of an approved education had its own techniques of generating agreed knowledge, the scholastic devices we met above. They were not needed to force compliance upon a sceptical student body, but to solve problems that arose during teaching or to make teaching easier. To the extent that they contributed to the world view of educated men, they were devices for producing a consensus and, as we shall see, for changing it. The disputant who sustained his thesis before a crowd of his peers was adding authority to the piece of knowledge he had borrowed for the occasion. The teaching master as a commentator who resolved apparent differences between two authorities strengthened them both in the eyes of his pupils. The author who overcame every possible objection to a piece of knowledge he had sponsored was adding to the consensus of his readers. Although the humanists of the fifteenth and sixteenth centuries made a display of attacking some of these scholastic devices, they nevertheless remained available for those authors who wished to convince their readers. Their readers too would know the forms and procedures of argument, and we as historians have to be sensitive not only to the writer's intentions and techniques, but also to the reader's expectations.

# 2 Harvey's sources in Renaissance anatomy

### Introduction: anatomy and the Renaissance

Harvey's natural philosophy, particularly that part of it related to anatomy and medicine, was formed partly by his reading. Before giving his own lectures on anatomy, he read widely among the anatomists of the previous seventy years or so. That period saw a great development in anatomy as a discipline within the schools. It had also seen the Reformation and the Renaissance. All three changes were linked. We shall see in a later chapter that the religious questions of the Reformation were important in determining how Harvey's doctrine was handled in the universities, and the origins of such attitudes lie in the earliest days of this period of change. Natural philosophy could not remain unaffected by these changes.

We shall look in this chapter primarily at authors whom Harvey read and quoted, and from whom he might therefore have taken components of his natural philosophy and material for his anatomy lectures. We shall not be concerned with wider questions about Renaissance anatomy unless they touch in some fairly direct way upon Harvey and the circulation. Among the authors that Harvey read, Vesalius occupies first place. Harvey quoted him more than forty times, more than any other modern author; moreover, Vesalius was personally responsible for much of the shape of Renaissance anatomy. He wrote at a time when the changes of the Reformation were becoming apparent.

### Anatomical demonstration

To highlight what was new in Vesalius' treatment of anatomy, we must first look briefly at the state of the discipline in the earlier part of the sixteenth century and in doing so we go back briefly beyond the authors cited by Harvey, whose work otherwise shapes this section. The authoritative text on anatomy was that of Mondino, completed in about 1316. This text was generally (except in France, where they preferred to follow Gui de Chauliac) specified by statute, for example in Padua,[1] and teaching took the form of commentary on Mondino's words. We have a student's account of Curtius' commentary on Mondino while the young Vesalius performed the accompanying dissections, in Bologna,[2] and perhaps the best-known early sixteenth-century anatomist, Berengario da Carpi, a successor to Mondino as the *practicus* at Bologna also made a commentary on Mondino his major work. Berengario's commentary follows the high scholastic model (described above) of the thirteenth and early fourteenth centuries closely.[3] What is of interest here is how, as an anatomist, he sought to convince his readers.[4]

Berengario had read almost all the extant anatomical literature, and part of his job as a commentator was to 'determine' between opposing views. He was also an energetic dissector and had a Renaissance confidence in his own anatomical discoveries. In both cases he needed ways of persuading his readers. He deliberately excluded from anatomy what could not be seen (for instance things that were invisibly small) and just as deliberately drew a line between 'philosophy' and anatomy, to exclude such procedures as inferring the existence of structures by the 'eye of reason' (which for example demonstrated the presence of a part from a consideration of function).[5] Much of traditional dialectical reasoning was thus closed to him as he was dealing with things rather than words. In particular the demonstrative proof by which Aristotle showed that a thing could not be otherwise was inadmissible in anatomy, and Berengario had to look elsewhere for means of 'proving' his opinions to the reader.

[1] *Statuta almae universitatis D. artistarum et medicorum Patavini Gymnasii*, Venice, 1589. The yearly anatomy receives considerable attention: (p. 42r) the preamble speaks of the benefit that accrues to the human race and to the Paduan scholars as a result of the dissection. The statutes specify that before the end of February the Rector and each *consiliarius* shall arrange for a body to be delivered from the town authorities. They also select two *massarii* of anatomy – medical students of two years' standing who have already seen an anatomy – to provide the instruments and other necessities. Attendance was limited to those concerned with medical education – including, at some point, intending surgeons. One of the extraordinary doctors attending would 'recite' the text of Mondino (as any extraordinary lecturer would give the text to be studied) while an ordinary doctor gave his commentary, in which the body was shown to agree with Mondino's words: 'qui declaret sententialiter dictum textum et literam occulate fide monstret, et verificet in ipso cadavero' (p. 42v).

[2] B. Heseler, *Andreas Vesalius' First Public Anatomy at Bologna*, ed. and trans. R. Eriksson, Uppsala and Stockholm, 1959. The statutes of Bologna claim the right to secure from the *podesta* of the town two bodies annually for dissection, preferably one of each sex and from a distance greater than thirty miles. See C. Malagola, *Statuti delle Universita e dei Collegi dello Studio Bolognese*, Bologna, 1888, p. 318.

[3] Jacopo Berengario da Carpi, *Commentaria cum amplissimis additionibus super Anatomia Mundini*, Bologna, 1521.

[4] R. K. French, 'Berengario da Carpi and the use of commentary in anatomical teaching', in A. Wear, R. K. French and I. Lonie, *The Medical Renaissance of the Sixteenth Century*, Cambridge University Press, 1985, pp. 42–74.

[5] Berengario, *Commentaria*, pp. 4r, 83v, 259v, 434v, 443r are a few examples.

It seems to have been for this reason that he chose the commentary form. He was addressing an academic audience who had expectations about the form the argument would take. Berengario must have chosen the rigour of academic presentation to try to convince his readers. The format he adopted allowed him to introduce his own discoveries at only two places, at the end of his determination of disputed questions from the authors, and in the summing up at the end of each comment. His readers would have expected some form of proof on these occasions, especially when Berengario's anatomical novel opinion – such as his denial of the Galenic *rete mirabile* in the human brain[6] – necessarily brought him into conflict with authority. Berengario introduced his novelties as propositions, as though they could be handled dialectically. To a certain extent they could be, and Berengario can proceed by the technique of *distinctio*, drawing out different meanings from a term, and comparing different meanings of the term in different authors. But there was a limit to these primarily verbal techniques in anatomy. Berengario relies in addition on 'demonstration', *demonstratio*. He uses it in a way that we might call 'physical logic'. Although the practice derived from the simple *ostensio* of the public anatomies, the word 'demonstration' carried over something of the force with which it was used in dialectic. Berengario applied it to the proposition that composed his opinion or discovery and used it as 'proof' by exposing the structure in question to the sight and touch of his audience. In the printed commentary Berengario 'demonstrates' the part in a way that enables the reader to perform the same dissection and employ his own senses in a repeated demonstration. In Berengario's language, sense, *sensus*, will be the master: that is, he who provides the determination in a disputation.[7]

The illustrations that are a novel feature of Berengario's work are another way of demonstrating structure to the reader. Berengario uses them when the complexity of the shape of the part is such that it cannot be easily described in words. Although such a shape, or discovery was indemonstrable in a verbal way, it had the advantage of being for the same reason defended against dialectical attack.[8] In short, in an *ostensio* before an audience at a dissection, and to the eyes of his readers observing the woodcuts, many eyes make proof. If the eyes belonged to distinguished people originally present at the dissection, so much the better. Galen had 'proved' some of his medical opinions by

---

6  Ibid., p. 459r.
7  Ibid., pp. 351r, 438r–v, 450r, 479v.
8  Where in his commentary he says that complexity of shape cannot be described in words he is of course denying the possibility of a dialectical demonstration. The shape of the vertebrae, he says (p. 494r), cannot be written, and the anatomist must visit a cemetery and investigate vertebrae by sight and touch. In other words the shape so perceived has the standing of an *indemonstrable* axiom or principle, akin to the starting points of demonstrative arguments. While a description in words is open to criticisms of being a variant particular, the woodcut assumes an authority.

vivisections carried out before Roman notables, whom he names, and Renaissance anatomists most likely took Galen as a model.[9] Berengario's audience consisted mostly of students who if not always distinguished were at least in a position to spread his 'proved' discoveries. We might call this the jury, or forensic, principle of demonstration.

The purposes and structure of the commentary necessarily meant that it gave minute attention to larger or smaller fragments of the text. Humanists and those who thought that all good things had come from the Greeks – Hellenists, like Leoniceno[10] – made fun of the repeated *ibi . . . ibi* (here . . . here) where the commentator broke up the text for individual treatment, and preferred to allow the text to stand in its entirety, to allow the author to speak for himself. To do away with commentary was also to do away with the scholastic 'physical logic' of authors like Berengario and to rely instead on the *authority* of the ancients. Their preferred authors were of course Greek and their efforts were directed to the recovery, in the case of anatomy, of the texts of Galen. His *On the Use of the Parts* had been available in a Latin translation since just after Mondino finished his *Anathomia*, but it generally proved too complex a text to be used in teaching.[11] Half of Galen's *Anatomical Procedures* had also been known in a Latin version in the Middle Ages, but this was no more suitable for teaching. In the 1520s both Galenic texts appeared in humanist versions and allowed Galen to 'speak for himself', at least to those whose interest in anatomy extended beyond the statutory four-day dissection of the 'three venters' of the body.[12] These dissections began with the abdomen for the strictly practical reason that the guts began to putrefy first. The thorax and then the head were opened next. This sequence could be defended philosophically because the nutritive faculty, located in the abdomen, was taken to be a prerequisite for the existence of the vital faculty in the thorax and this faculty in turn was necessary for the existence of the rational faculty in the head. The anatomist

---

[9] For Galen's experiments see D. J. Furley and J. S. Wilkie, *Galen on Respiration and the Arteries*, Princeton University Press, 1984, esp. p. 48; the two anatomy texts, *On the Usefulness of the Parts of the Body*, trans. M. T. May, 2 vols., Cornell University Press, 1968 and *On Anatomical Procedures*, trans. C. Singer, Oxford University Press, 1956 (books 1–9, which alone were available in the Renaissance), esp. 8.12, the vivisection of the heart. After 1525 Galen's discussion of the opinions of Plato and Hippocrates was available, which contains experimental treatment of the nature of the heart and brain as principal organs. See the edition and translation by P. de Lacy in the *Corpus Medicorum Graecorum: Galen on the Doctrines of Hippocrates and Plato*, 3 vols., Berlin, 1978–80.

[10] See R. K. French, 'Pliny and renaissance medicine', in R. K. French and F. Greenaway, eds., *Science in the Early Roman Empire*, London, 1986, pp. 252–81; 271.

[11] They used in preference an abbreviated and corrupt version: R. K. French '*De Juvamentis Membrorum* and the reception of Galenic physiological anatomy', *Isis*, 70 (1979), 96–109.

[12] Galen, *De usu partium corporis humani libri XVII*, Paris, 1528 (Sylvius' revision of Nicholas of Reggio's translation); Berengario's edition: *Galeni Pergameni libri anatomici*, Bologna, 1529. The Aldine *editio princeps* appeared in 1525.

was thus following the sequence adopted by nature in constructing the body. But Galen had written his anatomy cumulatively from many dissections (of animals) and had not been constrained by the need to show all parts before putrefaction ended the dissection. So he began with the hand, the organ by which man's superior intelligence was demonstrated in the world. The humanists would have preferred to have forgotten about Mondino and three-venter anatomy, and to replace the brevity and usefulness of his text they wrote short digests based on strictly classical sources.[13]

The humanists' desire to return to classical sources and allow the texts to stand on their own without commentary is paralleled by the Reformers' desire to allow the text of the Bible to stand on its own, to be read freely without the interposition of an interpreting church. Ultimately, the Catholic reaction to this was to emphasise the history of the scholarship by which true doctrine had become known – even in Padua the university came to a halt in the celebrations in which St Thomas Aquinas was remembered.[14] The Protestants, in turn, began to see such scholarship, antedating the Reformation, as Catholic, and like the humanists they had another reason to avoid the commentators. These were general trends, and we shall see some of their specific results later, when we consider the reception of Harvey's doctrines. Only hints of such things can be found among Harvey's renaissance authors.

Harvey does not mention Berengario, and probably had not read his commentary. But he did read the textbook of Nicolo Massa, which developed a central feature of Berengario's book and which may well have helped to shape the nature of the anatomical part of Harvey's natural philosophy.

Massa worked in Venice and was not a university teacher.[15] He had access

[13] For example J. Guinter of Andernach, *Institutionum anatomicarum secundum Galeni sententiam, ad candidatos medicinae, libri quatuor*, Paris, 1536; J. Sylvius, *In Hippocratis et Galeni physiologiae partem anatomicam Isagoge*, Venice, 1556.

[14] The Paduan *Statuta* (1589), p. 46. Aquinas became an official Doctor of the Church only in 1567, which suggests a Counter-Reformation move. See Peter Dear, 'The church and the new philosophy', in *Science, Culture and Popular Belief in Renaissance Europe*, ed. Stephen Pumphrey, Paolo Rossi and Maurice Slawinski, Manchester University Press, 1991, pp. 119–39; 123. See also p. 126 for the learned tradition and the Protestants' reading of the Bible. Although this is not the place to argue it at length, it is very significant for the story of natural philosophy that in the early thirteenth century the fourth Lateran Council, deeply concerned about the other-worldly heresy of the Cathars, first defined the central ceremony of the bread and wine in the worldly and concrete Aristotelian terms of substance and accident. (The bread and wine took on the essence of the body and blood of Christ but retained the accidents of bread and wine.) No other heresy was so dangerous for the church until the Reformation, when the Council of Trent met intermittently from 1545–63. Now the church insisted on the *miraculous* transubstantiation of the bread and wine in order to deny the Protestant claim that the age of miracles was over and to show the limitations of a philosophical (Aristotelian) view of nature.

[15] On Massa (d. 1569) see Lind, *Pre-Vesalian Anatomy* and C. Singer and C. Rabin, *A Prelude to Modern Science. Being a Discussion of the History, Sources and Circumstances of 'Tabulae Anatomicae Sex' of Vesalius*, Cambridge University Press (for Wellcome), 1946, where

to bodies in the convent and the hospital of St John and St Paul and had local legal backing to perform post-mortem dissections.[16] He was not therefore subject to university statutes about dissections and did not have to provide or answer disputed questions. Unlike university anatomists, he had plenty of female and foetal material.[17] He seems to have dissected a great deal in the 1520s (he mentions the appearance of emaciated bodies in the famine of 1527)[18] and in 1536 produced an introductory textbook of anatomy. In many ways it was very different from what had gone before. It was not a commentary replete with learning, like Berengario's, and nothing like the even bigger compilation of Zerbi. It was essentially a practical work, explaining in an introductory way how to see as much as possible in a single dissection; it resembled Mondino's text more than any other. Massa complained that other anatomists of the time (he must mean primarily Zerbi and Berengario)[19] were too much concerned with authorities and too little with the actual processes of dissection and observation; this is why his own text is abundantly practical.[20]

But like Berengario, Massa was much taken with the problem of the validity of anatomical knowledge. Where Berengario had made a great deal of *anatomia sensibilis*, the anatomy of the perceptible, and had deliberately excluded from anatomy rational ways of establishing structure, Massa went a stage further and wrote an anatomy of structure that had actually been seen, *anatomia sensata*.[21] While Berengario was exercised to mark out the medical

---

Massa's birth is variously given as *c.* 1500 (p. iv) and *c.* 1480 (p. xxxiv). He began reading medicine in 1521, the date of Berengario's commentary on Mondino, so almost certainly *c.* 1500 is more probable. Lind says that the edn of 1559 was a second, changed in a few pages only from the earlier edn which seems, however, to be rare: N. Massa, *Liber introductorius anatomiae*, Venice, 1559.

[16] Massa, *Liber introductorius anatomiae*, pp. 25v, 26r.

[17] University anatomists most often received the bodies of executed criminals, normally male. Pregnant female criminals would anyway rarely have been executed. Massa was able to dissect pregnant females and once performed a Caesarean section on a dead mother and saved the children (p. 43r). From a lot of experience of female material (pp. 14r, 15v, 41v, 44v, 45v) he was able to deny the existence of seven cells in the uterus.

[18] Massa, *Liber introductorius anatomiae*, chap. 2.

[19] His attack on his predecessors does not mention names, but at p. 10r he makes a big claim to be the first to see the *panniculus carnosus* after Avicenna, and he denies what Zerbi and Berengario had to say.

[20] He gives details of the manual operation of dissection, such as that in which the body is suspended by one foot (p. 38v) or is made to sit up (p. 26v). Those concerned with the purely verbal aspects of anatomy and the dispute between authorities, he says, 'chatter like birds' (pp. 3v, 4r). He expressly follows Mondino, p. 5r.

[21] He uses the phrase first in a significant place in addressing pope Paul III. Having announced the religious and philosophical purposes of anatomy and having dismissed the 'glosses and distinctions' with which the anatomists tried to reconcile the traditional 'disputes' between Aristotle and Galen, it is clear that *anatomia sensata* is going to be Massa's method of achieving these purposes and avoiding such disputes. Massa, *Liber introductorius anatomiae* (the address to Paul III is dated 1536), p. 3v; see also pp. 4v, 71v. *Sensata* is clearly his key-word: he applies it in the same general direction to *cognitio* (pp. 18r, 39t), *res* (p. 32r),

and anatomical area of natural philosophy and argues to keep the philosophers out of it, Massa makes no arguments and assumes that the anatomist is a specialised functionary with his own field; he uses the term *anatomista*,[22] as others used 'artist' and 'humanist'. No doubt (although educated in Padua) he was less exposed than Berengario, in a university, to pressures from philosophers to justify his study.

For our purposes, in looking at what Harvey might have seen in Massa, it is Massa's emphasis on what has been *observed* that is important.[23] In writing an introductory book Massa was concerned to explain what could be seen in a single dissection, which is the most that the bulk of his readership probably experienced. It is for these reasons that, despite his own experience being extensive he does not claim to be exhaustive in this text and necessarily omits much that can only be seen in repeated dissections, for in exposing the major organs much is necessarily destroyed in a single dissection.[24] So what is *seen* here is not what Massa has in his memory but what is seen in a single dissection: seen by the bystanders. In concentrating on what has actually been seen Massa can also escape the usual philosopher–physician disputes by insisting that what relates to 'discourse' rather than observation is not the province of the anatomist of *anatomia sensata*. For example, of the traditional rote of observables in the dissected body, Massa omits 'complexion' because, although fundamental in the natural philosophy of the body, it cannot be seen by the senses.[25] While Berengario argues with all the learning and most of the apparatus of the schools for a separate territory for an *anatomia sensibilis*,

---

*speculatio* (p. 34r), *corpora* (p. 66v), *notitia* (p. 28r–v), [*sensatum*] *experimentum* (p. 34v) and perhaps above all to *veritas* (p. 79r). It is practised by the *oculatae anatomistae*, the 'observant anatomists' (p. 31r).

22  At pp. 9v–10r the modern *anatomistae* include Zerbi and Berengario.

23  That is, it is claimed here that the sensory derivation of anatomical knowledge in Massa was more important for Harvey than, for example, what Massa had to say on the motion of the heart. Although Massa claims to be the first to notice (p. 55v) that one of the three *hostioli* of the aorta is structurally different from the others and so allows spirit into the arteries, he does not in Harvey's terms have a clear notion of the action of the valves, for the right auricle is said to act as a reservoir for blood ejected from the ventricle at constriction (p. 54r) and air cools the heart in the *right* ventricle (p. 55v). Part of his concern seems to have been to explain, by a flux and reflux in the vessels, a Hippocratic pangenesis, and sterility from phlebotomy in the neck (pp. 34v, 35r). His metaphor of the heart as king (p. 49r) is not uncommon and does not signify any significant new interest in the organ.

24  Massa, *Liber introductorius anatomiae*, pp. 5r, 25v. It is in effect an *historia*, a noteworthy description.

25  Ibid., p. 11r. He was aware of the variability of human organs and part of his message was to perform many dissections in *anatomia sensata* to get an idea of what was normal: pp. 22r, 25v (guts), p. 27v (liver). In a related way he follows the sequence of dissection necessary to reveal the parts, not a sequence indicated by theory (p. 38r) such as (we can guess) a 'synthetic' mode of presentation, following nature's scheme in putting the body together, or a philosophical scheme (as for example following Galen in beginning with the hand, the sign of the practical application of man's intelligence).

Massa's *anatomia sensata* confidently inhabits that territory. Where Berengario had angled for some link between his 'physical logic' and a more formal 'demonstration' to persuade his audience, Massa uses *sensata demonstratio* in a more confident appeal to their senses.[26]

So, although Massa does not struggle in the same way as Berengario to capture his audience with some form of demonstration inherent in the academic rigour of a commentary, he still has to persuade them. Like Berengario he names his 'jury' and tries to impress the reader with their probity. He gives the year in which he made some demonstrations, to add to the historical verisimilitude.[27] An important part of his claim about the importance of sensory perception is that as a method it had ancient authority. The two anatomy texts of Galen represented the medical and anatomical rationality that had made Galen urge his readers to see for themselves. It was also an experimental method. Massa draws too on the animal books of Aristotle, and was particularly taken with the methodological point that Aristotle made about gaining knowledge: discussing bees, Aristotle observed that too little was known to come to firm conclusions, and that sensory observation had to take precedence over theory in gaining new knowledge. Massa's two main predecessors, Zerbi and Berengario, had also read their Galen and Aristotle and also stressed the need for personal observation. Even Zerbi's text, outwardly a scholastic compilation, was written to accompany dissections and is based expressly on Galen's procedures. By Massa's time then, anatomy was seen by its practitioners as a well-defined territory with a special sensory epistemology; techniques like inflation of hollow parts to demonstrate their connections and shape in life were essentially experimental.[28] Like other anatomists Massa marked anatomy off from medicine by giving it firstly a religious and secondly a philosophical purpose. He does so twice, first in addressing the pope and second in beginning the text.[29]

Thus, in his reading of the anatomists of the previous century (we know he

---

[26] p. 88r: *sensata demonstrationae* (*sic*, for *demonstratione*). It is useful to remember that in an educational context Massa's epistemology would have been quite opposed to that of those whom he called (p. 62v) the *grammatistae*, who believed that the best recognition of things lay in their names; Massa, recognising that names changed over time (p. 66r), thought true recognition of things lay in the knowledge of their formal and material parts, all the way down to the elements. Despite his protestations, this is essentially an Aristotelian view and one that despite himself leads to a theoretical discussion (p. 28r–v) of the philosopher–physician dispute over the origin of the veins.

[27] p. 31v; chap. 20. On p. 7v he explains his habit of demonstrating the separability of the skin to bystanders; on pp. 9v–10r he names the jury that serves him throughout the book (e.g. p. 57v), a small group of men 'very learned' or 'learned in both languages' or possessing a law degree, or serving notable persons. At p. 90r he claims to have shown Galen's *rete mirabile* to his audience, although admitting that it is sometimes too small to be moved.

[28] p. 35.

[29] p. 4v.

read Massa, if not Berengario), Harvey would have seen how they made anatomy an autonomous and practical business. He would also have seen how they made it an experimental affair. To see how, we must take a preliminary look at Vesalian anatomy; we shall see later how people reacted to it.

In vigorously pursuing what he saw as faults in Galen's anatomy, engendered by Galen's dissections of apes (not man) Vesalius' anatomy was largely concerned with structure. At the end of the last chapter of the last book of the *Fabrica* Vesalius spent five pages explaining that the anatomist's task was also to consider function, which could only be obtained from vivisections (see fig. 4).[30] It is not an afterthought, for he knew that to perform vivisections adequately one must have experience of dissection and the structure of the animal in question, and this is what the bulk of the volume is about (although the animal in question is here man). In contemporary terms, dissection of the dead body revealed (says Vesalius) the number, site, figure, property of substance and composition, after which function was to be sought. (That is, this was the traditional rote of observables, used by anatomists since Mondino.) But function is not of prime interest to Vesalius. He chose to arrange his book by dealing first with the 'similar' parts, and he gives predominant attention to bones and muscles. Although bones have a clear function as the support and hinges of the body, and while we can see their function from accidents such as fractures, yet vivisection cannot add a great deal to our knowledge of them. The same may be said (and Vesalius says so) of cartilage. The use of tendons, another similar part and one that joined muscles to bones, can actually be demonstrated in the dead body and while Vesalius says that cutting them in the living animal helps demonstrate their function, again vivisection is not of prime importance. Vesalius saw little point in making a vivisectional study of the major viscera. One can see motion in the intestines of a recently fed dog, he says, but the liver, kidneys and spleen are just as well studied in the dead (his only live experiment is to see that the dog lived for a few days without its spleen or kidneys).[31] Many vivisections, says Vesalius, are more useful for manual training, learning how to deal with dislocations, and about the action of medicines than for searching out function.

When vivisections are important to Vesalius it is because Galen had used them to considerable effect. Vesalius cannot deny Galen's experiments as he denied Galen's morphology. He uses Galen's term, *administrationes*, for his vivisectional experiments and descriptions. Vesalius describes how to expose the nerves leading to muscles and how to ligature or stimulate them and observe the result in the muscle. The example of the recurrent laryngeal nerves

---

[30] A. Vesalius, *De fabrica corporis humani*, Basle, 1543, pp. 659–63 (the latter misnumbered as 659)

[31] Ibid., p. 660.

Fig. 4. A pig prepared for vivisection, from Vesalius' *De humani corporis fabrica*. The illustration is rather a celebration of Galen's vivisections in Rome than a report of those of Vesalius, who preferred to use dogs.

confirms that this is basically drawn from Galen. Galen had done it on a pig, and Vesalius' little woodcut shows a pig tied down to a board in preparation for the experiment (see fig. 4). But Vesalius preferred a dog, and perhaps this departure from Galen shows that he had in fact done the experiment. He gives plenty of practical advice, from describing how to tie the animal down to a table with holes in it for the ropes, to explaining how to expose the nerves.[32] Likewise his description of the sectioning of the spinal cord with the resultant loss of motion and sensation from the lower parts of the body is directly Galenic. So is his investigation of the nervous control of the diaphragm and intercostal muscles in respiration. When he says that his practice was to take his audience first through the anatomy of a dead animal so that they may understand the vivisections better, during which in any case there was little time for words, he is echoing a Galenic sentiment and following Galen's practice of demonstrating to a 'jury'.

It is perhaps ironic that Vesalius, following Galen closely on action and use, declared that vivisection was not very valuable in relation to the veins, for their function of nourishing the parts was seen well enough in the dead.[33] (We shall see how experiments with the living veins were very important for Harvey.) Nor was Vesalius convinced about the usefulness of vivisection in relation to the function of the arteries.[34] Again it appears with hindsight ironic that the experiments that Vesalius does mention in relation to the arteries have results that support a Galenic position (and with which Harvey came to disagree). It is

---

[32] Ibid., p. 658 (actually 662).
[33] 'Caeterum in venarum usu inquirendo, vix quoque vivorum sectione opus est.' Vesalius, *Fabrica*, p. 660.
[34] 'Item in arteriis vivorum sectionem vix requirimus.' Ibid., p. 660.

unlikely that Vesalius actually performed them, for he uses a style of writing (infinitives introduced by *Licebit*) that distances him from personal involvement; and by all accounts one of them was technically very difficult. They are again Galen's experiments: first, that by which Galen had shown against the Erasistrateans that the arteries contain blood (by ligating and puncturing them) and second (the difficult one), inserting a length of hollow reed into a divided artery. Tie the artery tight to the enclosed reed, says Vesalius, and you will see that the blood flows freely below the reed, but does not pulsate. Galen had used the experiment to prove that the pulse is carried in the arterial coats and so is interrupted by the length of reed; Vesalius says that when the ligatures are undone the pulse returns as strongly below the ligature as above.[35]

In contrast to such Galenic procedures that Vesalius may not have in fact performed, he certainly discovered a method of keeping the experimental animal alive by inflating its lungs. He was much taken by the recovery of the pulse as the faltering heart recovered when the lungs were ventilated, and he applied the practical medical man's terminology of the kinds of pulse to his vivisectional findings. He observed that the heart and arteries had the 'same rhythm' of pulsation, a phrase which would cover Galen's account of diastole and systole, but did not go further into the matter. He also paid a lot of attention to vivisections performed on pregnant female animals and on the foetus. With pigs and dogs, says Vesalius, it is particularly good to see – *iucundum est*[36] – how the foetus attempts to breathe as soon as it reaches the air. In an undisturbed foetus one may see through the thin membranes how the umbilical arteries pulsate and the foetus does not breathe. But when the uterus is removed and the foetus experimentally 'born' then while still within its membranes it struggles to breathe and will suffocate, says Vesalius, unless the membrane is punctured and air is allowed to reach its mouth.

In short, Vesalius' prime concern was with the errors of Galen's morphology and with restructuring anatomy. He was less concerned with function and by and large agreed with what Galen had said. Vesalius' vivisections are not designed (as is the rest of his text) to disprove Galen and indeed are largely inspired by Galen's own vivisections. Vesalius saw that vivisections like dissections could be usefully made in front of an audience, and saw that reports of vivisectional experiments could convince his readers; for example he uses the present tense in each of the subsequent stages of an experiment to heighten

---

35 It is not clear from Vesalius' words whether he envisaged the artery being opened with a longitudinal incision to allow the insertion of a reed, or the two ends of a transversely divided artery being connected by a reed. Probably the former, for then the argument about the ligatures stopping the pulse in the tunics of the arteries (but not stopping the blood) would be intelligible. But on the whole it seems unlikely that this is an 'administration' of Galen that he had in fact repeated.

36 Vesalius, *Fabrica*, p. 660.

the effect of the direct narrative. In a number of experiments, like those on the heart and vessels, he did not see any need to confirm or question by closer analysis the accepted account of function. He was perhaps more interested in the changes that took place in the foetus at birth. In all of this, from the discovery of function to the motion of the heart and the changes at birth, Vesalius was more experimental than his predecessors and less analytical than his successors; but above all it was clear that anatomical research now had to be experimental on the Galenic model.

Vesalius was followed at Padua by Realdo Colombo,[37] who developed his experimental methods. It is very likely that Harvey profited from both Vesalius and Colombo. Harvey was familiar with Colombo's book, quoting it on the movement of the diaphragm, the pulsation of the vessels of the lungs and on the alternate 'systole' of the living heart and arteries.[38] Colombo thought that Vesalius' treatment of Galen had concentrated too much on structure. Harvey's teacher Fabricius also thought so, and this too was important for Harvey, as we shall see. Both men, and Harvey, saw that only vivisection can supply knowledge of action and function. It is clear that Galen was the model for Colombo's experiments on action and function. Much more than the simple demonstrations of hollow organs by inflation, Colombo's experiments are vivisections, like Galen's. Colombo dedicates a whole book (14) to his vivisections, where Vesalius had given only a chapter to his. Both called the experiments 'administrations', a term that recalls Galen's most practical anatomy book, the *De anatomicis administrationibus*, a text that had been translated by Guinter and revised by Vesalius.[39] Colombo has to explain that he prefers dogs to pigs, the animal used by Galen, because he found pigs too fat to demonstrate the recursive nerves, Galen's discovery. He had begun, then, by attempting to reproduce Galen's famous demonstration that he could control the voice of the pig by compressing the recurrent laryngeal nerves. Like Galen, he did it before a group of distinguished observers (including his friend Valverde and a member of the Borgia family) but irked by the pig's squeals and fat subsequently used dogs with long necks.[40]

---

[37] On Vesalius, Colombo and the pulmonary transit see J. J. Bylebyl's useful PhD dissertation (Yale University, 1969: available from University Microfilms International), 'Cardiovascular Physiology in the Sixteenth and early Seventeenth Centuries'.

[38] W. Harvey, *Praelectiones anatomiae universalis*, facsimile edn of Harvey's MS. for the Royal College of Physicians, 1886. Harvey's folio numbers are followed; pp. 70v, 72v, 77r, 78r. See also G. Whitteridge, *The Anatomical Lectures of William Harvey. Prelectiones anatomie universalis de musculis*, Edinburgh and London, 1964.

[39] Before this the text was known as the *De anatomicis aggressionibus*, and so the 'administrations' seems to be a considered humanist usage for the method of anatomy. R. Colombo, *De re anatomica*, Venice, 1559. Book 14 begins at p. 256. The numbering of the pages loses its sequence here, so that book 15 on rarities seen in dissections is also numbered 256. It should be 262.

[40] Ibid., p. 257.

For Colombo this is *anatome viva*. He presents it as a course of experiments based on the vivisections of six dogs. Each demonstrated before it died an aspect of the functioning of the body: the control of the voice; the motions of the lungs, heart and aorta (decide whether the arteries swell as the heart contracts, says Colombo); the heat of blood inside the left ventricle of the heart (be careful not to scald your fingers, he warns);[41] the contents of the venous artery (does it contain air?). Much of this is directed against the Aristotelians who claimed that the voice comes from the heart and that the blood in the left ventricle was cooler than that in the right, and Colombo's fifth dog served to disprove the Aristotelians' assertion that the heart was the centre of life, as it ran barking across the room after Colombo had removed its heart. Almost certainly this was inspired by similar experiments made by Galen and available to Colombo in an edition of Galen's *On the Opinions of Hippocrates and Plato*.[42] Very probably the same can be said of Colombo's sixth dog, which demonstrated the generation of animal spirits in the exposed and pulsating brain.

These vivisectional experiments, performed before a notable audience, were clearly a convincing form of anatomical demonstration. 'Proof!' exclaims a marginal note in Colombo's book where the text describes the puncturing of the venous artery.[43] Moreover, the sequence of exposition of the whole work is governed by a desire to 'demonstrate' anatomy in a rigorous way. While the practical Massa and Berengario copied the 'three-venter' sequence of dissection of the equally practical Mondino, Colombo, like Vesalius, begins with the bones and other similar parts, which build up as the book progresses to the complete body. Anatomists called this a 'synthetic' mode of procedure and its use in teaching was that it followed the order which Nature or God had followed in assembling the body. In a sense Colombo, in starting from Nature's first principles, or 'what is first in nature' as the Aristotelians said, is *demonstrating* his anatomical knowledge. This is what Colombo called his *universa anatome*:[44] he means anatomy in general, as distinct from the vivisections of book 14, but the phrase carries some of the meaning of 'universal' in a philosophical sense. He tells the reader that he has had more than fifteen years' experience in dissecting the human body in Pisa, Padua and Rome and in one year he dissected more than fourteen. He also claims to have inspected 600

---

[41] Ibid., p. 261.

[42] *De Placitis Hippocratis et Platonis* was printed in 1526. See V. Nutton, 'De Placitis Hippocratis et Platonis in the Renaissance', *Le Opere Psicologiche di Galeno. Atti del terzo Colloquio Galenico Internazionale*, Pavia, 10–12 September 1986, ed. Paolo Manuli and Mario Vegetti, pp. 281–309.

[43] 'Probationum sanguinis, an aer in arteria venali contineatur.' Colombo, *De re anatomica*, p. 261.

[44] Ibid., address to the reader.

skulls in the Campus Sanctus (the cemetery of the common people in Rome) and in the Hospital of St Mary the New in Florence. It follows that what he wrote in his anatomy he considered to have been distilled from long experience and represented the human body in a pure form, shorn of individual peculiarities. These latter, indeed, he collected up separately for the last book of the work, on monstrous and pathological things. Having separated these from 'the human body' as it was meant to be (by Nature or God), it becomes a 'universal', capable of demonstrating anatomy in an authoritative way. In short, both Colombo's *universa anatome* and his 'administrations' are a parallel and perhaps a contribution to the Galenic, medical and experimental side of Harvey's natural philosophy.

## Vesalius and the battle for and against Galen

So now we are in a position to appreciate the change Vesalius made in anatomy. The humanists, Hellenists and even Berengario the scholastic had sought out pristine texts. Religious changes were beginning to contribute to this change in how people thought about ancient authority, the learned tradition and devices of teaching. The newly restored anatomy texts of Galen had nothing comparable to the 'physical logic' of the commentary and its demonstration; and instead relied on the standing of the authors as ancients. In fact these texts had a brief life as undisputed Authority. By 1539 Vesalius began to suspect that they were factually erroneous, and shortly afterwards he guessed that Galen had never dissected a human body, and had been misled by 'his apes'.[45] In principle, *all* of Galen's anatomy could be wrong, and the programme for

---

[45] Vesalius says in the dedication to the *Epitome* that Galen had never dissected the human body. See *The Epitome of Andreas Vesalius*, trans. L. Lind, New York, 1949. Vesalius also says this in the *Fabrica*, p. 275, where he constantly attributes Galen's errors to his apes; see for example, pp. 45, 81, 85, 233, 234, 246, 274, 299, 307. Very characteristically Vesalius attacks Galen vigorously for deriving his anatomy from *suis simiis* (e.g. pp. 299 and 631) and denying the human anatomy of earlier anatomists like Herophilus, Lycus, Andreas 'and other Alexandrians'. Characteristically also, Vesalius is being less than fair to Galen, who in the place referred to (the *Anatomical Procedures*, chap. 9, p. 143, in the 1956 edition by Singer), is explicit that he is dealing with apes. (I am grateful to Andrew Wear for reminding me that Vesalius discussed some of the matters arising from this text with John Caius, who was editing it for his edition of 1544. See C. D. O'Malley, *Andreas Vesalius of Brussels, 1514–1564*, University of California Press, 1965, p. 105.) Galen's reference to apes here may well have prompted Vesalius' guess that Galen had never dissected man. (A similar case occurs in relation to the axillary vein, Vesalius, *Fabrica*, p. 286.) Nor could Vesalius have made any judgment about the accuracy of the anatomy of Lycus, Marinus or Andreas. Vesalius' tone varies from sarcasm to denouncement. He gratuitously inserts a word into the title of Galen's little book on the blood vessels, making it 'The Dissection of the *Simian* Arteries and Veins' (*Fabrica*, p. 52). He constantly refers to Galen being misled by his imagination, for example when he ridiculously 'invented' pores in the cribriform plate (*Fabrica*, p. 641). It is the misrepresentation of Galen by Vesalius, as well as the latter's tone of criticism, that offended many of Vesalius' contemporaries.

anatomy was now in Vesalius' eyes to identify all of Galen's errors. It followed that the commentators who had relied on Galen's authority could no longer be read with faith. Vesalius put a humanist framework round his programme and claimed to be restoring the older and purer human anatomy of the Alexandrians Herophilus and Erasistratus (about which in fact little was knowable).

Vesalius' book of 1543 was shaped by the belief that drove him, that Galen had been describing simian anatomy. In correcting Galen's errors, Vesalius was obliged to keep very close to Galen's exposition. Because the differences between the anatomy of men and apes is one of structure (rather than function), Vesalius' treatment is almost entirely a *historia*, an account of the 'fabric' of the body: *De fabrica corporis humani*. Its numerous and impressive woodcuts are visual *historiae*.[46]

We must pause a little while considering these *historiae*, particularly when bearing in mind that Harvey would have seen that some anatomists continued to write without using illustrations while others developed the technique. Harvey had no reason, in viva voce lectures at an actual dissection, to procure illustrations, but he must have seen the impact of Vesalius' illustrations. We should note firstly, that because they were illustrations of structure, Vesalius' woodcuts could not present knowledge of a proper philosophical kind, which included knowledge of function. Printed *historiae* did not reveal *actio-usus-utilitas* or knowledge *propter quid*, both of which were techniques of producing knowledge of purpose, true causal knowledge. Yet Vesalius' woodcuts had undeniable impact. They struck the observer with their authority. Vesalius' illustrations were in fact built up over a number of dissections and from numerous sketches; but whether or not his readership recognised this, it remained the case that for them the illustrations did not appear as the result of this or that dissection, a 'particular' of observation, but represented 'the human body' in some general way and accordingly exhibited some of the authority of a universal, somewhat in the manner of Colombo. We have seen that Berengario published some of his woodcuts of 'the human body' for the use of artists,[47] knowing that words could never furnish an adequate description: the woodcut was a 'universal' exemplar, to be modified as necessary for the particular needs of the artists. Vesalius in a related way added immeasurably to his own authority by using woodcuts derived from artists of great skill and considerable anatomical knowledge.

Secondly, a woodcut, unlike a verbal description, is not open to dialectical

---

[46] Vesalius' attention to *historiae* is best seen in the *Epitome* and in his demonstrations in Bologna, in the first of which in particular he is less concerned to pick fault with Galen. There is a convenient edn of the *Epitome* by P. Paauw, Amsterdam, 1633; and see Heseler, *Andreas Versalius*.

[47] Berengario, *Commentaria*, f. 520v.

attack, and no equivalent graphical technique of criticism was available. Vesalius' pictures, although philosophically limited, acted powerfully on the senses and like Berengario's acted in practice like some sort of universal (see figs. 5 and 6). These woodcuts *demonstrated* the anatomy of 'the human body'. Harvey, with a sensory epistemology in a dominant place in his natural philosophy, probably saw this.

So energetic was Vesalius' attack on Galen that many sprang to Galen's defence. The language they used drew upon a religious vocabulary, and we are again reminded of the religious dimension of anatomy and its natural philosophy. Undoubtedly many observers saw parallels between what was happening in medicine and in the Reformation, as they did when they called the unorthodox Paracelsus the *Luther medicorum*. It is unlikely that Vesalius, who went on to serve the emperor, was reformist in the religious sense. The published *Fabrica*, however, was so hostile to Galen, so committed to replacing his authority and so much a book that would attract attention, that it might well have been unwelcome in some quarters where respect for authority played an important part in men's lives. Just as Ramism, which sought to replace Aristotle's philosophy, was unwelcome in many universities because of its ability to create disturbances, for example at disputations, so an anatomical text that ran counter to the statutory sources of the subject might cause trouble. Stability was essential within universities in the midst of the changes of the Reformation, up until (as we shall see) the middle of the next century.

Whether or not Vesalius, in Padua, foresaw problems is not clear. He did, however, take the unusual step of sending the manuscript and the wood blocks of the *Fabrica* to Basle to be printed, rather than following the obvious course of taking them to Venice, where he could have safely delivered the manuscript, have seen it through the press and have been assured of a product at least as impressive as that of the Basle publishers. Vesalius may have heard that censorship was afoot. In 1543, the year the *Fabrica* appeared in Basle, the Roman Inquisition came into being. At the same time the files of the compilers of the Index of Prohibited Books were opened. Books to be printed in Catholic countries had to be examined before publication. The church's permission gave the bookseller a ten-year monopoly, provided that the book contained nothing 'contrary or prejudicial to the Christian faith, to public behaviour or to princes';[48] that is, that it served to conserve the *status quo* in the religious,

---

[48] A specimen privilege in these words is found in another anatomy text important for Harvey, that of Colombo, *De re anatomica*. Eustachio's anatomical work (note 61 below), which favours the ancients against Vesalius, contains an elaborate apparatus of permissions: his publisher was negotiating a batch of educational works through the authorities for sale in Catholic countries and he gained the privileges of the pope, the king of France (his *Catolica et Caesarea* majesty), the Senate of Venice, the Duke of Venice, the Inquisitors and certain

Fig. 5. Berengario's woodcut of all the muscles of the back immediately under the skin. Where words could not adequately describe the shape of the muscles, Berengario relies on a visual image. He intended the illustration to be of use to artists in drawing the body and so clearly meant it to be *the* human body, a sort of universal.

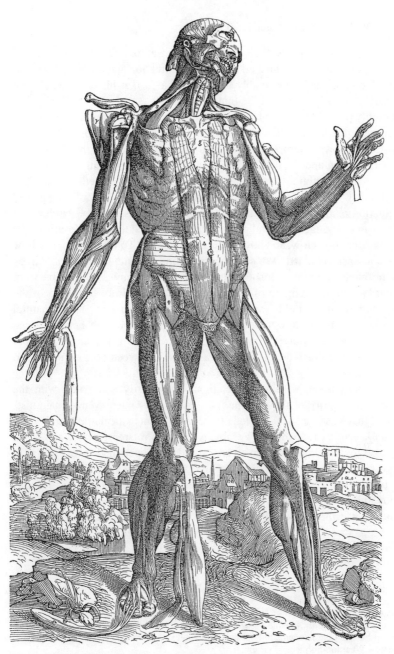

Fig. 6. The fifth table of the muscles from Vesalius' *De humani corporis fabrica*. The artist has given immediacy to the *historia* of the muscles by placing the figure in a landscape, but the authority of the figure as an anatomical statement lies in its representation of the human body in general.

social and political aspects of sixteenth-century Catholic life. Infringement of the monopoly was to be punished by excommunication and a fine of 500 gold ducats. Vesalius may conceivably have anticipated that his book would not have safely passed the eyes of the Inquisitor.[49]

Certainly part of the general – mostly later – reaction of the Catholic church to Protestant claims and behaviour was to restate the validity of its historical authorities, its own interpretative role and the faith that bound the authorities, the interpretation and the faithful together.[50] Without supposing that Vesalius was any form of religious protestant, it was nevertheless something very like this faith that Vesalius' critics accused him of breaking. In the following brief examination of the arguments for and against Vesalius we shall explore the mechanism of change in natural philosophy and related matters. Vesalius' was the New Anatomy. How, and how far, was it adopted? To what extent and how was a consensus reached? We shall begin to find, as with the case of Harvey himself, that the natural philosophy that underlay anatomy is inseparable from religion. Where the religion of the Protestants turned away from that of the older church, we would expect the religious dimension of its natural philosophy to differ. It would be easy to overstate the case here: in what follows it is argued only that in turning so readily to a language of *odium theologicum* Vesalius' opponents saw a parallel between philosophical and religious dissent.

The attacks upon Vesalius were, then, only partly concerned with the technical superiority of the anatomy of Vesalius or Galen. Many anatomists regretted that Vesalius' zeal had led him to overestimate the number and extent of Galen's errors (undoubtedly Vesalius very often misrepresents Galen); and many also regretted that such an attack should have been made at all. It was in attacking the 'Prince of physicians second only to Hippocrates' that Vesalius had 'broken the faith' that bound all anatomists to their teacher. Jacobus Sylvius in Paris was outraged, not because his pupil Vesalius had denied him, Sylvius, but rather Galen, the teacher of all medical men. In a language common to that of Bartolomeo Eustachio at the Sapienza in Rome, Sylvius deplored Vesalius' lack of 'piety' and 'faith'. Sylvius' attack on Vesalius, the

---

'commissars' (*per commissarios*). The publisher's monopoly was intended to be secured by the usual threats of excommunication and fines, and by the vigilance of archbishops, bishops and local clergy; informers were to share one-third of any fine imposed, the magistrate who tried the case another third, while the last went to the Venice arsenal.

49  In fact his book did not come to be listed on the index of prohibited books (I am grateful to Andrew Wear for this piece of information).

50  Signs of Counter-Reformation activity in the period after the middle of the sixteenth century were the appearance of many chairs of theology in the Italian universities, and the founding by the Jesuits of the Collegio Romano. See C. Schmitt, 'Science in the Italian universities in the sixteenth and early seventeenth centuries', in his *The Aristotelian Tradition and Renaissance Universities*, London, 1984, pp. 35–56 (item xiv).

*Vaesanus*,[51] 'madman', is addressed three times to the 'pious reader' where 'candid' would have been expected. Medical piety in Sylvius' eyes was due in the first place to the 'divine' Hippocrates, the godlike mortal instigator of the art of the gods Apollo and Aesculapius. Galen is then the *pius* interpreter of Hippocrates, and is too to be regarded as a god of medicine.[52] The laudatory verse that concludes the book likewise deals with the divinity of Hippocrates, the piety of his followers and the impiety of others. How odious to gods and men is impiety! exclaims Sylvius, emphasising his own *summa pietas*.[53] His attack on Vesalius, the madman and calumniator, is sharpened by more than the use of the vocabulary of a theological *odium*. It is that Vesalius has breached an observance that is at root religious. In abandoning respect for the Hippocratic spirit of the ethical works (says Sylvius) Vesalius has broken faith with real medicine. For it is in the ethical works that 'real', Hippocratic, medicine is defended against sophistical and professional opponents of the time, and this medicine could easily be seen as *divine*, having been revealed to the first practitioners by the gods of medicine themselves. This divine medicine is medical knowledge together with techniques for extending it; and the ethical duties of the Hippocratic physician include the protection of this knowledge from outsiders and the maintenance of the purity of mind necessary for its cultivation. 'Holy things are revealed to holy men' is one of the messages of the ethical works. Sylvius sees that this revelation has passed down from Hippocrates to all true medical men, and he sees himself in that tradition. He calls it the *res medica* and defends it passionately. He calls himself the Royal Interpreter of Medicine, perhaps a conscious echo of his epithet for Galen, the pious interpreter of Hippocrates. Sylvius' special business was the *res anatomica*, the restoration, according to their own canons, of the anatomy of Hippocrates and Galen. Vesalius was therefore a special enemy, and Sylvius called for help in rebutting him. 'You reborn and pious Asclepiads of France, Germany and Italy!' he cries. Rally to the defence of your teachers![54]

So for Sylvius, piety and faith are more than simple respect for age and authority. He is surely expressing the deep conviction of the Hellenist in the superiority of Greek culture and the humanists' passion for the classical. Piety and faith are the very mechanism by which Renaissance society received its culture and so held together: 'If we deny this faith in them [the ancient authors] we must accept almost all the writings of the great as fables', says

[51] J. Sylvius, *Vaesani cuiusdam calumniarum in Hippocratis Galenique rem anatomicam depulsio*. I have used the edn of Venice, 1555, where it is continuously paginated with Renatus Henerus, *Adversus Jacobi Sylvii Depulsionum anatomicarum calumnias pro Andrea Vesalio apologia*.

[52] Sylvius, *Vaesani*, p. 73.

[53] Ibid., p. 74.

[54] Ibid., p. 134.

Sylvius;[55] everything said and done in history would have to be denied, and all anatomy set aside. Moreover, without this faith, continues Sylvius, posterity will deny even the anatomical observations that we set down for them; without it the progressive nature of the *res anatomica* would be impossible. So important was this faith for Sylvius that he attributed the discrepancy between Galen's anatomical descriptions and the appearance of the body to degeneration of the body since Galen's time.

But more even than articulating an attitude to the ancients that was not often articulated, although very widespread (and with which it is difficult for us today to empathise), Sylvius is surely showing a religious horror at the apostasy of the Calumniator, whose impious tongue and sacrilegious mouth are agents of deception, and who grunting and stamping pollutes the pure founts by which ancient knowledge flows down to us.[56] To summarise, the medicine that Sylvius was defending had, like a religion, its divine and revealed sources of knowledge and procedures; it had its sacred texts, too holy to be discussed in the same breath as the Calumniator; it had, like the church of Rome, a history of commentary, authorities and interpreters; its practitioners had observances to hold to, mysteries to be understood and kept; it had a piety and faith binding the whole together; and Sylvius wanted it to have processes to deal with unbelievers. Sylvius also uses the religious language of Judgment when declaring that the greater rewards for reverence to Galen lay in the future; a future that would deal hardly with those who used impious language to impress the ignorant, who 'magnify these studies of impiety' and, throwing down their weapons, desert to the camp of the impious, ignorant of where they are going.[57]

Sylvius' call for a crusade was answered perhaps only in Paris. Even before Vesalius had published, his open rejection of Galen had called forth a reply from Ludovicus Vassaeus (Loys Vassé),[58] Sylvius' pupil; and afterwards the defence of Galen was carried on up to Harvey's time by the anatomists André du Laurens and Jean Riolan the younger. Elsewhere, and probably mostly in Protestant countries, Sylvius was ignored. Leonard Fuchs[59] had already

---

[55] Sylvius, *In Hippocratis et Galeni*, f. 7v.

[56] Ibid., f. 13v.

[57] Ibid., f. 11v.

[58] L. Vassaeus, *In anatomen corporis humani tabulae quatuor*, Paris, 1540. Vesalius is not named, but a calumniator of Sylvius, even as early as late 1540, is unlikely to be anyone else. Vassaeus' defence is of the medical tradition rather than of Sylvius himself. The text is said to have been the first summary of Galen's anatomy after the *Opera omnia* editions. See Le Roy Crummer and J. B. de C. M. Saunders, 'The anatomical compendium of Loys Vassé', *Annals of Medical History*, 3rd series, 1 (1939), 351–69.

[59] Fuchs was a Reformist doctor (MD 1524) who was prevented from resuming his position at Ingolstadt because of his religious stance. With the help of the Duke of Württemberg he was installed in a chair at Tübingen. See the *Nouvelle Biographie Universelle*, Paris, 1852 (henceforth *NBU*).

produced an epitome of Vesalian anatomy, and when he was criticised by Sylvius, Fuchs' pupil Renatus Henerus of Lindau came to his defence. Addressing Joseph Trapp, he scorned Sylvius' talk of piety and of 'I know not what gods', adding that one should not trust a Frenchman, German or Italian if they put their faith more in authority than in their own senses.[60] In contrast, in such a Catholic place as Rome, if there was not actually a crusade against Vesalius, there was sympathy for Galen. Eustachio[61] recognised that anatomy could grow and develop, and that Galen being human could be in error. But he did not on that account, argued Eustachio, relinquish our respect; he was still the Teacher. The point of defending Galen was not to try to demonstrate that he had not made mistakes, but to show that he still deserved faith. There may be errors in Galen's works, said Eustachio, but never deceit.[62] In a very similar way the lawyer Collenuccio had defended Pliny against the Hellenist Leoniceno, arguing that in a court of law the defendant – Pliny – should escape without penalty if he were a sufficient ornament to society in his sphere of activity. Pliny's business, to Collenuccio and the academics who did not share the Hellenists' *Graecitas*, was the *res Latina*, nothing less than Latin culture, of which Pliny was indeed an ornament.[63] Sylvius and Eustachio use *res medica* and *anatomica* with the same force: it was the whole medical tradition, at the head of which Galen should remain. In a similar way, but using the terminology of Catholic practice, Eustachio pleaded for 'indulgence', *venia*, for Galen in view of the faith that was owed him. This faith did not depend upon Galen being wholly factually correct; it was of a different sort. Eustachio continues with language that would have been significant in post-Reformation Catholicism: to sin, *peccare*, is Vesalius' vice, not Galen's, and it consisted in having bad faith rather than good faith, *mala* rather than *bona fides*, or not faith at all, *nulla fides*.[64] In a similar way Realdo Colombo used Sylvius' term *res anatomica* for the very title of his book.[65] It is a weightier

---

[60] R. Henerus, *Adversus Iacobi Sylvii Depulsionum anatomicarum calumnias pro Andrea Vesalio apologia*, Venice, 1555.

[61] Bartholomaeus Eustachius (Eustachio), *Opuscula anatomica*, Venice, 1563, introductory material and, for example, the sixth *antigramma*. Eustachio's alternate *syngramma* and *antigramma* is a format devoted to the defence of Galen and an attack on Vesalius. Eustachio makes much of his own reverence for the ancients (Galen is a *dux*) and Vesalius' 'false piety' (*antigramma* 2) but is not prepared to accept Sylvius' claim that the body has changed since Galen's day. When he wrote this book Eustachio had been professor of medicine at the Sapienza in Rome for about a year.

[62] Eustachio, *Opuscula*, p. 263.      [63] See French, 'Pliny'.

[64] This is Eustachio's *Examen ossium et de motu capitis*, in the *Opuscula* at pp. 165; 166, 168, 173. See also *syngramma* and *antigramma* 9, p. 282.

[65] Colombo, *De re anatomica*. It is in addressing the reader at the beginning of the book that Colombo announces that his 'administrations' consist of his vivisectional experiments. (See also pp. 256, 259.) While Galen is still the leader, *dux*, of anatomists, yet Colombo sides with Vesalius in assuming that Galen had never dissected a human body. This identified an area for progress, but Colombo does not make clear how his vivisections of animals will correct Galen.

phrase than merely 'the business of anatomy', just as *respublica* is weightier than 'public business'. Colombo saw it as progressive in an accumulative sense within a tradition, and felt that he was making additions to it by his vivisectional experiments, by his studies of strange things sometimes seen in dissection and by his reworking of 'general anatomy'. Colombo saw that Vesalius 'burned with incredible cupidity in attacking Galen and noting his errors'[66] which to an extent vitiated his anatomy. Colombo's book no doubt helped to strengthen the early seventeenth-century notion that medical experimentation was a valuable mode of procedure.

All in all, then, Colombo, Sylvius and Eustachio found authority in a number of things outside the strict morphology of the human body by which to oppose Vesalius. Harvey did not take sides in the Vesalius–Galen affair, and as a natural philosopher with an Aristotelian bias he read these authors for what, in their discussions of structure and function, could be used in his natural philosophy. But we shall see that these issues of faith and authority were important for those who read Harvey and made judgments upon his doctrines.

## Galenic, medical anatomy

An aspect of Vesalius' breaking faith with Galen that was particularly resented was his claim that Galen had never dissected a human body. In attempting to rehabilitate Galen on this and other issues, some anatomists later in the century undertook what might almost be called a 'Galen project'. Based on Galen, the dissector of human bodies, this made anatomy a human and medical affair.[67] For du Laurens, man – the measure of all things[68] – is the centre of the world, and all sublunary things were created for him. Du Laurens[69] (cited more than twenty times by Harvey), reminding his reader that the human body is the image of God, tells him that the reasons for doing anatomy are, in this order, to learn more about oneself, to learn more about God, to provide material for

---

[66] Colombo, *De re anatomica*, chap. 2 (p. 4).

[67] It is of course quite true that the medical men had had a traditional battle with the philosophers since the Middle Ages (although the prominence of the issue is due very much to the fact that the necessary university disputations could readily be constructed out of the differences between Galenic and Aristotelian doctrine) and that an anatomist like Zerbi had a long time before Vesalius pointed to the medical and human centre of Galen's anatomy in contrast to the philosophical and animal anatomy of Aristotle. The point here is that the Renaissance and Reformation gave added sharpness to the weapons used by the philosophers and physicians. See Gabriele de Zerbi, *Liber anathomie corporis humani et singulorum membrorum illius*, Venice, 1502, proem.

[68] A., Laurentius (du Laurens), *Historia anatomica humani corporis et singularum ejus partium multis controversiis et observationibis illustrata*, Frankfurt, n.d. (1600? *Ad lectorem* dated 1599). The edn of 1602 may thus be the second. See the address to the reader.

[69] Du Laurens, *Historia*, the address to the reader.

philosophers, both natural and moral, and also, lastly, to provide material for the medical man. Necessarily a body that was the image of God differed from the body of animals. Du Laurens explains that there was some similarity in the digestive organs, for all animals and man had in common a nutritive faculty. But Galen is the principal source for the argument that man is fundamentally different in other parts of his body. Although the neoterics, says du Laurens, attack Galen's style of exposition in *On the Use of the Parts*, yet it is here that Galen so excellently begins with the human hand, the organ that puts into practical effect the uniquely human reasoning power of the brain. Such knowledge could only come (claims du Laurens) from Galen's frequent dissections of man. To be sure, things have been discovered after Galen's time, just as Falloppio corrected and added to Vesalius' anatomy: while anatomy can progress, yet Galen is still the giant on whose shoulders we stand.

Such a Galenic, medical and human anatomy was in contrast to any anatomy derivable from Aristotle (and thus to Harvey's philosophical anatomy) and du Laurens' drive to rehabilitate Galen seems to have involved playing down the importance of Aristotle. Indeed, for du Laurens, natural philosophy (for him Aristotelian) was suspect, because pagan:[70] true philosophy is religious. Conceding value only to the *Physics*, du Laurens stressed that it was Aristotle who had not dissected the human body and was consequently ignorant of much of human structure. Du Laurens even maintained that the *Parts of Animals* and the *History of Animals* were largely derived from other authors. Du Laurens' anatomical argument runs from the body to man's soul and from there to God. His argument is not the simpler and Protestant search for signs of God in the Creation (which we may see in the work of the sixteenth-century Protestant natural historians) nor is he, as Aristotle was, looking for causes. The soul, indeed, is a Trinity, about which mere philosophers are in the shadows, he claims. His 'true philosophy' is closer to that of the Galen he was defending than to Aristotle's, and in particular, to the natural theology of Galen's *On the Use of the Parts*. Man's centrality in this text is brought out by du Laurens' philosophical consideration of animals, which are of interest only in illuminating the perfection of man. As Galen said, the ape, the animal most like man, is simply a laughable imitation of him; and other animals, as progressively less perfect than man, are of decreasing interest to the philosopher of du Laurens' kind and to the physician.[71]

This Galenic natural philosophy and the belittling of Aristotle's view of the physical world (correct in generalities, obscure in its brevity and erroneous in its particulars, says du Laurens) led du Laurens on to think, like Galen, in terms of a Platonic picture of the world. 'Nature' for du Laurens was not the

[70] Ibid., pp. 7–9.
[71] Ibid., pp. 9–14.

impersonal nexus of causality of Aristotle's *physis* but the Demiurge who in the Galenic and Platonic view had designed and built the human body and who, at least for Galen, was the source of its 'natural' faculty. Du Laurens and others rely on Galen's acceptance not only of factual information, like the location of the soul and faculties, but on modes of argument taken from Plato. Almost certainly the vehicle for these opinions was Galen's *On the Doctrines of Hippocrates and Plato*, which had first caught the attention of Western readers along with the Platonic texts brought to Italy by Byzantine emigrés in the late fifteenth century.[72] When it was made generally available in the middle of the sixteenth century, it was much used as a source of medical theory (for example by Fernel)[73] and of material that was useful to those who wished to argue against Aristotelian texts.

In considering Galenic anatomy we can add Riolan's commentary on Galen's book on the bones[74] to the *Historia anatomica* of du Laurens. For Riolan, as for his countryman Sylvius (whom he deliberately follows), Galen is the pure fount of all anatomy. It was human anatomy, to be defended from the *novatores* like Vesalius. Riolan had long believed that Galen had dissected the human body and that it had, however, degenerated since his time. This explains why our bodies (says Riolan, following Sylvius) are different from Galen's descriptions. But Galen remains the pure fount of anatomy, even though in need of interpretation: Riolan wishes no more than that his own anatomy should be regarded as such an interpretation.[75]

The religious dimension of anatomy and its underlying natural philosophy was expressed clearly in the anatomical textbooks. (Texts in anatomical 'administrations', like Colombo's, express it less clearly.) Caspar Bauhin was one author of such textbooks and he drew extensively on du Laurens, whose fight to rehabilitate Galen he shared. Bauhin was the author most extensively

---

[72] See V. Nutton, 'De Placitis Hippocratis et Platonis in the renaissance'.

[73] Fernel's general inclination was, much more than his contemporaries, to favour modern authors. Of course in practice he could not do without the ancients, and of them his preferred source was Plato. Not only did Platonic knowledge derive from more ancient sources still but the late Platonists, says Fernel, took much from the early Christians and so improved their philosophy. See J. Fernel, *De abditis rerum causis libri duo*, p. 5, in his *Universa medicina*, Geneva, 1643. The use of Platonism in Fernel's medical theory is set out in dialogue form in *De abditis rerum causis*, e.g. pp. 13, 17, 45, 88, 94. J. Riolan (the elder), *Opera cum physica, tum medica*, Frankfurt, 1611, p. 94, contains an attack on Fernel in which it appears that medical Platonists believed in the power of incantations and a non-substantial transmission of diseases.

[74] J. Riolan, *Opera anatomica*, Paris, 1649, p. 433: 'In librum Galeni de Ossibus, ad tyrones Commentarius.'

[75] Riolan (the elder), *Opera cum physica*, contains the younger Riolan's *Anatome*, intended as an introduction for students in Paris. Here the younger Riolan's distaste for vivisection of animals is evident, fuelled by the stories of human vivisection by Vesalius and (from Falloppio) by Berengario, who is said to have hated Spaniards, vivisecting twins who were suffering from the French disease.

cited (after Vesalius) by Harvey. His textbook[76] was probably the most widely used in the period immediately before Harvey, and together with the works of du Laurens, it characterises late sixteenth-century anatomy. Although some of the features of the textbook as such can be found in earlier anatomical writings[77] on anatomy generally, yet as in other fields like natural history,[78] the Renaissance classicism of the middle of the century gave way to something approaching natural theology. Man is very much the centre of the stage, partly no doubt as a result of the medical arguments used by the defenders of Galen, and partly for religious reasons. Bauhin says the body is the temple and simulacrum of God: it is the image of God, Who can be seen in it as Caesar's face is seen in coins.[79] Indeed, says Bauhin, this perception of God in His Creation is rationality itself (which by implication is no longer restricted to syllogism or dialectic as a whole). Man's rationality is divine, continues Bauhin, and because of it man is a miracle, a second god.[80] Materially, man is Adam, the protoplast of God. It follows that the anatomist, in approaching the body to dissect it, is undertaking a religious observance of a kind. But in no way does that distance anatomy from natural philosophy: Bauhin tells his reader that anatomy is an *ancilla* of natural philosophy, and moreover that natural philosophy is a revelation of God[81] (and a more personal revelation than had generally been argued for in the middle of the century).

---

[76] The *Theatrum anatomicum*, Frankfurt, 1605. There is also C. Bauhin, *Institutiones anatomicae corporis virilis et muliebris historiam exhibentes*, published by J. le Preux, n.p., 1604. Harvey, who was to lecture to a college of physicians, does not appear to have used this text, which was addressed to beginners. But it is of interest to see that Bauhin too saw himself as partaking in a 'Galen project' in which Galen's methods could be used to discover things unknown to Galen: the results were to be truly Galenic, and he takes exception to those who criticised these results simply because Galen did not see them.

[77] For example that of Zerbi, whose text is not mentioned by Harvey and should not divert our attention here.

[78] Many of the texts in these areas in the middle of the century seem infused with the philological concerns of the humanist and Hellenist. By the end of the century there appears to have been some sort of Christian reaction against the paganism inherent in a thoroughly restored classical text. Philemon Holland had grave doubts on this score about translating the pagan Pliny (see J. Newsome, ed., *Pliny's Natural History: A Selection from Philemon Holland's translation*, Oxford, 1964) despite the fact that a century before at the Protestant university of Wittenberg it had seemed like a good idea to try to derive a study of the natural world from Pliny rather than from an even more pagan Aristotle.

[79] C. Bauhin, *Theatrum anatomicum*, Frankfurt, 1605, dedication. Compare the edn of Basle, 1621.

[80] Bauhin, *Theatrum anatomicum* (1621 edn), p. 4.

[81] C. Bauhin, *Corporis Humani Fabrica*, Basle, 1590, prologue. Up until about the middle of the sixteenth century learned discussions were customarily graced with references to the classical pantheon (for example Fernel slides without difficulty from the pagan gods to the ancient medical men and to the *Deus Optimus Maximus* of the strictly Christian tradition. See his address to Henry II in his *Universa medicina*; I have used the edn of Geneva, 1643). The convention of allegory had for a long time enabled the use of pagan gods even in calculating the date of Creation in a Christian sense: see for example J. Grunpeck, *Tractatus de*

We shall see that Harvey used a Platonic mode of argument in a significant place. The Platonism that gave some of our medical authors (but not Harvey) an alternative to Aristotle is further evident in another author whom Harvey read, Salomon Alberti. Indeed, Harvey's Platonic argument comes immediately after his citation of Alberti and was prompted by it.[82] Alberti, from Nuremberg, had been one of the German pupils of Fabricius of Aquapendente at Padua, and had taken his degree in medicine at the university of Wittenberg. When he wrote the book that Harvey read he was a public professor of medicine at the same university. Like Fernel, du Laurens and Bauhin,[83] Alberti uses the Platonic key-word *ergastulum*, 'workhouse', to describe the body as the container of the soul.[84] We are far from Aristotelian Form and Matter, from Actuality and Potentiality: the soul, says Alberti, was compelled down from its celestial origin and forced like an oyster into a shell. But it burns with a desire to know, at first frustrated by the material sense, as is said in the *Timaeus*. Then it begins to recollect what it brought with it from its celestial origin into this colony, the body. That is, wisdom for Alberti was gained by reflection upon Platonic innate ideas rather than by learning by way of the senses.

Such a doctrine, distinctly unAristotelian in its dismissal of sensory knowledge, seems to have offered something that some found wanting in Aristotle in the late sixteenth century. Both Catholics and Protestants found the Platonic system sympathetic. Alberti published most of his books in Wittenberg, the arch-Protestant university where earlier in the century Aristotle's natural philosophy had come under attack because its search for causes was considered Godless. It was thought that a better physics could be derived from Pliny.[85] Alberti's Platonism was as agreeable to his keenly

*pestilentiali scorra sive mala de Franczos*, Augsberg, 1496. But by the early seventeenth century, no doubt as a result of the troubles of the Reformation, this was less frequent. We shall see that a somewhat fundamentalist reading of the Old Testament gave Fludd and Sennert a new view of 'soul' and Protestants in general sought God rather than causality in nature. In natural history the move away from classicism is clear in E. Topsell, *The Fowles of Heaven, or the History of Birds*, ed. T. P. Harrison and F. D. Hoeniger, University of Texas Press, 1972.

[82] Alberti was discussing the relative size of the caecum in the foetus and adult, and Harvey recognised the value of studying the same thing in different contexts: the 'rule of Socrates' that he invokes here is discussed in chap. 4 below. For Harvey's use of Alberti, see his text as published by Whitteridge, *Anatomical Lectures*, p. 86.

[83] Du Laurens, *Historia*, book 1, chap. 5; Bauhin, *Theatrum anatomicum* (1621 edn), dedication.

[84] Salomon Alberti, *Tres orationes . . . Tertia de disciplina anatomica et quomodo sensim aucta, et ad posteros transmissa sit: tum de Galeni libro, qui de ossibus inscribitur, et tyronibus nuncupatur*, Nuremberg, 1585. The term *ergastulum* is used also in his *Historia plerarunque partium humani corporis*, Wittenberg, 1595, which, addressed to beginners, makes anatomy a very religious exercise.

[85] See Pliny the Elder, *Liber secundus, de mundi historia cum erudito commentario v Cl. Jacobi Milichii*, without notice of place or date, but derived from Milich's public lectures at Wittenberg. See also my discussion in 'Pliny and Renaissance medicine', in French and Greenaway, *Science*, pp. 252–81, esp. 263; and Eastwood's discussion of Nauert's thesis in the same volume. The authority behind the attempt to use Pliny may have been Melanchthon's; see

Protestant religion as it was to du Laurens or Fernel in France. His reason for philosophising was, like that of so many before him, that natural philosophy was a religious business. It composes and brings the soul to blessedness, says Alberti; only by its discipline can the soul overcome the flux of matter that causes it to forget (and which disturbs it through the senses) and so attain wisdom. He asks, did not Christ pay more attention to the soul than the body? However, it is unlikely that Harvey was much taken with Alberti's form of religion or his practice of philosophy; he was probably more interested in the valves of the veins and gut, which Alberti was credited with discovering before Fabricius, Harvey's teacher.[86]

In Italy Constantius Varolius[87] was another anatomist to express himself in this Platonic way: he used an elegant image of the soul in its *ergastulum* as a man locked in a library. He is able to see the world, but incompletely, through the library windows, the material senses and the *sensus communis* of the soul. His immediate companions, the books in the library, are the Platonic Ideas of celestial origin. They do not, however, as in Alberti's case, give direct wisdom, or knowledge of God directly, but indirectly. They represent learning and interpretation. This indirect knowledge, says Varolius the anatomist, is to be made direct by inspection of the Creation outside the library windows.

Moreover, it seemed that by way of Plato one could reach older and therefore even more authoritative knowledge, and a *philosophia* even more *prisca*. Alberti thought Plato was retailing Pythagorean knowledge.[88] Du Laurens' and Bauhin's admiration for the noble ensouled animal, man, is derived, they say, from Zoroaster and the thrice-great Mercury (that is, Hermes).[89]

### Catholic anatomy

One of the most recent authors whom Harvey read before writing his anatomy lectures was Archangelo Piccolomini.[90] Both authors called their lectures *praelectiones* and while Harvey's are notes for lectures, Piccolomini's are the

Stephen Pumphrey, 'The history of science and the renaissance idea of history', in *Science, Culture and Popular Belief in Renaissance Europe*, Manchester University Press, 1991, pp. 48–70; 61. See also in the same volume Peter Dear, 'The church and the new philosophy', 119–39; 125.

[86] On Alberti and the valves see J. O. Leibowitz, 'Early accounts of the valves of the veins', *Journal of the History of Medicine*, 12 (1957), 189–96. According to Albrecht von Haller, *Bibliotheca Anatomica*, 2 vols., Tiguri, 1774–7, vol. I, p. 251 Alberti was a pupil of Fabricius; but *NBU* denies that he went to Italy.

[87] C. Varolius, *Anatomiae, sive de resolutione corporis humani*, Frankfurt, 1591.

[88] Alberti, *De disciplina anatomica* (delivered 1578).

[89] This form of Hermeticism became increasingly common by the early seventeenth century, as we shall see in the case of Robert Fludd. Bauhin, *Theatrum anatomicum* (1621 edn), dedication; du Laurens, *Historia*, book 1, chapter 1.

[90] Archangelus Piccolomineus (Piccolomini), *Anatomicae praelectiones*, Rome, 1586.

more formal records of a lecture series that had been delivered. Both relate directly therefore to viva voce proceedings, and Harvey may have found Piccolomini's book particularly interesting for that reason. But Piccolomini's anatomy is very different from Harvey's. Published in Rome and dedicated to the pope, these lectures show what it was in anatomy that was attractive to a Catholic view of the world. Piccolomini is confident, even aggressive, about his world. His argument about how anatomy fits into it is, as we would by now expect, centred on the soul. The body is both the (Platonic) vehicle of the soul and its (Aristotelian) instrument. But the soul is above all the immortal soul of Christian tradition. Its presence in the body is a reflection of its Maker, says Piccolomini, adding, like du Laurens, that it is for this reason that man is so admirable and so different from the imperfect animals.[91] Piccolomini saw and admired the wisdom and ingenuity with which the body had been put together, but for him (unlike the Protestants)[92] this was not direct evidence of the reason and providence of God. Rather, it is clear that for him knowledge of God came through the church. He addresses the pope as the Christ-appointed governor of the world of man, the 'microcosm'.[93] Anatomy was part of man's activities and so part of this microcosm. Like Sylvius and Eustachio, Piccolomini calls it the *res anatomica*, a phrase used by all three to emphasise the cultural role of anatomy. Like them too Piccolomini says that the *res anatomica* develops progressively, and so has a history, marked by its authorities and commentators, by their discoveries and faults. Progress in anatomy according to Piccolomini is to be made by improving on the style, language, intentions and accuracy of the authors. This can be helped by avoiding calumny (Vesalius' attacks on Galen are implied). It can also be helped, continues Piccolomini, by disputation, and one of the reasons he gives for preserving the lecture format is that it presents the opportunity for disputation. Clearly Piccolomini did not see himself as a reformer or a humanist reaching back across an unfortunate intervening age of commentary and disputation to the authoritative ancient texts in order to allow them to speak for themselves. The emphasis on an uninterrupted growth of scholarly interpretation is surely a Catholic one, and in Piccolomini's case, entirely confident: Piccolomini commits his book to the

---

[91]  Piccolomini, *Anatomicae*, address to the reader.

[92]  The major divide here is between the Protestant natural historians of the middle of the century, for whom animals have a philosophical importance in an Aristotelian way and a religious importance as direct evidence of Creation, and the rather later man-centred Galenic anatomists who saw man as a second God and who gave no importance to animals. Since we are here looking at authors read by Harvey for their part in forming his anatomy and natural philosophy, we cannot develop this distinction here, since Harvey does not discuss the natural historians or the religious dimension of anatomy.

[93]  Other authors invariably use 'microcosm' for the body of man, not for the world of man; Piccolomini's usage fits entirely his view of the relationship between God, church and individual.

pope not only for protection against enemies, but as part of the preparation for the coming (seventeenth) century, when (he says) the painful and calamitous events and heresies of the present century will be forgotten and eradicated under the pope's leadership. In other words the wrongs of the Reformation will be righted, and all souls will return as one flock under one shepherd, the pope. Piccolomini's dedication reads like the declaration of a programme to make anatomy, based on a true doctrine of the soul, a wholly Catholic enterprise.

Piccolomini's text is designed to show how his view of anatomy is appropriate to this exercise. As a medieval commentator would, he begins with God as the ultimate cause of everything that exists, including the human body.[94] This is not only to follow Christian belief, but to follow (he says) the philosophical method from universals to particulars – from God to the details of the body, which can then be seen and understood in the light of their divine cause. In a strong sense, this is a form of *demonstration*, causal knowledge of a thing. In contrast, the Protestant[95] use of the same Aristotelian doctrine was to stress first the particulars of the created world in the senses that then lead to the great Universal in the mind.

In ensuring that his natural philosophy is suitable, Piccolomini also uses a medieval device that had been employed to Christianise Aristotle's uncreated, eternal world. That is, it was argued that God is the only true eternal Being, to whom time did not apply, and that what He created *ex nihilo* was in some measure contained within time. The things created after time had begun were souls, intelligences, the heavenly bodies, the elements, and 'the seeds of things to be generated'.[96] These seeds were the species of animals and plants, which unlike the individuals making up the species, were not mortal but potentially at least, immortal. In this way Piccolomini is able to cite to the same end and without conflict Aristotle's eternal world and Genesis.[97]

These sempiternal things are the only *direct* result of God's causality, says Piccolomini. The human body, material and corruptible, is the result of indirect causality from God. It is not the parents who cause the foetus,[98] not the semen and blood of Galen's account or the matter and form of Aristotle's, but the soul, carrying the chain of causality down from God.[99] This is, to be sure, the *vegetative*[100] soul of the medical and natural-philosophical traditions and

---

[94] See R. K. French, 'Gentile da Foligno and the via medicorum', in J. D. North and J. J. Roche, eds., *The Light of Nature. Essays in the History and Philosophy of Science presented to A. C. Crombie*, Dordrecht, 1985.

[95] See note 92 above.   [96] Piccolomini, *Anatomicae*, pp. 9, 10.

[97] Piccolomini's second lecture, pp. 5ff.

[98] Piccolomini, *Anatomicae*, p. 7.

[99] Ibid., pp. 4–6 or lect. 1 and esp. lect. 3.

[100] The vegetative soul, which alone plants had, was responsible for growth, nutrition and generation. The sensory soul, which in addition animals possessed, gave motion and perception to them; while man had both these souls and also the rational soul.

derived from sources in Aristotle, Plato and Galen; and Piccolomini uses these sources and traditions to support his Christian position. In this way, the vegetative soul, naturally devoid of reason, is said by Piccolomini to have been directed, *instructa*, by God to generate the body in a rational and providential way.[101] The action of the parents (he continues) is simply to prepare the matter for the action of the soul. Once acted upon, the laws of matter and motion control the development of the foetus like so much clockwork.

Of all the authors we have considered in this chapter, Piccolomini has the most sophisticated synthesis of Aristotle's nature, *physis*, and the Christian Creation.[102] He takes as his beginning the formula *natura naturans* and *natura naturata* that had been used by Aquinas to express the relationship between God and His Creation in a language accessible to Aristotelian philosophy.[103] For Piccolomini *natura* (that is, *naturata*) was at the lowest level the elements, and the laws that govern them, as a source of motion and quiet. Above this in Piccolomini's scheme is nature as a higher level of activity, not rational but infallibly obedient, concerned with the action and preservation of living things. The generation of creatures had since the Middle Ages been the special preserve of 'nature', often allegorically framed to fit without problems into the relationship between an omnipotent God and His Creation, and Piccolomini seems to be drawing on such doctrines.[104] At the highest level, of course, was God in all His omnipotence, *naturans* and supplying the rationality and providence lacked by mere generative 'nature'. Piccolomini claims that this is what the philosophers mean when they talk of nature governing everything. In this way, for Piccolomini, all the apparatus of the philosophers fits into a Christian metaphysics: in the chain of causality from God to the structures of the body, matter receives substantial forms, which in the case of the similar parts are identified with Aristotelian 'essences' and are intertwined with the whole Galenic–Aristotelian doctrine of complexion, temperament, action and use. Certainly for Piccolomini, as for Aristotle, the body is the instrument of the soul, but for Piccolomini it is so for religious reasons; characteristically he returns to a scholastic formula, 'the whole of the soul is in the whole of the body and wholly in any part of the body', to argue here for the instrumentality of the body.[105] Dissection is the means whereby the soul and its functions – the faculties – will be *shown* to be 'wholly in any part of the body'. In short,

---

101 Piccolomini, *Anatomicae*, p. 11 (lect. 3).
102 Ibid. It is mostly dealt with in lecture 3.
103 See for example J. Weisheipl, 'Aristotle's concept of nature: Avicenna and Aquinas', in L. D. Roberts, ed., *Approaches to Nature in the Middle Ages*, New York, 1982.
104 His notion may also draw upon the Stoic conception of a creative nature and perhaps also the middle of the three souls of Plato.
105 Piccolomini, *Anatomicae*, pp. 214–15. The doctrine of the soul as 'tota in toto et tota in qualibet parte totius' was not uncommon. See for example P. Duodus, *Peripateticarum de anima*, Venice, 1575; M.-A. Biondo, *De anima dialogus*, Rome, 1545.

the soul brings God's instructions to matter, and in the making of the body the faculties of the soul are made partly material in the organs that fulfil those functions.

The soul dominates structure in another way, too. The soul is partly Aristotle's Form: the what-it-is-to-be-a-man is to be rational. The rational creature of natural philosophy seeks its creator; the rational soul's highest and religious duty is to revere God. To do so, explains Piccolomini, it needs organs, the brain, nerves and sense organs, to perceive and contemplate the world as God's handiwork. This religious duty is achieved in line with the principles of Aristotle's philosophy, for, says Piccolomini, there is nothing in the mind that was not first in the senses: the mind must first see the Creation. In furtherance of this purpose, it was necessary for the brain to be defended within bony walls, and the sense organs must be carried about within the world to perceive the particulars of Creation. This is Piccolomini's reason for the existence of bones, cartilages and muscles. In a similar way, the whole body must meantime be maintained, which is why the digestive organs were added by the soul as it built the body. The generative organs have the purpose we have already met, of helping to preserve the continuity of God's original creation, the species, which repeats the religious duty of observing Creation and revering God in every generation.

So Piccolomini's anatomy has a very clear religious dimension. But although he is explicitly Catholic this is not necessarily reflected in the morphological details of his anatomy. It would be difficult, for example, to find a Protestant anatomy to contrast to it. A contrast can be contrived with the rather earlier Protestant natural historians, who differ mostly in that the thrust of their argument is from the particulars of Creation to God, while Piccolomini's is the reverse. While they were not concerned with the human body and although Harvey does not discuss them,[106] the religious differences they reflect came to be important in the period when Harvey's doctrines were being accepted or rejected. We shall examine this in chapter 6 and later chapters, having now seen something of their origins.

---

[106] The basic Protestant position was the religious duty to learn about God by investigating the physical creation. Of the well-known natural historians only Salviani and Aldrovandi were untouched by religious dissent and in the case of the former it is arguable that his treatment was appropriately different. Rondelet was reckoned a member of the Protestant community by 1563 (*Dictionary of Scientific Biography*, ed. C. C. Gillespie, New York, 1970–4) (*DSB*). Belon had been educated 'among heretics' in Brittany and continued his studies at Wittenberg (see G. Sarton, *The Appreciation of Ancient and Medieval Science in the Renaissance*, University of Philadelphia Press, 1953, p. 55). Turner protested too much to be allowed to stay in England (*DSB*). Clusius was a Protestant and close relatives were burned for the same reason (see A. Arber, *Herbals. Their Origin and Evolution. A Chapter in the Evolution of Botany, 1470–1670*, 2nd edn, Cambridge, 1953). The botanists Brunfels, Boch and Fuchs were Lutherans or other kinds of Protestants (Arber, *Herbals*). See also Sarton, *Ancient and Medieval Science*.

To summarise, while Harvey read the authors we have now mentioned largely for the details about form and function that they supply, he must have been aware of the partisan nature of their reasons for writing. No one in Harvey's position could fail to see the religious nature of Piccolomini's anatomy or Alberti's reasons for practising philosophy. It would have been strange if Harvey failed to detect the *odium theologicum* of those who attacked Vesalius, or had not noticed the attractions that a newly vigorous Platonism had for Christianity. He was certainly aware of the censorship of books both in Catholic Italy and in Protestant London. It must therefore have been a considered tactic to avoid involvement with these things and maintain a natural philosophy that was largely Aristotelian and an anatomy that did not give first place to religious reasons for its practice. We shall see why in the next chapter.

# 3    Harvey's research programme

## Harvey, Cambridge and Aristotle

Harvey's natural philosophy, and the research programme that – it will be argued here – he derived from it, had Aristotle as its main source. Harvey would have first made acquaintance with Aristotle's philosophy at Cambridge. Natural philosophy was, of course, a traditional part of the arts course: in thirteenth-century Cambridge they spent the third and fourth year reading the *libri naturales* of Aristotle, the Europe-wide *corpus* of natural philosophy.[1] The Edwardian statutes of 1549 also specify two years of philosophy, including moral philosophy, politics and 'problems' from Aristotle, Pliny or Plato. Perhaps the intention was to reinforce the old system of teaching[2] after the uncertainties of the Reformation. Henry VIII had abolished the teaching of canon law and as a consequence civil law also suffered something of an eclipse in the universities. Medicine had never attracted large numbers at either university and the remaining higher faculty, theology, or now rather divinity, became an important instrument in the perpetuation of the new faith. Much more than before, the universities in England became predominantly schools of philosophy and divinity.

But in Mary's reign the universities reverted to the Catholic church, and the papal legate, Cardinal Pole, removed the Edwardian statutes.[3] Under Elizabeth the Edwardian statutes of Cambridge were renewed (1559) in a modified form. Now natural philosophy was included in the studies for only the last year of the four, between the BA and MA. Further statutes of 1570 followed nervousness that Puritans were about to take over the university, and they resulted in political power in the university moving out of the hands of the regent masters

---

[1] For the Cambridge statutes, see the anonymous *Collection of the Statutes for the University and the Colleges of Cambridge*, London, 1840; *The Commission of King Edward the Sixth for the Visitation of the University of Cambridge AD 1549*; G. Dyer, *The Privileges of the University of Cambridge*, London, 1824, 2 vols., esp. vol. I, pp. 157ff.; and especially B. M. Hacket, *The Original Statutes of Cambridge University*, Cambridge, 1970.

[2] We shall see below that both before and after the Reformation Aristotle represented stability in education.

[3] M. H. Curtis, *Oxford and Cambridge in Transition 1558–1642*, Oxford, 1959, p. 52.

51

to the heads of the colleges. This was coincident with the growth of the colleges at the expense of the medieval halls and with a growth in college teaching. By the time Harvey was in Cambridge (Michaelmas 1593) college tutors were probably numerous enough to undertake a great deal of the teaching, leaving the university with the responsibility only for conferring degrees and supervising the academic 'exercises' that took place three times a week in the schools.[4] The statutes specified (in 1586) that – to avoid trouble– disputing bachelors had to use Aristotle as their only authority.[5]

But the statutes were hardly enforceable, and were often disregarded. Those of Oxford, at least, said that students had to wait for the lecturer at his college and escort him to the schools,[6] but by the 1590s many were prepared to pay the fine of twopence regularly rather than hear the lectures. Moreover, as the students increasingly came from families higher in the social scale than previously, and needed qualifications less, so many left the universities before taking the MA, the preparation for which included reading natural philosophy. Many, indeed, left without taking any degree. Clearly such students had no need to follow a statutory reading list, and could increasingly dictate the kind of education they wanted, since it was essentially a private contract between a gentleman and his tutor. Often enough he wanted natural philosophy. From what we know of collegiate, 'private' natural philosophy in Cambridge in the seventeenth century, some of it was very different from the long-lived commentary on Aristotle that the statutes specified.[7]

So how much Aristotle Harvey was taught in Cambridge depended largely on his tutor, and we can form little idea of it. (His tutor was George Estey, a clergyman and lecturer in Hebrew.[8]) What is clear, however, is that school natural philosophy changed less over the course of the sixteenth century than one might have expected. Given that natural philosophy had religious dimensions, that universities were instruments for the maintenance of orthodoxy, and that their control passed through radically different hands, it might have been supposed that what was taught altered as radically. But in fact school natural philosophy remained long after Harvey's time essentially a commentary on the Aristotelian physical and sometimes metaphysical

---

[4] K. Charlton, *Education in Renaissance England*, London, 1965, p. 143.

[5] J. M. Fletcher, 'The Faulty of Arts', in J. McConica, ed., *The History of the University of Oxford*, vol. III: *The Collegiate University*, Oxford, 1986, pp. 157–99; 177.

[6] A. Clark, *Register of the University of Oxford*, vol. II: *1557–1622*, part 1: 'Introduction', Oxford, 1887.

[7] Some such process helped to create the class of amateurs of natural philosophy known as the *virtuosi*.

[8] We shall see below that interest – including linguistic – in the Old Testament played a particular role in some schemes of Protestant thought. There is no evidence that Harvey's later placing of the soul in the blood owed anything to the Old Testament or to Estey. But undoubtedly the biblical sources were important for figures like Fludd and Sennert.

works.[9] Much of this commentary was Catholic and even Jesuit. For example, although Suarez's book on the defence of the faith had been burned in Protestant London,[10] Cambridge academics accepted, through texts like these philosophy books, a number of his doctrines.[11] One of them was that the intellect knows primarily the singulars of experience, and forms proper concepts of them. This differs from the view of Thomas Aquinas that the intellect knows primarily universals;[12] such views were not without importance in the reception of Harvey's doctrines.

Harvey took his BA in 1597. By statute, he would by now have been familiar with Aristotle's dialectic at least, and this was surely the case, even though like others at the time his graduation documents record that the statutes had not been followed in every particular. But Harvey was in Cambridge for a good part of the next two years (he had periods of illness).[13] Since he did not

---

[9] Twenty or thirty years after Harvey left Cambridge there was a revival of arts course teaching, or at least a new agreement among teachers, and Cambridge was flooded with textbooks from largely Dutch and German sources. However agreeably Protestant they were, the content of the philosophy texts was still largely traditional and even Catholic commentary on the physical and metaphysical works of Aristotle. For example the third edition of Daniel Sthal's *Axiomata physica*, published in Cambridge in 1645, was put together in disputational form for the benefit of young students preparing for examinations (and not for young gentlemen's private reading) and was based largely on Suarez, Fonseca, Zabarella, Mendoza, Vasquez and so on. Clearly this text is not a re-thought Reformist natural philosophy (although there are some hard things said against Bellarmine on the temporal power of the pope, pp. 88ff.). See also W. T. Costello, *The Scholastic Curriculum at Early Seventeenth Century Cambridge*, Harvard University Press, 1958. This remained the case until philosophy was replaced in the universities by new Enlightenment studies like Natural Law. (A guide to books printed in Cambridge for the use of the university may be found in R. Bowes, *A Catalogue of Books printed at or relating to the University Town and County of Cambridge from 1521 to 1893 with Bibliographical and Biographical Notes*, Cambridge, 1894. Compare F. Madan, *Oxford Books*, vol. I, Oxford, 1895.) A large number of textbooks on natural philosophy and related subjects came into Cambridge in the earlier seventeenth century, and those of Keckermann, Burgersdijk and Heerebord were particularly popular. This increase in the number of books available coincided with the growth in student numbers. See L. Stone, 'The size and composition of the Oxford student body', in F. Madan, ed., *The University in Society*, vol. I: *Oxford and Cambridge from the Fourteenth to the Early Nineteenth Century*, Princeton University Press, 1974, pp. 3–110. Several textbooks are listed by P. Reif, 'The textbook tradition in natural philosophy', *Journal of the History of Ideas*, 30 (1969), 17–32.

[10] Costello, *Scholastic Curriculum*, p. 95.

[11] The mutual acceptability of Aristotelian scholarship among the different Christian confessions, and in particular that even Luther's and Melanchthon's followers came to believe Aristotle had to be the basis of education, is noted by Luce Giard, 'Remapping knowledge, reshaping institutions', in Stephen Pumphrey, Paolo Rossi and Maurice Slawinski, eds., *Science, Culture and Popular Belief in Renaissance Europe*, Manchester University Press, 1991, pp. 19–47; 43–4.

[12] We shall see below that Harvey's view of the generation of knowledge of universals from particulars was closer to Suarez's than to Aquinas. There is no evidence that Harvey read Suarez.

[13] Sir Geoffrey Keynes, *The Life of William Harvey*, Oxford, 1966 (repr. 1978), p. 19, believes that Harvey suffered from malaria.

take his MA (which would have been evidence of his following the statutes) it is not certain what he was doing in these years. Perhaps he was reading for the master's degree and was prevented by ill health from taking it. If so, then by statute he would have been reading natural philosophy. The nearest we can get to what kind of thing he might have been taught in this circumstance is probably the contemporary textbook by John Case in Oxford, or that of Magirus, which was to become a textbook in Cambridge (Newton had to read a later edition of it).[14]

It is worthwhile pausing to look briefly at these textbooks, not only to acquaint ourselves with the statutory natural philosophy of the universities in Harvey's time, but to see how it was that the academic study of natural philosophy had also a social and religious function. This is most apparent in the text of the Oxford teacher John Case, published in Oxford in 1599.[15] Case's text is a compendium drawn from Aristotle, rather than an analysis of 'the eight books of the physics'. In terms of knowing what Aristotle had written, Case's antecedents in Oxford were doing better 300 years earlier. Case's work is defensive from the outset, refusing to allow anything other than a thoroughly Christianised Aristotle to emerge.[16] Perhaps aware of the charm of neoteric thinking to young minds, he excludes it, 'lest the Christian philosopher should be a heretic'. What he is looking for is peace and certainty in philosophy: the fantasms of the contentious are to be pruned from the tree of philosophy so that the flower of truth may flourish; all dishes at the Philosophical Feast are to be equally digestible, not generating poisons. More directly, no disputations are to be allowed unless a full reply is known to be possible. The result of disputing major paradoxes would be the ruin of divine and human philosophy, concludes Case.

---

[14] Cited by Schmitt from A. R. Hall: C. Schmitt, 'Towards a reassessment of renaissance Aristotelianism', in his *Studies in Renaissance Philosophy and Science*, London, 1981, pp. 159–93; 191. See also R. H. Kargon, *Atomism in England from Hariot to Newton*, Oxford, 1966, p. 1.

[15] J. Case, *Ancilla philosophiae, seu epitome in octo libris physicorum Aristotelis*, Oxford, 1599. See also Charles Schmitt's learned treatment, *John Case and Renaissance Aristotelianism in England*, Kingston and Montreal, 1983. It seems likely that such texts were designed to meet the statutory requirements for natural philosophy. For Harvey's contemporary Brian Twyne, a scholar at Corpus Christi, who read his natural philosophy 'privately' with his tutor from the Greek Aristotle, see M. H. Curtis, *Oxford and Cambridge in Transition 1558–1642*, Oxford, 1959, p. 108, and H. Kearney, *Scholars and Gentlemen. Universities and Society in Pre-industrial Britain 1500–1700*, London, 1970, p. 64.

[16] Case was very much an Oxford product, having been a chorister, scholar and fellow of St John's College (MA 1572). He was 'popishly affected' according to Wood and taught philosophy mainly to Catholics, apparently outside the regular university system. By 1599 this might well have made him feel in a minority position and so defensive. Since he had by now made money by the practice of medicine and was in receipt of a stipend as canon of Salisbury, his textbook looks much like an *apologia vitae suae*. He died in 1600: see *Dictionary of National Biography (DNB)*.

Case does not say who the contentious men are, but they are likely to include the Ramists and the neoterics of the 'new philosophy', whom he has read but does not wish to identify. His enemies included the medieval nominalists who dealt, he said, only with the shadows of things, and the Epicureans, who denied purpose in nature.[17] Christian metaphysics is the basis of philosophy for Case. Not only is God the source of philosophy, He is the unmoved mover of the created things that are the subject of philosophy, and contemplation of Him is the ultimate purpose of doing philosophy; the very name 'philosopher' is divine, says Case, having a divine subject (the mind), a divine object (truth) and a divine purpose (God).

Case's philosophical axioms are as defensive as his introduction. 'Nature does nothing in vain', 'in every action of nature something new arises', 'there is a necessary connection between cause and effects' and 'the law, order and purpose of nature are certain' (because whatever depends on the First Cause is inevitable) are 'axioms' for Case and so the basis for the use of the philosopher's main tool, the demonstrative syllogism. But more fundamental to natural philosophy, Case told his students, are the Principles of physics, Matter, Form and Privation. These, he insisted, have to be handled with rules of personal and almost moral behaviour: the learner *must* believe these Principles; he must *not* enquire into the reason for them; and he must *never* dispute with anyone who does not believe them. For Case, the ability of the mind to believe in the Principles *without* the use of reason is the 'faith of the philosophers', clearly akin to religious faith. Those who do not believe the Principles are 'ignorant or impudent, spurning what has been held for so long by the agreement of great men'. Perhaps Case was still fighting his old enemies, the Ramists,[18] who denied privation, or perhaps the threat he saw came from the new natural philosophers who were flirting with atomism. The whole thrust of Case's work is to identify natural philosophy with the religious and academic world as he knew it – late sixteenth-century high-church Oxford – for their mutual support. Thus – in a final example – for Case it is blasphemy as well as philosophical vanity to claim to know the powers of the stars by means of amulets. (Yet Case allows that amulets can be used to summon demons, which God allows when man, in an act equivalent to the physical principle of privation, turns away from God and becomes superstitious and full of fantasies.)

Case sets out the fundamental physical principles of school natural philosophy, the principles which came to be challenged during the lifetime of Harvey and his natural philosophy. Natural motion in mobiles, said Case, using

---

[17] Case, *Ancilla philosophiae*, p. 42.
[18] Case had attacked the Ramists in 1582. On Ramism see Kearney, *Scholars and Gentlemen*, esp. p. 64.

the language of medieval commentary, derives from an internal principle of motion, Nature. Natural motions on earth are in a straight line – up and down – and other kinds are violent. An important category of violent motion is attraction, *tractio*.[19] We shall see how the challenge to these fundamentals extended into the argument for and against Harvey's doctrines, and the attack was well under way by Case's time, as he reveals in dealing with another Fundamental, the question of the void. Case admitted that 'some philosophers' say that 'vacuum' is a place, devoid of body. Case denied this, on the Aristotelian principles that there is no place without body and that motion in a vacuum would be instantaneous (because, on peripatetic reasoning, there would be no resisting medium). Case also draws on 'common experience' to deny the existence of a vacuum, pointing to the fact that water will not pass through its orifice in a water-clock unless air is admitted above it, so preventing a vacuum. He also pointed to the medical experience with the cupping-glass, which on cooling *attracts* blood from the skin in order to prevent the formation of a vacuum.[20]

Johannes Magirus was a teacher of natural philosophy in Marburg[21] and an author of textbooks available in Cambridge. Like Case, he denied the existence of a vacuum and allowed 'attraction' as a species of violent motion. Where Case does not name Ramus, Magirus is explicit: Ramus had denied the Aristotelian commonplace that Nature was the internal principle of motion in mobile things. Ramus used as an example a clock, which he argued was clearly artificial, not natural, yet with an internal principle of motion. Both Magirus and Case bring forward the example for refutation, maintaining that the clock's principle of motion is in fact external. The image of the clock was a troubling one, for while man-made and so not natural, yet all of its parts in their actions were purposeful and co-ordinated, like the parts of the natural world, and the whole had a purpose – to tell the time. So in one sense a clock was a purposeful thing. But in what sense could 'purpose' be said to reside in the simple wheels and weights that made up the clock? It was with the notion of nature not only as a moving, but also as an *organising* force that Magirus and Case insisted that the clock was unnatural, with an external moving principle. Axioms about Nature doing nothing in vain, being provident, and wise, clearly did not apply to clocks. But both authors have also to meet objections that these axioms did not apply even to *Nature*. Thus Magirus[22] faces the objection that Nature does not use reason in her actions, for example, the stomach does not *know* that it prepares food, and so has no goal, *finis*.

---

[19] Case, *Ancilla philosophiae*, p. 53.
[20] Ibid., p. 67.
[21] J. Magirus, *Physiologiae peripateticae libri sex*, Wittenberg, 1609. There was a Cambridge edition of 1642.
[22] Magirus, *Physiologiae* (1609 edn), p. 23.

Magirus solves the problem by distinguishing 'to act by reason of an end' (that is, towards a goal) from 'to act with deliberation' (where the goal is consciously known). Case also meets the objection that Nature is not possessed of conscious reason and does not make plans. His answer is that Nature works with 'natural reason' for the mutual good, being 'instinct with divinity'. Magirus adopts the related Protestant device of referring to the passages of Paul in which it is said that the presence of God in nature is such that we can almost reach out and touch Him: the visibles of the world giving us knowledge of the invisibles. Like Bauhin and the Protestant 'natural historian' Gesner,[23] Magirus found himself in a theatre of Creation, the stage 'properties' leading him to God.

In short, it was very important for the natural philosophy of Case and Magirus that Nature should not be seen as working like a clock, that is, by imposed motion and without any internal purpose. As we shall see, objections similar to those made by the opponents of our university philosophers about the local sentience and rationality of nature were being made against the natural principle of *horror vacui*.[24]

Such are examples of school natural philosophy available in the English universities when Harvey was a Cambridge student. If Harvey was not absorbing his natural philosophy from some compendium such as these, but was reading in college with his tutor, it may have been something rather more elaborate; Twyne, his contemporary in Oxford, was reading natural philosophy with his tutor, and wrote to his father asking for a copy of Aristotle's *Physics*.

---

[23] C. Gesner, *Historiae animalium. Liber 1 de quadrupedibus viviparis*, Tiguri, 1551: the address to the reader.

[24] Both Magirus and Case follow the pattern of quoting Catholic commentators freely. Only in his teaching text on moral philosophy (*Corona virtutum moralium*, Frankfurt, 1601: dedication and introduction) does Magirus have hard words for canon law and the conflation by the 'scholastics' (Catholics) of Aristotle and church doctrine. (He also has harsh words for those Protestants who behave well in this life simply for a hope of eternal reward.) Another textbook of natural philosophy in use in mid-seventeenth-century Cambridge, and printed there by the University Printer, was that of the Parisian Cistercian, F. Eustachius, *Summa philosophiae quadripartita*, 1648. The dedication preserved Eustachius' praise of his patron's efforts in spreading the Catholic faith, but even so appears not to have been found objectionable in interregnum Cambridge. (In a similar way the book on meteorology by the Catholic Libert Froidmont (we shall meet him in connection with the Harvey affair), printed in London for use in Cambridge, praises in generous language the links between his patron, the pope, a cardinal and canon law: *Meteorologicorum libri sex*, 1656). Indeed the mid-century edition of Magirus and that of Eustachius, from opposite ends of the religious spectrum, are very similar. They also share features with anatomy texts of similar date, including the image of the theatre and the passages from Paul. There is a new, hermetic Platonism in these books which eclipses (explicitly in Eustachius' case) the Christian Aristotle of the earlier part of the century. The social role of philosophy in Eustachius' book is very clear. Not only is moral philosophy a guide to public and private action, but a strong parallel is drawn, based on the *Republic* of Plato, between the philosopher and the magistrate: the man well educated in philosophy is a member of a stable society.

He seems to have read it in Greek.[25] On the other hand, the Parker scholarship, Harvey's source of funds, was intended to prepare the scholar for a medical education, and Harvey continued to draw his stipend to the end of 1599. This is when we would have expected him to finish his time in Cambridge, that is, after the statutory seven years of the arts course. Probably Harvey in those last two years was reading some medical texts together with the natural philosophy on which they depended. Certainly Sir Charles Scarburgh, who followed Harvey as Lumleian lecturer in anatomy at the College of Physicians, said that Harvey had read philosophy and medicine while at Caius.[26] Since he spent only two years in Padua, where the statutes specify three,[27] it seems very likely that he was able to count a year's reading medicine in Cambridge to make up his total. There is evidence that suggests Harvey may have seen a dissection while in Cambridge.[28]

## Disputation and authority

We must here note a characteristic of Harvey's natural philosophy. In the first place, as a product of the schools, it was adversarial. Disputation was perhaps the most characteristic activity of the academic. We have seen that the English universities, even when the statutes were sometimes ignored, could, and did, insist on the performance of disputation. Disputations occurred at all levels: visiting royalty was entertained by grand disputations, and the junior students' first hurdle was a disputation with their fellows. In Cambridge in Harvey's time each student had to dispute at least twice, and reply once to a class 'exercise' – *exercitatio* – before becoming a bachelor. As bachelors they took part, with bare heads, in the disputations of the masters.[29] Three such responses to a master, two more to *exercitationes*, and a declamation were needed to proceed to the master's degree.

The large numbers of artists in the university meant that disputations were frequent events. Masters' disputations occurred four times a week.[30] They lasted for two hours, and masters were obliged by statute to attend for four years. Bachelors' disputations were fitted in on other days. The theses to be defended were posted on the door (*in valvis*) of the schools eight days ahead of the disputation to allow prospective opponents to work out strategies of attack.

25 Kearney, *Scholars and Gentlemen*, p. 64, and see note 15 above.
26 Keynes, *William Harvey*, p. 14.
27 *Statuta almae universitatis d. artistarum et medicorum Patavini Gymnasii*, Venice, 1589, p. 44v.
28 P. M. Jones, 'Thomas Lorkyn's dissections, 1564/5 and 1566/7', *Transactions of the Cambridge Bibliographical Society*, 9 (1988), 209–29.
29 Dyer *Privileges*, pp. 157, 164.
30 Ibid., pp. 173–8.

Although disputations could be very ceremonial affairs, they were keenly competitive and often dealt with unorthodox views or novelties. Tempers could rise. In the later 1590s, when there was excitement in Cambridge over Ramist logic, one disputation ended in uproar when the moderator, unable to answer the interjection of a Ramist, boxed his ears. Much of the dislike that Ramism attracted, indeed, was due to its ability to provoke conflict.[31] Whatever views prevailed in the universities, they prevailed by disputation. The formal structure of argument and counter-argument was never far below the surface of the minds of university-educated men. This was to be of significance for Harvey and his philosophy.

Harvey would also have disputed in Padua. The emphasis the statutes laid on disputation suggests that those involved were often reluctant. To make sure they were observed, the statutes themselves were to be read out aloud in Italian to the sound of trumpets; and in an unusual preamble to the regulations to disputations, it is said 'Disputations lead not only to knowledge of the truth, but also to exercise, to promptitude and care in things that are taught, and to boldness in scholars.'[32] And elsewhere: 'Every day teaches how much profit there is in *exercitatio.*'[33] In Padua as elsewhere they might also lead to unruliness, and the rector had the power to impose fines in such cases.

Whatever the detail of what Harvey was taught, it would have been very largely consistent with what he was to face in Padua. The major difference was that in Cambridge he would have met the dialectical arts, the moral philosophy and the physical works of Aristotle; in Padua in addition he made the acquaintance of Aristotle's works on animals.[34]

### Padua

Having become familiar with the arts course and almost certainly the basis of medicine, Harvey left Cambridge for Padua.[35] It was the natural choice for an able and ambitious medical student. A Paduan degree was recognised at home,

---

[31] Fletcher, 'The Faculty of Arts', p. 178.

[32] *Statuta*, p. 38v.

[33] *Statuta*, p. 40v. These *exercitationes* were 'circular disputations', occurring every day in the *apotheca*. We shall see below in connection with Berigard that similar 'circular' events took place in Pisa, and provided a format for the discussion of Harvey's doctrines.

[34] As for possible other Paduan influences on Harvey, see C. Schmitt, 'William Harvey and Renaissance Aristotelianism', in C. Schmitt, *Reappraisals in Renaissance Thought*, London, 1989, pp. 117–38, who thinks that the parallels between Harvey's 'method' and that of Zabarella are very close indeed. But since Harvey did not rely on syllogistic argument, and Zabarella did not dwell on personal observations, it is difficult (as Schmitt says) to argue for a profound influence.

[35] On medicine in Padua, see J. Bylebyl, 'The School of Padua: humanistic medicine in the sixteenth century', in C. Webster, ed., *Health, Medicine and Mortality in the Sixteenth Century*, Cambridge University Press, 1979, pp. 335–70.

either directly by the College of Physicians, or by incorporation at the universities. In either case it would make possible a rewarding practice in London. It was also a natural choice, as it was the most famous medical school in Europe, the school of Vesalius, Colombo and now of Fabricius of Aquapendente.

Harvey's experience in Padua and with Fabricius was important in the development of his natural philosophy, and we must briefly look at the nature of studies in Padua. Padua had been controlled by Venice since 1405 and its *riformatori dell studio* were Venetian from 1517.[36] What Harvey was joining was an incorporation for learning very different from the Cambridge he had just left. In Padua he entered a *universitas* that had been originally a grouping of students foreign to Padua who had come together for their mutual benefit. The group retained its power to elect its own leader, the rector, and although its powers to determine the nature of what was taught and the persons of its teachers were somewhat eroded by the civil authorities, it still retained many features of an autonomous incorporation.

It was an incorporation of students in arts and medicine. Sometimes the students gave attention to arts before medicine, but more often the two studies ran in parallel. The incorporation set up its own statutes. They give little attention to the teaching of theology, save to establish that Thomist and Scotist theology should be taught in parallel. The statutes also controlled the powers of priests and regular clergy among its members: they were allowed to vote in the case of the moral philosophy lectures, but not for those on topics occupying more time in the curriculum.[37] This secular feel to the arts-and-medicine *universitas* may have been encouraged by the civil authorities, for Venice as a great trading city was as aware as any other town of the commercial advantages of a famous school inside its area of influence. In particular, Venice had valuable trading links with German-speaking lands, and it may have been partly as a result of this that between 1546 and 1630 some 10,000 German students matriculated into the two German nations in Padua.[38]

In other words, the student *universitas* and the civil authorities of the Veneto who paid the salaries of teachers like Fabricius found no difficulty in accepting Protestant students. When there was friction between Fabricius and his German students it was not religious, but because he gave them philosophical animal anatomy instead of the commercially valuable human anatomy they

---

[36] See H. B. Adelmann, ed. and trans., *The Embryological Treatises of Hieronymus Fabricius of Aquapendente*, 2 vols., Cornell University Press, 1942/1967; vol. I, introduction.

[37] *Statuta*, pp. 6r, 33v.

[38] Adelmann, *Embryological Treatises*, vol. II, p. 653. While lecturing on the organs of speech he explained why it was that his German students had a poor Latin accent: they hold their lips too stiffly, he said, and give wrong values for the consonants, rendering 'qui bonum vinum bibit diu vivit as qui ponum finum pipit, tiu fifit'. Adelmann, vol. I, p. 15.

wanted, and because he made fun of their Latin accents. But taking degrees was a different matter. Examination and graduation with a degree was the business of the Paduan College of Philosophers and Physicians. This was a civil, professional body of doctors, controlling local practice and consisting of Paduan practitioners, not all of whom were teachers. Conversely, the teachers within the student's *universitas* were often not Paduans and so not members of the college. In essence the authority of the college to give degrees rested on the authority of the bishop, to whom the college was an advisory committee.

Although nominally the two incorporations together constituted the *studio* of Padua, the links between the doctors' college and the student's *universitas* were limited to examination and graduation. In the 1560s indeed the students nearly succeeded in replacing the Paduan College with the medical College of Venice as their graduating authority, and a proportion of Paduan students regularly went to Venice for this purpose. While the Paduan College derived its authority from the bishop, that of Venice had been empowered by the pope (Paul II in 1470) to give degrees (of all kinds) directly. The parish priest acted as an apostolic chancellor. It was not however in the interests of the church to grace Protestants with a degree backed by the authority of the Catholic church, and in 1564 Pius IV insisted that all candidates for the degree should take an oath of allegiance to the Catholic faith. Protestants like Harvey and Fabricius' German students had to take what were essentially private degrees from the Counts Palatine.[39]

So again Harvey's education is less historically visible than we might wish. Almost certainly he followed the statutes of the *universitas*, but since these must have been framed with an eye on the expectations of the degree-giving colleges, it is not clear how far they related to degrees given by the count or even the emperor. If Harvey was examined in the same way as candidates at the college, he would have been given locations, *puncta*, to explain in a basic Aristotelian logical text and in the *Physics*, followed by more in the *Posterior Analytics* and the *De anima*, and by medical questions from book four of the *Canon* and from Galen's *Tegni*. That he obviously paid a great deal of attention to what Fabricius was saying on Aristotle and the animal books indicates that he was reading outside the statutes or was not bound by them.

Before examining Harvey's use of the Aristotelian animal books, we must explore the one hint we have of his use of the physical works. Later in life, when defending his ideas on the acquisition and use of knowledge, he quoted a fragment of Aristotle that has been identified as coming from an edition by Guilio Pace, or Pacius.[40] Pace, who had worked with Zabarella, was in Padua while Harvey was there. Of course, when Harvey wrote this in *De generatione*

[39] See R. Palmer, *The* Studio *of Venice and its Graduates in the Sixteenth Century*, Padua, 1983.
[40] C. Schmitt, *The Aristotelian Tradition and Renaissance Universities*, London, 1984, p. 305.

*animalium*, it was many years after he had left Padua, after the discovery of the circulation and when he may have felt that his methods in natural philosophy were threatened and had to be defended. He may well not have known Pace and his Aristotle when in Padua.[41] But it will broaden our picture of contemporary natural philosophy to look briefly at Pace's work.

He was a productive writer of school texts. There is even a very small and basic 'Institutes' of logic that was printed in Cambridge in 1597.[42] Pace changed his religion more than once, but it is probable that there was enough in common between both forms of Christianity to support without conflict his vision of natural philosophy. We have already seen that Protestants happily read Catholic texts, and we shall see below that both sides of the religious divide had their reasons, concerned with the stability of society, for using Aristotle as the authority in education. The mutual support that could be offered between natural philosophy, religion and society is expressed by Pace in addressing Frederick, Count Palatine, Elector, and granter of degrees, before beginning the *Physics*.

For since God and nature have wished you to be the legitimate and greatest prince, renowned in power and virtues, patron and defender of the Republic, Church and Academy, what more suitable than this work can I offer you? For in these volumes is contained that knowledge in which, by the principles of Nature, we proceed as far as is humanly possible to recognition of God Himself; through this knowledge we hear the heavens, along with the prophets, describing the glory of God; and by it too we can see with our eyes, as the apostles saw, the power and divinity of God which does not fall under our [untutored] vision.[43]

Nevertheless, Pace's view of natural philosophy is not the religious one of John Case. This is part of a new, Paduan, look at the words of Aristotle. Here as

---

[41] Since in this book we are concerned with the *fortuna* of Harvey's natural philosophy we should not be diverted to make internal comparisons between his and other philosophies where there is no evidence of interaction. Thus, while Harvey's exposure to the 'intellectual atmosphere' of Renaissance Italy was undoubtedly of importance, it is beside our purposes to examine the similarity of his doctrines and that of possible 'predecessors', like Cesalpino. For an account of such similarities, see W. Pagel, 'The philosophy of circles – Cesalpino – Harvey. A penultimate assessment', *Journal of the History of Medicine*, 12 (1957), 140–57 and Pagel's other scholarly work on Harvey, a good guide to which is R. Frank's essay review of G. Whitteridge's *William Harvey and the Circulation of the Blood*, in the *Journal of the History of Biology*, 5 (1972), 189–204. J. Bylebyl argues that 'it becomes highly unlikely that Harvey did not know of the work of Cesalpino'. See J. Bylebyl, 'Cesalpino and Harvey on the portal circulation', in Allen G. Debus, ed., *Science, Medicine and Society in the Renaissance. Essays to honour Walter Pagel*, London, 1972, vol. II, pp. 39–52; 47. But even this is too slender a basis for a digression from the argument of this book.

[42] *Iul. Pacii a Beriga Institutiones logicae*, Cambridge, 1597.

[43] J. Pacius, ed., *Aristotelis Stagiritae, Peripateticorum principis, Naturalis auscultationis libri VIII*, Frankfurt, 1596. In essence this is the first volume of a series dealing with the physical works as a traditional collection. The series continues with *Aristotelis de Caeli lib. IIII de Ortu et interitu II Meteorologorum IIII de Mundo I Parva (ut vocant) Naturalia*, Frankfurt, 1601.

elsewhere the traditional Latin names of Aristotle's *libri naturales* appear to have been seen as unsatisfactory, perhaps because associated with an old-fashioned form of scholarship: the entirely traditional *libri octo physicorum* becomes in Pace's edition *Naturalis auscultationis libri viii*. The new scholarship is partly philological: Pace refers to Johannes Casimir working with Greek manuscripts in Heidelberg, and his own commentary is sprinkled with Greek and references to the old (Greek) Aristotelian commentators. It is an 'analytical' commentary in dealing with the text syllogistically, much in the manner of the scholastics. There are postils, lemmata, *dubia* and division of the text (*primo . . . secundo . . .* ) and no attempt at all to Christianise Aristotle, even on the question of the eternity of the world.[44] Indeed Pace defends Aristotle against those who said that his doctrine of chance contradicted divine providence. Chance, said Pace, was due to the operation of secondary causes, not God's action. In other words Pace 'saves' Aristotle and distances God from the world.[45] It was in an entirely different spirit that Magirus argued that chance *was* the action of God, particularly indeed when any secondary causes were unknown to us.[46]

So Pace's commentary represents one of the new ways of looking at Aristotle. The attention to the Greek text, the use of the old commentators (Ammonius and Philoponus for example), the logical analysis, the replacement of the vulgar old Latin titles are all events happening at the same time as new textbooks were being written in a variety of subjects[47] and when the Portuguese Jesuits were very productive. One religious dimension of this new use of Aristotle is discussed below.

The last thing we need to note about Pace is what he has to say on one means of gaining knowledge. This is not a claim that what Pace said here had any effect on Harvey; it is simply another detail of a natural philosophy contemporary with Harvey, and one that was certainly used by some of those who discussed Harvey's doctrines. It is Pace's report of a technique commonly used in the schools (he says), the *regressus*. This was used when the normal principles of demonstration were unknown. The process was threefold, beginning with reasoning directed to discovering causes from effects. Part of this is the resolution, or analysis, of composite things into first principles. The second stage is a 'negotiation' of the intellect by which the principles so discovered are rendered better known to the mind. The third stage is the reverse of the first, to go from the first principles back to the effects. This is a true demonstration, says Pace, one based on causes, or in Aristotle's phrase, *to dioti*.

---

44 Pacius, *Aristotelis Stagiritae*, p. 420.
45 Ibid., p. 45.
46 Magirus, *Physiologiae* (1642 edn), p. 25.
47 For example Caspar Bartholin, father of Thomas, wrote not only an anatomy textbook, but also one on metaphysics, appended to the Cambridge edn of Magirus' text on natural philosophy.

Another aspect of Paduan Aristotelianism in Harvey's time is that of Cesare Cremonini, another of his teachers.[48] Cremonini was a philosopher, and although he taught medicine as well as philosophy at Padua (from 1590)[49] he disapproved of the anatomy-based rationalism of the Galenic doctor.[50] His revived Aristotelianism – they called him *Aristoteles redivivus*[51] – emphasised the fundamentals of Aristotelian philosophy at the expense of both the theory of medicine and the emerging neoteric philosophy. He even followed Aristotle into areas that got him into trouble with the Inquisition. Cremonini's book on innate heat[52] was not published until 1626 and is defensive in particular against neoteric chemists.[53] The Aristotelian principles of soul, Act and heat – instrumental to the soul and located in the heart[54] – would surely be what Cremonini taught when Harvey was in Padua (and when Harvey came to write on the generation of animals he agreed with Cremonini on the nature of the heat of the blood).[55]

These principles are also precisely what the new philosophers objected to (we shall meet some of them below). And they objected to more: Cremonini's defence of substantial forms was but part of scheme in which the soul, as Form, uses the body instrumentally in its Acts (for example in the senses). 'Act' for Cremonini is a local and *purposeful* motion, a faculty of conserving and perfecting the parts it governs. Nutrition and attraction[56] are parts of such purposeful actions deriving from a *principium*, the soul. Such actions are analogous to the control of the world by the greatest *principium*, God, without whose purpose and attention the world would fly apart into chaos.[57] Lastly, Cremonini interpreted Aristotle in such a way as to decide that a universal is known through the senses from particulars. Although Harvey came to read Aristotle in a similar way, we cannot tell if he had Cremonini's example in mind.

We can now return to the use of Aristotle's animal books in Padua and the nature of Fabricius' programme of 'research' in which they were used. First let us pause and realise how novel this use of the animal books was. We have seen that school natural philosophy was based on the Aristotelian physical, or

---

[48] See C. Schmitt's essay review of R. Frank's book on Harvey in *Isis*, 73, 3, 268 (1982), 432–3.
[49] See *Nouvelle Biographie Universelle (NBU)*, Paris, 1852.
[50] See Bylebyl, 'School of Padua', p. 364.
[51] See G. Whitteridge's edition of Harvey's *De generatione animalium*: W. Harvey, *Disputations Touching the Generation of Animals*, trans. and ed. G. Whitteridge, Oxford, 1981, p. 376 and the editor's note in the index.
[52] C. Cremonini, *Apologia dictorum Aristotelis de Calido Innato*, Venice, 1626, pp. 19–21.
[53] Ibid., pp. 38ff.
[54] Ibid., pp. 19–21.
[55] Harvey, *Generation of Animals*, p. 376: he particularly admires Cremonini's Aristotelianism.
[56] Cremonini, *Apologia*, pp. 24, 33
[57] Ibid., p. 28.

natural works. These *libri naturales* included the work on the soul and other short works – the *parva naturalia* – in aspects of its behaviour, such as perception, memory, sleeping, dreaming, life and death and even respiration. But they did not include the works on animals, although the soul was the principle of animal life. Perhaps this was the case simply because the animal books were too big, for they include the *Historia animalium, De partibus animalium, De generatione animalium* and two works on the motions of animals. But perhaps also it was because these books differ in an important respect from the didactic treatises in which Aristotle lays down the principles and examples of natural motion. The difference is that the animal books, more than the other physical works, represent not a finished doctrine, but a programme of acquiring knowledge.

Let us look at this a little more closely. The *Historia animalium* is a collection of information on the different kinds of animals, their parts and behaviour. It has an empirical air, even sometimes appearing as a collection of anecdotes by travellers and fishermen. But Aristotle is in fact careful to list only those accounts that he knows will later fit into a rational scheme of explanation. All such explanation he withholds for inclusion in *De partibus animalium*. Here it is plain that what he was looking for were the differences between animals that illuminate the special nature of each. He was not looking for or at 'nature' in an abstract or even generalised sense, but at the nature-of-the-thing of each animal. The important question for him was how that nature expressed and perpetuated itself. So the practical questions he asked related to the embryological development of the 'nature' of the animal and how the adult reproduced itself. Maintenance of the individual was an important part of the perpetuation of the kind, and Aristotle routinely asked questions about the organs of nutrition. Locomotion followed as a means of achieving nutrition and generation.

Aristotle's answers to these questions were of the general kind that the nature of an animal used the available material to the best advantage for that animal. A well-known example is that animals whose hard material is partly used in horns cannot have a full set of teeth and consequently need a more elaborate digestive system. But Aristotle was aware that in many cases information was simply too sketchy for the philosopher to come to conclusions. What he is doing in the animal books, then, is to set up a scheme whereby such causal knowledge about the purposes of the animal's nature can be generated when information about their parts and behaviour becomes available: the *Historia animalium* is the repository of selected empirical facts and *De partibus animalium* begins a causal account of the differences between the parts of animals which is continued, in line with Aristotle's interest in the nature-of-the-animal, into the generation and the motion of animals.

In other words, Aristotle's animal books represent one of the Lyceum's research programmes. This seems to have been newly recognised in the Padua of Harvey's time. Although the practice of natural philosophy in the Middle Ages threw up disputed questions in abundance, it did not have what we would recognise as a 'research' component, with the expectation that new knowledge could be regularly generated. A second source for the notion of a research programme in Padua was the agreement among anatomists after Vesalius that knowledge of the human body could be refined and added to (some of them produced monographs on particular parts of the body).

It is argued here that Harvey's programme of 'research' which he called into operation when faced with a particular anatomical problem (we shall meet it below) was derived ultimately from Aristotle. Because this book is about William Harvey's natural philosophy, and because 'natural philosophy' is being used here in a strict sense, it is necessary to be clear about what was happening at this important period in Padua. The teaching of school natural philosophy – the physical principles and examples of the *libri naturales* – included the commentaries of the masters and so could range widely from Aristotle's texts. But we cannot include the animal books in school natural philosophy. They were rarely specified by statute; they were being taught by Fabricius, a teacher of medicine, to medical students and not in the arts course; they represented a programme for the generation of knowledge, not didactic texts for bachelors hoping to become masters; and they were probably not being taught in this way anywhere else. Even negatively, when school natural philosophy came to be attacked, it was for its physical principles, not for the teleology of the animal books. Harvey adopted the programme of the animal books; and in the natural philosophy that resulted, he extended the traditional techniques of acquiring and validating knowledge (those of the disputation and commentary) to the parts, differences and causes of animals.

It seems clear that Harvey's model was his teacher in Padua, Fabricius of Aquapendente. Fabricius developed in Padua what has been called the 'Aristotle project'.[58] Fabricius' programme of 'research' was directed towards 'an account of the structure of the whole animal', *Totius animalis fabricae theatrum*. By *theatrum* he meant, like the anatomist Bauhin, a collective display. It was a display for which Fabricius constructed a physical theatre, the first permanent anatomy theatre, designed to allow as many people as possible to view the dissection at the same time. The *theatrum* 'of the whole animal fabric' was in Fabricius' case much more than a display of structure and more indeed than a display of *human* structure. Like Harvey, Fabricius saw that the anatomy of his time had been begun by Vesalius; but Fabricius saw also that

---

[58] See A. R. Cunningham, 'Fabricius and the "Aristotle Project" in anatomical teaching and research in Padua', in *The Medical Renaissance of the Sixteenth Century*, ed. A. Wear, R. K. French and I. Lonie, Cambridge University Press, 1985, pp. 195–222.

Vesalius' work had been vitiated by the passion of his attack on Galen. It was not that Vesalius had 'broken faith' with Galen, as other anatomists claimed; for Fabricius Vesalius' fault was that his pursuit of Galen had limited his attention to *structure*. Fabricius saw his own task as going beyond the minor improvers of Vesalius – Colombo, Falloppio (Fabricius' teacher), Eustachio and Jasolino – and supplying what was missing, an account of the *action and use* of the parts. But this account was not to be limited, as Galen's had been, to the human body, and was to be extended to animals. This was not comparative anatomy, in the way Galen the doctor had used animals, but was an exercise in natural philosophy, searching, as Aristotle had searched, for structure-and-function in 'the animal'.

The fullest expression of Fabricius' programme is found in his *On Speech and its Instruments*. The title itself, like those of the works on vision (*De oculo, visus organo*), on voice and hearing, and on the 'speech' of animals, on respiration (*De respiratione, et ejus instrumentis*) and on the local motion of animals, shows that he chose a function and explored the organs that served it. It is noteworthy that the function he chose was at a high level of complexity, needing several organs for its fulfilment. This goes beyond the traditional concerns of anatomy with the structure of the similar and organic parts and the 'action' of the similar parts and 'use' of each of the organs. Fabricius' concern was in fact to begin with *historia*, that is, dissection and description (including the qualitative nature of the parts). This is what he believed was Aristotle's purpose in the *History of Animals* and Galen's in the *Anatomical Procedures*. The next stage in the programme for Fabricius was to give an account of 'action' (or sometimes 'use'),[59] as Aristotle had done in *On the Soul* and *The Generation of Animals*, and Galen in *On the Natural Faculties*. Use, said Fabricius, was elicited from structure 'as from a very rich fountain'. Fabricius' *historia* is closer to Aristotle's rather than Galen's in being concerned with the dissection and description of a range of animals rather than only with man. Fabricius wanted to know, for example, what kind of thing a stomach was. He investigated a number of animals and, following Aristotle's technique, sought to explain how the variety of structure was correlated with the different diets, habits and dentition of the different animals. The final stage was the discovery of 'utility', the (Aristotelian) final cause of the organ. The final cause, like speech, respiration or local motion then became the organising principle of Fabricius' exposition. As we have seen, this final cause or utility may involve several organs and so is at a higher level than simple 'organic' use.

Fabricius' 'new Aristotle' is the Aristotle of the animal books and clearly (because the animal books were not statutory components of natural

---

[59] H. Fabricius, *De omento*, in the *Opera omnia anatomica*, Leipzig, 1687.

philosophy) Fabricius thought he was extending natural philosophy. The kind of reasons he used and the conclusions he came to were much more Aristotelian than Galenic. Galen's world, for example in *On the Use of the Parts*, was a providential created world in which the subject-matter that he claims will be of interest to philosophers is close to a natural theology which reveals the success of a divine nature (which is not far removed from a Platonic demiurge) in handling recalcitrant matter. Fabricius in contrast is concerned with Aristotle's *physis*. Fabricius wants to find rules that govern the variation seen in the same organ in different animals. His method is to construct inductive syllogisms to discover significant relationships between related organs in animals (for example between the stomach, teeth and horns of ruminants). Some relationships, he says, are simply accidental correlations, and should be disregarded (such as the true but not significant observation that all animals with kidneys also have a head). Where correlations are significant for Fabricius, it is because they reveal the causes of things. These are the four causes of Aristotle's *physis*, the nature-of-the-thing, not the providential and wise actions of 'nature'. The end result of Fabricius' method is, then, to produce *causal* knowledge of a part. According to Aristotle only causal knowledge is true knowledge, true *scientia*. In this way Fabricius has 'proved' his case. His search has produced universals, the what-it-is-to-be-an-organ, which lies behind the particulars of observation (how the organ varies in each animal).[60]

Fabricius also brought his natural philosophy newly into line with medicine. The differences between the philosophers and the physicians had since the Middle Ages been a rich source of disputed questions; Fabricius seems to have selected anatomy as the field where the two disciplines most satisfactorily met. Anatomy, he said, was a perfect goal of natural philosophy, and was also the basis of medicine.[61]

### Harvey's programme in practice

Harvey adopted at least three major points from Fabricius, the 'new Aristotle', the emphasis on 'utility' and the search for the identity of organs among animals. We shall look at these in more detail when considering Harvey's anatomical lectures. Here we can discover more about his own 'Aristotle programme' by looking at what he wrote on the motions of animals: *De motu*

---

[60] It would be fanciful to suppose that the similarities between Fabricius' method and the *regressus* of Pace, mentioned above, are due to any specific borrowing. It may well however be somehow related to the new way of looking at Aristotle that is evident in Padua.

[61] On Fabricius see also A. Pazzini, 'William Harvey, disciple of Girolamo Fabrizi d'Acquapendente and the Paduan school', *Journal of the History of Medicine*, 12 (1957), 197–201.

*locali animalium.*[62] Harvey's notes on this topic seem related to, and were perhaps intended as an introduction to, his lectures on the anatomy of the muscles of man. Harvey can thus be seen, like Fabricius, to be bringing natural philosophy closer to a medical, Galenic field, for Harvey's treatment in these general considerations is very Aristotelian. Indeed what makes this a programme of *research* is that Aristotle, although having written on the motion of animals, was ignorant of the nerves, did not think of the muscles as contractile and gave an account of the source of animal motion that was difficult to reconcile with Galen's sophisticated vivisectional demonstrations of the relationship of nerves and muscles.

Harvey's problem was therefore to bring Aristotelian physical principles to bear on an area well marked out in the medical literature. He does so in a characteristic way. The first six chapters comment on Aristotle's doctrine of motion and the movement of animals. Harvey begins with an account of motion that relies on the *Physics*. It is *physis*, Harvey's 'nature', that is the source of all motion. Aristotle's explanation of animal motion relies on the general principle of the relationship between the unmoved mover and the moved. The nature of the animal desires the Good, and the Good acts as the unmoved mover that attracts the animal. So Harvey has selected a level of explanation that is not vitiated by Aristotle's ignorance of nerve or even muscle. And Harvey can bring his natural philosophy closer to medicine by conflating the Aristotelian notion of pursuit of Good and avoidance of Evil with the Galenic notion of the Naturals and the Contranaturals.[63]

There is another way too in which Harvey brings his natural philosophy closer to medicine, although not deliberately. When Harvey used the Latin term *natura* he meant what other Englishmen meant in the seventeenth century: very largely 'nature' in the sense we use it today, as 'the natural world' or 'mother nature' as a personalised organising and productive principle. It is in this sense that *natura* was used to provide a Latin translation of Galen's *demiourgos*, 'nature' or the creator of the body. But Aristotle's *physis* was the nature-of-a-thing, not a generalised or personalised principle. It was for Aristotle the nature of the *animal* that desired what was good and avoided what was evil for that animal. In this way Harvey is interpreting Aristotle in a way consistent with seventeenth-century medicine.[64]

---

[62] W. Harvey, *De motu locali animalium 1627*, ed. and trans. by G. Whitteridge, Cambridge, 1979.

[63] The 'naturals' were the components and actions of the body, while the 'contranaturals' were those things that disturbed them.

[64] When Harvey, discussing the disposition of the guts, says 'Natura romidg as she can best stow, as in ships propter motus agilitatem', it is clear that he is using *natura* in Galen's personalised sense, despite Harvey's own Aristotelianism and Aristotle's meaning of *Physis*. See G. Whitteridge, ed. and transl., *The Anatomical Lectures of William Harvey*, London, 1964, p. 72.

Harvey's discussion does not introduce the notion of 'muscle' – in man and the animals – until the conclusion of chapter 6. Having identified the source of animal motion Harvey then goes on to discuss the nature of 'muscle' (and to try to demonstrate that Aristotle in fact knew such structures). Harvey moves through the parts of anatomy, beginning with *historia*, the parts of muscle (he follows an *accessus*-style list of observables) and proceeding with the *actio* of muscle, which is contraction or tonic motion. The result of contraction is *usus*, or first-order function, the motion of bone (or perhaps the closing of a sphincter). 'Utility' is the specific function of one or a group of muscles that results in a motion useful for the animal. This hierarchy is not very different from that of Fabricius which we met above.

Another feature of Harvey's natural philosophy is the absence of natural-theological arguments. Harvey did not share Galen's abundant wonder at the skill of a creator, or at least he did not express it when arguing about the action of the heart and the motion of the blood. Nor did he express the feeling shown by others[65] of being in a theatre of creation, able to read the nature of the Creator from the objects of creation. Unlike most other anatomists, he did not put in first place a religious justification of anatomy. The reason is no doubt that Harvey adopted what he saw as Aristotle's method in the books on animals. Aristotle's world was eternal, and did not reflect a creator; his natural philosophy was a search for causes within the operations of the nature of things.

---

[65] For example by the Protestant natural historians.

# 4    The anatomy lectures and the circulation

On his return to England from Padua, Harvey set about building a career. He first needed membership of the College of Physicians, which controlled the practice of internal medicine in London. He accordingly applied to the college in 1603 and in the next year became a licentiate. In 1604, too, he married a girl whose father was well placed to help Harvey in his career. But his father-in-law, after failing to secure Harvey at post at court, died in 1605.[1] But by the time Harvey was a Fellow of the College he had secured enough influence at court to secure (in 1609) the position of physician to St Bartholomew's Hospital. Harvey also pursued his career in the college with vigour, becoming a censor for the first time in 1614 and an elect before he published his first book. Like the rest of the Harveys, William was able, energetic and did not look down his nose at the material rewards of life. This was important, for it was only by having the financial wherewithal and leisure that Harvey could put his research programme into practice.

Another move made by Harvey to further his career was to accept in 1615 the position of Lumleian lecturer in the college. This was a stipendiary position, and it had been intended by Lord Lumley, in setting up the lectureship in 1582, that the lecturer should receive the equivalent of a university stipend. Harvey no doubt welcomed the money and probably too the opportunity of pursuing human anatomy on an Aristotelian–Fabrician model. This seems to be why he turned the lectures, founded to improve the practice of surgery and to be directed partly in English to surgeons, into philosophical lectures for physicians. There is no evidence that Harvey lectured on the specified surgical texts, and he later styled himself 'professor of anatomy' in the college. What was most important for him was the five-day dissection of the body in the winter that followed the year's lectures.

Because the college had another anatomical demonstration, it was arranged

---

[1] Harvey married Elizabeth Browne, daughter of Dr Lancelot Browne, who had been physician to Queen Elizabeth and was now physician to James. While Lancelot named his daughter after his queen, he named his son after the prince of professional physicians and called him Galen Browne. See Sir Geoffrey Keynes, *The Life of William Harvey*, Oxford, 1966 (repr. 1978), p. 48.

that this should alternate with the Lumleian, and Harvey gave his lectures first in 1616, again in 1618 and so on for a good part of the twenty-eight years for which he held the post. Harvey was not content – as lecturers regrettably often can be – to repeat his lectures year after year, but modified them after they had been heard and commented upon. This was of the greatest significance, as we shall see.

We have no reason to suppose that Harvey, as a recently appointed lecturer composing a course of lectures, should have had a special interest in the heart. It was, to be sure, an important organ of the body in the normal run of things, the fundamental organ for the Aristotelians and one of the three fundamental organs for the Galenists. The differences between the philosophers and the physicians on this point had indeed been a useful source of *dubia* for school disputations since Alfred of Shareshill, one of the first Aristotelian commentators, wrote a *De motu cordis* at the end of the twelfth century.[2] Another was written by Aquinas;[3] and more characteristic of Harvey's time, over three centuries later, André du Laurens,[4] one of Harvey's preferred authors, added a section of disputed questions, 'controversies' to each of his anatomical descriptions, no doubt also for their academic usefulness. It was not an uncommon practice.[5]

So Harvey too had to address himself to disputed questions. Not to have done so would have been to have failed to meet his audience's expectations. They too were educated, and knew the proper academic format and what it was to discuss a question properly. Another disputed question which must have been closer to his interests was: what *kind* of motion does the heart have? Galen had shown that voluntary motion depended on nerves and muscles. Even respiration, although largely automatic, could be modified by the will, and again some of Galen's most spectacular vivisections were concerned with the

---

[2] C. S. Barach, ed., *Excerpta e libro Alfredi Anglici de motu cordis item Costa-Ben-Lucae de differentia animae et spiritus*, Innsbruck, 1878/Frankfurt 1968. These two texts were part of formal philosophy as taught in the mid-thirteenth century. Their purpose was to clarify what was to be understood in a Christian context in a variety of ancient authors, most notably Aristotle and Galen, by such terms as 'spirit' and 'soul' and to explain their workings in the body, especially the heart. That Alfredus Anglicus or 'of Sarashel' was really 'of Shareshill' is argued by J. K. Otte, 'The life and times of Alfredus Anglicus', *Viator*, 3 (1972), 275–91. Otte accepts 'Shareshull' from Russell, but the modern name of the place is Shareshill, in Staffordshire.

[3] See V. R. Larkin, 'St Thomas Aquinas on the motion of the heart', *Journal of the History of Medicine*, 15 (1960), 22–30.

[4] A. Laurentius (du Laurens), *Opera anatomica*, Hanau, 1595; *Historia anatomica humani corporis*, Frankfurt, 1599. Both books contain – separate from and following the descriptive text – *controversiae* or *commentatiora*, consisting of *quaestiones*. *Quaestio* 10 of the *Opera anatomica* (p. 442) concerns the motion of the heart, and follows the established pattern: only after subjecting the opinions of Aristotle and Averroes to a proposition–objection–solution discussion does du Laurens give his own opinion, which is then developed in the same way.

[5] Cf. T. Knobloch, *Disputationes anatomicae et psychologiae*, n.p., 1612.

nervous and muscular control of respiration. But in the Galenic scheme of things the heart expanded forcibly and did not contract like a muscle, and did not appear to have nerves that controlled its action from some other centre (as voluntary muscles did). The heart was therefore not a muscle. The universities traditionally disputed, therefore, whether the heart had 'natural' or 'vital' motion, that is, they asked from what faculty of the soul its motion came.

It is unlikely that Harvey was seeking an answer to this question (but we shall see that it was of interest to those who reacted to his work). Rather, Harvey would have wanted in an Aristotelian way to give an account of the heart's action as part of proper knowledge about it.[6] He probably anticipated no problems. Harvey duly began his account of the heart (with the pericardium as its first visible part) and moved on to its size, shape, use, usefulness and dignity, ending with problems and observations.[7] He was, in other words, employing a form of the anatomical *accessus*[8] which asked the same routine questions of all bodily parts in turn. We have seen that this had been a usual procedure with anatomists since Mondino. In putting problems and observations in last place, Harvey was following in addition the procedure of academic commentary, the last stage of whose complex structure was the treatment of *dubia* in a disputational way. We have seen that it was *only* at this point that refutation or confirmation could be aided by an appeal to sensory experience – Harvey's 'observation'. (Sometimes the arguments in favour of an observed anatomical novelty served to resolve the whole disputed question.)

When we know this structure of exposition, we can see more clearly what it was to be an anatomical lecturer in the early seventeenth century. Although in a sense Harvey was giving his audience his own opinion throughout the lectures it was mostly an opinion that agreed with one or more of the authorities he was citing; but he also had to give opinions with which he did not agree. This was partly because the job of a commentator was to acquaint his audience with the literature of the field, and partly because the disputational–commentarial mode of exposition required the destruction of false opinions in the process of establishing true opinions. On much rarer occasions Harvey gave his audience opinions which were unique to him (the 'observations' mentioned

6  See also A. R. Cunningham, 'William Harvey: the discovery of the circulation of the blood', in *Man Masters Nature*, ed. Roy Porter, London, 1985, pp. 65–76.
7  W. Harvey, *Praelectiones anatomiae universalis*, facsimile edn of Harvey's MS. for the Royal College of Physicians, 1886, p. 72 (the pagination of Harvey's MS. is followed); G. Whitteridge, ed. and trans., *The Anatomical Lectures of William Harvey*, Edinburgh and London, 1964, p. 244.
8  Renaissance anatomists commonly looked for six visible *occasiones* in the body that had been listed by John of Alexandria in his commentary on Galen's *De sectis*. This literary technique was a form of *accessus* derived from the tradition of Aristotelian commentary; it came to be applied to the physical process of dissection. See R. K. French, 'A note on the anatomical *accessus* of the middle ages', *Medical History*, 23 (1979), 461–8.

above). But how was he able to convince his audience? He was not an 'author', *auctor*, like Galen or Aristotle in whose ancient name lay 'authority', *auctoritas*, but more akin to a university regent master, merely interpreting a text through commentary. To be without authority yet to convince an audience Harvey had to stick closely to accepted and rigorous modes of presentation and argument. It was in this process that his first *dubium* about the motion of the heart became a book about the circulation of the blood.

Harvey the lecturer 'determined' some frequent questions about the heart much as a master settled a disputation between students. His Determinations in this pre-circulatory period were largely in favour of the Aristotelian position: the veins do not arise in, or function from, the liver (but from the heart); the heart is the centre of heat in the body, and its interventricular septum is not porous.[9] Likewise in distinguishing 'use' from 'usefulness' of the heart, Harvey was in an unexceptional way pointing to the Aristotelian doctrine that true knowledge of a part depends on a knowledge of its function, as well as to the Galenic distinction between the simple qualitative 'action' of a part and its purposeful 'use' in the co-ordinated activity of the whole body.[10]

But Harvey was doing more than dealing with a *dubium* when considering the question of diastole and systole. He left it until last in his discussion of the heart, so it concerned his own observations rather than the confirmation of someone else's. His audience would have expected some novelty. Harvey, no doubt mindful of Aristotle's dictum that knowledge of a part rests upon knowledge of its function, had prepared for the lectures by performing vivisections. Perhaps too he had in mind the differing accounts given of the heartbeat by Aristotle and Galen. At all events, what he found when he observed the heart of living animals was not at first at all helpful to a man who wanted to give a good lecture. Instead of expanding and contracting as the heart ought to have done in diastole and systole respectively, it instead rose up with a vigorous motion and then relaxed, changing shape, but without any obvious change in size. He watched, and felt, a beating heart for hours, but was unable to make up his mind in which of these two motions the heart was expanding.

Unable to succeed by sensory observation, Harvey approached the matter from theory. Again, the doctrine that every organ had its own Action and Use meant that mobile organs had a characteristic motion, their own, proper motion by which they achieved their use of function (and which was distinguished from *common* motions shared with others, for example when the whole animal moved, and from *accidental* motions received from elsewhere). Of the two motions it seemed clear to Harvey that the vigorous erection of the heart was

[9] *Praelectiones*, p. 74.
[10] See for example the discussion by E. T. May in her translation of Galen's *On the Usefulness of the Parts of the Body*, 2 vols., Cornell University Press, 1968; vol I, p. 9 and the text there cited.

its characteristic act (and, by implication, that the period of relaxation was 'accidental'). Because Galen has taught that diastole was vigorous, the common opinion was, as Harvey told his audience, that the heart's forceful erection, during which it seems to strike the wall of the chest, was expansion, diastole (see figs. 7 and 8).[11]

Harvey had finally made up his mind that the common opinion was in fact wrong, and that the heart was undergoing a forcible contraction, systole, as it sprang up. In presenting this conclusion to his audience Harvey, for the reasons we have discussed, proceeded carefully. In order that this anatomical novelty could be discussed with proper academic rigour, he put it forward in the form of a proposition, to be understood and judged by his audience, 'quare vobis cernendum et judicandum proponam', 'whereby I offer it to you to perceive and judge'. In expressing himself in this way, Harvey was doing more than merely inviting his audience to 'see for themselves' (he was in no position to enable them to see forceful systole in the cadaver) and was putting to them what amounted to a *practical* proposition. As we have seen, anatomists for some time had recognised that there could be no strict logical demonstrative proof of an anatomical statement, but at the same time, because they were men of the schools and were addressing colleagues, they felt the need of some kind of recognisable confirmatory procedure. Such 'physical logic' often took the form of autopsy before a select audience. Just as Galen had performed vivisectional experiments before named and distinguished citizens of Rome,[12] so as we have seen Renaissance anatomists demonstrated their anatomical discoveries to a distinguished audience, some of whose names appear in the subsequent anatomy texts for the purpose of validating the anatomist's discoveries.[13] The procedure was similar – as perhaps hinted in Harvey's words – to the presentation of a case to a jury. The principle of the jury in Roman law was to collect together men with special knowledge of the facts of the case. To convince them, as to convince the anatomist's distinguished audience, was to 'prove' one's case. Finally, both procedures have points of similarity to the university disputation, in which assertions and counter-assertions are made and the matter is settled by the *praeses* – usually the master in charge – in front of an audience. All three are procedures in which someone is seeking to convince others of his truth. If he succeeds, then to a greater or lesser extent a consensus

[11] *Praelectiones*, p. 77.
[12] Galen, *On Anatomical Procedures*, trans. C. Singer, Oxford University Press, 1956, pp. 2, 212 (*Claudii Galeni Opera Omnia*, ed. D. C. G. Kühn, vol. II, Leipzig, 1821–33, pp. 218, 667); *De praecognitione*, chap. 5 (in the *quarta classis* of the Junta edition of the *Opera*, Venice, 1625, p. 215v).
[13] For these purposes, for example, Niccolo Massa names nine habitual and notable observers of his dissections: N. Massa, *Anatomiae liber introductorius*, Venice, 1559, p. 10. Likewise Benedetti lists the knights, senators and patricians attending: A. Benedictus, *Anatomice, sive de Historia corporis humani libri quinque*, Strasburg, 1528.

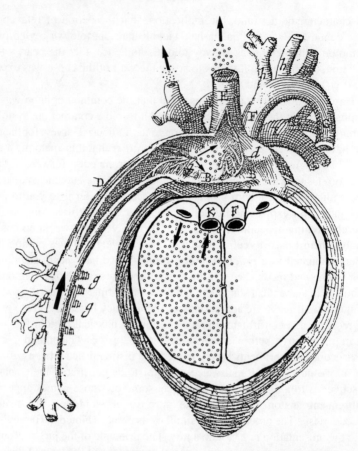

Fig. 7. The Galenic heart (i).

Galen believed that venous blood, produced in the liver, moved from there to the heart by way of the lower vena cava, D. From the right auricle, B, some of the blood passed along the upper vena cava, E, in order to nourish all parts of the body. The remainder of the venous blood passed from the auricle into the right ventricle (traditionally pictured here as seen in dissection, with right and left reversed). Galen held that the ventricle filled itself by forceful expansion, and the venous blood is represented here in the full ventricle by small circles. Note that this side of the heart was entirely nutritive in function. In addition to the venous blood of the vena cava and auricle, the ventricle further concocted and refined its contained blood, which left the heart in the arterial vein, KK, to nourish the lungs. A little blood filtered through the holes in the interventricular system, but otherwise the right-hand side of the heart was a self-contained nutritive system of veins and cavities linking the source to the destination of venous blood.

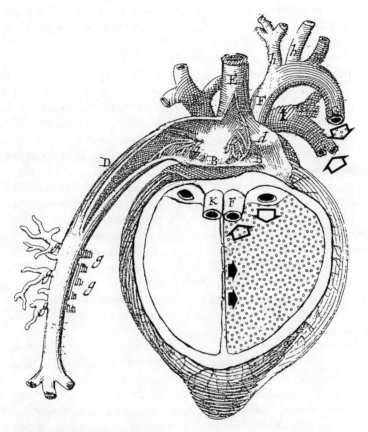

Fig. 8. The Galenic heart (ii).
In contrast to fig. 7, the left-hand side of the forcibly expanding heart, according to Galen, drew in air from the lungs through the venous artery, L. There, by the exercise of the vital faculty, the venous blood crossing the septum and the incoming air were concocted to form arterial blood, which was hot and full of vital spirits. Arterial blood left the left ventricle by way of the aorta, FF, to vivify and warm all parts of the body. This side of the heart was a system of arteries and cavities serving the separate function of respiration: the transmission of the spirit of the air to the parts. In the case of nutrition as well as respiration the prime force moving the fluids was attraction, whether formally a faculty of the soul or some kind of *fuga vacui*.

has been achieved and his subject has been changed a little. It is in this sense that Harvey and the anatomists sought 'understanding and judgment' from their audiences.

Harvey's proposition was 'It seems to be that what they call "diastole" [i.e. erection] is rather contraction.'[14] It followed that 'they' had defined 'diastole' wrongly, said Harvey. As we would expect in the commentary form, Harvey next puts the opposing views. The first is that of those who say that the heart gets bigger in erection by the expansion of its flesh. The second is that of Colombo, whose physical description of events was essentially the same as Harvey's, but with the labels 'diastole' and 'systole' reversed. Harvey used these different views to show the practical difficulties of settling the question. By reversing Colombo's use of the terms 'diastole' and 'systole' Harvey then achieves a *resolutio* of the question and produces four corollaries: the contracting heart becomes hard; the hardness and motion of the contracting heart make it feel bigger to the touch;[15] the arterial pulse is felt during the erection of the heart; the auricles clearly forcibly contract as they eject blood into the ventricles.[16] Finally he brings forward further evidence from vivisection: the ventricles of the heart continue to beat when separated from the auricles, the (simpler) hearts of fish clearly become smaller in ejecting blood and finally, blood flows out, *profluit*, from a perforated ventricle during erection of the heart.

This then was Harvey's earliest statement about the forceful systole. He had come to this conclusion before writing out the notes for his lectures, and he had compared it with the common opinion and with Colombo's. Having written out the notes and probably having given some of the lectures for the first time, Harvey made some additions to the notes, indicating that he was continuing to think about his new doctrine, and probably also continuing to do more vivisections. On the back of folio 78 of the notes he inserted a question about the possible pulsation of the pulmonary artery. In Galenic theory this was a vein, albeit one that looked like an artery, and so did not pulsate with arterial pulse, which was carried, according to Galen, along the arterial coats. (In contemporary terminology it was the *vena arteriosa*, the 'arterial vein'.) But if Harvey's new idea was right, then the heart in systole not only expelled blood

---

[14] 'videtur mihi potius aut quum appellat diastolen esse Contractionem cordis et proinde male definitam aut X esse quae dicunt', *Praelectiones*, p. 77. Whitteridge (Harvey, *Anatomical Lectures*), observes that Harvey's X indicates his disagreement.

[15] '2o. ex Molli enim fit durum ut nisi dum Erigitur non sentitur vel Maior Apparet', *Praelectiones*, p. 77v. Whitteridge (Harvey, *Anatomical Lectures*, p. 267) renders *vel* as *vena*, which destroys the sense.

[16] Since Harvey's use of Colombo's passage is partly to show the difficulty of describing the heartbeat, there is no need to assume that in it *systole* is a misprint for *diastole*, as Whitteridge does in arguing that Colombo, like Harvey, had an essentially modern view of the heartbeat. See G. Whitteridge, *William Harvey and the Circulation of the Blood*, London, 1971, p. 71.

forcibly into the aorta, but very likely also into the pulmonary artery. This note reads like a reminder to himself to find out, and contains hints on how to do so. His technique was to be vivisection, by which Vesalius and Colombo had made observations on the pulse.

Harvey clearly acted on his own suggestion and conducted more vivisections. His conclusion – that the pulmonary artery does pulsate – was inserted later into the completed notes, between the lines at the point where he had originally noted that the blood flows from a perforated heart during its erection. Indeed, to the original *profluit* he now added the stronger *prosilit*, 'leaps out', to emphasise the force of the emerging blood. A few words later he added a new sentence: 'ex arteriis prosilit et ex vena arteriosa', 'blood leaps from the arteries and from the arterial vein' (see fig. 9). So clearly in new experiments he had punctured arteries and the 'arterial vein' and found that blood sprang from both. This comes shortly after his statement that the pulse is felt in the arteries at the moment – the erection of the heart – when blood is expelled from the heart in forceful systole. The conclusion is clear: the pulse is *caused* by the forceful ejection of blood into the arteries, including the pulmonary artery, during systole of the heart.

Although we cannot be certain, it seems likely that it was in response to interest in, and opposition to, his notion of forceful systole, that Harvey performed these later experiments. Certainly it was after completing the notes and most likely after having given the course of lectures for the first time. We know that much later on in the cycle of lectures, Harvey met and overcame objections to the circulation, and it seems very likely that his lectures provided the usual academic opportunities for *dubia* and *quaestiones* to be disputed. We should also remember that Harvey prepared his case with great care, using a model of academic procedure that was not only prepared for challenge, but which could hardly convince his audience in the absence of challenge. To put it another way, Harvey could not establish his own opinions unless there were others to destroy: some of these he incorporates and destroys, as a device to convince, in his own text; and it would be unlikely that the learned minds listening to him in the college could not find further objections.

All this is clear when Harvey, having noted down the results of the vivisections mentioned above, turned a fresh page and announced his view of the heartbeat, and now the pulse, as a major new discovery.[17] It overcomes an error, he said, that had been current for a very long time, during which it had been discussed by very great men. It is not only that everyone had previously been wrong about diastole and ignorant of the forceful systole, but that they had with Galen misconceived the nature of the pulse. Taking the pulse of course was a very important diagnostic technique, and Harvey's new doctrine carried

[17] *Praelectiones*, p. 78r.

important implications (which he does not mention) for the practice of medicine. Harvey clearly saw the radical nature of his doctrine of the pulse and, as he had done in the case of the forceful systole, in order to convince his audience he was obliged to proceed in the strictest way. Harvey uses the phrase *obsignatis tabulis* to indicate this strict procedure. It is a phrase used by Cicero and Gellius to mean 'with properly attested evidence' or 'in strict accordance with proper procedures'. For Harvey this meant at the lowest level that the doctrine had been accessible to school dialectic, and he accordingly presents his case in the form of propositions. They are essentially what we have seen already about the forceful systole as the heart's *propria motio*, but to them is added the important proposition that during this motion blood is expelled from the heart into the arteries. The pulse of the arteries is therefore caused by the influx of blood, just as a glove may be inflated by blowing into it: 'as in a glove', said Harvey, breaking into English. It follows, according to Harvey, that Erasistratus' account of the heartbeat and pulse is to be preferred to Galen's: the pulse is not carried as a wave of expansion along the arterial coats (and that Galen's experiment to prove it was must have been wrong).

Harvey's notes for his lectures are not of course verbatim and are often little more than topic-headings. We cannot tell, therefore, what *obsignatis tabulis* meant in detail. But the formality of Harvey's treatment is apparent in his numbering of the supporting arguments. He has ten of them, four drawn from observation and six from reason. The point of numbering them was to emphasise that each was part of a series and that therefore, as in academic practice, anyone attempting a refutation of the single thesis would need to refute, piecemeal, the ten supporting arguments. (It was a contemporary practice for readers to number the arguments they found important in another author's text, even if the author had not done so himself.)

Harvey's formal arguments include those we have met above, and they add to them the observational argument that the cardiac valves prevent a reflux of

Fig. 9. The Harveian heart.
Harvey's first thesis was that the action of the heart was forcible contraction, expelling blood through the aorta, OO. It therefore seemed as though the pulse was due to the motion of blood, and was not a wave of expansion carried down the arterial coats, as Galen had said. When Harvey looked for and found a pulse also in the arterial vein, NN, he judged that this too was caused by expulsion of blood from the heart. He satisfied himself of this by puncturing the vessel and seeing that blood sprang from it with some force. But this meant that the arterial 'vein' was unlike any other vein in pulsating, and both sides of the heart were now seen to generate a pulse. Now the arterial vein not only looked like an artery but acted as one. The fluids in the Harveian heart moved not by attraction but by force: in Harvey's image, like blowing into a glove.

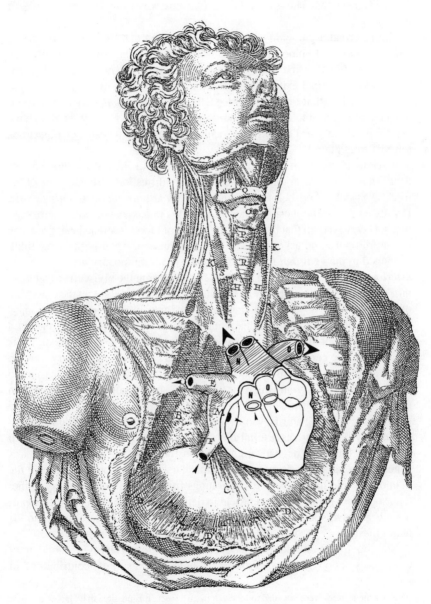

Fig. 9

blood from the arteries to the heart and that the arteries have thick walls (we can guess that Harvey explained that this was to resist the pressure of blood).

These formal arguments *include* the observation that the pulmonary artery pulsates, and emits blood through a wound while doing so. Clearly Harvey wrote this *after* the first draft of the earlier part of the notes, after the subsequent vivisectional experiments, and after the insertion of the results of the experiments into that first draft. Indeed, the *obsignatis tabulis* argument would not have been possible without those experiments, which Harvey seems to have been running in parallel with the lectures, perhaps as a result of objections raised during them.[18]

It seems likely, then, that Harvey's description of the pulse (the object of the *obsignatis tabulis* arguments) was a later modification of the doctrine of the forceful systole. And before he wound up his arguments *obsignatis tabulis*, Harvey extended the thesis further, to include the passage of blood across the lungs. Having shown that the forceful ejection of blood from the heart produces the arterial pulse, he asked himself, as we have seen, whether the same thing happened to the vein *that looks like an artery*, our pulmonary artery, his *vena arteriosa*. He had Colombo in mind when performing the vivisection that gave him his answer; but Colombo had been interested in the vessel on the other side of the heart, the *arteria venosa*, the artery that looks like a vein, our pulmonary vein. Colombo's argument at this point was to prove that spirit was generated in the lungs, not the left ventricle of the heart, as in Galenic theory. His vivisectional experiment was therefore to puncture the pulmonary vein to discover its contents. If air or sooty wastes, then it would have been possible to defend Galenic theory, in which air (or at least some quality of air) was drawn down to the left ventricle, and fuliginous vapours, a waste product of the process of producing spirits, were expelled upwards to the lungs. But Colombo found only blood. It was arterial blood and so, to Colombo, full of spirits. It seemed to him that he had amply demonstrated his thesis that spirit was generated in the lungs. It was a minor corollary that the blood he found in the pulmonary vein had come across the lungs from the pulmonary artery, rather than somehow from the left ventricle in defiance of the functional direction of the mitral valve. Colombo adopted the corollary simply to give weight to his major thesis.

Not too much should be made of the idea that Harvey's adoption of Colombo's notion that blood crossed the lungs was a sort of 'contribution' or

---

[18] Since the lectures were intended to be given twice a week, it is possible that Harvey had time to do vivisections while still on the topic of the heart, but he was hardly likely to have time to have done so during the five-day demonstration. On the whole it seems more likely that he made his experiments and modified his lectures in the year between the alternate courses, probably 1617 and 1619.

stepping-stone to Harvey's final discovery of the circulation.[19] There is no evidence that Harvey was interested in Colombo's thesis about the generation of spirits, and as we have seen, he disagreed with Colombo over the identity of diastole and systole. What Colombo's argument confirmed for Harvey was the utility of vivisection and perhaps that the Galenic doctrine of the heartbeat was wrong. In experimentally discovering a pulse in the pulmonary artery, Harvey was not confirming a detail of the pulmonary transit, but was extending his own doctrine that pulsation was due to the forceful injection of blood from the heart into a vessel that now had to be regarded simply as an artery. Harvey was now showing that *both* ventricles of the heart produced his new kind of pulse. As with Colombo, for Harvey the passage of blood across the lungs was a secondary corollary, not the point at issue.

Harvey used the phrase *obsignatis tabulis* at another place in the lectures, close to the beginning, where he announces the 'canons of general anatomy'. These canons are partly practical advice for conducting an anatomy expeditiously (begin with the abdomen, show as much in one demonstration as possible, do not show by dissection what can be shown without it) and partly an account of the purposes of anatomy. The overall purpose of anatomy, said Harvey, was to generate knowledge of the parts of the body, a knowledge of interest in itself for the philosopher and of practical utility to the physician. It was knowledge too that provided for the refutation of errors and the solution of problems: dissection illustrated and confirmed established knowledge, and provided the opportunity of making discoveries. Personal knowledge, added Harvey, was to be increased by re-thinking one's own opinions and those of others, '*vel obsignatis tabulis in aliis Animalibus agere secundum Socratis regulam* where it is farer written'.[20]

So here, *obsignatis tabulis*, 'in strictest form', is not the formal presentation of a concatenation of arguments that Harvey used in demonstrating the nature of the pulse, but a 'rule of Socrates' to be observed in making investigations into 'other animals'. What is clearly implied is that great care should be used when employing animals in anatomy. But what is the rule of Socrates? And does it help us to understand Harvey's mode of procedure, his natural philosophy?

To find an answer we should start from the fact, well known to historians, that Harvey's use of animals was unusually extensive. The very title page of his book of notes for the anatomy lectures carries a quotation selected by Harvey from Aristotle: 'The inner parts of man are uncertain and unknown wherefore

---

[19] This point is also made by D. Fleming, 'William Harvey and the pulmonary circulation', *Isis*, 46 (1955), 319–27 (re-published in I. B. Cohen, ed., *Studies on William Harvey*, New York, 1981).

[20] *Praelectiones*, p. 4r.

we must consider those parts of other animals which bear any similarity to those of man.' But surely there is something odd about Harvey's choice of quotation? It was well known to anatomists of his time that Aristotle had no opportunity to dissect the human body and indeed that anatomy had progressed a good deal since Aristotle's day. Yet here was Harvey with a human cadaver in front of him and a learned tradition in human anatomy behind him. What ignorance about the insides of man did he need to excuse?

Harvey the philosopher knew that true knowledge of a part included knowledge of its function. His terms *actio, usus* and *utilitates proper quid* were all parts of our 'function', which combined with simple descriptive and morphological *historia* to constitute anatomical knowledge. 'Use', 'function' and 'purpose' in the early seventeenth century included what the organ was *for* – its final cause, and knowledge embodying causes was true, demonstrated knowledge, *scientalis* as the anatomists called it.[21] Knowledge of action, use and purpose among the body's hierarchy of organs could be gained by vivisectional experiments, which could be performed *only on animals*. Half of Harvey's anatomical knowledge of man had to come from non-human sources.

It is implicit in this view of anatomical knowledge that the organs of animals are similar to those of man. Harvey probably derived such an assumption from Aristotle, no doubt by way of Fabricius in the 'Aristotle project' in Padua. It was not Aristotle's or Fabricius' purpose to pursue comparative anatomy, but to enquire into what it was to be an organ, wherever it appeared.[22] This we may call a natural philosophical position, in contrast to the medical position of Galen, for whom animals became increasingly less interesting and useful the more they differed from man.

So, Harvey's business among the animals was to look for the function of the parts. But what 'rule of Socrates' was he using? The clue comes when Harvey again uses the phrase in the anatomy lectures when discussing the variability of the caecum in a wide range of animals, including man. Here he says '*Hinc Socratis regula per similitudinem* in a great print.'[23] It seems certain that Harvey had in mind the passage in the *Republic* where Socrates is proposing a method of enquiry which will render the obscure clear,[24] just as an inscription *in large letters* and close at hand is clearer than one in small and distant letters. Socrates is about to argue that in seeking to gain a knowledge of 'justice' we should look in a city, where by virtue of its size, we can see justice more clearly than in an individual man. What is sought in both cases is, however, similar,

---

[21] See the discussion of du Laurens in chap. 2 above.
[22] Cunningham, 'William Harvey'.
[23] Whitteridge's edn, p. 86. Whitteridge inserts '[should be set up]' in her translation to make sense of Harvey's Latin. This is unnecessary when the Platonic text is considered.
[24] II, 368; for example in the edn of F. Cornford, *The Republic of Plato*, Oxford University Press, 1941, p. 55.

and Harvey's rule of Socrates *per similitudinem* appears thus to be a rule about looking for the same thing in different contexts to see it more clearly.

It is likely that Harvey met this rule of Socrates through Galen, who turned it to medical uses. Harvey was familiar with Galen's *De placitis Hippocratis et Platonis*,[25] and it is here that Galen takes his reader through the simple compare-and-contrast technique that is the *per similitudinem* method.[26] Galen had found it both in the *Republic* and in the Hippocratic surgical works and he links both to a more elaborate double process he saw in the *Phaedrus*. Here, Socrates is searching for the true meaning of 'love', and he first collects together all the varying usages of the term to form a 'single generic term'. Galen calls this process 'synthesis'. Socrates then found that the generic term had natural articulations, which supplied a more satisfactory idea of the meaning of 'love'. Taking the generic term apart to see how its natural parts related to one another was a process Galen calls 'analysis'.

We can now see what Harvey meant by the 'rule of Socrates'. His anatomical knowledge was incomplete without a knowledge of function, which could be found only in animals. Many animals had to be investigated to form a comprehensive composite term for the thing being investigated, in this case the heart. *Per similitudinem* is the search for similarity of function; in Aristotelian terms, the what-it-is-to-be-a-heart. Harvey found that while morphologically the hearts of different animals varied considerably yet in the even more important question of function *all hearts served to eject blood in forceful systole and in so doing generate the pulse* (see fig. 9 on p. 81).

## Disputation and *De motu cordis*

Harvey repeated the anatomy lectures in 1618 and on subsequent occasions. In 1628 he published *De motu cordis*, which contains his account of the circulation of the blood. The moment of discovery surely came while he was thinking on anatomical matters, and almost certainly then, during the course of the lectures. In trying to reconstruct how the discovery came about, we must use evidence from *De motu cordis* and also reflect on the state of Harvey's knowledge during the anatomy lectures.

It is evident from both that Harvey distinguished three components of his 'discovery': the true motion of the heart, the nature of the pulse, and the arteries-to-veins transit of blood, the 'circulation' itself. He had discovered the first two first and announced them to his audience with a considerable

---

[25] W. Harvey, *Exercitatio anatomica de motu cordis et sanguinis in animalibus*, Frankfurt, 1638, p. 31.

[26] Galen, *De Hippocratis et Platonic Placitis*, book 9, chap. 2 (Kühn, *Galeni Opera Omnia*, vol. V, p. 720).

flourish. When he came to write out the final formal account of discoveries, he did not call his book 'On the Circulation of the Blood' but 'An Anatomical Exercise on the *Motion of the Heart and Blood* in Animals'. Its first seven chapters do not mention the circulation and are taken up with establishing what he has demonstrated *obsignatis tabulis* in the anatomy lectures.

This difference between the three components of Harvey's doctrine is the difference between *motus* or *actio* on the one hand and *usus, utilitas* or *functio* on the other; at the beginning of the proemium of *De motu cordis* Harvey says his subject is the 'motion . . . action, use and utility' of the heart and arteries. We have already seen that for Harvey these terms imply a hierarchy of increasingly directed motion, derived not only from Aristotle, but from Galen's distinction between the simple qualitative 'action' of the simple parts of the body and the purposeful function of the organic parts. The simple 'action' or 'motion' of the heart was for Harvey its forceful systole. The *purpose* of this motion was in the first place to produce the pulse, and the circulation followed upon that. To express these higher-level motions, Harvey uses *usus* or something similar. But still the distinction between the pulse and the circulation is maintained, for Harvey even uses *functio* (of the heart) to mean 'pulse' rather than 'circulation'.

So when Harvey referred back (in 1628)[27] to his first announcement, in the anatomy lectures, of the 'simulque motum, et usum cordis, et arteriarum', he had in mind the forceful systole and the nature of the pulse. He certainly may (in 1628) have meant to imply also 'circulation' in *usum*, and that is how the word is normally read by modern historians, for whom the *circulation* is Harvey's topic. But we have seen that his first announcement, *obsignatis tabulis*, was to do only with the systole and pulse. It is also argued above that Harvey as a natural philosopher was investigating in a way that was both Aristotelian and Socratic *what it was to be a heart* in a wide range of animals. This programme of 'research' was completed, but not otherwise changed, when Harvey discovered the circulation of the blood. It was the action of the heart, not the circulation of the blood, that Harvey was at first defending in the anatomy lectures.

It was not a straightforward process. To begin with, he had to have the courage to announce a radical opinion (he says he did not fear to do so). He did so privately, among friends (perhaps at first) and then publicly, *Academico more*, in the anatomy lectures.[28] 'In academic fashion' can only mean 'by disputation', and obviously his academic colleagues raised objections to Harvey's new doctrine. The result was not entirely favourable. Some accused

---

[27] Harvey, *De motu cordis*, p.21.
[28] 'Ex quo non solum privatim amicis, sed etiam publice in praelectionibus meis anatomicis, Academico more, proponere meam in hac re sententiam non verebar.'

him (as others had accused Vesalius) of 'breaking faith' with all anatomists. Others suspended judgment until Harvey had explained the matter more fully. The image this supplies us with, of Harvey disputing with his colleagues in the more or less formal manner of universities everywhere, agreed not only with the 'strictest form' with which he presents the matter in the anatomy lectures, but also with his words in the address to Argent at the beginning of *De motu cordis*. Harvey says that he had 'many times' made known his ideas to Argent and the physicians of the college, and had for more than nine years[29] confirmed it by ocular demonstration. Here is the 'physical logic' of the anatomists, and the distinguished audience, centred on Argent. Harvey adds to this that the topic was 'illuminated by reasons and arguments, freed from the objections of learned and skilled anatomists' and that he had 'proposed it to you, confirmed it by autopsy [that is, to the eyes of the "jury"] responded to your doubts and objections, and accepted the favourable judgment of the distinguished President'. Altogether this adds up to a picture of full and frequent disputations in which Harvey's thesis was attacked and defended before an audience and finally 'determined' in an academic way by Argent, who was *praeses* of both the college and the disputation, just as a university master as *praeses* would determine a disputation.

At the very least, this process of disputation obliged Harvey to refine his thesis and assemble the most telling arguments in his favour. We shall be concerned later in this book with how Harvey's doctrine became widely accepted, how, that is, a consensus was reached. That process must have started with Harvey convincing his colleagues and his president, a process that lent shape, and conviction, to *De motu cordis*.

But almost certainly the significance of the disputation process at the college is greater than that. If, as argued above, Harvey's first announcement was about the forceful systole and pulse alone, then it seems extremely likely that it was in the process of defending his position that Harvey discovered that the blood circulates. The lectures, vivisection and disputation are the three keys to Harvey's discovery.

It is, then, of considerable interest to try to reconstruct the objections that were made to Harvey's thesis, and to see how he overcame them. The first objection made to Harvey's doctrine that we can identify is not, as we might have thought, concerned with defence of the accepted Galenic system, but with an opinion so different that Harvey can use Galen's words to refute it.[30] It was a new doctrine. It maintained that the arteries, pulsating with the innate faculty

---

[29] Possibly 'nine years' is a literary phrase meaning simply 'a long time', but if taken literally it takes the discovery either to 1619, when Harvey may have been doing experiments in preparing for the lectures of 1620, or to the lectures of 1618, when Harvey had already faced and overcome objections made in the first course of lectures.

[30] He does so in the introductory discourse of *De motu cordis*.

of the coats, ventilated the heart with air drawn in from the pores of the skin in the same way as the heart drew in air from the lungs. Respiration and pulsation were thus held to serve the same function. Certainly Galen had held that the fine ramifications of the arteries can absorb spirit from the air,[31] but, as Harvey pointed out, Galen's business was very much more to show that the arteries contained blood and not air or spirit, and that they served to carry arterial blood and heat away from the heart.

Harvey used much more space in refuting this scheme than he did in rejecting Galen's. The reason seems to be that the new scheme was used as an objection against Harvey's doctrine of the forceful systole and 'injected' pulse. Harvey makes no mention of the new doctrine of ventilating, respiring arteries when dealing with the pulse in the fullest possible manner in the anatomy lectures, so it seems it was used as an objection to his own doctrine at some later point, no doubt during the disputations he refers to. Harvey was obliged, therefore, to deal with the matter in De motu cordis. Arteries that actively drew in air from the outside through the skin were inimical to Harvey's view of the pulse, because it seemed like an extension of the Galenic doctrine of the active action of the arterial tunics. Harvey rejects the opinion partly by referring back to the demonstrations in the anatomy lectures in which he showed that the arteries were filled passively, like leather bags.[32]

Harvey's opponents had found support in, or derived their case from Fabricius' new book on respiration, published in 1615.[33] This was before or while Harvey was writing the anatomy lectures, and the new book was probably not seen by him or his opponents until after the lectures had begun for the first time in the spring of the next year. This would explain why the lectures are silent on the topic and why Harvey had to spend so much space in De motu cordis in refuting the new ideas of his old teacher.

There were two other contemporary objections Harvey had to meet. The first was again an attack on Harvey's doctrine of the forceful systole and pulse. It was an objection raised by those who adopted – as Harvey suggests – the notion of Vesalius that the heart contracted along its straight fibres only, and that as a result diastole was a forceful motion in which the base of the heart was drawn to its apex, pushing the walls of the ventricles out, and so increasing the volume of the heart. Harvey countered the objection simply by asserting that contraction takes place in all fibres.[34]

The second objection was that blood could not pass through the substance of

[31] De usu pulsuum, Kühn, Galeni Opera Omnia, vol. V, pp. 165–6.
[32] Harvey, De motu cordis, pp. 13, 14.
[33] See Whitteridge's note in her translation of De motu cordis: W. Harvey, An Anatomical Disputation Concerning the Movement of the Heart and Blood in Living Creatures, Oxford, 1976, p. 22.
[34] Harvey, De motu cordis, p. 23.

the lungs. The force of this objection seems to have been that the blood could not therefore reach the heart in a quantity sufficient to account for the forceful systole. Harvey answered that no one doubted the passage of fluids through the much denser substances of the liver and kidney.[35]

Harvey reserved the first part of chapter 10 of *De motu cordis* for the formal rejection of objections to the entire scheme of circulation, the exposition of which he had now completed. But again, the most important of them was an objection to the forceful systole and pulse. It was undoubtedly a real objection, made to Harvey during discussion, and not merely a literary device used by Harvey to strengthen his case. The objection said that blood did not leave the heart at all. This was the strongest of the possible objections to Harvey's doctrine of the forceful systole. The alternatives were to assert that blood left the heart in passive systole (the Galenic position), in active diastole (as Colombo appeared to say) or in passive diastole (which had no precedent in the anatomical literature). But that blood did not leave the heart at all, or in very small quantities, could be suggested by reading a number of authors. It was a powerful objection to Harvey's original idea of the forceful systole, and it seems very likely that in overcoming it Harvey was compelled to recognise that the blood circulated.[36]

The essence of this objection was that the heat of the heart made the blood boil up like milk in a pan, occupying a very much greater volume than when cold. The alternate motions of the heart could then be explained as alternate heating and cooling of the blood, without any necessary motion of blood into or out of the heart. Such a notion could be derived from Aristotle and the commentators, and it is clear that at first, in the anatomy lectures, Harvey did not find the idea of blood effervescing in the heart inconsistent with his own idea of forceful systole. He even thought the boiling motion of the blood and the forceful systole might have a ventilating function.[37] When looking for other purposes of the forceful systole, however, he did indeed reject Aristotle's notion that diastole is a passive or accidental result of the 'boiling pottage' in the heart. Harvey's rejection is based on the observation that a punctured heart emits blood, not vapour. Perhaps this is evidence that Harvey changed his mind. He certainly changed it when the 'boiling milk' argument was used against him.

Since it was an argument against the forceful systole, the 'boiling milk' objection may well have been used against Harvey during the disputations that

---

[35] Such a reply may suggest that the force of the objection was actually against the arteries-to-veins transit described by Harvey. If so, it was unusual. Harvey, *De motu cordis*, p. 37.

[36] Harvey formally recognised this as an objection in chapter 10 and had already referred to it in chapter 9: 'Nec est dicendum, quod cor in sua contractione aliquando protrudat, aliquando non, vel quasi nihil, et imaginarium quid' (p. 44).

[37] *Praelectiones*, p. 73r.

arose from the anatomy lectures, before he discovered the circulation. James Primrose,[38] the first opponent of Harvey to publish, makes it clear that the objection was made to Harvey before 1628, at least. If Harvey at first accepted the ebullition theory and then denied it on vivisectional grounds when he found it being used against him, then a third stage was Primrose's rejection of Harvey's experiment. Puncturing the living heart, he says, is unnatural: it provides a route for the blood to escape that the undamaged heart did not have. In a state of nature, he continues, blood is motionless in the heart, just as wine is in a barrel. Puncturing the ventricle is like tapping the barrel, when the blood and the wine emerge with some force. In a state of nature, he concludes, no significant quantity of blood leaves the beating heart. Although Primrose did not publish this until 1630, it is this final form of the argument that Harvey replied to in 1628. Its early stages surely date back to the anatomy lectures and the period before Harvey had discovered the circulation.

We have now looked briefly at all the early objections to Harvey's ideas that can be reconstructed. Since all of them were united in denying a forceful systolic pulse, it is natural to think that Harvey sought to emphasise, first, the *force* of blood emerging from the heart. We have already seen that he changed the weak *profluit* to the stronger *prosilit* when he discovered that the forceful systolic pulse was present in the arterial vein as well as the aorta and arteries. When his opponents tried to insist that little or no blood emerged from the beating heart, it was natural that Harvey should concentrate, second, on the *quantity* of blood leaving the heart. On the basis of his notion of forceful systole, Harvey made a rough estimate of the amount of blood in a distended, diastolic, ventricle of the heart. He compared that with the amount estimated to be in the ventricle at systole, and concluded that the difference between the two estimates was the amount of blood ejected in each forceful systole.

Harvey made some such calculation before he discovered that the blood circulated, as he tells the reader in chapter 9 of *De motu cordis*. It is a calculation that lies at the centre of that discovery, not only historically, in Harvey's own thought, but in its power to convince others. Let us recall that Harvey was seeking to defend his thesis of the forceful systole by showing that blood emerged from the heart with some force and in some quantity. If only as little as one-eighth of the contents of the ventricle – perhaps a drachm in weight – was ejected at each systole, then in the course of half an hour, 1,000 heartbeats later, 1,000 drachms of blood will have been ejected from the heart, argued Harvey. Clearly in a comparatively short space of time the whole of the blood contained in the body must pass through the heart. When this realisation first came upon him, Harvey was at a moment of crisis. The defence of his new

---

[38] J. Primrose, *Exercitationes, et animadversiones in librum, De motu cordis, et circulatione sanguinis*, London, 1630, pp. 71, 74.

thesis of forceful systole had led him into impossibility and threatened the very credibility of the thesis itself. If so much blood passed out of the heart, where did it all go? Why were the arteries not distended with blood? How could the flesh absorb so much nourishment? And where did all this blood come from? Could such a large amount be produced from the ingested food, as Galen said it did?[39]

This moment, when Harvey was struggling to defend his first thesis from its own impossible consequences, is the moment he refers to autobiographically at the beginning of chapter 8 of *De motu cordis*.

Truly when I had often and seriously considered with myself, what great abundance there was, both by the dissection of living things, for experiment's sake, and the opening of arteries, and many ways of searching, and from the Symetrie and magnitude of the ventricles of the heart, and of the vessels which go into it, and go out from it, (since Nature, making nothing in vain, did not allot that greatness proportionably for no purpose, to those vessels) as likewise from the continued and careful artifice of the doores and fibres, and the rest of the fabrick, and from many other things; and when I had a long time considered with myself how great abundance of blood was passed through, and in how short time that transmission was done, whether or no the juyce of the nourishment which we receive could furnish this or no: at last I perceived that the veins should be quite emptied, and the arteries on the other side be burst with too much intrusion of blood, unless the blood did pass back again some way out of the veins into the arteries and return into the right ventricle of the heart.

I began to bethink myself if it might not have a circular motion.[40]

This somewhat rationalised, *post hoc* account nevertheless still provides us with an image of Harvey labouring under grave doubts about the thesis of the forceful systole, which he had proudly presented and demonstrated in the most rigorous fashion in the anatomy lectures. Then suddenly he had the answer. He remembered (he later told Robert Boyle) that the valves in the veins all seemed to point *to* the heart; if they were valves as Harvey understood valves, this meant that the motion of blood in the veins was *to* the heart, *from* the finest ramifications of the veins, where they collected the blood that had been driven to the finest ramifications of the arteries by the forceful systole and pulse.

---

[39] Some instances of the use of quantitative arguments like Harvey's but earlier have been collected by Bylebyl: those of Sanctorius, Parigiano, Cremonini and Hofmann. J. Bylebyl, 'Nutrition, quantification and circulation', *Bulletin of the History of Medicine*, 51 (1977), 369–85. There is no evidence that Harvey knew of these.

[40] This is the English of the translation of 1653, used and cited by G. Whitteridge, *William Harvey and the Circulation of the Blood*, London, 1971, p. 125. It is used here as it follows the sequence of Harvey's Latin better than a number of more recent translations and was made by a translator with intimate knowledge of seventeenth-century usage. Harvey's Latin sentence, long and somewhat rambling, has given trouble to many translators. Whitteridge gives a detailed analysis of the problem in her own translation: Whitteridge, *Harvey, An Anatomical Disputation*. The latest and most detailed analysis of the situation has been made by Don Bates, 'Harvey's account of his "discovery"', *Medical History*, 36 (1992), 361–78.

This passage, in which Harvey keeps the narrative running through a long and complex sentence, is central to the story of the discovery of the circulation. Translators, struggling with Harvey's Latin, have often allowed their conceptions of philosophical or scientific method to inform their renderings. Willis looked to nineteenth-century inductive science in beginning: 'And sooth to say, when I surveyed my mass of evidence, whether derived from vivisections . . . ' Franklin seems to have had in mind the image of the quantitative science of *his* generation when he began: 'In attempting to discover how much blood passes from the veins to the arteries, I made dissections of living animals . . . ' In giving careful consideration to the technical details of the Latin, Whitteridge appears to have felt that the historically important thing was Harvey's modern method: 'Now truly, when I had many times and seriously considered with myself the varied means of searching, and how many there were! both from the dissections of living creatures . . . ' Now, Harvey did not come to the notion that the blood circulated by making inductions from a mass of evidence and neither was he making quantitative experiments to discover how much blood passed from veins to arteries. Somewhere deep in the modern historiography of Harvey scholarship is the notion that Harvey's method was important because it was quantitative, like modern science.[41] Undoubtedly Harvey's estimate of the amount of blood ejected from the heart helped to convince some of his readers of his case. But it was hardly scientific. As a 'quantitative method' it was far less precise than those of Sanctorius and van Helmont; it was not an experiment or even an observation, but a mode of argument, or rhetoric. To contemporaries like Hofmann it was an accountant's trick, incapable of true demonstration. To another, the student Conring, Harvey's whole case lacked

[41] Harvey's use of quantity has been discussed by F. R. Jevons, 'Harvey's quantitative method', *Bulletin of the History of Medicine*, 36 (1962), 462–7, who points to wide agreement among historians about the significance of Harvey's quantitative method. Indeed, probably no topic in the bulk of Harveian scholarship has attracted so diverse a range of comment. A little space must be given here to an explanation of why the present book is not in this tradition. The Harveian literature is instinct with the notion that Harvey, having made so momentous a discovery, must have had a superior method, indeed, a scientific method. For example, Pagel begins one of his learned articles thus: 'William Harvey established by a scientific, i.e., quantitative demonstration . . . [and] became the most important among the founders of modern Physiology and Medicine'. Although Pagel wanted to see this in relation to the 'ideas' of the time, in fact it remained programmatic for his work on Harvey. See W. Pagel, '"Circulatio" – its unusual connotations and William Harvey's philosophy', in Cohen, ed., *William Harvey*. Sometimes this 'scientific method' is conflated with Merton's thesis about method in Padua (for example by F. G. Kilgour, 'Harvey's use of the quantitative method', in Cohen, *William Harvey*, p. 411). The reading back of characteristics of modern science into Harvey's words makes every scholar see Harvey in his own image. The true significance of Harvey is thus seen variously in his comparative anatomy, his hypothetico-deductive method, his zero-level statements and first-level hypotheses, his contribution (even) to a modern philosopher's attempt to analyse modern scientific method. None of this is helpful in the present attempt to describe how William Harvey's natural philosophy led him to his discovery and how other people's natural philosophy made them accept or reject that discovery.

demonstration. Neither meant the traditional demonstration syllogism, but ocular demonstration, *autopsia*. James Primrose likewise thought that Harvey's quantitative argument was elegant and ingenious but based on 'likely conjecture'[42] rather than on *autopsia*. For such people (we shall meet these three again later on) geometry had a power of demonstration, but the arithmetical side of mathematics did not. For many contemporaries, that Harvey's account of the blood ejected from the heart was quantitative gave it no special demonstrative power. Many agreed with Aristotle that mathematics simply described the appearance of things and did not deal with essences and causes. It is important to remember that mathematics was not part of traditional natural philosophy. It was taught in the arts course of the university as part of the quadrivial subjects of the older seven liberal arts. Mathematics had an ambivalent position with respect to *physical* truth and demonstration, part of natural philosophy. To the peripatetic schoolman mathematics contained no final causes and so was not part of natural philosophy. This is a point made by Antonius Scaynus, who was writing texts based on Aristotle at the same time as Case and Magirus.[43]

In short, a number of Harvey's opponents did not accept Harvey's quantitative argument because they did not recognise what kind of argument it might be. It had no place in the contemporary categorisation of the modes of reaching knowledge. On the other hand, we shall see that a number of those who were convinced by Harvey said that the quantitative argument played an important role in their conversion. They felt its force but could not categorise it any more than their opponents could. They saw, however, that it was the essential link between the idea of forceful systole and the circulation.

---

[42] Primrose, *Exercitationes*, p. 73: 'verisimilis conjecturae'.
[43] A. Scaynus, *Paraphrasis cum adnotationibus in Lib. Arist. de Anima*, Venice, 1599, pp. 1, 2. However, Scaynus wanted to give an unAristotelian importance, within philosophy as a whole, to mathematics and 'divine philosophy'.

# 5   The structure of *De motu cordis*

### Introduction: exercises and declamations

Harvey's task in presenting his case in print was to convince his readers. We can assume that he adopted what he thought was the most appropriate style of presentation to achieve this. The Harvey who had given much thought to presenting his discovery of the forceful systole with the utmost rigour, *obsignatis tabulis*, to the audience at his anatomy lectures in the college, would be unlikely to be more casual in announcing it, together with the discovery of the circulation, to the whole learned world in a printed work. He succeeded in the task of persuading his readers to the extent that by the end of his life the circulation of the blood (at least) was generally admitted.[1] There was a consensus.

In beginning to write *De motu cordis* Harvey was not in a strong position. He wanted to tell the world that he had discovered the true *actio* and *utilitas* of the heart. As a modern, he did not possess the authority of the ancients, whose opinions, indeed, he was trying to overturn. Although discussions of 'action and use' were recognised parts of 'anatomy', Harvey's task was not the simpler one of some of his anatomical predecessors of announcing a new discovery in morphology. But he shared their disadvantage of not being able to 'demonstrate' the discovery in a proper logical way 'so that it could not be otherwise'. The 'physical logic' available to anatomists was indeed even weaker in attempting to demonstrate function than it was in showing structure. Nor was Harvey writing in other recognised modes, such as the commentary or the textbook, in which the author's business lay principally with the words of others and consequently followed accepted dialectical procedures. Faced with these difficulties, Harvey no doubt thought carefully about how to proceed.

---

[1] It was clear to Hobbes in 1655 that it was given to only very great men to see the acceptance of their works in their own lifetimes. See R. Frank, 'The image of Harvey in commonwealth and restoration England', in *William Harvey and his Age. The Professional and Social Context of the Discovery of the Circulation*, ed. J. J. Bylebyl, Johns Hopkins University Press, 1979 (Supplement, n.s., no. 2, to the *Bulletin of the History of Medicine*), pp. 103–43.

So what can the historian learn about Harvey's persuasive techniques from the structure of his book? How did the book succeed in introducing such a fundamental change into natural philosophy? Harvey knew that the readership of his book would consist of learned men. They would have shared with Harvey notions about the nature of knowledge and how it was acquired and demonstrated. They were familiar with academic exercises. In choosing for a second time to find the most rigorous form of procedure for his discoveries, Harvey responded to the expectations of his audience and to his own training and wrote an academic exercise. This is precisely what he called it, *An Anatomical Exercise on the Motion of the Heart and Blood in Animals* (*Exercitatio anatomica de motu cordis et sanguinis in animalibus*). It will be recalled that the *exercitatio* was demanded of the student by statute in the Cambridge of Harvey's time, even when teaching was moving into the colleges and other statutes were losing some of their force. 'Exercises' in general were adversarial classroom activities and the term included disputation and 'declamation'. A declamation was a speech (the forerunner of the undergraduate essay) based on such a topic as an event in classical history, often expressed in question form. The declamation was essentially an expansion and defence of the topic, giving the student an opportunity to display relevant learning and a good Latin style. Although the declamation included the removal of objections it was not primarily a dialectical exercise, seeking for demonstrative proof, but was 'judicial' or 'deliberative', the arguments being partly quotations from the authors (corresponding to the 'authorities' of a dialectical disputation).[2] But the declamation was similar to the disputation in being a defence of a disputable question. A declamation of course was something that a student could, like a lone author, do on his own, without opponents and moderator. This 'exercise' thus could be either a group and oral activity, as appears in the Elizabethan statutes or, when teaching became a college affair between tutor and pupil, it could be private and written.[3]

Harvey's *exercitatio* can be thus seen as the defence and amplification of a disputable question following academic protocol. Harvey used the term *exercitatio* not only in his reply to Riolan,[4] but also for his work on the generation of animals,[5] and we can glance briefly at these to help us understand what Harvey meant by *exercitatio*. In the case of the *Exercitationes de generatione animalium*, each of the comparatively short chapters is an anatomical 'exercise'. Collectively they present Harvey's argument, but individually they are parts of academic anatomy: the *historia* of structure, the

---

[2] W. T. Costello, *The Scholastic Curriculum at Early Seventeenth Century Cambridge*, Harvard University Press, 1958, p. 53.

[3] Ibid., p. 58.

[4] W. Harvey, *Exercitatio anatomica de circulatione sanguinis*, Cambridge, 1649.

[5] W. Harvey, *Exercitationes de Generatione Animalium*, London, 1651.

action, use and function of the parts, the setting up and overturning of other opinions, the resolution of objections and the citation of authorities. (The 'what' of generation, like the action of hearts in *De motu cordis*, is the egg.)

The similarity of structure of these publications – a structure seen at its clearest and most formal in *De motu cordis* – indicates what an 'exercise' was in anatomical matters. An anatomical exercise was philosophical as well as physical, structured dialectically as well as with 'physical logic'. The title of Harvey's book ('The motion of the heart and blood *in animals*') makes it clear that it is an exercise in natural philosophy, not medicine. Harvey was not searching in 'comparative anatomy' for elucidation of what was happening inside man. (As a number of his critics – we shall meet them below – were to point out, the book could be seen as a hindrance to medicine, particularly practical medicine.) Rather, Harvey had wanted to know, and has now found out, what hearts do, and how blood moves, 'in the animal'. The book is the result of an ultimately Aristotelian programme designed to explore 'what it is to be a heart'. But Harvey's programme had to go beyond what Aristotle had said, both because Aristotle, to seventeenth-century medical eyes, had been vague about the vessels of the heart, erroneous on the number of its ventricles, and ignorant of its valves; but also because Harvey saw the advantages of extending his investigation into a number of small animals which Aristotle had not dealt with.

In the light of these considerations about the nature of Harvey's programme and the structure of his book we must regretfully dismiss the interesting suggestion that *De motu cordis* consists of two books written at different times on different topics and later joined together by Harvey to form a single work. Nor can we accept an alternative proposal that *De motu cordis* is a disputation.[6]

To take the second suggestion first, although of course containing dialectical components *De motu cordis* is more than a disputation. A disputation was oral, with proponent and at least one opponent, together with (most often) a moderator with the power of intervening and the duty of summing up and providing a final conclusion. None of this applies to Harvey's book, which has, moreover, experimental material inappropriate for a

---

[6] J. J. Bylebyl, 'The growth of Harvey's *De Motu Cordis*', *Bulletin of the History of Medicine*, 47 (1973), 427–70. Bylebyl's claim that the first half of *De motu cordis* was written before Harvey had discovered the circulation was rejected by G. Whitteridge in the introduction to her translation of the text, which – in a counter-assertion – she claims is a disputation. W. Harvey, *An Anatomical Disputation Concerning the Movement of the Heart and Blood in Living Creatures*, trans. G. Whitteridge, Oxford, 1976. The dispute has been continued: G. Whitteridge, '*De Motu Cordis*: written in two stages?' and J. Bylebyl, '*De Motu Cordis*: written in two stages? Response', *Bulletin of the History of Medicine*, 51 (1977), 130–9 and 140–50 respectively. Whitteridge is perfectly correct to see the discussions referred to by Harvey in his preface as disputations, but it is not possible to accept the entire text as a disputation, together with what Whitteridge calls demonstrative proof.

disputation. Moreover, disputations could make abundant use of arguments that were demonstrative in the philosophical manner, which was not sought for in a declamatory exercise and which was not possible in an anatomical exercise.

Secondly, the difference between the two halves of Harvey's book, which make it look as if they are about different things that Harvey discovered at different times, is due to the structure of the *exercitatio* form that Harvey chose, and to the expectations of Harvey's audience, who also knew what an exercise was.

The nub of the matter is this: unless Harvey adopted some accepted academic format, his audience would not have recognised his work as an argument. It was the essence of an academic presentation that it proceeded by a concatenated series of arguments, each with a proposition, by the meeting of objections (if none were made they had to be invented; Harvey does so in the exercise to Riolan) and with a final restatement of the proposition or disputed question in a positive form. Questions demonstrated in this way as positive conclusions were then taken as further propositions for a new argument until the final conclusion was reached. To have introduced the final conclusion before its support was established in this way would have been to confuse the reader by an unusual and unskilful practice. We shall see below that one of Harvey's readers marked the formal stages of Harvey's argument in his copy of *De motu cordis* in order to follow its argument more lucidly.

The same point can be made from Harvey's second *exercitatio* to Riolan. (We shall examine it in more detail below.) Its introductory paragraph posits the circulation as the question under discussion, but it is not mentioned again until Harvey has reported on some experiments that support the forceful systole and pulse, the necessary condition for demonstrating the circuit of blood. Here too he expressly recapitulates the arguments used in *De motu cordis* and preserves the academic order of an exercise:[7] he first deals with the filling of the right auricle with venous blood and the forceful transit of blood to the ventricle, lungs, left ventricle, aorta and arteries. Here he pauses, as he had paused in *De motu cordis*, at the point of wondering why the arteries did not burst with the quantity of blood. Rather than proceed directly to the transit of blood from the arteries to the veins, Harvey instead continues to add to the reasons on which that final statement will be made, that is, that the ventricles, like the auricles, do not in fact burst. This is followed by evidence pointing to the centripetal flow in the veins and finally, in its proper place, the recapitulation, to the circuit of blood.

In this recapitulation Harvey says that in *De motu cordis* he was trying to confirm the matter not from causes and principles but in an anatomical way

7 Harvey, *De circulatione sanguinis*, p. 101.

*–Anatomico more* – from observation and experiment.[8] In traditional academic form this was closer to the exercise (which also did not rely on dialectical demonstration) than to the disputation. When Harvey is not arguing in a formal way, he says so, and the difference is striking; while discussing the activity of the blood itself, in the second exercise to Riolan he says he is putting it forward simply as a thesis,[9] without any kind of demonstration and without the objections by the overturning of which could his arguments be constructed. Indeed, he asks for such objections to be made.

Now we must turn our attention to the structure of Harvey's book itself.

## Chapters 1 to 7

*De motu cordis* begins with a long proem. It is longer than any other chapter of the book except the last, which rounds off the whole exercise. The purpose of the introduction is twofold. In the first place Harvey is setting out, as Aristotle often did, to discredit the opinions of others, and so strengthen his own. Secondly, by doing so, Harvey is showing the reader that there is in fact a problem to be solved. Most of his readers, particularly the practising physicians and surgeons, had no reason to suppose that there was any grave difficulty about understanding the motion of the heart. They were aware of course that where ancient or modern accounts differed from that of Galen there was a fertile source of material for disputation. But the same could be said of many other form-and-function questions in anatomy. Apart from those few actively engaged in education and looking for theses to sustain or material with which to oppose a thesis, the medical man in practice found that his knowledge of the heart served him pretty well.

So Harvey played on the differences between the various theories of heartbeat and pulse. He begins with a rejection of Fabricius' new book on respiration,[10] which had developed the notion that the arteries draw in air from the skin. Such a notion was antithetical to Harvey's doctrine of the pulse, and as we have seen, it may have been used against him before the publication of *De motu cordis*. Harvey makes much of the differences between the views of Erasistratus, Galen and Colombo, largely by the technique of asking rhetorical questions about various impossible consequences that would follow from a development of these views. Indeed, he formalises the picture by listing five questions that cannot be answered by current theories. How can two structures so similar as the two ventricles of the heart have such different

---

[8]  Ibid., p. 105.
[9]  Ibid., p. 115.
[10]  Fabricius' work on respiration may be consulted in the collected works: H. Fabricius, *Opera omnia anatomica*, Leipzig, 1687, p. 161.

functions? The current consensus – except for those who accepted Colombo's assertion that blood moved across the lungs from the right side of the heart to the left – was that the right ventricle served to concoct venous blood to nourish the lungs and the left ventricle generated arterial blood and spirit, and initiated the pulse of the arteries. How is it that the valves of the left ventricle are almost identical to those of the right, but are said to control the flow of spirit and not blood, as in the right ventricle? As in the first question, Harvey is arguing from the anatomical principle that structure and function are closely related: different functions demand different structures. Harvey's third question is related to the same principle: since the arterial vein is so similar in its connections and size to the venous artery, why is it that the former (our pulmonary artery) has a 'private use', the nourishment of the lungs, and the latter a public use (helping to prepare spirit for the whole body)? Moreover, the size of the arterial vein, says Harvey, is bigger than both femoral branches of the vena cava taken together: why do the lungs need so much nourishment? And why is a second, pulsating ventricle needed to enable this nourishment to reach the lungs, given their proximity to the heart, their mobility and the size of the connecting vessel?

In this way all five of Harvey's formal list of questions are concerned with the principle that different uses are achieved by different structures. Only his own theory of the forceful systole and pulse (which he announces here) does not involve incongruence between structure and function. His attack goes on with the rhetorical questions (the printer failed to include a number of the question marks): how does blood seep through the dense septum between the ventricles? (Galenic theory asserted that this was the only pathway for the blood from the liver (where it was made) and the veins to the arteries.) *Deus bone!* 'Good God!' cried Harvey, 'How does the mitral valve hinder the return of air, and not of blood?' To understand Harvey's exasperation, we must recall that it was part of the Galenic consensus that air moved down from the lung to the heart in the venous artery to help in the concoction of the blood that had seeped through the septum, in order to generate arterial blood and vital spirit. The mitral valve was believed to prevent the reflux of air. But the concoction generated sooty wastes that had to be expelled through the lungs, which needed also their share of the newly produced arterial blood. The incomplete closure of the mitral valve was held to allow reflux of blood and sooty wastes, but to prevent that of the air.

To recapitulate, Harvey has begun his *exercitatio* by establishing that there is a problem to be solved, by rejecting, Aristotle-fashion, the views of others (and by doing so on the anatomical principle of congruence between form and function) and by announcing his thesis, the forceful systole and pulse. Chapter 1 sets the tone for the rest of the book. The 'logic' of his presentation is not demonstrative, as might be sought in disputation, but perhaps more 'judicial' or 'deliberative', as declamations in Cambridge were. To the 'physical logic' of the anatomists, Harvey adds a strong historical account of what he has done. What convinced Harvey will, he hopes, convince his reader, when suitably presented. This contributes largely to the structure of the book.

In this way in chapter 1 he tells the story of his personal first reaction to the problem (which he had set up generally in the proem) that of the true nature of the heartbeat and pulse. This was Harvey's first problem, and his solution to it is the first thesis to be sustained in the *exercitatio*. It was prior to Harvey's second problem, that of the quantity of blood emerging from the heart, both in time and logically, as we have seen. The answer to the second problem was the circuit of blood from arteries to veins, and this is the second thesis to be sustained in Harvey's exercises. The logic of the situation, whether dialectical or 'physical', did not allow Harvey to introduce the second problem or the thesis derived from it, before he had fully dealt with the first. Harvey's historical mode of exposition adds strength to the logic of the case.

This is why the first half of the book is 'silent' about the circulation. It is instructive to compare the book with Harvey's treatise on the local motion of animals, which we glanced at in an earlier chapter.[11] Here too, a strict regard for the sequence of exposition leads Harvey to write six chapters on the prior principles of motion before using the word 'muscle', the agent of motion. That the first six chapters are silent on 'muscle' does not mean they are part of another enterprise.

Having described the disputations that took place in the College of Physicians following his announcement of the forceful systole and pulse, and having given his reasons for writing (to present misrepresentation of his case) Harvey proceeds in chapter 2 to describe how he first interpreted the alternate motions of the vivisected heart. What he was looking for in the first instance was the *motus proprius*, the heart's own, characteristic motion. It was again a question of the congruence of form and function: the heart was an organic part of the body and therefore had an *actio* of its substance and a *usus* in the workings of the body. These were components of the heart's *motus proprius*, its reason for being a heart. But from vivisection Harvey could only tell that the heart repeatedly lifted itself up. He decided that this action of rising was the heart's proper motion because it happened less often when the animal began to die: in death – the absence of any function – the heart was stationary in the relaxed, not the elevated position.

Harvey's analysis is therefore of the rising motion of the heart, and he sets out four cardinal observations to support his thesis. They are that the heart's forcible elevation can be felt from the outside of the chest; that this elevation is a contraction, primarily from side to side; that in elevation, the heart becomes

---

[11] W. Harvey, *De motu locali animalium 1627*, ed. and trans. G. Whitteridge, Cambridge, 1959.

hard, like the muscles of the arm when the fingers are moved; and that in cold-blooded animals the heart grows paler as it contracts and ejects blood. Many of Harvey's opponents would have agreed that the elevation of the heart, because of its vigour, was the heart's 'proper motion'. But Galen had said that diastole, expansion, was the vigorous proper motion of the heart, during which it drew in blood from the vena cava. To his opponents, then, elevation of the heart was diastole.

Harvey's third chapter deals with the necessary consequence of the forceful systole, that is, the arterial pulse. Again he has a numbered list of cardinal observations: the pulse is felt in the arteries (including the arterial vein) while the heart contracts; it stops when the contraction of the heart stops; and blood spurts from a punctured artery during the contraction of the heart. What follows from this is the second half of Harvey's first thesis, that is, that the pulse is the forceful motion of blood from the right ventricle to the arteries. Using the analogy he had used in the anatomy lectures, he explains that the pulse was essentially simultaneous in all parts of the arteries, as the fingers of a glove arise together when one blows into the hand of the glove. Harvey is here overcoming a possible objection to his theory of the pulse, namely that a delay would be expected as the blood travels along the artery, carrying the pulse with it. It is not possible to say whether this was a real objection made to him before publication or a device to disarm his readers.

In the next chapter (4) Harvey elaborates his description of the motion of the heart by distinguishing that of the auricles from that of the ventricles. These chapters are short and to the point. Harvey writes of the results of his vivisections in a wide range of animals. More than one of his opponents[12] admitted that Harvey's knowledge of different animals impressed the reader of the book, and we must regard it as one of the reasons why Harvey was able to convince some of his readers. It is of course the Rule of Socrates in operation, finding out what it is to be a functioning heart. But Harvey was not only looking at functional hearts in a wide range of animals, but at the heart in the *embryonic* animal. Here (looking forward for a moment to chapter 6), as in different adult animals, the particular circumstances of the animal determined the nature of its heart. Embryonic mammals cannot respire air, and do not use their lungs *in utero*. Their arterial blood is derived in some manner from the mother by way of the placenta, which has vascular arrangements very different from that of the lungs. But as in the adult, all parts of the foetus need both arterial and venous blood. These circumstances and needs are different embryonic functions which must be congruent with different structures: the

---

[12] J. Primrose, *Exercitationes, et animadversiones in librum, De motu cordis, et Circulatione sanguinis*, London, 1630, p. 54. More opponents of Harvey are considered in the following chapters.

embryonic heart has two openings, a *foramen ovale* and a *ductus arteriosus*, which close at birth. Galen knew all this as well as Harvey, but for Harvey it is additional evidence of what the Rule of Socrates had told him already: that the *action* of all hearts is to eject blood and create an arterial pulse in cardiac systole; and that the *form* of different hearts varies with the circumstances and needs of their possessors.

Harvey continues his exercise with a plain summary (in chapter 5) of the preceding stages of the argument. This is followed by his account of why other people have been wrong. This section serves the same purpose as Harvey's opening tactic of dismissing opposing views and so strengthening his own. It is the argument that most investigators have been concerned primarily with the dead human body rather than also with a range of simpler, living animals. Harvey remarked that the shortcomings of such a method (we can think of it as medical, or Galenic, rather than Aristotelian) was that it amounted to an attempt to syllogise about a universal form from a particular proposition (like a man who pretended to know about agriculture because he knew a single field, said Harvey). Harvey is really promoting his own use of the Rule of Socrates, here in conjunction with the text where Harvey found it, the *De placitis Hippocratis et Platonis*. In the passage cited by Harvey,[13] Galen rejects the views of Erasistratus on the flow of blood, and Harvey's point is that the proximity and vascular connections of the lungs to the heart in man confused even Galen. Let us recall that Galen adopted the not uncommon Greek notion that blood was produced in the liver from ingested food. The blood itself was the food of the body and had to be distributed to all parts. But Galen had become engaged in a fierce controversy with the followers of Erasistratus,[14] who maintained that the arteries contain air, or spirit. Galen's vivisections settled the question to his satisfaction, showing that the arteries in fact contain blood; there was, however, no obvious anatomical pathway from the vena cava, the main route of distribution of blood from the liver, and the aorta, the source of all the arteries in the body. Galen's answer was that the septum between the two ventricles of the heart was perforated by invisibly small pores. Harvey's argument is that the picture was confused by the presence of two large vessels, the arterial vein and venous artery, which leave the heart and disappear, *obliterari*, into the lungs. In other words, these two vessels did not seem to Galen and all who followed him, as they now did to Harvey, to provide a route for the blood from right to left.

Harvey's next task, consequently, is to demonstrate that blood does indeed

---

[13] W. Harvey, *Exercitatio anatomica de motu cordis et sanguinis in animalibus*, Frankfurt, 1628, p. 31.

[14] Galen, *An in arteriis natura sanguinis contineatur*, in *Claudii Galeni Opera Omnia*, ed. C. G. Kühn, vol. IV, Leipzig, 1821, p. 703.

move from the vena cava via the right ventricle to the lungs, and from there to the left ventricle and arteries. His argument is again the Rule of Socrates: in fish, which have no lungs and consequently only one ventricle of the heart, the auricle is clearly seen sending blood into the ventricle which in turn can be seen (by puncturing the artery) to send the blood into the artery. Rather different animals, like frogs, toads, snakes and lizards 'which are said in a manner of speaking to have lungs, since they have a voice', have different habits (they live partly at least out of water) and the different action of their parts requires different structure. The difference, says Harvey, is not great, for these animals have 'as it were' a single ventricle, as if the dividing septum of a twin-ventricle heart had been removed, and the motion of blood is seen almost as easily as in fish. Had other investigators examined such living animals, says Harvey, they would not have fallen into error; moreover, such animals greatly exceed in number those with more complex hearts, so the forceful systole and pulse is admissible in general. It is here (as we saw above) that Harvey considers the case of the foetal stages of animals with lungs. He is not only extending the Rule of Socrates to animals with different needs. He is showing that different animals with the same needs have similar (if not identical) structures. Here he equates adult animals without lungs to embryonic lunged animals that do not use their lungs. In both cases there are open and clear pathways for the blood from the veins through the heart to the arteries. What we call the *ductus arteriosus* (Harvey's *canalis arteriosa*) connects the foetal arterial vein to the aorta, so that the contracting right ventricle sends blood not to the lungs but to the arteries. In other words, says Harvey, the two ventricles beat as one, having the single function of sending blood into the arteries, and thus acting in an exactly analogous way to the *quasi unus* ventricle of amphibians that looked like a twin-ventricle heart with the dividing septum removed. Moreover, our *foramen ovale* (in Harvey's words 'foramen amplum patens, ovali figura')[15] joins the vena cava to the venous artery and so provides a clear route for venous blood to cross to the left-hand side of the heart and be sent to the arteries. Not only are these pathways clear and large, says Harvey, but the valves of the heart ensure the direction of flow. All in all, as Harvey concludes, the state of the foetus of an animal having lungs but not using them is the same as that of the adult animal not having lungs; the 'same thing happens' in the hearts of both (because the needs of the animals are similar). Nothing could be a more dramatic vindication of the relationship between form and function inherent in the Rule of Socrates than the moment of birth of an animal with lungs: in a new environment with new needs the lungs become functional by the sudden closure *and ultimate disappearance* of the two foetal openings. The structure alters radically because of radical new needs,

---

[15] Harvey, *De motu cordis*, p. 34.

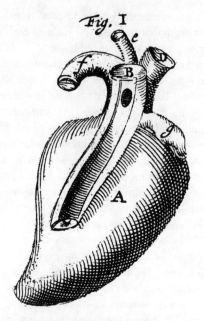

Fig. 10. The embryonic heart (i).
Fig. I (the lower figure in Bartholin's table) shows an embryonic heart, A, with its attached great vessels, the vena cava, B, the ascending aorta, D, and descending, f (and e is the axillary artery, g the right auricle). Directly below B is the foramen ovale.

and blood passes across the lungs to the left auricle and ventricle (see figs. 10 and 11).

Harvey refuses to be drawn into a digression on the purpose of the blood passing through the lungs and contents himself with demonstrating that it can happen and that it does happen. That is, despite the *actio–usus–utilitas* structure of his anatomical method, Harvey is here pragmatically stating that it does not vitiate the demonstration to stop before reaching the final stage, or the discovery of the final cause. He shows that the blood passes through the lungs in chapter 7, by pointing to examples in the body of commonly agreed cases where fluids pass through substances even denser than that of the lungs. He also quotes Colombo and an extensive passage from Galen[16] on the fine communicating channels between arteries and veins. It is the final extension of his argument of the forceful systole and pulse, the argument that has given structure to the book so far. Let us remind ourselves that the important stages

---

[16]  Ibid., p. 38.

## II

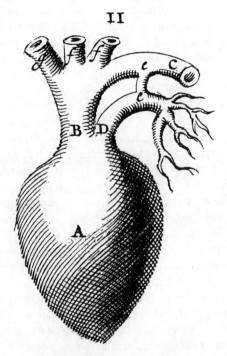

Fig. 11. The embryonic heart (ii).
Fig. II in Bartholin's table represents at A the 'little heart', *corculum*, of the embryo. B is the aorta with the subclavian and carotid arteries (g, f, f) and C is the descending aorta. cc is the 'canal' linking the arterial vein, D, to the aorta.

in the argument are the identification of the *proprius motus* of the heart as systole, the recognition that blood is emitted during this motion, the description of the result of this emission – namely the true nature of the pulse, first in the arteries and second in the arterial vein, and finally the continued motion of the blood from the arterial vein – across the lungs to the venous artery.

### Chapters 8 to 13

This sequence of argument seems to follow approximately the chronology of his observations and discoveries. The exception is Colombo's description of the flow of blood across the lungs, which Harvey almost certainly knew about before the anatomy lectures, but which fits most naturally into his argument in a late position. Harvey has now reached a critical stage. In his *exercitatio* he has sustained one thesis – the forceful systole – and its consequences, and he must now take the argument one important stage further. He is essentially introducing another thesis, although it is a consequence of the first. His exercise is about two things, the forceful systole and the circuit of blood, and the disjunction that Harvey makes between them is not so much logical as rhetorical. He maintains the narrative mode of presentation into the second half of the book, and the hesitation he expresses at the beginning of chapter 8, in which he is to argue for the circuit of blood, reflects the problems he had actually faced in wrestling with the idea of the quantity of blood emerging from the heart, the radical nature of the solution of those problems and the opposition he had met and expects to meet in the future. He tells the reader what his problems were, and what else was in his mind when he was labouring with them: the symmetry and size of the vessels of the heart and the structure of the valves. The centrepiece of the chapter is the announcement of the resolution of his problem: the circulation of the blood. The exposition is autobiographical and the rhetoric high flown: the valves are elegant and careful contrivances; the circular motion of blood is like the cycles of Aristotle's meteorology: the moist earth is warmed by the sun, vapours arise, condense and fall again as rain, making the soil fertile; did not Aristotle himself compare this to the circular motions of the heavens? Does not the circular motion of the sun generate storms and meteors? In this way, continues Harvey, the circulating blood is restored and perfected in the heart, which is the treasure-house of life, the sun of the microcosm, the fountain of the body and its domestic deity. Harvey's rhetoric here is close to the student's use, in his declamation, of elegant pieces from classical sources, which 'will furnish you with quaint and handsome expressions for your Acts to qualifie the harshness, & barbarisme of Philosophical termes'.[17]

'Acts' in Cambridge were degree-disputations, bristling with the barbarisms of dialectic. Harvey now drops his rhetoric, and his narrative style, and becomes more formally dialectical. Chapter 9 sets up three propositions, the proof of each of which contributes to the demonstration of the circulation. The 'proof' of these propositions structures the book up to chapter 13 (chapter 10, as we have seen, is given over to resolving objections). The first proposition is that the blood is moved by the heart from the vena cava to the aorta in quantities too great to be supplied by food. It is here that Harvey uses the quantitative argument in estimating the weight of blood to be ejected at every systole. It was a convincing argument, according to a number of contemporaries, but there is no reason to suppose that quantification was a special part of Harvey's natural philosophy.

The second proposition is that the amount of blood reaching the body by way of the arteries is greater than needed for nutrition. Proof of this proposition on

---

[17] Costello, *Scholastic Curriculum*, p. 32.

its own, says Harvey, will demonstrate the circulation, and even more so if taken in conjunction with the first proposition, about the quantity of blood passing from the heart in relation to the quantity of food consumed. So how does Harvey 'prove' his proposition and so – he hopes – convince the reader? As observed above, proof in the geometrical sense or in Aristotle's meaning of demonstrative proof that a thing cannot be otherwise, was not available to Harvey. The best he can do is to 'strengthen' or 'confirm' his propositions: he regularly uses the verb *confirmare*.[18] He does so in this chapter (11) by recreating for his readers a series of experiments. They are experiments in our sense for Harvey, and for his readers they would also represent experience, both covered by Harvey's use of the word *experimentum*. These are experiments with ligatures, which were used in medicine for phlebotomy, amputation and the removal of certain tumours. Many of Harvey's readers would have been medical men and perhaps all of them at one time or another had been bled, and so Harvey is making them re-live their experiences.

Ligatures, explains Harvey, are of two sorts. Tight ligatures compress the limb so tightly that there is no arterial pulse on its distal side, which becomes cold. Such ligatures are used in amputations, the removal of some tumours and the castration of animals. Medium-tight ligatures allow some arterial pulse to penetrate. Those for bloodletting were commonly tied above the elbow, resulting in the swelling of the veins *below* the elbow. This was called 'drawing' (Harvey uses *attractio*). Harvey then invites the reader to follow a series of experiments. First, let a tight ligature be put upon a man's arm, and the reader will see that the artery on the proximal side of the ligature will swell and beat more violently, while distally the arm becomes cold and without pulse. Arterial blood is not passing through the ligature. When the tight ligature is loosened to one of medium tightness, then blood can be felt, both by the experimenter and his subject, to flow down the artery. Being unable to return in the veins compressed by the medium ligature, the blood accumulates in the lower arm, which becomes swollen and hot. Harvey invites his readers to inspect the swollen veins of the lower arm, and to try to push their contained blood past the ligature into the upper arm: it can only be done using considerable force. When the ligature is removed altogether, continues Harvey, the lower arm subsides and becomes paler in colour as the blood moves back towards the heart in the veins. Moreover, if the medium ligature has been in place for some little time, allowing the stationary blood in the lower arm to grow cold, then the patient will feel the coldness of the blood pass up his arm when the ligature is removed. Harvey guessed that this was the reason why even strong men sometimes fainted after phlebotomy.

---

[18] E.g. Harvey, *De motu cordis*, p. 48.

So Harvey is forcibly reminding his readers of the experience of blood-letting. Most of them knew that a medium-tight ligature 'drew' the blood, and Harvey has to convince them that his explanation of 'drawing' was better than theirs.[19] Harvey here allows that heat and pain attract blood. (We shall see below that the whole question of attraction, both in and out of the body, was a major topic for dispute in the natural philosophies in which Harvey's claims were considered.) Harvey's argument here is that given a Galenic centrifugal flow in the veins, it would be impossible for the veins on the far side of the ligature to swell with excess, attracted blood. The swelling should be on the near side. The argument is lucid throughout the whole *experimentum*: the blood flows through a medium-tight ligature in the arteries by reason of the force of the pulse, but cannot return again in the veins having crossed into them through small anastomoses or the pores of the flesh.

The third proposition, that the veins carry the blood back to the heart, is dealt with without leaving the image of a bloodletting experience that Harvey has conjured up for his reader. Indeed, Harvey now reinforces this image with four figures of a ligated arm, the only illustrations in the text of *De motu cordis* (see fig. 12). Prepared for phlebotomy, the swollen arm (preferably of a rustic) shows in its extended veins various nodes, which contain valves. Harvey knew that there were valves not only in the veins of the limbs but also in the renal, mesenteric and jugular veins.[20] What they had in common was not only their structure (Harvey used *valvula* for what we call the 'flap' of a valve) but their disposition: they all 'looked' towards the heart. And for Harvey the common use of *all* valves, the what-it-is-to-be-a-valve, was to impose unidirectional flow. Fabricius and the others who had described the valves were therefore wrong, concluded Harvey, in deciding that their function was to delay the descent of blood. This could not be the case with the valves of the jugular veins which 'looked' down (that is, to the heart).

Harvey introduces the matter with an account of his exploration, in dissection, of the function and direction of the valves, but the main thrust of his argument is concerned with further *experimentum* of the ligated arm. Harvey tells the reader directly to press the blood away from a valve by a firm stroking movement of a finger towards the hand. 'You will see', says Harvey 'that no blood can follow, because of the intervening valve.'[21] The empty vein remains flat and invisible (see the second of Harvey's figures in fig. 12, p. 109). Any attempt to fill it by forcing blood from the higher part of the vein past the valve will fail (Harvey's figure 3). Lastly, if the vein is blocked by pressure from a

---

[19] J. Bylebyl, 'The medical side of Harvey's discovery: the normal and the abnormal', in Bylebyl, *William Harvey*, pp. 28–102.

[20] Harvey's view of the valves is dealt with more extensively below, chap. 11.

[21] Harvey, *De motu cordis*, p. 56.

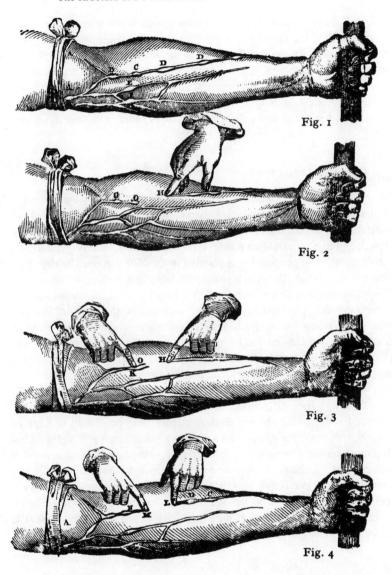

Fig. 12. Harvey's illustration of the ligatured arm in *De motu cordis*.

finger (L in Harvey's figure 4) and the blood squeezed out *towards* the heart, then having pushed the blood past a valve (N) it will not return, and the vein remains flat. It will fill again, of course, if the finger at L is removed. In a second quantitative argument Harvey invites the reader to estimate the amount of blood that enters when this is done, and how much blood must be moved if the operation is done a thousand times ('Iam si rem supputaveris . . . ').[22] Again, the quantity is too great to explain on any basis other than that the blood circulates.

### Chapters 14 to 17

Having in this way supported his three propositions, Harvey has finished the formal defence of his 'thesis', and chapter 14 is a brief 'conclusion of the demonstration' of the circulation. By *conclusio* Harvey means that the argument has closed, and that as usual in a formal academic exercise, the original thesis, disputable question or proposition is restated in the affirmative as having been in some sense proved. By *demonstratio* he does not mean 'demonstrative proof'[23] but something closer to the ordinary English word 'demonstration',[24] here involving the 'physical logic' of the anatomists, the experiments and experiences he wants the reader to re-live and copy, so that he can share in them, and the arguments he can bring to bear from the relationship between form and function. Chapter 14 consists of three sentences, one of which announces the purpose of the chapter and the other two restate the thesis.

Thus, having concluded the formal part of the argument, Harvey in chapter 15 brings forward a different *kind* of reason, less formal and less experimental – those that are *verisimiles* or 'probable' according to three of Harvey's translators.[25] He opens with a sentence not as clear as it might be but which almost certainly means that he intends now to show that circulation is 'convenient and necessary' within certain accepted systems of thought.[26] The most important of these is that of Aristotle, and Harvey shows that circulation is necessary and convenient to the Aristotelian doctrine that the heart is the centre of the body's heat (which the circulating blood distributes). Heat is necessary to the body for as Aristotle says, lack of heat is the cause of death.

---

[22] Ibid., p. 57.
[23] Whitteridge translates it in this way: *Harvey, An Anatomical Disputation*, p. 107.
[24] See also A. Wear, 'William Harvey and the "way of the anatomists"', *History of Science*, 21 (1983), 223–49.
[25] *The Works of William Harvey, M.D.*, trans. Robert Willis, London, 1847, p. 68; Whitteridge, *Harvey, An Anatomical Disputation*, p. 108; W. Harvey, *The Circulation of the Blood and Other Writings*, trans. J. K. Franklin, London, 1990, p. 108.
[26] Whitteridge, *Harvey, An Anatomical Disputation*, p. 108, translates 'communes quasdam ratiocinationes' as 'certain processes of formal logic', which is surely not what Harvey intended.

The rapid recovery of people blue with cold, says Harvey, can only be explained by the return of the almost congealed blood to the central source of heat: Aristotle is cited once more. In contrast, should the heart be chilled or damaged in some way, then the whole body will suffer and become corrupt: as Aristotle says, nothing can come to the aid of a damaged *principium*.

In a not dissimilar way, Harvey's next chapter explores less formal evidences for the circulation from another area. This area is that of unsolved problems (*problemata*, which we can think of as another kind of disputable question) which Harvey argues become clearer if one assumes that the blood circulates. As a mode of proof, it is not very strong, and of the title that Harvey gives the chapter, 'Sanguinis circuitus ex consequentibus probatur', we cannot translate the last word as 'proved' but rather as 'probed' or 'approved'. Harvey himself opens by saying only that such a way of proceeding is 'not useless as an *a posteriori* way of producing belief'.[27] It is then, another technique to persuade his readers. Harvey gives it as much logical form as it will bear, if not more: he treats the *problems*,'shrouded with great ambiguity and obscurity' as *consequences* of the circulation. He can then say that circulation provides the 'reason and causes' of the problem and so explains it. Such problems are: how in contagion do symptoms appear distant from the point of infection? How do external medicines have internal effects? How do the mesenteric veins carry chyle in one direction and blood in another? All these are 'problems' in the sense that Harvey can usefully extend the doctrine of circulation into them. Harvey recognised that such a programme was necessary to take circulation into every detail of medicine. But he recognised also that this was not the place even to begin such a programme, and he announces, in approaching his final summing up in the last chapter, that he prefers anatomical arguments to take first place, that is, those that relate to the structure, use and true causes of the heart and arteries.

Finally then, in the last and lengthy chapter Harvey summarises his evidence from anatomy, considered in a natural-philosophical way. Firstly (pp. 64–5), he considers the relationship between form and function in a range of animals, beginning with those that are so like plants that they do not have hearts, like sponges and some kinds of worms and caterpillars. Harvey prefers to think that in such animals the whole animal acts as a heart, distributing its food by its motion. Such a view preserves better his Rule of Socrates, and it is this Harvey is following in proceeding to deal with increasingly complex and more perfect animals, from those whose heart is seen only with a glass, like flies and bees, up through the fish, frogs and warm creatures. This is a scale of complexity where the more elaborate complexity and needs of the higher animals demand

---

[27] This may be compared to the use of *a posteriori* methods by Francis Glisson, Harvey's colleague: see chapter 10, below.

a more elaborate heart: greater heat requires finer nourishment, which in turn requires a lung, which in its turn requires a second ventricle in the heart. Most elaborate are the hearts of the hottest animals, where much force is needed to push the blood through the lungs: Harvey takes from Aristotle the basis of his description of the sinews and other structures within the hearts of the largest animals. Again Harvey (pp. 65–6) takes his Rule of Socrates as the principle that explains how the very different circumstances of the foetus and the adult demand a very different structure of the heart and vessels in each, yet in both the same action forcefully expels the blood in systole. Harvey even extends the principle a little, observing that while in the foetus both ventricles have the common purpose of propelling blood into the body through the aorta, they are both similar in appearance. But after birth, with the closure of the foetal vessels and the blood passing from the right ventricle through the lungs, the right ventricle has a lighter burden than the left and so comes to have a lighter structure.

Secondly, Harvey discusses the valves in the same way. Where the ventricle exerts a major force in expelling its blood, says Harvey, then the valves are made very accurately and entirely prevent a reflux. But where the need for a powerful expulsion is less, then nature has been less precise and even negligent in the degree of precision with which the valves close (p. 67). Like hearts, valves vary in structure according to their circumstances.

Harvey is not here trying to convince the reader by a narrative of discovery, by high rhetoric, by experiments or experience, but by arranging his anatomical material into what we might say was first in nature rather than first in his experience: the nature and distribution of hearts, the action and use of their parts, the nature of the pulse and arteries and particularly of the venous artery. The spirit of his enquiry and the way he expresses his results here are Aristotelian. Like Aristotle, he has been looking for significant correlations between parts of the body, and here expresses them in an Aristotelian way. 'So in whatsoever creature there are lungs, the heart has two ventricles . . . and wheresoever there is a right ventricle there is also a left.' The significant correlations that Harvey is making had not been made by Aristotle (who believed that the heart had three cavities and who was ignorant of its valves) and so there was an 'Aristotelian space' in which Harvey's research programme could operate, and here come to an end.

But the natural philosophy of Harvey's research programme was not entirely Aristotelian, and we have seen that he expressed his search for the essence of an organ among a wide variety of animals as a Platonic Rule of Socrates. This probably came to him through the medical side of his education, by way of Galen. And from Galen and seventeenth-century society Harvey too had a rather unusual idea of 'nature' that was not at all Aristotelian. Aristotle's *physis*, generally translated as *natura*, was the essence of the animals, its 'nature' in a wholly local sense. Galen conflated it with the notion of a demiurge, drawn from Plato. But while Aristotle's *physis* and Galen's 'nature' both used the available matter in the best possible way for the benefit of the animal, Harvey thought that nature was sometimes a less than perfect worklady. Although traditionally she 'makes nothing in vain',[28] yet in what she did make there were sometimes signs of carelessness. She 'rummages as she can best stow', he said of the way the guts were packed into the abdomen, and he thought some of the valves were rather slipshod.[29] Even man's degeneration since classical times is something that nature has not put right (even though her business was the preservation of the original species of animals). This is closer to the *natura* of Pliny, which was personalised to the extent of arranging spectacular fights between large animals to amuse herself, and who played games in the generation of animals, producing monsters, *ludi naturae*.

In short, we can see that Harvey's natural philosophy owed much to classical sources, interpreted individually. We have seen how it led him to tackle a problem in a particular way and how it structured his results and the way he expressed them. Aristotelian, Platonic–Socratic, vivisectional in the manner of Galen and the recents, even Plinian, Harvey's natural philosophy is used here in the last chapter of *De motu cordis* as a personal amalgam that encouraged him to express the circulation in terms of what was first in nature: the physical structures, principles and necessities on which it was based.[30]

---

[28] 'nihil faciens frustra', Harvey, *De motu cordis*, p. 69.

[29] 'sed in aliis exactius, inaliis remissius et negligentius', Harvey *De motu cordis*, p. 67.

[30] *De motu cordis* is also structured by rhetoric in the formal sense. Again, we must assume that Harvey gave careful thought to what he wrote and anticipated what his audience's expectations and reactions might be. They like him were learned men and had been taught Latin at an early stage in their lives. The Latin masters taught them not only grammatically correct Latin but Latin with the elegance approved in the day. Either at school or early in his arts course at university Harvey would have been taught Aristotle's rhetoric. This had two parts, demonstration (one's own view) and refutation. It is easy enough to see these in Harvey's writing; but Harvey appears also to be following Aristotle more closely. Aristotle advised the rhetor to show his own character in a good light, with good sense, goodwill and good moral character: do not create objectionable suppositions about yourself. This is at least consistent with Harvey's unpretentious mode of writing, his evident respect for authority (the king, Argent, Aristotle) and his generous treatment of other anatomists: the sixth of Harvey's 'general canons' for an anatomy is 'Not to prayse or disprays, for all did well' (G. Whitteridge, ed. and trans., *The Anatomical Lectures of William Harvey*, Edinburgh and London, 1964, p. 16). Vesalius, Bauhin, Riolan are all praised. Metaphor and simile are also parts of Aristotle's rhetoric, by which, he says, the subject-matter can be elevated. We have noted Harvey's use of these devices in chapter 8, where the newly announced circulation is compared to the great cycles of the macrocosm, the great process of the world that Aristotle himself had described. While the fact of the circulation and its discovery are to be elevated in the reader's mind by these comparisons, yet in demonstrating its details Harvey keeps his similes concrete and practical. The operation of firearms, the filling of leather bottles, the pulling of cords and ship's ropes, the passage of blood past gatekeepers (the valves): all are firmly based in the experience of his readers and lend a concrete, even mechanical image to the circulation. See P. W. Graham, 'Harvey's De Motu Cordis: the rhetoric of science and the science of rhetoric', *Journal of the History of Medicine*, 33 (1978), 469–76). The question of machines and the use of mechanical analogy is further explored below.

# 6    Early reactions in England

## James Primrose

The first published opposition to Harvey's doctrines[1] was that of James Primrose. The son of a Reformist Scot, Primrose was brought up in Bordeaux. Younger than Harvey, he took his MD, at Montpellier, in 1617.[2] He had also studied with Riolan in Paris.[3] He chose to incorporate at Oxford – in 1629 – and was admitted as a licentiate to the College of Physicians later in the same year, Harvey being one of the examiners.[4] He seems to have been an ambitious man, and it was not long before he had persuaded the king to allow him to give a public lecture on medicine.[5] The embarrassed college put a stop to it, claiming that Primrose (still a licentiate) was not qualified. It may be that his book

---

[1] Convenient guides to the bibliographical history of Harvey's works and to published reactions are Sir Geoffrey Keynes, *A Bibliography of the Writings of Dr William Harvey 1587–1657*, 2nd edn, Cambridge University Press, 1953; and E. Weil, 'The echo of Harvey's *De Motu Cordis* (1628) 1628–1657', *Journal of the History of Medicine*, 12 (1957), 167–74.

[2] J. Primrose, *Academic Monspeliensis a Iacopo Primirosio Monspeliensi et Oxoniensi doctore descripta*, Oxford, 1631. This volume gives the questions and theses with which Primrose proceeded to the doctorate in May 1617. He incorporated in Oxford in March 1628/9. See Falconer Madan, *Oxford Books*, Oxford, 1895, vol. I.

[3] See the *Dictionnaire de Sciences Médicales. Biographie Médicale*, vol. VI, Paris, 1824; Keynes, *Harvey*, p. 188. Primrose's family were Calvinist, and while this is consistent with his education in Bordeaux and at Montpellier, it is less so with his allegiance to Riolan in Paris. His use of the learned tradition from Aquinas to Turrisianus and the Jesuits has almost a Counter-Reformation feel, especially when he discusses with apparent approval the sentence of excommunication offered by the Council of Tours for priests who practise medicine, and is prepared to accept points of doctrine from a pope. See his *Popular Errours. Or the Errours of the People in Physick*, trans. R. Wittie, London, 1651, p. 14 and his *Destructio* (see notes below) of Plemp's textbook, p. 237. Yet he married in the Huguenot church in Soho Square (O. P. Grell, personal communication) and the evidence is that he remained an orthodox Calvinist. As we have seen, Protestants and Catholics could often share the same philosophical language.

[4] *DNB*.

[5] Primrose may have had ambitions at court. His father Gilbert had been a chaplain to James I in London and his grandfather had been his principal surgeon in Scotland. But Harvey had been physician extraordinary to James I since 1618 and remained at court to attend Charles I after James died in 1625. After his marriage in 1640 and his father's death about a year later, Primrose abandoned his ambition in the capital and moved to Hull to settle in medical practice (*DNB*).

114

against Harvey (it appeared in 1630) was also conceived as a way of publicising himself. Historians have been uniformly negative about Primrose's writings, either because of aspects like this of his personality or because he appears to have been so wilfully blind to the truth. But for us Primrose is interesting as one of those who was not convinced by Harvey's research and presentation: his natural philosophy. A study that seeks to explore the fate of Harvey's doctrine – and in this chapter we are concerned with its early *fortuna* – rejections are as important as modifications, misunderstandings and acceptances.

Primrose heard some anatomy lectures 'as a new member' of the college. These must have been either the 'extraordinary' lectures of the college, given for the last time in December 1629, by Helkiah Crooke, or Harvey's 'ordinary' lectures, completed in the college by 26 February 1630. Primrose mentions hearing the lectures when he addresses Harvey, and so perhaps it was Harvey's lectures he heard. Certainly the circulation must have been discussed, for Primrose records that everyone was pleased and rated the matter of the lectures as equal to any new discovery. He also records that (as we have seen in earlier years) not everyone was convinced and a rumour was being circulated that Harvey had been refuted by someone (wishing to defend the ancients) in Germany. But 'an old man, speaking gravely and proudly like an oracle' defended Harvey by saying there was no one in Germany capable of it.[6] This seems to have annoyed Primrose, who thought the old man had had the temerity to say that since he was not able to refute Harvey himself, then he thought no one else could. This, and the President's encouragement, prompted Primrose (he says) to study Harvey's book. A between-the-lines interpretation of Primrose's account of this occasion might be that after a sharp exchange on the likelihood that Harvey was right, Primrose was put firmly in his place by Argent and told to go away and read Harvey's case.[7] He did so, and in a very short time had composed his answer. He called it 'Exercitations and animadversions' upon Harvey's book, and also referred to it as a 'little disputation', *disputatiunculum*. It is indeed closer to a disputation than was

---

[6] J. Primrose, *Exercitationes, et animadversiones in librum, De motu cordis, et circulatione sanguinis adversus Guilielmum Harveium Medicum Regium, et anatomes in Collegio Londinensi Professorem*, London, 1630: the dedication to Harvey. The volume used to belong to Alexander Read and is now in King's College Library, Aberdeen.

[7] On the other hand it is clear that Harvey did not convince everyone in the college, which as a body did not want to appear to have given the imprimatur to Harvey's book. Primrose, Drake and Parigiano all in fact thought that the college had in some way authorised Harvey's book. C. Webster ('William Harvey and the crisis of medicine in Jacobean England, in J. Bylebyl, ed., *William Harvey and his Age. The Professional and Social Context of the Discovery of the Circulation*, Johns Hopkins University Press, Baltimore, 1979) suggests that the difficulties faced by Primrose in gaining admission to the college turned him against Harvey, one of its senior members. If Primrose did have ambitions at court, his book against Harvey could be seen as a self-promoting claim of orthodoxy, against a powerful rival.

Harvey's book, and a purely verbal one; it is shaped by the sequence of Harvey's own formal exposition; and Primrose often structures his own replies in a repeated proposition–objection–resolution format. He dedicated it partly to Argent, perhaps because Harvey had done so, and perhaps as a personal reply to the confrontation at the anatomy lectures. Like others, he thought that Harvey's book had been published under the College's auspices. Primrose's argument is that anatomical novelties like Harvey's destroy traditional medicine. He urges the king, in his other dedication, to restore the medicine of Hippocrates in the *academiae* that enjoy royal support. In doing so, he was at least sensitive to the political advantages of maintaining the intellectual and academic tradition that now appeared to be threatened. Primrose doubtless chose Hippocratic medicine rather than Galenic because he saw it as practical and useful, while that of Galen had a large theoretical component which added little to practice. Primrose thought that the medical teaching of the universities and the college was seduced by novelty, with the very students resonant with circulation, lacteal veins and the statical art (of Sanctorius) none of which, he complained, helped the doctor to heal. Unable to get a straight story about the circulation from such tyros, Primrose decided that the medicine of his old teacher Riolan could not be bettered.

We have already met Riolan as a defender of Galen, and of course when it came to disputing with Harvey on technical grounds, it was to Galen that Primrose necessarily had to turn. Indeed, he represents Harvey as breaking faith with Galen, just as others had accused Vesalius; he also represents his own task as the humanist one of restoring the pristine doctrines of the ancients.[8] Riolan saw himself in a tradition of medicine stretching from Cos to Paris, in which too his father had been part; and Primrose, whose grandfather had been a notable Scottish surgeon, may also have had family reasons for feeling part of the same tradition.[9] As for Riolan, so for Primrose, the argument is that the doctrines of the forceful systole and of circulation add nothing to benefit practice and indeed destroy the foundation of practice. Thus in an important diagnostic technique, the doctor believed that the pulse he felt at the wrist was more or less directly the vital faculty in operation in the heart and arteries. If Harvey was right, and the *propria motio* of the heart was systole and the filling of the arteries was passive, then the doctor was simply feeling the result, which was in Aristotelian terms merely accidental.[10] Again, in the very frequent

---

[8] Primrose, as a medical humanist, cites Galen over sixty times, three times as many as Aristotle. Of the moderns (after Vesalius) his most-used authors are the French Galenists Riolan and du Laurens.

[9] James Primrose's grandfather Gilbert (see note 5 above) had also been Deacon of the Incorporation of Surgeons of Edinburgh in 1581–2 and 1602. See D. Guthrie, 'The Harveian tradition in Scotland', *Journal of the History of Medicine*, 12 (1957), 120–5; 121.

[10] Primrose, *Excitationes*, p. 49.

therapeutic technique of bloodletting, circulation of the blood would destroy the basis of revulsive and derivative bleeding,[11] the theoretical basis of which had been fought over so energetically in the previous century.[12] (The argument was over techniques that diverted blood flow from or to a diseased organ; circulation would make such a distinction meaningless.) Any circulation, said Primrose, would be positively dangerous in putrid and continuous fevers, for the putrid matter would be spread all over the body and the moving blood would prevent concoction and expulsion of the noxious matter.

In a number of places Primrose's words allow us to see that Harvey's methods of exposition had some force, either to Primrose or to others. It is clear, for example, that Primrose has no notion of the method that lay behind Harvey's use of so many animals,[13] but he saw that others were impressed. He observes that there are so many names of animals in *De motu cordis* that many of Harvey's readers thought he was a *summus investigator* of things natural, and consequently admired him and treated his words 'as if they came from an oracle'. Clearly Harvey had chosen wisely in using the Rule of Socrates and the Aristotle Project.

It is evident too that Harvey's quantitative argument about the amount of blood leaving the heart had power to convince. In dealing with it[14] Primrose invokes the *ars statica*. He has already identified this as another fashionable novelty, and he is certainly referring to the work of Sanctorius, whose *De statica medica* appeared in 1614. Sanctorius used measurements of weight to find out how much 'invisible transpiration' was lost through the skin. Although one Harvey scholar can see not 'the slightest resemblance'[15] between Harvey's and Sanctorius' measurements, it is clear that Primrose naturally associated them and saw that one fashionable novelty could be used in support of another. Harvey's readers may indeed have been 'sensitised' in this way to arguments based on measurement. In any case it is clear from the amount of space Primrose devotes to the quantitative argument that he felt its strength; it is, he says, elegant and ingenious. But he argues (and not without force) that Harvey has not based the argument on observation, *autopsia*, but on a likely conjecture, *verisimili conjectura*. He is referring to Harvey's rather wide range of postulated quantities of blood ejected by the heart at each beat. Primrose even accepts that the heart would be moving in vain if it merely expanded and contracted without some blood emerging, but using the argument we have met

---

[11] Ibid., p. 79.
[12] See O'Malley's explanation of Vesalius' 'bloodletting letter': C. D. O'Malley, *Andreas Vesalius of Brussels 1514–1564*, University of California Press, 1965, pp. 95–7.
[13] Primrose, *Exercitationes*, p. 54.
[14] Ibid., pp. 73ff.
[15] See W. Harvey, *An Anatomical Disputation Concerning the Movement of the Heart and Blood in Living Creatures*, trans. G. Whitteridge, Oxford, 1976, p. 84.

above about spumification of the blood, he argues that the amount is very small. In a sense he has seen the force of Harvey's quantitative argument but has drawn its teeth by altering his figures.

Occasionally – but less often than most of Harvey's readers – Primrose misunderstands the point at issue, and so has another kind of reason for not accepting what Harvey has to say. He treats Harvey's description of the forceful pulse as if it were concerned with projectile motion. He refers to those natural philosophers who were concerned with such problems (a traditional one in Aristotelian commentary) and argues that the projectile force of blood entering the aorta would rapidly be lost in the ramifications of the arteries.[16] His assumption is that the *motus projectorum*, the term he gives to Harvey's *impulsum*, would have to remain in the blood until it reached the ends of the arteries (which he held was impossible). No, he insists, the blood is moved by an internal principle, that is, an immanent and continuous force (see fig. 13). A related argument that Primrose uses is that if the arteries are filled passively by the active heart,[17] there should be a delay as the blood and pulse pass along the artery. Harvey may have thought this worth responding to (but without dignifying it by attaching Primrose's name) for he later explained how the pulse is instantaneous on the analogy of a long bladder filled with water, which transmits a 'pulse' instantaneously when tapped at one end.

Primrose, as we would expect of an educated man, recognised and accepted the formality of Harvey's arguments. Harvey was here successful in marshalling his arguments in that Primrose agrees that all hangs on the three propositions – and particularly the first of them – which Harvey sets out in chapter 9 of *De motu cordis*. The first proposition maintains that the amount of blood passing through the heart to the arteries is far greater than can be

Fig. 13. Primrose's proof that the pulse was not due to the impulsion of blood was the Galenic experiment – *administratio*, Primrose called it – of inserting a hollow reed in the artery. Primrose follows Vesalius' account and his diagram shows the artery, B, ligated between A and F, and G and C. When it is punctured between the ligatures the only blood to emerge is that between the ligatures (so blood is clearly not flowing along the artery). Then the rigid tube, ED, is introduced into the artery through the cut, and two ligatures tied above it at F and G. Then the first two ligatures are untied, and according to Primrose the blood flows freely through the artery and tube but *without* a pulse in the part below the tube (where the ligatures were thought to intercept the pulsific expansion of the arterial coats). Harvey thought the experiment too difficult to perform, and there is nothing in Primrose's words to suggest that he had done it himself.

16 Primrose, *Exercitationes*, p. 89.
17 Ibid., p. 23.

res *Harveis* non minùs curiosi id fecerunt: Audi *Vesalium* qui aliàs *Galeno* non solet favere,quoties vel minimam habet reprehendendi occasionem; Sic itaque ait, *capite ultimo suæ Anatomes: Vt cer-. tiores fiamus pulsandi vim non arteriæ inesse,aut con- tentam in arterijs materiam pulsuum opificem existe- re, verùm à corde eam virtutem pendere, præterquam quòd arteriam vinculo interceptam non ampliùs sub vinculo pulsare cernimus, licebit inguinis, femorisve arteriæ longam sectionem inducere, & canaliculum ex arundine tam crassum assumere, quanta est arteriæ ca- pacitas, & illum ita sectioni indere, ut superior canalis pars altiùs in arteriæ cavitatem pertingat,quàm secti- onis superior sedes, & ita inferior quoque canalis pars deorsum magis ipsa inferiori sectionis parte protruda- tur, ac dein vinculum arteriæ circumdetur,quod ipsius corpus super canalem stringat. Quum enim id fit, san- guis quidem & spiritus per arteriam ad pedem usque excurrit, verùm tota arteriæ pars canali subdita non amplius pulsat, soluto autem vinculo arteriæ pars ca- nali subdita non minùs quàm superior pulsat.* Non fecit id *Harveius*, sed *Galenus* & *Vesalius* fecerunt, quibus magis credendum. Sed fieri non posse pu- tas ob sanguinis impetum. Accipe igitur à nobis administrationem anatomicam, arteriam liga in- ter F A, & G C, acuto scalpello sectionem faci- to in B, nullus sanguis profluet, nisi qui consistit intra vincula, tum canalem D E indito, ut docet *Vesalius*. Liga iterum arteriam super canali in F & in G, tunc solve priora vincula quæ arteriam stringebant inter *A F*,[& *G C*, sanguis liberrimè per canalem profluet ad extremas usque arterias, nec

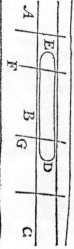

Fig. 13

supplied from the food consumed. Primrose again invokes the spumification theory, and insists that the quantity of blood is very small. He goes on to maintain that nutrition is achieved by each part *attracting* what it needs in the quantities it needs from the blood, and that Harvey is consequently wrong in relating nutrition to a motion of the blood that has been *imposed*. Indeed, he often returns to the Galenic faculty of attraction in criticising Harvey, and to him indeed it looked as if Harvey was denying this (and a large number of other principles of theoretical medicine). That blood could be moved without a faculty of attraction might well have been part of the reason why (as we shall see) Descartes and others became interested in Harvey's doctrines. We shall also see that the denial of attraction became an important feature of those who opposed traditional natural philosophy.

Here, it is part of Primrose's attack on Harvey to reaffirm the learned tradition in natural philosophy and medicine. For him, the tradition was based on Galen (whom he quotes more than sixty times) and to a lesser extent on Aristotle (a third as much). Vesalius and the modern anatomists (but not Colombo) appear in Primrose's words less often than Aristotle, but enough to show that he accepted recent developments in anatomy. So much could be said of most authors of his time, but where he differs from most is in accepting the medievals as a useful part of the learned tradition. No humanist or reformer of the earlier period would have found it useful to identify Harvey's view of the forceful systole with that of Turrisianus, the *plusquam commentator* and arch-scholastic in the eyes of a Hellenist like Leoniceno.[18] Primrose also cited Nicholas of Florence and relied on a series of authors between Aquinas and the sixteenth-century Portuguese Jesuits.[19] Primrose maintained his devotion to the learned tradition for another quarter of a century, and in 1657, the year of Harvey's death, he was still deep in an old battle with Fortunatus Vopiscus Plemp of Louvain (who is considered below), a Harveian convert. In this tract Primrose says he prefers the old commentators, Gentile da Foligno, Ugo Benzi, Jacobus de Partibus, Jacobus Forliviensis, Thomas de Garbo and Nicholas of Florence, to the moderns (except for his teachers).[20] By now he had come under heavy attack from the *circulatores*, he says,[21] and as we shall see indeed the controversy had been effectively settled in Harvey's favour. Primrose was now

---

[18] Ibid., pp. 23, 76. (The identity Primrose mistakenly finds in the views of Aristotle, Harvey and Turrisianus is a spumification of blood in the heart.) For the attack on Turrisianus see for example N. Leoniceno, *Opuscula*, Basle, 1532, p. 5r (the attack on Pliny) where the work of the commentators is said to be 'all exposition and of little use'.

[19] See below, chap. 8.

[20] J. Primrose, *Destructio Fundamentorum medicinae Vopisci Fortunati Plempii in Academia Lovaniensi medicinae professor*, Rotterdam, 1657, p. 1. Plemp came back readily two years later with a *Munitio* to defend his *Fundamenta* and in the same year G. Blasius fired off an *Impetus* against Primrose's involvement in the Plemp affair.

[21] Primrose, *Destructio*, p. 86.

ready to accept a pulmonary transit.[22] In doing so he preserves what he can of the Galenic system by having the sooty wastes from the heart expelled through the pulmonary artery, not the traditional venous artery (pulmonary vein). But still he demands that nutrition of the flesh can only occur by the exercise of the faculty of attraction, drawing from blood that is often still and certainly not circulating.

### Thomas Winston

Primrose's articulate reaction to Harvey's book was the beginning of a continuing campaign on Primrose's part, which we shall follow in subsequent chapters. A more usual reaction to *De motu cordis* was to ignore it. John Collins, the Regius Professor of Physic at Cambridge from 1626 to his death in 1634, took no notice of Harvey or the circulation.[23] He had taken his MD twenty years before Harvey published and was not inclined to alter his ideas. He had been a fellow of the college since 1613 and so undoubtedly knew of Harvey's demonstrations; but as censor (1615) and lecturer on anatomy (1624) he had professional reasons to preserve orthodox Galenism, the touchstone of learning within the college.

Such also was the case of Thomas Winston, an almost exact contemporary of Harvey and Professor of Physic at Gresham College from 1613 to 1643, a period, that is, that included Harvey's anatomy lectures, the publication of his book and the controversies of its early career. Like Harvey, Winston had been to Padua and had heard Fabricius. Winston was also a Fellow of the College of Physicians from 1615 and must surely have been aware of Harvey's doctrines from their first announcement. But Winston was also a censor of the college from 1622 to 1624 and again from 1630 to 1637.[24] In this position he was responsible for helping to assess candidates for the licence and fellowship, and as we shall see below the criterion on which they were judged was their learning, in other words, their Galenism. Winston had a professional obligation to be a Galenist, and in addition seems to have had no inclination as an individual to follow Harvey. Having spent some time in France, he was again Professor of Physic at Gresham from 1652 until his death in 1655.

His Gresham anatomy lectures were published in 1659, but it is not

---

[22] Ibid., p. 86.

[23] *DNB*; H. Bayon, 'William Harvey, physician and biologist: his precursors, opponents and successors', *Annals of Science*, 3 (1938), part II, p. 83.

[24] *DNB*; see also Sir H. Rolleston, 'The reception of Harvey's doctrine of the circulation of the blood in England as exhibited in the writings of two contemporaries', in *Essays on the History of Medicine Presented to Karl Sudhoff on the Occasion of his Seventieth Birthday*, London, 1924, pp. 247–54; 250.

known to which period of his teaching they relate. He refers to anatomical observations made in 1628, and to another made by Riolan in 1624,[25] but the bulk of his authorities belong to the previous century. His anatomy is of the 'public demonstration' style, concerned with the three venters rather than the limbs, aimed at displaying the seats of disease within the format of a traditional accessus of observables. There was no place for 'controversies' in a teaching-course at this level, and Winston expressly excludes them, addressing his remarks 'to that which you pleas'd to command us; that was, the History of parts for structure and use'.[26] Nevertheless, he reports quite fully on the older dispute about the passage of blood across the lungs and on new opinions about the generation of arterial blood in the spleen. He offers no 'determination' or personal opinion on these matters; but accepts that the pores of the septum, difficult to see in the dead human body, are revealed in the boiled ox-heart. His mention of Aselli and of the observations of 1624 and of 1628,[27] makes it likely that the lectures were not complete by the time Harvey's book appeared, but were not modified subsequently. Indeed, the problematic anatomy he decided to leave to another place was very probably in fact the circulation: he consequently gives a standard account of the heartbeat, based on the action of the fibres in producing natural motions.[28]

In short, Winston could not have been convinced by Harvey, for he had ample opportunity even before 1628 to teach the new doctrine. His refusal to discuss it in his lectures was no doubt prompted by the recognition that it was a controversy of much greater dimensions than that of the septal pores and would need much re-thinking of the way in which the body worked. But neither was Winston a determined enemy of Harvey's doctrine, for these lectures also gave him the opportunity for battle. That he did not publish the lectures himself also suggests that he had no anti-Harveian axe to grind. No doubt like other practitioners such as Primrose and Read (as we shall see) Winston could see no practical use to the practitioner of a knowledge of circulation, nor any function indeed of the blood itself circulating. The same can be said of one of the most famous practitioners of the seventeenth century, Thomas Sydenham. Harvey's work on the pulse and circulation was seen by Sydenham as precisely the kind of speculative reasoning that he disliked. Moreover, his practice was among 'the vulgar' who, as Evelyn tells us, thought

---

[25] T. Winston, *Anatomy Lectures at Gresham College, London*, 1659, p. 74. Winston here quotes Riolan's pathological observations: 'fit stuffe for a Lawyers heart' he observes (p. 182), upon Riolan finding a bone in the heart of a legal man.

[26] Ibid., p. 82. That these are Winston's Gresham lectures is in fact the supposition of their publisher, who signs himself 'F.P.'. The table of contents, the title and the postils are in Latin; the lectures, at least as published, in English.

[27] Ibid., p. 83.

[28] Ibid., p. 174.

Harvey crackbrained. To have shared that epithet would have done Sydenham's reputation no good at all.[29]

## Robert Fludd and the Rosy Cross

Another colleague of Harvey who saw his demonstrations and heard his lectures, almost certainly at the same time as Primrose, was Robert Fludd. Unlike Primrose, Winston and (as we shall see) Alexander Read, Fludd agreed with Harvey that the blood circulated. But like these three, what determined Fludd's attitude to Harvey's opinions was his own scheme of things. The religious nature of Fludd's world-view is more evident than that of other natural philosophies that Harvey met during his life. It was also a minority view, seen by the major religious sects as eccentric and perhaps dangerous.[30] In a number of places in this book we see how people's religious convictions, because so important to them, determined whether they found anything useful in Harvey's doctrines. This is true of Fludd, and we must pause to examine his position.

Fludd was a Rosicrucian, a 'Brother of the Rosy Cross'. The brothers had no formal organisation and their doctrines became apparent in a number of individuals in the early seventeenth century.[31] Although they often claimed a lineage for their doctrines back to a pre-Reformation figure with the name of Rosenkreuz, by Fludd's time the movement was clearly Protestant. Two seminal Rosicrucian works appeared in 1614 and 1615, causing a stir

---

[29] On Sydenham see A. R. Cunningham, 'Thomas Sydenham: epidemics, experiment and the "Good Old Cause"', in R. K. French and A. Wear, *The Medical Revolution of the Seventeenth Century*, Cambridge University Press, 1989, pp. 164–90.

[30] It must have been seen as dangerous in that the Rosicrucians had no formal organisation and so were difficult for the orthodox authorities to suppress. Moreover the Brothers (as Fludd describes them in the *Clavis*), grasped by an inner conviction, were little concerned with the outward ceremonies and observances that characterised the Christian sects. As a result they readily adopted the external forms of worship wherever they happened to be, and so must have been seen as dangerous from within. Likewise, this inner conviction, based on an understanding of God's mystery, led Fludd to believe that the Mosaic law, introduced as a guide to the troubled post-Adamite world, was merely external and as such was the basis of the 'external' religions of the world, those of the Jews and Muslims, as well as of the Christian sects, the Lutherans, Calvinists, Catholics, Arians, Brunists and Anabaptists. R. Fludd, *Clavis philosophiae et alchymiae Fluddianae, sive Roberti Fluddi armigeri et medicinae doctoris, ad epistolicam Petri Gassendi theologi exercitationem responsum*, Frankfurt, 1622, p. 46. This was printed by Fitzer, the printer recommended by Fludd to Harvey and who published *De motu cordis*; Fitzer explains to the reader that wartime conditions and opposition to Fludd delayed the appearance of the book by about two years. On the Rosicrucians and on the central question of whether they did in fact constitute a secret society, see Frances Yates, *The Rosicrucian Enlightenment*, London, 1972.

[31] See A. G. Debus, *The English Paracelsians*, London, 1965. See also W. Pagel, 'Religious motives in the medical biology of the xviith century', *Bulletin of the History of Medicine*, 3 (1935), 265–312.

throughout Europe as they addressed working scholars with a call for a substitution of Greek learning with a Christian view of nature.[32] Published anonymously and simultaneously in five different languages these works prompted a great deal of correspondence and publication. In Fludd's hands the essential feature of Rosicrucian thinking was a rejection of school natural philosophy as pagan and the adoption of a Mosaic, cabbalistic and hermetic philosophy.

He had spent six years among continental Paracelsians after going down from St John's College, Oxford in 1598,[33] which undoubtedly gave him his spagyric interests. These caused trouble for him when in 1606 he twice failed the college's examination. It was not that he was unlearned, it is recorded,[34] but too chemical in his medicine. His contempt for Galen was felt as a piece of insolence by a college for which Galenism was the professional touchstone of knowledge and qualification. After a difficult period he became a fellow in 1609, and was a censor in 1618 and 1627. As such, he himself sat in judgment on candidates, and so had either swallowed his contempt for Galen, or was bringing the college round to accepting chemical remedies. It was probably the former, for he could hardly have rejected Galenism. Indeed, a year after becoming a censor for the first time he published a book partly structured by the centrally important Galenic categories 'contranatural', 'nonnatural' and 'natural'. To this he added the Rosicrucian category of 'supernatural',[35] which suggests that he wanted to modify Galen's pagan philosophy in his own Christian way.

Fludd is said to have been a friend of Harvey,[36] and was present at many of his dissections. He expressed this as a search by Harvey and others for the cause of circulation, and so he is probably referring partly at least to the period after the announcement of Harvey's doctrines, shortly before Primrose joined the audience. Fludd emphasises the number of bodies dissected and the unremitting search that did not lead to the discovery of septal pores, but only to weariness: further evidence of Harvey's repeated demonstration and discussions before his colleagues and president. Fludd insists on the certainty of knowledge that derived from the repeated dissections, scrutinised by men with eyes like lynxes'. Of course, he says, nature varies in her productions, and

---

[32] These works were the *Fama fraternitatis* and the *Confessio*. See A. G. Debus, 'Harvey and Fludd: the irrational factor in the rational science of the seventeenth century', *Journal of the History of Biology*, 3 (1970), 81–105; 84.

[33] Debus, *The English Paracelsians*, pp. 106–12.

[34] *The Roll of the Royal College of Physicians of London*, 2nd edn, vol. I, London, 1878 (i.e. Munk's Roll).

[35] W. Shumaker, *The Occult Sciences in the Renaissance*, University of California Press, Berkeley, 1972, p. 13: Fludd's *De supernaturali, naturali, praeternaturali et contranaturali historia* of 1619.

[36] Debus, 'Harvey and Fludd', p. 82.

we may sometimes see a body with only one kidney, or without a spleen; and so the single dissection at Aix, when, as we shall see, Gassendi claimed to have seen a hole in the septum, could not be made into a general statement any more than a single swallow makes a summer.[37]

Fludd's book on the pulse, finished in 1629, is the first positive reference to the circulation.[38] Meanwhile his religious philosophy of the world had attracted the critical attention of Mersenne and Gassendi, and he was drawn into a network of correspondence that included neoteric philosophy and religious matters.[39] Gassendi, drawing Peiresc's attention to Harvey's book in 1629,[40] was critical of Harvey's denial of the septal pores, a denial shared by Fludd.[41] Gassendi attacked Fludd on the question of the pores and on the nature of his philosophy.[42] Again we see that what such men made of Harvey's doctrines depended on what was in their minds before they read about the circulation. A major point of Gassendi's view of the body was that the arterial blood was the same as the venous, and since he did not accept the circulation, he argued that blood crossed, largely unchanged, through the pores. Fludd, despite approving of circulation, had a philosophy of nature that made it imperative that the arterial blood was distinct. To explain the significance of Gassendi's complaints against Fludd's 'etherial spirits' of the arterial blood, and indeed to understand why Fludd so readily adopted Harvey's doctrine we must begin at the beginning of his religious philosophy.

We can best do so by looking at Fludd's reaction to the criticisms of Mersenne and Gassendi.[43] As a Rosicrucian, Fludd thought that the natural philosophy of Aristotle should be rejected on two counts. It was in the first place pagan, or heathen, *ethnica*.[44] Secondly, it was in any case a human contrivance. In its place Fludd wanted something that more truly reflected the power of God in His created world. What he chose was the philosophy of Moses, not only older and more authoritative than that of Aristotle, but closer to the will of God. Moses was not only the law-giver, but was also the biblical authority on the Creation, an essential topic for any philosophy or religion that

---

[37] Fludd, *Clavis*, p. 34.

[38] Debus, 'Harvey and Fludd', p. 82.

[39] Mersenne had attacked Fludd's 'black magic' in his *Celebrated Questions on Genesis* of 1623. In 1628 he sent a number of Fludd's works to Gassendi, along with Harvey's book on the motion of the heart. Gassendi quickly composed a refutation of Fludd (published in 1630). The work examined here is Fludd's summary of a complex of charge and counter-charge, described by Debus, 'Harvey and Fludd'.

[40] R. Descartes, *Oeuvres*, ed. C. Adam and P. Tannery, Paris, 1896–1913; reprinted 1956, Vol. I, p. 264.

[41] Also P. Gassendi, *Viri illustris Nicolai Clausii Fabricii de Peiresc, Senatoris Aquis Extiensis Vita*, 3rd edn, The Hague, 1655, p. 137.

[42] P. Gassendi, *Opera omnia*, 6 vols., Florence, 1727; vol. III, p. 218.

[43] Fludd, *Clavis*, the address to the reader.

[44] Ibid., p. 56.

took account of the natural world. Fludd relies heavily on Old Testament sources for his world-view. But not all that Moses knew or said was represented in the Bible, held Fludd; nor was it all said directly and plainly. There was in other words an oral tradition stemming from Moses, which, being expressed obliquely, needed interpretation. As Fludd says,[45] this is a cabbalistic tradition. Fludd gives space to the views of Leo Hebraeus who taught that the ultimate origin of this 'vocal tradition' was Adam[46] (to whom of course God gave the power to name things).[47] The study of Hebrew was central to this concern for words, and Fludd's text is as sprinkled with Hebrew characters as those of the classical humanists of an earlier generation were sprinkled with Greek.

The interpretation that the cabbala needed, according to Fludd, was that described by Reuchlin (alias Capnion, the pre-Reformation German humanist) and largely resided in a complex treatment of symbolism. Words and particularly names were potent symbols, and the re-arrangement of their letters and an analysis of their numerological value was part of the business of the cabbalist. Reuchlin, who had also faced those who thought the cabbala heretical and diabolical, presents well the case for rejecting the school-authorities: the cabbala, he said (according to Fludd),[48] is not to be understood in terms of coarse senses or by imperious logic, but is to be understood in a third region of thought, where reason is not dominant, where the demonstrative syllogism does not reign and where in its place a more noble awareness, the light of the mind which is higher than the intellect, brings free-will to belief.

Naturally enough, this kind of thing was not agreeable to the university teachers of arts and theology (whom Fludd readily dismisses as scholastics),[49] for whom there was no higher logical demonstration than the demonstrative syllogism, and who professionally separated arts-course logic and natural philosophy from theology. For Fludd it is *all* theology, and all the traditional concerns of natural philosophy are for him explicable in terms of the direct action of God. The early seventeenth-century schoolmen knew that their Christianised but still very Aristotelian world-picture, on which their society rested, would be threatened by the adoption of such a view. Neither Mersenne nor Gassendi were teachers of this kind, but were clearly uneasy about Fludd's views. They could not agree that he was an atheist, but had no trouble in labelling him a heretic and black magician.[50] No doubt to an orthodox Catholic

---

[45] Ibid., p. 17.
[46] Ibid., p. 44.
[47] The tradition was held to have passed from Adam to Noah to Enoch. The cabbalists attempted to remedy the confusion caused by the Fall (Fludd, *Clavis*, p. 44).
[48] Fludd, *Clavis*, pp. 21–2, 45.
[49] Ibid., p. 16.
[50] Ibid., p. 38.

Fludd's determinedly individual reading of the Old Testament, the cabbalistic tradition, the rejection of Aristotle and the school commentators, must all have seemed conspiratorial and subversive. Even Mersenne and Gassendi, who did not want to retain Aristotle, must have shared this feeling. Other parts of Fludd's scheme in contrast were openly opposed equally to both orthodox Catholicism and the new philosophy, in which Mersenne and Gassendi were so interested. Gassendi argued[51] that the scriptures were to be read for their history and their laws, and not for any physical account of the world (the province, that is, of the new philosophy). But for Fludd, Gassendi and Mersenne's new philosophy was an unfortunate and excessive reliance on secondary causes, which distanced God from the workings of the created world.[52] Moreover, said Fludd, they belonged to a 'political' church, a church concerned only with outward display, with the maintenance of morality and the governance of institutions, without an understanding of God's mystery.[53] No, said Fludd, there is more in the Bible than history and law, and it is to be read in a symbolic way. It also, said Fludd, contained true physical knowledge. (In particular its 'meteorology' was far superior to Aristotle's.)[54] This symbolic interpretation led Fludd to argue that Christ's reference to the bread and wine as His flesh and blood was metaphorical.[55] It followed that the Catholic doctrine of transubstantiation, the Aristotelian terminology of substance and accident that it used and the tradition of Thomistic scholarship that reinforced it, were meaningless.

Fludd's rejection of the Aristotelian apparatus of secondary causes and his insistence on the direct action of God in the created world led him to a radical theology. God, he said, is everywhere in the world, in His omnipotence needing no instruments for the operations of the world. The divine spirit animates everything: even the metals of the earth are alive. Even local actions are caused directly by God, the *forma informans*,[56] the *natura naturans*. As Protestants now had done for a long time, Fludd held with St Paul that God is so instinct in the world that one can almost reach out and touch Him.[57] Another Protestant commonplace that Fludd uses is that the invisible things of God are made known through the visible. In perhaps a conscious parody of the Aristotelians' definition of nature as an internal principle of change, Fludd asserts that God is the actor and motor within natural things.[58] Fludd also has

51 Ibid., pp. 44–6.
52 Ibid., p. 63.
53 Ibid., p. 58.
54 Ibid., pp. 13–14; 45–6; 54–5.
55 Ibid., pp. 47, 48.
56 Ibid., pp. 14–16.
57 Ibid., p. 16.
58 Ibid., pp. 52–3.

the Protestant view that it is a duty to come to know God from His creatures – necessarily, he says,[59] it can only be done *a posteriori*.

So Fludd would replace all of Aristotle's local causality with the direct action of God. No doubt Galen's faculties were threatened with a similar fate in Fludd's view, which the college had said was contemptuous. But Fludd as a Rosicrucian was not content to replace the traditional *ethnicae* authorities with a directly religious authority, but instead invoked alchemy as a system of thought in place of school and medical natural philosophy. He is at pains to point out that this is not vulgar alchemy. It has no common fire, no artificial furnaces, no silver or gold of the common alchemist (all of which are 'dead' or simply superficial). It is indeed not a practical subject at all, but a symbolic use of language. Rosicrucians were actually hostile to the ordinary alchemical books, criticising the obscurity of their terminology, their concern with sordid gain and their impious use of the name of the Trinity.[60] Their own use of alchemical symbols was religious, and according to Fludd the all-important image of alchemy was that of purification. Just as in vulgar alchemy the preparation of gold was a question of releasing it from clinging impurities, so the symbolic alchemist separated good from evil, pure from impure, subtle from gross, precious from excremental and true from false, all in number, weight and measure.[61] 'Transmutation' was not of base metals into gold, but the purification of the individual. The philosophers' stone was not an agent in the search for gold, but the spiritual Christ, the rock upon which the true church is built.[62] Fludd calls his synthesis *mea Philosophica sacra*[63] and the notion of the sacred runs through his symbolism: alchemy is an art, and arts imitate nature; nature is the image of the word of God, in which eternal wisdom lives and moves, purifying, rarefying and condensing. In other words God uses macrocosmic alchemy in regulating the world.[64] Fludd explains how baseless is Aristotle's explanation of the changes, 'meteorology', that happen in the world. Aristotle's explanation, involving vapours from land and water attracted by the heat of the sun and forming clouds in the middle air, on which generations of arts course students had been brought up, was for Fludd alchemical: the middle air was an alembic, the alchemical fire was the sun, God's temple, and the clouds and rain the distilled liquors. For Fludd also the process of Creation had also been alchemical, for God had used spagyrical powers to separate the light from the dark (Fludd is not far from his ever-present notion of purification) and the earth from the waters. He was surely

---

[59]  Ibid., pp. 53–4.
[60]  Ibid., pp. 80–4.
[61]  Ibid., p. 77.
[62]  Ibid., p. 46. Fludd's term is the *lapis angularis*.
[63]  Ibid., pp. 14–16.
[64]  Ibid., pp. 77–8.

heterodox indeed in asserting that in doing this God was not creating *ex nihilo* but from pre-existing matter.[65]

It has been necessary to set out so much of Fludd's vision in order to explain what it was that made Harvey's doctrines attractive to him. Pursuing his alchemical symbolism, Fludd sees the action of God in all things primarily as the divine light;[66] in its presence the etherial spirit becomes a world soul or divine spirit. Entering into all things, this becomes specific and directs their actions, especially in maintaining their individual character.[67] Its entry into animals is through the inspired air. This air thus carries a food, *pabulum*, as necessary for the life of the animal as the solid ingested food. In both cases what enters the body is subjected to an alchemical process of purification – which in its technical details is not in fact far from a Galenic concoction.[68] As Servetus had thought, for related reasons,[69] and like Colombo, Fludd held that it was appropriate that the incoming spirit should enter the blood in the lungs, and that its centre of distribution for the vivification of the body by way of the arteries should be the heart. It was consequently necessary for Fludd that the blood crossed the lungs; and for this an impervious cardiac septum was equally necessary. Departing from the somewhat submerged Galenic frame-work into which Fludd squeezes his alchemical purification of spirit, he also says that the blood itself is condensed air, and the flesh concreted blood.[70] Harvey's notion that the blood circulated could be happily accommodated to such a view,[71] for the arterial blood took life and substance to the parts of the body and returned through the lungs for further supplies. But it was the pulmonary transit – the route of the divine spirit into the body – which was more important to Fludd, and it was the impervious septum which he defended most vigorously as a necessary part of that transit.

This minority view was in some ways radically Protestant.[72] For Gassendi,

---

[65] Ibid., pp. 16–19; 69, 72, 77.

[66] Ibid., p. 84.      [67] Ibid., pp. 32–4.

[68] Ibid., pp. 32–3.

[69] Servetus had been a medical student with Vesalius and their teacher, Guinter, recommended him for his knowledge of Galenic anatomy. It was a necessary part of his belief about the entrance of the divine spirit into the body that the blood crossed the lungs, much as in Colombo's case. Servetus fell foul of the Reformers and was burned at the instance of Calvin in 1553. See C. D. O'Malley, *Michael Servetus*, Philadelphia, 1953.

[70] Fludd, *Clavis*, p. 32.

[71] Indeed, Fludd had already described a spiritual and chemical 'circulation' of the blood in his *Anatomiae amphitheatrum* of 1623: see Debus, 'Harvey and Fludd', p. 83. Almost certainly by the time Fludd had finished the book (in 1621) Harvey had described the circulation in his anatomy lectures.

[72] Gassendi (Fludd, *Clavis*, p. 48) expressed his distaste for Fludd's esoteric language by saying that as a Rosicrucian he cried in public 'Bahal, Bahal', as if expecting a *deus ex machina*. Fludd was stung to reply that, in contrast, Gassendi the papist 'trembled in dark papal shadows', 'palpat in densis Papatus tenebris', praying to painted images and statues of wood and stone of mortals and manufactured saints.

Fludd's alchemy linked him to Paracelsus, the *Luther medicorum*[73] and fundamental Rosicrucian texts also spoke approvingly of Paracelsus.[74] The rejection by many Protestants of the learned tradition,[75] now seen as Catholic, the emphasis on personal reading of the scriptures, which so often led to personal interpretation, the preference for the Old Testament in place of the *ethnicae* authorities, led Fludd, as it seems to have led his Protestant contemporary Daniel Sennert (at Wittenberg), to abandon the complex of Greek philosophical ideas about soul, *anima*, or *psyche*, that had come into Western Christendom as Augustine and the Greek Fathers strove to give a rational, philosophical understanding to Christ's words about eternal life. In place of the Platonic or Aristotelian *psyche*, Fludd and Sennert saw the soul in Old Testament terms as the blood. Such a position is not distant from Harvey's later opinion, although we cannot tell if any religious concerns were important to him. But it is significant that in the cases of Servetus, Colombo, Fludd and Sennert it was a similar religious concern that led their attention to the animation of the blood. For Fludd the blood was symbolic. He defined the true Rosicrucian as he who knows what he is in his heart and its deepest blood – *profundo sanguinis illius* – in which inheres the divinity of life.[76] At the very least, this could be seen as consistent with Harvey's view of the blood, and may have encouraged Fludd to see Harvey's doctrines in a sympathetic light. In any case his microcosmic alchemical model of repeated purifications matched closely Harvey's belief that the blood returned to the heart for renewal. Like all chemists he was already familiar with the *circulatio* of distillation, and more than most he was ready to appreciate Harvey's macro–microcosmic parallels.

The natural philosophy of the chemists was another which Harvey met and was of course one which determined how its practitioners viewed Harvey's doctrines. There were perhaps two main responses of this kind to Harvey's doctrines. The first was that in England at least chemistry was part of an alternative to classical medicine, along with Platonic and Hermetic doctrines. Many of these had micro- and macrocosmic schemes of correspondence, of which circularity was often a feature. Not only was Harvey, as censor of an increasingly defensive college, acutely aware of the power of such systems, but – it has been argued – they prepared the ground for Fludd's synthesis and for the reception of Harvey's doctrine of circulation. It was from such Platonic and alchemical sources indeed that Walter Warner, in the group round the ninth

---

[73] Fludd, *Clavis*, p. 11. Fludd remarks favourably on some Paracelsian remedies.
[74] See Debus, 'Harvey and Fludd', p. 85.
[75] I am grateful to Andrew Wear for pointing out that Calvin did not reject it.
[76] Fludd, *Clavis*, p. 46.

Earl of Northumberland,[77] described a circulation in the body as part of a general circulation.[78]

The second reaction of the 'chemists' to Harvey's views derived from the fact that many of them drew some support at least for their doctrines from Paracelsus. He had rejected classical medicine because it was pagan – Greek – and had wanted to develop instead a Christian and inspired medicine. Doctors were born, not made, said Paracelsus,[79] created by God to serve man by using the God-given natural remedies. Many of these could be recognised by their 'signatures' and the 'essences' of their virtues could be separated and concentrated, the chemists claimed, by distillation. That is, Paracelsus rejected the traditional rationality of the learned physician, which as we have seen rested on anatomy and the *actio-usus-utilitas* rationality of the parts, so fundamental to Harvey's work. This meant that for the chemists, traditional anatomy had no function, and they preferred to talk in terms of 'cosmic' anatomy, in which the parts of the body corresponded to features of the heavens. Thus the English sectarian John Webster, although accepting (perhaps as an aid to overthrowing traditional views) that the blood circulated, complained that Harvey used 'vulgar anatomy' rather than 'mystical'.[80] Likewise Oswald Croll dismissed 'local anatomy' in favour of 'essential and elemental' anatomy of man and the world.[81] Such a medicine had a clear political and religious position. The preparation of medicine from freely available materials and the absence of a need for traditional learning meant that ordinary people could heal themselves without recourse to a learned physician and his monopolistic Latin books. As a Reformer, Paracelsus wanted every person to have at their disposal the means of taking responsibility for their own health.

Paracelsian medicine appealed to those who disliked medical monopoly and authority. In England it made little headway before about 1640[82] but was attractive to some Puritans, who thought that classical medicine had failed in the same way as the established church, and that its scholastic dress was close to the doctrines of the church that had been rejected at the Reformation.[83]

---

[77] This was Henry Percy, the 'wizard earl', whose patronage of non-university natural philosophy was important in early seventeenth-century England. See R. H. Kargon, *Atomism in England from Hariot to Newton*, Oxford, 1966.

[78] For Warner, see Webster, 'William Harvey'.

[79] Compare Albert Kyper, *Institutiones medicae, ad Hypothesis de circulari sanguinis motu compositae. Subjugitur ejusdem Transsumpta medica, quibus continentur Medicinae fundamenta*, Amsterdam, 1654, p. 4.

[80] Debus, 'Harvey and Fludd', p. 97.

[81] C. Webster, *The Great Instauration. Science, Medicine and Reform 1626–1660*, London, 1975, p. 286.

[82] Ibid., pp. 273–6. More recently Webster has given greater prominence to early seventeenth-century chemical medical practice; Webster, 'William Harvey'.

[83] Webster, *The Great Instauration*, p. 274.

Chemical medicine was also attractive to those practitioners without access to the college. The troubling paganness of Greek medicine could be avoided by accepting the authority of the Bible in place of that of the ancient authors. This led to differences of emphasis, with Paracelsus and others finding a model of healing in Christ and the New Testament while others like Fludd found that the Old Testament had a more holy and more ancient authority than the Greeks.

While it is possible to see some links between Harvey's natural philosophy and chemistry (for example he uses the notion of distillation and compares the lungs to an alembic),[84] yet there is no doubt that chemistry, partly developed as an alternative to Aristotle, was alien to Harvey's natural philosophy. For a variety of reasons then, chemical practitioners of medicine were unlikely to agree with Harvey.[85] They contrast as a group on almost every particular with the traditional physicians, where perhaps Harvey was most readily received. The physicians were learned in a traditional way, most of them having Oxford and Cambridge degrees. They were members of a medical monopoly, the college. Some, like Glisson and for a while Harvey himself, worked within a university. They were largely Anglicans and Royalists.[86] They were less interested than those working for further Reform in gaining control of the natural world and more interested in how God had put it together; they more readily accepted Harvey's doctrines and made experiments with animals one of their chief concerns. Harvey was one of them. He was no religious or political radical. He disliked religious enthusiasm and the religious and political atmosphere in Cambridge made him change his mind about endowing a chair of natural philosophy.[87] He was a Royalist, a traditionalist and he did not think much of the chemists.[88]

---

[84] W. Pagel, *William Harvey's Biological Ideas*, Basle, 1967, p. 192 and other writers have taken up his use of the analogy of distillation.

[85] Some instances of the chemists' rejection of Harvey's philosophy are listed by Robert G. Frank, *Harvey and the Oxford Physiologists. A Study of Scientific Ideas*, University of California Press, 1980, p. 17. Van Helmont's *Ortus medicinae* of 1648 does not mention Harvey or the circulation (Bayon, 'William Harvey', part II, p. 93). Like Paracelsus, van Helmont found Aristotle pagan, and he sought an alternative metaphysics in a created world. See W. Pagel, 'The reaction to Aristotle in seventeenth-century thought. Campanella, van Helmont, Glanvill, Charleton, Harvey, Glisson, Descartes', in *Science, Medicine and History*, Oxford University Press, 1953, vol. I, pp. 489–509.

[86] In Oxford Thomas Clayton, the professor of anatomy, formed the Royalist Legion. Thomas Willis joined it in 1643. See Audrey B. Davis, *Circulation Physiology and Medical Chemistry in England 1650–1680*, Kansas, 1973, p. 15.

[87] 'I might just as well have made Anabaptists, fanatics and every kind of robber and parricide my heirs.' L. M. Payne, 'Sir Charles Scarburgh's Harvean Oration', *Journal of the History of Medicine*, 12 (1957), 158–64; 163.

[88] See Sir Geoffrey Keynes, *The Life of William Harvey*, Oxford, 1966, p. 372; it is one of Aubrey's stories.

## Corporations and Galenism

When Harvey, about to announce the fact of the circulation in chapter 8 of *De motu cordis*,[89] expressed his fear not only of evil from the ill-will of certain people but even of making all men his enemies, he had in mind more than the deep-rooted respect for the ancients which he knew, and said, was widely cultivated. He also knew there were external reasons for preserving Galenism.

In the early seventeenth century, learned medicine was the business of the medical faculties within the universities, of professional groupings like the College of Physicians in London, of the Colleges of Doctors in the Italian university towns, which were not coterminous with the faculties, and to a lesser extent of the professional groupings of surgeons. Another specialist group was that of the apothecaries, incorporated largely within the guild structure of the towns. The primary purpose of such groupings was to act for the benefit of their members. Thus the College of Physicians in London, Harvey's professional body, had in principle a monopoly of internal medicine in London, backed by parliament, and the routine business of the college was the suppression of illicit practice. Their monopoly did not conflict with the claims of the two universities to give licences to practise. Rather, their co-operation was mutually supportive. The universities had long since defined what learned medicine was and they supplied also the people – the lawyers, members of parliament – who would argue for the maintenance of the monopoly of learned medicine. When in 1620 the college forgot to pursue the confirmation of their charter in parliament, Harvey and others hastily lobbied the universities' MPs. They got what they wanted, and the MPs in turn sought closer links between the college and the universities.

What constituted illicit practice was in effect defined by the college itself. To see how this had come about we must briefly look at the earlier history of the college. Its ultimate origin was Henry VIII's legislation (1511) for the control of medical practice in London by a system of licensing by the Bishop of London or the Dean of St Paul's, and in the country by the bishops. The prelates were to act on medical and surgical advice. However, the system did not appear to be very successful and in 1518 Henry and Wolsey set up a College of Physicians. This was basically a group of eight physicians who took over the bishops' power of licensing. They were also able to fine unlicensed practitioners and, under Mary, imprison them. The eight physicians of the college were the 'Elects', and one of them was Thomas Linacre.[90]

---

[89] W. Harvey, *Exercitatio anatomica de motu cordis et sanguinis in animalibus*, Frankfurt, 1628, p. 41.

[90] On the College of Physicians see Sir George Clark, *A History of the Royal College of Physicians*, vol. I, Oxford University Press, 1964.

The College was thus founded at a critical time in the history of medicine, just as the humanists had succeeded in their campaign against the scholastics. The printing history of the *Articella*, the medieval textbook of medicine, came to an abrupt halt in the 1530s. In its place appeared humanist translations of Hippocrates and Galen and somewhat later digests – more suitable for teaching – of classical authors.[91] Linacre and the humanists knew exactly what medicine was. It was Greek; and the practical and aphoristic Hippocrates was to be interpreted rationally as Galen the great commentator had interpreted him. The humanists did not succeed in removing Avicenna from the medical curriculum, but they greatly fortified the presence of Galen.

We have already seen that in becoming a university subject medicine became increasingly rational, in the sense that its theory became an important characteristic, identifying this kind of medicine. It was this kind of medicine of which the university faculties attempted to keep a monopoly. One of the arguments they used was that learned medicine was more effective than any other medicine. It was therefore (they argued) in the public interest to suppress other kinds of practice. To the extent that they succeeded, practitioners of empirical medicine, a recognised sect in antiquity, became quacks. The rational physicians also claimed a large measure of control over the surgeons and apothecaries. The statutes of Padua employ very strong language in urging the town authorities to act against empirics.[92] The preamble tells of the many empirics who without shame, skill or learning, call themselves physicians; the apothecaries, the barbers and the *mulierculae* apply internal remedies without understanding; to stop them is to protect the public and maintain the dignity of the faculty; Padua and district should be rid of all practitioners except those who have studied medicine for three years. As in the case of the college in London, the faculty in Padua claimed the right to grant a licence to illicit practitioners (at least in surgery) after an examination.[93]

The touchstone of learned, rational medicine was, then, that its practitioners had spent a number of years at a university, learning medicine and the arts, including a natural philosophy that provided a good deal of the learning that constituted the theory of medicine. The claim that other kinds of practitioners were not qualified was a claim that they did not have this learning, in strict medical terms, of Hippocrates and Galen. The very process of becoming a physician involved learning a great deal of these two authors; correspondingly, the test of medical qualification was to enquire into the classical learning of the

---

[91] For example, the anatomical digests of Sylvius, *In partem . . . Isagoge* (1556) and J. Guinter, *Institutionum anatomicarum secundum Galeni Sententiam, ad candidatos medicinae, libri quatuor*, Paris, 1536.

[92] *Statuta almae universitatis D. artistarum et medicorum Patavini Gymnasii*, Venice, 1589, p. 69r.

[93] *Statuta*, p. 42v.

candidate. The language of learned medicine was Latin, and the physicians took care that it should remain so. Surgeons and apothecaries were normally taught in the vernacular, and had little access to the medical texts.

So in examining unqualified practitioners the President and Censors of the College of Physicians first discovered whether or not the examinee could speak Latin. In 1614, a Dr Eyre 'making use of a language very like Latin' gave insufficient answers to his questioners. In 1624 a protégé of the duchess of Richmond claimed to have forgotten all his Latin following a fracture of the skull; another candidate in the same year claimed to be able to understand, but not to speak Latin. In 1627 John Lambe was asked to 'read a little in a Latin Galen', but could not.[94] If they passed the language barrier, the examinees were then quizzed on their knowledge of Galenic theory. Dr Eyre did not know what the seven 'naturals' were, and showed generous ignorance about elements and temperaments. One of the texts the candidates may have been expected to know was Linacre's translation of Galen's *On Temperaments* and *Unequal Temper*, to the understanding of which a Dr Boet proved unequal in 1632, in Harvey's presence. By 1676 the examination ranged in order over three main areas, the form and function of the body, pathology and therapeutics.[95] Rational medicine, as observed above, had anatomy as its starting point, and in 1608 the college had announced 'our Statutes require that every Fellow of the College be deeply studied and soundly learned in physick, that he be well read in Galen and Hippocrates, that he be able to read a lecture in Anatomy'.[96] Fines could be imposed for unorthodoxy.[97]

Harvey's own career in the college illustrates the pressures on the physicians to preserve their Galenism. He was a censor in the college for the first time in 1613, when he was a philosophically inclined physician who (on the evidence of the anatomy lectures) might be inclined to adopt a peripatetic position rather than a Galenic one in some traditional disputed questions, but whose Galenic orthodoxy was otherwise intact. But when he became censor for the second time in 1625 he believed that the blood circulated, and two years later, censor for the third time, he was close to writing *De motu cordis*. He was censor again in 1629, the year after the book appeared and Harvey was in the anomalous position of a radical innovator examining candidates for the orthodoxy on which the college insisted, and imposing penalties upon illicit practitioners. These penalties were not light. Just before Harvey's time one John Lumkin was fined £20 and imprisoned. In 1610 Stephen Bredwell appeared before the full Comitia of the college, including Harvey, on a charge of publishing a pamphlet

[94] Keynes, *William Harvey*, p. 152.
[95] Ibid., pp. 36–42.
[96] Ibid., p. 137.
[97] Ibid., p. 95.

attacking the college. It also contained, however, material from Sambucus Hispanus, who had criticised Hippocrates and Galen. The attack upon themselves and upon Hippocrates and Galen struck at the very heart of the college's activity in maintaining their monopoly of learned medicine in London. Bredwell was fined £4.[98]

So how could Harvey reconcile his own radical innovation with his professional activity as an enquirer into other people's orthodoxy? It could not have been easy; and (as we shall see) the college did not like being seen as endorsing Harvey's book, and it soon tightened up the rules about fellows publishing. It seems likely that Harvey saw his work on the heart and blood as philosophical rather than medical. As his opponents argued loudly, the circulation had no medical use. Harvey made little attempt to explain the medical significance of circulation, and conspicuously avoided building up a system on it in the years after 1628. In other words he separated the truth of his philosophical novelty from the professional business of making sure that practitioners had an appropriate level of learning in medicine. He may have believed that at the level of practice Galenic medicine worked well enough, despite his own modification of one of its theoretical principles.

Similar external forces were acting in universities like Paris. Sir Theodore Mayerne, Harvey's colleague at the college, was accused by the faculty in Paris of neglecting Hippocrates and Galen. What they may have been concerned about was his espousal of chemical medicines. The danger here was the potential development of a chemical medicine as a whole alternative practice, over which the colleges and faculties would have no control. Here was an additional reason to insist that real medical training was reading the ancients. De Mayerne wrote a defence in answer to the charge, the only book he published during his lifetime.[99] We have also seen Paris as the centre of the defence of Galen's anatomy, and Harvey himself came to see (as he told Schlegel)[100] that Riolan, as Dean of the College of Paris had external and professional reasons for defending Galenism.

These then were the circumstances and pressures upon Harvey when he decided to write the book. The pressure for orthodoxy must have become greater when Harvey became an elect of the College in 1627, a year in which he was again censor and we can understand his hesitation and the fears that he expresses in chapter 8. Would Harvey, as censor for the first time in 1613, before his discoveries, have then admitted into a fellowship a candidate who believed in such non-Galenic things as a forceful systole and an artery-to-veins circuit of blood? In 1616 in the anatomy lectures Harvey himself argued (like

[98]  Ibid., p. 64.
[99]  Ibid., p. 137.
[100]  See Harvey's letter to Slegel: Harvey (1963; Everyman edn), p. 185.

Sylvius) that the body had changed since Galen's day, perhaps in order to escape being fined for unorthodoxy by the college.[101] It is possible that Harvey had his book published abroad so as not to appear to be speaking with the voice of the college, which had good reason to remain Galenic and could have been embarrassed. It was no doubt to avoid any such embarrassment that the college decided in 1635 that all books published by the fellows had first to be inspected by the president and censors. When Roger Drake in 1641 wanted the college's approval for the re-publication of his thesis, a defence of Harvey against Primrose, the imprimatur was not forthcoming. Drake was in fact allowed to publish it, but the college's refusal to give its name to the book suggests either that Harvey still had opponents within the college, or that the college did not wish to become involved in controversies that might tarnish its orthodox image.[102] Indeed, Drake discovered that the college wanted to make it clear that it had not at all lent its corporate name to Harvey's book.[103]

It is even possible that Harvey would have run into difficulties had he tried to publish in London. In 1614, for example, the Bishop of London sought the advice of the college on whether he should give a licence for Helkiah Crooke's anatomical textbook to be printed. The problem was partly that it was in English, and partly that it had illustrations of the male and female genitalia. The college was against publication in an unmodified form, but the bishop did not take their advice and publication went ahead. After 1625, when Laud became Charles I's religious adviser, control of book publishing became tighter. Harvey might have had the embarrassment of his very unorthodox book being sent by the Bishop of London to his own college for assessment of suitability for printing.

To have looked at these pressures acting on Harvey and indeed on many medical men is helpful in two respects. Firstly, it helps us understand Harvey's research, his 'Aristotle project'. There was clearly an 'official Galenism', indeed a statutory Galenism, of the medical institutions[104] which throws into

---

[101] Keynes, *William Harvey*, p. 95.    [102] Ibid., p. 282.

[103] R. Drake, *Contra Animadversiones Iac. Primirosii in theses quas ipse pro sanguinis motu circulari, sub Praesidio Io. Walaei, in celeberrima Leidae Academia, publico examini subjecerat Vindiciae*, p. 238, in *Recentionum disceptationes de motu cordis, sanguinis, et chyli, in animalibus*, Leiden, 1647.

[104] In the London college, the new statutes of 1647 retained an insistence on rigorous examination for new members in Hippocrates and Galen. Yet this was not seen as inconsistent with novelty of belief within the college, and Baldwin Hamey gave pro-circulatory anatomy lectures in 1648, as Harvey had done thirty years before. See T. M. Brown, 'Physiology and the mechanical philosophy in mid-seventeenth century England', *Bulletin of the History of Medicine*, 51 (1977), 25–54. In Padua the statutes set out with some urgency the reasons for maintaining the monopoly of internal medicine in the hands of university-educated physicians. They argue that unlearned internal medicine is dangerous to the public and to the Faculty's dignity. Like the London college, the Paduan physicians claimed the power to summon and fine misbehaving surgeons. *Statuta*, p. 42v.

relief Harvey's natural philosophy, based on Aristotle and progressive in nature. Secondly, these pressures had a significant part to play in determining how Harvey's doctrines were taken up, and how a consensus was formed or prevented.

### Surgery and Alexander Read

During Harvey's lifetime the physicians, by constant action, maintained their monopoly of internal medicine based on anatomical and rational principles. Harvey himself was instrumental in the political battle of the physicians to maintain dominance over the surgeons.[105] So much so that the Lumleian lectures, endowed as surgical lectures with the intention that the partly English lecture should be derived from the big Latin surgeries, was turned by Harvey's time into a mostly philosophical anatomy.[106] Even the old anatomy demonstrations at Surgeons Hall could involve a lecture by a physician.[107] The surgeon's work was practical, his writings technical rather than theoretical and in English. We would not expect that there was much in Harvey's doctrines to command the surgical interests of surgeons.

One surgeon who did concern himself with Harvey's doctrine was Alexander Read.[108] He indeed lectured on anatomy at Surgeons Hall, in the years immediately following the publication of De motu cordis.[109] He can hardly have been ignorant of the Harvey affair and, as a fellow of the college, had a number of professional links with Harvey himself.[110] We can reconstruct with some certainty how he reacted to Harvey's book, because his copy of it, bound with Primrose's attack on it, survives in Aberdeen University Library. Indeed Read gave the whole of his library to King's College, and we can therefore also see how he reacted to other contemporary and related publications.

Read gave 113 books to King's. Over seventy of them were published after 1600 and almost all the rest in the last three decades of the sixteenth century. It looks, then, like a working library built up by Read himself rather than one he had inherited or one that he had been given. If this is so then it is clear that he had, apart from the anatomical and surgical works we would expect, a considerable interest in the new chemical medicine. He was also interested in

---

[105] Keynes, William Harvey, p. 69.

[106] Ibid., p. 85.

[107] See also P. Allen, 'Medical education in seventeenth century England', Journal of the History of Medicine, 1 (1946), 139.

[108] See R. K. French, 'Alexander Read and the circulation of the blood', Bulletin of the History of Medicine, 50 (1976), 478–500.

[109] See the slightly differing accounts by D'Arcy Power, William Harvey, London, 1897 and W. Menzies (on which see French, 'Alexander Read').

[110] He and Harvey together examined the Lancashire witches for morphological peculiarity. See K. Keele, William Harvey, London, 1965, p. 71.

contemporary debates and in contemporary assessment of ancient medicine. Of the ancient texts themselves he had few. The only Galenic text he owned, but one that befitted a surgeon, was that on bones. The four volumes of Hippocrates (with an emphasis on the *Aphorisms* and *Prognostics*) form only a skeletal classical foundation of medicine. The four volumes of the works of Caspar Hofmann are largely commentaries on Galen and represent up-to-date assessment of the ancient author. The eight volumes of Hieronymus Mercuralis and the eight of Daniel Sennert, both modern unorthodox authors, testify to Read's interest in contemporary authors.

So Read was no defender of the ancients, and was apparently attracted to recent developments in medicine. Yet an examination of his own printed works and of the notes he made in his copies of Harvey's and Primrose's books show that ultimately he did not find the doctrine of circulation attractive. Why not? As in the case of Primrose, it is important to discover the reasons behind people's rejections, as well as acceptances, if we are to understand the mechanisms of consensus.

Read was primarily a surgeon. He had, it is true, been created MD of Cambridge by letters of James I (whose Latin Secretary was Read's brother Thomas). It is also true that Read was well educated, for his was a Latin library, and his Greek was better than, for example, Harvey's.[111] But it may be that his surgical background and long experience did not endow him with that respect for the 'official Galen' of the faculties and of the college. He would have been about fifty when he was made MD (in 1620) and it was four years later that he was elected fellow of the college.

The story of Read's anatomy publications (in which his reaction to the circulation appears) is a continuation of that of Helkiah Crooke's. We have seen the college hesitate in 1614 over the publication of Crooke's *Microcosmographia*, partly because it was in English. Almost certainly the college objected because publication represented a breach of the medical monopoly of Latin. The publisher, W. Jaggard, had in fact spotted a gap in the market. There were anatomy books aplenty in Latin, liberally supplied with illustrations,[112] but few in English. The illustrations could be copied readily by a wood-engraver, and Jaggard needed only a medical man to compose an English text from fragments of the Latin of a number of originals. The Jaggard–Crooke partnership (Keynes said they were 'in league') was a good one, and the early seventeenth-century English reading market supported an enlarged second edition of Crooke's book in 1631. This must have been at least partly a surgical market, for the new edition carried notes on the use of over fifty

[111] Keynes, *William Harvey*, p. 95.
[112] The college had complained of Crooke's book that it exposed the private parts of both sexes in its illustrations. The fact that Latin texts did the same implies that the college's real objection was to the use of the English language.

surgical instruments. That it was a surgical market is also indicated by the fact that after both editions Jaggard sought out the surgeon Read to make an abbreviated version of Crooke's longer (and more expensive) book. Read complied, and the first result, his first publication, of 1616, is simply a series of notes attached to the illustrations from the larger book. Read called it Ευματογραθια Ανφρπινε or *A Description of the Body of Man*. This was also the year in which Harvey, still of course in ignorance of the circulation, began his anatomy lectures in the college.

So the story we must pursue here begins in 1628 with the publication of Harvey's book. As a fellow of the college since 1624, Read surely knew of the arguments for and against Harvey's doctrines even before 1628, and certainly had not accepted them. He did not buy a copy of Harvey's book until 1630 or even later, and waited until Primrose had published his attack on it. He then devoted a great deal of care to reading the jointly bound volume.

We can tell a great deal about Read from his inscriptions in the books of his library, and first we must look at the nature of these inscriptions. This will mean a little digression, justified by the uniqueness of Read's position (his closeness to Harvey, the extent of his inscriptions and the survival of his library). It will also be justified in showing us other aspects of contemporary natural philosophy.

Read marked his books in a characteristic way, scoring important words above and below in red ink. His marginal postils summarise important stages in the author's argument. Sometimes, as in the case of Harvey and Primrose, he lists these postils in an alphabetical index in the rear flyleaves of the book, almost exactly as the disputed questions and *dubia* of a medieval commentary were often listed separately. Occasionally – as in the case of Spiegel's anatomy textbook, the *De humani corporis fabrica*[113]– he describes the content of each of the major sections of the work on a slip of paper glued to that section and projecting above the top of the book. The purpose of the scoring and the postils is not to express agreement or disagreement, but to list the important arguments. He is in fact behaving exactly as an academic expositor would, in mapping out the 'logical morphology' of the author's arguments (see chapter 1 above). His over- and under-scoring, so often at the beginning of sentences, corresponds to the 'points' at which the commentator broke up the text (see fig. 13). His postils are located in the margins to connect to and expand the word or phrase scored in the text, in precisely the manner that university students had been doing for centuries in the wide margins of their textbook of natural philosophy.

These postils of Read's often follow the sequence of a disputation. The topic will be written in the margin as though it was a thesis, sometimes as a question,

[113] Frankfurt, 1632.

beginning *An* . . . and sometimes just *Dubium* or a proposition couched in the infinitive. Then opinions of various authors are numbered, including that of the author, arguments are listed and numbered, problems and solutions likewise. So natural is this approach to a text to Read that he often sees structure in argument where the modern reader does not because it is slightly below the surface in the author. Read often writes down the stages of the argument by a marginal Roman number when the author – for example Harvey – has expressed himself simply with something equivalent to 'if': Harvey's 'si enim . . . Et si in Diastole . . . Similiter . . . Quomodo . . . Et si in Systole . . . ' are the scored 'divisions' of Harvey's text that Read marshals numerically in the margin to support his own marginal proposition 'Pulsum et respirationem iisdem usibus non inservire' ('Pulse and respiration do not serve the same purposes'). What might appear to us to be easy rhetorical phrases like 'Of course you might say that . . . however . . . ' become for Read the formal *objectio* and *solutio*, as indeed they were surely intended to be by the author. It is argued above that Harvey's *De motu cordis* is an academic exercise like a declamation, with its disputational techniques. Read's markings show that the formality of the argument was what the contemporary reader did indeed see. The success of Harvey's text in convincing people must have depended partly on his structure of argument (see fig. 14).

Structure of argument was an important part of contemporary natural philosophy. It was this structure of argument that mediated between on the one hand the expectations and conceptions of the audience about anatomy (in this case the audience was Read) and on the other Harvey's attempt to persuade. Read's own education at King's College would have included or indeed have consisted of an arts course that after the troubles of the Reformation had become as Aristotelian as any university course.[114] Here he would have encountered the dialectic and disputational principles with which all university-trained men became familiar.

It will be noted that while Read does not go beyond the *expositio* stage and

---

[114] There survives in King's College Library, Aberdeen, a student notebook (MS. 150) containing much of the arts course as written down by John and William Moir. John was a fourth-year student in 1619 and his course included a discussion of anatomy, which the reformers had inserted into the Scottish universities' arts curriculum; it is taken largely from Bauhin's *Institutiones anatomicae*. John Moir and his fellow students were thus listening to anatomy lectures in Aberdeen while Harvey was giving his anatomy lectures in London; and although Harvey's were at a different level, both sets show the place of anatomy in the received scheme of knowledge. John Moir learned that anatomy was part of self-knowledge and that it was useful in a number of ways: to supply and explain vocabulary that is encountered in good authors and in natural philosophy, to explain how the body was an expression of the powers of the soul. The medical usefulness of anatomy, as in Harvey's similar introductory remarks, is only third on the list. John Moir was also taught that anatomy was useful in ethics (for behaviour follows the temperament of the body) and in theology. See R. K. French, *Anatomical Education in a Scottish University, 1620*, Aberdeen, 1974.

begin a commentary proper, yet we can nevertheless form some notion of what his preferences were. He contents himself with listing the important arguments, but he only does so when the proposition they were designed to support was interesting. Arguments that were not interesting, even in support of an interesting topic, were not marked by Read (he was after all making his *expositio* for himself only) and it is hardly to be supposed that they convinced him. Thus his copy of Bauhin's very orthodox *Theatrum anatomicum* has very few marks, even though he must have agreed with most of it (and it was of course the ultimate source of the anatomy of his own publications). The *Theatrum* does not, for example, subscribe to the theory of pulmonary transit, which Read found interesting and came to accept.

The care with which Read read Harvey's book is shown by his emendations: he supplies a fragment of text lost by clipping when the two books were bound together, and either from the rare erratum-sheet (not now present in this copy) or from his own close reading he corrects a large number of misprints, to say nothing of his own insertions where the typography is particularly bad or Harvey's style more than usually obscure (for example on p. 27). So we would expect his postils and analysis of the argument to be equally careful. He starts with the example given above, systematising Harvey's arguments (in the Proemium) for the proposition that respiration and the pulse do not serve the same purpose. He has little interest in Harvey's preceding dedications or the following account of his reasons for writing. He is at once struck, however, by Harvey's use of animals, which is evidence to support Primrose's grudging admission that Harvey's readers were generally impressed by his knowledge of animals. (Read in particular took note of Harvey's description of the way some

Fig. 14. Alexander Read's annotations on the second page of Harvey's proem. Read acted as a medieval expositor in analysing Harvey's text. He first identifies Harvey's proposition and writes it in the margin. He scores in red ink above and below each *puncta* or *lemma* where Harvey begins a new stage of the argument, and numbers it formally with Roman numerals in the margin (there are ten of them here, continued over the page). Harvey has not broken up his prose to indicate these stages of the arguments formally, but simply introduces them with *Si enim . . . Et si . . . Similiter . . .* , and so on. Likewise Read (but not Harvey) formally labels Harvey's sentence beginning *Dicere vero* as a refutation of an objection, an essential stage in scholastic procedure. Read continues in this fashion through the whole of Harvey's text and that of Primrose's rejection of it. At the end of each he makes an alphabetical index of all the propositions he has listed in the margins, just as medieval disputed questions were listed separately from the commentary, for the convenience of those contributing to disputations. In other words contemporary readers saw a great deal of structure in Harvey's text, a structure that shaped their reaction to it. We in turn need to understand that structure if we are to understand the reaction.

## PROOEMIVM. 11

*similiter Arte, iarum pulsus, & vsus, à pectoris & pulmonum. Si enim ijsdem vsibus inseruiant pulsus, ac respiratio, & in Diastole introsumant aërem in cauitates suas arteria (vti vulgo dicunt)& in Systole per eosdem poros carnis, & cutis fuligines emittant, nec non medio tempore inter Systolem, & Diastolem aërem contineant ; & quouis tempore aut aërem, aut spiritus, aut fuligines. Quid itaque respondeant Galeno, qui librum scripsit, Natura sanguinem contineri in arteriis, & nihil praeter sanguinem, nimirum neque spiritus, neque aërem, sicut ab experimentis, & rationibus in eodem libro facile colligere licet. Et si in Diastole replentur arteriae ab aëre introsumpto, in maiori pulsu, maiori subeunte aëris copia : ergo magno existente pulsu, si totum corpus in balneum immerseris, vel aquae, vel olei, necesse est pulsum statim aut minorem esse, aut tardiorem multo : cum per corpus ambientis balnei, aërem intra arterias permeare difficilius sit, si non impossibile. Similiter, cum omnes arteriae tàm profundae, quàm cutaneae, eodem tempore, & pari velocitate distendantur; quomodo poterit aër tàm libere, & celeriter per cutem, carnem, habitumque corporis in profundum pertransire, quam per cuticulam solam. Et quomodo Embryonum arteriae forinsecus in cauitates suas aërem per ventrem maternum, & per corpus vteri attrahant? Velquomodo Phocae, Balenae, Delphines, cetaceum omne genus, & pisces omnes in profundo maris arteriarum suarum Diastole, & Systole, per immensam aquae massam celeri pulsu aërem introsumunt, & emittunt. Dicere vero quod aërem implantatum in aqua absorbeant, & in aquam fuligines suas reddant, figmento haud absimile. Et si in Systole arteriae per poros carnis, & cutis, fuligines è cauitatibus illorum expellunt, cur non item spiritus, quos dicunt etiam in illis contineri, cum spiritus multo tenuiores fuliginibus sint. Et si cum in Systole, tum in Diastole aërem arteriae accipiunt, & reddunt, vti pulmones in respiratione; cur non & hoc faciunt inflicto per*

B 2 *arterio.*

Fig. 14

animal hearts turned pale as they ejected blood.) 'All animals have a heart' notes Read (p. 28) and he scores and postils all the important points in these early chapters where Harvey is establishing the action of the auricles, the forceful systole and the passive, glove-like inflation of the arteries.

But Read passes over, without note or marking the arguments, the passage (p. 33) where Harvey explains that the reason why everyone else has been confused about the true nature of the heartbeat and pulse was the proximity of the heart and lung in the human subject. Read's silence is probably due to Harvey's use of the 'dispute' between Galen and Erasistratus, together with a large quotation from Galen's *On the Opinions of Hippocrates and Plato*. Read, whose interest in modern medical topics we have noted, generally ignores discussions based on ancient authorities. If Harvey had hoped to convince by this device, he had here failed. Perhaps it is partly again a case of a surgeon, Read, not having excessive respect for the official Galen of the medical institutions.

It is not that Harvey's style of exposition is inappropriate for Read's attention as an expositor, for this chapter (5) cries out for the formalisation that Read often employs elsewhere. Moreover, Read has with his usual care (on p. 32) added an ablative sign to give (needed) clarity to Harvey's words, so he has not let his mind wander. The basis of his 'silence' is that he does not think these arguments are worth pointing out. To this extent of course his silence implies non-assent. It continues, at all events, through chapter 6 where Harvey is building up the case for the pulmonary transit, largely from the relationship between the heart and lungs in animals. Read notes only the arguments drawn from the vascular arrangements of the foetus and the final answer – the pulmonary transit – to the question that headed the chapter. Again, Harvey's arguments about the blood permeating through the substance of the lungs have been left unmarked by Read except that he has noted 'The use of the valves' against the very large quotation that Harvey has taken from Galen's *On the Use of the Parts*.

In short, what Read has found interesting in Harvey's book is firstly the distinction between respiration and pulse. Secondly, he followed Harvey carefully on the forceful systole and the nature of the pulse. But he does not seem to have found the arguments for the pulmonary transit very interesting and almost certainly at this point in his career, in the early 1630s, he did not accept it. Harvey's position is that if a link in the argument about the pulmonary transit is broken, the conclusion about the arteries-to-veins circuit cannot follow. Consequently Harvey's report of the problems he wrestled with, of his fear of opposition and his rhetorical justification of circular motion with which he introduces the notion of circulation in chapter 8 are all ignored by Read. He notes only 'The difference between arteries and veins' (p. 42).

So again, if Harvey thought he could carry the reader along with him with these devices, in this case he was wrong. In marked contrast to this silence Read the expositor returns to business with Harvey's sober return to dialectical exposition in chapter 9. Here Read scores the three propositions with which Harvey intends to demonstrate the circulation he has just announced. What particularly interests him is Harvey's quantitative argument. Read's postil reads: 'Quantum sanguinis singulis pulsibus protrudatur in habitum corporis' ('How much blood is propelled into the substance of the body at each pulse'). He scores Harvey's conjectural quantities of blood emerging from the heart at systole, and treats them as two of the four stages of the argument that leads to the conclusion (towards the bottom of p. 44) which is the accumulated quantity resulting from 1,000 pulses. Read leaves the rest of the chapter clear, even though Harvey himself sets up straw 'objections' to be 'resolved'. It is here that Harvey leads from the quantitative argument to the circulation. Read did not think it worthwhile to identify and mark the argument.

His interest returns in the tenth chapter, where Harvey counters objections. We may suppose that it was his personal interest as a surgeon that caused him to note down in postils the experiments with the ligatures with which Harvey offered some visual demonstration of his second proposition in chapter 11; and why fainting sometimes happens after blood has been let (p. 51). He scores some of Harvey's argument only. Again in chapter 12 (Harvey is arguing that blood emerging from a vein must ultimately have come through the arteries from the heart) Read's interest is a surgical one, in why blood sometimes emerges with greater force in phlebotomy (partly from fear, he notes from Harvey). We can note here too Read's interest in the practical medical problems by the solution of which Harvey hoped to confirm the circulation (chapter 16). Like other practical medical men Read would have wanted to know whether a circulation was compatible with practice.

Read was distinctly interested in valves. His half-dozen postils on the valves of the veins – their discoverers, their position, Harvey's rejection of their apparent function, their true 'causes' and Harvey's experiment (with the probe) – end with 'sanguinem per venas in cor fluire, non autem contra' ('Blood [is said] to flow through the veins into the heart, not the other way round'). The infinitive indicates that Read is using a sort of *oratio obliqua* or is treating the sentence as a proposition rather than a conclusion, and in either case is not committing his own opinion. But it is clear that Harvey's argument and experiments on the valves are significant for Read.

Read marks the text most consistently in the last chapter, where Harvey, having maintained his thesis in a partly narrative way, now summarises his conclusions as a sequence of events of the heartbeat, pulse and circulation: this seems to have been more attractive to Read. Running Read's postils together, we can see the stages of the exposition of the argument that Read read into Harvey's text:

Some animals do not have hearts . . . and in others there is a certain pulsating part that corresponds to the auricles of the heart. The differences between the hearts of animals. The dignity and function of the left ventricle. The function of the sinews of the heart . . . their difference . . . some animals do not have them. The substance of the left ventricle; how the substance of the heart relates to that of the body generally. The use of the sigmoid valve [and] of the tricuspid or mitral . . . The right auricle of the heart is the first living part and the last to die . . . the large auricles of the foetus . . . the structure of the heart in the foetus. The different kinds of fibre in the heart and their use. The heart is the principal part of the body. Problem 1 . . . problem 2. Why the arterial tunics are finer towards the extremities. Why the tunic of the arterial vein is not so thick as that of the aorta. Why the lungs have such large vessels. Why similar blood is found in the right and left ventricles of the heart. Why the arterial vein has the structure of an artery and the venous artery that of a vein.

In short, Read had picked up fragments of Harvey's Aristotelian/Socratic method, which showed how a 'heart', wherever found, in different animals or in the foetus, has the same action, an action which, as Read notes with interest but not yet conviction, includes pressing the blood through the lungs.

It is not so easy to interpret Read's inscriptions in Primrose's attack on Harvey. His 'silences' here may represent lack of conviction of the arguments of either the original author or his critic, or may simply be that Read did not want to repeat himself. The topics he picks out may be those he found interesting in Harvey's text, or may be those in which he found Primrose's replies interesting. It is often difficult to tell. But where – very unusually – he inserts a new heading into Primrose's text, *Contra circulationem sanguinis* ('against the circulation of the blood') (p. 79) it is part of his systematisation of Primrose's argument, with which he must have been largely in agreement.

So the treatment given by Read to Harvey's book, probably in 1630 or soon after, shows us that he was interested in the forceful systole, but was probably unwilling to accept the pulmonary transit. Perhaps he read the books while preparing his own lectures for the barber-surgeons in 1632. By then he was sixty-two and had for two years been acting as his own executor (he said)[115] in giving away his books to his old college in Aberdeen. He must have felt that he was nearing the end of a working life. 'The Hour-glass hasteneth and but few sands remain unrun', he was to write.[116] He was not disposed to accept much of Harvey's four-year-old anatomical novelty.

Few historians have missed the parallel and the contrast between Read and Harvey: While Harvey was lecturing on anatomy in the college, his co-fellow Read was doing the same in the Barber-Surgeons' Hall; they knew each other

[115] Read's words are reported in the *Deeds of Foundation of Bursaries at the University and King's College*, Aberdeen (printed by order of the Senatus Academicus), 1857, p. 18.
[116] A. Read, *The Manuall of the Anatomy or the Dissection of the Body of Man*, London, 1638: address to the reader. Read died in 1641; the third edition of the work appeared a year later: I have used the apparently unchanged fourth edition of 1650.

well, yet Read failed to mention the circulation. That at least is the usual interpretation, which carries with it the express condemnation of Read.[117] But Read was not 'doing the same': Harvey was lecturing, probably in Latin, on a largely philosophised anatomy to an audience of educated rationalist physicians; Read (as appears from the publications that arose from the lectures)[118] was lecturing in English to surgeons on tumours, ulcers, muscles and surgical technique.

In 1634 Read published the second edition of the Ευματογραθια and at the same time prepared a discursive work on anatomy, *The Manuall of the Anatomy or the Dissection of the Body of Man*. This was a development of the Ευματογραθια, containing some re-cut figures and new text. It was printed in the same year, after Archbishop Laud's office had scrutinised it. Read's interest remained largely surgical, and the bulk of his output of publications was on surgical technique, tumours, ulcers and muscles. The anatomy text – the *Manuall* – represented as it were the 'theory' of surgery and was heavily derivative, being drawn ultimately from Crooke's account of the body and of the surgical instruments appropriate for operations upon it. Crooke had made no secret of the fact that his book was derived from the books of Bauhin and others – indeed the very market he and Jaggard were aiming for wanted the best Latin authors in English. The same is true of the *Manuall*, which is 'collected out of the best authors'. In 1634 discussion of Harvey's discoveries would have fitted better into the learned discussions in the controversy literature than into digests of accepted Latin authors directed at beginners and dedicated to the Company of Chirurgeons, as the *Manuall* was. Read was probably preparing the book while still giving the anatomy lectures, and all the evidence shows that his anatomy was entirely orthodox (save for his interest in Harvey's forceful systole).

But the more he read the more he was inclined to believe that one component of Harvey's doctrine, the passage of blood through the lungs, must represent reality. Almost certainly by the mid 1630s he had read Spiegel's anatomy text of 1632, the *De humani corporis fabrica*. He had also read Hofmann's two books of 1625 and 1628, that is, the commentary on Galen's anatomy, *Commentarii in Galeni de usu partium corporis humani* and the original work on the thorax, *De thorace*. He could not have done so before 1630 (they are bound with, and annotated with, a book of that date) and internal evidence suggests that he read them after the publication of the first

---

[117] Thus Read is criticised by Pagel, *William Harvey's Biological Ideas*, p. 350; E. Wiel, 'The echo of Harvey's De motu cordis', *Journal of the History of Medicine*, 12 (1957), 167–74; L. Chauvoius, *William Harvey*, London, 1957.

[118] Read's surgical works were *The Chirurgicall Lectures of Tumours and Ulcers*, London, 1635, followed by *A Treatise of all the Muscles of the Whole Body*, London, 1637 and *A Treatise on the First Part of Chirurgerie*, London, 1638. They were based on his lectures to the surgeons.

edition of the *Manuall*, some of the opinions in which he now changed. Read's annotations in Speigel's *De humani corporis fabrica* are dense, particularly where Spiegel denies the porosity of the interventricular septum and the presence of air in the pulmonary vein and comes forcefully to the conclusion that blood passes across the lungs. Spiegel also describes a forceful systole and a forceful diastole: Read scored these passages heavily, and altogether we seem to have here one of the sources for the mixture of things that made up Read's final account of the motion of the heart and blood. Something similar may be said of Read's treatment of his copy of Hofmann's commentary (1625) on Galen's *On the Use of the Parts*.[119] Not much more of it than book 6, on the motion of the heart and blood, has been marked by Read. The latter's attention is again given to the pulmonary transit, which Hofmann demonstrates partly by showing how the *vena arterialis* and *arteria venalis* cannot have a function consistent with their structure and size. In particular Read scores the passage in which Hofmann, dwelling on the quantity of blood that moves from the right to the left side of the heart, insists that it must pass through the lungs.[120]

Read's copy of Hofmann's commentary is bound with Hofmann's book on the thorax in the edition of 1628.[121] Here again Hofmann deals with the quantity of blood passing through the lungs, and as before he is taken with the size of the pulmonary vessels. He agrees with Colombo and Arantius that in man the arterial vein is big enough to take two fingers: Hofmann cannot believe this is needed simply for the nourishment of the lungs. Once more Read shows by his postils that the argument was not lost on him.

So when he came to prepare the second edition of the *Manuall* (it appeared in 1638) Read had read three modern authors arguing for the pulmonary transit. He now accepted it as orthodox enough for this *compendiolum* designed for *tyrones*. Read describes the transit of blood through anastomoses of the lungs and the action of the cardiac valves, and denies the passage of air from the lungs to heart. He has incompletely edited the text of the first edition, for he later speaks of air reaching the heart. The action of the heart is partly the Galenic forceful diastole, in which blood is attracted into the heart from the vena cava (and air from the lungs). But for Read now systole is also a forceful motion, compelling venous blood to enter the lungs by way of the *vena arterialis*, spirits to enter the aorta and, strangely, arterial blood to move up the pulmonary vein, the *arteria venalis*, to the lungs.

---

119 C Hofmann, *Commentarii in Galeni De usu partium corporis humani*, Frankfurt am Main, 1625.
120 Hofmann, *Commentarii*, p. 113 (Book 6): 'Mens non satis acquiescit, quomodo brevi adeo temporis spatio, quantum ab una cordis diastola ad alteram est, tantum sanguinis transfundi possit quantum opus est?'
121 C. Hofmann, *De thorace*, Frankfurt, 1628. Read's scoring is on the passage in book 3, chap. 11. This passage is on p. 93 of the edn of 1627; I have not had the opportunity of re-consulting the unique copy in King's College Library, Aberdeen.

Read must have prepared the third edition by or before 1640. 'This shall be the last that shall be published in my life-time', he wrote, 'which is not far from its period.' He died in the following year and the edition appeared in 1642. The section on the thorax had been rewritten and it must therefore represent Read's last thought on what was appropriate for beginners; he did not expect his text to be useful for those who had made 'a reasonable progress' in anatomy. He is now certain that the septum between the ventricles of the heart is impermeable, which confirms his earlier account of the pulmonary transit. Now, in the third edition, Read adds that the forceful systole moves arterial blood (rather than spirit, as before) into the aorta. He does not explain what happens to the arterial blood and does not describe, or indeed deny, an arteries-to-veins transfer. He seems in fact to have been careful not to involve himself in a discussion of the topic. In short Read, like many others who read Harvey's book, divided Harvey's doctrine into two parts and handled each separately. He found the forceful systole and pulse (to which he attached the pulmonary transit) a doctrine proper for beginners, but not the circulation of the blood.

# 7    Overseas

## Introduction: Descartes and Bartholin

Many people did not first encounter Harvey's doctrines in his book, but by reading or hearing other people's reports or versions of them. There were two main vehicles of this sort that carried the forceful pulse and circulation over Europe. One was Descartes' new mechanical natural philosophy. We shall examine it in the next chapter. The other was the report by Joannes Walaeus on experiments he had made to support Harvey's conclusions. This report first appeared as appendix to an anatomy text which had been written by Caspar Bartholin and was being brought up to date by his son Thomas. In one form or another Walaeus' report reached at least eleven editions, and Thomas' book, favourable to Harvey and often carrying Walaeus' appendix, was translated into all European languages and even into Chinese. It clearly had an important role in the ultimate acceptance of Harvey's doctrines: we must look at the genesis of Bartholin's book.

## Communication and consensus: two controversies

In England Harvey, Read, Primrose, Winston, Fludd and others were known to each other and were in a position to discuss the circulation. Overseas, however, the formation of any consensus depended upon means of communication, which become important in our study.

Travel was important in communication. Harvey himself travelled widely in Europe (but not for academic reasons) and found himself arguing about the circulation from time to time. More characteristically, students travelled to one or more distant universities, and sometimes young men whose formal education was complete would take something of a Tour. Our purpose here is to look more closely at the communications between England and, in the first place, the United Provinces, which made possible a growth of consensus there. The United Provinces were in fact the biggest battleground for and against Harvey's views. Apart from the disputations which are described later, there were, between 1628 and 1671, seven Dutch editions of *De motu cordis* and only two English and two Italian.[1] Correspondence was also important in sustaining a network of information and in feeding anatomical 'controversies'. Thomas Bartholin's book was founded on his correspondence and talks with a very wide variety of men and owed much of its success to that fact.

Two 'controversies' preceded that on the circulation and had an important bearing both on Bartholin's book and on the *fortuna* of Harvey's doctrines, and we must briefly examine them.

The first is that concerned with the existence of vessels in the body which appeared to carry not blood but some kind of white liquid. The lacteals which were described by Aselli before Harvey published on the circulation were perhaps more vigorously debated in the north than in Italy, and when Rudbeck described the lymphatics it is clear that in terms of anatomical novelty the northern countries were the more active. Thomas Bartholin had a special interest in these vessels and historians have made claims of priority of discovery for him;[2] at all events the controversy over these vessels is part of the story of this book. The problem at the time was firstly to assign a function to these vessels. They were clearly involved in the processes of nutrition because of their connection with the intestines, but nutrition had been thought of as the generation of blood, conspicuously absent in these vessels. After Harvey had suggested that the blood circulated, the old picture of sanguification was again threatened and any successful neoteric formulation had to include both circulation and lacteals. By the time Harvey had finished publishing his work the dispute over the lymphatics was probably more fierce than that over circulation; but it largely took the latter as proven, and when it was itself settled the circulation was thereby strengthened.

The second of these disputed questions asked whether it was in fact true, as Galen had said, that the wall between the two ventricles of the heart was perforated with small holes. This was an important question in the reception of Harvey's doctrines, because a belief in the existence of the septal pores meant that there was no need of a pulmonary transit of blood to explain how blood came to be in the arteries. The pulmonary transit was part of Harvey's complete scheme, which was not, then, consistent with the septal pores. Doubts about the septal pores often caused those who read Harvey's work, like Alexander Read, to disarticulate Harvey's doctrine into its two natural halves, the forceful systole and the circulation. The controversy over the pores followed Colombo's claim that the blood passed across the lungs and not through the septum. Like other controversies, it gave opportunities for publishers to put out

---

[1] See Sir Geoffrey Keynes, *A Bibliography of the Writings of Dr William Harvey 1573–1657*, 2nd edn, Cambridge, 1953.
[2] See for example the biography attached to T. Bartholin, *Vasa Lymphatica. Edited on the Tercentenary of the Birth of Thomas Bartholinus*, ed. Vilhelm Maar, Copenhagen, 1916.

collections of opposing material.[3] It was a controversy that threatened a central feature of Galen's scheme of bodily function and was often contested. It was contested often enough with demonstrations directed to the senses of the audience. As a part of anatomy teaching it normally took the form of demonstration on the heart itself. While the textbooks normally side with the old opinion,[4] and some give details of how to see the pores in a long-boiled ox heart, the porosity of the septum was being demonstrated to classes of medical students before Harvey published *De motu cordis*. The anatomy teachers, like Fabricius, often demonstrated the porosity of the septum by pushing a probe through it. Petrus Monavius watched him do so in 1576, 'simply, as if there were no controversy'.[5] But there was a controversy, which is probably why the anatomy teachers took care to demonstrate the pores. Monavius remembered that three years before in Heidelberg he had watched the Italian Pigafetta showing, in the course of a dissection, how thick the septum was. Pigafetta denied that the blood passed across the septum. Also present on that occasion was a Spaniard, whose name Monavius could not recall, and who argued that the blood went through the lungs. It must have been Valverde, Colombo's student and the man who some believe discovered the pulmonary transit first.[6]

After Harvey the question became more controversial than ever, and for this reason Gassendi wrote down what he remembered of the controversy in the pre-Harvey days. While at Aix Gassendi was often in the anatomy theatre to observe the frequent dissections and he recalled that over many years, when the dissectors had a heart in their hands, they always pushed a slightly blunt probe through the septum, and so concluded 'with the medical men' that the blood passed across. Gassendi's language suggests that the dissectors were not learned in medicine. If so, they were clearly in no position to offer contro-

---

[3] For example T. Knobloch, *Disputationes anatomicae et physiologiae*, n.p. (pub. P. Helvigius), 1612.

[4] Doubts about the septal pores had been expressed by Vesalius in the second edition of the *Fabrica*: see W. Pagel, 'Vesalius and the pulmonary transit of the venous blood', *Journal of the History of Medicine*, 19 (1964), 327–41. As in the controversy over the circulation, those who joined in that over the pulmonary transit disarticulated its parts, here the transit of blood from the pores of the septum. J. C. Arantius, *De humani foetu* (I have used the edn of Leiden 1664, pp. 56–60), was hesitant on the question of the septal pores (and of course did not allow a pulmonary transit in the foetus); C. Varolius, *Anatomiae sive de Resolutione corporis humani*, Frankfurt, 1591, pp. 291–2, denied the pores and constructed a theory of the heart that derived arterial blood from a symmetrical flow in both arteries and veins; and L. Botali denied the pores because he thought he had found a separate vessel for the blood to pass between the ventricles: as his later editor observed, Botali 'straight away, with Archimedes, cried Eureka! but it was a Triumph before a Victory': L. Botali, *Opera omnia*, ed. van Horne, Leiden, 1660.

[5] The story is reported by J. Astruc, *De morbis venereis libri novem*, Paris, 1740, p. 537.

[6] Valverde knew of the pulmonary transit before 1556, when he published an account of it in Spanish. It is argued by F. Guerra, 'Juan de Valverde de Amusco', *Clio Medica*, 2 (1967), 339–62, that the notion that the blood crosses the lungs was originally Valverde's rather than Colombo's (whose book did not appear until 1559).

versial views. The controversy was left to the teachers and students of medicine and often enough took the form of a disputation. Gassendi was present at one in which the surgeon Payen undertook to demonstrate the existence of the pores. Gassendi describes how he brought the probe obliquely to the septum, gently pushing its point sideways, up, down, always patiently twisting and exploring. Finally the point of the probe emerged from the other side. The audience claimed that he had ruptured the septum,[7] so Payen delivered the heart to be cut by someone else, who showed the audience, convincing Gassendi that nothing had been ruptured and that the passageway could be seen meandering through the septum, lined with a fine and shining membrane. Gassendi was writing to refute the notion of Fludd about the role of an etherial spirit in the generation of arterial blood, and these details of the apparent channel through the septum seem designed to reinforce the standard account of the production of arterial blood.[8]

In the Low Countries the teachers Valckenburg and Heurnius made similar demonstrations in their public teaching, as noted by Diemerbroeck, probably in the year Harvey's book appeared.[9] Walaeus recalled having often penetrated the septum with a stylus like, he says, Gassendi's surgeon; but after adopting Harvey's view he came to believe the hole so revealed had always been unnatural, produced by the instrument.[10]

### 'Our North': Walaeus and Bartholin

These two controversies form part of the background to the story of how Harvey's doctrines were accepted or rejected. The location of the story is in the first instance within the universities of the Low Countries or, more precisely, the United Provinces. This was no accident, for there were growing ties between the Provinces and England. Leiden was becoming increasingly attractive to English medical students, possibly because of the congenial political and religious tone of the place and because by now Padua was in decline. Indeed a significant proportion of correspondence on these controversies and especially that about the circulation was now crossing northern

[7] See P. Gassendi, *Opera omnia*, 6 vols., Florence, 1727; vol. III, question 16, p. 218.
[8] Fludd replied in 1631, suggesting either that Payen had used force, or that the heart was pathological, that is, a 'particular' of observation and not a universal.
[9] G. A. Lindeboom, 'The reception in Holland of Harvey's theory of the circulation of the blood', *Janus*, 46 (1957), 183–200; 190.
[10] J. Walaeus, *Epistolae duae: de motu chyli et sanguinis. Ad Thomam Bartholinum, Casp. filium*, p. 38. I have used the text published in the *Recentiorum disceptationes de motu cordis, sanguinis, et chyli, in animalibus*, Leiden, 1647, and in the edition of 1651: *Anatomia, ex Caspari Bartholini Parentis Institutionibus, omniumque recentiorum et propriis observationibus tertium ad sanguinis circulationem reformata*, Leiden, 1651; the text seems to be unchanged and the letters bear the original date.

Europe. 'Our North' Bartholin called it, writing to Walaeus in 1642.[11] Thomas Bartholin's uncle, the Copenhagen professor Oluff Worm,[12] wrote in 1630 to his countryman Jacob Svabe in Leiden asking how the doctrine of circulation had been received. Svabe consulted his fellow student Herman Conring, who said it was heretical but fascinating; titillating in its newness, he thought it elegant and probable and wished that Harvey had shown it to be true by autopsy and demonstration. (By the time he had become professor of philosophy in Helmstadt in 1632 he was the first to defend the circulation in German-speaking countries.) His teachers, also consulted by Svabe, were appropriately more sober in their assessment. Valckenburg and Heurnius, still demonstrating the pores in the septum, urged caution in adopting new ideas, a caution that Worm still employed in 1640 (he thought that if blood left the arteries to pass through the pores of the flesh before entering the veins, as Harvey suggested, it would coagulate).

In the meantime, Worm's nephew Thomas Bartholin was continuing his education in Europe. He travelled extensively in France, Italy and the United Provinces for ten years, from 1637. He went first to Leiden and was taught by Walaeus for three years.[13] (From 1643 he studied with Severino,[14] having visited Montpellier.)[15] Clearly the young Thomas was being put through an ambitious and expensive programme of learning. His circle at Copenhagen was that of the university elite and it was expected that he would follow the path taken by his uncle and his father. His father, Caspar, had published an anatomical textbook, the *Anatomicae institutiones*, in 1611, before the controversies on the lacteals and circulation. To bring it up to date seemed like a good idea to a number of people: to Thomas for reasons of filial piety (he said),[16] to Walaeus, who had a professional interest in anatomy and who urged Thomas to publish, and to the publisher, who saw an opportunity to cover the new and marketable doctrine of the lacteals and circulation and asked Bartholin for an account of them.[17] But Bartholin was not sure that the blood circulated and hesitated to disturb his father's words on the heart and blood. He therefore asked uncle Oluff, who was equally uncertain. So Bartholin turned to Walaeus

---

[11]  T. Bartholin, *Epistolarum medicinalium a doctis vel ad doctos scriptarum, Centuria I et II*, Copenhagen, 1663, p. 113.

[12]  I adopt the spelling of E. Gottfredsen, 'The reception of Harvey's doctrine in Denmark', *Journal of the History of Medicine*, 12 (1957), 202–8; 202.

[13]  R. Descartes, *Oeuvres*, ed. C. Adam and P. Tannery, Paris, 1896–1913; reprinted 1956, vol. XII, p. 25.

[14]  C. Schmitt and C. Webster, 'Marco Aurelio Severino and his relationship to William Harvey: some preliminary considerations', in *Science, Medicine and Society in the Renaissance. Essays to Honor Walter Pagel*, ed. A. G. Debus, 2 vols., London, 1972; vol. II, pp. 63–72; p. 67.

[15]  Gottfredsen, 'Harvey's doctrine in Denmark', p. 205.

[16]  Bartholin, *Anatomia*, the address to the reader.

[17]  Gottfredsen, 'Harvey's doctrine in Denmark', p. 204.

and asked him for an account of both controversies. Walaeus replied with two letters, one giving an account of the motion of chyle in the new vessels and the other supporting a Harveian account of the circulation. Still unwilling to disturb his father's words more than necessary, Bartholin added these two letters to the book as an appendix.

We cannot tell precisely when Walaeus was first convinced of the circulation. He first heard of it from Vesling,[18] the German anatomy professor at Padua, and was at first energetically opposed to it. It was perhaps during Thomas Bartholin's stay in Leiden that he came to believe in the circulation, for in April 1640 Bartholin wrote to Worm saying that 'at last' Walaeus had been convinced by seeing a series of experiments, which Bartholin had also seen. Worm had not seen them and was not convinced: he told Bartholin so in the following month, and instead waited to see the re-issue of Caspar's book, which was clearly in preparation. Walaeus dated his epistolary appendix to the book in December.

The experiments witnessed by Bartholin and Walaeus which convinced Walaeus at least were those performed by Franciscus Sylvius. For our purpose Sylvius is best considered as part of the story of Descartes rather than Bartholin's handling of Harvey's doctrine, and we need note here only that Sylvius, arriving in Leiden in the autumn of 1638, soon began to argue for the circulation. In little over a year Walaeus first attacked circulation, saw Sylvius' vivisections, was converted, made a series of experiments himself, had his English student Roger Drake defend a thesis in February 1640 (both before crowds of students) and wrote his letters for Bartholin.

Before looking at Bartholin's book as a vehicle for Harvey's doctrines, we must then look a little more closely at Walaeus, whose name was linked so much with Harvey's. Descartes thought that Harvey was using Walaeus as an agent to spread his doctrines in the universities; and while Harvey remained silent on the controversy it seemed to many that Walaeus was the principal protagonist of the circulation. Walaeus had taken his MD at Leiden[19] three years after the publication of Harvey's *De motu cordis*. Others like him were not exposed to Paduan Aristotelianism or the anatomical tradition of Vesalius and Fabricius. Possibly, as Padua lost its pre-eminence in medical matters, it tended to emphasise its continuing links with its own past and to discourage innovation. For whatever reason, Walaeus and others did not find Padua attractive enough to go there. He became an extraordinary professor in Leiden in 1633. In 1634 the young Franciscus Sylvius de la Boe was involved in a

[18] T. Bartholin, *Epistolarum medicinalium a doctis vel ad doctos scriptarum, Centuria [I–IV]*, The Hague, 1740, vol. I, p. 115.

[19] J. Schouten, 'Johannes Walaeus (1604–1649) and his experiments on the circulation of the blood', *Journal of the History of Medicine*, 29 (1974), 259–79.

disputation about the pulmonary transit of blood and Walaeus was drawn into medical controversies.[20] Sylvius too was a product of the north, having studied in various Swiss and German universities before taking his MD at Basle in 1637. He returned to Leiden in the following year and, now convinced of Harvey's account of the circulation, he began to demonstrate it privately. The doctrine of the circulation was still highly controversial and there was undoubtedly considerable excitement in the crowds of students who are reported to have been present during these experiments and disputations.

Because disputations were important opinion-formers and could lead to a consensus within a faculty or university, it is of interest that the theses of one of Walaeus' students survive. From them we learn not only that the student was prompted towards defending the theses by Walaeus, but that it was only through Walaeus that he had come to hear of Harvey's book (together with Primrose's refutation), some six months earlier. Clearly a teacher in a university could widen the readership of Harvey's book as well as concentrate the minds of the young on the arguments for and against Harvey's doctrine.[21]

From these theses, together with Walaeus' letters to Bartholin, we can reconstruct a little of Walaeus' teaching on the topic of the circulation. While the disputation was a major way of settling such disputes, yet by its nature it was dialectical and formal and not practical. But as seems to have been the case here, it could act as a formal statement of a course of teaching – that of Walaeus – which had been practical and indeed experimental. The issues involved, then, were more than the dialectic and the authorities used in the disputation, and reflected a whole course of lectures and experimental demonstrations.

The student was the Englishman Roger Drake. In opening his defence, Drake noted its importance and its controversial nature, some (he said) having adopted the circulation as dogma; others, wishing to be more prudent, taking it as mere commentary for rejection. Drake's treatment in this disputation of Walaeus' teaching and experiments is very much a school exercise. It admits very little of neoteric traditional natural philosophy and is using it to defend an experimental and anatomical novelty which he has met in his later medical course. He sees that the 'circle' of circulation is metaphorical, like the cycle he had met in the meteorological part of his natural philosophy in which rain is produced from the condensation of rising vapour from the sea, itself fed by rain. He also compared the metaphorical circle of blood, with its alternate rarefaction and condensation, to the repeated distillations of the chemists.

Having pointed out such similarities in the wider field of philosophy, Drake

---

20  See Schouten, 'Johannes Walaeus', p. 259.
21  R. Drake ['author and respondent'], *Theses de circulatione naturali seu cordis et sanguinis motu circulariu pro Cl. Harveio*, published in *Recentiorum disceptationes de Motu cordis, sanguinis et chyli, in animalibus*, Leyden, 1647, p. 238. See also J. Schouten, *Johannes Walaeus*, Amsterdam, 1972, which contains a facsimile of the theses.

sets up the problem in traditional natural-philosophical terms. Circulation is motion; in any motion, four things have to be considered, the moving, the moved, the path and the destination. Drake proceeds through his categories: the path is the arteries and veins (including the traditional path of newly generated blood from the liver to right ventricle); the moved is the blood. The mover is double, being the faculties of attraction and retention, located in the veins and arteries respectively. The major part of the moving force, however, is located in the heart, which for Drake has a powerful attractive diastole (theses 5 to 8). 'Attraction' therefore, remained a major category in the world-view that Drake was summoning in order to defend his thesis.

Fundamental to his argument is that God and Nature do nothing in vain and that it would therefore be insulting to both if the heart's action were without purpose (thesis 9). This leads Drake directly to what Harvey had largely avoided, the purpose of circulation. In seeking to defend a formal thesis in a traditional way, Drake was of course under considerable pressure to produce a final cause for, as his audience knew, no traditional demonstration was complete without one: here is another way in which Harvey's doctrines were 'misunderstood'. The final cause that Drake came up with was double, to preserve the blood itself by constant motion and to nourish the parts. This leads Drake at once to assert the basic identity of venous and arterial blood, which had possessed different functions in the Galenic scheme of things. Drake does so characteristically in traditional natural-philosophical terms, allowing only that the two kinds of blood differed in their 'accidents', not their essence.[22] It followed that all parts of the body could be nourished by the same elementary parts of the blood as a whole.

On the critical question of the quantity of blood passing from the heart Drake formally divides his defence into two, reason and sense. The rational component is Harvey's quantitative argument, and the sensory simply that the quantity of each amount is perceptible. While this is hardly experimental, it is evidence that sensory observation of the physical world could have a legitimate place in a formal disputation (and this is a very formal one, the arguments ending with the medieval formula 'ergo etc.' customarily used to introduce the last stage of a syllogism).[23] It seems probable that Walaeus and Drake found, like many others, that the quantitative argument was Harvey's most convincing. At least, it was seen as critical, for if it could be defeated it would be very difficult to defend circulation. One objection made to Drake during the defence of the thesis was in fact that the small amount of blood ejected at each beat of the heart could not possibly fill the arteries. This was a real field of misunderstanding of what Harvey had said, and different readers of Harvey's text

[22] Thesis V.
[23] Thesis X.

could not understand how the pulse, but not the blood itself leaving the heart, could reach the ends of the arteries at every pulsation. Drake seems to have felt himself on dangerous ground here and, struggling to make a joke of it, said that the objection 'goes for the jugular of our case'.[24] The force of the objection compelled him to make another change in Harvey's scheme and argue that the blood, heated and excited in the heart, is converted into a spirit and forcibly expands the heart and arteries, causing the pulse.[25] Looking sideways at other neoteric ideas, Drake compares this expansion to that of spirits of nitre or gunpowder. In short, Drake, like many others, accepted Harvey's account of the circulation but could not accept that of forceful systole. In order to render the notion of circulation acceptable in this disputation, Drake tried to show that in fact circulation was compatible with practical medicine, such as the letting of blood and the treatment of fever. For the same reason he fitted it out with a final cause and decorated it with some other self-evident facts from philosophy in order to strengthen it. It was a disputation like many others in the universities, but the issues involved were given a longer life by Primrose's attack on it, published in Amsterdam in the same year.[26]

Primrose's purpose of course was to defend medicine as he saw it, practical and largely traditional. Since he had read Harvey, he understood fairly clearly what the issues were. Since he totally opposed Harvey, and had no intention of making the circulation fit some scheme of his own, he had no need to modify what Harvey had said. Anyone who had not read Harvey's book would gain a better idea of what it contained from Primrose's rejection of it than from almost any piece of writing in which the circulation was accepted. He was not sympathetic to 'chemical' explanations of the working of the body, as Sylvius was, and could not see why they should be invoked in a discussion he took to be about Harvey. For him there was no point in comparing the circulation to the repeated distillation, *circulatio*, of the chemists. He saw in the comparison merely a similarity of names: Harvey's *circulatio* was imaginary, that of the chemists real, a process that would in fact destroy blood; in any case Harvey did not mean distillation.

---

[24] Thesis X. The objections made to Drake's thesis included the notion that the heart's shape, but not the internal volume of its ventricles, changes as it beats. In this case, by reason of *horror vacui* no blood would leave the heart.

[25] The theses defend the doctrine of circulation not only from the attacks of Primrose, but of Parigiano. Here Drake refutes Parigiano largely by insisting on the efficacy of the valves. He refers to Harvey's experiments with a ligature, and claims to have performed one himself. He uses it also to reject an opinion voiced by Plemp (see below) before Plemp became converted to circulation. The remaining objections are largely concerned with the medical implications of circulation.

[26] J. Primrose, *Observationes in Johannis Wallaei medicinae apud Leydenses Professoris disputationem medicam quam pro circulatione sanguinis Harveana proposuit: cui addita est ejusdem de usu lienis adversus medicos recentiores sententia*, Amsterdam, 1640.

Fundamental to Primrose's attack was an antipathy to vivisections. Not without ingenuity, he could use experimental evidence of others, and he argued that separated and still beating hearts (he is using Harvey's evidence) neither attracted nor expelled, yet still moved. Clearly (he says) expulsion is not a necessary part of the heart's action. He argued instead that the heart altered shape but not volume as it moved, and that the narrow exit provided by the valves meant that no more than a drop of blood left the heart at each beat. Primrose repeats here the charge he made earlier against Harvey's vivisections, that they were unnatural. Thus when Drake described the experiment in which the vena cava is ligated and the heart empties itself into the arteries, Primrose replies that the ligature prevents the spirits in the vein coming to help the injured heart, which therefore acts unnaturally. Underlying this reply is Primrose's belief that the nobility of the heart cannot be investigated by such ignoble means. To try to do so is merely *taediosa*.[27]

Both Drake's disputation and Primrose's attack on it were purely verbal affairs and cannot tell us directly about Walaeus' course of experiments, in which he claimed to have dissected and vivisected a hundred dogs.[28] This teaching itself was a way of convincing people of the circulation, but it could contribute only indirectly to the traditional, formal and dialectical defence of a thesis by which Drake carried the message of that teaching. Walaeus, as a practical and experimental teacher, therefore resented, as he wrote to Hofmann at the end of that year,[29] being attacked in a literary way by Primrose. Primrose had assumed that Drake was simply the mouthpiece of Walaeus and attacked the latter directly, which Walaeus also resented. In writing the two letters to Bartholin (they reached their eleventh edition by 1650)[30] he makes it clear that he allowed his students a considerable degree of liberty in defending theses. It was not the habit at Leiden for the defending student simply to act as the mouthpiece of his teacher in disputations. (For most other universities Primrose's assumption would have been correct.) For both reasons Walaeus felt it necessary to explain that much of what Drake had said was his own, and these two letters to Bartholin set out Walaeus' own position. The most obvious thing about this was that it was indeed experimental. The vivisections had been witnessed by Bartholin, Sylvius, van Horn and other learned men.[31] It seems to

27 Ibid., section 11.
28 G. A. Lindeboom, 'The reception of Harvey's theory of the circulation of the blood', *Janus*, 46 (1957), 183–200; 193–8.
29 G. Richter, *Epistolae selectiores III Mantissae sex IV spicilegium*, Nuremberg, 1642: p. 809, Walaeus to Hofmann, Leiden, Dec. 1640.
30 Lindeboom, 'Reception', 197.
31 Sylvius claimed to have been the first to demonstrate the circulation in Leiden, and that at first Walaeus was unconvinced and attacked the doctrine in public. Sylvius further claimed that it was his experiments that finally convinced Walaeus. All of this was in front of a crowd of students, and we are reminded again of the role of the disputation and experiment in the

have been these people who, crowding round to see Walaeus cut the tip from the ventricle of a dog's heart, were drenched in blood as it spurted four feet from the unfortunate animal. 'Unde evidens est', remarked Walaeus, 'sanguinem a parte propelli'.[32] It was natural that he should emphasise the force of the circulating blood, and its speed (he thought the whole mass would circulate in a quarter of an hour). The object of this experiment was to determine whether the blood in the heart was indeed in a vaporous state (as Drake believed). Its unlooked-for result allowed no dissent: there is a conviction arising from being covered in blood that recognises no philosophical opposition.

Although he sometimes vivisected geese, the experiment he particularly valued for the purposes of demonstration was that on the crural veins of a dog, where he used ligatures in a Harveian way (see fig. 15). He also made estimates of the amount of blood ejected from the heart of a rabbit and a dog at each beat, in order to reinforce the quantitative argument from Harvey. Like Harvey, Walaeus thought Galen's reed-in-artery experiment, designed to reveal the nature of the pulse, too difficult. He tried it in a rabbit, but the animal died before he could complete it. He did not repeat the attempt, arguing that it was difficult to find an appropriate artery and that the abundance of blood and the convulsions of the dying animal made it impossible. Although he mentions Colombo in relation to the terminology of the pulmonary veins, it is obvious that the bulk of this experimental practice is derived from Harvey. This is set out most clearly in the second of the two letters. Having left the refutation of Primrose (he says) to Drake, Walaeus simply addresses himself to the description of these experiments and the refutation of objections. Some of the objections are in fact Primrose's, like the small aperture of the valves (Walaeus' reply calls upon vivisection) and others are straightforward views about how and in what quantity the liquids of the body flow in relation to ligatures, incisions and so on. He spends much space on again refuting the notion that the blood vaporises in the heart[33] and, as arguments both for and against, admits only those that are experimental and ideally vivisectional.

It is clear that as the middle of the seventeenth century approached, a great deal of animal experimentation was going on in the Low Countries and in England. Much of it was directly Harveian and was used in investigating and teaching the circulation. But it was not limited to that, and Walaeus for example extends the technique to another controversy so often linked to that of the circulation, the movement of chyle in the lacteals (in the first letter).

formation of a consensus. See Lindeboom, 'Reception', 193. Walaeus merely adds Sylvius to the list of anatomists who lent credence to his own experiments by witnessing them: *Epistolae duae*, p. 71.
[32] 'Whence it is evident that blood is propelled by the part': Walaeus, *Epistolae duae*, p. 59.
[33] Ibid., p. 58.

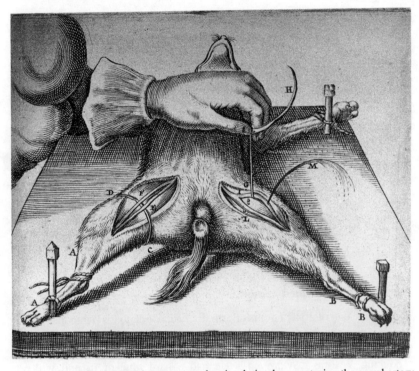

Fig. 15. Walaeus demonstrates the circulation by puncturing the crural artery of a dog.

Walaeus performed a number of experiments on dogs, dissecting them at different periods after a meal to see how long digestion took for different foodstuffs. He then vivisected them and experimented by ligating the lacteal, mesenteric and portal veins. He continued with similar experiments on the vena cava, the pulmonary vessels and the aorta. In other words his experiments covered two controversies and linked them not only with the same investigative technique, but as parts of an extended physiological scheme reaching from digestion of food through the generation of blood to the pulmonary transit and the nourishment of the parts.

Such experimentation was done privately, before a few friends, or publicly, before colleagues and students. As we have seen, the importance of an audience was not only that they might be convinced by the experiment, but also that, if distinguished, they could be cited as reliable witnesses when the experimenter came to express himself in words. The words might be in the form of letters – part of the network of correspondence – lectures, disputation or textbook. The experiments were generally undertaken to demonstrate a belief or to prove an opponent wrong. More of these experiments are described in a later chapter, and here we need note only that they had now become part of the language of natural philosophy.

Indeed, so much had experiment become a part of natural philosophy, particularly that part of it concerned with animals, that often enough a purely verbal treatment was felt to be inadequate. When replying to Primrose[34] Drake upbraided him for never doing even the simplest experiment with a ligature, let alone vivisections. In the absence of experiment, even to speak as though from an oracle, says Drake, is no way to convince people. To attempt to do so would be like 'that grave theologian' who tried to refute all the work of Bellarmine (Galileo's accuser) by saying only 'Bellarmine, you lie.'[35]

Walaeus also pointed to the absence of vivisections in Primrose's case and imputes to him the belief that 'the mind grasps things more surely than the eye can see them'.[36] This was a phrase used by an opponent[37] of Harvey and may have been currency among those who opposed the experimental method and its sensory epistemology.

### The 'Reformed anatomy'

Thus by the end of 1640 Thomas Bartholin had a book to his name that at least in part supported the circulation. Probably Bartholin had now accepted some form of circulation, for moving on to Montpellier he defended circulation by producing Vesling's *Syntagma*.[38] He had a hard time of it, and wrote to Walaeus in 1641 complaining that the Montpelliards were all Galenists and did not perform experiments.[39] Experiments, they thought in the north, were of the

---

[34] R. Drake, *Contra Animadversiones Iac. Primrosii in theses, quas ipse pro sanguinis motu circulari, sub Praesidio Io. Walaei, in celeberrima Leidae Academia, publico examini subjecerat vindiciae*, in the *Disceptationes*, p. 189. See also p. 179.

[35] The bulk of Drake's reply to Primrose, apart from a re-assertion of the details of circulation, is directed at Primrose's logic and his behaviour during the controversy. Primrose raised the image of Roger's namesake, Sir Francis Drake, as the putative 'circulator' of the macrocosm, and treats Roger as the lesser and attempted circulator of the microcosm; Drake replies with the remark (attributed as we have seen to Eustachio) that he (Primrose) would rather be wrong with the ancients than right with the moderns. Here the scornful remark is attributed to Sennert, the well-known neoteric.

[36] See the fifth edition of the letters in Bartholin, *Anatomia*.

[37] It was E. Leichner: see chap. 9 below.

[38] Gottfredsen, 'Harvey's doctrine in Denmark', p. 204: Bartholin was 'hated and feared' by the Galenists.

[39] Only in 1650 did Riverius in Montpellier publish in favour of circulation. Bartholin in these letters takes up the gossip of the day. He took up and discussed Walaeus' suggestion that Father Paolo Sarpi of Venice had first discovered the circulation and that Harvey had taken it from him. See Walaeus, *Epistolae duae*, p. 49, and Bartholin, *Epistolarum medicinalium*. We might note a Henricus a Mönichem who wrote from Padua in 1655 describing experiments made by A. Molinetti and P. Marchetti with pumps and warm water to demonstrate the circulation in a cadaver. Bartholin, *Epistolarum medicinalium*, p. 599.

essence. Bartholin also argued against the scheme of bloodflow drawn up by the Italian Fortunio Liceti (whom we shall meet below) because it was not experimental. He thought the whole controversy was a matter for vivisections and what Worm (in 1643) called *ocularis demonstratio*.

But Bartholin never fully accepted a Harveian position. He wrote to Harvey in 1642 with some misgivings, one of which was derived from Scribonius Largus' account of venesection, in which blood is said to be best taken from a swelling *above* the ligature[40] (in Harvey's account the swelling is below and the blood does not come from an incision above the ligature). By 1643 he seems to have accepted the forceful systole and he was arguing that only the arterial blood nourishes, both parts of his final version of circulation. It was only in the edition of his father's text in 1651 that he publicly accepted a form of circulation (and followed it by enthusiastic letters to Harvey).[41] In essence, Bartholin waited until he saw that the circulation controversy was almost settled in Harvey's favour before accepting, because so many others were doing so, that it represented truth. Then it became important for him to weave it into his textbook.[42]

This was a *very* successful textbook. It does not have a message about Bartholin's own discoveries, nor does it preach a new method. It does not even depart from his father's words where they can be left.[43] New material is added in square brackets so that the reader can see where the original has been supplemented. And what has been added is vast. He is proud of his ten years of travel and meeting people and of a longer period of writing to them and to others. He lists many of them in addressing the reader. Opinions are given even when Bartholin has to throw doubt on their accuracy. He reports dispassionately.[44] There is no talk of an anatomical faith to be kept or broken, no institutional defence of the ancients of the kind that was still to be found in Paris. He uses a traditional *accessus* of observables for convenience of teaching and learning. He looks in a traditional way for causes, but there is no

---

40 Ibid., vol. I, p. 10.
41 Bartholin to Harvey, May 1652: '[of circulation] qua nihil elegantius, utilius nihil, nihil verius mortalis industria invenire potuit'. Bartholin, *Epistolarum medicinalium*, p. 478. He not unreasonably claims to be the cause of the pro-circulation consensus in Copenhagen and refers to his many disputations in other countries. See p. 479.
42 ' . . . et quod caput rei est, ad *sanguinis Circularem motum* ab *Harvejo et Wallaeo* propugnatum, jamque apud plerosque receptum', 'and what is of chief importance, [the book is modified],in line with the circular motion of the blood, supported by Harvey and Walaeus, and now accepted by many'. (The address to the reader.)
43 His father's was also a successful book, going through six editions before Thomas began to edit it. This was another reason to leave much of it clearly intact. See Bartholin, *Vasa lymphatica*.
44 Bartholin's philosophical range was wide. He uses the Platonic image of the soul in its earthly *ergastulum*, the body (in the address to the reader) and adopts a Helmontian doctrine of 'lucid spirit', *Lumen spirituum*, which remains in the living body from its seminal origins and which in the heart contributes to its motion (p. 256).

suggestion that not to find causes is to invalidate knowledge. He does his best (he tells the reader) to reconcile the opinions of major teachers like Riolan and Hofmann. He calls the book a *messis*,[45] a 'harvest', a crop taken from the anatomical literature from Hippocrates to Harvey. Above all it was a useful, synthetic and a safe book, accommodating recent developments but without commitment to a system, so that for example Descartes' anatomical statements are noted (and gently reproved) without any enthusiasm for or discussion of mechanism as a whole.[46]

Even though the title page[47] proclaims that this anatomy is 'reformed' by the circulation it is a reformation only of two chapters on the heart in one of the four books. The rest is presented in a framework entirely traditional in anatomy texts. Definitions of 'part' are taken from authors from Hippocrates to Fernel: similar, dissimilar, principal, serving, contained, containing, public, private. Like Mondino, he organises his book round the three cavities (and adds another discussion of the limbs). Any other book on anatomy his readers had read would find some echo here, and each reader would find a systematised and systematic presentation of the literature. Its tacit assumption of the value of modern as well as ancient anatomy and its overall air of confidence about future progress perhaps added to its attractions. There is no vestige of the battle for and against Galen, and in fact, in line with medical thinking generally, Galen is less popular and cited less than he would have been a generation earlier. Above all, what Bartholin does is to take as central anatomical facts on which most authors agreed. The format, with its square brackets, was indefinitely modifiable to accommodate new findings: that consensual fact could change had been demonstrated in a striking way by Harvey and those involved in the discovery of the lacteals. These discoveries dictated the mode of exposition adopted by Bartholin.

In such an undertaking it is not to be expected that Bartholin entirely accepts the account of the circulation as given by Harvey. Harvey would not have agreed for example that he had said (as Bartholin claimed)[48] that the heart was the instrument of the soul. In a manner appropriate for a textbook, Bartholin

---

45 Compare the 'Golden Harvest' of Hemsterhuis, which was a publisher's opportunity to cover the marketable doctrines of Pecquet, Bartholin and Rudbeck on the lacteals and lymphatics. Siboldus Hemsterhuis, *Messis aurea triennalis, exhibens anatomica: novissima et utilissima experimenta*, Leiden, 1654. Perhaps *Tirennialis* indicates that the publisher hoped to be able to crop such a harvest every three years. It is notable that *Experimenta* form part of the attraction of the title.

46 Like others, Bartholin found it difficult to accept the Cartesian doctrine that heat is a greater motion of ultimate particles. Bodily heat, he said (p. 241) is seminal in origin and exists in the body *before* motion, and motion serves only to preserve it. The heat of the heart therefore is something other than the motion of its parts, and contributes directly to the concoction of the blood.

47 *Anatomia ex Caspari Bartholini Parentis Institutionibus, omniumque recentiorum et propriis Observationibus tertium ad Sanguinis circulationem reformata.*

48 Bartholin, *Anatomia*, p. 240.

breaks down the subject into the usual parts – the structure, action and use of the heart and its vessels. In each case Bartholin gives greater or lesser credence to the doctrines to be found in the literature. Characteristically he takes a 'middle way', 'Nos media via incedimus',[49] and attempts a compromise. A good example is his treatment of the pores of the septum. His father believed that they existed and Bartholin can find many authorities from the sixteenth- and seventeenth-century controversy who agreed with him. He accordingly leaves his father's words untouched but brings them up to date by a large section in brackets which includes the pulmonary transit. Brackets enclose Colombo's finding that the septum was dense and also van Helmont's description of the pores as like triangles, with an invisibly small opening at their apex in the left ventricle, and with obvious broad bases in the right. Bartholin recounts Gassendi's story from Aix and declines to doubt someone as *oculatus* as Gassendi and as dextrous as Payen. Bartholin himself had seen a hole in the septum of a young pig big enough to admit a pea and others with valve-like flaps.[50]

Bartholin accordingly does not abandon the old doctrine of blood passing through the pores of the septum but rationalises it by distinguishing between the blood that crosses the septum (it is more subtle) from that which goes across the lungs (it is coarser and needs further refinement in the lungs and left ventricle). It is also rationalised by Bartholin emphasising the differences in the amount of blood crossing the septum (it is tiny) compared with that crossing the lungs (he develops Harvey's quantitative arguments): the result does not interfere very seriously with the plumbing of Harvey's circulation. Thomas also edits in modern opinions that Caspar would have been ignorant of or disagreed with, like the descent of blood in the venous artery:

*Usus* [of the left ventricle] est, spiritum vitalem cum sanguine arterioso elaborare ex duplici materia, I Ex sanguine in dextro cavitate preparato, & per septum [pulmonesque] transmisso. II Ex aere per os & nares inspirato, in pulmonibus preparato, & per arteriam venosam [cum sanguine] in cordis sinistrum ventriculum misso, [ad flammae suscitationem, & ventilationem . . .

That is,

---

[49] p. 241: he is here reaching for a mutual understanding between two radically different opinions that supported sanguification in the heart and liver respectively. These are Aristotelian and Galenic positions, but Bartholin does not use the terms and does not add to the conflict. Instead he uses the new doctrines and characteristically uses a *distinctio* made possible by them to resolve the old problem. Much sanguification (he says) happens in the liver, and the blood so made goes to the heart, where it is perfected; but the heart also deals with venous blood returning from the circulation and restores that to perfection. So the heart also has an important role of sanguification, although of a rather different sort.

[50] Bartholin, *Anatomia*, p. 266.

Use: to make the vital spirit and arterial blood, from two substances: I from blood prepared in the right cavity and transmitted through the septum [and the lungs]; II from air inspired through the mouth and nose, prepared in the lungs, and sent [with blood] through the venous artery to the left ventricle of the heart [to maintain and ventilate the flame] . . .

where the bracketed 'and the lungs' and 'with blood' add most of what is needed to compromise between the old and the new. Bartholin also has to explain how the fuliginous vapours escape from the heart, since (he does not emphasise the fact) the traditional route, along the venous artery to the lungs, was closed by his adoption of the pulmonary transit. He therefore argues that they escape from the *right* ventricle rather than the left, along the arterial vein, to the lungs. He also adds a new doctrine that other impurities sweat through the wall of the heart and condense in the water in the pericardium to be finally removed from the circulating blood by sweat and in the urine.

Another example of Bartholin's treatment is the question of whether the heart is a muscle. The issue was clearly drawn. Galen had said that muscular activity was voluntary and mediated by nerve, and that the motion of the heart was neither. Hippocrates had said the heart was a muscle. Shall we say then, asked Bartholin, that the heart is a muscle with *natural* rather than *voluntary* motion? Or better, with others, that it is a collection of muscles? Or best, with Walaeus, that it is like muscles spread amongst fibres of flesh? So, the issues are reported, the moderns shown in a good light, a compromise is indicated and a conflict avoided.[51]

Nor can Bartholin bring himself flatly to deny Aristotle's account of the three ventricles of the heart, even though there is no way in which a three-ventricled heart would fit into the principle of Reformed anatomy, the circulation. He explains how the problem has been explained by Galen, Sylvius, Liceti, Cesalpino, Vesling, Conring and Riolan (a modest list for Bartholin): some think the pores in the septum constitute the third ventricle, and Walaeus found a sinus in an ox heart that was big enough to take a finger, which he took to be the extra ventricle.[52] Bartholin's even-handed treatment includes his attachment to the teaching of Folli, who described pores in the septum between the two *auricles*. Bartholin says he has seen them, and he supplies a drawing of a probe penetrating them.[53]

Bartholin's treatment of Harvey's quantitative argument also illustrates his methods. Perhaps because he was also a mathematician (he briefly occupied the chair at Copenhagen) he did not share the suspicion of mathematical

[51]  Ibid., p. 239.
[52]  Ibid., pp. 265–8.
[53]  Bartholin (1651), p. 259; the drawing is at p. 273. Bartholin also repeats Botali's account of a duct between the two auricles, which Walaeus took to be a persisting foramen ovale, and which Bartholin thought was a coronal vein.

arguments that some of Harvey's opponents had. He accordingly assembles a number of the authors who had discussed Harvey's estimates of the amount of blood ejected during systole, and considers their estimates of the amount of blood contained in the left ventricle, the amount ejected and the number of beats these authors thought the heart made in an hour. There is little critical assessment of the likely truth of these figures: they are reports from people who had become involved in the dispute. Bartholin then made calculations in each case to show for each author how long it would take for all the blood in the body to circulate. The answer was, in all cases, not very long: from a quarter of an hour to two hours. The conclusion was Harvey's: that this quantity could neither be generated from food nor absorbed as nourishment by the flesh, and so the blood must circulate. Bartholin has given Harvey's conclusion backing by making it also a large consensual fact established in an apparently rigorous way from a table of differences. He excluded only Riolan's estimate that the blood did not circulate more than twice a day as too small. But he did not dwell on the differences between Harvey and Riolan.

One of the major ways in which Bartholin diverged from Harvey is his account of what happened in the heart. Two of the doctrines he could not reconcile, despite his best efforts, were those of Descartes and Harvey. He has read Descartes and his followers Regius and Hogelande (whom we shall meet in the next chapter) and their doctrine that the forceful vaporisation of drops of blood entering the hot heart causes the expansion of the heart and the pulse in the arteries.[54] Bartholin attempts another *via media* by allowing some effervescence of blood in the heart, but cannot allow that it exists in a vaporous state. For once he is firm. He has in mind one of Walaeus' experiments, in which the blood in a very liquid state leaped four feet from a punctured ventricle: there was simply no time for it to have condensed from a vapour to a liquid by the coldness of the air, and it must have been liquid inside the heart.[55]

There were other reasons why Bartholin could not accept a theory of inflation to explain the heartbeat. One was that separated pieces of the living heart continue to move. More important was that any such mechanical cause lacked a controlling power. Without a pulsific faculty, he argued, the heartbeat would always be irregular, depending only on the quantity of blood entering the heart. So there must be a faculty, perhaps mediated by spirits; it is in any case appropriate for the nobility of the heart that it should be moved by an internal principal rather than violently, from an external cause. Bartholin argued that the faculty was manifested by the lucid spirit, which moved the heart and blood almost instantly. No elementary cause could do so, he claimed,

54  Bartholin, *Anatomia*, p. 253.
55  Ibid., p. 254.

for elements always move in straight lines, while light was often manifested by orbs, appropriate for circulation. Bartholin appears to be drawing on van Helmont here, and is clearly distant from Harvey's natural philosophy.[56]

One of the ways in which Bartholin tried to keep to a *via media* and avoid philosopher–physician disputes was to sidestep the doctors. He asserted that the whole study of man, *anthropologia*, was constituted of anatomy and *psychologia*, the study of the soul. Anatomy was then part of natural philosophy, *physica*. For this reason it was concerned with animals as well as with man; and Galen, with his medical anatomy, Bartholin leaves in the hands of the medical men and their professional interests. It is a broad gesture, and Bartholin is going beyond his anatomical predecessors who had only wanted that all anatomy should be a philosophical operation; he claims indeed that anatomy is the part of natural philosophy to be learned *first*, without which no one could call himself a *physicus*. But this is too firm a position for Bartholin to hold. In practice, he says, we give most of our attention to man. There are so many animals, it would take centuries to cut them all up; man is anyway the perfect animal, the guide to the imperfect; the philosophical imperative to Know Oneself cannot be satisfied with animals; and lastly there is, after all, some medical use in knowing human anatomy. Thus has Bartholin again embraced differing and even opposing views. Some he shared with his father, some not. It is his assertion that medical anatomy should be left to the Galenic 'administrations' of the medical men; but it is also his, characteristically, that there was some use in them. Here he cites the legendary Democritus *physicus*, the dissector of animals, Aldrovandi, Severino and the vivisections of Aselli, Harvey and Walaeus. In a way not foreseen by his father, experimental vivisection was for Thomas Bartholin *the* important research technique in the progressive anatomy of mid-seventeenth century.

### Ent and attraction

Harvey's doctrines were also taken up by men with a view of the world radically different from that of Bartholin. This view was a new form of natural philosophy, largely independent of the universities, not yet with a comprehensive explanation of the natural world, but with articles of faith about the fundamental nature and movement of things that seemed to hold out much promise to those who no longer trusted school natural philosophy. Some contemporaries saw the new mechanical philosophy as a largely Dutch affair. Men who held some form of this philosophy accepted or rejected Harvey's doctrine because it could, or could not, be made to fit this philosophy. We need

---

[56] Ibid., pp. 251, 255. Bartholin's Faculty included Attraction in a fairly traditional way, directly opposed to the system of Descartes and Regius: p. 257.

to look here at some of those who had espoused some form of this new natural philosophy. Here again the United Provinces were an important centre, and we shall find that the story ultimately leads us (in the following chapter) to Descartes' activities there. Here we must look at another example of the links between the United Provinces and England. While Roger Drake had taken his medical education in Leiden, George Ent travelled in the opposite direction and came to Cambridge for part of his education. The son of a Low Countries merchant, he had been taught in Isaac Beeckman's school in Rotterdam (from 1620 to 1624) and was part of a circle of correspondents that included Mersenne and Descartes. Some such circle brought news of Harvey's book to Rotterdam, for the Rotterdamers Zacharias Sylvius and Jacobus de Back were part of the local pro-Harveian consensus that had formed by 1633, and collaborated with Arnout Leers, a publisher who specialised in English medical works: of the seven Dutch editions of Harvey's book, four were published by Leers. Much of Ent's natural philosophy must have been gathered from Beeckman and this circle, and when he came to live in England he found many with a sympathetic ear for it. Having met opposition to Harvey's doctrines while in Padua (he took his MD in 1636, after Cambridge) Ent decided to defend Harvey in his adopted homeland. He did so with a natural philosophy wholly different from that of Harvey.

To understand what it was, let us look first at his teacher, Isaac Beeckman. It was in the 1620s[57] that he was co-Rector of the Latin School of Rotterdam[58] and from 1627 he was Rector of the Dordrecht Grammar School, a colleague of Beverwyck, who corresponded with both Harvey and Descartes on the subject of bloodflow. Gassendi visited him in 1629, Mersenne in 1630.[59] All of these men were to be involved in discussing Harvey's doctrine, and all were ready to listen to Descartes, another member of the circle. Such circles, indeed, these schools, were important groupings in which a consensus could flourish. Beeckman kept an intellectual diary for thirty years, from 1604. From this we can see that, as with others who were involved in the changes within natural philosophy, he was motivated by a dissatisfaction with school physics before a comprehensive alternative was available, and it is with this background that we must treat of his reaction to the circulation controversy. Beeckman was one of a small number of people with radical new ideas about the nature of the physical world: the new philosophy of mechanism. By 1613 he was noting down queries about heavy objects being lifted by *fuga vacui*, nature's proverbial abhorrence of a vacuum. Was there some sort of *power* in a

---

[57] M. J. van Lieburg, 'Zacharias Sylvius (1608–1664), author of the Praefatio to the first Rotterdam edition (1648) of Harvey's De Motu Cordis', *Janus*, 65 (1978), 241–57.

[58] Sylvius was a master at this school while studying medicine.

[59] M. J. van Lieburg, 'Isaac Beeckman and his diary-notes on William Harvey's theory on blood-circulation (1633–1634)', *Janus*, 69 (1982), 161–83.

vacuum? wondered Beeckman. And why do bodies move *in order* that a vacuum should not occur?[60] His answer (by 1615) was that motions apparently due to avoidance of a vacuum were actually due not to an attractive power from within the vacuum but to pressure from the air towards it. His answer was thus expressed in terms of the inequality in the pressure of air as the parts of the apparatus – no doubt some form of pump – were moved. Magnetic attraction was also considered under this head.[61]

By 1620 Beeckman was thinking about 'attraction' in a medical context, linking it to Erasistratus and the fear of a vacuum.[62] He probably had in mind Galen's account of how the followers of Erasistratus, who believed that there was not blood but only *pneuma* in the arteries, explained the bleeding that followed the incision of the living artery: the *pneuma*, they said, was so subtle that it at once escaped from the punctured artery, leaving a vacuum behind, which attracted blood across fine anastomoses from the veins.[63] Denial of forces of 'attraction' came to be a major article of manifestos of the new philosophies, and attractive forces within the body were central to the debate between the old and the new. Clearly Beeckman was hoping to explain the body in mechanical terms, based on atomism (partly from Erasistratus) and on denial of attraction and *fuga vacui*. In other words he was looking at medicine in part as a vehicle for his natural philosophy.[64] Beeckman first mentioned Harvey in 1633 – apparently the date of the Rotterdam consensus – and approved of his experiments.[65]

Clearly Beeckman accepted Harvey's doctrine because it could be made to agree with and therefore support an incipient mechanical natural philosophy that Beeckman was already formulating. In line with one of the principles of that philosophy Beeckman was anxious to refute a current idea that the liver drew chyle from the intestines by a form of attraction that resembled magnetism. 'Attraction' was inadmissible to Beeckman as to other New Philosophers because it seemed to imply action at a distance and some sort of mysterious force or 'virtue'. By adopting Harvey's description of the direction of bloodflow in the veins, Beeckman was able to invoke his preferred

---

[60] C. de Waard, ed., *Journal tenu par Isaac Beeckman de 1604 a 1634*, 4 vols., The Hague, 1939, 1942, 1945, 1953; vol. I, p. 26.

[61] De Waard, *Beeckman* (1939), vol. I, pp. 36, 101.

[62] De Waard, *Beeckman* (1942), vol. II, p. 122.

[63] P. Brain, *Galen on Bloodletting. A Study of the Origins, Development and Validity of his Opinions with a Translation of the three Works*, Cambridge University Press, 1986, p. 10.

[64] As we shall see below, Descartes also sought to use medicine as a vehicle for his new philosophy. Beeckman met Descartes in 1618 or 1619. Born in 1588, Beeckman was prepared for a career in the Reformed church, but took a medical degree at Caen in 1618 (*DNB*).

[65] De Waard, *Beeckman*, vol. III, pp. 292, 297, 298. Beeckman probably heard of the Harvey affair before 1633, for he was in Cambridge (where he would have found an increasing number of Dutch textbooks in use) when Harvey published his book.

explanation of pressure, so that the pressure of the air (ultimately from the mouth) is said to *push* the chyle (eventually to the heart).[66] The circulation of the blood presented the related problem of how the venous blood, having no pulse, moved into the heart. To meet this problem Primrose had spoken of the 'attraction' produced by the forcefully expanding heart; but to Beeckman this also was inadmissible and in disagreeing with Primrose he agrees with a Harvey who is made to argue that pressure-contact compels the blood to enter the heart in a forceful diastole. As was very often the case with others, in accepting Harvey's doctrine in outline Beeckman here modified its detail to fit it into his philosophy.

About five years after returning home – which was now England – from Padua, Ent decided to defend Harvey against the attack he had learned of (probably) in Padua. It was that of Parigiano, whom we shall meet in a later chapter. Ent's defence,[67] published in 1641, took the form of a promotion of a new natural philosophy rather than a rebuttal of an old. So different is the language and philosophy of Ent from that of Parigiano that it is more convenient for us to treat of Ent as part of the Anglo-Dutch story than as part of that of more distant continental reactions. Moreover, much of what he has to say that interests us is set out in formal 'digressions' which have almost nothing to do with Parigiano.

Some people who belonged to groups of one sort or another, in which a consensus might form, were aware of and explicit about the groups they belonged to and the beliefs the members had in common. Ent clearly felt that those like him who accepted the circulation of the blood were in a minority. He represented knowledge of the circulation as elite, the true knowledge, held by only a few great men. It was true knowledge precisely because the perspicacity of the great and few rose above the mediocrity of common opinion. It was the consensus of those who counted. For Ent the common opinion was not only old fashioned – indeed ancient – but held by old people, and he represented himself as the young champion of the great and the few. (He was now thirty-seven.) The common opinion was seen by Ent and by others as *vulgar*: it was in fact the natural philosophy of the schools, and the schoolmen and their traditional pupils were another group with a ready-made consensus. Because this group was far larger than Ent's, he had to be clear

---

[66] In a similar way, his account of action-by-contact enabled him to meet an objection to Harvey made by Primrose, who had imagined Harvey to have said that all the arteries were filled in a moment by the heart. Beeckman points out that the heart emits only a small amount of blood, which moves further on the blood already contained in the arteries. De Waard, *Beeckman* (1945), vol. III, p. 298.

[67] G. Ent, *Apologia pro Circulatione sanguinis: qua respondetur Aemilio Parisano Medico Veneto*, London, 1641. It was dedicated to the nobleman Theophilus Clinton, within whose areas of interest such matters lay; perhaps he was one of the new virtuosi.

about how the knowledge of his own group was superior. We do not need a plebiscite in order to be able to know, he says; and so the vulgar forum of the mob is to be dismissed in favour of the theatre of the true philosophers.[68] In pursuing the matter of elite and vulgar knowledge, Ent nicely distinguishes between the political aspects of the formation of a consensus, 'in which [vulgar] people ask "What is said?" and the [truly] philosophical, where they ask "What is true?" '. What Ent meant by his elite knowledge was of course the circulation expressed in terms of the new and largely mechanical natural philosophy, and not that of Harvey, Drake and Walaeus.

So Ent thinks of himself as full of true, youthful, dangerously controversial (he says),[69] select and new knowledge; his fellow-philosophers in whose theatre this was generated are also new, and are opposed also to another group, more learned than the vulgar mob, but with related vices. This group for Ent contained people like Parigiano, who accepted the teachings of the old writers because the latter represent the authority of teaching, not of (sensory) demonstration.[70] Ent saw this authority – the consensus of this group – as residing in a learned tradition, a tradition in which an anatomist like Eustachio (said Ent)[71] could claim that it was better to be wrong in the company of Galen than to be right in following this or that modern master.[72]

While Parigiano and Primrose, the enemies of both Harvey and Ent, wished to squash Harvey's doctrines under the weight of a coherent and massive world-picture, Ent as a self-perceived radical and reformer, could only chip away at particulars of this opposing world-picture. In doing so he gives the appearance of the revolutionary who is guided by the promise of an idea – that nature is mechanical – which is not yet as comprehensive as the world-picture he is trying to replace. For this reason Ent focusses his attack on a particular topic rather than on the fundamental principles of the opposing world picture. This topic had been important to Beeckman and came to serve as a central issue in the new philosophy, attraction. We have seen that attraction was objectionable to the new philosophers partly because to accept it would seem to be accepting action at a distance, which was incompatible with a natural philosophy based on particles in motion and in contact. Partly also it was objectionable because it was often explained on the basis of *horror vacui*,

---

68  See Ent's second dedication, to Harvey.
69  Ent, *Apologia*, the dedication to Harvey.
70  Ent, *Apologia*, p. 25.
71  Ibid., dedication to Harvey.
72  Like Severino and Gassendi (whom we shall meet below) Ent somewhat metaphorically identifies Democritus as the ancient figurehead of the new philosophy. Congratulating Harvey on his 'golden book' Ent observes that medical men 'wonder how so great a truth [as circulation] could be hidden so long in the well of Democritus'. He is not advocating the atomism or particularism of the new philosophy, but is referring to 'Democritus *physicus*', the philosopher of nature often cited by Pliny.

nature's way of arranging things so that a vacuum would not occur. There were a number of reasons why it was commonly held that a vacuum could not exist, many of them derived from Aristotle and contained in the philosophical textbooks of the universities.[73] But perhaps because these textbooks were short digests, which had replaced the traditional text-of-Aristotle-with-commentary format of earlier teaching materials, they did not retain the force of Aristotle's arguments. It was now possible to attack these digests as representing the *horror vacui* principle as a sort of local sentient action. By what messenger, asks Ent, thinking of a pump, does the water perceive the departure of the air and so rise up to replace it? Ent preferred to think – in another example – that when the neck of a cooling vessel was lowered into water, the water rose not with the *purpose* of preventing a vacuum, but because it was driven by the water below (see fig. 16). Indeed, in such cases it was possible to generalise and say that everything that seemed to move of its own accord, *sua sponte*, was in fact driven by something else. The same was true, he thought, of the barometer.[74] In no case was a vacuum the cause of motion, because a vacuum was nothing, and could not act. The notion of local, sentient and purposeful action now looked *vulgaris*, an opinion of the common crowd, not of the elite band of philosophers.[75]

But it was more difficult to generalise about motions within the body. Attempting to do so Ent said there were five kinds of 'attraction' inside and outside the body, commonly thought to be caused by *fuga vacui*, similarity of substance, heat, pain and faculty.[76] Let us glance at them in turn. 'Similarity of

---

73 See also the discussion of Case and Magirus, above, pp. 54–6. On vacuum experiments, see C. Schmitt, 'Experimental evidence for and against a void: the sixteenth-century arguments', in his *Studies in Renaissance Philosophy and Science*, London, 1980, pp. 352–66. Schmitt's observations that Aristotelians valued experiments more highly than their opponents would be consistent with the Aristotelianism of Harvey and Fabricius. Thus the positions of those defending the existence of a vacuum were generally theoretical. The 'armchair' experiments described by Schmitt are of course rhetorical devices, for example the 'experiment' based on the assumption that water shrinks as it freezes, leaving a 'vacuum' above it in a rigid container. See also Schmitt's 'Experience and experiment: a comparison of Zabarella's view with Galileo's in *De Motu*', in the same volume, pp. 80–138.

74 'vitris illis diariis (quibus tempestatum vicissitudines notantur)'. Ent, *Apologia*, p. 29. The context (air pressure) suggests that these glasses were barometers rather than thermometers. But he may be referring back to this location when he later (p. 31) talks of a *thermoscopium*.

75 Ent rejected it also in a philosophical language that, however, retained some Aristotelian terminology; it is foreign to true philosophy, said Ent, ti take a final cause (the ultimate reason for an action) for the efficient cause (here the local and sentient action).

76 G. Ent, *Apologia pro circulatione sanguinis*, 2nd edn, London, 1685, p. 37: he accuses Pecquet of stealing his discussion. Attraction was also the subject of an experiment by Fludd: a burning candle standing in a saucer of water is covered by a bell-jar. As the candle burned lower and was extinguished, so the water rose in the bell-jar. Fludd argued, in 1617, for chemical purposes, that the air had been consumed and that the water rose to prevent a vacuum. By 1631 the Aristotelians were using the same experiment to argue that heat attracted water. See A. G. Debus, *The English Paracelsians*, London, 1965, p. 118.

substance' was a traditional explanation of 'sympathy' between the parts of the body, where organs of the same constitution suffered pathologically in the same way, although distant from each other. Such sympathies were a kind of attraction.

Apart from this, there were three distinct medical contexts in which the question of attraction was discussed. One of them (it is the last on Ent's little list) was the traditional and fundamental business of the Galenic faculties, one of which was the power exerted by the straight fibres of hollow organs, the faculty of attraction. The second was the question of how blood entered the heart. This was a problem mostly for those who adopted Harvey's scheme of bloodflow, for those who did not had a consistent Galenic account of the matter (it included attraction).[77] Many who did adopt a version of Harvey's scheme were those who had adopted the new philosophy and so denied attraction.[78] Yet it seemed that the forceful systole, producing the arterial pulse, was a cause of the blood's motion in the arteries only. The blood seeped across the pores of the flesh or through very small vessels into the veins, which were without pulse. Yet somehow, in the absence of attraction, the blood moved through the tributaries of the vena cava to the right auricle. The third medical context also related to the motion of the blood, for it had been commonly asserted before Harvey that the swelling of the veins on the wrong side of a medium-tight ligature was due to a power of attraction, the 'drawing', generated by the heat and pain (the other examples listed by Ent) of the ligatured part.[79]

Doubts had been expressed by medical men on attractive 'drawing' for perhaps half a century. Daniel Sennert, the Protestant professor at Wittenberg, recorded in 1611 that many of the recent authors denied that heat, pain and even the vacuum could exert attraction.[80] By 1615 (and in a medical context in 1620)

---

[77] Thus J. Primrose, *Exercitationes, et animadversiones in librum, De motu cordis, et circulatione sanguinis adversus Guilielmum Harveium Medicum Regium, et Anatomes in Collegio Londinensi Professorem*, London, 1630, has the active arteries attracting the blood (p. 22) and finds in attraction the reason why two substances can move in two directions in the same vessel – the venous artery (p. 41). Nourishment was attracted to the parts, not squeezed into them by the heart (p. 71) and the heat and pain of a ligature attract blood (pp. 85, 89).

[78] Thus Beeckman, in denying the attraction posited by Primrose. See van Lieburg, 'Isaac Beeckman', p. 169.

[79] J. Primrose, *Destructio Fundamentorum medicinae Vopisci Fortunati Plempii in Academia Lovaniensi medicinae professor*, Rotterdam, 1657, p. 90, continued to assert that the swelling on the wrong side of the ligature was due to the otherwise very slow-moving blood moving out of the small branches of the veins into the larger channels. Primrose also (p. 88) restated the apparent Harveian 'problem' of how the blood in the vena cava moves towards the heart. See also J. Bylebyl, 'The medical side of Harvey's discovery: the normal and the abnormal', in J. Bylebyl, ed., *William Harvey and his Age. The Professional and Social Context of the Discovery of the Circulation*, Johns Hopkins University Press, 1979, pp. 28–102; 57.

[80] Sennert's *Institutionum Medicarum Libri V* was first published in 1611. See Sennert, *Operum Tomus I [–III]*, Paris, 1641: *Institutionum . . .* , book 2, part 2, chap. 11 (p. 347).

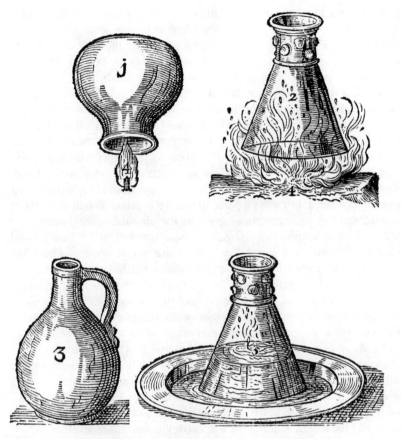

Fig. 16. Attraction in a medical context.
A simple and basic image around which circulated discussions of 'attraction' and *fuga vacui* was the medical cupping glass. Whether it was a *cucurbita* or a *scypho* (the top two figures) the glass was heated and placed on the skin, often after scarification. As it cooled, the traditional doctors said, it 'drew' blood to the surface of the skin. No, said the New Philosophers, the blood is *pushed*, in the same way as the external air pushes water in a dish into the cooling *scypho* (in the last figure of the four).

Isaac Beeckman was prepared to believe that there was no inherent power of attraction in a vacuum, but rather a pushing from the weight of the ambient air.[81] We shall see that attraction was a central point at issue in Henricus

---

[81] However, he retained the term *fuga vacui* and applied it to the motion of chyle from the intestines to liver and heart. De Waard, *Beeckman* (1939), vol. I, pp. 26, 36, 101; vol. II (1949), p. 122.

Regius' disputations on the circulation in Utrecht and the subsequent controversy with Primrose,[82] and we shall look at Glisson's sarcastic rebuttal of local sentience in apparent cases of attraction in the blood vessels. Sometimes attempts were made to explain attraction within the body by means of magnetism. (Beeckman[83] and Regius[84] toyed with the idea.)

Clearly Ent wanted to believe that all apparent instances of 'traction' inside the body could be explained in the same terms as the motions of weatherglasses and pumps outside the body. It was for him difficult to think of 'attraction' within the body, like the commonly asserted cases of blood moving into the heart or chyle to the liver, as a category of motion; in particular, said Ent, we cannot imagine an efficient cause for such motion. Rather than 'attraction' or 'faculty' (said Ent) we must think in terms of 'propulsion'. Indeed, Ent was prepared to believe in propulsion in the body as an act of faith in the new philosophy, in the absence of any intelligible causality. In justification, he sets out the basic physics of his new natural philosophy. Gravity and levity (he begins) are not absolute qualities but relative; *everything* tends to the centre of the world, but the heavier displace the lighter. But for this displacement, by contact, all matter would remain in the same state (of motion or rest). Ent cannot offer a cause for these motions, and presents them as simple facts of observation. It is in this framework that in Ent's explanation air presses down upon water to force it into the pump or cupping-glass that the air itself cannot reach. A central example is the thermometer, *thermoscopium*, in which, upon the cooling of the fluid, a space is left that the air does not reach. Ent does not discuss whether this space is a true vacuum, but it is clear that some two or three years before Torricelli's famous experiments the newly vigorous dispute about the possibility of a vacuum and the nature of attraction was becoming open to experiment.[85]

The principal example of attraction that Ent was anxious to discredit was that traditionally exercised by the fibres of the body, one of the four Galenic faculties of attraction, retention, assimilation and rejection. The term 'faculty' itself was naturally a butt of the rhetoric of the new philosophers, and Ent devotes a great deal of space to being sarcastic about it. To use 'faculty' was like calling upon the gods in the theatre when the plot in a play got into difficulties, he said. Above all, for Ent, the blood did not enter the heart by attraction, was not propelled along the arteries by a faculty in their coats, and

---

[82] Regius' *Spongia* in *Recentiorum disceptationes de motu cordis, sanguinis, et chyli, in animalibus*, Leiden, 1647, p. 152.
[83] De Waard, *Beeckman* (1945), vol. III, p. 298 (1633): if Harvey is right, wrote Beeckman, then we must stop discussing the 'magnetism' by which the liver draws the chyle.
[84] Regius, *Spongia*: see Regius' clash with Primrose, chap. 8 below.
[85] Ent, *Apologia*, p. 31. See also the discussion by S. Shapin and S. Schaffer, *Leviathan and the Air-Pump. Hobbes, Boyle and the Experimental Life*, Princeton University Press, 1985.

was not attracted to the parts by the faculty of assimilation – indeed, it did not nourish the parts.[86] So great was Ent's resistance to the notion of faculty that he could not accept Harvey's account of the heartbeat. Perhaps he felt that a forceful systole was too close to a pulsific faculty. Perhaps he adopted Descartes' notions as more suitable to the new philosophy (we shall meet them below). Certainly, in following Beeckman and resisting the idea that blood entered the heart by attraction, he came to believe that the blood became ebullient in the heart and forced its way into the arteries. The arterial pulse was, consequently, simultaneous with the cardiac. The advantage of such a scheme was that he could also deny those who claimed that the arteries too had a pulsific faculty. Secondly, the heat of the heart (the same thing as its spirits, said Ent) provided a non-facultative explanation of the entry of blood into the heart: it moves, he said, to the heart as the oil in a lamp moves to the wick, by pressure of surrounding parts, to avoid a vacuum. This heat, or flame,[87] was supplied by the fatty part of the blood itself, together with the *nitrum*, or 'nitrous virtue' of the air.[88]

Ent's natural philosophy was not simply a particulate and mechanical view of the world on the lines of that of his teacher, Beeckman. It included much 'chemistry' derived from authors like Quercetanus, and much on the generative power of salts and dew.[89] Nor was his natural philosophy close to that of Harvey. Again, it was in a severely modified form that Harvey's doctrines were being propagated. Ent was a significant figure in that propagation: he corresponded with other non-traditional physicians, like Severino;[90] along with Glisson, Scarburgh and Merrett, all of whom were physicians and "protégés of

---

[86] The question of whether the circulating blood nourishes the body was a few years later disputed in the traditional manner in Cambridge by Glisson (see chap. 10 below).

[87] Ent, *Apologia*, pp. 92–7.

[88] Ibid., p. 18. We have seen that this idea appealed also to Drake, the rest of whose natural philosophy was so different to Ent's. 'Aerial nitre' was a notion used by Fludd and the alchemists (see A. G. Debus, 'Harvey and Fludd: the irrational factor in the rational science of the seventeenth century', *Journal of the History of Biology*, 3 (1970), 81–105; 88) and it came to be used by the Oxford 'Harveians'. (See Robert G. Frank, *Harvey and the Oxford Physiologists. A Study of Scientific Ideas*, University of California Press, 1980.) Since the attacks on school medicine had largely destroyed 'faculty' as a source of motion, Fludd used this spirit in its place, and the alchemists and the Oxford group used 'nitre' as a source of local spontaneous action (as in gunpowder).

[89] In connection with this he reports (*Apologia*, p. 139) that Harvey in his public lectures said he could find no semen in the female deer after coition. Clearly Harvey was working on generation at an early date and was teaching at least part of it, apparently in the anatomy lectures. This would confirm Webster's argument that the work for and writing of Harvey's book on generation were largely complete at a comparatively early date and helped to shape Harvey's reply to Riolan and his doctrine of the primacy of the blood. See C. Webster, 'Harvey's *De Generatione*: its origins and relevance to the theory of circulation', *British Journal for the History of Science*, 3 (1966–7), 262–74.

[90] See C. Schmitt and C. Webster, 'Harvey and M. A. Severino. A neglected medical relationship', *Bulletin of the History of Medicine*, 45 (1971), 49–75.

Harvey',[91] he became a member of the so-called 1645 group, which contained men interested in the new philosophy; he was later, like other members of the 1645 group, a founder member of the Royal Society. Like Glisson (whom we shall meet below as another Harveian activist), Ent held the Goulstonian pathology lectureship in the College of Physicians[92] and eventually became its president. Ent and Glisson were key figures in putting the seal on the English consensus.

[91]  C. Webster, *The Great Instauration. Science, Medicine and Reform 1626–1660*, London, 1975, p. 55.

[92]  P. Allen, 'Medical education in 17th century England', *Journal of the History of Medicine*, 1 (1945), 115–43; 138.

# 8 Two natural philosophies

## Descartes reads *De motu cordis*

For Harvey's doctrines to be rejected, or sufficiently accepted to form the basis of a new consensus, they had to be known. Some people read *De motu cordis*, others heard or read about its contents at second hand. What they made of it depended upon what was already in their minds; and however direct or indirect their knowledge of the book, almost everyone modified or misunderstood Harvey's doctrine. Such misunderstandings are basic to the processes by which a consensus came about and to its nature once formed.

As we saw in the last chapter, personal communication[1] played a large part in people's knowledge of new works in natural philosophy. Gassendi read *De motu cordis* in the year after it was published. He thought the doctrine of circulation was attractive, but accepted the medical view that the septum between the ventricles of the heart was porous.[2] The heart could not therefore work as Harvey had claimed. Gassendi sent his opinions to Mersenne. Mersenne in turn discussed the topic with Descartes, who seems to have read the book by 1632. Mersenne was at the centre of a circle of correspondence concerned primarily with philosophical issues.[3] Safe postal systems had

---

[1] Patronage was also important. In the Gassendi–Descartes–Mersenne circle, Peiresc was a 'Maecenas' in for example paying for the printing of Aselli's book on the lacteals in 1627 (H. P. Bayon, 'William Harvey, physician and biologist: his precursors, opponents and successors', part 5 (*Annals of Science*, 4 (1940), 328–89; 370)). Gassendi recommended Harvey's book to him either in the year of its publication, 1628 (Gassendi to Peiresc): R. Descartes, *Oeuvres*, ed. C. Adam and P. Tannery, Paris, 1896–1913; reprinted 1956, vol. I, p. 264) or in 1629 (P. Gassendi, *Viri Illustris Nicolai Claudii Fabricii de Peiresc, Senatoris Aquis Extiensis Vita*, 3rd edn, The Hague, 1655, p. 137).
[2] Descartes' letters are very revealing about his attempts to promote his philosophy in the universities. See Descartes, *Oeuvres*, ed. Adam and Tannery, vol. I, p. 264. An earlier version of this chapter ('Harvey in Holland: circulation and the Calvinists') appeared in Roger French and Andrew Wear, eds., *The Medical Revolution of the Seventeenth Century*, Cambridge University Press, 1989.
[3] See R. Frank's essay review of G. Whitteridge, *William Harvey and the Circulation of the Blood*, London, 1971, in *Journal of the History of Biology*, 5 (1972), 189–204, where he points out that a huge amount of material is extant relating to the centres of correspondence in Leiden, Amsterdam, Paris, Rome, Florence and Padua.

been developing in Europe over the previous century and now allowed a comparatively rapid means of communication, by letters and the dispatch of books.

Descartes was familiar with *De motu cordis* by the end of 1632.[4] He too modified Harvey's doctrine. This modification is doubly important for the story of this book. Firstly, part of Harvey's doctrines became firmly tied to some of those of Descartes and may thereby have reached a wider, or at least a different audience, albeit in a modified form. Secondly, Descartes' natural philosophy was radically different from that of Harvey and had a great impact on the way in which Harvey's doctrines were understood from the 1630s on. Descartes' natural philosophy is probably the biggest single issue in the story of the acceptance or rejection of Harvey's doctrines.

Let us reflect on the fundamental differences between the two men and their natural philosophies. Harvey had been educated at Protestant Cambridge and the religiously tolerant Padua. He had taken up the most recent development of an ancient philosophy and had used it in teaching another traditional subject, anatomy, with unexpected results. Descartes had been educated by Jesuits and had reacted against conventional education with a doubt so fundamental that it questioned his own existence and that of God. In reconstructing his own existence and that of God Descartes was, to use his own analogy, pulling down the house of thought in which he had lived and beginning again entirely afresh. Following a kind of self-evident metaphysics, Descartes proved himself to be an autonomous being by the very act of doubting his own existence. It followed that God existed because he (Descartes) as an imperfect being could not be the cause of his own (perfect) idea of God as a perfect Being. God as perfect must be the cause of this idea; and likewise God as perfect would not deceive Descartes in any perfectly clear and simple idea that he might conceive.

On this basis Descartes developed a philosophy largely concerned with the nature of man and the natural world. Its principal feature was that in descending from first principles to the laws of physics each step was a clear and simple idea which cumulatively excluded all the moving principles of traditional natural philosophy: forms, potentiality, final and formal causality, qualities, faculties – and especially attraction – privation and the rest. All matter was particulate and all motion by particle-to-particle contact.

By 1630, having taken himself from his native France to the Low Countries, Descartes believed that he had developed a new philosophical method. He had decided that the laws that God had made for the natural world – the laws of physics – had been so impressed on the human mind as to be almost

---

[4] Descartes, *Oeuvres*, ed. Adam and Tannery, vol. I, p. 263. Descartes is said to have accepted the circulation before reading Harvey's book. See J. A. Passmore, 'William Harvey and the philosophy of science', *The Australian Journal of Philosophy*, 36 (2) (1958), 85–94; 86.

innate.[5] It was this that made the philosophical method universal in application and, by the time Descartes had finished his brief flirtation with university studies at Franeker and Leiden,[6] he believed he had also a complete scheme of results of applying the method to the natural world. These results were the basis of his *Le Monde*, finished in 1633 (but withdrawn from publication when Descartes heard of Galileo's condemnation). By 1632, when he read *De motu cordis*, Descartes had finished the part of *Le Monde* that dealt with man – 'L'Homme' – but he revised it by adopting part of Harvey's doctrine.

But Descartes did not publish his new doctrines at once. It was not until 1637 that he published his *Discourse on Method*, which contained a part – the action of the heart and the motion of blood – of the earlier work on man. This publication is significant in a number of ways. Firstly, he chose his description of the motion of the heart and blood as the most notable example of the results of his new philosophy. And while he carefully presents most of his new teaching as a construction, he is unusually confident and dogmatic about the motions of the heart. Indeed, he said that if what he wrote about the heart was wrong, then so was the rest of his philosophy.[7] Secondly, he modified Harvey's doctrine in accordance with his own purposes and beliefs: in brief he adopted the circulation of the blood, but dismissed Harvey's account of the forceful systole. Thirdly, the *Discourse* as a whole was intended as the centrepiece of the new philosophy, the central statement of Descartes as the new Philosopher.

## Replacing Aristotle. Descartes as the new Philosopher

We have already seen that Aristotle remained the basis of the university arts course up to and past Harvey's and Descartes' time. After the Reformation both Catholics and Protestants had their own reasons for basing an education on Aristotle. Bacon's philosophical programme called for a new departure from scholastic Aristotelianism. He did not call directly for the abolition of Aristotelianism, because he saw its social function in the society of his time. Instead, he hoped it would be simply left behind with the adoption of his own methods. Thus the *Novum organum* was to replace the organon, Aristotle's tool or method of the logical and analytical arts. But ultimately Bacon provided no concrete teachable alternative: in natural philosophy, no systematic account

---

5 See T. A. McGahagan, 'Cartesianism in the Netherlands, 1639–1675; the New Science and the Calvinist Counter-Reformation', University of Pennsylvania PhD thesis, 1976 (University Microfilms International), Ann Arbor and London, 1980, pp. 108–32.

6 See G. A. Lindeboom, *Descartes and Medicine*, Amsterdam, 1978, pp. 5–8, 17.

7 R. Toellner, 'Logical and psychological aspects of the discovery of the circulation of the blood', in *On Scientific Discovery. The Erice Lectures 1977*, ed. M. D. Grmek, R. S. Cohen and G. Cimino, Dordrecht, Boston and London, 1977, pp. 239–59; p. 249.

of what the natural world was.[8] As Harvey said, it was Lord Chancellorish philosophy. The 'new philosophy' of Bacon and, often enough, Gassendi, was on the whole attractive to those with tolerant views in religion, like the Arminians. It is often said too that the practical usefulness inherent in Bacon's conception of understanding and controlling nature appealed to the 'work ethic' of some forms of Protestantism. In contrast those at the further sides of the religious spectrum, the Jesuits and Calvinists, found what they wanted in Aristotle.

Descartes may have aimed his new philosophy at the broad, tolerant church, where some form of new philosophy had already found a market. It is sometimes said that he chose to go to the Low Countries for the sake of a religious toleration that he hoped would enable him to develop his unorthodox ideas. Whether so or not, Descartes' activities suggest that he was putting into operation a plan to have himself accepted as the Philosopher in place of Aristotle.[9] First, although the *Discourse* was published anonymously, Descartes took care to send out a number of copies to physicians and philosophers for comment. V. F. Plemp of Louvain received three; Mersenne probably more, because he forwarded back to Descartes some critiques by others; the university teachers Sylvius and Regius almost certainly received copies; the Jesuit P. Vatier certainly did[10] (he sent it on to his doctor); and Descartes' countrymen Petit and Libert Froidmont (a teacher of Plemp) also had copies and like all those above sent comments back to Descartes.[11] In the *Discourse* itself Descartes asks (by way of his publisher) for criticisms and comments to which he hopes to reply. He also asks his friends to undertake further experiments in order to leave his own time free for thought.

In other words, for a man who was nervous, in the shadow of Galileo's condemnation, of publishing philosophical novelties, this was an aggressive programme for the promotion of his own doctrines. The second point that suggests that Descartes' plan was to supplant Aristotle is that the *Discourse on Method* was to play the same role as Aristotle's own 'method', the universal arts that were applicable to all 'sciences' but not of them. For about four centuries the university student in the arts course had first been taught the general principles of argument, the logical, dialectical and rhetorical arts. Subsequently he learned how the (broadly speaking) dialectical art was used in specific subject areas. The Aristotelian *Physics* first discussed the general

---

[8]  As Bacon said, the task was to start again. See J. Devey, ed., *The Physical and Metaphysical Works of Lord Bacon*, London, 1853, p. 381.

[9]  This was a considerable undertaking, for the pressures on universities to retain Aristotle were great. Opposition to Aristotle could in the France of 1624 lead to exile: see Lindeboom, *Descartes and Medicine*, p. 8.

[10]  Descartes, *Oeuvres*, ed. Adam and Tannery, vol. I, p. 561.

[11]  Ibid., vol. I, p. 377; vol. II, p. 343.

principles of motion, and following texts were examples of the application of these principles to classes of natural objects of increasing complexity, from the *Meteorology* and *On the Heavens* to the works on animals and their actions. If Descartes were to destroy Aristotle's philosophy he would have to replace it with something of the same curricular shape: the *Discourse on Method* was to replace the universal arts, and the treatises published with it were what Descartes called essays in the application of the Method. They were the *Meteorology*, the *Dioptrics* and the *Geometry*, which like Aristotle's physical works take the general principles to different sets of physical circumstances. In accordance with Descartes' first principles, the *Geometry* for example is a 'science' based on the mathematical metaphysics of particulate motion.

Additionally, the constraints of the university system (which it was not in Descartes' interests to challenge) demanded that an arts course could be used as a basis for the advanced subject medicine (and required that it was not inconsistent with the study of law and divinity). But medicine was thoroughly based on Aristotelian–Galenic natural principles. Descartes could not replace the arts course on its own. He needed a Cartesian medicine. In fact in many ways such a thing can be seen as his ultimate objective, to be begun after the completion of the *Discourse*.[12] Indeed, he concluded that work with a declaration that the rest of his life would be devoted to developing a firm basis for medicine. We can see Descartes' attempts to produce a cartesian medicine in his choice of a medical man to promote his doctrines in the universities[13] and in his friendship with the medical man Cornelis van Hogelande (as we shall see shortly). It is clear from the *Principles of Philosophy* (1644) that he saw an improved medicine as one of the chief benefits of his new metaphysics and physics; the *Passions of the Soul* is concerned with a physiological understanding of the emotions; and the unfinished *Description of the Human Body* is wholly concerned with the structure and action of the body.[14] 'Where the philosopher finishes, the physician begins' was as true for Descartes as for the centuries before. If Descartes' whole philosophy from metaphysics to practical morals and medicine was to replace Aristotle's, it had to occupy the same pedagogic niche in the same institutions, the universities; it had to rely on valid first principles and be subject to academic procedures.

---

[12] R. Descartes, *Discourse on Method, Optics, Geometry and Meteorology*, ed. P. J. Olscamp, Indianapolis, 1975, p. 50.
[13] During this campaign Descartes' letters show that he was actively seeking medical knowledge, including the mechanism of fevers, the ontology of disease and coagulation of the blood. He told Huygens he was undertaking a survey of medicine; it probably included his look at botany and chemistry. See Descartes, *Oeuvres*, ed. Adam and Tannery, vol. III, pp. 443, 456, 457, 459, 462.
[14] I am grateful to M. Shulman for useful discussions during the writing of her Cambridge MPhil dissertation 'Descartes' Philosophy of Medicine' (1989).

## Descartes, Harvey and the universities

The story of this book is how Harvey's natural philosophy led him to the discovery of the circulation and how other people's natural philosophy enabled them to accept or prevented them from accepting that discovery. As we have seen, the chief of these other people was Descartes. It was not only his campaign to become the new Philosopher that was important, of course, but also the content of his natural philosophy. We can begin the story of his campaign with an examination of his handling of Harvey's doctrine.

We have reached the year 1637, in which Descartes published his *Discourse on Method*. It is here that Descartes says that the house of traditional learning must be demolished and a fresh start made. The result is Descartes' particulate-plenum world and he selects as its principal example the workings of the heart. While Descartes covers the whole work with the careful disclaimer that it is not meant to describe the real world directly, yet in section 5, his account of the heartbeat, he is unusually dogmatic. He claims that the disposition of the parts makes his explanation the only one possible, so that as in a clock the motions necessarily follow the shape and position of the parts. We have seen above how the clock provided a troubling image for the natural philosophers of the schools, and here the issue is articulated very clearly by Descartes. This clockwork is Descartes' 'mechanism', which for the moment at least, we can more usefully think of as 'natural necessity'.[15]

Descartes accepted from Harvey that the blood circulated round the body. It was an acceptable idea because it could be seen as consistent with what Descartes had in his mind already. By viewing the blood as particulate, Descartes could see its motion as derived from a single source – the heart – and transmitted particle to particle. Since the blood circulated, this motion reached all parts of the body and was responsible, when transmitted to the parts, for all actions, such as secretion, perception and other localised motions. This removed at a stroke any need for old explanations of attraction, faculties, qualitative action and the actions of the vital and nutritive faculties of the soul, which Descartes' mechanism had rigidly excluded from the animal body.

But Descartes could not accept Harvey's doctrine of the forceful systole. Let us remind ourselves that Harvey had presented his case in *De motu cordis* in a carefully reasoned way. The forceful systole, the question of quantity and the resultant circulation were both a historical and logical sequence that had convinced Harvey and which he hoped would convince his readers. He anticipated, no doubt, that his readers' preconceptions would not largely differ

---

[15] So central was the example of the heartbeat to Descartes that he said that if what he had written about the heart was wrong, then so was the rest of his philosophy. See Toellner, 'Logical and psychological aspects', p. 249.

from what his own had been before he had made his discovery, and his arguments were measured accordingly. But in natural philosophy Descartes was from another world. It is argued below that he would not have agreed with Harvey on the very criteria by which knowledge was defined, and it is not to be expected that Descartes, with his head full of an exciting new metaphysics of nature, would have followed Harvey's argument that the circulation was a conclusion deriving from earlier premisses, largely the forceful systole. Instead he picked the circulation out of its context. In doing so he 'misunderstood' Harvey by dividing Harvey's message at the articulation where so many others were to divide it. While Alexander Read, for example, picked up the first half of the message, Descartes adopted the second.

The principal ground for Descartes' rejection of the forceful systole was probably that contraction of the heart, its *propria motio* in Harvey's natural philosophy, could be seen as a kind of *attraction* in which the parts of the heart came closer together. This would have looked to Descartes like a local source of motion, an attraction which was entirely at odds with his first principle that all motion was transmitted, particle to particle, from a pre-existing ultimate source. So it was important for Descartes that the heart was the sole source of motion in the body and equally important that it was not self-generated motion. He therefore concluded that the motion of the heart was derived from a natural (not 'innate' or 'native') heat implanted by God in the heart, a fire without light, or heat of the kind that arises naturally in hay cut and stacked too green. This heat, he concluded, was great enough to vaporise the 'very large' drops of blood entering the heart from the veins.[16] The result was a forceful diastole of the heart, powered by the expanding vapour that forced its way into the aorta and pulmonary artery and condensed into blood again in the arteries and lungs.

Descartes' natural philosophy aroused much interest and criticism. The motion of the heart and blood remained, as Descartes had intended it to be, the most potent example of his natural philosophy's ability to explain the nature of the machine of the body. It was in association with his idea of forceful diastole that many people met the second half of Harvey's doctrine, the circulation. In Descartes' campaign to insert his natural philosophy into the universities the importance of the example of the motion of the heart and blood was that Descartes could fight his battle on the medical front as well as in the arts course (with his physics). In 1638, the year following the publication of the *Discourse on Method*, Hendrik de Roy – Regius – was appointed extra-ordinary teacher of medicine in Utrecht, and he wrote to Descartes to express his admiration of the latter's physics. As a physician he was particularly interested in the circulation (in Cartesian dress) and asked Descartes about the reception of the doctrine. Descartes took his opportunity. Here was an admirer

---

16 Descartes, *Discourse*, p. 40 (p. 49 in the edn of 1637).

with a voice in a university who could be used to cultivate Cartesian natural philosophy in his teaching.

And so from April 1639 Regius, now as ordinary professor, began to teach a course that included Cartesian physics. Descartes was on hand to offer advice. Now, while lectures, such as the 'ordinary' lectures of Regius, could be largely controlled by statute, disputations were a different matter. Although the university authorities could refuse to allow the defence of a thesis, there was nothing predictable about where the argument from even a safe thesis might lead. Disputations were public, adversarial, partisan and they attracted attention. A series of related theses defended over a period might develop a personal or idiosyncratic theme on the part of a teacher whose students defended the theses; and often having 'proved' his opinions by successful defence in this manner, the teacher might publish his textbook on the subject.[17] This, the disputation, was to be the route by which Descartes planned to take his natural philosophy into the universities, as indeed he told Mersenne. Sylvius and Walaeus in Leiden had also chosen (in 1639 and 1640) disputation as the arena in which to discuss circulation, and Regius in Utrecht differed in having Descartes in the background as adviser and indeed as patron.

Disputed questions had no natural role in Descartes' natural philosophy, which drew its strength from its first principles. In contrast, as we have seen, formal modes of argument were central to the presentation of Harvey's natural philosophy. A second difference between the two philosophies was that while Harvey's first principle of procedure was a mode of observation, comparison and experiment that he variously called Socratic or Aristotelian, in contrast these modes are generally held to have a place in Descartes' natural philosophy only when the deductive descent from first principles ramified to the extent that the mind was unable to choose on *a priori* grounds the course that nature had chosen. But in fighting for his natural philosophy within the university of Utrecht Descartes had to tackle directly both disputation and observation, including experiment.

Disputation was central to the adoption or rejection of Harvey's and Descartes' doctrines, both separately and when conjoined. A publicly and successfully defended thesis went some way at least to generating a consensus, the necessary precondition for a change in natural philosophy. The importance

---

[17] The practice was common. Sylvius worked his theses up into a textbook, and Regius himself produced a text that owed a lot to his theses. On Sylvius, see A. Gubser, 'The Positiones Variae Medicae of Franciscus Sylvius', *Bulletin of the History of Medicine*, 40 (1966), 72–80. His textbook is *Opera medica, hoc est disputationum medicarum decas*; I have used the edition of Geneva, 1693. The disputations proceed from digestion to chylification, sanguification and circulation. Some such sequence was not uncommon, and it was designed to replace the old doctrine of 'concoction' and to take in the new discoveries of Aselli and Harvey. Compare Regius' sequence of topics, below.

of the disputation justifies a closer look at what one would have consisted of at this time in the Dutch universities. One of the few formal descriptions of the disputation was published by Adriaan Heerebord in Leiden in the middle of the century.[18] Heerebord taught logic in Leiden and was part of a new movement in the arts course of the northern Protestant universities. Even the fact that Heerebord felt it desirable to set out the form of the disputation, taken for granted for centuries elsewhere, indicates that a fundamental review of arts teaching was under way. In Heerebord's case there was a religious dimension to this, and as we shall see, part of the task he saw himself doing was to rescue a pristine and Reformed Aristotle from the clutches of the scholastic Catholics. Important teachers like Heerebord and his predecessor Burgersdijk taught throughout the arts course, from logic to moral and natural philosophy, and their consistency of purpose and exposition made their textbooks attractive particularly in the English universities.[19]

Heerebord's description of the structure of the disputation undoubtedly reflected practice in the Dutch university in the period we are discussing and had not inconsiderable influence in the English universities, particularly Cambridge. While disputations sharpened students' powers of argument, and were also ceremonies that attended graduation, they were much more. We have seen that they could be used to promote a teacher's interpretation of a topic, and they were also held to be a mode of discovering truths, including those of the physical world. A full disputation centred on a number of theses addressed to a particular topic or theme. Heerebord said that a thesis was a 'germ of truth', and the disputation was therefore the defence, expansion and proof of this truth. According to Heerebord a thesis could be arrived at in one of three ways. The first was from the words of a teacher: this no doubt reflected the common practice of a teacher arranging for his pupils to defend his own opinions and so 'prove' them. The second source for a thesis, in Heerebord's view, was from

---

[18] A. Heerebord, Ερμηνεια Logica: seu explicatio tum per notas tum per exempla Synopsis Logicae Burgerdicianae . . . accedit ejusdem Auctoris Praxis Logica, Leiden, 1650, book 2, chap. 23, p. 176. Eleven editions of this text came into Cambridge University Library between 1650 and 1694, some measure of the attractions of the Dutch universities for Cambridge.

[19] Students coming up to Cambridge would already have done some logic and would be introduced to Burgersdijk's 'Institutes' of logic (2nd edn 1642) and his metaphysics, and Heerebord's Annotamenta. See W. T. Costello, The Scholastic Curriculum at early Seventeenth Century Cambridge, Harvard University Press, 1958, p. 45. For Burgersdijk's natural philosophy, see E. G. Ruestow, Physics at Seventeenth and Eighteenth Century Leiden. Philosophy and the New Science in the University, The Hague, 1973, pp. 16, 17. Textbooks available in Cambridge indicate the popularity of Burgersdijk's moral and natural philosophy. See R. Bowes, A Catalogue of Books Printed at or Relating to the University Town and County of Cambridge from 1521 to 1893 with Bibliographical and Biographical Notes, Cambridge, 1894, e.g. under 1631, 1637. Burgersdijk's works were also extensively printed and used both in Oxford and Cambridge, and there remain ten edns of Heerebord's commentary on Burgersdijk's logic in Cambridge University Library.

the meaning of words. This was the analysis of terms within a proposition or of the argument that followed, and had been the basis of disputation since the twelfth century. Thirdly, Heerebord allowed that the 'germ of truth' might be obtained by the senses from observation of the physical world. Such a thesis could also be defended by arguments from 'problems in nature'. Heerebord rates such natural theses and arguments lower, for student use, than the dialectical, but they still had an important role to play. Moreover, argument from authority, said Heerebord, was to be encouraged only in theological disputations.[20] Put into the context of medicine or the natural part of the arts course in Utrecht or Leiden, this meant that the student would often be defending his own or his teacher's opinions on some natural point largely by dialectical and natural arguments. The procedure was that the theses were published in advance of the disputation to allow the opponent to study the form of the proposition and to construct his reply, the antithesis. The opponent's first attack would be on the logical form of the proposition. If unsuccessful he would then press upon the substance of the proposition. If the proponent had used authority then it was legitimate, said Heerebord, for the opponent to quote 'another man equally distinguished and learned'. In the disputations we are considering, it was at this point that the opinions of Descartes, Harvey and others would be introduced. So too would be their experimental results, particularly when the thesis had been a germ of truth derived from observation.

In the case of Descartes and Regius the overall purpose of the series of disputations was the promotion of a Cartesian natural philosophy within the university by means of theses mostly concerned with the circulation of the blood. Successful defence of the theses would have cleared the way for the publication of a Cartesian physics and a Cartesian medicine.[21] While at the junior level (according to Heerebord) the proponent always successfully defended his thesis (and the *praeses* could intervene to ensure success) at the level at which Regius had his students dispute a real battle was inevitable. Medical theses contrived by Regius were provocative, and their advance publication allowed partisan feeling to develop. In particular there was antipathy between the theological and the medical students. This was inevitable, given the strong theological component of the natural philosophy, whether Cartesian or Aristotelian, that underlaid medicine.

At first Regius and Descartes carefully collaborated on the theses before they were published. Sometimes Descartes revised Regius' suggestions in two

---

[20] Heerebord, Ερμηνεια *Logica*, p. 10.
[21] According to Heerebord, ibid., p. 20 and item xxiv, the thesis was defended by a *respondens superior* (the *praeses*, normally the determining master) and the *respondens inferior* (his student); opposing both was the *opponens*. The determined theses, such as Sylvius' pro-circulatory *Disputationes medicae* of 1639 (Keynes (1966) p. 449) could be offered as a teaching text. I have used Sylvius' edn of 1693: see note 17 above.

stages, as projected theses and in a later and more complete draft stage.[22] In all cases he carefully monitored Regius' interpretation of his natural philosophy. The theses proposed for disputation on 10 June 1640 at 'Medico-physiological disputations for the circulation' reached Descartes from Regius in late May. Descartes carefully distinguished between effervescence and rarefaction within the heart and corrected Regius' interpretation of the Cartesian ebullition theory of forceful diastole.[23] In the accompanying letter to Regius Descartes reminded him that his new natural philosophy, including the motion of the heart and of the air particles in respiration, was based on the existence of God. He also removed the names of Harvey and Walaeus from the theses: not only did he want to keep the new natural philosophy in all its departments Cartesian, but he imagined that Harvey was attempting to promote his doctrines in the university of Leiden by using Walaeus as his agent, just as Descartes himself was using Regius in Utrecht.

Descartes was fully prepared when 10 June came. He had revised the theses and had reminded Regius of the very basis of the new natural philosophy. Descartes clearly saw the outcome as critical for the advance of his doctrines in the university, and he made arrangements to go to Utrecht and observe the proceedings secretly from a hidden room.[24] He duly heard Regius as *praeses* and John Haymann as *defendens* present and maintain the new mechanical workings of the body.[25] Regius began with nutrition, in which the blood had its traditional role as the nutriment of the body. But the change from blood to flesh and bone was not (said Regius the opponent of the ancients) a change in substantial form but a mechanical adaptation of the particles of the blood. The term 'mechanical' here is Descartes' modification of what Regius had proposed, and in a similar way Descartes abandoned Regius' term 'spiritual juice', which could only be ambiguous in a mechanical process (which is how Descartes presents the traditional 'concoction').[26] Descartes was also very careful in introducing, in the manner described above, his observations and experiments into the disputation. Where Regius had included a reference to the newly discovered lacteals in his discussion of concoction, Descartes removed it, because he had not personally seen these vessels.

The ultimate stage of Descartes' mechanical 'concoction', a process of the perfecting of blood that begins in the intestines and proceeds in the liver, takes place in the heart, as Descartes said directly in the second thesis. Here, in the heart, the circulating blood returns and mingles with the newly produced chyle, the penultimate stage in concoction. The 'pulsific ebullition' of the heart is the

---

[22] Descartes, *Oeuvres*, ed. Adam and Tannery, vol. III, p. 455.
[23] Ibid., vol. III, p. 440.
[24] Ibid., vol. III, p. 70.
[25] Ibid., vol. III, p. 63; vol. XIII, p. 6.
[26] Ibid., vol. III, p. 67.

final act, completing the concoction of the blood and at the same time causing the active diastole that drives the circulating blood. By now Descartes had modified somewhat his simple notion, expressed in the *Discourse on Method*, that the heart was inflated by the vaporisation of the entering blood meeting the heart's natural heat. Now the motion of the blood seems to be closer to a 'fermentive' ebullition, for which it was necessary that a trace of blood should be left in the heart from one beat to the next. We shall see below that this change may have been forced upon Descartes by his brush with Plemp, in Louvain. It may also be partly a change to answer Regius, who in the thesis originally submitted to Descartes had also cast some doubt on the ebullition of blood within the heart. He probably wondered how the heart could contract at the end of diastole if still full of vapour: certainly Descartes' reply proposes that the impetus of blood leaving the heart is such that all of it (except the fermentive trace trapped by the closing valves) emerges into the vessels. It is very clear that Descartes was busy with dissection (he claimed to have had eleven years' experience)[27] and vivisection, and that the results had a proper place in university disputations. As in the case of Harvey's anatomy lectures, the criticisms of others resulted in the refinement of the investigator's first idea.

## Natural philosophy and theology

So what Regius and Descartes were promoting in Utrecht was a mechanical and modified version of Harvey's doctrine of circulation. Not only was the circulation novel, but the natural philosophy in which it was expressed was radically different from anything before. These theses promoted the destruction of many traditional categories, like the 'concoction' mentioned above. Another was the faculty of 'attraction', and Regius and Descartes give an elaborate mechanical account of how the blood moves from arteries to veins and how air enters the lungs in respiration in the absence of attraction. Neither the circulation nor mechanism were of direct interest to the theologians of Utrecht. But both were grounded in natural philosophies which were, like all natural philosophy, God-centred. Even though Harvey's anatomy had a smaller religious dimension than that of others, yet the natural philosophy of which it was a part was firmly tied to an Aristotle who reciprocally supported and drew support from the church. Descartes' natural philosophy was centred in a very direct way, as we have seen, on the existence of God. While the disputations in Utrecht remained on a medical topic, and while Descartes' connections with the theses were (almost certainly) unknown, the theologians made little attempt to suppress them. It is true that the rector, hearing of the theses of June 1640,

---

[27] Lindeboom, *Descartes and Medicine*, p. 37.

had suggested that Regius should not dispute, or at least should defend the theses as a mere intellectual exercise in a corollary, but the professor of theology, Voet, approved Regius' published reply to the criticisms of the theses made by Primrose, and so seems far from condemning the new doctrines.

But it soon became clear that the mechanism of the circulation theses was Cartesian, and the theologians became less happy. Regius, having wriggled out of the rector's efforts to stop the disputations, received from him and the university Senate a formal warning against sowing dissension in the university. Moreover, Regius had been unable to maintain an aloof and impersonal tone when replying to criticisms from Primrose, and probably as a result Voet obtained from the curators a decree banning the discussion of 'novelties'.

What was at stake of course was much more than whether blood circulated or the body was mechanical. In looking at the response of Voet and the theologians to Harvey's doctrine in its Cartesian disguise we are in the same position as we are in attempting to discover how medical men and philosophers handled these new doctrines when they came across them. In Voet's case too we must see what was in his mind, intellectual or not, that made him select and interpret, to 'misunderstand' the new doctrines. What Voet was interested in was the stability of the university, of orthodox Calvinism and ultimately of Dutch society. This stability, he thought, could easily be damaged. The United Provinces, after all, were still in the process of rejecting the absolute and Catholic rule of the Spanish king. The process had left pockets of Catholics here and there, besides minority groupings of the broad-church Arminians. No doubt Voet felt that the price of maintaining orthodoxy was eternal vigilance. The Arminians were a case in point: preaching religious toleration and emphasising points of doctrine and piety common to each extreme of the religious spectrum, they seemed to the Calvinists dangerously lax in doctrine. To close such a possible arena of conflict that might threaten the very stability of Dutch society, the Calvinists secured the suppression of Arminianism at the Synod of Dort in 1618. Even by then the Arminians had looked favourably on their new philosophies of Bacon and Gassendi, and where their religious attitude prevailed – and that of the related Cambridge Platonists – philosophical novelties like Cartesianism were viewed sympathetically. It was these novelties, with all this in mind, that Voet as the leader of the Calvinists wanted to stop. He was horrified that the whole of Descartes' natural philosophy was founded on a doubt about the very existence of God. Voet believed that a knowledge of God was inherent in every man, and that deliberately to suppress such knowledge was atheism. For Voet, then, Descartes had been an atheist, deliberately doubting the existence of God. Moreover, Descartes had proceeded to prove the existence of God on the basis of reason, not of faith. In fact Voet made the powerful connection between atheism and social revolution,[28] arguing that some atheists wanted to overthrow both the natural order and the order of society. He held that the great danger of a purely rational system of the world was that there was no moral control over where it might lead. For this reason Voet held that the theologians had the right and duty to question the use of reason in philosophy. His series of disputations on atheism in 1639 were perhaps prompted by the dangerous laxity of the successors of the Arminians or those who were seen as embracing new philosophy, perhaps Regius himself.

So when Regius began to prepare some more theses on circulation in April 1641[29] he was working in a tense situation, of which Descartes at least was well aware. Again revising the theses before publication, Descartes made sure that his views on the nature of the soul were correctly represented. Regius had used the traditional conception of a triple soul – vegetative, vital and rational – but Descartes was anxious to explain that his thinking-substance soul was the single immortal entity of church doctrine. But so completely had Greek – Aristotelian and Platonic – doctrines of soul been assimilated to the Christian doctrine of immortality that Descartes now faced criticism of men like Voet and Froidmont that to deny the role of the soul in the actions of the body like the beating of the heart was to belittle the nobility of the soul. Nor did Voet agree with Descartes, who appeared to locate the soul in the pineal gland.

During 1641 Regius maintained at least five sets of theses in favour of Cartesian circulation. It was at this time also that he and Descartes were building up a Cartesian medicine which, as we have noted, was an important strategy in Descartes' campaign for his natural philosophy. In November of that year one of Regius' pupils inserted a corollary about the circulation into a mathematical thesis, secretly substituting Regius' name for that of Harvey. It was a provocative act, and it duly provoked Regius, who found that he had to dispute in defence of circulation in another faculty, something he appears to have agreed not to do, and it also provoked shortness of temper among the other professors.

It was in this atmosphere that Regius made a strategic error. Preparing still more theses for December, he had in mind what Descartes had written to him, in April, about the singleness of the immortal, immaterial and thinking soul. Developing the notion that a soul of this kind and the material and unthinking body are mutually exclusive categories, Regius came up with the thesis that man, composed of both mutually exclusive categories, was a unified being only *per accidens*. But this time Regius published the theses without first consulting Descartes. It was a fatal mistake. When Descartes read them, he was horrified. He saw, as perhaps Regius did not, that this would be too much for the

28 McGahagan, 'Cartesianism', p. 162.
29 Descartes, *Oeuvres*, ed. Adam and Tannery, vol. II, p. 370.

theologians. He wrote desperately to Regius, pointing out that the thesis was difficult, offensive and even criminal.[30] He urged Regius to insert a corollary to say that *per accidens* was meant relatively rather than absolutely, and to agree that the soul is ideally suited to the body in its union with it.

Descartes' fears were realised. At the disputation there was shouting and stamping as one medical student argued for the new philosophy and another opposed it. The same thing happened when Regius' pupil, defending the new medicine, was attacked by a theology student. Finally Regius' students made such an uproar, intimidating the opposition with aggressive displays, that the theology student could not be heard. Even Regius said it was an insult to the university, and lost his temper. The rector and other professors marched out; and the disputation, and with it Descartes' attempt to insert his natural philosophy into the university, effectively came to an end.

Although Regius struggled on with more disputations, Voet now saw Descartes as the real enemy and began a campaign against him. His own series of theses on aspects of the old philosophy such as substantial forms was part of this campaign (and Descartes and Regius collaborated on the replies). But now the battle between Descartes and Voet was also waged in an overtly political way. Descartes represented Voet as a rabble-raiser, a potential theocratic dictator. He also thought he could win over the magistrates, whose own position would be threatened if such a potentiality became actual, and who were as a class distinctly less Calvinist than Voet, who thought they were tainted with Catholicism. But Descartes miscalculated, and the magistrates saw him as a Jesuit and a threat to the university. The university Senate agreed: quite apart from anything else, the new philosophy would have destroyed the usual curriculum, they said, and would have prevented students from following related subjects. As we have seen, medicine in particular rested on the philosophy of the arts course and could not flourish without it. There could be no piecemeal replacement of traditional curricula; and Descartes' and Regius' mechanical medicine was still in its early stages.

### Circulation in Louvain

Descartes had sought to promote his view of the motion of the heart and blood as the prime example of his natural philosophy not only by disputation in Utrecht but also by other means, mostly by letter, in other places. These too were means by which the learned world could reach some sort of consensus on circulation and the mechanical philosophy. One of the people he wrote to was Jan Beverwyck, who had written to him in 1643 asking for the mechanical demonstrations by which Descartes had strengthened the theory

---

[30] Ibid., vol. III, p. 459.

of circulation.[31] Here as elsewhere Descartes' and Harvey's doctrines were inextricably bound together, perhaps to their mutual advantage: Beverwyck also wrote to Harvey to say that 'everyone here' accepted the circulation.[32]

Descartes' letter to Beverwyck sets out a problem he had met in Louvain. One of the people to whom Descartes had sent 'review copies' of the *Discourse on Method* and its essays in 1637 had been Fortunatus Vopiscus Plemp, a medical teacher in Louvain, whom Descartes had met sometime before 1632.[33] Plemp is a striking instance of an apparently conservative man who was converted to Harvey's views. He had been educated at Bologna, Louvain and Leiden and wrote conservatively on medical topics.[34] When Plemp received Descartes' book, he was for the second time Rector Magnificus of the university and was busy writing his own textbook of medicine; he did not believe that the blood circulated or that the body worked mechanically. His doubts about Descartes' scheme may have been reinforced by correspondence with one of his teachers, Libert Froidmont, who had also been sent a copy of the *Discourse* and who told Plemp that he thought the heat of the heart, described by Descartes as similar to that of wet hay, would not be great enough to rarefy the blood. Indeed, Froidmont believed that the lower part of the soul played its traditional role in the heartbeat and that to deny this involved the risk of attributing the same function to the immortal soul and being seen as a materialist. For Froidmont the mechanism of Descartes was an ignoble cause of the heartbeat.[35]

Still busy with his book, Plemp forwarded these criticisms to Descartes, and received in reply a lengthy exposition on the basis of his natural philosophy, a justification of the immateriality of the soul and the opinion that blood vaporises at a lesser heat than other fluids. Now free to turn his attention to the matter, Plemp did some experiments. Removing the heart from a living animal, he cut it into pieces. For a while, the pieces continued to beat. He concluded that Descartes' theory of diastole-by-inflation was untenable, and that in any case the heart was not hot enough to vaporise the blood. He wrote to Descartes to tell him so in January 1638.[36]

---

[31] J. Beverovicius (Beverwyck), *Epistolicae quaestiones cum doctorum responses. Accedit ejusdem necnon Erasmi, Cardani, Melanchthonis Medicinae Encomium*, Rotterdam, 1644, p. 118.

[32] J. Beverovicius (Beverwyck), *Exercitatio in Hippocratis Aphorismum de Calculo. Accedunt doctorum Epistolae*, Leiden, 1641, p. 190.

[33] See Descartes, *Oeuvres*, ed. Adam and Tannery, vol. I, p. 399 (Plemp to Descartes).

[34] He defended a thesis at Leiden in 1622 on angina, and wrote a 'prolix and scholastic' *Ophthalmographia* in 1632. See *Dictionnaire des Sciences Médicales. Biographie Médicale*, vol. VI, Paris, 1824.

[35] Descartes, *Oeuvres*, ed. Adam and Tannery, vol. I, p. 402.

[36] Ibid., vol. I, p. 496; Beverwyck, *Epistolicae Quaestiones*, p. 122.

Descartes was somewhat taken aback.[37] He prepared his answer to Plemp by vivisecting the hearts of fish (because they continued to beat for longer out of the body) in the manner adopted by Plemp. In the isolated heart Descartes claimed to see that pulsation was prompted by blood dropping from some higher part to a lower. Even in the separated pieces of the heart some similar processes occurred, said Descartes: the descending drop of blood was activated by a 'ferment' which lay in the substance of the heart. The result was a 'fermentive' ebullition, a (purely mechanical) change like that sometimes seen in the mixture of two liquids. He added that since the heart had been habituated to contract since its embryonic period, only very small amounts of the fermentive liquid are needed.[38]

This was a major change in Descartes' account of the forceful diastole. In the *Discourse* he had said that the blood enters the heart in large quantities, as indicated by the large size of the vessels; and that the diastole was simple inflation by the vaporised blood. Now, in replying to Plemp, Descartes emphasises the smallness of the quantity of blood entering the heart: the merest drop will suffice for pulsation, particularly because of the habitual character of its motion. Moreover, inflation is no longer the answer, but fermentation.

Descartes clearly took a great deal of trouble over this reply to Plemp (mid-February 1638). The letter is long, elaborate and not always plain. It was not only that Plemp's arguments were difficult to refute (Descartes told Mersenne he thought Plemp had used every conceivable argument against him)[39] but also that Plemp would have been a most useful ally. Like Regius, Plemp was a university teacher and so well placed to act as a point of dissemination of Descartes' doctrines. For Descartes, the most deductive of natural philosophers, to have bloodied his fingers with the vivisection of fish, it must indeed have been important for him to adopt the techniques of the medical men in order to convince them. Indeed, Descartes vivisected not only fish but dogs (which proved unsatisfactory because of the shape of the heart) and rabbits. It was in the latter that Descartes performed his 'most certain experiment' by exposing the living heart and a length of the aorta, which he ligated at some distance from the heart. He then punctured the aorta between the heart and the ligature and claimed that blood emerged while the heart was in diastole. Harvey had done this experiment, while preparing the anatomy lectures, to show just the opposite, that blood emerges from the artery as the heart is contracting. It is perhaps fruitless to discuss which of them was the most acute

---

[37] Ibid., vol. II, p. 192.
[38] Beverwyck, *Epistolicae Quaestiones*, p. 127. See also F. V. Plemp, *Fundamenta Medicinae*, Louvain, 1654, pp. 128–30.
[39] Descartes, *Oeuvres*, ed. Adam and Tannery, vol. II, p. 192.

observer, although it is worth remembering Harvey's report of the technical difficulties of observation of the motion of the heart in warm-blooded animals – Descartes was using a rabbit – and his consequent choice of the slower-moving hearts of cold-blooded creatures.

Plemp replied to Descartes in the following month.[40] He attacked all of Descartes' major arguments. Fermentive actions, he maintained, were slow and quite different from the action of the heart; it was absurd to claim that the cold hearts of fish vaporised their blood when our hands, hotter than the hearts of fish, did not; and no blood could be seen to Plemp's eyes dropping from one part of the vivisected heart to another, causing pulsation. Plemp's conclusion, like that of Froidmont and many of his medical colleagues, was that it was indeed the soul that was the cause of the motion of the heart. But in resorting to experiment to try to defeat Descartes, Plemp made trouble for himself. If the pieces of a dismembered heart continued to beat because of the soul, was then the soul divisible along with the physical body? Plemp concluded that the soul remained in the body and was not present in the separated heart, where its functions were continued for a while by its agents, the spirits.

Descartes did not give up. But neither did he stand his ground. His second reply to Plemp is even more involved than the first and in it he reduces the part played by fermentation and inflation. As Harvey had done, Descartes was refining his ideas in the face of criticism. In fact, just as Primrose had attacked Harvey's experiment of puncturing the living heart and arteries as unnatural, and therefore as throwing no light upon what happened in a state of nature, so Descartes now said that the vivisected and divided heart was behaving unnaturally. Under this cover, Descartes felt free to modify further his thinking on the nature and causes of the heartbeat. He now distinguishes between the action of the auricles of the heart and that of the ventricles. The former is not caused by inflation or effervescence of blood, for by cutting off the tip of the ventricles normal blood could be seen entering the ventricles from the auricles. Of course, the heart is mutilated and thus not acting naturally, but Descartes seems to want to restrict his inflative–fermentive theory to the ventricles alone. He also refines the fermentation theory to explain the mechanism of both natural and unnatural pulsation. Firstly, it is the blood in the small vessels of the heart that is responsible for the fermentive action. Its motion is habitual and so occurs even in the vivisected heart, but in a different way: the blood emerges from the vessels on a cut surface of the vivisected heart like sweat and gradually builds up into discrete drops, which account for the separate beats of the heart. Early in the morning before writing to Plemp he had cut the heart from a young eel. Its separated right ventricle did not begin to beat until the drying blood on its surface began to form a skin. His explanation – secondly –

<hr />

[40] Ibid., vol. II, p. 52; Beverwyck, *Epistolicae Quaestiones*, p. 139.

was that before becoming dry the open vessels of the cut surface allowed free passage for the fermentive 'vapours' and it was only when some resistance had been formed by the skin of blood that the pulsations began, like the alternate rising and falling of the bark on a piece of green wood in the fire as the steam from the sap alternately builds up and escapes below it.

In short, Descartes modified his account of the heart's motion to meet criticism. What remained constant in the change from inflation to fermentation, in the distinction between natural and unnatural motion and between that of the auricles and ventricles, was that all motion was of course mechanical. It was this that antagonised Plemp. At this stage in his life we can make a useful comparison between Plemp and Primrose. Both objected to what they saw as unnecessary and speculative novelty, Primrose in Harvey and Plemp in Descartes. Both took the view of the businesslike practical medical man with a deep respect for the utility and importance of the ancient authors. Both had what amounts to a Counter-Reformation view of medical scholarship.[41]

We need to look at these things in a little more detail in Plemp's case. Plemp saw medicine as a professional and autonomous preserve, based ultimately on Hippocrates and concerned above all with practice. Reading medical authors was to be supplemented by medical experience and training, and medicine as an activity included the teaching that passed on both the authors to be read and the professional training to be experienced. Plemp would have seen philosophical novelty of Descartes' kind as obtrusive and damaging to medicine. In addition, Plemp's respect for the autonomy of medicine and the transmission of its practices coincided with the Counter-Reformation's perception of the value of a continued tradition of scholarship (and Catholic Louvain was a natural centre for such a view; the Catholic Plemp was 'summoned' to Louvain).[42] The humanists of the Renaissance had, they believed, recovered a pure (and pagan) *prisca scientia* of the Greeks. Medical humanists gave their attention to Hippocrates, Galen, Celsus, Paulus and

---

[41] Primrose, as a member of the French church in London, almost certainly remained a Calvinist. His respect for the learned tradition, the commentators and even authorities within the Catholic church seem to be the result of personal conservatism rather than religious inclination (which is what is suggested at first sight). In fact it is clear that at the philosophical level Catholics, Calvinists and others spoke the same language. The present study shows for example that writers of letters and textbooks often agreed on the nature of natural philosophy despite religious differences. Where these differences were important was in teaching, where the youthfulness of the audience and the unpredictability of disputations posed threats to stability. For Primrose's conservatism see his attack on Plemp: *Destructio Fundamentorum Medicinae Vopisci Fortunati Plempii in Academic Lovaniensi Medicinae Professor*, Rotterdam, 1657, pp. 128, 237. Both Primrose and Plemp are listed in the *Dictionnaire des Sciences Médicales. Biographie Médicale*, Paris, 1824. Lindeboom, *Descartes and Medicine*, no doubt thinking of his use of authorities, represents Primrose as Catholic.

[42] See G. A. Lindeboom, 'The reception in Holland of Harvey's theory of the circulation of the blood', *Janus*, 46 (1957), 183–200. See also Ruestow, *Physics*.

others, while the medical Hellenists restricted their admiration to the purely Greek component of the ancient legacy. What they had in common was the belief that the age of commentators lying between themselves and the ancients was a regrettable lapse, a perversion of the true ancient message. In a similar way the Reformers gave their attention to the sacred texts and dismissed the commentative and interpretative role of the Catholic church. In reaction, the Catholic church gave a new emphasis to the tradition of learning which reached back to the early Christian centuries, which continued to refine the knowable truth and which was an answer to the deplorable and heretical novelties of the Protestants.[43]

A similar reaction to novelty is discernible in the philosophical and medical world. Primrose found it natural to use the opinions of medieval commentators in his attack on Harvey. Plemp found it natural to produce for the medical tradition of scholarship a new translation of parts of the *Canon* of Avicenna.[44] In doing so he had to defend himself against the Hellenists of his day, who regarded Avicenna as a mere commentator and, as Arabic, a barbaric one. Their preferred medicine relied on highly systematised presentations of the Greek authors. To this Plemp objected that the Greeks had not written like that, but – in a telling analogy – discoursively, like hunters who had not yet found their quarry. To Plemp, the hunt had to be continued by later scholars in the tradition of medical scholarship of which he felt himself to be part.

Within this tradition, Plemp felt that the Hippocratic texts were comparable to the scriptures in containing revealed knowledge. To make the comparison effective, Plemp played down the pagan nature of the Hippocratic texts. This indeed had been emphasised by the Hellenists he so disliked and who indeed had often seemed more Greek than Christian. This revealed knowledge was the foundation of all medicine for Plemp, who set down his version of it in his own *Fundamenta medicinae*,[45] just as the foundations of health and salvation – both are *salus* – are found in the scriptures. Plemp extends the analogy: Galen, the verbose, prolific and unsystematic interpreter of Hippocrates, was paralleled by St Augustine, whose treatment of the scriptures was similar. Avicenna, who gave system and order to Galen's medicine, making it so authoritative and efficient in teaching, was matched in Plemp's analogy by Thomas Aquinas and his treatment of Augustine.

In both religion and medicine the continuity of the learned tradition was

---

[43] Louvain had remained in Spanish hands during the rebellion against Philip II. Both sides saw the advantages of securing the universities as centres of correct doctrine. Leiden was founded in 1575 by William of Orange; Philip II established the university of Douai in 1562 to counteract the influence of the Calvinist Academy in Geneva. See Ruestow, *Physics*.

[44] V. F. Plemp, trans. Avicenna, *Canon medicinae*, Louvain, 1658; prologue to the reader. (The work consists of books 1 and 2 only, together with the 'de febribus" of book 4.)

[45] V. F. Plemp, *Fundamenta medicinae*, Louvain, 1654, pp. 129–30.

important for Plemp. As part of that tradition he was concerned with explaining it and passing it on. The teaching devices that the Hellenists and the humanists tried to banish are well represented in his books: the translation of the *Canon* has scholia and the apparatus of academic teaching and the *Fundamenta medicinae* is expressly designed 'for the schools'. This scholasticism is Counter-Reformation, reflected by the woodcut of Aquinas, the Avicenna of religion, that decorates the title page of the translation of the *Canon*[46] (see fig. 17).

The continuity of the learned medical tradition was also important to Plemp because of his conception of the nature of medicine itself. As a cumulative and collaborative enterprise, it needed the work of many hands. While as a *scientia* it was demonstrative in an Aristotelian sense, yet as an art it was an area outside the competence of the philosophers. There was no certain way, save experience, he insisted, of coming to a knowledge of how one pain differs from another for example, or how a drug will act by its 'whole substance'.[47] Galen and Celsus had made it clear that there are few sure precepts in medicine, said Plemp: the accumulated experiential knowledge of the centuries was important. We can see that with all this in his mind when he received review copies of the *Discourse on Method* from Descartes, he was unlikely to have been persuaded of its radically new and dogmatic message about the mechanical motion of the heart. Descartes' first principles, from the demolition of the old house of learning to the laws of mechanism, were utterly foreign to Plemp.

Yet by 1644, in the second edition of his textbook, Plemp was an advocate of the circulation. What had happened? What made Plemp add his name to the consensus that ultimately agreed with Harvey? The answer is that he untied the circulation and the motion of the heart from Cartesian mechanism. He read *De motu cordis* (nothing else would explain his knowledge of Harvey's case) and was persuaded by Harvey's presentation. In considering what made him accept Harvey's case we should begin with the most general reasons. He was, in the first place, broadly in agreement with Harvey's natural philosophy. He was at home with its first principles. Secondly, he responded to Harvey's mode of presentation. The tradition of learned medicine in which Plemp saw himself had since the Middle Ages commented on texts and opinions, had raised *dubia* and *quaestiones*, and had developed elaborate techniques for examining and justifying knowledge. In writing a textbook Plemp's job included putting forward conflicting views in order to inform his reader about the nature of the

---

[46] A similar device is on the title page of Plemp's *Fundamenta medicinae* in the edn of Louvain, 1654 and on that of the accompanying defence of Plemp against a critic by Daniel Vermostius.
[47] For the category of 'whole substance' see L. Deer Richardson, 'The generation of disease: occult causes and diseases of the total substance', in *The Medical Renaissance of the Sixteenth Century*, ed. A. Wear, R. K. French and I. Lonie, Cambridge, 1985.

subject, to show him the nature of the resolution of such questions and to provide disputed questions and authorities for use in disputation. Harvey's book would have fitted naturally into these procedures. Moreover, as we have seen, Harvey adopted an academic exposition in anticipation of an academic audience.

In short, Plemp accepted Harvey's book in the way Harvey intended. What he found difficult about it at first (and he said that many contemporaries found the same thing) was the conclusion that all parts were nourished by the same blood.[48] This was an unnecessary disturbance of the accepted system. But also from the start, Plemp found it difficult to argue away Harvey's quantitative argument. Plemp gives the reader a little autobiographical account of how he was in the end convinced by Harvey, and we can see that many of the arguments that went through his mind have parallels elsewhere. For a long time, he says, he wrestled with himself in an attempt to defend the ancients, and found it difficult to abandon his old conceptions. His first idea was to deny Harvey's quantitative argument and to assert either that little blood left the heart on pulsation or that, as in the severed but still beating heart, no blood entered it. Or again, he wanted to believe perhaps that the blood in the heart became much distended with spirits when the heart was in diastole and so occupied much space with little substance. As he says, any such explanation would have left him free to maintain the old system that blood was generated in the liver, that the pulse was in the arterial coats and that little blood passes into the arteries.

Plemp found it equally difficult to argue away Harvey's demonstration that the veins swell up on the wrong side of the ligature. He tried again to defend the ancients by imagining the existence of some sort of bladders that were closed by the ligature. For some time he continued to teach the traditional account, incorporating such defences of the ancients against Harvey's new doctrine. This teaching appears to have been his formal lecture course, for he ways it was *e cathedra auditorio*, where such defences were adequate because nothing could be examined minutely. But on later occasions he grew 'more desperate' in his defence of the ancients and 'more vehemently denied' the circulation. Here probably he was involved in disputation, where his logic and authorities were exposed – much more than in lectures – to critical analysis.[49] Ultimately he found that he could not sustain his defences of the ancients. Harvey was right.

In a sense Plemp had been brought to agree with Harvey by denying Descartes. The resources he had were taken in two ways from what we might call the medical tradition. First, vivisections provided experiential knowledge.

48  Plemp, *Fundamenta*, p. 131.
49  Ibid., pp. 128–30.

Fig. 17. St Thomas Aquinas, the Counter-Reformation 'Sun of the Church', took his place on the title page of a number of books published in Louvain. Here (i) he appropriately decorates Plemp's edition of book 1 of the *Canon* of Avicenna, which Plemp thought had systematised Galen's diffuse writings just as St Thomas had done to Augustine's. A similar device (ii) adorns Plemp's *Fundamenta medicinae*.

Galen's vivisections and other experiments on animals were known to the anatomists of the seventeenth century and the technique was used deliberately as a source of demonstration and argument. Plemp thought of Colombo as the leader of the moderns and he repeated Colombo's experiment of opening the pulmonary vein in a living dog, in order to confirm the pulmonary transit of blood. Moreover, he added the extra precaution of ligating the vessel before incising it, making sure that it retained its original contents. To confirm that the pulse was caused, as Harvey said, by an inflow of blood, Plemp inserted a small sponge into an artery, showing that the pulse disappeared below the sponge and was not transmitted by the still intact arterial coats. Such experiential knowledge corresponds to Plemp's conception of the 'art' of medicine.

Second, Plemp also sought rational knowledge of the heartbeat and circulation from within the medical tradition. Here he acted in accordance with his belief that medicine as a *scientia* is 'assent to the conclusion of a demonstrative syllogism'.[50] The premises of the syllogism were the self-evident facts of universally accepted medical or natural-philosophical belief, such as the number and nature of the elements, the action of the qualities, the antipathy of opposites and so on: precisely the kind of self-evident truth that Descartes had denied. This is essentially how Galen had rationalised the medical writings of the Hippocratics and it remained a valid medical way of arguing in the Renaissance. Plemp uses such reasoning when arguing that all bodily motions have a source, a *principium*, and that the *principium* of the motion of the heart is the vivifying vital faculty resident in the heart.

### Rotterdam and Leiden

Thus far we have looked at the reaction to Harvey's doctrines in Utrecht and Louvain, and we have seen that this reaction varied with the extent to which Harvey's work was associated with that of Descartes, and with the religion of those who reacted to the circulation.

The same factors were at play in other places. It is instructive to compare Plemp's conversion in Louvain with that of Jacobus de Back. De Back was a product of Rotterdam, where he was a physician, and Rotterdam was an important centre for the new philosophy. The Latin school there undoubtedly played a part in making it so: as we have seen, Isaac Beeckman was co-rector of the school in the 1620s and George Ent was a student there from 1620 to 1624.[51] Zacharias Sylvius (van den Bossche) was its master, while studying medicine, and some form of the new philosophy informed his medicine and his

---

50 Ibid., p. 172.
51 See M. J. van Lieburg, 'Zacharias Sylvius (1608–1664), author of the Praefatio to the first Rotterdam edition (1648) of Harvey's De Motu Cordis', *Janus*, 65 (1978), 241–57.

later acceptance of the circulation. It was Ent who later told Beeckman about Harvey's work, and by 1633 both of them, and their fellow citizens Sylvius and de Back, had come to accept the circulation. So the Rotterdam consensus about the circulation was partly an academic one because of the school, but was not, unlike others, a wholly university affair. De Back, who had taken his MD at Franeker in 1617, had been in practice some sixteen years when he became acquainted with Harvey's doctrine,[52] so his conversion must have been prompt. De Back describes his moment of conversion in an essay appended to the 1648 Rotterdam edition of Harvey's book, to which, also, Sylvius added a preface.[53]

De Back first describes how he was educated with the doctrines of the ancients.[54] It was the Hippocratic ethical works (with their injunctions about the respect due to teachers) that generated within him, as with many others, a feeling of respect for the ancients. It was something more than respect and admiration, for there was something of faith in it. It was 'almost a religion', *quasi religio*, he said, to defend the doctrines of the ancient medical Heroes. (At the other end of the volume, introducing Harvey's work, Sylvius echoed the sentiment, declaring them right who revere the ancients *religiose*.) De Back then recalls how, about fifteen years earlier (in 1633) Harvey's book came into his hands. Its doctrines were widely thought at this time (he says) to be 'heretical' (that is, to be opposed to the faith and 'religion' attached to the old writers). At first he thought it would be easy to refute them, but when he came to do so, weighing them 'in a just balance' and giving due importance to sensory observation, he found that Harvey had convinced him. Almost certainly the story of Plemp's conversion helped to convert de Back; Sylvius retells it in his preface and certainly the two fellow citizens would have discussed it.[55]

While de Back was now convinced that Harvey's doctrine was 'to be embraced with both arms' his problem lay with his attachment to the old authors. Was he to abandon Hippocrates and Galen? Like many others, including Riolan, whose own (much more limited) conversion was very close in time to de Back's, he could not. We still 'belong' to them, he said; and the fact that the doctrine of circulation has clearly overturned some of their teachings has (he continues) caused much confusion in the academic world. In

---

[52] See B. Lake, 'A Discourse on the Heart by James de Back', *Medical History*, 10 (1966), 60–90.
[53] I have used the edition of 1650: W. Harvey, *Exercitationes anatomicae, de motu cordis et sanguinis circulatione*, Rotterdam, 1650.
[54] De Back had studied at Leiden. See Lake, 'Discourse'.
[55] Sylvius is also more robust on the question of the reverence due to the ancients. Do not overdo your religiosity, he advises, 'for this is the liberty of wisdom, that being oblig'd to none, It's under it's own command and jurisdiction; in her Common-wealth it's permitted to abrogate, derogate, and search without prejudice to any'. The rather political flavour of Sylvius' words no doubt owes something to his interregnum English translator, with whom, perhaps, Sylvius, as a Huguenot, would have been in sympathy. See also Gubser, 'Sylvius', 72–80.

the words of the English translation of two years later:[56] 'all the order of teaching is troubled, and the doctrine of Physick is endevourd and learned altogether preposterously and confusedly, without any certain method'. This is a very apt description of the state of things in the universities of the United Provinces, as Cartesians battled with Aristotelians, using Harvey's doctrines as weapons. De Back's purpose in writing was to bring order to the chaos.[57]

In this way some sort of consensus was reached about Harvey's doctrines by leading medical citizens of Rotterdam. We have also seen how in different circumstances some people accepted and others denied the circulation in Louvain and Utrecht. We must now look at Leiden, another Dutch university from which emerged publications on the Harvey affair, where the intellectual and religious atmosphere was like that of Rotterdam, and very different from that of Louvain. The university was founded during the revolt against Philip II (in a period when both sides saw the advantages of doctrinally correct universities) and remained aggressively Protestant until the Peace of Munster in 1648.[58] There were other differences too, more directly concerned with Harvey's doctrine. In Leiden Descartes did not have an agent in the university, as he had in Utrecht, and the circulation of the blood was not thereby linked to Cartesian mechanism. As with Plemp in Louvain, so in Leiden there were reasons, some of them to do with religion, for keeping circulation and mechanism separate.

We can see how religion, natural philosophy and Harvey's doctrines interacted in the case of Heereboord, whose model of disputation we have examined. At his inaugural lecture of 1641[59] he gave a new and Protestant view of the use of Aristotle in teaching. Aristotle represented truth, not only in his teaching but in his method: like him, we should follow nature and not mere human 'opinion'. But for Heerebord the 'opinion' we must eschew is that of the scholastics. He does not mean those of the Middle Ages alone, but those who had resisted the Reformation. It is, he says, the commentaries of the scholastics that have perverted the meaning of Aristotle just as they had

---

[56] *The Anatomical Exercises of Dr. William Harvey . . . with The Preface of Zachariah Wood . . . To which is added Dr James De Back, His Discourse of the Heart . . .*, London, 1653. The English translation differs from the Latin original, for example in omitting some five pages on the Galenic notion of the richness and wisdom of nature, and all of de Back's dedication to Harvey. (In it de Back claims that Harvey's fame has spread as far as India.)

[57] He followed this policy in later editions. The fourth, the separate *Dissertatio de corde*, Rotterdam, 1671, brings in a lot of the later literature. He tries to accommodate Harvey's *De generatione animalium*, and the work of Pecquet, Rudbeck and Highmore. It is an attempt to put the circulation in its context of sanguification, nutrition and respiration. He denies the later Cartesian synthesis of Regius and tries to reintroduce the soul into an explanation of the motion of the heart. De Back and the Rotterdam College of Physicians also gave their attention to correcting the many printer's errors of the text of the first edition of Harvey's book.

[58] Ruestow, *Physics*, p. 4.

[59] McGahagan, 'Cartesianism', p. 221.

infected theology. His model of philosophy was that of the humanists of the Renaissance and the Hellenising Byzantine emigrés of the fifteenth century. For him the Reformation was a continuation of this Renaissance, but (he said) it had not yet reached philosophy, which was still informed by authors like Fonseca and Suarez, the Portuguese Jesuits. Heerebord's 'new Aristotle' whom Heerebord saw as now standing revealed beside a pristine theology, was Reformed and Humanised. He had a natural philosophy in which (said Heerebord) it was important to work from a study of nature to a knowledge of God.

In Leiden, as in Utrecht, the advantage of Aristotle was that he represented stability in philosophy. The Leiden theologians Revius and Trigland were, like their counterparts in Utrecht, concerned with the integrity of Calvinist belief and with the stability of the social order in the face of the wiles of the Jesuits and the laxity of the Arminians. Philosophical novelty, often associated with Arminianism, seemed to threaten this stability. Descartes became involved in the situation in Leiden, although less directly than in Utrecht, urging the Curators that the case for his philosophy should be judged by the magistrates, not by academics. He secured the political help of the Prince of Orange and of the French ambassador. But he was robbed of the help of both of them by historical accidents in 1647. Giving up his attempt to become the Philosopher, he committed his papers to the discretion of his friend Hogelande and departed for Sweden.

Yet in Leiden, Heerebord's New Aristotle became a little too new. Even at the end of the Descartes affair, the Curators warned him (as Regius had been warned in Utrecht) to adhere to Aristotle. In fact Heerebord increasingly wanted to show that the natural philosophy of Aristotle could be reconciled to that of Descartes. He thought the Protestant view that knowledge of God could be gained from nature was like the claim of Descartes that his own natural philosophy showed the direct action of God in the world. When Adam Stuart, a rigid Scots Presbyterian, was promoted over Heerebord's head, he became even more Cartesian. In 1646 he defended a thesis on the Cartesian claim about the necessity of clearing out of one's mind all traditional knowledge. The theologians objected on the grounds that this involved the notorious *cogito ergo sum* which rested on a doubt over the very existence of God. Heerebord answered that it could apply equally to his new Aristotle as to Descartes; but there were riots on the Utrecht scale when Stuart disputed against such a notion in 1647 and 1648. The university's reaction, as in Utrecht, was to return to Aristotle.

So in Leiden, the argument for and against Descartes' natural philosophy involved Harvey's doctrine of circulation to a lesser extent. Had it been accepted, of course, then it would have taken with it the circulation of its mechanical form, for the motion of the heart and blood remained Descartes' most potent example of the new mechanism. But since the university had returned to Aristotle for its arts course philosophy, if the doctrine of circulation was to enter the university, it would have to be by another route. An obvious route was medicine and one of the men who did in fact argue in favour of Harvey was the medical man Franciscus Sylvius. ('Sylvius' was a name coined by transnomination in the Hellenistic manner from a vernacular surname meaning 'of the wood'. This is why the Rotterdamer Zacharias van den Bossche called himself Sylvius and why his English translator called him Zachary Wood; it is also why Franciscus de la Boe, also 'Sylvius' should not be confused with him.)[60]

Franciscus Sylvius had studied at several universities in Switzerland and Germany and had taken his MD at Basle in 1637. Along the way he had picked up some theory of a new natural philosophy[61] – it was partly chemical – but was not sympathetic to Descartes' mechanism.[62] Before he arrived in Leiden in 1638, not a great deal of interest had been shown in the question of the circulation. Sylvius was already a convert, however, and in some private capacity began to demonstrate the circulation by experiment.[63] It is possible that Descartes witnessed these[64] but more important is that Walaeus was convinced by these experiments or by Sylvius' disputations, between 1639[65] and 1640 when Walaeus wrote his two letters to Bartholin. Sylvius left to practice medicine in Amsterdam in the following year. Sylvius had read the *Discourse on Method* and most likely also *De motu cordis*. Like many others he 'misunderstood' Harvey by disarticulating his doctrine between the motion of the heart and the circulation. He seems to have done so because he saw no connection between Cartesian mechanism (in the *Discourse*) and the circulation (in *De motu cordis*).

Let us see why this should have been so. Sylvius was interested in natural actions which we may call for convenience 'chemical'. For him, motion in the body was not transmitted particle to particle from a single source but arose locally, like the fermentation of plant juices or the ebullition of chemical substances: these were different kinds of motions, not different manifestations of an increased intestine, particular, motion. Like any medical teacher, Sylvius

---

[60] On van den Bossche see M. J. van Lieburg, 'Zacharias Sylvius (1608–1644), author of the Praefatio to the first Rotterdam edition (1648) of Harvey's De Motu Cordis', *Janus*, 65 (1978), 41 and on de la Boë see Lindeboom, 'Reception', p. 193.

[61] McGahagan, 'Cartesianism', p. 13.

[62] Descartes, *Oeuvres*, ed. Adam and Tannery, vol. III, p. 440.

[63] Our evidence for this comes from Bartholin's funeral eulogy of his teacher Walaeus. See Descartes, *Oeuvres*, ed. Adam and Tannery, vol. XII, p. 25.

[64] Lindeboom, *Descartes and Medicine*, p. 32.

[65] This date is given by Sir Geoffrey Keynes, *The Life of William Harvey*, Oxford, 1966, p. 449. Sylvius arrived in Leiden in the autumn of 1638. See Lindeboom, *Descartes and Medicine*, p. 32. The first edition seems to have been in 1663.

wanted to present a coherent account of the actions of the body. The central demand upon a teacher in that position was to explain how the ingested food was converted into the substance of the various tissues, which (it was assumed) needed constant replenishment. Essentially this demand had been set by Galen, whose microcosmic physiology had centred on the continuous processes of purification which the food was subjected to as it generated the blood (the nutriment of the body), the humours and the spirits. In a new age when Galen's account had been destroyed by Harvey, Aselli and Rudbeck, nutrition still remained the *explanadum*, and Sylvius, like many others, treated Harvey's account of the motion of the blood as part of the bigger scheme of sanguification and replenishment of the tissues.

His series of disputations accordingly begins with the fermentation of food in the stomach.[66] Sylvius maintained that this fermentation, like that of fruit juices, was then an entirely different kind of motion to that produced by the ebullition of chemicals. It was the first stage of sanguification and a necessary preliminary to his account of the action of the heart. The heat of the heart, the central activity of the living body, is the next agent of sanguification in Sylvius' view: the incoming chyle, produced from the food, blood circulating in the body, and lymph in the lacteal veins are all moved towards the heart, where the right auricle contracts and forces them into the ventricle. There the 'fire' rarefies components and produces an impure blood that is tempered and completed by passage through the lungs and left ventricle.

Sylvius was thus sympathetic to Descartes' account of ebullition of blood inside the heart, which he was content to believe was a source of heat. But this was not Descartes' 'natural' fire-without-light, but an 'innate fire', fed by the perfected blood itself and no doubt chosen by Sylvius because of the apparent agreement between modern 'chemical' explanations with Descartes and also with ancient descriptions of the heat of the heart. According to Sylvius, the blood rarefies and expands in the heart, causing diastole, but this, he says, is followed by a muscular contraction of the ventricles, causing the expulsion of blood. Sylvius probably took this muscular contraction from Harvey, and argues simply that not all of the blood is used in nutrition, and much returns to the heart to take part in the sanguification process once more. As with so many others, Sylvius had found it undesirable to forget the ancient doctrine about the heat of the heart, and this is what made him change Harvey's doctrine.

In other words Sylvius fitted both descriptions, of ebullition and muscular

---

[66] Sylvius did not publish the disputations until 1663, when he had gone back to Leiden as professor of practical medicine. There may therefore be an element of *post hoc* rationalisation, but it is not very evident. Franciscus Deleboe Sylvius, *Opera medica, hoc est Disputationum medicarum decas*, Geneva, 1693.

contraction, into the framework of the theory of medicine, which he was unwilling to disturb. Like Harvey, whom he quotes here, Sylvius felt the need to identify the *propria motio* of the heart, the action whereby it discharges its function. For Sylvius this was muscular contraction at systole, which was an 'animal' function. In contrast the expansive diastole was merely a 'natural' action that served only to return the heart to the state where it could again discharge its function. These are the terms of the disputed question about the motion of the heart that was not infrequent in the anatomical literature at Harvey's time and which had been asked on occasions since the Middle Ages. ('Natural' motion belonged to the lowest group of faculties of the soul, 'animal' to the higher.)[67] Sylvius was obeying the law of intellectual economy and fitting Harvey's doctrines into his existing intellectual furniture with a minimum of damage to both. Accordingly (and unlike Harvey) Sylvius retained notions of spirits activating the muscles of the heart and the heart's link to the soul.

In contrast, Descartes' doctrines simply would not fit. Descartes recognised this. Having objected that there could be no 'animal' function in a piece of a heart of an eel, separated from the soul that Sylvius considered to exercise this function,[68] Descartes saw that he would not success with Sylvius, and urged Regius to be gentle in further correspondence with him (Descartes marked the difficult passages for Regius' convenience).[69]

Our final look at Leiden is through the later textbook of Albert Kyper, the ordinary professor of medicine (and rector) there. In 1654 he produced an 'Institutes', a systematic treatment, explicitly founded on the circulation of the blood.[70] Clearly a consensus had finally been reached in favour of Harvey. Attached to Kyper's book are the fundamental physical principles on which medicine is founded: we shall meet both texts again when considering the role of observation and experiment in natural philosophy. The context in which this book has to be understood is the troubles in philosophy following Descartes'

---

[67] Strictly, *animalis* meant 'rational', in the case of motion, voluntary; but by Sylvius' time it could simply mean (the motion) of an animal.

[68] Descartes, *Oeuvres*, ed. Adam and Tannery, vol. III, pp. 444, 445.

[69] Ibid., vol. XII, p. 25.

[70] Albert Kyper, *Institutiones medicae, ad hypothesi de circulari sanguinis motu compositae. Subjugitur ejusdem Transsumpta medica, quibus continentur Medicinae fundamenta,* Amsterdam, 1654. Kyper (1605–55) was also First Physician to the House of Orange. Kyper's attack on Vopiscus Plemp's text on the foundations of medicine was answered by Vermostius in Plemp's second edn (1644). Kyper replied with his *Institutiones physicas. In fine adjecta est Confutatio pseud-apologematis, quod Plempius Fundamentis suis medicinae subjunxit,* 2 vols., Leiden, 1645–6, which seems to include Kyper's first acceptance of the circulation (pp. 397–9). It also demonstrates his adherence to the faculty of attraction. These works sparked off another polemic exchange of pamphlets on the topic of circulation, but one which takes us beyond the *terminus ad quem* of this book. See *Nouvelle Biographie Universelle,* Paris, 1852 (*NBU*).

attempt to remove Aristotle, and the political and religious troubles of the United Provinces. While Regius' textbook was a final attempt to promote the mechanical medicine that he and Descartes had been trying to establish by disputation, Kyper's is an attempt to build stability in a very uncertain time. Addressing a group of prominent lawyers in Leiden, he praises Aristotle and Plato as cultivators of 'civil prudence' and the ideal state. It is, he says, by the exercise of such ideals that the Leideners have now thrown off the Spanish yoke; now is the time to practise the right (Protestant) *cultus* of God, together with true learning.

In other words, Kyper's textbook was designed to give a firm lead in an education that was to ensure stability by inculcating proper doctrine. It is accordingly not a radical book but is tradition brought up to date. Cartesian mechanism is eschewed and a picture of the body is gradually built up, from the elements, similar parts, organic parts and spirits, which a Galenist would have been comfortable with. The soul has its traditional faculties providing growth, nutrition, sensation and generation.[71] His scheme of microcosmic physiology includes innate heat, but he relates this more directly than had been done in the past to the element fire. He also departs from tradition by replacing the traditional theory of humours with a more structural account of the body, based on the qualities of the elements. Fernel and other neoterics are drawn upon to provide a widely acceptable notion of what a 'part' is, and to distinguish 'organic' from 'inorganic': an up-to-date idea.

Kyper's address to the Leideners is another expression of the often-met idea that social stability was to be ensured by tight alliance between the political, religious and educational aspects of society. Early in the Reformation Fuchs had addressed the Duke of Bavaria in very explicit terms, saying just this; and here it is repeated as the last of the physical disturbances of the Reformation were coming to an end. Sometimes the Protestants expressed at the same time their sense of freedom in the intellectual and civil worlds, the micro- and macrocosm. Sennert makes the parallel strongly in appealing for rational and civilised debate: in a republic, *res publica*, there are free votes and we must expect different opinions; likewise in the world of learning, *res literaria*, where we are looking at nature's obscurities.[72] The same sense of independence of the 'Commonwealth' of letters is expressed in the English translation of de Back's treatise on the heart, quoted above; and we shall meet something similar in Glisson's disputations.

---

[71] These topics are discussed in the first book, in what Kyper calls the 'college' of general theory.

[72] Sennert, *Operum Tomus I in quo continentur Epitome physices Hyponemata physica, Institutionis medicae, Tabulae institutionum de consensu chymicorum cum Galenicis*, Paris, 1641, p. 3.

## Pamphlet war

In the previous chapter we looked at Primrose's attack on Drake and Walaeus in Leiden. We must now return to Primrose, for he commented too on the Utrecht theses that we have now discussed, and his consistent and persistent attack on the doctrine of circulation continued for much of the period covered by this book.

By the time the Utrecht theses were being disputed, ten years had passed since Primrose made his first attack on Harvey, and he was known as someone with a finger in the heartbeat-and-circulation pie. The network of correspondence that had taken knowledge of Harvey's book to Descartes and Descartes' to his 'reviewers' now brought Primrose back into the fray. It was Regius who sent him copies of his own Utrecht disputations. Again, it is worthwhile looking at Primrose's reaction, not because he was wilfully blind to the truth, or was unable to see it when it was in front of him, but because his truth, like that of others, was what he found worth fighting for and was part of his overall interpretation of the world. Primrose's world was that of the practical doctor. Practice was the purpose of being a doctor. Having failed in his early ambition to draw attention to himself in the capital, he settled in Hull to practice. His ten years of practice was for him the real source of medical wisdom, and he viewed the questions in the theoretical medicine of the universities as internal squabbles of a speculative nature: the academic mind, he says, is naturally drawn to the contentious and to disputations, which he scornfully dismisses as 'frequent games'. Games such as these disputations, says Primrose, take only a few hours of the time of a truly wise doctor to refute; and he had dismissed even Harvey's book, he was fond of saying, in only a couple of weeks back in 1630.[73] But Primrose, now older and still wiser, also sees danger in such academic extravagance, danger that real medicine, that originated by Hippocrates and Galen and confirmed by practice, would suffer. Indeed, he sees the medical world as already split, part of it led astray by an irrational fashion for novelty, subtlety and a desire to be conspicuous, all vices of academic medicine and all fuelled by Harvey's doctrine.

In reading the Utrecht theses, Primrose was in a position which differed from that of the other authors we have considered. Like Plemp he had reasons to want to preserve the learned tradition of medicine, but unlike Plemp he was not obliged to handle Harvey's doctrine in lectures and was not exposed to attack in disputation. He did not feel the need of experiments. He did not have a new doctrine of his own to promote, as did Descartes. Indeed, Primrose said that

---

[73] J. Primrose, *Animadversiones in theses, quas pro circulatione sanguinis in Academia Ultrajacensi D Henricus le Roy, ibidem medicinae professor, disputandas posuit*, Leiden, 1640, preface.

before reading the Utrecht disputations (of June 1640) he had not heard of Descartes. It is small wonder then, that Primrose should be unaware of the part played by these disputations in the battle for and against Descartes' natural philosophy. He did not know how Harvey's doctrine had been 'misunderstood' and misrepresented in Utrecht. Primrose, who thought he was commenting on theses that had been promulgated on Harvey's doctrines, could not see why the original account of the forceful systole had been omitted and some explanation about vaporised blood substituted. Primrose's misunderstanding related to the purpose of these disputations and consequently of their content. No wonder that for him such 'games' were absurd and ultimately dangerous.

The battle continued when Regius prepared a 'sponge' to wipe away Primrose's attack.[74] It is a piece of propaganda for the new natural philosophy which sets out its characteristics, as seen by Regius, in a clear fashion. Regius calls it the Intelligible Philosophy, *philosophia intelligibilis*. By this he means that the mind can follow the motions of particles as they move by contact. Other causes of motion, such as that prompted by *horror vacui*, are simply not Intelligible and are (he says) forbidden in natural philosophy. Fear of the vacuum was a species of attraction, all kinds of which were to Regius equally not Intelligible. Impulsion, on the other hand, was very Intelligible and could easily explain the apparent attraction of the air in respiration. (But Regius is obviously in trouble in explaining the attraction exerted by the magnet and amber, two of Primrose's examples. He is even prepared to believe that blood might be attracted to the tissues by a kind of magnetism.) Also Intelligible was the structure of the body, the disposition of nerves and muscles, on which alone the non-voluntary motions depended. Such motions happened in man as automatically as in an automaton, and Regius says they could equally be called 'natural', since nature is no more than 'the temper and conformation of the parts of our body'. Regius makes an elaborate analogy between the wheels and weights of a clock and the purely mechanical driving of the spirits from the heart to the brain and from the brain to the nerves controlling 'natural' respiration.

Naturally enough, Regius found that Primrose's description of faculties (including that of attraction) were 'inexplicable', 'imaginary' or 'occult'. His inability to understand such things was of course assumed. He was old enough to remember what the world was like before he came across Descartes, when he had probably believed in faculties himself. His attack on Primrose was made lest such systems should stand in the way of the great potential that the new

---

[74] H. Regius, *Spongia, qua eluuntur sordes Animadversionum, quas Iacobus Primirosius, doctor medicus adversus theses pro circulatione sanguinis in Academia Ultrajectina disputatas nuper edidit* in the *Recentionum disceptationes de motu cordis, sanguinis et chyli in animalibus*, Leiden, 1647, p. 159.

philosophy and medicine were offering. Descartes' method could offer mathematical certainty on such matters, said Regius; and the new mechanical circulation, far from being medically useless, was to be the entire foundation of a new Rationalist and Dogmatic medicine.

Primrose was not to be silenced and continued the pamphlet war with an 'antidote' to Regius' 'poisoned sponge'.[75] We might have expected the quarrel at this stage to have degenerated into personal wrangling and counter-assertion over details, but in fact Primrose makes a full and clear statement of his position. It is true he begins with a slighting reference to Regius as a recently elevated schoolmaster who as a new professor of medicine 'thinks himself among the Greeks', but this helps us to understand Primrose's position. He saw himself as on the side of the 'Greeks', indeed almost as a Greek in his learning, his knowledge of the valued, old and right medicine. His scorn for Regius' 'grammar-school philosophy' has intellectual, social and religious components. It is summed up in his attack on Regius, who had denied the existence of substantial forms in concoction, by his use of a passage from Suarez:

This doctrine of forms is so well received in philosophy that it is not possible to deny it without showing great ignorance, and so agreeable to Christian truth that its certainty is no little increased on that account.

In fact Primrose now calls to his aid the whole tradition of philosophical learning, from the medieval schoolmen Aquinas and Scotus[76] to the Paduan Aristotelians and the Portuguese Jesuits of Coimbra. Zabarella, Javellus, Toletus, Pereira, Soncinas, Smiglecius: all are witnesses for Primrose that the Intelligibles on which Regius based his whole philosophy were no more than accidents. The point is central. Discussing the nature of concoction, Regius had made it a matter of moving particles which undergo a series of Intelligible changes, largely in shape and colour, that make the food fit for assimilation by the tissues. But the very Intelligibility of these changes makes them, in Primrose's eyes, precisely what comes first in the senses. They may look important – and so deceive Regius – but Primrose had the whole learned tradition behind him to support the Aristotelian position that what is first in the senses is last in nature. To understand what is really going on, says Primrose, we must discover what is first in nature, the principles and causes. Then it is plain that concoction is a change of substantial forms, and that what was

---

[75] J. Primrose, *Antidotum adversus Henrici Regii Ultraiactensis medicinae professoris venenatam Spongiam*, Leiden, 1644.

[76] In a similar way he used the names of the surely obscure commentator Nicholas of Florence, and of the arch-commentator Turrisianus, otherwise known as Plusquam Commentator, whose commentary on the *Tegni* was specified in the Paduan statutes. See J. Primrose, *Exercitationes, et Animadversiones in librum, De motu cordis, et circulatione sanguinis*, London, 1630, p. 13 and the *Statuta almae universitatis D. artistarum et medicorum Patavini Gymnasii*, Venice, 1589, p. 38r.

occupying Regius' attention is merely a series of accidents.[77] Primrose here writes with clarity, vigour and utter confidence. What stimulated this full response seems to have been Regius' claim that the doctrine of the circulation as put forward by Descartes was more than useful to medicine and was in fact the very basis for the new rationalist medicine. Primrose now returns to his old complaint that circulation is destructive to traditional medicine and attacks Regius' new rational medicine with the whole weight of the learned tradition. This is where his confidence lies, and it must have been similar thoughts that prevented many others from adopting Regius' and Descartes' mechanism and thereby also their version of Harvey's doctrine of circulation. It seemed obvious to these people that changes like the production of blood were more than the shuffling around of accidents, and involved Forms and their changes in the Generation of Substance and the exercise of faculty in that substance; and in fact the whole apparatus of Galenic medical theory and Aristotelian natural philosophy. To disprove Regius' assertion that heat is no more than the motion of small particles, Primrose adduces forty-nine cogently linked philosophical principles that ramify through and draw support from the complete Aristotelian world picture. To deny faculty, especially that of attraction, said Primrose, is to deny all ancient and modern philosophers; and the burden of proof must lie on the shoulders of those who wish to make the change. In the face of Regius' mechanism Primrose reformulates the Galenic argument from generation-substance-faculty to produce an anti-mechanical aphorism: singular parts, separately or together, have no force of action from number, position, shape or size; if a thing does not have an active power, it will not acquire it from these. No mere machine can have a pulse.[78]

When he compares Regius' material particles to Democritean atoms, Primrose is pointing to the lack of purpose in an atomic view of the world, a view traditionally regarded with suspicion by the Christian learned tradition. It is clear from his quotation of Suarez that he closely identified medical and religious learning; he consequently saw dangers to both from different forms of attempted Reformation.[79] When Primrose came to systematise his medical

---

[77] Harvey seems to be reacting against corpuscular mechanism when he said of the neoterics that it was an error to derive the diversity of parts from the diversity of their matter. See W. Pagel, 'The reaction to Aristotle in seventeenth-century thought. Campanella, van Helmont, Glanvill, Charleton, Harvey, Glisson, Descartes', in *Science, Medicine and History*, Oxford University Press, 1953, vol. I, pp. 489–509, p. 501. In direct contrast people like Hobbes saw 'substantial form' in natural philosophy as part of the superstitious language by which priests had bullied and deceived the people. See S. Shapin and S. Shaffer, *Leviathan and the Air-pump. Hobbes, Boyle and the Experimental Life*, Princeton, 1985, p. 92.

[78] A pulse in a machine would be a mere accident, medically useless: Primrose, *Exercitationes*, p. 49.

[79] In Oxford, where Primrose incorporated, the Catholic philosophers Fonseca and Toletus were read in conjunction with the *libri naturales*. See M. H. Curtis, *Oxford and Cambridge in Transition 1558–1642*, Oxford, 1959, p. 111. Perhaps this contrasts with the new Dutch texts in Cambridge.

thinking[80] in his *Encheiridium medicum. Sive brevissime medicinae systema*, many of the inferences we have made about his views become apparent. He dwells on the medical tradition, its divine origin, its sects and its history. Galen is the rationalist systematiser of Hippocrates' art. Criticism is aimed only at the medical sects, who are to blame for the lack of stability of the medical art. He sets up a traditional natural philosophy as supplying physiology and pathology: 'physiology is properly speaking natural philosophy put to medical use'. This is where the philosopher ends; and the medical man begins with semiotics.[81]

## Mechanism and knowledge

The two natural philosophies, Harvey's and Descartes' were mutually exclusive. They were based on quite different first principles. It was impossible for anyone to adopt parts of one into the framework of the other without considerable damage to the coherence of both. In the last analysis, the two differed in what constituted knowledge.

Let us remind ourselves that Harvey had sought knowledge within the framework of an 'Aristotle project' that was intended to uncover the what-it-is-to-be-a-thing: in Harvey's case the parts of the body. His natural philosophy told him that knowledge of a part could not be gained except by a study of form and function in some such hierarchical series as *actio*, *usus* and *utilitas*. What was discovered was purpose in what we now think of as a teleological sense or, in Aristotelian terms, the cause: Aristotle's natural philosophy could readily be seen by its seventeenth-century followers as a search for the causes of things. We have also seen that Harvey related this theory of knowledge to the real world by employing the 'rule of Socrates', the synthesis of a compound image (by a kind of induction) which is then disarticulated into its natural parts.

Descartes and his followers expressly denied the validity of knowledge derived in this way, and developed a concept of 'knowledge' that had no validity in Harvey's natural philosophy. One of Descartes' followers, Cornelis van Hogelande, expressed this very clearly in discussing 'what it is to think mechanically'. His discussion was prompted by thinking about the valves of the heart,[82] for he was struck by the way in which the blood itself, by pressing back upon the aortic valve after its ejection from the heart, closed the valve mechanically (see fig. 18). That is, there was no *purpose* in the closing of the

---

[80] J. Primrose, *Encheiridum medicum. Sive brevissime medicinae systema*, Amsterdam, 1650.
[81] Primrose, *Encheiridum*, preface.
[82] C. ab Hogelande, *Cogitationes quibus Dei existentia; item animae spiritalitas, et possibilis cum corpore unio, demonstrantur: necnon brevis historia oeconomiae corporis animalis proponitur, atque mechanice explicitur. Hic accedit Tractatus de predestinatione*, Leiden, 1676, dedication. The text of this edition (used here) seems to be identical with that of the edition of 1646.

valve, which was simply following the laws of mechanics. So for Hogelande 'thinking mechanically' excludes 'reasons sought from purpose'[83] (or in Aristotelian language, causes). No more than Descartes would Hogelande have denied that God had used purpose in creating the structure, for the very foundation of their natural philosophy was God the Creator. But for Hogelande the clear and distinct ideas with which in Cartesian fashion we see the world are the laws of mechanics and to argue mechanically – *mechanice* – is the only valid form of reason and demonstration.

Harvey would also have disagreed strongly with Descartes that such laws of mechanics were almost innate in the human mind. Harvey's experiential model of the generation of knowledge not only had a long history in Aristotelian natural philosophy and Galenic medicine, but in the latter was closely related to a history of experiment and anatomical demonstration. Descartes' natural philosophy, in contrast, was not yet a basis for a theory of medicine, was deductive and gave no important place to experiment (although as we have seen he was compelled to indulge in experimentation in battling for the success of his natural philosophy; in a similar way Descartes' natural philosophy, unlike Harvey's, had no inbuilt formal mode of argumentation, but in practice was compelled to enter the arena of disputation).

Following Hogelande's thought on these matters illustrates some of these points. He was a friend of Descartes and claimed that what he wrote was entirely consistent with Cartesian principles. Descartes in turn used some of Hogelande's medical knowledge to help build up a mechanical medicine. Hogelande lived near Leiden and no doubt followed the progress of Descartes' natural philosophy in the universities, modifying his own opinions accordingly. His book on the mechanism of the body appeared in 1646 and being concerned very largely with the motion of the heart and the circulation of the blood looks like an attempt to continue the fight for Cartesian natural philosophy after it had been all but lost in the universities. Of all the authors we are examining who wrote for or against Harvey, Hogelande is the most 'Cartesian', but as we shall see, he departed from Descartes' opinions in some significant ways.

Hogelande's version of Descartes' natural philosophy begins, naturally enough, with a rational demonstration of the existence of God. Man, according to Hogelande, has been created as the image of God's wisdom, and remains linked to Him by means of the immortal rational soul. This connection meant also for Hogelande that the (Cartesian) clear and distinct ideas have a divine guarantee of truth. They are of course concerned with the categories of extension, motion and thought. It is very notable that Hogelande did not base his natural philosophy on a doubt about the existence of God, no doubt because of the hostility that Descartes had met from the university theologians on this

[83] Hogelande, *Cogitationes*, pp. 122–5.

account. In its place Hogelande uses the argument from design, principally in relation to the structure of the heart. Nor does Hogelande dwell on the fact that in Cartesian natural philosophy the body and soul are mutually exclusive categories. This had led to Regius' disastrous *per accidens* thesis, to the subsequent riots and to further hostility from the theologians. In its place Hogelande emphasised the role of the soul as part of the image of God's reason. He also has a large and speculative passage on a possible substantial way in which the soul might be linked to the body, which also looks like an attempt to avoid the difficulties of Cartesian dualism. A number of topics that Hogelande deals with are those which had been used against Descartes in the disputations, and almost certainly Hogelande had followed them and was furthering the defence of Descartes' natural philosophy.

Another major way of defending this natural philosophy occurred to Hogelande after his book had been printed. Again we may suppose he had been following the fate of Descartes' mechanical circulation in the universities and had seen how it had succumbed to the attacks of the theologians, largely Calvinist. There was little in common in terms of belief between a Catholic like Hogelande and the Calvinist opponents of Descartes, but Hogelande found a doctrine that would put mechanism on a religious basis that would appeal, he hoped, to both sides of the religious divide. It was predestination. This was a doctrine that was available to orthodox Catholics as a development of Augustine's teaching on fore-ordination, God's foreknowledge of those who are to be saved. The Calvinists gave emphasis to predestination and indeed it was for this reason that many more latitudinarian groups had broken from

Fig. 18. The machinery of the heart.
Regius followed Descartes in making the action of the heart and motion of the blood the most notable examples of the new mechanism. Since for them the explanation of the motion of the heart did not lie in a faculty, spirit or soul, but in the material construction of the heart, it was important to show this structure in order to make the motion of the heart (as Regius would say) Intelligible. His illustrations show (i) a heart divided to demonstrate the two ventricles, G and H, the auricles and great vessels, A, B, C, D. (ii) shows how the blood enters the heart from the vena cava, AB. The tricuspid valves are KLM. The mechanism that ensures the passage of blood through the lungs is shown in (iii), where the arterial vein (now coming to be called the pulmonary artery) is shown at CD and the semilunar valves at EFG. (iv) shows the descent of the blood through the pulmonary vein, H, into the left ventricle across the mitral valves IK, which prevent its regress. The semilunar valves BCD likewise prevent reflux when the blood at the end of the cycle flows into the aorta, A. The whole machine is illustrated in the final figure (v): the vena cava is NX (the latter at the bottom of the figure), the pulmonary artery K, leading to the lungs, YZ. The blood returns to the heart through the pulmonary vein, HGF, and thence into both branches, RP, of the aorta, O.

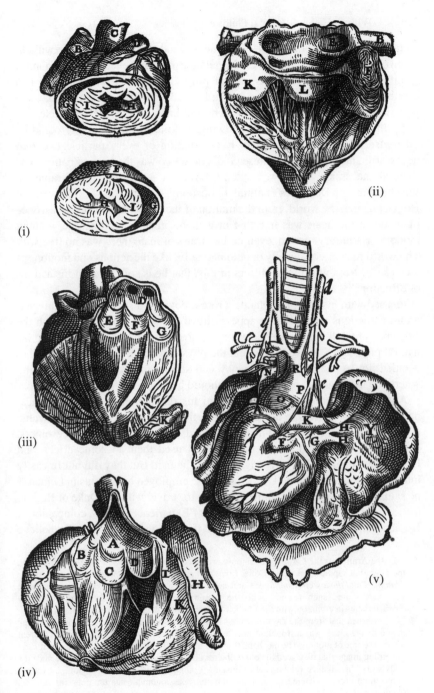

(i)

(ii)

(iii)

(iv)

(v)

Fig. 18

them, preferring to believe that a lifetime of good works could not be without significance in one's salvation.[84] Hogelande now believed he had found a significant way of relating his natural philosophy to his religion: God had created the world of particles in contact; He had also made motion and laws to govern it. Moreover He was omniscient and knew where every particle was and what law of motion it was following. It followed that nothing could be otherwise than as in God's plan. Every motion of every particle occurred necessarily, but naturally, because God's directive was the laws of nature. The 'natural necessity' that we noted above as sometimes preferable to 'mechanism' in Descartes' natural philosophy is here too. It followed for Hogelande that the world, from the motion of the heavens to the effervescence of blood in the heart was like that of a great predestined machine, without random or arbitrary motion, even in the affairs of man: there was no free will. The world runs 'mechanically or automatically, like the actions and motions of a clock . . . from which man differs in this, that he is conscious of his actions or affections'.[85]

Pleased with his idea, Hogelande wrote it down and sent it to his publisher, with instructions that it should appear directly after the opening essay on the existence of God. Hogelande clearly now thought of it as the major link in his natural philosophy between God and the physical world. (His frugal publisher decided not to disturb the typography and simply inserted a note indicating where the new tract on predestination should go.)

Another afterthought of Hogelande in his defence of his and Descartes' natural philosophy was to do some vivisections. He no doubt saw their value as confirmation of one's own doctrine and as devices to convince others. Harvey, Descartes and Plemp had after all used them to some effect, and Hogelande could not have been ignorant of the fact. But they did not fit easily into his natural philosophy. Using the phrase employed by Sylvius in Leiden,[86] he said it was his method of philosophising to 'travel with the Duke of Reason (*dux*, leader) in the company of the Count of Experience (*comes*, companion)'. He accordingly sneered at the critics of the Rational Method 'who believe

---

[84] Like the Arminians the Cambridge Platonists rejected predestination and were sympathetic to the new philosophies. See R. L. Colie, *Light and Enlightenment. A Study of the Cambridge Platonists and the Dutch Arminians*, Cambridge University Press, 1957. While the Cambridge Platonists shared such features with the Arminians, Voet and his followers had many characteristics in common with the English Puritans (McGahagan, 'Cartesianism', p. 4).

[85] We have seen that from the days of Ramus and the late sixteenth-century commentators, the image of the clock was a troubling one, as unnatural, yet purposeful and with an apparent internal source of motion. The mechanists removed the difficulty by making it their central and governing image that displaced the old problems about nature and purpose. For Hogelande the body works 'mechanice vel automatice, instar actionum motuumque horologium . . . a quibus homo in eo proprie differe videtur, quod actionum passionumque suarum conscius sibi sit', *Cogitationes*, p. 143.

[86] Sylvius, *Opera medica*, p. 3.

nothing without experience'. His inspiration was not only Descartes but Plato: the soul, incarcerated in the body, is often misled by the senses and can even be deprived of its reason by its association with the material body. The business of philosophy, says Hogelande, is indeed to overcome these defects by the use of reason, the soul's image of God. His deductive argument, from God to the nature of the soul to the beating of the heart is so strong for Hogelande that he says that it might seem like mere curiosity rather than necessity to examine the question of at what point in the heartbeat the blood emerges. As in the case of Descartes, so deductive, so Rational is the philosophy that it seems clear that the necessity of performing experiments was the necessity of persuading one's opponents.

So Hogelande reluctantly turned to experiment. As observed above, it was an afterthought. He had already sent the manuscript of his book to the publisher, who had set most of it up in type. Then Hogelande decided to vivisect the heart of an eel. He became increasingly engrossed. He began to note down his results, and wanted them included in his book. The typesetter stopped where he was, in mid sentence, and began to set up the new material in a 'digression' that finally ran for twenty-six pages, with its own title page. The 'digression' is essentially a scholastic disputed question. It offers an *ordo tractandi* in a thoroughly academic way and begins with a series of definitions.[87] We can assume that Hogelande, like Harvey, had good reason to adopt a formal mode of exposition, and there is no doubt that he expected to be able to convince by means of it. The definitions and his search for the *propria motio* of the heart (it is a fermentive diastole) preclude a Harveian resolution to the question. No doubt he too undertook the vivisections as devices to convince, following Harvey, Descartes and Plemp. But his conclusions are by no means clear-cut evidence in favour of a Cartesian fermentation–inflation. He found that contraction of the heart did not always look 'accidental' but forceful. In a number of places he says the ejection of blood from the heart is 'possibly' helped by contraction. Such contraction might indeed result from a fermentive change in the substance of the heart that brings the walls of the ventricle forcibly together. Finally he claims that fermentive–inflationary schemes apply only to quadrupeds, which have also, however, some measure of forceful contraction, and that in fish, like the eel he was vivisecting, contraction is 'more natural'.

Without doubt, Hogelande's experiments made him seriously modify the Cartesian position, even though it looks very much as though he had begun

---

[87] Hogelande, *Cogitationes*, p. 50. The *ordo tractandi* is the commentator's way of handling the sequence of the author's argument. It was part of the preliminary apparatus that told the reader what was going to happen in the commentary and was normally paired with an *ordo tractatus* that described the arrangement of the text.

them as confirmatory and persuasive devices. The doctrine of Hogelande that got into the anatomical literature was 'Hogelandian effervescence' of blood in the heart.[88] Whoever was responsible for creating the phrase had not taken notice of the 'digression' and Hogelande's vivisections. Finally, Hogelande in the digression gives generous praise to Harvey, seeing his arguments about the size of the vessels, the auricles and the quantities of blood ejected at every beat as entirely mechanical.

This brings us back to the question of the validity of knowledge. Hogelande and the Cartesians could only see Harvey as rational when he appeared to be describing a mechanical system. All of the search for the causes of things, the purpose inherent in the *historia-actio-usus-utilitas* could reveal nothing to a Cartesian. For Harvey knowledge could only be gained by considering purpose in conjunction with form. No reductive mechanism of the Cartesians could ever generate knowledge for Harvey. Perhaps what he felt about the neoterics was part of the evident antagonism shown by Aristotle and Galen for the ancient atomists who denied purpose in nature. Perhaps he had Descartes in mind when he advised John Aubrey (as Aubrey says) to 'goe to the fountain head & read Aristotle, Cicero, Avicen., & did call the neoteriques shitt-breeches'.[89]

### Heart, soul and machinery

The question of what moved the heart was one where religion and medicine were firmly bound together. The Greek notion of a physically active soul had come into the West with Plato, Galen and Aristotle, and was taught in the university arts course in texts like Aristotle's *De anima* and the shorter text on the 'Difference between the soul and spirit', in which were collected together some ancient opinions arising from the terms *anima, spiritus, psyche* and *pneuma*. We have seen that Alfred of Shareshill wrote a *De motu cordis* probably in the first years of the thirteenth century and that Aquinas wrote another, treating the Greek *psyche* as the Christian immortal soul. The standard doctrine of sixteenth-century Catholicism, to be found in pocket manuals of systematic theology like that of de Combis, was that the soul was located in the heart and exercised its functions by means of the three faculties that Galen had identified in the process of nutrition, of which the first was attraction.[90]

---

[88] See E. de Meara, *Examen diatribae Thomae Willisii, doctoris medici et professoris Oxoniensis, de Febribus,* London, 1665, p. 3: the heartbeat arises perhaps *ex Hogelandico fermento* or from Cartesian 'fire'. Better known but not better informed were the series of editions of the anatomy textbook of Thomas Bartholin, which identify the views of Regius, Descartes and Hogelande, speaking of the vaporisation of one or two drops of blood. See Descartes, *Oeuvres,* ed. Adam and Tannery, vol. XII, p. 29.

[89] Keynes, *William Harvey* (repr. 1978), p. 434.

[90] Johannes de Combis, *Compendium totius theologicae veritatis,* Venice, 1554, pp. 75v, 103v.

De Combis, citing yet another *De motu cordis*[91] shows how readily the *anima* of ancient philosophy was identified with the Christian soul as described by the church Fathers. To put it another way, the purely theological account of the soul from sources like Augustine took on physical attributes and functions.

Like de Combis, the near-contemporary philosopher and physician Michaelangelo Biondo took the Christian doctrine of the soul as a spiritual substance capable of reason and of perceiving revelation, always mobile and alive. Aristotle could be made to agree with the Fathers in saying that the soul – rational and immortal – was not a dimensional substance and so could not be located, but was present through its actions principally in the heart. This is the part of the body, says Biondo, that was specially prepared for the creation of the soul, which God makes *in situ*. The heart is the first to live and the last to die, an appropriate organ for the soul's actions. Biondo tackles the traditional question about how the early embryonic heart can live without the nutritive faculty of the as-yet-unformed liver, and answers that the heart contains within itself the faculties of nutrition, the first of which is attraction. This Galenic faculty, which was to be so strongly opposed by the new philosophers of half a century or so later is essentially for Biondo a divine action, for the soul is the image of God in the body.[92] He does not reject the view that the soul itself is the agent that forms the heart. It was some such feeling for the divinity of actions in the body that informed the anatomical views that we have met of Piccolomini and Parigiano, and prompted the dissatisfaction shown by some of the critics like Froidmont of Descartes' opinion on the motion of the heart.

Doctrine as set out by de Combis and used by Biondo was pre-Reformation and would have been difficult to oppose as doctrine was strengthened in the Counter-Reformation period. Disputed questions on the soul and its location routinely drew from biblical as well as medical sources as doctrine was reconfirmed to face the Protestant threat. That of Nicholas de Nancel, published in a volume devoted to the topic of the immortality of the soul,[93] is an example. De Nancel was a Counter-Reformation figure who after teaching the classical languages in Paris turned to medicine. Before his studies were complete he was driven out of Paris by the religious disturbances and took up a position in Douai, the Catholic school founded by the Spanish monarch. By 1565 he was able to return to Paris, took his medical degree and became

---

[91]  The author was 'Alexander': de Combis, *Compendium*, p. 73r.
[92]  Michael Angelus Blondus, *De anima dialogus*, Rome, 1545: 'in which are damned the false opinions of the early philosophers'. The work is a dialogue between Blondus the father and his son Scipio. Blondus describes himself as a *physicus*, a philosopher of natural things. The work is unpaginated. Biondo, who was born in 1496 in Venice, practiced medicine in Rome and Naples and wrote extensively on medical subjects. See *NBU*.
[93]  N. Nancelius (de Nancel), *Problema, An sedes animae in cerebro? an in corde? aut ubi denique?* In *De immortalitate animae*, Paris, 1587, pp. 60r–78r.

physician to the royal family.[94] His disputed question on the seat of the soul uses sources in the Old and New Testaments together with the Fathers, the Greek medical writers and the philosophers up to Aquinas, to show that the soul is in the heart. This is the learned tradition of a unified knowledge. Even though de Nancel claims to be writing philosophically as a *physicus* – the term used also by Biondo – the biblical sources are extremely important for him.

De Nancel's attention was given primarily to the immortal part of the soul. But the orthodoxy that he drew on insisted that the soul of man was single and faculties of nutrition, growth and generation, while like those of animals and not immortal, were nevertheless faculties of a single soul. Many scholastics had argued that the soul in all its faculties was spread over the entire living body. The argument was that the lower faculties are seen in all parts; and that the rational, immortal soul had no physical dimensions and could therefore not be located. This argument was adopted by one of Harvey's opponents, Fortunio Liceti. Like Biondo, Liceti says that the lower faculties in man, and when present as separate souls in animals, are drawn from matter, while the rational, immortal soul is given by God. For Liceti, the lower faculties are controlled by the rational soul, which is thus effectively spread with them through the body. Liceti argues that Aristotle did not want to *locate* the soul in the heart:[95] it was simply that the heart, as the first to live and the last to die, was a notable example of an organ that contained the coextensive soul;[96] and of course many of the body's most notable actions occur in the heart, so the soul is more obviously there than in other organs. Liceti is arguing against the notion that the heart is a principle *from* which flow powers to the rest of the body. The whole of the body, he says, is like a circle drawn by geometer, without a source and destination, without beginning or end.

It was almost universally agreed that the means whereby the soul achieved its purposes in or through the heart were by means of the faculty of attraction (and the others) and by means of heat. The medical view of this is exemplified by Julius Caesar Claudinus – Claudini or Chiodini in the vernacular – a well-known professor of medicine at Bologna. (He died in 1618, but seems to have been a pupil and friend of Caspar Hofmann, who published some of his opinions.) For Claudini the heat of the soul in the heart was the same at the heat by which nourishment is said to be digested in some of the Hippocratic writings. It is also innate heat: these actions of heat in the body are one of the reasons why the topic of innate heat became something of a controversy in the early seventeenth century; and because heat was fundamental to nutrition as

[94] For de Nancel (1539–1610) see *NBU*.
[95] Fortunius Liceti, *De animarum coextensione corpori*, Padua, 1616, p. 74.
[96] Ibid., p. 61.

well as to the motion of the heart, disputes on the motion of the blood were often linked to those on nutrition. Claudini has his own scheme of things, for he believed that blood moves *from* the heart to the liver to complete its sanguification, because the liver on its own was not hot enough. As Aristotelians were wont to do, Claudini makes the heart central, analogous to a king in the macrocosm and even to God in the universe.[97]

In complete contrast to these developments of the learned tradition were the doctrines of the new philosophers, particularly in respect of the soul, innate heat and the faculty of attraction. Either shortly before or after Descartes had left for Sweden, and towards the end of the period considered in this book, some of the disputants we have met above produced systematic accounts of their medical-philosophical positions. One of them was Regius' textbook of natural philosophy,[98] the *Fundamenta physices* of 1646. It is an attempt to give an entirely Cartesian picture of the natural world. To this end it goes from fundamental physical principles through the actual world of elements, mixtures, qualities, meteorology, generation and corruption, plants, animals and man. Whatever the details of the physical actions that are here taught in an ascending order of complexity they make up an Aristotle-shaped replacement for Aristotle. The replacement is more or less complete. The fundamental law of nature, the *lex naturans* (says Regius) is that, with God's concurrence, things stay as they are unless moved by something else. Nothing stops, moves or 'receives' except by external action. The agent of this law is 'nature', traditionally the internal moving principle of things, but here essentially corporeal. It follows, in Regius' argument, that things with an incorporeal internal source of motion – God and the angels – are *supernatural*. They have no part in the discipline that Regius prefers to call *physica* rather than natural philosophy. This is in marked contrast to the very widespread principle that natural philosophy *began* with God.

While the Aristotelian commentators of a generation earlier (as we have seen) were worried by the image of the clock as an object with purpose and an internal principle of motion, yet unnatural, Regius relished it.[99] The 'form' of the steel that composes it, he says, is entirely 'accidental' to the steel (in being imposed artificially) but 'essential' to the clock. In other words, the Aristotelian terms, here in inverted commas, are but guises for a new view of nature: the clock is like other things in running according to the nature of its parts, not according to an internal and non-corporeal principle of motion. The shift is part of Descartes' banning of the soul in any traditional form from

---

[97] J. C. Claudinus, *Quaestio, an facultates principes animae secundum sedes distinguantur in cerebro?* Published by Caspar Hofmann in his *Pro veritate opellae tres*, Paris, 1647.
[98] H. Regius, *Fundamenta physices*, Amsterdam, 1646.
[99] Ibid., p. 6.

active involvement in the actions of the body: the soul is for Regius a corporeal principle. In Cartesian fashion, but quite unlike the soul of tradition, it does not produce motion in the body (which arises from motion transferred from Cartesian subtle matter). Nowhere was the action of the soul more central than in the motion of the heart, and this is one of the reasons why Regius chooses the production and circulation of the blood as the main example of his new *physica*[100] (see fig. 19).

The action of the heart Regius describes is what we would expect from someone who had been in close contact with him as Descartes changed his notion in the face of criticism. It includes both inflation by the vaporisation of the large drops of blood entering the ventricles and a fermentive action of spirits. It has nothing whatever to do with the soul.

We have seen that some of those who first had a view of Descartes' ideas on the heartbeat, like Froidmont, were disturbed that the noble action of the soul had been usurped by machinery in Descartes' account. He therefore retained the traditional view that the soul moves the heart. So did Kyper, in the textbook we have looked at: the soul as a whole is the form of the body and the vegetative and sentient souls are subordinate forms. Kyper saw the soul as an integral part of man, the rational animal, and not only in these Aristotelian and scholastic ways, for he also saw it as the Hippocratic *impetum faciens*, the source of motion in the solid and liquid parts of the body.[101] Likewise de Back, some time after the disputations in the Dutch universities, expressed the view that the soul moved the heart, and was not even to be put off by Plemp's argument that since a separated and divided living heart continued to beat, it could not be moved by the soul (which would therefore also have to be separated and divided). De Back's argument was religious, not physical.[102] The question of the soul of animals was acute as the implications of Descartes' programme were worked out. Descartes said that animals did not have souls, and that even their apparently mental faculties such as memory, perception and imagination (strictly, the forming of images) were entirely material. Few wanted to attribute immortal souls to animals, of course, but outside France there was a general resistance to the idea that machinery could produce perception and memory. To put it another way, Descartes and his followers came to accept the equivalence of mind, soul and conscious reason.

But few others did. An example is Daniel Sennert. He lived and worked in one of the centres of the Protestant world, Wittenberg, where he had taken his MD in 1601 and where he continued as professor of medicine until his death in 1637. He was the first to introduce chemistry in its Paracelsian and Protestant

---

[100] Ibid., p. 174.
[101] Kyper, *Institutiones Medicae*, p. 4.
[102] J. de Back, *Dissertatio de corde*, 4th edn, Rotterdam, 1671, p. 203.

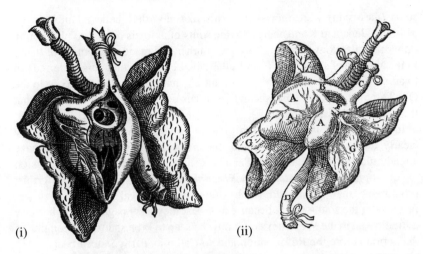

(i)                                        (ii)

Fig. 19. The mechanics of foetal plumbing.
When Regius systematised his Cartesian natural philosophy in his
*Fundamenta physices*, like Descartes he chose the heart as the principal
example of mechanism. It was in the heart that traditionally the soul had acted
in producing motion, warmth and spirits, and here, then, that the mechanism
was most strikingly different. In (i), Regius shows the cavities, vessels and
valves of the heart and in particular at 4 the foetal foramen ovale. In (ii), F is
the ductus arteriosus. Regius' argument, like Descartes, is that as a result of
the disposition, size, motion and shape of the parts of the heart the blood
*necessarily* flows in a certain direction: it is not through *purpose* that these
foetal vessels close at birth and drive the blood through the lungs.

form into Wittenberg and the enthusiasm he put into developing innovations
looks like an attempted Reform of medicine. In direct opposition to the
Cartesians he believed that God had created animal souls *ex nihilo* and with
special powers (the traditional faculties). He was attacked by another energetic
Protestant, Johannes Freitag, professor of medicine at Helmstadt and then
Groningen, and an enemy of what he saw as the pernicious new sect of
Sennerto-Paracelsians.[103] Freitag said that God has used pre-existing
elementary matter and that animal souls were therefore elementary in nature
and without special, supra-elementary powers. Sennert wrote indignantly to a
number of German theology faculties and received a reply in his favour from
eight of them. The Leipzig theologians ruled that God had indeed created
animal souls *ex nihilo* to be propagated in the usual way by animals. These

---

[103] *NBU*. Freitag, 1580–1641, preferred a chemistry that was closer to Aristotelian matter-theory;
he was opposed, as was Sennert, to Descartes.

souls (they said) were mortal. For this reason – they believed in Leipzig, Marburg, Jena and Königsberg[104] – the souls of animals related to philosophy rather than theology, and this was why Luther had made no mention of them. In the absence of a directive from Luther, the Leipzig theologians preferred not to adopt the 'vulgar and scholastic opinion' (that is, Catholic) but to go to the Old Testament, where Genesis and Leviticus could be read as indicating that the soul is in, or is, the blood.[105]

In other words, in the question of what moves the heart we can see very clearly how religious and medical matters were closely related. We have already glanced at Fludd's and Sennert's fundamentalist Protestant views on the question of the soul and blood. What made them possible was a Reformist programme that questioned some Greek philosophical ideas – the lower faculties of the soul – partly because as Greek they were pagan, partly because as traditional in the West they could now be seen to Protestants as belonging to the period before the Reformation and so Catholic, partly indeed because the Counter-Reformation now emphasised this learned tradition, and partly because the Old Testament – available to anyone in new versions of the Bible – seemed to represent knowledge that was older and more authoritative than that of the pagan Greek philosophers or the medieval commentators. The mechanism of the Cartesians cut right through these differences, being radically different from both in its very fundamentals. These are major events and attitudes of the middle of the seventeenth century, and they were fundamental to the way in which men noticed and interpreted Harvey's doctrine of the action of the heart and motion of the blood.

[104] *Regiomontana.*
[105] Sennert, *Opera tomus I*, pp. 1–18.

# 9 Circulation through Europe

We have now looked in some detail at the way people reacted to Harvey's doctrines in England and the Low Countries and at some of the mechanisms operating for and against the formation of a consensus of opinion. Comparable stories could be told about the other countries of Europe. In Spain, with one exception, the physicians remained Galenist until well after the middle of the century, and so beyond the timescale covered in this book.[1] We have already glimpsed the Danish reaction. What follows below is a brief examination of how Harvey's doctrines were treated in Italy, France and the Germanic lands.[2]

Harvey's doctrines were, for his opponents, novelties that did not agree with an extant scheme of things and were therefore, they concluded, wrong. It followed for them that Harvey's *method* of producing these novelties, what we are here calling his natural philosophy, must also have been at fault. It was Primrose's complaint that Harvey took no note of medicine as an autonomous activity: of how the thought of its founders had been bound into an intelligible

---

[1] J. M. L. Piñero, 'Harvey's doctrine of the circulation of the blood in seventeenth century Spain', *Journal of the History of Medicine*, 28 (1973), 230–42; 231–2. See also H. E. Bayon, 'William Harvey, physician and biologist: his precursors, opponents and successors', *Annals of Science*, 3 (1938), part, 59–118; 99, who argues that Gaspar Bravo was influenced by Harvey, perhaps when the latter was in Spain with the Duke of Lennox. Bravo's book of 1649 has been elusive even to Spanish scholars: See J. J. Izquierdo, 'On Spanish neglect of Harvey's "De Motu Cordis" for three centuries, and how it was finally made known to Spain and Spanish-speaking countries', *Journal of the History of Medicine*, 3 (1948), 105–24; 106. Bravo, 1610–83, was at the University of Valladolid.

[2] In publishing his book through Fitzer in Frankfurt Harvey might have been taking advice from his friend Fludd and so getting it printed cheaply (see W. Pagel, *William Harvey's Biological Ideas*, Basle, 1967, p. 118) or he may have been aiming at a European market by way of the Frankfurt book-fair. But publishing in the German towns was difficult in wartime (see Fitzer's address to the reader in R. Fludd, *Clavis philosophiae et alchymiae Fluddianae, sive Roberti Fluddi armigeri et medicinae doctoris, ad epistolicam Petri Gassendi theologi exercitationem responsum*, Frankfurt, 1633 and Hofmann's correspondence). At all events, *De motu cordis* was a cheap job. Harvey often complained of the errors it contained and thought that some attacks upon his doctrine arose from them. (See M. J. van Lieburg, 'Zacharias Sylvius (1608–1664), author of the Praefatio to the first Rotterdam edition (1648) of Harvey's De Motu Cordis', *Janus*, 65 (1978), 241–57; 249.) An erratum sheet was printed but is not present in most copies.

and trustworthy system of understanding and, importantly, practice, which circulation could only disturb.

## Circulation in Italy: Parigiano's attack on Harvey

These sentiments and others that we must consider were developed a few years after Primrose's first attack by another opponent of Harvey, Emilio Parigiano, Latinised as Aemylius Parisanus.[3] Parigiano was a Roman, thought of himself as a philosopher as well as a physician, and practised in Venice. There he was a member of the council (he was *consiliaris*) of the Venetian College of Physicians. So there were parallels between him and Harvey, as well as differences. The differences were that they were born and worked in different parts of Europe and doubtless practised a different form of religion. But both were practising and philosophically inclined doctors and each a respected member of his important professional body. Moreover, like Harvey, Parigiano had his own anatomical novelty – very different from Harvey's – to defend and promote.

Parigiano saw these similarities and differences. He understood Harvey's dedication of *De motu cordis* to Argent and the doctors of the college to be the college's seal of approval for the book. For him it was their book as much as Harvey's, in which they expressed the common view of London doctors, or at least, thought Parigiano, they were united in their protection of Harvey.[4] This was not the case, of course, for as we have seen voices were raised against Harvey, and Primrose with equal freedom made the same dedications as Harvey. Moreover, the college later, and perhaps because of Parigiano's view of the matter, became cautious about what was published apparently in their name and as we have seen even refused to commit themselves to Harvey's view, which was rapidly becoming accepted.[5]

That the College of Physicians seemed to endorse the book, and so

---

[3] W. Harvey, *De motu cordis et sanguinis in animalibus, anatomica exercitatio. Cum refutationibus Aemylii Parisani Romani, philosophi, ac medici Veneti et Iacobi Primirosii in Londonensi Collegio doctoris*, Leiden, 1639. (These *Refutationes* of Parigiano are henceforth referred to as Parigiano, *Refutationibus*.) According to Keynes' bibliography, there was an edition of Parigiano in 1635. See Sir Geoffrey Keynes, *A Bibliography of the Writings of William Harvey 1573–1657*, 3rd edn, revised by G. Whitteridge and C. English, Winchester (St Paul's Bibliographies), 1989. (I have mostly used the 2nd edn, Cambridge University Press, 1953.)

[4] Parigiano, *Refutationibus*, proemium; pp. 40, 243.

[5] Roger Drake, arguing with James Primrose, accused him too of seeing collegiate support for Harvey in the dedication to Argent. Drake made enquiries and found that the college did not endorse Harvey's views: *minime subscripsisse*, he said. R. Drake, *Contra animadversiones Iac. Primirosii in theses, quas ipse pro sanguinis motu circulari, sub praesidio Io. Walaei, in celeberrima Leidae Academia, publica examini subjecerat Vindiciae* in *Disceptationum Recentium* (1647), p. 167.

constitute a professional London consensus, made it a bigger threat to Parigiano, and his rhetoric is designed to draw its sting. He tells the reader that he admired the faith of Harvey's followers and was astonished at the consensus in the college, but that gradually doubts set in about this *maxima novitas* of Harvey. His weapon for fighting it was to be in the first place the same as what he saw as Harvey's, the support of his own college, that of the Venetian College of Physicians and Philosophers. His doubts about Harvey's doctrine turn into a rhetoric of sarcasm as throughout the book he wonders why it is that things visible and audible in London are invisible and inaudible to anatomists in Venice.[6] His own dedication to his college becomes an elaborate metaphor of a grand battle between the two groups.

Undoubtedly what prompted Parigiano to write the book was that he had already begun his own programme of work, and had indeed already published, on sanguification and the motion of the heart. Believing that arterial blood was generated in the spleen and transmitted to the heart by way of the arteries, he necessarily disagreed with Harvey's conclusions.[7] It followed too that Harvey's natural philosophy was in error, and the main thrust of Parigiano's attack was to show how Harvey's underlying principles and the method built on them were unsatisfactory. He saw his own system as a refinement of the Galenic system, and consequently found that he could attack Harvey equally effectively by defending the sanctity of the learned tradition within medicine. Like Primrose he felt that the effectiveness of practical medicine lay in the authority of the ancient texts, and that any radical departure from this linked understanding and practice must be destructive.

Parigiano found Harvey's 'Aristotle project' deeply unsatisfactory. We can recall that Harvey's method was to look for the quiddity of the heart's action wherever hearts were found. Undoubtedly an Aristotelian technique, a search for causes among the parts of animals, Harvey allied it powerfully to the 'rule of Socrates' by which the true nature of a term was discovered. For Parigiano, the practice of the method in *De motu cordis* was deeply flawed. As a worthy of the professional body of the Venice physicians, there were institutional reasons why Parigiano defended Galen and the medical learned tradition rather than Aristotle and the philosophical. Indeed, Parigiano asserts with confidence that he is in the 'Galenic *schola*'.[8] We have examined some of these institutional reasons in relation to other figures already, and we are reminded that the major difference between the two in the anatomical part of natural philosophy was that the physicians saw the purpose of all anatomy as

---

[6] See also Parigiano, *Refutationibus*, p. 106.
[7] See also J. Bylebyl, 'Nutrition, quantification and circulation', *Bulletin of the History of Medicine*, 51 (1977), 369–85, who sets out the context of Parigiano's view of blood flow through the heart.
[8] Parigiano, *Refutationibus*, p. 212.

understanding man, while the philosophers sought knowledge for its own sake also from animals.[9] Indeed, in the medical tradition from Vesalius onwards the study of animals had always had the notoriety of being the very thing that had misled Galen.

Parigiano had no interest in animal anatomy for any other reason than to know about man. For him man was the 'exemplar, norm and goal (*finis*) of all animals',[10] the rule by which others are judged.[11] The only, but useful, purpose of dissecting animals, he says,[12] is to place the structure of these imperfect creatures alongside the perfection of man, to bring out the truth and demonstrate the excellence, perfection and divinity of man. Man's nobility was a newly emphasised feature of anatomy texts of the late sixteenth and early seventeenth century, used to add to the dignity of anatomy. Parigiano seems to be drawing his material here from Bauhin or du Laurens. In such a comparison between man and the lower animals, the least perfect and lowest are disgusting indeed: the most vile, the most helpless and useless, the coldest and smallest.[13] Harvey is tainted, according to Parigiano, by working with such creatures, the frogs, toads, snakes and eels that fill his book.[14] Harvey has 'fished out' a theory: abandoning the waters that are fished by the wise, says Parigiano, Harvey has gone to an easy river, but has only landed the faeces of animals and the *pisciculos*, eels and frogs.

It is not only that Harvey, for Parigiano, was tainted by such creatures, but that by them the 'senses are poisoned and the intellect damaged'. It was, he said, precisely because of their imperfection, their distance from man, that no valid knowledge could be derived from their hearts: Harvey's method was fundamentally at fault. Cold, slow-beating and devoid of spirits, such hearts were essentially different to the human heart.[15] Moreover, adds Parigiano, these hearts are seen only after the animal has been opened and practically eviscerated; or even when cut out of the animal entirely. 'Good God!' he cried,

---

[9] Primrose indeed reported that those who were impressed by Harvey's animals were not medical men. (J. Primrose, *Exercitationes, et animadversiones in librum, De motu cordis, et circulatione sanguinis adversus Guilielmum Harveium Medicum Regium, et Anatomes in Collegio Londinensi Professorem*, London, 1630, p. 54.) Harvey made use of about a hundred animals (F. J. Cole, 'Harvey's animals', *Journal of the History of Medicine*, 12 (1957), 106–13: Harvey mentions 128 'types of animal life', 49 of which are in *De motu cordis* and the reply to Riolan). This must have appeared strange from a medical viewpoint.

[10] Parigiano, *Refutationibus*, p. 244 and compare A. Laurentius (du Laurens), *Historia anatomica humani corporis et singularum ejus partium multis controversiis et observationibus illustrata*, Frankfurt, n.d. (1600? *Ad lectorem* dated 1599), p. 9.

[11] Parigiano, *Refutationibus*, p. 118.

[12] Ibid., p. 117.

[13] Ibid., p. 70. Primrose felt the same about Harvey's animals, but his words admit that Harvey here had power to convince others, who thought him the *summus investigator* of natural things, with oracular authority. Primrose, *Exercitationes*, p. 54.

[14] Parigiano, *Refutationibus*, p. 45.

[15] Ibid., p. 46.

is this a valid mode of experience, when the hearts of these creatures have been torn from their bodies, exposed to the air, lacerated and are lying exhausted and half dead on the table or in the hand, devoid of blood and spirits? In a similar way, as Primrose had done, he criticised Harvey's experimental vivisections as unnatural: producing results that did not occur in nature and did not illustrate nature's mechanisms. The emergence of blood from the hole Harvey made in the ventricle of a living heart was for Parigiano an artefact produced by unnatural intrusion into the workings of the heart and therefore 'greatly repugnant to reason'.[16]

The essence of Parigiano's attack on the 'Aristotle-project' part of Harvey's natural philosophy was that there was no quiddity, no what-it-is-to-be-a-heart throughout a range of creatures. For Parigiano man's structure defined what 'heart' meant and everything else was imperfect and incapable of generating useful knowledge. Indeed, so far was the 'heart' of some of Harvey's creatures from normality that it could not be called a heart at all. If the 'heart' of some small creatures did not beat in the winter, as Harvey admitted, yet they remained alive, clearly they were being nourished by other means and their 'heart' could not be a heart at all (because its function was nourishment). Even more tellingly, where Harvey described a simple heart in some creatures as a single pulsating bladder, Parigiano declared that such a thing would be part of a heart only, and a part existing and operating without the whole was unthinkable.[17] Moreover, at the earliest stage of their embryological existence, says Parigiano, even more perfect creatures do not have hearts, and so there cannot be any such principle that all animals have hearts.[18]

Whether or not Parigiano recognised the nature of Harvey's 'Aristotle project' he clearly saw that many of the differences he had with Harvey lay in what he saw as Harvey's claim to be an Aristotelian.[19] Parigiano had already written on the development of the chick in the egg and had come to a Galenic conclusion that the rudiments of the heart were simply spermatic fibres, which did not become a heart until literally fleshed out with a parenchyma derived from the blood. The heart was not, then, the first part of the body to live and the last to die, as Aristotelians maintained. Believing that Harvey was an Aristotelian on this point, Parigiano became highly indignant at Harvey's observation that in the dying heart it is the auricle that beats a few times after the ventricle has stopped; moreover Harvey's account of the heartbeat made it clear that the beat of the auricle was prior to that of the ventricle. But for Parigiano the auricles were mere appendages, secondary organs, yet Harvey

[16] Ibid., p. 49.
[17] Ibid., p. 255.
[18] Ibid., p. 99.
[19] Ibid., p. 212.

seemed to be saying they were the first to live and the last to die. Is the auricle the principle of principles, asked Parigiano, the source of motion and spirit, the author of our actions and preservation: No; these are vile, cold, inept bladders of the heart; indeed, he concludes, with a return of his sarcasm, man would simply be a bladder, if these London Ears, *auriculae*, hear acutely in the distance (that is, if Harvey and the college are right).[20]

For these reasons, Parigiano explains, his own method will not be to look at imperfect animals, nor to vivisect. Rather he will begin with the heart of a calf where everything is easy to see.[21] What is observed, in fact, is no less than the perfect *oeconomia* of provident nature. Here too Parigiano draws upon the medical Galenism of the professional doctor. Nature's 'economy' is more however than the wisdom, skill and foresight that Galen's *physis* or demiurge used in constructing the body:[22] it is the whole functioning of the body (according to Parigiano's refined Galenism) in which the centrally important soul owes as much to Parigiano's time and place as to Greek philosophy. It is this 'economy' that Harvey's doctrine threatened, and which Parigiano is defending. It is an economy that depended on what had been made 'sacred'[23] by the medical learned tradition. This economy was ordered on an essentially hierarchic system. The importance accorded to organs reflected their function in nature's overall purpose, the protection of the individual and the continuation of the race. It is these considerations, according to Parigiano, that provide irrefutable reasons for the actions of each particular organ and part. So complex and interdependent are the actions of the parts in pursuance of these goals that reason and sense seem mutually to support the system. 'Just as in the best-established republic', says Parigiano, so in the well-ordered body, some stand above others in the hierarchy.[24] In his own scheme, the spleen makes nourishment for itself and the heart (as noble organs) and in distributing what remains to the other parts, it has a public function (as no doubt members of the republic in Parigiano's analogy could have public functions).

In such an elaborate 'economy of nature' within the body, Harvey's scheme cut across too many relationships, denied too many places in the hierarchy and replaced them with nothing. To the extent that Parigiano felt that there was a relationship between the body and society, Harvey was a revolutionary. Perhaps the most dangerous of all Harvey's suggestions was that all parts are

---

[20] Ibid., p. 97.
[21] Ibid., p. 71.
[22] See Galen's *Du Usu Partium Corporis Humani*, M. T. May, ed. and transl., *Galen on the Usefulness of the Parts of the Body*, 2 vols., Cornell University Press, 1968, especially the final book.
[23] Parigiano, *Refutationibus*, proem.
[24] Ibid., p. 200. Compare the body–society analogy of Glisson in interregnum England, chap. 10 below.

nourished by the same, circulating, blood. Just as it would not be proper, says Parigiano, to serve to a king the same food and drink as one would offer to his servant or his tailor or a rustic, so in the body each organ in the hierarchy requires its own nourishment, produced by its related organs. Yet in Harvey's scheme, continued Parigiano, all is chaos and confusion, with pure blood mingling with coarse, phlegmatic with melancholic, spirituous with unconcocted: all would be indecent and would deny the highest and best reason and order of provident nature.[25]

Parigiano's 'economy of nature' was not only paralleled by civil life, but both hierarchies were based on divine order. Much more explicitly than Harvey's, Parigiano's natural philosophy rested on God. As we might expect of someone who was expressly Galenic, the providence of nature is important for Parigiano (as it was in Galen's *On the Use of the Parts*). We would also expect a Galenist to favour the brain as the chief organ of the hierarchy of the body (as Galen had done in opposing Aristotle in his *On the Doctrines of Plato and Hippocrates*). But more than being Galenic in these two ways, Parigiano gives his natural philosophy a distinctly Christian character. Like Piccolomini, whom he often cited, Parigiano gave his attention to the brain as the prime organ of the hierarchy because it was the seat of the immortal soul of Christian doctrine. It was the soul that generated the body and the soul that gave the heat that moved the growing and adult heart. By implication at least it was the soul that carried out God's instructions, the providence of nature, for making the body, as Piccolomini had explicitly described. The importance of the motion of the heart for Parigiano was that it distributed vital spirits – life itself – to the parts, and above all to the brain, where animal spirits were generated for the benefit of the nerves and, at the highest point of the hierarchy, the rational soul.[26] The heart was made only for the benefit of the 'nobler operations of the soul'.[27] It was this that made the study of man important. The perfection of man in comparison to the lower creatures was ultimately to give glory to God.[28]

So Parigiano's attack on Harvey was more than that of an affronted professional Galenist of an important college who had just read a new opinion that did not agree with his own account of bloodflow and the action of the spleen. There was an important way in which Parigiano saw Harvey as attempting to overturn the rationality and providence not only of nature, but of

---

[25] Ibid., p. 168.
[26] According to Galen, the basic living function of the body was the purification and concoction of ingested food to produce nutriment for the body. The first result of this process was the venous blood, carried to the tissues in the veins. A further concoction produced vital spirits in the heart which warmed and vivified the parts by way of the arteries. The animal spirit was a third stage, produced from arterial blood in the brain and giving function to the nerves.
[27] This is number 56 of the 'knots' that Parigiano set at the end of his treatise for Harvey to solve.
[28] Parigiano, *Refutationibus*, p. 117. It is also the explicit of the entire book.

God. It was Harvey's sin – *peccat Harveius*[29] – to refuse to see the immense providence and rationality of nature in the vascular arrangements of the foetus or in the structure of the whole adult.[30] Harvey indeed would have nature do things in vain,[31] says Parigiano. To avoid all this, he further explains in a somewhat elaborate metaphor, he will lead us away from Harvey's fishponds and vivaria, from his disgusting animals, towards a crossroads: here the way is dark and we need candles to help. But Parigiano will lead us not to the left, through the dark woods and shadows, where one simple mistake (Harvey's forceful systole) will lead to greater mistakes later on (the circulation) if we recede from the works of God; but to the right, where on the straight Roman road in the light of day Parigiano will overturn all errors by 'divine demonstration' of wisdom and providence, congruent to sense and reason.[32]

Finally, whether or not Parigiano thought a straight road to Rome was an appropriate one for Harvey and the college of Protestant London to take, it is abundantly clear that Parigiano's main complaint against Harvey is that his natural philosophy contained the wrong kind of interpretation of the way in which God had put the world together. It will be useful to bear one last example in mind. Like almost everyone who had written on them, Parigiano expressed wonder and admiration at the purposefulness and the skill that could be seen in the action and structure of the valves of the heart. Harvey's language on this topic is characteristically restrained, observing that the force of the blood in the aorta acts to close the valve.[33] Their closure was part of the rapid sequence of events that Harvey compared to the firing of a flintlock firearm. This was unacceptable to Parigiano, who saw it as a blind and necessary sequence imposed by an external force, while in the body 'all things move separately and singularly by their own actions and for a proper and concerted purpose, that of nature; not by force or coercion or in any way from anything outside'.[34] There was nothing mechanical in Parigiano's nature.

### Parigiano's natural philosophy

Underlying Parigiano's detailed refutation of Harvey was his natural philosophy, a brief look at which will help us to understand his reactions to Harvey and *his* natural philosophy.

We can conveniently go back to 1623, when Parigiano published *Twelve*

---

[29] Ibid., p. 120.
[30] Ibid., pp. 121, 122.
[31] Ibid., p. 119.
[32] Ibid., p. 125.
[33] W. Harvey, *Exercitatio anatomica de motu cordis et sanguinis in animalibus*, Frankfurt, 1628, p. 30.
[34] Parigiano, *Refutationibus*, p. 106.

*Books of Noble Exercises on Subtlety*.[35] The 'subtlety' of the title is a conscious reference to the works of Cardano, Scaliger and Fernel. In all four authors 'subtlety' is a departure from what was increasingly seen as the gross and 'vulgar' Aristotelianism of the schools. While none of them departed entirely from the basic peripatetic principles of form, matter and causation, yet it was felt that these could explain only the major and obvious changes in the natural world. Subtle changes required subtle explanations, whether the sympathies and antipathies of Cardan and Fracastoro, or the occult qualities and 'whole substance' actions of Fernel and Parigiano's contemporary, Sennert.[36]

For Parigiano, the subtleties that needed explaining were almost all concerned with the human body and his mode of explanation was almost entirely religious. He explains as much – it is to be a Christian philosophy – in his dedication to the emperor, Ferdinand II. (It was a successful dedication, for Parigiano was later decorated by Ferdinand.)[37]

Parigiano's departure from Aristotle was, then, because Aristotle was pagan and not aware that he was dealing with God's Creation. But it was much more than the traditional offence caused by Aristotle's assertion of the eternity of the world: Parigiano's whole concept of knowledge is religious. True knowledge and the desire to know were given to Adam, he says, but subsequently corrupted by passing through the hands of the Egyptians and Hebrews. But the Greeks were worse: Orpheus covered his knowledge with fables, Pythagoras with numbers.[38] Plato adopted both coverings, and Aristotle, although removing the covers, made his writings deliberately obscure from the pride of vanity; and of all things, he was most obscure on what Parigiano calls 'our subject', the soul.

Parigiano the physician could not depart entirely from Aristotle nor, *a fortiori*, from Galen, whose side he often takes. Indeed, Galen, as a doctor who was concerned with the body of man, and as a philosopher who revered

---

[35] A. Parigiano, *Nobilium exercitationum libri duodecim de subtilitate*, Venice, 1623.

[36] H. Cardanus, *De subtilitate libri XXI*, Nuremberg, 1550; H. Cardanus, *De rerum varietate libri XVII*, Basle, 1557. That Cardano's work was attacked by Scaliger served to make it better known: J. C. Scaliger, *Exoticarum exercitationum liber quintus decimus, de subtilitate, ad Hieronymum Cardanum*, Paris, 1557. H. Fracastorius, *Opera omnia*, Venice, 1555 (includes the work on sympathy); J. Fernel, *De abditis rerum causis* in his *Universa medicina*, Geneva, 1643; D. Sennert, *Disputatio medicina, qua suam de occultis, seu totius substantiae quas vocant morbis sententiam defendit*, Wittenberg, 1616.

[37] Parigiano's work on subtlety was continued in two further volumes, largely taken up with the controversies prompted by the first volume and his attacks on various neoteric opinions. The *De microcosmica subtilitate pars altera* was published in Venice in 1635 and includes the attack on Harvey. Lastly, the *Nobilium exercitationum de subtilitate pars tertia. De semine a toto proventu. De principiis generationis. Singularis Certanimis Lapis Lydius . . . De visione* appeared in Venice, 1638. For Parigiano and Ferdinand see the address in Parigiano, *Pars tertia* by J.-B. Dolionius, who also congratulates Parigiano on having bound Harvey 'with Hippocratic bonds'.

[38] The discussion about the decay of knowledge is at p. 2 of the 1638 volume.

the wisdom and providence of the demiurge, was a model for Parigiano. In particular, Galen's natural-theological peroration to his anatomy text, *On the Use of the Parts*, was a model for Parigiano's 'Epilogue'. This was an 'Epilogue on the epilogue of God', where God's epilogue was man. Man: not merely the last thing to be created, but the purpose of the entire creation; man, the image of God, and his soul His habitation; man, the miracle of nature – 'O homo magnum Naturae miraculum' cries Parigiano.[39] He felt these things keenly, indeed personally: his address to his son in the second part of the work becomes a prayer;[40] not an entreaty to the Almighty but a paean of celebration of the right-thinking religious philosopher. 'I am God's image', he declared, 'his *archetypus*; God has created the entire world *propter me*; indeed *"God has been thinking about me since eternity"*.'[41] The right-thinking religious philosopher was of course Christian, and the less fortunate Jews, Arabs and Turks did not have access to proper knowledge. Nor indeed, adds Parigiano, do the 'heretics' who, because they are not 'Italian and Roman'[42] must have been the protestants of Parigiano's time. So long and so passionate is Parigiano's celebration of the nature of man and his relationship with his Creator that it is easy to see that he would have no pre-formed sympathies with a Protestant London doctor and his ideas. For Parigiano man was the measure of all things; Galen came nearer than the old philosophers – especially Aristotle – to seeing this; man was the purpose of Creation and the animals were only understood in terms of their utility to man: nothing could be further from the eccentric, perhaps impious, and certainly limited and wholly useless description of the body's plumbing by Harvey, based on little animals and Aristotle.

For Parigiano anatomy was a religious exercise. But it is not the Protestant exercise we saw in chapter 2, where the anatomists felt a religious duty to explore the way in which God had put the body together. Rather, it is a Counter-Reformation assertion that God has granted true knowledge to the right people. In terms that recall those of Piccolomini, Parigiano explains that it is the soul that is central to anatomy. It is through the soul that God governs the body, its spirits being His secondary causes. It is as God's Creation that the body has subtleties.[43] To examine it, Parigiano starts with its primordium, the semen. It is this, not the heart, that is the first part of the animal to live. It is this, not the individual, that is immortal, preserving God's Creation, the species. Parigiano takes as his text God's words 'Go forth and multiply':[44] only by

---

[39] The same sentiments can be found on a much smaller scale in the prefatory material of the earlier anatomy texts (see chapter 2 above) of du Laurens and Bauhin, to whom Parigiano seems particularly close in quoting the 'thrice great Mercury'.
[40] Parigiano, *Pars altera*.
[41] Ibid., the address to his son. (My italics.)    [42] Ibid., the address to his son.
[43] Parigiano, *Nobilium Exercitationum*, address to the reader.
[44] Parigiano, *Pars tertia*, p. 5.

following the scriptural path can we understand the nature of generation and the bodies it produces. Only in this way can we resolve the traditional dispute between the philosophers and physicians and dismiss the heart as the central organ. Only thus can we explain the transmission of original sin. It is to conform with these constraints that Parigiano describes non-Aristotelian 'subtleties' that involve the new action of the spleen, a new flow of blood and the generation of spirits; it is his religious certainty and his intellectual investment in physiological subtleties that prevented him from having sympathies with Harvey's doctrines.

### Argoli, Severino and Berigard

In the years between Parigiano's attack on Harvey (1633) and Riolan's (1649), and while Regius and Descartes were conducting their campaign in the United Provinces, a number of other Italians besides Parigiano reacted strongly enough to Harvey's work to go into print. There is little agreement between their handling of the motion of the heart and blood, and not all of them agreed with Harvey. It is not however without relevance to this that they all lived in an Italy that for centuries and up to Harvey's time there had been the home of the most prestigious medical school in Europe. Parigiano was at the very end of that tradition, for by the 1640s human dissection was no longer practised in Padua, and Italy was in economic decline. A professor from the north, Vesling, occupied the chair of anatomy in Padua.[45] The Harvey controversy was European; when Colston, an English medical student in Padua, wanted to know about its latest development, he had to write home, to London. It was also Counter-Reformation Italy, where the Inquisition decided what was fit to be published. Theology grew at the expense of the physical aspects of natural philosophy in the period after the Council of Trent.[46]

It was no doubt for some of these reasons that Harvey's book did not appear at first on its own in Italy, but with Parigiano's refutation of it.[47] At first it was

---

[45] Vesling was born in Westphalia in 1598 and having spent some time in Egypt, went to the chair of anatomy in Padua in 1632. He died in Padua in 1649.

[46] See C. Schmitt, 'Philosophy and science in sixteenth-century Italian universities', in his *Aristotelian Tradition and Renaissance Universities*, London, 1984, pp. 297–336. From 1564 Pius IV insisted that candidates for degrees at Venice should take an oath of allegiance to the Catholic church. The only way to avoid this was to take the degree privately from the Count Palatine. See R. Palmer, *The Studio of Venice and its Graduates in the Sixteenth Century*, Padua, 1983, p. 35. See also J. Gascoigne, 'A reappraisal of the universities in the scientific revolution', in D. C. Lindberg and R. S. Westman, eds., *Reappraisals of the Scientific Revolution*, Cambridge University Press, 1990, pp. 207–60; p. 236.

[47] C. Schmitt and C. Webster, 'Harvey and M. A. Severino. A neglected medical relationship', *Bulletin of the History of Medicine*, 45 (1971), 49–75, 57. As in England, editions of standard textbooks appearing after the publication of *De motu cordis* in 1628 ignored Harvey and the circulation; for example, the tables of Casserius: *Iulii Casserii Placentini olim in Patavino*

almost absorbed into another and home-grown controversy about the passage of blood from one side of the heart to the other. This had been begun by the anatomist Leonardo Botali, a pupil of Falloppio in the previous century.[48] Botali claimed to have found a passageway from the right to the left auricle, much bigger and more obvious than the pores in the septum and providing an alternative route for blood from its site of generation, the liver, to the arteries. Vesling's pupil Cecilio Folli of Venice showed (probably in early 1640) something similar, called by historians a persisting foramen ovale,[49] which allowed him to make claims about Galen's knowledge of the motion of blood.[50] A controversy began within a few months, with the appearance of pamphlets for and against Folli's position[51] (see fig. 20). The dispute has not been studied in detail, but its significance for the story of Harvey's discovery is that if blood could be shown to have a ready passage from right to left through the foramen ovale, then there was no need of a route either through the lungs or through the pores of the septum. At least part of Harvey's scheme could be demolished if such a thing were accepted; and if Galen could be defended then the entire circulation was at risk.

Another figure to enter the story briefly is Andrea Argoli, who mentioned the circulation approvingly in a book on critical days published in Padua in 1639.[52] He was the public *mathematicus* in Padua, that is, the astronomer/astrologer, and his interest in critical days stems from prognostication by numbers. Circulation of the blood has no medical bearing on this for him, and he adopts it because it is consistent with the analogy he develops between the human body and the macrocosm. The world is round, its axis like an umbilicus.[53] Man is the little world, his head is heaven, his arms the wind. His belly is the mixture of qualities, his urinary tract the shores of the sea. His body, built upon bony stones, is covered with the hair that represents trees, and

---

*Gymnasio Anatomiae et Chirurgiae Professoris celeberrimi tabulae anatomicae LXXIIXX*, ed. D. Bucretius, Frankfurt, 1632. At p. 132 a pre-circulatory account of the vena cava is given.

[48] We met Botali in an earlier chapter; here it should be observed that although related the controversy over his work was distinct from the earlier disputes over the pores in the septum and the pulmonary transit.

[49] Schmitt and Webster, 'Harvey and M. A. Severino', 49–75.

[50] Bayon, 'William Harvey', part 2, p. 88.

[51] Part of the story is summarised in the anonymous tract *Sententia Apollinis super aliorum sententias de facile reperta via sanguinis confluentis a dextra in sinistram cordis regionem*, Venice, 1640.

[52] Andrea Argoli, *De diebus criticis et de aegrorum decumbitu*, Padua, 1639.

[53] Ibid., chap. 1: *De universo*. The macro–microcosm analogy was a natural one, used by Harvey himself. That the macrocosm was encircled by rotating spheres made it easier to believe in a microcosmic circulation, not only for Fludd, but for Sir Thomas Browne. See F. L. Huntley, 'Sir Thomas Browne, M.D., William Harvey and the metaphor of the circle', *Bulletin of the History of Medicine*, 25 (1951), 236–47 and in I. B. Cohen, ed., *Studies on William Harvey*, New York, 1981. The principal scholar to have used such arguments is of course Walter Pagel; they are not reduplicated in this book, the aims of which are rather different.

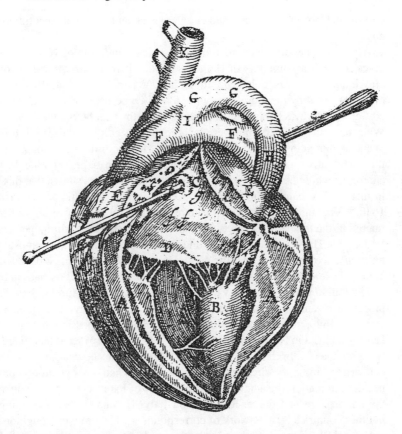

Fig. 20. Bartholin's illustration of the 'duct of Folli' demonstrated with a probe.

contains rivers in its veins. 'It is observed by those skilled in dissection' that the blood moves in a circle like the stars, which seem to irrigate the heavens with their light. In these terms Argoli accepts that the blood circulates; it seems rational, he says, for otherwise the blood would stagnate in the vessels and not follow the 'roundness' in Vitruvius' description of the body. He also notes that circulation is consistent with the weakening of the whole body from the local letting of blood. Argoli uses *vena* indifferently for either kind of blood vessel, as in classical or poetic usage, and the valves that he says the anatomists have seen are those of the aorta, preventing reflux to the heart. In short, Argoli's interest – it would be too grand to call it his natural philosophy – is in the correspondences between the heavens and earth, which enable the astronomer to make and explain his predictions. A macro-microcosmic analogy is a natural part of such correspondences, and circular shape and motion are central to that analogy.

Argoli returned to the circulation later, in his *Pandosion* of 1644, where he gives an accurate summary of Harvey's book.[54] Perhaps Argoli learned of the circulation from his colleague in Padua, Vesling, who had finally been convinced of it by meeting Harvey in 1637.[55] Or perhaps he had read the new edition of Harvey's book, published in Padua in the year before the *Pandosion*. Walaeus' letters to Bartholin were included in this edition, and Argoli follows Walaeus more closely than he does Harvey. He also follows, on the matter of the quantitative experiments for the circulation, an experimenting Paduan anatomist whom he calls J. G. Verden. It has recently been shown that this was in fact J. G. Virsung, who practised in Padua after taking his degree there in 1630.[56] Virsung knew many of the combatants in the Harvey affair, collected many of the books and tracts for and against the circulation, performed Walaean or Harveian experiments (and used their techniques in demonstrating his own discovery, the pancreatic duct). He died in 1643 and must be reckoned among those who would have liked to have seen a Harveian consensus in Italy.

The Italian who took Harvey most seriously was Marco Aurelio Severino,[57] professor of anatomy and surgery in Naples. He was converted to Harvey's views by 1640, perhaps by his students, or perhaps by a possible meeting with Harvey and Ent in Naples in 1636 and 1637. He certainly met at that time John Houghton, a Cambridge medical student who he later said was an influence in converting him to the circulation.[58] Severino, who had other heterodox beliefs besides circulation (he admired the philosophy of Paracelsus),[59] was uneasy in the atmosphere of Counter-Reformation Italy. He knew what was going on in other countries by a network of correspondents. He wrote to Houghton and to Samuel Remington, another Cambridge student he had met. He wrote to Ent, Bartholin and to Harvey himself. He was loud in praise of what he saw as Harvey's circle of fellow workers, prefixing to his account of the seal a list of the most distinguished men in the *scientia* of nature.[60] There was indeed an

---

[54]  W. Pagel and N. Poynter, 'Harvey's doctrine in Italy: Argoli (1644) and Bonaccorsi (1647) on the circulation of the blood', *Bulletin of the History of Medicine*, 34 (1960), 419–29; 420.

[55]  Pagel and Poynter, 'Harvey's doctrine in Italy', p. 419.

[56]  See A. Gamba and G. Ongaro, '"Anatomes Peritissimus": Johann Georg Wirsung's unknown experiments on the circulation of the blood', forthcoming in *Physis*, 1993 (second issue).

[57]  Severino has been discussed by Charles Schmitt and Charles Webster, 'Marco Aurelio Severino and his relationship to William Harvey: some preliminary considerations', in *Science, Medicine and Society. Essays to Honor Walter Pagel*, ed. A. G. Debus, 2 vols., London, 1972, vol. II, pp. 63–72; and Schmitt and Webster, 'Harvey and M. A. Severino'.

[58]  Schmitt and Webster, 'Harvey and M. A. Severino', p. 59.    [59]  Ibid., p. 61.

[60]  M. A. Severinus, *Phoca illustratus anatomicum Aytosxediasma*: it is the third item, separately paginated in M. A. Severinus, *Antiperipatias, hoc est adversus Aristoteleos de respiratione piscium diatriba*, Naples, 1659. The list of notables is: Harvey, Ent, Conring, Nathaniel Highmore, Thomas Bartholin, Rolfink, van Horn, Plemp, G. E. Scheffer, Petro Castello.

'international network of medical intelligence':[61] in the terms being used in this book, a pre-requisite for the formation of a consensus. But at home Severino had trouble with the Neapolitan Inquisition. He could not publish his views in Italy, and asked Houghton whether he thought they might be acceptable in England. In the event, he chose Germany for one of his most radical works, which we shall meet in a moment. First we should briefly note how the church had an obvious role in the production of knowledge. No open consensus on radical points could be reached in Italy. In Severino's case it was less perhaps the circulation that was objectionable (for Argoli's book passed the censors) than his inclination towards a Paracelsian sort of chemistry. What was wanted by the Inquisitors and the *Riformatori* of the universities (both groups put their names on the licence to print in the books of Argoli and Berigard) was that the book should contain nothing against the Catholic faith, against princes or against public behaviour. What worried them was thus explicitly just what worried the Calvinists in the United Provinces, namely that the status quo and even the stability of society would be threatened by the introduction of novelties. For Voet in Utrecht as for Berigard (whom we shall meet below) in Pisa, the answer was the same, to return to Aristotle. It was undoubtedly because Severino explicitly denied the truth of Aristotle's natural philosophy that he was unable to publish in Italy.[62] His efforts were in fact directed towards creating a new natural philosophy. He published largely on that section of it concerned with living things. By looking briefly at this we can compare Harvey's natural philosophy with another that dealt with novelties and see in what ways they agreed.

They agreed principally in seeing animals as objects worthy of study. Severino took the direction opposite to that of Parigiano, who had derided the imperfections and ugliness of the animals investigated by Harvey. Severino would almost certainly have known Parigiano's attack on Harvey, for *De motu cordis* was first published in Italy together with Parigiano's attack on it.[63] The two philosophies disagreed most, perhaps, in the attitude of their promulgators to Aristotle. Harvey said that he never cared to depart more than necessary from Aristotle, while Severino wanted to remove Aristotle as the Philosopher

---

[61] The phrase is Schmitt and Webster's 'Harvey and M. A. Severino', p. 649.

[62] Local control over the printing press had existed even in the fifteenth century, and papal jurisdiction was exercised even in pre-Reformation England and Scotland. After Luther civil unrest was feared and control became tighter; even Henry VIII had a list of prohibited books drawn up. Not all of this was effective, but by the early seventeenth century control was tighter. In some Catholic countries some books were banned on the grounds that they were translations made by Protestants, and in 1601 the Congregation of the Index banned the printed catalogues of the libraries of Oxford and Cambridge. See Paolo Rossi, 'Society, culture and the dissemination of learning', in *Science, Culture and Popular Belief*, ed. Stephen Pumphrey, Paolo Rossi and Maurice Slawinski, Manchester University Press, 1991, pp. 143–75.

[63] Schmitt and Webster, 'Harvey and M. A. Severino', p. 57.

and to replace him with Democritus. This is why he called his book *Zootomia Democritaea*.[64] He does not intend to make natural philosophy atomic;[65] rather, he sees Democritus as the true father of the knowledge of animals. This is the traditional 'Democritus Physicus', whose fellow citizens were said to have thought him mad when he retired into the woods to investigate the nature of animals, and who to philosophers in the late Renaissance seemed to avoid many of the vices of Aristotle. The woodcut on the title page of Severino's book shows Democritus Physicus seated in his sylvan hovel, surrounded by living animals and their dead remains (see fig. 21). At the front of the book, this 'Democritus the Philosopher' is made to address Hippocrates to symbolise the utility of the new natural philosophy to medicine. (Democritus explains, to Hippocrates' evident satisfaction, how he has discovered the cause of madness by dissecting animals.) Indeed, although Severino insists he is writing not medically but 'physically'[66] (philosophically), medicine occupies the biggest place in the tabulated scheme that he supplies to show the relationships of his new natural philosophy with other branches of the whole conspectus of human knowledge. Another part is the knowledge of morals, including civil law and piety, that is, the recognition of the providence of God. Even though Democritean, *zootomia* is also Christian. Severino believed that Paracelsus had developed a true method in seeing in the world, directly and without an apparatus of learning, what God had put there for man's use. He also has an almost Protestant feel for the perception of God through his creatures, and part of his task was to be to build on the work of the sixteenth-century 'natural historians'. With more than hints of Protestantism, Paracelsianism and with an explicit rejection of Aristotle, it is easy to see why the book was unpublishable in Italy.

Severino introduces the work in a very defensive way. The real objections he had met from others while preparing the work are related to those made against Harvey, and so are informative. The most serious seems to have been that 'zootomy' was not a proper art. Clearly something new (as Severino intended), it did not fit into the contemporary picture where all the arts were defined and defended, each with its proper methods and aims.[67] A related objection was that zootomy was useless to medicine and to itself, having frail

---

[64] M. Aurelius Severinus (Severino), *Zootomia Democritaea: idest, Anatome generalis totius animantium opificii*, Nuremberg, 1645.

[65] When he says (p. 36) that zootomy involves the cutting of animals down to their indivisible parts, which he indeed sometimes (p. 42) calls atoms, he does not mean the atoms of the Greeks, but the 'similar', homogeneous parts, which are incapable of being divided into anything else (p. 37) and so are *atomos*, 'uncuttable'. Other divisions of the body stop at the smallest functional unit.

[66] Severino, *Zootomia*, p. 8.

[67] Those who made the objection presented themselves as atomists, and Severino vigorously rejects the purposelessness of an atomic world.

Fig. 21. 'Democritus Physicus' sits in his sylvan retreat, investigating animals by dissection. Severino adopted this traditional image of Democritus in developing a non-Aristotelian natural philosophy. The figure approaching is probably Hippocrates, who traditionally found Democritus to be saner than the citizens he shunned.

rationality and being concerned with despicable subject-matter. We have seen that Harvey's doctrines attracted similar objections, for example from Primrose and Parigiano. Another objection was that the whole subject was the business of nature, not of man, and therefore unknowable to human faculties. All these objections are essentially variants of the first, and what lies behind them is this: a proper art has a purpose concerned with the benefit of man, like agriculture or navigation; because it is for the benefit of man, it uses faculties God gave man for the purpose; each art has some degree of nobility, and although less noble than the philosophies, does not entail the despicable; and the real arts have long been known. In his defence against these objections Severino had to bring forward some concrete purposes of zootomy. One of them was to repair the damage done to medicine by the virtual cessation of human dissection in Italy. But above all he has to insist that what he is doing is presenting a new programmatic natural philosophy: he is writing for the future,[68] the art will take long to mature,[69] and it will displace Aristotle and Plato.[70]

It is possible to make one or two suggestions about the sources of Severino's natural philosophy. First, his education had been somewhat unusual for a medical man, for he had taken a special interest in mathematics and juris-prudence (and had written a commentary on the *Pandect*). Moreover, one of his philosophy teachers had been Campanella, who taught him what he had himself taken from from Telesio. Both Campanella and Telesio were opposed to the natural philosophy of Aristotle and turned to other things, among them Platonism. We would not expect that the alternatives to Aristotle found by Telesio and Campanella would be the same as those selected by Severino at a later date, especially as Severino, unlike his teachers, has the Aristotle of the animal books so much in mind. But probably Severino shared with his teachers the view that a grave problem with school Aristotelianism is that it was insufficiently Christian. Clearly Severino wanted to outline a complete philosophy that was properly religious and took into account not only civil behaviour (where his legal studies would have been important) but also medicine and the study of animals.

In practice Severino is less radically anti-Aristotelian. He uses (without attribution) Aristotle's argument for the greater certainty of the knowledge derived from an immediate inspection of animals, compared with that of the distant stars.[71] What his new natural philosophy will discover, he says, is the uniform and the immutable in the small animals so often thought nameless,

---

68  Severino, *Zootomia*, p. 11.
69  Ibid., p. 7.
70  Ibid., p. 18.
71  Ibid., p. 6.

infinite in number and vague in form. In practice the 'uniform and the immutable' turn out to be more or less standard doctrines of the unity imposed by the soul, the faculties of which are exercised by the body, by the organic and similar parts and the four elements. He even appears to be pursuing an Aristotelian line of argument when he observes that organs are similar in animals with similar functions of the soul.[72] He sees a common plan for most animals, where wings in some may be analogous to legs in another. This is God's archetype,[73] and it is a 'law of nature' that animals have unity in diversity and diversity in unity.[74] He is somewhere between the Aristotelianism of Fabricius (whom he often quotes)[75] and a view that seems to combine a Plinian picture of a rich prolific nature with a Paracelsian view that nature herself contains demonstrations of how to think about Creation. While man is the image of God, yet the animals that God has given to man for his use also are parts of Creation and tell us more of the Creator. 'Nothing on earth is more gratifying to God than palpitating and respiring viscera', said Severino graphically if not very gracefully, and it followed that they should be treated with reverence.[76] Parigiano would have been scandalised, and would have cast Severino aside, into the Harveian camp.

Severino's book appeared some five years after he was converted to Harvey's doctrines, and it may be that Harvey's use of animals encouraged Severino to develop his new natural philosophy along these lines. If this is so, then in the story of the 'reception' of Harvey's doctrines, it is an unusual situation. But it seems more likely that Severino found Harvey's work attractive because it presented doctrines that did not agree with Aristotle on the heart and blood. He did not see Harvey as an Aristotelian and grouped him with others like Ent and Highmore, whose natural philosophy was far from being Aristotelian. Harvey therefore looked to Severino like a welcome anti-Aristotelian who seemed free of the apparatus of dialectical reasoning and the physical principles of form, matter, elements, qualities, final causality and so on. Harvey was in fact free of these things because his Aristotle was the author of the *History of Animals* and the *Parts of Animals*. Not being part of the natural philosophy curriculum of the schools, and being taught and explored in a radically new way by Fabricius and Harvey, this was almost an unAristotelian Aristotle. Severino, who draws upon Fabricius, and who had been taught by the anatomist Jasolino,[77] and who was aware of the medical tradition of dissection and vivisectional experiments, clearly felt that he like

---

[72] Ibid., p. 94.
[73] Ibid., p. 102.
[74] Ibid., p. 108.
[75] Severino, *Zootomia*, pp. 109, 119.
[76] Ibid., p. 22.
[77] Severino was nearly contemporary with Harvey and lived from 1588 to 1656.

Harvey was engaged in a zootomical and unAristotelian enterprise. If, as seems very likely, he had worked out his scheme before he read Harvey's book, then *De motu cordis* must have seemed like a triumphant vindication of his own method.

Another author of the period, publishing in Italy, whom we should consider is (in his Latin *persona*) Claudius Berigardus. He was actually a Frenchman, Claude Guillermet, seigneur de Beauregard. He had studied at Aix, spent some time in Paris and moved to Pisa in 1628, the year of *De motu cordis*. His mention of Harvey comes when he is discussing the soul in the course of a systematic commentary on the Aristotelian *libri naturales*. He has cast his discussion in the form of a dialogue and it is only one of the interlocutors who brings forward Harvey's name. The speaker does so only to show that the forceful systole of the heart and the pulse of the arteries are synchronous. The circulation is not mentioned. Berigard (as he came to be called in Italy) counts for little in our search for natural philosophies that opposed or welcomed Harvey's views. Nevertheless, his purposes illuminate some of the other philosophies that shared common (if disputable) ground with Harvey's, and they are therefore worth examining. In doing so we shall return to his views on the action of the heart.

Berigard taught philosophy in Pisa and Padua. He spent twelve years in Pisa having been attracted there, he said, by 'religion and philosophical certainty'.[78] This of course is just what the Inquisition sought to foster, especially in the two universities, Pisa and Padua, where Galileo had been making a name for himself as a dangerous neoteric. In 1632 Galileo published his dialogue on the two world systems, and at once Berigard published an attack on it, under the name Galilaeus Lynceus.[79] In this small way Berigard contributed to the church's attack on Galileo, who was condemned in the following year.

Berigard, the enemy of the neoterics, would probably not have agreed that the blood circulated and his silence on the topic indicates this. He was more concerned to refute new philosophies by re-asserting that of Aristotle. The Inquisition agreed, and Berigard's book on the *libri naturales* was published without problems. It was 'refereed' by a Paduan doctor of theology, who indicated that it contained 'nothing impure' to religion and that – significantly for our story – it freed peripatetic philosophy from error. The report by the Inquisitor-General of Padua, carefully defining the book by its incipit and explicit, repeats the formula that it contains nothing offensive to religion,

---

[78] Claudius Berigardus (Berigard), *Circulus Pisanus . . . de veteri et peripatetica philosophia in priores libros Phys. Arist.*, Utini, 1643.

[79] This was the *Dubitationes in Dialogum Galilei pro terrae immobilitate*, Florence, 1632. Galileo was then in Florence, where his dialogues were published.

princes and morals; Berigard's dedication to the local prince, Ferdinand II,
Duke of Etruria, reinforced the acceptability of the book. The other signatory
of the licence to print was another Inquisitor-General. Finally the licence to
print was endorsed by the Paduan *Riformatori*.

This entirely acceptable book is essentially a commentary on Aristotle's
works in nature.[80] Berigard had first made acquaintance with natural philosophy
in Paris, and spent his dozen years in Pisa teaching the 'eight books of physics'.
The commentary he now presents from Padua was distilled from his Pisan
experience, and its title, *Pisan Circles* (1643), refers to the disputations which
played such an important part in the teaching. 'I have seen no other shorter,
easier and safer method of manifesting truth than that which is presented in
this kind of disputation', he observed in the proem.[81] They had 'circular
disputations' too, every day in the *apotheca*,[82] in Padua, where the statutes
dwell on the importance of such *exercitationes* for the development of the
scholar.[83] At a number of points in this book we have seen that disputations
have been important in the generation and validation of knowledge, both
deliberately (as in the case of Regius and Descartes and, as we shall see,
Riolan) and accidentally (as when Harvey made a second discovery in
defending the first). In Berigard's case we see the Counter-Reformation church
defending its own: Berigard, of Paris, Pisa and Padua belonged to a Catholic
world where control of knowledge was tight. Some in the Pisan 'circles'
expounded Aristotle syllable by syllable, says Berigard; the circles were, to use
his words, 'safe' because the Platonic kind of dialogue used prevented radical
departures from the subject-matter, 'easy' with the familiarity of technique
which made people attentive and ready to use defensive arguments, and 'short'
because there was little repetition. Little chance here, then, of the riotous
disputations of Utrecht. Stability is to be given by safe discussion of the eight
books of physics, which were to be modified only when they were in conflict
with Christianity.[84] This is the 'middle way' of teaching natural philosophy,
following Zabarella's *De inventione aeterni motoris* ('already approved by
the Holy Office'). To retain the link to the Pisan disputations Berigard presents

---

[80] The volume as commonly found contains four separate paginations, each with its own title
page. Each contains a discussion of some of the physical works, beginning with the *Physics* and
ending, in the fourth pagination, with *De anima*.
[81] Berigard, *Circulus Pisanus*, p. 1.
[82] Literally, 'storehouse'.
[83] *Statuta almae universitatis D. artistarum et medicorum Patavini Gymnasii*, Venice, 1589,
p. 40v.
[84] Berigard, *Circulus Pisanus*, pp. 4–5. The most obvious errors of Aristotle in this respect for
Berigard are the eternity of matter and the (Averroistic) notion of a single active intellect given
to all men by the lowest sphere. Otherwise he follows Franciscus Piccolomineus and Thomas
Campanella in condemning other errors of Aristotle (which are also rather Averroistic) like
God not knowing the inferiors, souls being perishable forms, there being no reward or punish-
ment after death and that religion is a mere *inventio politica*.

his commentary in the form of a dialogue, between Aristaeus and Charilaus (Aristotle and the old (and mostly erroneous) philosophers). But each speaker quotes numbers referring to Aristotle's text, in just the same way as a medieval commentary quoted *lemmata* from the text, and the format is only superficially different from a thirteenth-century commentary. But of course there are modern sources for dealing with old disputes. In protecting Aristotle[85] from the neoterics who assert that there can be, after all, such a thing as a vacuum, Berigard describes a modern experiment. A closed cylinder, containing a little water, has been fitted with a piston. As the piston is drawn away from the closed end of the cylinder a space appears and effort is required to pull the piston.[86] (The device was a modified medical syringe, which Berigard calls a *sipho*.) The piston is the *manubrium* (see fig. 22). The neoterics, says Berigard, claim that a vacuum has formed (and that the piston tries to return to prevent it). Berigard claims that what is actually happening is that a very fine substance, whose nature it is to mix with other substances, is attracted through the glass and collects in the space above the water.

As we shall see below, the possibility of there being a vacuum was of course a serious threat to Aristotle's natural philosophy, and Berigard is obliged to spend much space in discussing it. Can things have weight in a vacuum? Some neoterics, says Berigard,[87] say that weight is the result of the motion of particles between the heavy body and the earth. But if there are particles, there is not a vacuum. Can there be motion, even of particles, through a vacuum? Berigard's answer is Aristotle's, that motion is by action of the medium, and therefore impossible in a vacuum. This leads him on to modern experiments designed to illuminate discussion of motion in general, mainly concerned with the relative speed of fall of balls of various materials and weight (Galileo is not mentioned by name). Berigard's final disproof of a vacuum is that God is everywhere, and that a vacuum that is truly empty would not contain God; it therefore cannot exist. He makes light of the whole business with a little play on words and passes on to consider time, the next topic in Aristotle's sequence of exposition.[88] It is clear then that Berigard is familiar with both the particulate (probably Cartesian) and the experimental (Galilean) forms of the new philosophy. As a product of dangerous neoterics, it is to be opposed with the use of Aristotle's natural philosophy, judiciously strengthened with the true doctrine of the church; that is to say, in circumstances very similar to

---

[85] Berigard, *Circulus Pisanus*, p. 57.
[86] This is what was in Glisson's mind when comparing the blood spurting from a punctured artery to water from a pump: the jet of liquid intensifies as the *manubrium*, or the heart, is in action. See chap. 10 below.
[87] Berigard, *Circulus Pisanus*, p. 61.
[88] Ibid., p. 62: 'Et haec de vacuo: ne vero in re inani inaniter teramurus tempus, temporis ipsius naturam potius investigemus.'

Fig. 22. The attraction of the vacuum: even the Aristotelian Berigard, presenting an essentially medieval commentary on Aristotle's physics, was obliged to employ a diagram of a piece of experimental apparatus to deny modern speculation that a vacuum might, after all, exist. C is a piston in a cylinder and over it is water, B. As the piston is drawn down by the weight, D (which in descending overcomes the 'attractive' force of the vacuum) a space appears at the top of the cylinder at A. Was this a true vacuum? Opinion was violently divided between the different groups of philosophers.

those in which natural philosophy was first invented. The medieval parallel is extended as Berigard in further volumes extends his coverage to more of the *libri naturales*.[89] His commentary on the last book of the *Physics* was published separately. Its proem supplies us with a most telling analogy. Coming to Padua, he says, he was determined to make it a seat of philosophy second to none. But there have been difficulties in his life as a philosopher, principally the perils of war. And just as he had hoped that truth would result from physical war, so he had set Aristotle to war with the ancient philosophers so that his truth would prevail. In other words, as the religious differences between the opposing sides

---

[89] C. Berigardus (Berigard), *Circulus Pisanus . . . de veteri & peripatetica philosophia in Aristotelis lib. de ortu et interitu*, Utini, 1643; C. Berigardus, *. . . in tres libros Aristotelis de anima*, Utini, 1643. All have separate title pages and pagination, but are bound together in the Cambridge University Library volume.

in the Thirty Years War were being settled by victory, so safe doctrine would be secured by education by means of the victory of Aristotle.[90]

Berigard's final collection of circles is that concerned with Aristotle's text on the soul, *De anima*. For Christian Aristotelians there could scarcely have been a more important text. It was not only the culmination of the physical works of Aristotle, where the physical principles were most abstracted from matter, but also the text that explained the process of intellection itself, and above all, it was the philosophical account of the vehicle of Christian immortality. It is indeed with the refinement of the combination of Greek philosophy and Christian belief that Berigard is concerned when he turns to the heart. His concern is to limit the number of 'faculties' said to be exercised by the soul. They were, after all, rather a Greek philosophical thing and Berigard is anxious to emphasise the direct action of God and the soul, rather in the way that we have noticed in Piccolomini and Parigiano. Because his purpose is to re-cement, in a new period of difficulty for the traditional Christian church, the interlocking of Aristotle and church doctrine, he returns to Aquinas and argues (it is Aristaeus speaking) that it was the Angelic Doctor himself who best followed the ancients and said that the soul moved the heart directly, *without* the aid of faculties.

Possibly Berigard saw the faculties as too Galenic and medical and therefore not appropriate to a true marriage of peripatetic philosophy and Christianity. Certainly his answer in both Christian, Aristotelian and in a sense surprisingly up to date. He argues that it is *the body* that is the 'faculty' of the soul. The soul shapes the heart and arteries and their actions follow accordingly. Thus in consonance can Charilaus invoke Aquinas[91] (in his *De motu cordis*) to say that motion comes directly from the soul, and Aristaeus can cite Zabarella to the effect that 'faculties' are merely states and conditions of substance that enable it to act.[92]

So it looks as though Berigard too wanted to get rid of the 'faculties' that were causing concern to the new philosophers. As we have seen, he was by no means ignorant of neoteric philosophy and seems to be reshaping the old alliance between the church and Aristotle to meet some such challenge. Even though he does not mention the circulation and probably did not approve of it (or this may simply be evidence of the fact noted above that the church had little interest in circulation as such) it is clear that Berigard knew of Harvey's contemporary reputation as an investigator of animals. He notes the insects and others that have to be examined with a microscope to reveal what it is in them

---

[90] C. Berigardus (Berigard), *Circulus Pisanus . . . de veteri & peripatetica philosophia in octavum librum physicorum Aristotelis*, Utini, 1643, p. 1.

[91] Berigard, *De anima*, p. 27.

[92] Berigard, *De anima*, p. 23.

that corresponds to a heart, and he dwells on those slightly larger animals that so disgusted Parigiano, in order to show that in all cases the hearts were fitted by their structure to cause movement of the blood without the intervention of any faculty.

In pursuit of the argument that the soul does not need a faculty to move the blood, Berigard adopts Harvey's argument that the active phase of the heart's motion is systole and that the arterial pulse is synchronous – that is, that a hand placed on the chest feels the systolic heart knocking on the wall of the thorax at the same time as the pulse is felt with the other hand at the wrist. He also adopts Harvey's experimental results about the blood springing from punctured arteries and heart (he credits the whole equally to Walaeus).

In short, Berigard's treatment of the forceful systole and pulse is but a very small part of his effort to make sure that a Counter-Reformation Aristotle could meet all demands made by neoteric philosophy. But following his efforts has added a little to our understanding of the pressures at work in the question of what was to be knowledge in one society.

### Letters and Liceti

We have seen that in the time between Fabricius and Berigard the intellectual atmosphere in Padua changed from a degree of liberality to one of considerable discipline. To control what was printed was to have some effect, however complex, on the formation of a consensus of shared knowledge. The complexity lies in the fact that the church had no special reason to disapprove of Harvey's doctrines as long as they were not associated with any other novelty that was seen as damaging. But often enough of course, Harvey's doctrines *were* taken up by people with other dangerous novelties, like Descartes and Severino. Nor was the Roman church the only authority to exert control over publishing. We have seen that the bishops were exercised about Helkiah Crooke's anatomy text in london, and when William Laud became archbishop the pressure for conformity became greater (we saw an example of this in the case of Alexander Read). The Archbishop of Canterbury tried to ensure that popish recusants or schismatical persons were not admitted to the College of Physicians,[93] and it is easy to see that such filtering of the entry to the college could have effects on the climate of opinion within the college.

This newly clear control of publication was matched by the increasing economic power of northern Europe. With this power came cultural resources, which grew outside the traditional centres of the Italian cities and Paris. While the Grand Tour remained culturally desirable, it was less necessary for ambitious medical students to travel to Italy. Increasingly, on medical

[93] Munk's Roll, vol. I, p. 121.

developments of the day, one could be kept up to date by writing letters (perhaps indeed to those on a Tour).

It is in this context that we should look at Fortunio Liceti, professor of the theory of medicine in Padua, the university where Berigard was a philosopher. We need to look at him partly because he was involved in this exchange of letters, some of them concerned with the circulation, and partly because his views were taken very seriously by those who were involved with the spread of Harvey's doctrines: his contemporary reputation was greater than we have supposed. In particular, what he had to say was given great weight by Harvey's major opponent, Riolan. For those who like Glisson (as we shall see below) were waiting for Riolan's descent into the arena in which the battle for and against the circulation was fought, Liceti's views were of significance.

Like Beverwyck in the United Provinces, Liceti wrote letters with more than half an eye on publication, linking his own name with those of the men whom he thought distinguished and who answered his letters. The mutual flattery in the letters when published did no one's reputation any harm and reflected on a grander scale what was happening informally. We have already seen that Mersenne, Gassendi and Descartes were exchanging letters on the circulation very soon after the publication of *De motu cordis*.

In 1641, as we have seen, Bartholin, apparently on a Tour, was in Montpellier, defending some form of the doctrine of circulation before Galenists. In 1643 he was in Padua, where Liceti wrote to him. Liceti wanted to know what Bartholin thought, not only of Harvey's doctrines but of his own, Liceti's, idea of the motion of the blood. (He also wrote to Vesling.) This scheme of Liceti's can be briefly put. He believed that the venous blood flowed from the right ventricle along the vena cava to nourish all the parts.[94] It then returned (he said) along the same route to the heart, where it received a further supply of spirits and heat. Such blood was necessary for the generation of semen, and was accordingly attracted to the testes from the heart again by way of the vena cava. A similar motion (continued Liceti) occurs in the aorta, which carries arterial blood to nourish the more spiritual parts, followed by a return to the heart and attraction to the testes.

What made Liceti describe this unusual – indeed unique – reciprocal flow of blood? The answer seems to be that it was his answer to a problem. It was now fifteen years since Harvey had published *De motu cordis*, but no general consent had been gained for or against the doctrine. It was however established as a major controversy, a major disputable novelty. Liceti in Padua could not ignore it any more (as we shall see) than could Riolan in Paris. A great teacher

---

[94] Fortunius Licetus (Liceti), *De tertio-quaesitis per epistolas clarorum virorum, medicinalia potissimum, et aliarum disciplinarum arcana postulantium, Responsa Fortunii Liceti Genuensis*, Utini, 1646, p. 135.

in a great centre of learning had above all to be able to settle difficulties of this sort: it was the meat or disputation and of the magisterial 'determination' that concluded it. And of course often enough the resolution of disputed questions was by 'distinction', showing by refinements of sense and usage of terms that what had looked opposed were merely complementary. To settle the circulation business was important to Liceti, and to adopt some form of circularity looked like resolving the question in this way. He denied Harvey's account of the circulation vigorously[95] but his own double reciprocation of blood seems designed to equate some form of a circulation with an Aristotelian position.

Keeping peripatetic philosophy whole was indeed important to him (he is explicit).[96] Keeping Aristotle alive was also the concern of the Holy Office, as we have seen in the case of our other Italians. The Inquisition had no particular concern with how the blood moved, and Liceti's book passed the censor. He was free to attempt to solve an important technical problem in his own field, which in his position he could be called on to solve, and he could re-generate peripatetic philosophy in his teaching. In pursuing the latter aim, he added to these letters an explanation of the apparent anomaly of Aristotle's description of three ventricles of the heart. It was of course a difficult problem for a peripatetic, as Liceti observes, but not at all for the medical men, who 'measure everything by sense' and simply deny Aristotle's account. For Liceti this medical habit of determining and judging by sense and autopsy is erroneously applied by medical men to things which are of their nature imperceptible.[97]

Thus the contrast between Liceti and Harvey is striking. Liceti was only a year older than Harvey and took his MD at Padua two years before Harvey took his. They must have shared a number of teachers and both found Paduan Aristotelianism attractive. If intellectual history was a question of influence, we might expect to see more similarities between Harvey and Liceti. But Liceti selected from what was available what suited him. He selected and taught the dialectical Aristotle in Pisa and Padua. He was Aristotelian in the same way as Cremonini, and when Cremonini died and Liceti did not get his chair, as he had hoped, he retired in disgust to Bologna. When he returned, it was to a chair of the theory of medicine.

Harvey in contrast had found the Aristotle of the animal books attractive. He was content with visual demonstration as a mode of knowledge, without demonstrative proof. While Liceti was a popular and prosperous teacher of logic and philosophy, Harvey was a practising physician and an anatomy

---

[95] See also Schmitt and Webster, 'Harvey and M. A. Severino', p. 57.
[96] Liceti, *De tertio-quaesitis*, p. 135.
[97] Ibid., p. 137.

demonstrator. His concern with anatomy was exactly what Liceti dismissed for its failure to grasp the imperceptible and what Cremonini thought pretentious for its claims to be knowledge.[98]

What do our Italians have in common? It is clear that they were working in a country where Aristotle was the approved philosopher. Just as the university authorities in the Low Countries linked academic and civil stability with their view of Aristotelian philosophy, so those who issued the *imprimatur* in Italy did not allow a departure from their own Aristotelian perspective. Neither view was static, for Heerebord's Aristotle, in becoming more and more Reformed, approached a Cartesian position, and Berigard's moved forwards to meet the problems of the new philosophy. It seems that novelty was less objectionable in the Protestant countries – Severino had to publish in Germany – but what was more important was whether novelty, such as the circulation, was tied to something that looked dangerous to the church. Argoli's mention of circulation was innocuous because it supported an accepted macro-microcosm analogy. Berigard's account of the action of the heart was acceptable because it supported the interpretation by Aquinas and others of an Aristotelianism that had since the time of Aquinas himself supported Christian doctrine. The defence of that Aristotelianism became newly urgent in the Counter-Reformation and Berigard's systematic treatment of the *libri naturales* is characteristic of the intellectual energy that went into that defence. The new ideas about bloodflow presented by Liceti and Parigiano show that anatomical novelty on its own presented few problems, if presented in an appropriate context. If the context was not appropriate the circulation was rejected, as when its Aristotelian context was found wanting by Parigiano and its Cartesian context was found objectionable to the theologians of the United Provinces.

### Harvey, Hofmann and the Germans

Opinions on medical controversies were spread not only by correspondence but by travel. We have seen the emergence of the medical 'Grand Tour' by students, in which the flow of medical intelligence was not always one way. Harvey's own travels with the Earl of Arundel certainly highlighted, wherever he went, the controversy of which he was at the centre.[99] There does not seem to have been a lot of background interest in Harvey's doctrines in the

---

[98] See also A. Wear, 'William Harvey and the "way of the anatomists"', *History of Science*, 21 (1983), 228.

[99] Thomas Howard, Earl of Arundel, was on an embassy to the Emperor Ferdinand to try to secure the claims of Charles I's nephew, Prince Charles Louis, as heir to Frederick of Bohemia. See W. Pagel and P. Rattansi, 'Harvey meets the "Hippocrates of Prague"', *Medical History*, 8 (1964), 78–84.

German-speaking countries, no doubt because of the devastation (which Harvey saw) of the Thirty Years war. The Frankfurt book fair seems to have come almost to a halt (Hofmann was unable to publish a book defending Galen).

Nevertheless, some individual reactions to Harvey's work are known to us. On his travels Harvey met Marcus Marci (also called 'the Hippocrates of Prague' and the 'Bohemian Plato') in April 1636. Marci was known to the English sectarians, like John Webster, as a welcome opponent of Aristotle. He had published on generation in the previous year, using optics to refute some Aristotelian notions. It is probable that Marci approved of the circulation, although as we might expect Harvey took no notice of Marci's opinions.[100] Much more important than Marci in terms of the assimilation of Harvey's doctrines was Johan Vesling, who was nominally professor of anatomy at Padua from 1632 to 1648[101] but who seems to have spent some of his time at Minden in northern Germany. It is likely that Harvey met him, in Germany, at the end of 1637. Vesling was well-disposed towards the nature of the pulse and the pulmonary transit as described by Harvey but hesitated to accept the circulation because he believed in the traditional difference between the venous and arterial blood and because he could not work out how the circulation took place in the developing chick. He was ultimately convinced by Harvey's letters (as he wrote to Liceti) and incorporated the circulation in his textbook, the *Syntagma anatomicum*, the authority of which was influential in achieving the Harveian consensus. In the Oxford of 1650, for example, the Principal of Hart Hall, Philip Stephens, prepared his students for a dissection by readings from the *Syntagma*.[102]

Harvey and Hofmann met in the previous year, 1636, a month after meeting Marci.[103] Caspar Hofmann was an important figure in the medical world of the mid-seventeenth century, and it is not surprising that Harvey tried to convince him of the circulation. As professor of medicine at Altdorf, Hofmann was in a position to broadcast his beliefs by means of lectures and theses published by his students. A great teacher was clearly important in forming a consensus within his university. Harvey had no such teaching position and might well have hoped that his doctrines would have been accepted and spread in this way by Hofmann.

---

[100] Ibid., p. 79. Marci was *praeses* for a disputation on the pulse by J. Forberger in 1642, which seems to have been in Harvey's favour. See W. Pagel, *William Harvey's Biological Ideas. Selected Aspects and Historical Background*, New York, 1967, p. 60.

[101] Sir Geoffrey Keynes, *The Life of William Harvey*, Oxford, 1966, p. 270.

[102] R. Frank, 'Science, medicine and the universities of early modern England: background and sources, part 2', *History of Science*, 11 (1973), 239–69; 243.

[103] E. V. Ferrario, F. N. L. Poynter and K. Franklin, 'William Harvey's debate with Caspar Hofmann on the circulation of the blood. New documentary evidence', *Journal of the History of Medicine*, 15 (1960), 7–21.

Harvey performed a demonstration of the circulation in Altdorf but Hofmann remained unconvinced and later wrote to Harvey to explain why. He seemed to see the force of Harvey's quantitative argument, for he said it was brief but weighty, 'Pauca verba, sed ponderosa!'[104] But the run of Hofmann's rhetoric is more clearly expressed in his dismissal of Harvey's quantitative argument as being merely arithmetical and not philosophical (we shall meet this again). The principal intellectual reason for Hofmann's rejection was that he, like others, could not see the purpose of circulation. It seemed to him that Harvey was attributing to nature the *stultitia*[105] of error, that is, perfecting the blood only to have it go to the body, degenerate and be obliged to return to the heart for a second perfecting. This meant for Hofmann that Harvey, in not finding final causes, was not a very good analytical philosopher. In other words, for Hofmann as for so many others a truth was what fitted with a whole system of natural philosophy, not only in terms of the account it gave of the parts of the world (such as the relationship of parts to causes) but also in terms of how knowledge was reached (analysis). Harvey naturally resented being called a poor philosopher. In replying he describes himself indeed as an analytical philosopher, practising an *analytica disciplina*. But for Harvey the business of such a person and of such a practice is to produce a description, *historia*, before giving causes or settling doubts. Harvey insisted in his reply that he had often praised nature's care, wisdom and industry, and that rather than saying nature has done something 'in vain', he had deliberately *avoided* discussing causes, especially final causes. Whether by choice or necessity, Harvey's natural philosophy now included the notion that reliable *historiae*, mostly experimentally produced, were of value on their own and constituted knowledge, without an intellectual link to a final cause. Harvey felt that the rhetoric of Hofmann's letter led Hofmann to ignore Harvey's experiments, no doubt those he had made in the demonstration at Altdorf.[106]

We can tell more about Hofmann's natural philosophy and the reasons why it led him to deny Harvey's doctrine by looking at what else he wrote. First, he had made a considerable investment of time and effort in work that would have

---

[104] This is taken from Hofmann's *Digressio, in circulationem sanguinis, nuper in Anglia natam*, printed by Riolan in his *Tractatus de motu sanguinis eiusque circulatione vera, ex doctrinae Hippocratis*, Paris, 1652, p. 357. Here it is announced as a chapter 48 of a manuscript on physiology and is in fact part of the *Apologia pro Galeno* that was to be published in 1668. It is very similar to Hofmann's letter to Harvey, the Latin and translation of which are included in Appendix 1 of G. Whitteridge, *William Harvey and the Circulation of the Blood*, London and New York, 1971.

[105] Hofmann's letter to Harvey and Harvey's reply also are given in a characteristic seventeenth-century collection of letters: G. Richter, *Epistolae selectiores III mantissae sex, IV spicilegium*, Nuremberg, 1642, pp. 806, 809.

[106] See the detailed survey in four parts by H. Bayon, 'William Harvey, physician and biologist: his precursors, opponents and successors', *Annals of Science*, 3 (1938), 59–118 and 435–56; 4 (1940), 65–106 and 328–9; 3 (1938), 91.

to be changed if he were to adopt the circulation.[107] His time and effort had gone into a complete scheme of body function which centred, as all such schemes did in the seventeenth century, on how ingested food became blood and nourished the parts. Before Harvey discovered the circulation, medical men and natural philosophers were arguing whether the blood was made in the liver (with Galen) or the heart (with Aristotle) and often enough the function of the spleen was involved in the discussion. Galenists said that it was the repository of black bile, produced during the generation of blood, but others preferred to think of it as analogous to the liver but producing arterial rather than venous blood. As early as 1613 Hofmann was defending in disputations his own idea of the function of the spleen[108] and later (1639) published it as a defence of Aristotle. Hofmann also came to make a special study of the heart and vessels as part of his scheme of body function: his work on the heart and blood, published in 1625,[109] concluded that the blood was made in the liver and perfected in the heart, which controlled the process *magistraliter*; the heart was the cause, the liver the *con*cause.[110] This is a strongly Aristotelian conclusion, and Hofmann added to it the Aristotelian doctrine that the nutritive faculty of the soul is located in the heart.[111] This was a part of Aristotelian philosophy from which he was unwilling to be moved by Harvey.

But as a good Aristotelian who adopted the methods but not necessarily the detailed conclusions of the Philosopher, Hofmann had become convinced of the pulmonary transit of blood. From an Aristotelian viewpoint he could see why nature had made two different kinds of vessel for the same purpose of carrying blood:[112] it was because there were two types of blood (which Aristotle did not suspect). In the same way he began to see the terms 'arterial vein' and 'venous artery' as anomalies[113] because they were simply an artery and a vein, carrying the two types of blood). He also concluded that the septum of the heart was not porous and this was an additional reason to think that

---

[107] In particular Hofmann had discussed the heart in his *Commentarii in Galeni De usu partium lib. xvii*, Frankfurt, 1625. Hofmann's defence of ancient opinion is the basis of his *Apologia pro Galeno*, not published until 1668 in Leiden. It seems to have been finished by 1640, when Plemp advised him that he thought it would be difficult to publish an account of the disturbed state of the German countries and the virtual disappearance of the Frankfurt book-fair. See Richter, *Epistolae selectiores*, p. 810.

[108] Hofmann, *Commentarii in Galeni*, p. 75.

[109] That is, the commentary on Galen's text on the use of the parts and the study of the chest.

[110] Hofmann, *Commentarii in Galeni*, p. 95.

[111] The theses defended by Hofmann's students at Altdorf show his Aristotelian orientation. They are concerned with the use of the brain (1617 and 1619), the use of the spleen (1619) and the generation of man (1629), all explicitly *secundum Aristotelem*.

[112] In 1627 he had Daniel Moegling defend a thesis in Altdorf 'cur natura fecerit duo vasa sanguiflua, venas and arterias'.

[113] Hofmann's student Tobias Pontanus defended in Altdorf in 1618 a thesis 'de usu arteriose et arteriae venosae'.

blood could pass from the arteries to the veins across the lungs.[114] This was consistent with the existence of the two different kinds of blood of Galenic theory, the arterial (on the respiratory left side of the body, from lungs to left ventricle and arteries) and the venous (on the nutritive side, from liver to right ventricle and veins). Hofmann would have also lost this distinction by following Harvey (who insisted that the blood was single).

In this commentary on Galen's book on the use of the parts of the body, Hofmann indeed saw that ancient knowledge was not invariably true – 'Facile enim dictu est, *Antiqua haec sunt*; at non facile scitu est, *Verane sunt*?' he said to the reader – 'For it is easy to say *These are ancient*, but not easy to know whether *they are true*.' His acceptance of the pulmonary transit of blood is repeated in his later textbook of 'institutes'[115] because it helped to explain the generation of the separate arterial blood.

In short Hofmann was a man who could not forget what he had written and read about ancient medicine. He was aware of modern thinking on procedure within natural philosophy and readily agreed that some modern anatomical novelties were acceptable. But at the time when he encountered Harvey and his doctrine, his own natural philosophy was inclined to solve controversies with an Aristotelian solution that embraced the Galenists as well as the moderns.

### Hermann Conring

Like Hofmann, Hermann Conring at Helmstadt was affected by the wars and felt himself fortunate to be in a university protected by God.[116] He took great advantage of the fact. With God's protection he published energetically on scores of things, promoting Protestantism and German nationalism, attacking the pope, commenting on Machiavelli's *The Prince*, on the French church, the Jews, Poles, Swedes,[117] Asians, Turks and Egyptians; he investigated academic and legal history and Roman antiquities. His views on politics and medicine were disseminated by his teaching and the defences he mounted for his students: he was *praeses* for at least 120 printed theses. He must be reckoned a major figure in the spread of Harvey's doctrine.

---

[114] It was even claimed afterwards that an experimenting pupil of Hofmann's, H. Dieterich, suggested to him in 1622 that the blood circulated. Hofmann replied that to believe that would make one a 'circulator', an itinerant quack. See Ferrario, Poynter and Franklin, 'Harvey's debate'. Critics of Harvey at home went so far as to suggest that Harvey had taken the idea from Hofmann.

[115] C. Hofmann, *Institutionum suarum medicarum epitome*, Paris, 1648, p. 85 (where the circulation is not accepted).

[116] H. Conring, *De sanguinis generatione, et motu naturali*, Leiden and Amsterdam, 1646, dedication, dated 1643.

[117] Conring was invited to Sweden by Queen Kristina in 1650, in the early part of which year Descartes had died there. Conring remained attached to the dukes of Brunswick and soon returned to Helmstadt.

Like Hofmann he tended towards an Aristotelian natural philosophy, and had no time for Cartesian mechanism. But the obvious difference between the two is the emphasis Conring put on experiment. He experimented with dogs in Helmstadt, defended eight theses based on the experiments, beginning in 1640, and subsequently – 1646 – published a book on the generation and motion of blood. It was probably by these experiments that Conring made up his mind that the blood circulated for, as we have seen, as a twenty-five year old student at Leiden with Svabe in 1631 he had been torn between the delights and dangers of novelty. Conring had become a teacher of natural philosophy at Helmstadt in the following year, and we may ask how an Aristotelian teacher of natural philosophy came to use medical experimentation.

Some clue to this aspect of Conring's natural philosophy is given by his *Introduction* to the subject, which appeared in 1638 and which includes the first book of his *Natural institutes*.[118] Perhaps the thirty-seven theses of which it consists were those sustained over the first six years of his Helmstadt teaching. They set out an Aristotelian natural philosophy in an aggressive and almost proselytising way, beginning with the early educational *paedeia* by which one – anyone – can tell if a *master* is teaching natural philosophy correctly. This is the 'universal logic' of Averroes and Conring identifies it with the analytical doctrine. This is not the analytic of Harvey and Hofmann, but the prior and posterior analytics of the early arts course. It is from Aristotle's remarks on induction in the *Posterior Analytics* that Conring seems willing to build a bridge to the medical experiments he was doing at the same time. Conring takes induction as a way of proving, or uncovering (they are not the means if *constructing* them) the principles of a *scientia*.[119] This induction, he says, is only to be gained by long personal experience, and as a result cannot be taught satisfactorily to the young. In particular, experience of complex natural bodies like animals is difficult to gain. Conring seems to be referring to the older students and particularly the teachers of medicine, the higher and progressive discipline in which *experientia* – no doubt including experiments – alone can enable a man to reach the highest rung.[120]

This emphasis on an experiential method in natural philosophy, although based on Aristotle, made it often necessary for Conring to depart from Aristotle's factual statements. Necessarily he had to do so when he agreed with Harvey in his *On the Generation and Natural Motion of Blood*, and when he says that the 'best disciples of Aristotle' do not always agree with the master, and never use his opinions in place of arguments, he may well have been

---

[118] H. Conring, *Introductio in naturalem philosophiam et naturalium institutionum Liber 1*, Helmstadt, 1638. It is unpaginated and the thesis numbers are quoted here.
[119] Conring, *Introductio*, theses 13 and 14.
[120] Ibid., theses 23 to 26.

thinking of Harvey.[121] But more than that, Conring's method meant that he sometimes had to change his mind about what he had himself previously announced. Like Hofmann, he had earlier been involved in the controversy over the spleen, but by now, unlike Hofmann, he was obliged (in view of Harvey's doctrine) to dismiss his earlier hypothesis as false.

Conring's commitment to Aristotle was greater than Harvey's, for he retained as the second leg of his method the kind of demonstration that he called apodictic, that is, from first principles. His confidence in experience and demonstration is as aggressive as his earlier claims about analysis and he demands of the readers the right to be judged by their own experience and apodictic demonstration. To do this the reader must be 'in council with his own senses' and must judge Conring according to the canons of 'our Aristotle'.[122] 'Our' Aristotle is not to Conring just the patron of philosophers, and not just an Aristotle interpreted in a particular way by Conring and his circle: it is an Aristotle who has true followers who are *germani*, not only 'children of the same father', and so 'true' (sons of Aristotle), but also 'German' in nationality. They are contrasted with the 'crowd of semi-learned', with an anxious and superstitious religion and observances. It may be that Conring is making an elitist philosophical sneer at the 'vulgar' crowd of school philosophers, but the pun on *germani* and their opposites does seem to suggest a religious division, perhaps prompted by the war.[123]

In reviewing the controversy Conring deals courteously with Plemp and Primrose,[124] but condemns Parigiano's attack as disgraceful and barbaric. Perhaps he thought Parigiano's barbarism was semi-learned, and that he was prejudiced by a superstitious religion; at all events he devotes this work to defending the truth from such attacks. In practice he gives almost as much space to Primrose as to Parigiano.

Conring largely agrees with Harvey on the physical details of circulation. He differs in insisting that heat (but not pain) is the cause of *attraction* in the body. The hottest part of the body is the heart, and so (he says) this attracts most strongly, the blood coming in from the vena cava from all parts, which are cooler.[125] So the forceful systole, ejecting blood from the heart, is a forced motion. He also differs from Harvey in attributing the contraction of the heart to a spirit becoming effervescent with the innate heat of the heart and activating the heart's fibres.[126] Conring believed that Harvey's account of

---

[121] See Conring, *De sanguinis generatione, ad lectorem.*

[122] All from Conring, *De sanguinis generatione, ad lectorem.*

[123] Ibid., *ad lectorem.*

[124] Ibid., p. 238.

[125] Ibid., p. 423.

[126] Ibid., p. 428. Elsewhere Conring was less enthusiastic about the role of spirits in the body and at least denied that they had a role in moving arterial blood in its circulation. See H. Conring,

forceful systole was not enough to explain the whole circulation of blood. To explain the matter he employed not only attraction, but the *horror vacui* that occurs in an 'inflexible siphon', that is, not a pump but the siphon of modern terminology in which the weight of fluid in the larger descending arm draws up and after it by apparent *horror vacui* the fluid in the shorter arm. Here the aorta and the vena cava act as the short and the long arms of the siphon. *Horror vacui* ensures continuity of blood in the vessels (but, adds Conring, it occurs only inside the body, not in the outside world). Gravity is an additional force to help the blood circulate.[127] Lastly, Conring needs to find a final cause for circulation. It is the distribution of heat and nourishment.

Conring's book of 1646 (on the generation and motion of blood) may be compared with that of Ecchard Leichner, published in the same year at Arnstadt (he was a new member of the Faculty at Erfurt).[128] Leichner was a teacher and like others of his kind he felt the need to pronounce upon the circulation controversy in order to bring stability into the business of the academic teaching of medicine. He writes[129] of the astonishment of the students at so great a novelty as circulation, and of the uncertainty caused by the refutations of Primrose and Parigiano. Leichner does not attempt to refute Harvey experimentally and his book centres on the dialectical treatment of five propositions which must, he argues, destroy Harvey's case when attacked. His argument is essentially the self-evident truth of traditional medicine. First, the traditional division between the three venters of the body and the separation of their faculties – nutritive, vital and animal – meant that the blood of the heart, the seat of the vital faculty, can have nothing to do with nutrition (the office of venous blood from the liver). Leichner was unwilling to disturb the traditional faculties, on which he had invested time and energy in an earlier thesis on generation. The faculty of attraction is not questioned. Ultimately all actions, he asserted – in the company of traditionalists like Froidmont – come from the soul, which supplies the agent faculty for every action. Thus an action like the pulse must arise from an internal principle and this must (as Galen said) reside in the arteries. Leichner had studied theology for two years before coming to medicine and no doubt, like Froidmont, this encouraged him to insist on the traditional powers of the soul – we have seen that the basically Greek

---

*De calido innato sive igne animali liber unus*, Helmstadt, 1647, p. 169. The question of animal heat was another controversy of the first half of the seventeenth century, no doubt because so central to the challenged traditional notions of soul and faculty. Conring examines the opinions of Fernel, Sennert, Cremonini and others. Hofmann also published on innate heat.

[127] Conring, *De sanguinis generatione*, pp. 432, 437.

[128] E. Leichner, *De motu sanguinis exercitatio anti-Harveiana*, Arnstadt, 1646. Arnstadt is here *Arnstadiae*, more usually Latinised as *Arnstadium*.

[129] Leichner, *De motu sanguinis*, sig. Ai.

notions of the physical activities of the soul in the body had become a formal part of orthodox theology. Like Liceti, Leichner believed that the soul was extended throughout the body.[130]

Yet Leichner's resolution or 'determination' of the circulation controversy was not simply a restatement of a previous consensus. Like others he felt the need to evaluate the validity of the opposing arguments. Leichner concluded that nature when disturbed made efforts, *conatus*, to defend herself in the body.[131] In the arteries this resulted in a motion from the centre to the periphery; in the veins however a disturbance like pain or a ligature resulted in an unnatural motion *towards* the centre. Thus can Leichner explain the swelling on the wrong side of the ligature and other phenomena which indicate a centripetal flow. Moreover, Leichner allows that venous blood may reach the arteries through anastomoses, by attraction, heat and even systolic motions. In other words Leichner admits the possibility of a circulation, but primarily as an unnatural event prompted by – indeed the creation of – experimental techniques. In such a circulation, Leichner emphasised, the returning venous blood does *not* become arterial and is not redistributed in the body: Galenic physiology is untouched.[132]

Leichner's teacher of medicine had been Werner Rolfink at Jena in the years 1636–8. Either Leichner disagreed with his teacher on the topic of the circulation, or Rolfink himself had not yet accepted it. But we know that Rolfink had accepted the circulation by 1653 at the latest.[133] Although older than Leichner, Rolfink was broader and more flexible in his interests. He had extended his education from Wittenberg to Holland, France, England and Italy and took his MD in Padua in 1625 (Leichner does not seem to have left Germany). He taught a wide range of subjects – botany, anatomy and chemistry, of which he held the first chair in Germany[134] – and wrote with much erudition (Leichner concentrated on logic, the soul and his battles with the neoterics).

In his travels Rolfink must have seen a great deal of the Thirty Years War, which had not long been over when he came to write on the heart and blood, back home in Jena. It is understandable that (like Paul Slegel of Hamburg, whom we shall meet in a moment as a pupil of Riolan), Rolfink readily slipped into a military metaphor. Doctors are generals, waging war on disease in the

---

[130] Leichner (1612–90) began his theology at Strasburg in 1631, studied medicine under Rolfink from 1636–8 and took his MD at Jena in 1643. He arrived in Erfurt shortly before publishing against Harvey (*NBU*).

[131] Leichner, *De motu sanguinis*, sig. Fi.

[132] Leichner seems to have resisted all manner of neoterics, and was opposed as much to Descartes and van Helmont as to Harvey. He continued a controversy over the circulation with H. Kipping down to the 1670s (*NBU*).

[133] See Bayon, 'William Harvey', 4, 90, 91.

[134] *NBU*. Rolfink lived from 1599 to 1673.

battlefield of the body;[135] the body is the camp of the enemy and its defences and layout must be known for strategic purposes. The anatomy that is seen in this somewhat aggressive way as the basis of medicine centres here on the structure and action of the heart. While Slegel was immersed in the battle surrounding Riolan's entry into the circulation controversy, for Rolfink, four or five years later – at the end of the period covered in this book – the battle for the circulation has been won. His book is not an argument for or defence of the circulation, but a triumph for the consensus that has been achieved. He has read very widely in the contemporary controversy and equally widely among the ancients, fragments of whose wisdom adorn his text. The heart, he declares, is the sun of the microcosm, the navigator of its ship, the driver of its horses, the king in its city, the general of its army, the demiurge – nay, the very God – of the body.[136] Inevitably in such a learned and elegant piece Harvey's message has become obscured. The septum of the heart is said to be porous.[137] Alimentary blood is generated in the heart. So are vital spirits.[138] If this represents consensus then as elsewhere it was a consensus that the circulation existed, not that Harvey's account of it was right.

In short, we have seen in this section that the universities were important places for the propagation or the suppression of novelty. At Jena, Altdorf, Helmstadt and Erfurt German-speaking teachers (and here we could include Vesling in Padua) had to make up their minds on the circulation controversy. Their pupils expected guidance on such a revolutionary doctrine, and it was a teacher's business to reach a determination. Having once decided, the teacher could promote his views in lectures, experiments and above all by a series of disputations in which his pupils defended linked theses, which might eventually be published in book form.[139] These were powerful forces in the formation of a consensus.

### France

The French reaction to Harvey's doctrines seems to have been rather hostile during the period of Harvey's lifetime. In Montpellier, where Bartholin was on his Grand Tour in 1641, they were as Galenist as in Paris, and consequently

---

[135] Guernerus Rolfincius (Rolfink), *Dissertatio de corde, ex veterum et recentiorum, propriisque observationibus concinnata, et ad circulationem accommodata*, Jena, 1654, introductory material. This book followed something similar on the liver in the previous year and in which he also accepted the circulation. See Bayon, part 2, p. 90.

[136] Rolfink, *Dissertatio de corde*, pp. 1–4. Rolfink allows from the mechanists the image of the heart as a spring – *aequipendium* – of a clock.

[137] Ibid., p. 74.

[138] Ibid., p. 47.

[139] Probably if the theses were individually printed, as seems to have happened most often in the German-speaking countries, the teacher did not follow them up with a book.

(according to Bartholin) neglected modern experiments and denied the existence of the lacteals and the circulation of the blood.[140] When Bartholin spoke up for the lacteals and the circulation, the Montpelliards invoked the authority of Padua. But Bartholin discomfited them by producing a copy of the *Syntagma* of the Paduan teacher Vesling, of which they had not heard and which had determined in favour of the circulation. Johann Vesling (from Westphalia) had decided in Harvey's favour in 1637, either on meeting Harvey[141] or by an exchange of letters with him (as we saw above). Here we meet the limits of the process of the spread of opinions by correspondence and travel. The network was imperfect. The Montpellier doctors remained Galenist at least up to 1650 – when Riverius was called on to resign for teaching the circulation[142] – despite the visits of Bartholin and his news of Vesling, and of Pecquet (in 1648) who made experiments relating to the circulation. In 1651 Riolan himself (see below) accused the Montpellier doctors of being old-fashioned in not understanding the (Riolanesque) circulation. Jean Martet, a surgeon in Montpellier, did accept circulation (and the lacteals), but his knowledge of it was no greater than that of his fellows, for he attributed it to Walaeus, without mentioning Harvey. At another boundary of the network, the Italian Bartholomeo Bonaccorsi thought Harvey was a Pisan and had discovered the lacteals;[143] it is Argoli who is mentioned in relation to the circulation. As we have seen, it was at yet another boundary of the network that the English student in Padua, Colston, had to write to London to discover whether Harvey had answered the Venetian Parigiano.

When Descartes set up his own network by sending out review copies of the *Discourse on Method* in 1637, he sent one, as we have seen, to his countryman Libert Froidmont, who refused to accept that the soul did not play its traditional role in the action of the heart. A dozen years later Froidmont was a doctor of theology, a Regius Professor in Louvain, a Dean of a collegiate church and the *praeses* of a seminary. It is not surprising that he maintained traditional and by now Counter-Reformation views on the soul and its actions. Indeed, he

---

[140] W. R. Lefanu, 'Jean Martet a French follower of Harvey', in *Science, Medicine and History. Essays on the Evolution of Scientific Thought and Medical Practice Written in Honour of Charles Singer*, ed. E. Ashworth Underwood, 2 vols., Oxford University Press, 1953, vol. II, pp. 33–40.

[141] J. D. Alsop, 'A footnote on the circulation of the blood. Joseph Colston and Harvey's discovery of 1642', *Journal of the History of Medicine*, 36 (1981), 331–4; W. Pagel and F. N. L. Poynter, 'Harvey's doctrine in Italy: Argoli (1644) and Bonaccorsi (1647) on the circulation of the blood', *Bulletin of the History of Medicine*, 34 (1960), 419–29 and G. Whitteridge, *William Harvey and the Circulation of the Blood*, London and New York, 1971, p. 157.

[142] Lefanu, 'Jean Martet', p. 35.

[143] Pagel and Poynter, 'Harvey's doctrine', p. 427.

made a point of writing about how the soul should be seen from a religious viewpoint,[144] one of the several textbooks he wrote for his students. They included a meteorology and it is clear that his development of the partly Aristotelian learned tradition (including the immobility of the earth) had an educational role.[145] In writing a Christian *De anima* Froidmont sought the support of a German elector of the Holy Roman Emperor, now a bastion of Catholicism where all around Froidmont saw the slide into 'heresy', Protestantism. In this book Froidmont again deals with the motion of the heart and blood, but is not now so dismissive as he had been before, either because he now sees that the Harveian circulation is not so mechanical as Descartes had made it, or (more clearly) because by 1649 the controversy was moving to a settlement in Harvey's favour. He saw that experiments (like the swelling of a vein on the wrong side of a ligature) were crucial and must be accepted or dismissed as a whole; he recognised too that Harvey's quantitative argument was prominent in the controversy. His hesitations were two. Firstly he questioned whether the blood could pass through the invisibly small channels or pores of the flesh. If, as the doctors say, it sweats across the flesh, how does the blood move in the veins? Secondly – and this unresolved doubt serves to indicate his position – he asks how the venous blood can be perfected into vital spirits and arterial blood in so fast a passage as set out in Harvey's quantitative argument. Clearly Counter-Reformation philosophy had no objection to the circulation as such, as long as it did not intrude upon its teaching on the soul, which Froidmont is here helping to establish.[146]

### Harvey and Riolan

Harvey's major opponent was Jean Riolan the younger. He made no sizeable attack on Harvey until 1649, over twenty years after Harvey had published *De motu cordis*. In replying, Harvey made the only extended defence of his doctrine, having remained aloof from lesser controversies. Not to have secured Riolan's agreement must have seemed like a major obstacle in the spread of his scheme. The two had met, not on Harvey's travels, but in England when Riolan attended the exiled Maria de' Medici. Riolan's rejection of the circulation was, at that period and like that of his pupil Primrose, that it was of no medical

---

[144] L. Fromondus (Froidmont), *Philosophiae Christianae de anima libri quatuor*, Louvain, 1649.
[145] The learned tradition for him included the medievals but not the modern followers of Bodin or Campanella. Froidmont, *Philosophiae Christianae*, address to the reader.
[146] On Froidmont see also E. Gilson, *Etudes sur le rôle de la Pensée Médiévale dans la Formation du Système Cartesien*, Paris, 1961, pp. 84, 127. Froidmont (1587–1653) defended the astronomy of Ptolemy against the Protestant minister Philippe Laensberg and so was clearly aligned among the enemies of Galileo. He wrote a tract on the immobility of the earth, and another on the anatomy of man, which does not seem to be available in Great Britain. See *NBU*.

use.[147] There are a number of things other than the technical problems of Harvey's description of the motion of the heart and blood that concurred in making Riolan act as he did. He was, firstly, a prestigious figure, physician to Louis XIII and the Queen Mother, and was obliged to defend the dignity of his own doctrines. He was Dean of the Medical Faculty of Paris, and as Harvey himself observed, had a duty to see that Galenic medicine was kept in good repair. We have seen already that the rational physicians of the universities were above all learned, where learning was both a means of attracting patients and a criterion in the suppression of unlicensed practice. From the establishment of medicine in the universities in the Middle Ages, no other form of learning was acceptable, at least in the theory of medicine, than Galenism (including its Arabic form). To be a learned physician was to be a Galenist, unless one were to tread the dangerous road of medical heresy.

Riolan had no heretical instincts. He was a classically minded humanist.[148] He was an enemy of the new chemistry. He wanted Paris to be the new Cos and Montpellier the new Cnidus. He saw himself within a tradition of excellence and sought to defend it. Defence of Galen in Paris went back to Jacobus Sylvius, and Riolan's defence shared Sylvius' nationalistic and religious sensitivities. As with Sylvius the old, true learning was that of religion – now Counter-Reformation Christianity – as well as that of medicine. When he understood Pecquet to say that the chyle must flow from the lacteals to the subclavian vein and thence to the heart, he was horrified: 'The true religion of our forefathers is destroyed, and the true old medicine, confirmed by the experience of centuries, is being corrupted' by the new figment, *novis figmentis opinionem.*[149] Of course, for Riolan the inheritance that we – he said – have received from the ancients should pass on to our descendants is progressive. That we should make additions to that inheritance is Riolan's jus- tification – made even some years before – for a quarter of a century's work at anatomising.[150] Progress, he thought, was based on the slow penetration of the complex mysteries of nature, or, in his words, that Jove did not choose to reveal all things at once. Outside anatomy, Riolan was much taken by the progress in astronomy and geography. He was not, therefore, simply a reactionary figure; and sometime in the 1640s he was obliged to admit that the fact of circulation was part of the progress of medicine. By early 1645 he had decided on a minimalist form of circulation, admitting the return of blood to the heart in

[147] See Nikolaus Mani, 'Jean Riolan II and medical research', *Bulletin of the History of Medicine*, 42 (1968), 121–44; 132.

[148] Ibid., p. 124.

[149] Ibid., p. 134.

[150] J. Riolan, *Anthropographia et osteologia. Omnia recognita, triplo auctiora, et emendatiora ex propriis, ac novis cogitationibus, et observationibus*, Paris, 1626, the address to the reader.

the major veins only, denying the pulmonary transit and that all the blood circulated.

To set out his position in February 1645 Riolan arranged a quodlibet disputation in which he was moderator and Jean Maurin,[151] a bachelor in Paris, was the *defendens*.[152] It proceeded in a formal manner, *juxta ritu Scholae*,[153] and Maurin's presence was of little significance, for Riolan was in tight control. The thesis was his: 'Given the circular motion of blood in the heart, must the Galenic mode of healing be changed?' It was his old worry, that a circulation would disturb traditional medicine. He had finally decided that a much-reduced circulation could be consistent with Galenic practice, and the disputation was to do a number of things for him. It was to show that he had made a Determination on the major medical controversy of the day. It was to show that he, rather than Harvey, was the originator of the true doctrine of circulation. It was to point the way to a whole new medicine, a major progressive step. It was to leave the medical tradition of practice unchanged. It was to provide Riolan with the apparent backing of the Paris Faculty to promote his new scheme and to attack Harvey.

Riolan defended his thesis first by an appeal to parallels between macro- and microcosmic circles. The simple circle of his scheme involved only the major portions of the aorta and vena cava, joined by anastomoses. This meant that almost all of Galenic medicine was preserved: the traditional generation of blood in the liver and its perfection in the heart remained, and with it the distinction between the two types of blood. The humours and residues produced during the generation of blood were still localised and were not threatened with mixture and confusion by the circulating blood. The old notion of assimilation of the tissues by the blood was preserved by the slow and non-circular motion of blood in the smaller branches of the great vessels. The same thing preserved also the localness of disease; while the traditional cause of fevers (unnatural heat reaching the heart) was untouched. Therapy was likewise unaffected. Bloodletting from the small and non-circulatory veins retained its ancient rationale. Purging, frictions, baths, sinapisms, percussions and gymnastics all remained valid techniques.

Riolan also recorded the objections that were made during the course of the disputation. Some of the objections were against the whole notion of circulation, and we see Riolan in almost an anomalous position of defending circulation in general against unbelievers. It is thus strange to see Riolan defending himself against the objection (number 24) that the vivisectional

---

[151] J. Riolan, *Opuscula anatomica nova. Quae nunc primum in lucem prodeunt. Instauratio magna physicae et medicinae per novam doctrinam de motu circulatorio sanguinis in corde*, London, 1649, p. 4.
[152] The disputation was written up by Riolan and published in the *Opuscula anatomica nova*.
[153] *Opuscula*, address to the reader.

experiments used to support circulation were entirely fallacious in being unnatural, the animal cruelly tortured and the heart as the principle of life drawing to itself in this emergency its blood and spirits. Precisely the same objection had been made to Harvey, and Riolan, who hated vivisections,[154] himself had used it.[155] Riolan here made a rather tame defence of other people's experiments by quoting Lucretius on the value of the senses. Riolan the late and reluctant circulator was also in a slightly odd position in replying to the first objection, which was simply that circulation was new, false, absurd and dangerous, attractive only to the vulgar taste for what is new and useless. His reply was that medicine could be added to, just as Galen had added to his inheritance, *patrimonium*, from Hippocrates.[156] That is, Riolan thought of his circulation as the latest addition to the learned tradition. To be sure, the fact of circulation was discovered by Harvey, said Riolan in response to the second objection, and must be believed because the blood that leaves the heart must be replaced. This is the barest hint that Riolan had been convinced of the circulation either by Harvey's quantitative argument (which Riolan severely modified) or by the action of the valves.

A number of other objections were raised about circulation which Riolan could reply to by arguing that they were real objections to Harvey's scheme but not to his own. These objections were, then, made by people like himself before he had come up with his own idea about circulation, and they suggest that it was in working out the difficulties presented to traditional medicine by circulation that Riolan devised his scheme. A major objection of this sort was that if the circulation were total, including the vena porta and the small vessels, there would be mixture, a confusion of the humours and a general dispersion of impurities through the body. Riolan's reply was that in his new circulation neither the vena porta nor the small vessels were circulatory; and that the heart was the location of purgation and the circulating blood carried impurities to the sites of evacuation (objections 4, 5, 10 and 27).

Another objection (the eleventh) claimed that if there was a circulation at all, it must be total, for all blood must pass through the heart, where alone it becomes red. The objector was arguing for an Aristotelian and central role for the heart as the organ of sanguification, for he had observed that some animals had white or green livers (and so no blood-making function). This was irrelevant to Riolan the medical Galenist, for whom animals were of interest only inasfar as they related to man. He dismissed the objection by observing that he was concerned only with terrestrial animals that resembled man. It is quite clear that he had been equally unimpressed with Harvey's use of animals

---

154 Mani, 'Jean Riolan II', p. 127.
155 *Opuscula*, p. 16 (response to objection 24).
156 *Opuscula*, p. 4.

and the Aristotelian research programme. Indeed his first task in defending the
thesis was to destroy the scheme of Harvey and 'bring back circulation to
medical use',[157] an echo of Primrose (and of Riolan's *Encheiridium*: see below)
which also reminds us that the medical Galenists' background, their natural
philosophy, was very different from Harvey's. As Riolan says, 'However,
since I am a medical man, I freely dissent from Aristotle.'[158]

Having devised his own scheme of circulation, Riolan began to incorporate
it in his publications. Three years after the disputation in Paris, Riolan
published a textbook on pathological anatomy, the *Encheiridium* of 1648.[159]
He intends, he warns the reader, to ignore the advice of the Spaniard Huartes,
who said that no one should write after the age of fifty: Riolan was three years
short of seventy, and clearly felt he had a lot to offer the learned world,
including his new circulation. His plan in this book is to give an account of
normal anatomy and then to show how this differed in cases of disease. His
knowledge was derived not only from his own long experience but from the
Parisian learned tradition.

If anyone should find in [my] pathology several things against the common opinion, I
shall reply that I know them ex Patradosi, or the secret tradition of the old medical men
of the School of Paris . . . I follow the example of Hippocrates, who urged medical
men to teach the art to sons of teachers, without payment, and to have them as
brothers.[160]

This, from the new Hippocrates of the modern Cos, is essentially the same call
for medical 'faith' as that made by the Parisian Sylvius. For Riolan it is the faith
that the entrant to medicine undertook to keep when swearing the Hippocratic
*Oath*, a faith that stretched all the way back to Hippocrates himself. The
learned tradition of which Riolan thought himself part was continued, he
thought, in the person of his teacher, the Regius Professor Simon Pietreius,
and perhaps also his own father.[161] Riolan dwells on the Christian piety of
Pietreius, to which he assimilates his own twenty years of teaching
Hippocratically and without fee. The natural philosophy which underlies
Riolan's notion of 'anatomy' is the Galenic-medical rather than Harvey's
Aristotelian-philosophical, and it has a clear religious dimension. It is
consistent with this first that he conceives of anatomy as being practised for
knowledge of God as *artifex* (in place of Galen's demiurgic Nature) and
second that it is practised for medical utility. Riolan's general precepts for

---

[157] *Opuscula*, address to the reader.
[158] *Opuscula*, address to the reader.
[159] J. Riolan, *Encheiridium anatomicum et pathologicum. In quo ex naturali constitutione
partium, recessus a naturali statu demonstratur, ad usum theatri anatomici adornatur*, Leiden,
1649 (first edn, Paris, 1648).
[160] Riolan, *Encheiridium*, address to the reader.
[161] On p. 2 of the *Encheiridium* he attributes part of his anatomical method to his father.

anatomy[162] dwell on the pre-existing knowledge that Aristotle had said was fundamental to every *doctrina*, and which for Riolan was the learned tradition. This human, medical and pathological anatomy for Riolan, centring on the dead body, excluded Action as a category. It is clear that this is one of the reasons why he 'misunderstood' Harvey, whose doctrine of the motion of heart and blood was not concerned with medical usefulness, did not demonstrate divine providence, did not belong to a learned tradition or to a complete system and included an indissoluble link between structure and action.

Riolan deals with the heart in book 3, chapter 8. There is nothing to suggest that this was an especially important chapter for him. His overall purpose is to locate the seats of diseases, and the anatomical part of this exercise does not involve a formal distinction between structure and function, so he has no reason to be particularly concerned with the action of the heart. In a book of over 470 pages, only four are devoted to the heart. Although consistent with his pathological purposes, it is yet surprising that he treats so cursorily an entirely new and unique system of circulation. Yes, he says, there is a circulation, discovered by Harvey and sharply defended by Walaeus.[163] But for Riolan, as in the disputation, so here too the blood does not go across the lungs, but through the cardiac septum; the circulation is limited to the major vessels, the vena cava and aorta, and does not occur in the smaller branches; and again Riolan claims that this avoids confusion of the humours and avoids the destruction of the old medicine. Also closer to the old medicine was Riolan's assertion that the heart admits only one or two drops of blood at every beat and that the total mass of blood that circulated does so only twice or three times a day.

The major vehicle for Riolan's attack on Harvey was the *Opuscula anatomica nova* of the following year, 1649.[164] Although it is a collection of different pieces, they are co-ordinated to promote Riolan's new scheme. He is aggressively on the attack. This is to be a 'Great Instauration' not only of medicine, but of natural philosophy – *physica* – itself. The means of achieving this is to be the new theory of circulation, 'never before published'. It includes a critical evaluation of most of the recent textbooks on anatomy, those of du Laurens, Bauhin, Spiegel, Bartholin and Vesling as authorities alternative to his own. The collection begins with the Paris thesis of 1645 and its objections and their solutions. To this Riolan has now added a large section on new proofs of the New Circulation.[165] From this it is tolerably clear what events led to Riolan's position when writing. We have seen that his first reaction to the idea

---

[162] Riolan, *Encheiridium*, p. 55 (the beginning of book 2).
[163] Ibid., p. 220.
[164] *Opuscula*, address to the reader.
[165] *Opuscula*, p. 20. The running head calls this section a *Liber de circulatione sanguinis*.

of circulation, expressed when he met Harvey, was that circulation had no medical purpose. He would surely have agreed with other critics of Harvey, like his pupil Primrose, in holding that circulation destroyed the ancient system of medicine. But the controversy refused to go away. Riolan had seen many distinguished people adopt some form of circulation. He is painfully aware that the doctrine of circulation 'excites great rumours and tumults in the universities':[166] it is painful that the old medicine is in danger and that a division is appearing within it. Riolan had to take it seriously, and above all, he had to be able, as a famous teacher, to pronounce upon it. He began to work out how some form of circulation could occur without damage to medicine as he knew it. We can guess from his new proofs of 1649 that the major stumbling block to accepting Harvey's account of a total circulation was that it seemed to make nonsense of the extremely important therapeutic device of bloodletting.

It was a difficult problem. Galen had set up an anatomically specific account of phlebotomy, in which anatomy told him which veins should be opened to lessen the quantity of blood in a particular part of the body. It was an essential part of his whole scheme of an anatomically rational medicine. But according to Harvey, not only did blood circulate through *all* the parts, but the blood moved in the veins in the direction opposite to that of Galen's account. Moreover, the traditional medicine of Riolan's day had an elaborate rationale that distinguished revulsive from derivative bleeding, techniques with opposite effects. Riolan put a great deal of effort into solving the problem. By 1645 he was ready to reply to objections that circulation destroyed phlebotomy by giving further details of his New Circulation: the blood, he said, was forcibly ejected from the heart and so moved comparatively quickly in the arteries (although much slower than in Harvey's scheme). In the vena cava, on the other hand, the blood moved slowly and so, claimed Riolan, there was always twice as much of it as in the arteries. This slow-moving mass of blood acted as a reservoir from which blood could be drawn off against its natural direction of flow, in other words, as in traditional phlebotomy.

By 1649, in the *Opuscula*, Riolan had put an immense amount of intellectual labour into elaborating this scheme, as indicated by the size of the chapter (20) dealing with it. Riolan works systematically in this chapter, dealing with diseases of the body from head to toe, explaining in each case how bloodletting should be done in light of the circulation, or what is often the same thing, explaining how traditional practice was still effective. It is part of his doctrine that the traditional bloodletting veins are the smaller branches of the great vessels and so non-circulatory, and therefore function in a traditional way.

Let us look more closely at the question of why Riolan came to accept any form of circulation, each of which would be a radical departure from Galenic

[166] *Opuscula*, p. 22.

theory; and how he adjusted his philosophy to accommodate it. There is the possibility that he was convinced by Harvey's account of the amount of blood leaving the heart, or of the action of the valves. There is a strong possibility that during his years of silence, the topic had become immovably established as a 'controversy' (as it had for Liceti) which could not be solved simply by denial of one side of the question. And many public teachers – the English, French, Germans and *Belgae*, said Riolan – had adopted the doctrine; and 'that which many nations agree has the highest authority'. The consensus of learned men was a powerful force in compelling Riolan to agree, and a stout weapon of defence for his thesis once adopted. Riolan provides the reader with his view of the whole controversy in his brief critical history of it.[167] This enables us to form an idea of the consensus he faced, and provides another hint about his adoption of circulation. He deals sympathetically with Primrose, no doubt because he shared his views on the medical uselessness of Harvey's circulation. Parigiano comes in for a great deal of direct criticism by Riolan ('wordy, obscure, futile and arrogant in his usual way') and indirect, in Riolan's quotations from Primrose, Conring and Sinibaldi (all of whom agreed that Parigiano made up in arrogance what he lacked in understanding). Riolan gives a brief account of the views of Conring, Plemp, Ent, Leichner, Regius, Hogelande and Liceti (on whom Riolan dwells longer).[168] It is, he says, precisely because of the disagreements among these authors about the nature of circulation that others have rejected it entirely. This, he maintains, is a false reason for rejection. After all, he says, they all agree on the basic fact of circulation, that blood returns to the heart. Now, for Riolan, this is precisely that on which all nations agree and which has thus the highest authority (a principle that Riolan takes from Cicero). The names he has just mentioned are the 'public teachers' whose consensus he previously mentioned as being important for him. And Riolan's circulation is just what is common to all these opinions, that is, a simple return of blood to the heart, without a questioning of the septal pores, without the unresolved controversy of pulmonary transit, without the common dislocation of Harvey's two theses about the forceful-systole-and-pulse and the arteries-to-veins-transit of blood and without the idiosyncrasies of every individual's scheme as modified in the course of its adoption from its sources. Riolan's intellectual affiliations are clear from his sympathetic treatment of Primrose's subtleties, and his huge but not unfriendly critique of Liceti's 'subtle and ingenious' scheme.[169] He has no sympathy at all for 'The new Dutch mechanical philosophy' – 'Mechanicam illam

---

[167] Ibid., p. 20.
[168] He also attacks an anonymous tract in French which denied the circulation. This was that of Gassendi, as Riolan later discovered.
[169] *Opuscula*, p. 49.

Philosophicam Hollandicam' – that is, the adventures of Descartes, Regius and Hogelande in Holland. Riolan has technical arguments, partly quantitative, partly criticism of the vaporisation of blood, against these three, but is not touched at all by the exciting possibilities that Hogelande for example found in the radically new mechanism. In contrast, Riolan's much-heralded Great Instauration of *physica* is related closely to Liceti's attempt to defend Aristotelian natural philosophy. Riolan's Instauration in fact is little more than a peripatetic account of how the body works, and does not extend beyond the microcosm.[170] It is simply an account of how the body works that comes within the field of the natural philosophers, the medical details being omitted. He shows, with Liceti, how to see the three Aristotelian ventricles in the heart (but ultimately disagrees with Liceti) and is at particular pains to show that his own theory of circulation strengthens Aristotle's doctrine of the supremacy of the heart. Moreover, the long and slow growth of the learned tradition, the investment made by Galen of the Hippocratic patrimony and the final Great Instauration of *physica* and medicine, based on the new Riolanesque New Circulation, is given further foundations by showing that Hippocrates and Aristotle were not after all ignorant of the circulation, which was 'delineated' or 'adumbrated' in *Places in Man, On Disease* and *De generatione animalium*.[171] In modifying his view of the learned tradition in this way, Riolan is not only seeking to strengthen his case to the reader by constructing a history for it, but is also accommodating his view of his own place in that tradition to the fact of the circulation: he is changing his philosophy.

In short, the image of Riolan that appears from these texts is that of a man who was compelled to accept some form of circulation, who spent much energy and ingenuity in reconciling it with what he had previously believed, and who finally tried to turn compromise to his advantage by making great claims for his New Circulation. The same ingenuity and compromise is found in his account of how his theory of circulation could even explain Harvey's. In violent respiration, announces Riolan,[172] the rapidly beating heart takes into itself more blood that can be sent through the pores of the septum. The excess blood could only flow into the lungs (because of the direction of the valves) and from there to the left ventricle. In other words, for Riolan, the pulmonary transit, although 'violent' and 'unnatural' nevertheless occurred regularly in

---

[170] Ibid., p. 111.

[171] Riolan's claim that the circulation was known in antiquity was part of a strategy to strengthen the image of ancient medicine in disturbing times. It was also adopted by his countryman N. Papin of Blois who like Riolan selected as a prime candidate for proof of his opinion the well-known Hippocratic phrase 'Confluxio una, conspiratio una, consentientia omnia' (which was also being used by those who sought ancient authority for the doctrine of sympathy). N. Papin, *Cordis diastole adversus Harveianum innovationem defensa*, Alençon, 1652. Papin had also published against Descartes.

[172] *Opuscula*, p. 37.

heavy exercise, whether the body was ill or healthy. Like Leichner, who had made a related argument (and Riolan had read it) Riolan seems to have wanted to make the best of two worlds.

## Harvey's reply

Harvey's reply to Riolan's *Opuscula* and *Encheiridium* was made within a few months of their appearance and took the form of two 'exercises', published in the same year in Cambridge and in Rotterdam.[173] The purpose of this was almost certainly to provide further material and to prompt further discussion on the academic communities of both places. There were academic links between the two in addition to a common religious climate, and Dutch textbooks of philosophy were popular in Cambridge in the middle of the century.[174] Disputations had been held in both places for a number of years on the topic of circulation. Riolan's views of 1649 caused a stir in Cambridge[175] and it was clear from the words of both Harvey[176] and Riolan[177] that the doctrine of the circulation was still disputed.

It was Harvey's last attempt to promote his doctrine. He was now over seventy, and had seen his doctrine often accepted, but as often mutilated or dismembered. He had failed to convince important figures like Hofmann. He was surrounded by neoterics, of whom he did not approve and with whom he did not agree. He had seen his doctrine transmogrified into a particulate and mechanical scheme in Holland, and it was not clear yet whether the Dutch universities would settle for a mechanical circulation or for Aristotle. By now too the bulk of his book on the generation of animals was written, and he had been giving thought to the proper means of acquiring knowledge in natural philosophy, a philosophy which for him had led to the discovery of the circulation but which he now found he had to defend against very different natural philosophies. Finally, he found that Riolan presented his form of the doctrine of circulation in a book on pathological anatomy, a topic on which Harvey hoped to publish his own very different ideas. Harvey's *exercitationes*[178] were not so much an attempt to convince Riolan but to supply material for others who, prompted to interest themselves in the matter by the engagement of the prestigious Riolan in it, might dispute or write on the matter.

---

[173] W. Harvey, *Exercitatio anatomica de circulatione sanguinis*, Cambridge, 1649.
[174] For example, those of Adriaan Heereborde and Bartholomaeus Keckermann.
[175] See the section on Glisson below.
[176] The opening of the second exercise to Riolan, viz., 'Exercitatio . . . in qua multae contra Circuitum Sanguinis Objectiones refelluntur.'
[177] See the section above on Riolan.
[178] Harvey, *De circulatione sanguinis*, 1649.

Harvey's exercises do two things. Firstly, Harvey presents a survey of the course of the 'controversy'[179] and gives an account of how Riolan had come to occupy his present position. By showing (to the readership of the published exercise) that Riolan had other than philosophical grounds for writing what he did, Harvey can weaken his opponent's philosophical conclusions. Secondly, Harvey presents new experimental evidence. Both of these are of some importance.

When Harvey wrote the first exercise[180] he had received from Riolan only a copy of the *Encheiridium*. His reply is appropriate to the pathological context of Riolan's objection and Harvey argues largely from Riolan's words and his own earlier work. He shows that Riolan had listened to the authoritative voice of many nations and had accepted what was common to all the variants of the doctrine of circulation, namely the simple return of blood to the heart. Riolan, says Harvey 'speaks expediently', seeking to please many and annoy none. Harvey also sees that this expediency includes preserving old medicine and what Riolan had already published. For Harvey another part of Riolan's expediency or compromise was to use the authors in place of dissection, which for Harvey included the vivisectional techniques which as we have seen Riolan could not face. Clearly, Harvey thinks that the audience for the letters will see the force of the argument from experiment over that from authority. Having given thought to philosophical method in his work for *De generatione animalium*, Harvey can cogently apply it to experiments designed to confirm the circulation: all *scientia* comes from the sense, *cogitio*.[181] Dissection of healthy bodies leads to *recta physiologia* and to *philosophia*.[182]

When Harvey completed his 'exercise' to Riolan with a formally polite tribute to Riolan and the *Encheiridium*, and put his name at its foot, it was probably as much as he intended to write. But before he sent it to the printer he was able to read Riolan's *Opuscula*, with its major claims about the nature of the circulation and medicine, and Riolan's projected instauration of *physica*. So Harvey took up his pen again and wrote another exercise to Riolan. It is very different from the first and appropriate to the nature of Riolan's attack. Harvey has been prompted to make a major reply. In contrast to the first exercise, which was largely a verbal argument, the second exercise is heavily experimental, with new experiments[183] and Harvey's deliberations about

---

[179] This word is used here for the contemporary *controversia* because it retains the notion of the vigour of the dispute.

[180] W. Harvey, *The Works of William Harvey*, trans. R. Willis (1847), reprinted with an introduction by A. C. Guyton, University of Pennsylvania Press, 1989, p. 89.

[181] Harvey, *De circulatione sanguinis*, p. 2.

[182] Ibid., p. 3.

[183] p. 43: 'Exercitatio altera ad Johannem Riolanum in quae multae contra Circuitum Sanguinis Objectiones refelluntur.'

procedure in natural philosophy. It is a reply to Riolan's new *physica* and his non-experimental method. It is a major statement, not only to Riolan, but also, like the first *exercitatio*, to the readership, the potential converts, the people involved in the continuing controversy, who will be stimulated into discussion by this exchange between the originator of the doctrine and his noble opponent. Harvey's technique is to show how the controversy has arisen by the maltreatment of his original doctrine. It follows that if the faults of those who changed or rejected it are overcome – and identifying them and providing fresh evidence to overcome them is the point of this exercise – then the controversy will die down and a consensus will be established. For these reasons Harvey begins the second exercise with an account of the progress of the controversy. Every day, he says, indeed almost every hour, he hears something good or ill of the circulation. Some agree with his experimental observations (he says) while others think he has not yet proved it. Others have rejected the circulation because they cannot disagree with their teachers (perhaps he is thinking of the pupils of Hofmann) and some because they think it indecorous or even criminal to abandon ancient doctrines.[184] (He perhaps has Primrose in mind, and his words certainly capture the way in which such people – indeed, Riolan himself – spoke of a medical 'faith' to be preserved.) Others have scoffed at his use of frogs and snakes (he must mean Parigiano).[185] Harvey pretends a disdain for such critics, but his language is bitter. He justifies his use of small animals by the story of Heraclitus at the stove,[186] inviting in his hesitant friends because here too were gods. Harvey also uses the Christian, and probably Protestant view that God is often more visible in His lesser works. His target is surely Riolan himself when Harvey speaks of those who cannot adopt Harvey's doctrine because on its basis they cannot explain medical appearances.

In reviewing the controversy Harvey takes the opportunity to use evidence derived from earlier experiments and experiences. He refers to a post-mortem of the second decade of the century and to experiments performed before the king sometime between 1633 and 1636. The water pump to which he compared the heart came to be widely known in the late 1630s and early 1640s. He seems to rely to some extent on Walaeus' experiments, published in 1641. Lastly, he refers to his own 'medical observations' and other medical works which were lost from the palace of Whitehall during the occupation by the Parliamentarians. He may not therefore have been aware of their loss when writing, and it has been argued that this second essay dates from 1641–6, largely while Harvey was in Oxford.[187] No doubt Harvey had made notes in defence of the

---

[184] See the Willis trans. (1847), p. 123.
[185] Harvey, *De circulatione sanguinis*, p. 45.    [186] Harvey, *Works*, p. 110.
[187] See Robert G. Frank, *Harvey and the Oxford Physiologists. A Study of Scientific Ideas*, University of California Press, 1980, p. 33. I am grateful to Don Bates for drawing this problem of dating to my attention.

circulation as the controversy progressed; but what gave shape to them now and was the cause of Harvey publishing them was Riolan's *Opuscula*.

A frequent, and more telling argument, made against Harvey by Primrose, Parigiano and Leichner, was that vivisectional experiments were unnatural and produced unnatural results. Harvey cannot entirely meet the objection and contents himself with a limited reply: in the case of the divided vein, while it may appear unnatural that so much blood emerges from the distal side of the cut, nature, however much disturbed, does not close the proximal side. It was, in other words, from the proximal side, closest to the centre, that in traditional medicine a natural flow would have occurred. The argument about the unnaturalness of experiments was a difficult question to answer, being a piece of rhetoric useful for Harvey's opponents but with no arguable alternative except Harvey's implicit assumption that the vessels of the body continue to act as so much plumbing, pipes and pumps, 'sive natura turbatur sive non'.[188]

These then are reasons why his doctrines have been misunderstood. The rest of the exercise is taken up with Harvey's new experimental evidence, which we must take as the way he saw to remove misunderstandings and settle the controversy. As a means of persuasion the experimental method had its advantages and drawbacks. Its great advantage was the conviction that attached to knowledge gained by the senses. Harvey's answer to those who cannot leave the doctrines of the ancients is a form of this: nothing is older and with greater authority than nature, known to us by sense perception. The drawback of sense perception (to step for a moment out of Harvey's exercise) was that it did not lead infallibly to the discovery of final causes, to the system on which the world was built, or to a whole and satisfactory natural philosophy. For Harvey demonstration was that a thing was, not a showing of its final cause (as he had said to Hofmann). This principle of 'limited explanation' is how he here answers those who cannot accept circulation because they cannot see its final cause and ask *cui bono*?[189] Harvey's reply is *Prius in confesso esse debet, Quod sit, ante quam Propter quid, inquirendum*,[190] 'We should first ask of a fact that it is, before an account of what it is.'[191] This is Harvey's use of the medieval distinction between *quia* and *propter quid*, the equivalent of the more fashionable *to oti* and *to dioti*. Harvey illustrates his meaning by comparing the experimental method to astronomy, where causes, the *propter quid*, can only be investigated by reasoning from appearance. Actually to see the causes

[188] Harvey, *De circulatione sanguinis*, p. 73.
[189] Harvey, *Works*, p. 122. Franklin's trans., p. 156 (W. Harvey, *The Circulation of the Blood and other Writings*, trans. Kenneth J. Franklin, London/New York (Everyman's Library) 1963.
[190] Harvey, *De circulatione sanguinis*, p. 76.
[191] My translation of Harvey, *De circulatione sanguinis*, p. 76; cf. Willis' edn, p. 122. Franklin's translation (p. 157) does not here do justice to Harvey's Latin.

directly, the observer would have to be placed above the moon.[192] Harvey's meaning is clear: with animals and experiments we can actually see the causes, directly and without the need of reason; 'of those things that are subject to sense, nothing else can make a more certain demonstration, producing faith, than sense and autopsy'.[193] Harvey here has much rhetoric on the certainty and conviction carried by sense perception. How would you convince a person who has never drunk it of the sweetness of wine? Where reasoning follows such observation, says Harvey, it should be like geometry, which is a *demonstratio* from sensibles about sensibles.[194]

So Harvey, in bringing forward first Galen's experiment of inserting a reed into a cut artery, is calling on an approved technique of experimental demonstration, from sense and experience, not from first principles. Galen claimed to have done it and to have shown that where the rigid reed replaced the walls of the artery, the pulse (believed to travel along the arterial wall) could not be felt below the reed. Harvey had previously thought this experiment impossible to perform, but now reports that he found the pulse was present, but lessened, below the tube he had inserted into the artery. His explanation was that the tube formed a partial obstruction in the artery, which consequently swelled above it. This absorbed some of the 'shock' of the pulse but did not destroy it. It was after all, says Harvey, a difficult experiment, producing some confusion and a great deal of blood. The graphic language continues in Harvey's preferred experiment, which was to use the senses to see the transmission of the pulse and blood in an exposed artery. Blood from a punctured carotid artery, he reports, emerges with such force that it rebounds from the hand for four or five feet. This graphic image is an excellent rhetorical device. No one can doubt that Harvey, like Walaeus, was drenched in the animal's blood as he tried to fend it off with his hand. The same was happening in other places in Europe: real experiments were happening in a period when natural philosophy, partly on a medical model, was becoming experimental, and were reported in a powerful form of words.[195]

But when Harvey here takes the opportunity to reply to Descartes and those who had assumed that the blood boiled up in some way with the heat of the heart, Harvey could not give an experimental demonstration. Instead, he sets up a thesis for further discussion, asking for objections. It is based on his notion of the innate heat of the blood, the common instrument of all actions: it is the

---

[192]  Harvey, *De circulatione sanguinis*, p. 81.

[193]  Franklin (p. 159) here does not follow Harvey's punctuation and his translation differs somewhat from that given here; Harvey, *De circulatione sanguinis*, p. 81.

[194]  Harvey, *De circulatione sanguinis*, pp. 97, 98. Franklin's 'non-sensibles' is gratuitous. On Harvey's message here see also Wear, 'William Harvey'.

[195]  Another new experiment of Harvey is the demonstration that air forced into veins is stopped by the valves. Much of the remaining material in the letter is a reworking of old arguments.

blood that gives heat *to* the heart, through the coronary vessels, and so enables it to pulsate.[196]

## Slegel

There was extensive interest in the republic of letters, where the idea that the blood circulated was still a live controversy, at the entry of the great anatomist Riolan into the dispute. The English reaction, in the person of Francis Glisson, is discussed below, and here we can conveniently add to the German picture by following the controversy through the eyes of Paul Slegel, in Hamburg. Writing in 1649, Slegel records his delight at first receiving the works in which Riolan accepted the circulation.[197] He at once concluded that such was the authority of Riolan and so great the fame of the Paris school, the model for most of Europe, that at least the controversy would be settled and the truth of Harvey's doctrines would be accepted.

But his delight changed to dismay as he read what Riolan had written. He had enormous respect for Riolan and had indeed sought him out as a teacher in the early 1630s.[198] Yet here was Riolan setting out a scheme of circulation that differed extensively from Harvey's, in which Slegel was an early believer. He was at once plunged into a labyrinth of doubt. Had he been deceived by his first reading of Harvey? Had he been teaching an error for twenty years? His mind went back to his early medical education, when the controversy over *De motu cordis* was just beginning. In rethinking the arguments that had been brought forward on both sides as the controversy developed, Slegel began to rebuild his damaged confidence in Harvey's doctrine. His Ariadne's thread out his labyrinth (he says) was to commit to paper some defence of Harvey (which he sent to Riolan). In doing so, he provides us with a contemporary's view of the controversy, which we can briefly examine.

At its first appearance (begins Slegel) there was hardly anyone who did not consider Harvey's doctrine absurd.[199] It was, indeed, just the ridiculous kind of notion that ought to be kept out of the schools.[200] But, inevitably, there were those who were attracted by novelty, and these added their voice to the few who gave the idea serious attention. But (continues Slegel) more obvious were the enemies of the doctrine: Parigiano, whom Slegel dismisses as inept, and Primrose, learned and acute in his arguments. These two articulated the private

---

[196] Harvey, *De circulatione sanguinis*, p. 114.
[197] P. Slegel, *De sanguinis motu commentatio, in qua praecipue in Joh. Riolani V.C. sententiam inquiritur*, Hamburg, 1650, the preface to Schelhammer and Gartz.
[198] After that he spent time at Altdorf and also with Rolfink at Wittenberg and Jena. See Harvey, *Circulation of the blood*, trans. Franklin, p. 191.
[199] Slegel, *Commentatio*, preface (unpaginated).
[200] Ibid., p. 1.

doubts and suspicions of the majority – 'the chorus' – of medical men, who saw, Slegel records, that their practice of medicine would be disturbed by such a novelty. The majority remained silent, not choosing to air their suspicions or to embrace novelty publicly. Slegel's medical Grand Tour took him to Belgium, England, France, Italy and Germany. He took the opportunity to discuss the matter with learned medical men and anatomists and claimed to have found no one who could develop a good argument against circulation, even in public anatomies.

While in Montpellier in 1634, he persuaded 'the learned Scot', Alexander Fraser, to propose a thesis favouring the circulation. Slegel claims that in the disputation (under the auspices of Lazarus Riverius) Fraser was successful; or at least insofar as he won over some and was bitterly opposed by others. Slegel, who says that he fell in love with Harvey's doctrine while it was still in its swaddling clothes,[201] *incunabula*, conceived a missionary zeal in propagating it, largely by 'punctilious disputation' in a number of different places. Slegel was one of the few people to understand and not to modify Harvey's doctrine. He was convinced, as Harvey had hoped, by the quantitative argument, the direction of the venous valves and the experiments with ligatures.[202] He had no argument of his own to prefer to Harvey's, and took up Harvey's case energetically. He often uses a military metaphor to add colour to his description of the controversy: it was a battle, to be won by bringing opposing soldiers 'into our camp'.

One old soldier he could not win over was another of his teachers, Hofmann.[203] This saddened Slegel, because he knew that it was Hofmann's teaching on the structure and function of the heart and lungs (including, that is, Hofmann's acceptance of the pulmonary transit of blood) that had prepared his own mind for its grasp of the circulation. Slegel knew of Harvey's attempt to convince Hofmann, and indeed often made the same attempt when he stayed with Hofmann for some four months two years later, in 1638. Slegel recognised that Hofmann's refusal to accept the circulation had a great deal to do with the amount of his own previous theoretical work, which it would seriously damage; moreover, Hofmann was now old, and Slegel saw his resistance to undertaking new work. Nevertheless, Slegel claims that towards the end of his life Hofmann began to think better of the idea, and re-read works in its favour (he wrote to Slegel to say so). Slegel was sure that Hofmann would have come 'into our camp' had he lived longer.

As a missionary for the new idea, Slegel found converts particularly admirable. He accordingly saw Plemp, the man who changed his mind, as

---

[201] Ibid., p. 5.
[202] Ibid., p. 13.
[203] Ibid., preface and p. 10.

something of a hero. 'Verissima vox, et Philosopho digna!' cried Slegel in reply to Plemp's assertion that Galen can be defeated by sense observation.[204] In contrast to Plemp, Riolan was for Slegel the man who changed his mind not quite far enough. Everywhere he praises Riolan's standing as the prince, the coryphaeus, even the phoenix of anatomists, clearly the biggest prize of all, could he be brought into the right camp. Slegel is also full of admiration for his former teacher's intellectual honesty in changing his mind so far.[205] Like Harvey, he sees that Riolan had professional and institutional reasons for staying close to Galenism, for it seemed ordained that the doctors of the Paris school should defend Galen.[206] It was then for Slegel so much the greater pity that Riolan could not be persuaded of the Harveian circulation. Like Harvey, he is not addressing Riolan, nor (he says) the extremely erudite, but those who have not accepted the whole, Harveian, doctrine of circulation, and those who are disturbed by it.[207] Such people still seem to have been in the majority.[208] Just as the common people laugh at the idea that the earth moves round the sun, says Slegel,[209] so do the people among whom his missionary work lay deride the circulation.

Slegel's commentary on Riolan illustrates many of the constraints acting on the spread of novelty in medical knowledge. What was new did not have ancient authority, and most people laughed at it. Those who promoted novelty had therefore to derive authority from elsewhere. Often they chose sensory observation of nature. This had the advantage that support for it could be found in Aristotle and Galen, and so the neoterics could claim ancient authority of method, while discounting some ancient factual accounts of the world. Nature, too, could be quoted as authority (as Harvey did). But sense observation was uncomfortably close to empiricism, with all the attendant professional dangers, as we saw in an earlier chapter. Slegel saw the danger clearly, and refused to open the 'window of calumny' to the despisers of the ancients, such as the 'empirics and the pseudo-chemists'.[210] This is his reason for continuing to revere the ancients. This takes two particular forms. Firstly, he reports extensively on Riolan's claim that the ancients 'had not been ignorant of' or had 'adumbrated' the circulation without explicitly discussing it. This allowed the learned physician to maintain his claim to status and monopoly on the basis of ancient learning. Secondly, and again like Riolan, Slegel argues that

---

[204] Ibid., p. 4.
[205] Ibid., pp. 3, 6.
[206] 'Prima est ut Galenus veteraque dogmata defenderentur, pro more celeberrimae scholae Parisiensis: cujus doctoribus fatale esse Galenum tueri', Slegel, *Commentatio*, p. 21.
[207] Ibid., p. 5.
[208] Ibid., p. 124.
[209] Ibid., the preface.
[210] Ibid., p. 122.

adopting the circulation would mean little difference to the practice of medicine. We have seen that this was a frequent charge against Harvey's doctrine, and partly the efforts of Slegel and even Riolan were directed towards reassuring the waverers who thought this. But it is also a claim that old medicine was in fact still the best because the ancients had laid down rules that were consistent with the medical effects of circulation, even if they did not discuss it as a theoretical issue.

But the neoterics' insistence on sense observation not only looked empirical, but had severe limitations in practice. Only the vivisecting anatomist could properly put into practice the widely agreed precepts of observation. To communicate this knowledge he had to use words. The generators of knowledge were Harvey, Walaeus, Descartes, Hogelande, Plemp and others who vivisected. Riolan did not, and Slegel could do no more than recall the experiments he had made as a young man. The vast majority of their audience would never dissect or vivisect, yet were increasingly receptive to the rhetoric that said that true knowledge was to be gained only from the senses. How did a consensus come about? How did the medical missionaries convert the native population? We have seen that Slegel used disputations. When he also says by viva voce methods, he may mean lectures. As for the printed word, in this book he employs a particular use of the term 'experiment'. It is in vivisectional experiments that we have faith, *fides*, says Slegel,[211] the experiments that converted Plemp and which Riolan lacked. But it is not the visual or tactile perception, nor that of being covered in blood, that characterises the experiment on the printed page. Instead, for Slegel, they have another quality, an aesthetic character: they are elegant. Harvey's new experiments, produced in answer to Riolan's attack, were seen in this way by Slegel. 'Harveus', wrote Slegel, confirmed the pulmonary transit of blood 'certissimo et elegantissimo experimento'.[212] Elsewhere the term is used more generally for Harvey's experiments. Slegel's hero Plemp is equally elegant in a number of places. So for Slegel is Hofmann, in showing that air does not reach the heart.[213] The same feeling is evident in Slegel's description of Harvey's 'beautiful' demonstration of the passage of blood into the mesentery. The elegance of the experiments was matched for Slegel by the elegance of the conclusions. In contrast, Riolan's system, says Slegel, is founded upon a hypothesis rather than experiments, and forced on to the anatomy of the body. It is consequently clumsy: (i) it has many 'principal' organs – the liver, heart and the major 'circulatory' vessels; (ii) it has three or four different routes for the blood; (iii) it has three or four different kinds of blood (Slegel has detected different

211  Ibid., p. 22.
212  Ibid., p. 125.
213  Ibid., p. 64.

accounts in Riolan's different published works); (iv) it has many boundaries, and (v) contrary motions in the same vessels. In contrast, in each of these five cases, the characteristics of Harvey's scheme are simple. Harvey's scheme is 'simple, uniform, constant, rejoicing in the simplicity and order of nature and harmonious'.[214]

Slegel's reply to Riolan was in press when Harvey's own reply to Riolan arrived. Finding, after a moment of panic, that Harvey in fact used arguments that differed from his own, and that his own still therefore had value, he sent off a brief addition to be added by the printer. He sent a copy to Harvey, no doubt to seek his approval and perhaps as part of a method of establishing a network of contacts. Harvey wrote back in 1651,[215] sending a copy of his book on the generation of animals, the preparation of which, he said, had prevented him from replying to more criticisms from Riolan (no doubt made in reply to Harvey's exercises of 1649). Harvey uses the term 'sponge' with which he is to wipe away Riolan's criticisms: this is the language of pamphlet war, used elsewhere in the controversy over circulation, as we have seen. In answer to Riolan's continued insistence on existence of pores in the septum of the heart, Harvey now relates a new experiment, performed in the presence of colleagues. With an ox-bladder attached to a pipe, Harvey tried, without success, to force warm water from right to left ventricle of a recently hanged man, the pulmonary vessels having been tied. When these ligatures were removed and the experiment repeated the water flowed into the pulmonary artery, lungs, pulmonary vein and finally appeared mixed with blood in the left ventricle. This is more graphic language from Harvey who significantly chooses this place to highlight the absence of experiments in Riolan's account. Harvey again recognises that Riolan had professional reasons to stand with his colleagues, and as Dean of the Paris Faculty, defend Galen against novelty and leave the medicine and pathology of the ancients undisturbed.[216] Riolan acts as an advocate, says Harvey, with the demonstrative arguments of a philosopher: that is, from paper, not from experiments.

Riolan made a final attempt to promote his own views. In 1652 and 1653 he issued a flurry of booklets from Paris. He was now seventy-two (he died five years later, in the same year as Harvey) and clearly the time was past for any major effort to deny a total circulation. He first tried (arguing with the wisdom

---

[214] Ibid., p. 20.

[215] Harvey, *Works*, p. 596.

[216] Ibid., p. 598. Riolan's partisan attachment to Paris led him to attack vigorously the Faculty at Montpellier; ironically his charges include the assertion that the Montpellier doctors were not up to date and did not understand the circulation, 'qui est une demonstration tres-evidente' (t serves, he said, to prevent the blood putrefying and to control its heat). J. Riolan, *Curieuses Recherches sur les Escholes en medecine, de Paris, et de Montpellier*, Paris, 1651, p. 142.

of Solomon that there was nothing new under the sun)[217] to show that Hippocrates had known of the circulation.[218] Riolan meant his circulation, of course, not Harvey's, and by linking Hippocrates' name to it he could emphasise again that a Riolanesque circulation alone was compatible with the practice of medicine.

He also retained features of his own system that relate to the theory of medicine. The blood from the liver is still distinct from that of the heart. It is still the soul that directs the action of the heart.[219] In doing so, the heart uses spirit and heat as its instruments: not indeed elementary heat, but celestial. Here Riolan is being very French, preserving not only what he can of the learned tradition of Galenic medicine,[220] but apparently drawing upon Fernel, who was well known for his defence of the action of celestial spirits in the body.[221] (Harvey seems to have had Fernel in mind when attacking notions of spirits in the second exercise to Riolan.)

Riolan's second tract was a brief restatement of his argument for a limited circulation, directed against Harvey's first exercise against him (of 1649).[222] His refutation of Harvey's second exercise (which as we have seen contained some new experimental material) appeared in the next year, 1653.[223] (It is his fifth tract.)[224] In it, Riolan looks back at the course of the whole dispute, beginning with his meeting, in attendance upon his queen, with Harvey in London.[225] His summary of the whole affair, here essentially concluded, is that while Harvey was the Discoverer, the Christopher Columbus of the

---

[217] J. Riolan, *Tractatus de motu sanguinis eiusque circulatione vera, ex doctrinae Hippocratis*, Paris, 1652, address to the reader.

[218] The *loci* in Hippocrates include *Places in Man* (for anastomoses), *On the Heart* (for how long the circulation takes), *Insomnia* and *Fleshes* (that blood is always moving), *Nature of Bones* (that there is a flux in the body) and *Diet* (for circular motions in the world). Riolan, *De motu sanguinis*, p. 32. For good measure Riolan throws in a general account of circular motion from Plato and Aristotle (pp. 61, 65).

[219] Riolan, *De motu sanguinis*, p. 12.

[220] It is a learned tradition that includes, in a rather Catholic way, the authority of Thomas Aquinas in his *De motu cordis*. Riolan, *De motu sanguinis*, p. 13.

[221] See J. J. Bono, 'Reform and the language of renaissance theoretical medicine: Harvey versus Fernel', *Journal of the History of Biology*, 23, no. 3 (1990), 341–87. On Fernel see also L. Deer Richardson, 'The generation of disease: occult causes and diseases of the total substance', in *The Medical Renaissance of the Sixteenth Century*, ed. A. Wear, R. K. French and I. Lonie, Cambridge University Press, 1985, pp. 175–94.

[222] J. Riolan, *Notationes in primam exercitationem de motu cordis et sanguinis in animalibus*, with a separate title page, but without notice of date or place and with a pagination continuous with Riolan's *Tractatus*. It contains little that is new. The third tract is an examination of a work by Highmore (p. 151), and the fourth (p. 176) is a 'pneumatical anatomy', not obviously by Riolan, concerned with anatomical demonstration by inflation, and related material.

[223] J. Riolan, *Responsio ad duas exercitationes anatomicae postremas Guillelmi Harvei . . . de circulatione sanguinis*, Paris, 1653.

[224] It begins a new pagination and has a different date but is bound in a single volume in the British Library copy.

[225] Riolan, *Responsio*, p. 5.

microcosm, it was he, Riolan, who gave his name to the discovery, as Americus Vespucius gave his name to the New World.[226]

In summary, with Riolan's admission that the blood circulates, the controversy in Europe was practically at an end. It remained for Harvey's followers, particularly in England (and we return to Cambridge in the next chapter) to argue for a complete, Harveian, circulation in preference to the minimal circulation described by Riolan. Riolan had been compelled to agree some form of circulation essentially by a consensus that had been formed among his peer-group – the elite republic of medical letters consisting of major teachers in Europe – and in joining it he strengthened it. Even though his account disappointed the Harveians, it became more difficult for a sceptic to argue against circulation in some form or other. Lastly, Riolan's doctrine differed in a major way from that of other circulators: it was not experimental. We return to this topic in the final chapter.

---

[226] Ibid., p. 63. This tract continues with Riolan's defence against Gassendi (*Notationes in tractum clarissimi D.D. Petri Gassendi . . . de circulatione sanguinis* (continuous pagination)); his reply to Pecquet (*Opuscula anatomica, varia et nova*, Paris, 1652, but continuous pagination, (p. 137)); his defence against Slegel (p. 223). At p. 358 is Hofmann's attack on Harvey (in which he accuses Harvey of charging nature with incompetence). As for Harvey, his correspondence at this time on the Riolan affair and other matters shows some of the pattern of the mid-seventeenth-century network. In a major controversy like that of the circulation, a doctor with some learning or ambition might write to the major figures involved, asking their opinion perhaps also of some other controversy, like that of the lacteals (so often bracketed with the circulation) and enclosing a book. Harvey replied in 1651 to such a letter from J. Nardi of Venice, and sent a copy of *De generatione animalium* with his reply. (Harvey, *Works*, p. 603.) Robert Morison, in Paris, wanted to know Harvey's opinion of the lacteals, as did Johan Daniel Horst of Hesse-Darmstadt, who also wanted Harvey's opinion on the Riolan affair. (Harvey, *Works*, pp. 610, 612.)

# 10    Back to Cambridge

## Introduction

The Cambridge that had taught Harvey the philosophy of Aristotle was an important centre from which his views were subsequently disseminated. The story of the Oxford 'Harveians' has been told,[1] and in making a tentative beginning to a similar story in Cambridge, we are concerned with Francis Glisson, who was a generation younger than Harvey (he died in 1677).

Like Harvey, Glisson was a product of Caius College (MD in 1634), was a Fellow of the College of Physicians and lectured there on anatomy. From 1636 he was Regius Professor of Physic in Cambridge. He was therefore in a position to play an important role in determining how people reacted to Harvey's doctrine. Knowledge of the forceful systole and circulation was being generated both within the university and in the college, and a consensus in both institutions would have had an important influence on the English perception of Harvey's doctrine.

In Cambridge, Glisson gave lectures and, like other university teachers we have looked at, conducted disputations. He also seems to have given academic orations. Men graduating in medicine under Glisson – and so defending his theses – shared his beliefs about the motion of the heart, arteries and blood. (One of the earliest theses in favour of the circulation under Glisson, that of Wallis, was in 1641.)[2] In the College Glisson spoke in favour of Harvey from 1639, demonstrated the circulation as Goulstonian lecturer,[3] and as one of the

---

[1] See Robert G. Frank, *Harvey and the Oxford Physiologists. A Study of Scientific Ideas*, University of California Press, 1980, p. 22.

[2] Wallis himself maintained that it was the first defence of Harvey and that it took place in 1641. See Sir Geoffrey Keynes, *The Life of William Harvey*, Oxford, 1966, p. 451. H. P. Bayon, 'William Harvey, physician and biologist: his precursors, opponents and successors', *Annals of Science*, 3 (1938), part 2, pp. 59–118, 89, argues that it was earlier. From some dated disputations in the Sloane MSS. (see note 5 below) we can estimate very approximately that Glisson conducted about fifteen disputations a year in the 1650s.

[3] Theodore Goulston founded his lectureship in 1632. Glisson was followed by Ent as the lecturer; both were agents in forming the English consensus. See P. Allen, 'Medical education in 17th century England', *Bulletin of the History of Medicine*, 1 (1974), 115–43. See also Frank, *Harvey*. It is not clear whether Glisson's experiments to demonstrate the circulation took place

country's leading teachers played his part in the growth of a consensus. The same may be said of his membership of the '1645 group' (see below).[4]

But Glisson, like everyone else who had read Harvey's book – or read about it or heard about it – perceived Harvey's doctrine in a very personal way. Glisson too had his own natural philosophy, and circulation was made meaningful to him by it.

### Glisson's natural philosophy

We can reconstruct some basic positions in Glisson's natural philosophy by examining what he taught at those two places where knowledge of the circulation was generated for successive generations of students and doctors. The manuscripts produced in this process are closer to the mechanics of the generation of knowledge than are his polished published works, and what follows is based mainly on those gathered together in the Sloane collection.[5]

Glisson's natural philosophy begins, like so many others, with God. In taking his class through the physical principles on which rested natural philosophy and in turn the medicine derived from it,[6] Glisson found it natural and proper to begin with the traditional distinction between *natura naturans*, or God, and *natura naturata*, the creation, including the physical world. But in ordinary language, he warns, it is improper for us to use 'nature' to mean God, the angels and souls: strictly 'nature' is the essence of corporeal bodies, and it is over this nature that God rules as law-giver, *legislator*. Glisson saw his duty as a teacher of natural philosophy – even one who was simply making *Annotationes quaedam physicae* as a basis for medicine – to begin with a demonstration of the existence and nature of God. To the medieval distinction

---

in Cambridge or at the college. Henry Power reported an experiment in which Glisson filled a clyster bag with warm water and a little milk and forced the contents into the vena porta. Power said this washed out the blood from the vena porta and cava, right ventricle, lungs and left ventricle, demonstrating the circulation. Power saw that such experiments, and Harvey's, in their reliance on sensory observation, made the usual disputations for and against the circulation mere 'paper-skirmishes'. F. J. Cole, 'Henry Power and the circulation', *Journal of the History of Medicine*, 12 (1957), 291–324.

[4] C. Webster, *The Great Instauration. Science, Medicine and Reform 1626–1660*, London, 1975, p. 55.

[5] This section is based on Sloane 3307, 3309, 3310 and 3312. There are considerable difficulties involved in working with these MSS. There are few indications of date of composition, except for the dates of disputations and some internal references, for example to Riolan's book of 1649. Some of the disputations and their drafts are incomplete and some folios that have been bound out of sequence cannot easily be located in their proper places. Nor is it easy to tell in all cases if the MSS. belong to Glisson's activity in the college or at Cambridge.

[6] Sloane 3310, f. 226. (Glisson generally wrote on one side of the paper only. Reference to a verso side is included where he continued on the other side.) It seems likely that this is Cambridge material, more suitable for students than for the Fellows of the College of Physicians.

between knowledge of God revealed in the scriptures and that furnished by the book of nature, Glisson adds a distinction much more historically local, in which personal knowledge of God – a third category – is said to be different in those who expect to be saved and those who do not. Clearly, varieties of Protestant belief were important to Glisson's thinking at the deepest level.[7]

As a physician and natural philosopher, Glisson is most concerned with demonstrations of God from His creatures. The two ways in which, Glisson explained, this could be done relate to his beliefs about the acquisition of knowledge in general, as we shall see in relation to circulation. By analogy with creatures, argues Glisson, we may know about the nature of God either negatively or positively. Negatively by taking note of the imperfections of creatures and denying them to the Creator; positively by extending their perfections to the ultimate perfection of God. Since both methods are based on the results of God's Creation – His creatures – Glisson calls them a posteriori methods.

The results of God's Creation are described next by Glisson in a section on natural bodies. These bodies are of two kinds, being either corporeal or spiritual in substance. Spiritual substances are demons, angels and the separated human soul. All other substances are corporeal, including the spirits of the body – natural and vital – and spirits of wine.[8] It is difficult to date these *Annotationes* of Glisson, but the reader will see that Glisson was not anxious to embrace any of the more radical positions available in a period of great change in natural philosophy. The point here, however, is not to label Glisson as a conservative[9] or as anything else, but to show how his religious commitments had a determinative effect on his natural philosophy and hence on his treatment of Harvey's work.

The *Annotationes* form the basis for two disputations. That is, Glisson like other teachers used the disputation as a teaching method. As we have seen, it was among the purposes of a disputation to confirm the thesis by freeing it

---

[7] 'Deus omnia in se et totus omnium extra se. Deum intelligimus 1. Quod sit 1 ex testimonio spiritus sui 1 revelato in scripturis 2 revelato . . . in cordibus nostris 1 communo modo in iis qui ad electionem spectant 2 speciali in iis qui spectant ad electionem 2 ex creaturis . . . 2 Quid sit 1 Positive per analogiam . . . ', Sloane 3310, f. 226v.

[8] 'Corpus sic sumitur ut apponitur naturae spirituali qualis est Angelorum demonum et animae rationalis separatae quae substantiae quidem sunt sed non corpora sed . . . spirituales: quare formalis differentia hic quaerenda quae constituit corpus distinctum a substantia spirituali proprie dicta; est enim spiritus corporeus, et spiritus naturalis vitalis animalis spiritus vini, hi spiritus analogice tantum spiritus dicuntur quod ob subtilitatem et nobilitatem essentiae, proprius ad naturam spiritualem accedere.' Sloane 3310, f. 227r.

[9] As a teacher necessarily using the techniques of the schools, Glisson can indeed often look conservative in a time of change. He may himself have seen a virtue in not grasping at novelty: 'Non is sum qui novitatem verborum, aut etiam opinionem, nulla urgente necessitate affectem: quin potius veterum placita veterumque loquendi formulas quoad sine praeiudicio veritatis fieri potest amplector.' Sloane 3307, f. 2.

from objections. Glisson normally wrote out a brief sketch of the disputation, a side or two of paper with the thesis as a title and at least some of the major objections that could be made against it. Probably this corresponds to the thesis that was traditionally published before the disputation, and to the drafts sent by Regius to Descartes. But unlike Regius' disputations, those of Glisson were not controversial or noisy. Glisson was in control, and sometimes at least wrote out the disputation in full, supplying the speeches of the *respondens* and *opponens*, generally designated by the letters A and B; sometimes, as here, there is also a C. This corresponds to Heerebord's account (which we met above) of the form of disputation, where at the classroom level the teacher acted as *praeses* or 'senior respondent' and his pupil as 'junior respondent', both attacked by the 'opponent'. Glisson's technique was often to express a part of his doctrine in words that appeared to be contradictory to another part. In showing that the contradiction was only apparent – that is, in reaching a Determination – the doctrine was ultimately made to look stronger.

In these two disputations on the nature of matter and spirit the disputants assert the fundamentals of Glisson's world-picture: only God exists in a simple or absolute sense, and of His creatures, matter and spirit exist most simply, being the results of nothing but God's action in creating them by emanation. By analogy, argues the *respondens*, God is the substrate of all creatures, which perpetually depend on His will for their continued existence and operation.[10] God is to creatures as substance to accident, for accidents cannot exist without substance. Matter and spirit agree, then, also in being susceptible to accident; they agree as well in being composed logically from genus and differences; in being finite substances, created in time; in having parts (although those of spirit are not separable); in having boundaries in space and being incapable of shrinking to a mathematical point. Both agree in moving with finite speed: in the written-out text of the disputation Glisson supplies a diagram of a line, abc, from heaven to earth, arguing that an angel that could move in an instant from a to c would exist simultaneously along the whole line, and could even at the same time move on a new line from earth to heaven, ultimately occupying the entire universe, which was clearly impossible (see fig. 23).

---

[10] The *respondens* enlarges on this point, which is fundamental for the theological basis of Glisson's natural philosophy: 'Annotatio de concursu dei. concursus dei non est creatura sed ipse deus relative determinatus per voluntatem suam ad conservationem creaturae in esse et operari. ita ut per analogiam dicamus deum ipsum esse ultimum substratum omnibus creaturis: et ut substantia se habet ad accidentia, ita per similitudinem quandam se habet deus ad ipsas substantias; subtracta substantia cessant accidentia, substracto concursu dei annihilatur ipsa substantia converso substractis per impossibile forsan a substantia quavis omnibus ac solis accidentibus et concursu ad illa accidentia; manet tamen substantia manet deus concurrens ad conservationem dictae substantiae; sed subtracta dicta substantia manet solus deus sine voluntate concurrendi . . . ut in deum omnia ultimo resolvuntur ut primo a deo emanent . . . A.' Sloane 3310, unmarked folio, presumably 229.

Glisson's discussion of the finite speed of angels moving between heaven and earth might appear bizarre to a reader expecting to see signs of a 'scientific revolution' in the writings of those concerned with natural philosophy at this time. But such things really were fundamental to the way Glisson saw the world. Having told his class of the nature and source of the world, he can now proceed – in more notes or lectures – to the material part of it, his concern as a natural philosopher and a physician. In its nature the material part of the world is similar to the spiritual, as he has been at pains to point out, and a principal similarity is that motion is a property of both spirit and matter, and not something that is imposed from without. These were doctrines that Glisson later published as a book on the energetic nature of substance, and here in this Cambridge material we can see the religious and metaphysical foundation of his full doctrine.

The principal characteristic of that full doctrine was that matter was self-mobile, or 'energetic' in Glisson's terms. Deriving from his belief that matter was, like spirit, ultimately a divine emanation, Glisson's natural philosophy is radically different from that of the Cartesians, for whom all motion is derived from elsewhere and imposed on matter. Nor is there any suggestion that Glisson thought of matter as particulate or atomic – it was after all divine – and the purposelessness of an atomic world that had so offended Aristotle, the philosopher of causes, would have equally offended Glisson the Christian.

### Glisson, arteries and blood

It was probably because he saw in Harvey's account of the forceful systole a motion being *imposed* on the blood that Glisson could not agree with Harvey that the heart alone was the cause of circulation. It was a disagreement he shared with others who accepted that the blood circulated; his answer was of course individual. The problem was how the heart could move the blood all the way to the ends of the arteries. 'Prorsus', wrote Glisson, 'enim improbabile est cor posse traijcere sanguinem ad extremitates undique totius corporis',[11] 'For in short it is improbable that the heart can propel the blood to every extremity of the whole body.' It is not clear from these words what physical objections Glisson had in mind, but it was a topic on which many had real difficulty in understanding Harvey. Some imagined that he claimed that blood left the heart with sufficient projectile motion to carry it to the capillaries, and others that he claimed that the blood ejected from the heart reached the capillaries in a single beat. Glisson's answer was in two parts, that both the arteries and the blood actively participated in circulation. Both were active parts of the body and both

[11] Sloane 3307, f. 6r.

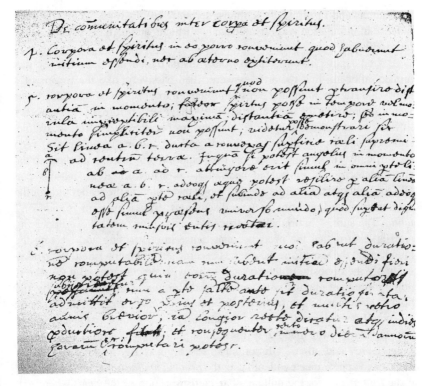

Fig. 23. Glisson's notes on the similarities between bodies and spirits, showing the diagram of a path of an angel travelling between heaven and earth, marked abc.

were species of corporeal substance of which motion (as in his physical first principles) was an inherent characteristic.

Let us look first at his account of the motion of the arteries. This is a lengthy piece at the beginning of one of the Sloane manuscripts.[12] Its thesis is that the heart and arteries become tense, and relax, at the same time. It thus relates to the first part of Harvey's doctrine, that of the forceful systole and the nature of the pulse. Its context, to which its opening words relate, is the traditional 'controversy' about the motion of the heart and pulse, listed as a disputed question in such collections as that by André du Laurens and now given new life by Harvey's conclusions. It is probably a comparatively early piece of writing by Glisson, because the non-Harveian views he attacks are those of

---

[12] Sloane 3307, f. 2. It is written out explicitly in defence of a thesis, but is not given over to alternate defences and objections.

du Laurens and Primrose. It is almost certainly before 1649, when Glisson's defence of circulation was directed against Riolan, and perhaps as early as the late 1630s.[13]

At first sight Glisson's thesis looks distinctly unHarveian. Harvey had argued, after all, that the arteries were filled passively, like the fingers of a glove that Harvey imagined himself blowing into. It followed that the arteries were expanding as the heart contracted. We have seen before that it was a very difficult business to untangle the relationships between such terms as systole, contraction, action, relaxation, diastole and expansion. We have also seen the difficulty Harvey had – and his final solution – in relating all these to the appearances of the vivisected heart. It is probably for these reasons that Glisson deliberately evolves a terminology that brings to the reader little of the connotations of the terms of past discussions.[14] His key term is 'tension', *tentio*. The short – but rather superficial – explanation of his thesis appearing nonHarveian is that the heart becomes tense in contracting and ejecting the blood and at the same time the arteries become tense in being filled. Relaxation is simply the opposite of tension and is likewise synchronous. But Glisson is doing more than playing with words and definitions. To understand why and how he spent a not inconsiderable amount of time and energy on this question (at some fifteen pages it is one of the longest pieces in these manuscripts) and how circulation was made to fit his natural philosophy, we must look deeper. Like Harvey and others, Glisson sought to bring clarity to the confusion of names and appearance by identifying the *propria motio* of the heart. He called it the *formalis actio*: the unique, characteristic action of the heart whereby it fulfilled its function in the body. It was matched by a less important or, in Aristotelian terms, accidental motion that returned the heart to a point where it could again fulfil its function. In doing this Glisson was fitting this part of Harvey's doctrine into a whole apparatus of traditional natural philosophy as it related to medicine: the Galenic distinction between action, use and purpose, the Aristotelian distinction between accident and essence, remote and

[13] Glisson's connections with Cambridge fall into two main periods. He lived in Cambridge as Regius Professor from 1636 to 1640, when he went into practice in Colchester. He was thus perhaps close enough to visit the university for lectures or graduation exercises. As a Royalist, Glisson was sent by Fairfax to parley with the Roundheads at the siege of Colchester (in which more than fifty houses in his parish were destroyed). He shortly afterwards settled in London, near Fleet Street, and may again have found time to visit Cambridge. But in 1654 he received five years' salary in arrears (see *DNB*) and was probably more actively involved in university life. Many of the Sloane MSS. derive from this period.

[14] Sloane 3307, f. 2. 'forsan enim fieri potest, ut formalis actio utriusque [sc. heart and arteries] sit eadem et simul, etiamsi eodem tempore cor contrahitur quo arteria dilatatur: formalem vero geminam cordis actionem tentionem esse dico, modo sano sensu tentio intelligatur. Inprimis igitur termini quaestionis nobis explicando veniunt, et quid sit tentio. vox a tenendo derivari videtur: siquidem quod tenditur extra istam po[r]tionem quam appetit vi tenetur. definitur autem tentio conatus trahendi [f. 2v] cum resistentia unde res sic tracta rigidior fit.'

proximate causes and (to which we shall have occasion to refer later) grades of nobility and natural necessity.

Glisson levered the Harveian doctrine of forceful systole into his natural philosophy with the aid of his commitment to the innate mobility of matter. He agreed with Harvey that the 'formal' motion of the heart was contraction, by which it expelled blood. This was a simple case of 'tension', on the part of the fibres of the heart. But for Glisson tension was not always simple. Four things were always found in cases of tension: flexible matter (stones cannot show tension), resistance (without which tension is mere traction), rigidity (the most certain sign of tension, says Glisson) and the effort of pulling, the *conatus trahendi*. This latter was the characteristically Glissonian view of the innate mobility of matter.[15] The disposition of these four components determined what actually happened in cases of tension. If the resistance was too strong, the effort of pulling did not succeed, like the tense but immobile strings of a musical instrument. Even here the strength of the effort of pulling resulted in greater rigidity.[16]

In Glisson's terminology tension is measured by the *conatus trahendi*, not the actual contraction made. Actual contraction is simply 'tension with victory', that is, over resistance. With this apparatus Glisson can say that both the heart and arteries have a 'formal motion' of tension, the purpose of which is the expulsion of blood. Both have this tension at the same time (his thesis) but only that of the heart is 'with victory', that is, in overcoming the tension of the arteries and filling them with blood. The situation is a dynamic one: the powerful heart first overcomes the resistance of the blood contained in its ventricles, and then the contractive tension of the arteries, which can only be tense-with-victory when the heart has finished contracting. The resistance in the arteries is double, that of the blood they contain at cardiac diastole and the fresh impulse at systole. When the arteries can follow their own tension in cardiac diastole, the blood is driven into the parts of the body. In defending this thesis Glisson allows the arteries to become flaccid as their blood is emptied. Elsewhere when insisting on the outward direction of

---

[15] Historians have found in Glisson an early expression of the 'idea' of irritability, often thought to have been put into a recognisable modern form by Haller in the next century. Pagel finds 'traces' of it in Glisson's work on rickets of 1650 and more in that on the anatomy of the liver of 1652. This geneticism of ideas is largely constructed on a modern medical category and is not part of the present story. But Pagel's chronology shows how the Cambridge disputations preceded the published works: W. Pagel, 'Harvey and Glisson on irritability with a note on van Helmont', *Bulletin of the History of Medicine*, 41 (1967), 497–514. For Glisson's 'vitalism' see T. M. Brown, 'The Mechanical Philosophy and the "Animal Oeconomy" a Study in the Development of English Physiology in the Seventeenth and early Eighteenth Centuries', PhD dissertation, Princeton, 1977, esp. pp. 50–7.

[16] *Tentio* is further divided by Glisson into contractive and expansive, and into violent, natural, and animal. Sloane 3307, f. 2v.

arterial flow, he insists that the arteries never reach the lower limit of their natural contraction but are always unsuccessfully pushing upon the contained blood.[17]

Glisson used his doctrine of tension in a disputation – probably at a graduation, and certainly in June 1653 – in which Robert Brady defended the thesis that the pulse in the arteries results from the force of blood coming from the heart.[18] Glisson prepared for the disputants different interpretations of his idea of tension, and finally resolved the differences, allowing the thesis to stand confirmed. Brady began with an analysis of the pulsific faculty, declaring that it was based on the structure of the heart and arteries and secondly on the 'mication' of the blood. Glisson's mication was an alternate ebullition and collapse of the blood itself, the result of a constant struggle between the innately mobile vital spirits of the blood and the blood's coarse component. The motion of the spirits was a kind of tension in Glisson's special sense, which was alternately exercised 'with victory' and without. This was the second major way in which Glisson's account of the action of the heart and arteries differed from that of Harvey's, and like the first (the active motion of the arterial walls) was based on Glisson's convictions about the basic mobility of matter.

The notion of mication was developed by Brady's opponent during the course of the disputation. He objects that mication cannot be the prime cause of pulsation, because a heart cut from a living animal continued to beat for a while, while yet deprived of blood. Brady's reply is that mication occurs in the substance of the ventricular walls as well as in the blood in the ventricles; and that the final cessation of motion of such a heart is due to the exhaustion of vital spirits. Such a position was not dissimilar to that of Descartes, who was driven to assert a local expansive force by a similar line of opposing argument; but of course Descartes' natural philosophical principles were not in the least like Brady's or Glisson's.

Brady's opponent further asserted that it was the micative expansion of blood in the ventricles of the heart that irritated the fibres in the walls of the ventricles by trying to stretch them; the ventricles in response contracted to expel the contained blood. The same thing happened in the arteries, but without 'victory', for the arteries were still expanding under the superior force of the heart. So mication was a 'tension' similar to that of the fibres (now called tonic motion). It is notable that Glisson rarely uses Harvey's quantitative proof

---

[17] Sloane 3312, f. 359: 'tamen etiam in quiete sua arteriae modice nituntur exprimere; adeoque ex positis partium huic nixui aequalis producit in arteriis quietam tonicam, aequaliter libratam ex nixu arteriarum et contra nixu partium'.

[18] The thesis and draft disputation are at Sloane 3310, f. 245; Brady's disputation is f. 252. Brady seems to be the later master of Caius, whom the old Glisson appointed as his deputy as Regius professor (*DNB*).

of circulation, no doubt feeling like others that volumetric considerations were inappropriate for an inherently expansive blood.

The disputation was 'determined' by an agreement between the 'erudite respondent' and his opponent that the force of the heart was indeed one of the causes of pulsation of the arteries, and that mication and fibrous tension of the blood and arteries respectively had their place in a hierarchy of causes.

### Glisson and Riolan

Glisson's doctrines of mication and tonic motion were developed much earlier than Brady's disputation in 1653, and probably date from Glisson's first reaction to Harvey's work. If interest in the action of the heart and arteries ever diminished in England after these early years, it was reawakened in 1649, when Riolan published his *Opuscula*. Glisson wrote that Riolan's opinion was seized upon eagerly by everyone, hoping for great things by so acute a man.[19] And Riolan was, as we have seen, a distinguished figure: Dean of the Paris Faculty, physician to the French Royal Family and the author of well-known anatomy textbooks. He was the only person to whom Harvey made a formal reply: a reply indeed that was prompted by this *Opuscula*. To publish an English edition (London 1649) of the *Opuscula* must have been seen as provocative, and undoubtedly it caused a stir in London and the universities.

But Glisson was disappointed in the opinions of the distinguished anatomist. Riolan's opinions were more like poetic fiction than solid experience, he said, recalling the fable from Aesop of the king of the frogs.[20] Glisson organised a disputation in Cambridge not long after reading the book,[21] designed to refute Riolan on the major points on which Riolan's account of the circulation differed from Harvey's. These, for Glisson, were two: that the blood passes from the major arteries to the major veins by anastomoses (and not through the substance of the parts) and from right to left ventricle of the heart by way of the traditional pores in the septum (and so not through the lungs).

What evil spirit could have made Riolan construct such a mutilated scheme? asked Glisson rhetorically. His answer is that Riolan was compelled to admit a circulation by the force of Harvey's anatomical demonstrations, but could not accept the destruction of traditional medicine that he believed would follow from the confusion of humours in a total circulation. As Glisson knew, Riolan's

---

[19] Sloane 3312, unnumbered folio, shortly before 119.

[20] In Aesop's fable, the frogs asked Zeus for a king. He sent them one: a block of wood. For a while they were happy but soon became discontented. When they asked him again he sent a water-snake (whose diet included frogs). Presumably Glisson intended to suggest that the famous Frenchman, 'the King of the Frogs', was somewhat wooden in his understanding of Harvey or an excessively aggressive leader.

[21] The thesis and draft are at Sloane 3312, f. 120.

stake in traditional medicine was by this time considerable, for he was a distinguished author. 'Believe me', said Glisson through his *respondens* to his audience, 'Mihi credite auditores', 'there is no greater bond than prejudice, and no greater prejudice than towards previously published opinions.'

Glisson's rejection of Riolan's scheme is simply to deny the existence of the 'manifest and conspicuous' anastomoses that would be required for a circulation between the major vessels. He and Harvey had been unable to find them, for anastomoses occur (he says) only in particular parts of the body and between minor vessels; Riolan does not in fact name any major anastomosis in the *Opuscula*, and in the *Anthropographia* admits anastomoses only in the spleen, plexus choroides and other 'remote' places where the circulation of Riolan does not anyway run; and, concludes Glisson, no help is available to Riolan from the texts of Galen, for who anastomoses were invisibly small.

Many more pieces in Glisson's manuscripts were prompted by Riolan's book of 1649. As we have seen, Riolan himself had defended his own doctrine in a quodlibet disputation in the Paris Faculty, and claimed a corporate authority for his thesis. Such authority derived from the objections that Riolan had successfully overcome, and it strengthened his case to repeat the objections and his response in the printed work. Many of these are listed also by Glisson, undoubtedly taken from Riolan's book, and perhaps for use in disputations in Cambridge.[22] To judge from the effort he put into refuting it, Riolan saw a great threat to his own system from that of Fortunio Liceti, who had proposed a reciprocating flow in the vessels. It may have been Glisson's examination of this text in Riolan's book that prompted Glisson to begin a separate piece 'On the motion of blood in general, and that it does not stagnate in the veins'.[23] His argument, from the nature of the parts (such as valves),[24] is that blood moves progressively and continually in an inward direction in the veins. Riolan as well as Liceti could be defeated by insisting on the quantity and speed of the circulating blood, which Riolan consistently denied. Glisson began to write 'Motion of blood . . . ' in the title, but thinking of the force and quantity of the motion of the blood in Harvey's scheme, changed it to 'Torrent . . . ', which he used consistently thereafter.

In promoting his own scheme of circulation, Glisson found it necessary to attack that of Descartes. Like Riolan, Glisson, with his belief in self-active

---

[22] For example 3312, f. 256. It is not easy to see what use Glisson put them to. Many were arguments against Riolan, but also against circulation; Riolan's responses defended circulation, but often attacked Harvey. Many of them reveal their French origin in their concern for the significance of circulation for practical medicine. The drafts for disputations at f. 359 may also derive partly from material found in Riolan's book. The points listed are almost all against circulation: it is as if only the *opponens* is being briefed by Glisson. Without the accompanying texts of the disputations it is difficult to see how the objections were used.

[23] Sloane 3312, f. 334. This was not a disputation and it is not clear who Glisson's audience were.

[24] Sloane 3312, f. 355.

matter, had no sympathy with 'the new Dutch mechanical philosophy', but – like Riolan again – his attack is not on the first principles of a radical and alien philosophy, but on some technical details of the circulation. It is as though our authors 'misunderstood' or did not recognise the scope and purpose of Descartes' programme.

In this way, for Glisson, Descartes' insistence that the heat of the heart is ordinary physical heat is simply his ignorance of the differences between innate and physical heat.[25] The simple relationship that Descartes had proposed between heat and rarefaction in the heart did not hold for Glisson, who pointed to rarefactions occurring without heat. He believed that rarefaction was a property of the matter on which the form of heat acted;[26] and that vital heat was the action of the vital spirits (as in mication). Glisson cannot wholly deny Descartes' account of the expansion of blood inside the hot heart, for it is not unlike his own idea of mication. But he denied that it was sufficient to explain the entire circulation; after all, his own theory relied on the activity of the blood and arteries to supplement the action of the heart. And worst of all,[27] Descartes had attributed the heat to the walls of the heart, while for Glisson it was the blood itself that was warm and mobile.[28] As others had done, Glisson dismisses Descartes' inflation-theory of the heartbeat by reference to a separated, and divided (and so bloodless) but still beating heart of an eel.

### Nobility and necessity

Two things must have been obvious to Glisson, as to anyone else who largely accepted what Harvey said. The first is that innovation was possible within that part of natural philosophy that related to medicine. The second was that experiment played a large part in establishing innovation.

But innovation, reinforced with whatever experiment, was only acceptable if consistent with what opinion held to be irrefutable truths of received natural philosophy. Such consistency was generally achieved by modifying the innovation rather than the philosophy, as we have seen in the case of the heart-beat and circulation. In this section we shall look at some of the truths of received natural philosophy that faced Glisson in arguing for his version of Harvey's doctrine. Secondly, we shall consider the place of experiment in this process of negotiation.

Glisson, through Thomas Barwell in June 1653, defended the thesis that the

---

25 Sloane 3309, f. 142. Glisson was familiar with the *Discourse on Method* and the *Passions of the Soul*, which had appeared in the same year as Riolan's *Opuscula*, 1649.

26 'quasi materiam circa quam forma caloris versatur'.

27 'turpiter Cartesius errat'.

28 The same MS., Sloane 3309, ff. 117, 139, contains Glisson's theses that the blood is more than the nutriment of the body, and alone is innately warm.

blood was the highest and principal part of the body. He was again exploring the consequences of Harvey's work, which was a 'handle for innovation' and the basis for the disputation.[29] Since the heart was now seen as providing the physical moving force – indeed as a pump – for the circulating blood that entered and left it, it could no longer be regarded as the *fons vitae* in the same way as the ancients had seen it, that is, as a source of a faculty and of a unidirectional flow of arterial blood. One of the truths of received natural philosophy was that the heart supplied heat and spirits to the parts of the body, and Glisson does not attempt to deny it. But he now sees the self-regenerating blood as the vehicle of the heat and spirits, indeed of life itself.[30] Consequently the blood must itself have 'original life' and must be the supreme part of the body.

But this would not fit with other truths of received natural philosophy. Many denied that the blood was part of the body at all, except in the wide sense of being covered with the common skin (but then so were food and faeces, which were clearly not parts). The serious argument against the blood being a part of the body was that it was 'similar ' – homogeneous and without subsisting structure. 'Similar' parts were distinguished from 'dissimilar' or 'organic', which were composed of several different 'similar' parts and which exercised a particular function or 'faculty' within the body (the similar parts had only simple 'actions' determined by their qualitative nature, such as Wet or Cold). Natural philosophy said that the soul was the Act of the organic body; that is, as (Aristotelian) Form, the soul informed the *organic* parts only. Blood, as a 'similar' part, was therefore not informed by the soul and so not animated. As a result it ranked low in the hierarchy of parts. Moreover, received philosophy said that blood was the nutriment of the parts, again hierarchically low.

The central issue here, and one which Glisson does not want to avoid, is that of nobility. It was another truth of received philosophy that the organs of the body existed on a scale of nobility. There are a number of connotations of *nobilitas* in this context. The first is Galen's scale of dignity in which the qualitative 'action' of the similar parts is inferior to the 'use' of organic parts, and in which both are subsumed in Nature's co-ordinated actions that preserve the whole body. Another is Aristotle's scale of perfection in natural things, where the more perfect things are those with the most elaborate Form. (In animals Form for Aristotle was soul, so a philosopher with a rational soul was superior to slaves, women and animals.) A third, and potent resonance of

[29] Sloane 3310, f. 228.

[30] A number of items in these MSS. are devoted to showing that the liver, no longer to be regarded as the root of the veins, was not the organ of sanguification, but merely of the separation of bile. Sloane 3310, ff. 277, 287.

the term is Plato's comparison of the faculties of the human soul with the construction of the state, in which the nutritive faculty and workers have the lowest place, and the rational faculty and the philosopher-guardians have the highest. The analogy from microcosmic body to macrocosmic society is explicit in Glisson's speech for Barwell.[31] The parts of the body live in a 'common society of life'; this is 'natural politics' in which parts can be carried from a lower grade to a higher. The case, says Barwell, is just the same in the 'civil republic' where it was 'not indecorous' for a citizen to be moved from a low function to one more eminent.[32]

This was at least a prudent thing to say in 1653, in Cromwell's republic.[33] When Harvey wrote De motu cordis in 1628 and Primrose replied to it in 1630, it was natural for both of them to make comparisons between the heart in the microcosm, the king in the civil macrocosm and the sun in the world. The king was not alone in believing he ruled by God's will, and in the order of society below him, in an age when nobility was associated with power, the hierarchical ordering of society must have seemed to many as natural and proper. At least it was worth preserving for fear of something worse and we have seen for example that the express purpose of prohibiting risky disputations at the Dutch universities was to prevent civil disorder. In the same way the Counter-Reformation societies defended their status quo by the Inquisition's insistence that published books should contain nothing against the faith, against princes or against civil behaviour. In a stable and hierarchical society each person had his trade or calling, in fulfilling which he contributed to the common good, and

---

[31] The analogy between the body and society was not uncommon in the earlier anatomical literature. Du Laurens thought that the relationship between the noble and ignoble parts of the body should be a model for the ruler and ruled in the state: the brain issues laws, the heart provides health and the liver provides nourishment 'like a generous prince'. The plebeians accept such rules and provisions, undertaking in turn to remove the waste. *Historia anatomica humani corporis et singularum ejus partium multis controversiis et observationibus illustrata*, Frankfurt, n.d. (1600? *Ad lectorem* dated 1599), p. 7. The parallel between the body and the 'best-established republic' was one of the reasons that led Parigiano to deny Harvey's account of how the body worked. The stability of the social order was reflected in Parigiano's account of the society of the body, where the noble organs like the lungs – like a king – cannot with propriety be supplied with the same food as the ignoble. W. Harvey, *De motu cordis et sanguinis in animalibus, anatomica exercitatio. Cum refutationibus Aemylii Parisani Romani, Philosophi, ac Medici Veneti et Iacobi Primirosii in Londonensi Collegio doctoris*, Leiden, 1639, pp. 168, 200. Compare Varolius' resolution of the traditional disputed question of the rival superiority of the heart and brain by means of an elaborate social analogy: C. Varolius, *Anatomiae, sive de resolutione corporis humani*, Frankfurt, 1591, p. 47.

[32] 'communis vitae societas'. The folio with the speech of the *defendens* follows 229 but is out of sequence. 'Etenim vel ea ipsa, crassiore illa portione sanguinis nondum spiritu vitae imbuta, nobiliora sunt. Neque in politia naturali absurdum putandum est, partes ab inferiori dignitatis gradu ad superiorem in eodem corpore pervehi: Quemadmodum in republica civili indecorum non est, eundem civem a munere viliore ad eminentius promoveri'.

[33] Compare Sylvius' introduction to the English translation of Harvey (1653) where he discusses the freedom of wisdom in a Commonwealth.

departures from which caused outcry. In just the same way in the microcosm each organ has its own motion, *propria*, or in Glisson's language, *formalis*. We have seen some of the relationships this had with Galenic theory and here we should note that these too had a hierarchy, some *propriae motiones* being more noble than others. Much material of this sort can be found in the anatomical textbooks with which Glisson and Harvey were familiar (and we have seen how the notion of a 'proper motion' was important in Harvey's discovery). These, of the late sixteenth and early seventeenth century, were very different to the humanist and classical texts of the middle of the sixteenth century, and insist more on the admirable nature of man's body, as a microcosm within a macrocosm and as the image of, or the temple of God. At least in the rhetoric of their introductory material, Plato is given a new attention and there could hardly have been a medical man who was not acquainted with Plato's account of nobility in the analogy of state and soul.

But Barwell was making his public speech in a world very different from that of 1628. Cromwell had risen from comparative ignobility to a position of great power. It was no longer clear that God had ruled through the person of the king. That the hierarchy of society could be unstable had been demonstrated in the most potent way in the Civil War. And Harvey had shown by the discovery of the circulation that the microcosm ordered its analogous society in a completely unexpected way. Barwell and Glisson, acutely aware of the analogy, must have wondered whether the microcosm of the body and the macrocosm of society were as parallel as people had believed in earlier times.

In one important respect Glisson now saw an important difference. While he still continued to be concerned with the concept of nobility of organs and actions – for example the veins were less noble than the arteries, and relaxation was less noble than the *formalis actio*, contraction, of the heart and arteries – yet he saw that the society of organs in the body did *not* act like a society of people in a state. While for Glisson, as in the medical tradition, Nature does nothing in vain (which in his time was closer to saying that God had created the body with prudence) yet the working of the body did not involve perception and rationality (which we see in human society). Here is Glisson addressing an audience in London or Cambridge on the supposed attraction exerted by a ligature upon blood:

Does the ligature know what is going on inside the body? Is the faculty of attraction to be extended to the ligature? Perhaps, you say, it excites attraction in the ligated part. What is this? It excites attraction by impeding? By blocking the very channels through which attraction occurs? You have in mind a wonderful attraction! . . . It may be objected that a part damaged by accident and in pain attracts blood to help itself; or that other parts send blood to the affected part to relieve the pain. A splendid thing to say! For the other parts, touched by there being a ligature in one, send blood to free it: you describe a wonderful prudence and rationality to the parts. Not only do they understand, but they come to help in a friendly and medical fashion![34]

Glisson goes on with a rhetoric that amounts to sarcasm, to enquire about the means whereby the parts communicate, understand and judge severity of the circumstances. Is this the economy of nature? he asks. His reply is no. All these things (which we might expect in a society of people) are conspicuously absent from the body. The actions of nature, says Glisson, are governed not by helpful plans, *consilia*, but by necessity. 'Natural actions are performed by the necessity of nature, not its judgment': 'naturales actiones ex necessitate naturae non eius arbitrio administrantur'. (The same point is made by the Cartesian Regius, but of course from a very different sort of metaphysics.)[35]

In denying the power of attraction to a medical ligature Glisson is using arguments similar to those that were used by others – for example Boyle – in denying attraction in the physical world. Boyle attacks the notion that nature's well-known abhorrence of vacuums caused parts to be attracted where a vacuum might form by reason of a certain consent among the parts that a vacuum should not occur. The resemblance is striking, but it is not clear at all that Glisson appreciated the particulate philosophy that made denial of attraction a point of faith.

We have seen that Harvey's presentation of the case for the forceful systole and circulation was a demonstration that it occurred and not a demonstration of its final cause, or purpose. Harvey himself remarked on this. Many of his opponents objected to what he wrote precisely because it did not fit into an existing scheme of natural philosophy, and did not present a new one. Harvey's refusal to build a system might even be called the principle of limited explanation: if the demonstration of a thing is valid, then it must be accepted irrespective of the consequences.

Glisson's *necessitas naturae* is something of the same kind; the examples he gives are local instances of nature acting necessarily, without regard to an overall plan or prudence. By the time he wrote on the generation of animals Harvey too was thinking along the same lines. While for him nature is still the principle of motion and quiet, and the vegetative soul is the efficient cause of generation, yet neither act as people do, with an acquired faculty and with

---

[34] Sloane 3312, f. 9: 'ecquid sapit ligatura eorum quae intus geruntur in corpore? An et facultas attractrix ligaturae etiam extenda est? a forte (inquies) excitat attractionem in parte ligata. Quid hoc est, excitat impediendo attractionem, nempe occludendo canales per quos fieret? miram attractionem memoras . . . At vero ex accidente quatenus pars dolere aut molestia afficitur attrahit sanguinem in subsidium, aut forte reliquae etiam partes eo transmittunt ad partem molestia affectam su[b]levandam. Splendidae haec dicta sunt! Primo ergo aliae partes tanguntur . . . ligaturae in hac, adeoque affundunt eo sanguinem ut literent; miram partium prudentiam et ratiocinium narras, non tantum intelligunt, sed et succurere amice medicantur.'

[35] H. Regius, *Fundamenta physices*, Amsterdam, 1646, p. 182.

prudence, but in accordance with natural laws. There is no plan, *consilium*, no discipline. Using similar language Glisson argues that necessity is derived from the structure and action of the parts: it is by the 'urgent necessity of the parts' that the arteries cannot drive blood inwards. (Glisson means the aortic valves and the tonic motion of the arteries.) That the arteries only expel blood is a 'law of nature', a term synonymous with 'necessity of nature'.[36] When the tension of the fibres of the heart is 'victorious', then *necessario* the ventricles contract and emit blood.[37] (The corresponding relaxation of the heart is equally necessary but much less noble.) The forced expansion of the arteries against their natural tension is the simple necessity arising from the superior force of the heart.[38] Two of Glisson's large formal defences of circulation depend entirely on the principle of local necessity. Having shown that the left ventricle emits blood at every beat, it is simple necessity that the heart becomes full again for the next contraction. The only available route is from the venous artery (a true vein, says Glisson) and so the left ventricle is, of the necessity of the valves, filled with blood in this way. But the venous artery does not remain empty and must of necessity be filled from somewhere. The only possible source is the substance of the lungs. In this way Glisson worked round the path taken by the blood showing that at each stage the local necessity of the structure and action of the parts determined what happened.

### The primacy of the blood

Glisson's emphasis on the blood as the principal part of the body was perhaps prompted by Harvey himself. By the time he replied to Riolan in the exercises of 1649, Harvey had come to give the blood a greater role than before among the causes of the circulation. It has been argued that Harvey's comparison, in 1628, between the heart and the king as rulers of their small and large worlds gave way to a perception of the primacy of the blood,[39] just as the power that had once resided in the person of the king was now distributed through the Commonwealth. A wider study of Harvey makes such an idea unlikely. It is more probable that Harvey's new emphasis was due to the work he had been doing on the generation of animals, for his book on the subject was by now

---

36  Sloane 3312, f. 357 (*lex naturae*).
37  Sloane 3310, f. 253.
38  Sloane 3310, f. 255.
39  C. Hill, 'William Harvey and the idea of monarchy', *Past and Present*, 27 (1964), 54–72. Hill's argument has met with brisk opposition from G. Whitteridge, 'William Harvey: a royalist and no parliamentarian', *Past and Present*, 28 (1964), 104–9. The extension of this dispute contains little of interest for the concerns of this book. A useful assessment of Hill's argument and the genre of history it represents is made by H. Kearney, 'Puritanism, capitalism and the scientific revolution', *Past and Present*, 28 (1964), 81–101.

almost complete.[40] The early appearance of the blood in the developing egg (which he continued to study during his stay with the Royalist party in Oxford) and the constant motion of the blood once formed persuaded him that the causes of the circulation could be traced back to the blood itself. A vital, constantly moving blood rendered unnecessary the notion of spirits, which had figured large in the schemes of many who had opposed Harvey or who had modified his doctrines in accepting that the blood circulated. Harvey insisted that it was the same blood that moved in the arteries and veins and that it was not the addition of spirits that made arterial blood different from venous. The innate mobility of the blood also distanced his views still further from the now widespread doctrine, largely derived from Descartes, that it was the heat of the heart that moved the blood. A primal, active blood was the start of the cycles both of circulation and of generation.[41]

This new insistence on the primacy of the blood led Harvey to say that its mobility included an expansive motion, which prompted the heart to contract and expel it. Probably he was thinking in part of what is seen at the beginning of the development of the egg.[42] He even likened this motion to the Aristotelian analogy of ebullient potage, because both motions depended on Aristotelian 'nature' as an internal principle of motion.[43] It seems as though the demands of the new emphasis on the primacy of the blood led Harvey close to an argument used against him by Primrose and others and taken from Aristotle himself. The expansion of the blood was also a common component of the systems of those who accepted the circulation component of Harvey's doctrines but who modified or misunderstood the rest. Glisson's 'mication' appears shortly after Harvey's reply to Riolan. Possibly the two men discussed the matter, for Harvey was now back in London, and Glisson spent some of his time in the College and some in Cambridge. Perhaps, in the end, Harvey had indeed found a sympathiser well placed in a university to spread

[40] See C. Webster, 'Harvey's De Generatione: its origins and relevance to the theory of circulation', *British Journal for the History of Science*, 3 (1966–7), 262–74. See also J. S. White, 'William Harvey and the primacy of the blood', *Annals of Science*, 43 (1986), 239–55. It has been argued that it was Harvey's view of the identity of the venous and arterial blood that gave him the idea of circulation. See Lord Cohen of Birkenhead, 'The germ of an idea or what put Harvey on the scent?', *Journal of the History of Medicine*, 12 (1957), 102–15.

[41] It is also possible to see the primacy of the blood as Harvey's reaction to those who had criticised him by pointing out that the heart in hibernating – but still living – animals is motionless. This meant that the motion of the heart, its ultimate quiddity, the result of his Aristotelian/Socratic search, was no longer a constant. In its place was the innately mobile and vital blood, possessed by all animals, the ultimate cause of circulation.

[42] In *De generatione animalium* Harvey says that the blood is prior to the heart embryologically and functionally. The image he uses for the expanding blood is of milk boiling. W. Harvey, *Disputations Touching the Generation of Animals*, trans. and ed. G. Whitteridge, Oxford, 1981, p. 242.

[43] G. Whitteridge, *William Harvey and the Circulation of the Blood*, London, 1971, p. 196.

the doctrine of circulation, just as Descartes, ten years earlier, had used Regius.[44]

If the entire circulation was the result of cumulated local necessity, how did Glisson deal with the category of 'usefulness', the Purpose that Galen had attributed to the organic parts of the body and which often coincided with 'faculty' in contemporary medicine? Robert Brady, Glisson's mouthpiece in the disputation of 1653, said that faculties were what he called 'relative qualities' or 'aptitudes', and not 'absolute things'. The pulsific faculty of the heart was simply a force based on the 'organic constitution', the structure itself of the heart,[45] combined with the mication of the blood. In contrast, continued Brady, actions – the example is pulsation – are absolute things, and occur necessarily from efficient causes (structure and action). So Glisson has done away with faculties as traditionally understood and substituted events linked necessarily to structure and action, the latter a form of tension. When Brady calls structure-and-action *organica sive mechanica*, he does not mean either the organic action of traditional theory or the mechanism that historians have seen in the new philosophies of the period. His mechanism is Natural Necessity, the law of nature that generally but not invariably acts for the preservation of the body.[46]

### Spirits

Despite Harvey, Glisson continued to give a major role to spirits, which were as we have seen a fundamental part of his natural philosophy. For Glisson the spirits in the body were the instrument of the soul and were informed by it; they were also the chief element of the blood.[47] The speeches for Brady's disputation on the arterial pulse are followed by a numbered series of notes that are Glisson's attempt to *demonstrate* the circulation in a *to dioti* way: from first

---

[44] The question of the primacy of the blood was related to the contemporary dispute about whether animals had souls. Since the Cartesians equated soul with reason, it followed that animals did not have souls; and to argue that they did seemed in addition to be impious. But many preferred to believe that animals were animated by something that approximated to the nutritive and vital principles of earlier times. Sometimes these could be derived from the Bible rather than from Aristotle, and the Old Testament could be read as indicating that the animal's soul was its blood. This was the position of Daniel Sennert, who sought defence for his views from a number of German theology faculties. D. Sennert, *De origine et natura animarum in brutis*, in the *Opera omnia in tres tomos distincta: Operum tomus I*, Paris, 1641.

[45] 'ipsa fabricata, structura', Sloane 3310, f. 252. See also f. 254.

[46] For example in the case of a ligature causing a swelling of the veins, the law of nature forces more blood into an already full part, causing pain and damage.

[47] 'Insuper demonstrari potest ex confessione tum medicorum tum peripateticorum, spiritus vitales qui princeps elementum sanguinis sunt ab anima informari Fatentur enim hosce spiritus esse primum instrumentum animae . . . ' Sloane 3310, f. 229.

principles.[48] These include the structure of the heart, veins, arteries and valves. That is, Glisson is saying, almost as Descartes had, that given this structure there can be no other way in which the blood can move. But quite unlike Descartes Glisson is also saying that these first principles of nature include purpose or 'cause' as in traditional demonstrative knowledge: the necessity of respiration and of life itself demand, and are the final cause of, circulation. It is in Glisson's view primarily the spirits circulating with the blood that have chief place here. The blood carries them to the extremities, a process that is essentially life itself. Glisson's beliefs about the spirits were in practice axioms that need not – perhaps could not – be demonstrated. His notes here contain a rare passage in English.

> De Corde
> Some thinges are here granted as
> 1. that the heart makes vitall blood & vitall spirit.
> 2. that it is the fountaine of heat in the body.
> 3. that it sends vitall blood to all parts.[49]

This vital spirit was drawn ultimately from the respired air, and acquiring it and distributing it after concoction in the heart were the purposes of respiration and pulsation in the heart: in Glisson's language the vital spirit is the single 'cause' of respiration and pulse.[50]

## Demonstration

When Glisson argues for the circulation on the basis of natural necessity he is arguing (to use his own words) a priori.[51] Let us recall that he had used such terms in setting out the fundamentals of his natural philosophy. God relates to the physical world a priori, as a revealed first cause. Likewise in the case of the circulation, Glisson is starting from first principles and showing what emerges from them. He also uses the term *to dioti* to mean the same.[52] He explains that he is not particularly anxious about method, because often enough discussion about method takes precedence over the actual investigation; but he recognises his audience's expectations and explains the difference between the two methods. A priori is demonstrable knowledge in the philosophical sense. What

---

48  Sloane 3310, f. 328r. 'Ordiendum videtur in to diote a fabrica cordis venarum ac arteriarum, earumque valvularum etc.'
49  Sloane 3310, f. 369r.
50  Sloane 3310, f. 372. This is followed by a series of theses on the relationship between the spirits and the vital faculty, and whether the faculty includes the power of attraction. There is no discussion and it is not possible to be certain whether these theses were duly sustained in disputation.
51  Sloane 3312, f. 334.
52  Sloane 3312, f. 393.

is a priori for Glisson is, like what is first in nature for Aristotle, not first in the senses but obscure and difficult[53] and open to the distortions of prejudice.[54] Yet the certainty that links first principles to the *explanandum* (Glisson uses a language of logical necessity that is close to that of Natural Necessity) makes the a priori method of demonstration superior to that a posteriori, just as the a posteriori method of knowing God can never be perfect. Glisson's complete demonstration of the circulation will – he says – rise from the a posteriori to the a priori. This is expressed in a connected series of pieces in the Sloane manuscripts in which he uses a number of ways of convincing his readership of the circulation. He carefully distinguishes the two methods, recognising the expectations of his readers. The a posteriori demonstration is a procedure of taking the results of experiments and inferring causes. It is explicitly analogous to the proof of the existence of God from His creatures that lies at the basis of Glisson's natural philosophy.[55] It is also very close to the various uses of the *regressus* technique, discussed elsewhere in this book and, moreover, gives a considered place to experiment, which is the subject of our final chapter.

The a posteriori method is best seen in Glisson's vivisectional experiments, accounts of which are also to be found in the Sloane manuscripts. They differ in a number of ways from the other pieces, such as the disputations we have looked at. It is partly that the language Glisson uses in them is strikingly different from both disputation and the monologue addresses of the manuscripts. These latter were sometimes lectures,[56] some of which were in English, and sometimes orations, formal and perhaps ceremonial academic exercises. As we have seen in the case of Harvey, formal academic exercises involved the deployment of rhetorical skills, which the audience expected. However ceremonial or formal they were still designed to win over the audience. In the formation of a consensus of belief, the inaugural lecture (let us imagine) of the Regius Professor of Physic at Cambridge would not be without influence. It is in what may be a lecture or an oration that Glisson employs his a posteriori method. He first sets about demonstrating that the blood always moves inwards in the veins: a first step in a systematic demonstration of the circulation. He does so in two ways, first without and then with arguments taken from dissection. He begins with an account of the experiment to which Harvey had attached the illustration in *De motu cordis*, on the external veins of the arm. Glisson describes how one may easily squeeze blood along a vein and through a valve towards the heart, but never back across the valve in the other

---

[53] 'a priori inquisitio remotius utplurimum est a sensu, adeoque obscurior difficiliorque et errari ob praeiudicium facilius exponitur'. Sloane 3310, f. 393.

[54] Sloane 3310, f. 393.

[55] Sloane 3310, f. 226.

[56] Sloane 3310, f. 374" 'I showed in my former lecture the distinction of the liver and the maner of passinge of blood through it . . . '

direction. As Harvey had done, Glisson exhorts his readers to do it a thousand times and consider the amount of blood that had passed to the interior of the body. For Glisson, beginning a verbal exercise, it is of course an 'armchair' experiment, a rhetorical device to persuade his audience.

The veins of the arm are the torrent of a river that we are investigating. In place of a dam, we place a moderate ligature above the elbow. It will be clear to your eyes that the veins swell outside the ligature. Why do you hesitate? Do you suspect some fraud? Try it at the wrist, in individual fingers and the thumb, at the feet, shin, and thigh, even at the neck (but beware the danger of suffocation that I have often encountered in venesection below the tongue): the veins always swell outside the ligature and collapse within. Do you still doubt the torrent of blood in these parts? Why should the veins swell outside the ligature, unless the torrent is inwards and now stopped by the ligature, as we said above about a flood? Why should they become empty inside the ligature, unless the flow is inwards? They are not filled as before from the veins now blocked by the ligature, just as in the dammed river we discussed. What? You will make the ligature not so tight that it cannot admit some blood running in an outward direction through the ligated veins? What kind of thing is this, that the flaccid veins would somehow expel their blood, notwithstanding the ligature, into veins already turgid? Do the poor, of their need, offer things to the rich? Nature is not so prodigal with her goods: it is the needy part that attracts, not the full; and the full that seeks where to empty itself, not the empty.[57]

Moving on to the arguments taken from vivisections – 'administrations' – Glisson's language changes strikingly. In terse, descriptive and prescriptive words he tells his audience to select the animal, divide its sternum with a suitable knife two to three fingers to one side of the centre line (taking care not to puncture the jugular vein). The assistants then step forward on either side of the animal to pull apart the divided sides of the sternum and reveal the contents of the thorax.

Glisson then describes two experiments in language which echoes the haste with which the experiment must be done before the animal dies. Displace the lungs to reveal the vena cava and azygos; ligate the azygos vein and note the swelling. Puncture it below the ligature and observe the quantity of blood

---

[57] Sloane 3312, f. 8. 'Sint venae brachij fluvij cuius torrentem quaerimus. Sit loco aggeris fluvio obducti ligatura supra cubitum moderata iniecta . . . Oculis cernas ab extra statim intumescere, ab intus subsidere. Quid haesitas? num qua fraudi subesse putas? Idem experire, in carpis vel in singulis digitis, polliceque, vel in pedibus, in tibijs, in cruribus, imo in ipso collo caveas de suffocatione (quae saepius vidi factum in sectione venarum sub lingua): Extra ligaturam venae perpetuo tument intra flaccescunt. Ad huc dubitas de torrente sanguinis in dictis partibus? Unde tument venae extra ligaturam nisi torrens sanguinis sit introrsum, et per ligaturam obstinctus, quemadmodum supra diximus deluvio? Unde detumescunt intra ligaturam nisi quod torrens eorum introrsum? non supple[n]tur ut prius venis extra ligaturam obvallatis, haud aliter ac in fluvio obstructo supra monuimus? quid? finges ligaturam non esse adeo arcta quin adhuc sanguinem extrorusm currentem per venas ligatas admittat? Qui sic? ut venae flaccidae exprimerent sanguinem non obstanta ligatura in venas prius turgentes? sive solent indigentes ex sua inopia divitibus ultro offere copias. At natura non suorum bonorum sic prodiga est. pars indigens attrahit non pars plena; pars plena quaerit ubi se exoneret, non pars depeleta.

that escapes (it can only come as a 'torrent' from the arteries). Ligate the vena cava just below the heart in such a way that the ligature can be tightened or loosened at will: you will see that (i) the whole vena cava swells; (ii) the blood in the vein above the ligature disappears into the heart; (iii) the beat of the heart begins to fail and will stop unless the ligature is loosened; (iv) when the animal dies you will see that the right auricle and ventricle contain no blood and the pulmonary vessels and lungs very little.

A number of things have combined to make Glisson's style so different here. In his own terms, he is now arguing a posteriori in describing experimental results and allowing the reader to infer (*inferas*, he says) conclusions (in all four cases that the blood moves inwards in the veins). The language is deliberately non-rhetorical and appeals only to the eyes and reason of the audience. As we have seen Glisson say elsewhere, it is this sensory evidence ('first in the senses' in Aristotle's phrase) that has the more immediate impact than the relatively hidden first principles that are the ultimate causes ('first in nature'). Causes can only be inferred from this visual impact, but the accumulation of consistent inferences seems to be what Glisson means by ascending from the a posteriori method to that a priori.

Glisson's language in describing these experiments seems naturally enough to us to be the language of experiments; this is what we are used to. But it is not entirely clear that Glisson has done the experiments, and less clear that he ever expected his audience to go away and do them. He is in any case presenting a purely verbal account, away from the dissection table. His use of language is in fact carefully studied and designed to appeal to some part of the sensibilities of his audience. Their eyes and reason are addressed, but no other part of their make-up. The gory spectacle, the pain and death of the dog or some other animal are not mentioned, although much could have been made out of the animal's sacrifice for the growth of knowledge in a rhetorical piece of writing. These things were real enough, and distaste for vivisection prevented Riolan and others from undertaking it.

So Glisson is using a certain mode of language for a certain purpose. He is taking his audience in spirit into the dissecting room as impartial observers and inviting them to witness experiments and make inferences. He is persuading his audience by making them in their minds witnesses of the experiments. To this extent he is using a device of speech by using experiments which he and his audience might well never witness: but he could only succeed if his audience recognised the value of such experiments, and knew that such things were done.

### Conclusion

Glisson was nearly twenty years younger than Harvey. That is not an explanation of why he accepted the circulation of the blood, but it helps us a little in understanding why he did so, for men young in 1628 more often did than those who were old. It may be that it also helps to recall that like Harvey, Glisson was English, a physician, a royalist, a Cambridge and Caius man, a fellow and censor of the College of Physicians, an anatomy lecturer, an experimentalist and an enemy of neoteric natural philosophy. These are not explanations either, and the evidence we have points – rather than to why Glisson should have accepted the circulation – to how he modified and propagated it in line with his natural philosophy. Firstly, his beliefs about how one could know God gave validity to parallel modes of knowing His creation, the natural world. The a posteriori mode was both observation of God's creatures and experimental discovery of their internal first principles. Secondly, his fundamental principle of the innate mobility of matter, based on its divine source, encouraged him to think of the vessels and the blood itself as causes of the circulation in addition to the heart. Thirdly, the innate mobility of matter, when that matter was configured in a certain way – as organs of the body – resulted in a natural necessity of action that replaced the old conception of 'faculty', by now difficult to defend. Fourthly, the same fundamental philosophical principles enabled him to make the 'spirits' of the body strictly corporeal and yet still innately mobile. We have seen in a little detail how in each of these cases he accepted, modified or disagreed with Harvey's doctrines. His agreement with Harvey was great enough to make his long career, partly in London and partly in Cambridge, and his disputations and other academic exercises undoubtedly significant in the formation of a consensus in Harvey's favour in the College of Physicians as in the University.

# 11  Harvey and experimental philosophy

## Harvey's natural philosophy

This story of Harvey began with the image of him raising his scalpel to begin the Lumleian lectures. It will be useful to return to that image in this final chapter. We have now seen how Harvey's dissection was related to his natural philosophy. We have also seen how his natural philosophy was based on an experiential Aristotelian model and a sensory and experimental practice that owed a little to Plato and a lot to Galen and the anatomists closer to Harvey's time. We shall be concerned in this chapter with an attempt to discover how important Harvey's experimentalism was for the new and much celebrated Experimental Philosophy of the seventeenth century.

The question is centrally one of the validity of experimental knowledge compared to that of knowledge derived from other sources. We must first therefore look at what Harvey thought on this matter. His natural philosophy, in the course of practising which he came to discover that the blood circulated, changed – at least in its external expression – over the period with which we are concerned. He began as an anatomy lecturer who used a scholastic apparatus that included the Aristotelian and partly too Galenic notion that knowledge of a part included and was partly drawn from knowledge of its purposes. Harvey as an anatomy lecturer dealt with a disputed question, a traditional *dubium*, in a slightly unusual way, by means of a simple experiment (he punctured the ventricle of the heart of an animal). This demonstration of the forceful systole sent Harvey further down the path of experiment that was already recognised in the medical tradition. He discovered the circulation as a result of experimentally establishing an earlier thesis and presented it with a confident experimental argument which was part of the natural philosophy that he had acquired during his education; he did not feel the need to justify it. Nor did he feel the need to find the purpose, or final cause, of the circulation as an essential part of 'knowledge' of it. While some of his enemies picked on this lack of justification of his natural philosophy and on the lack of a final cause of circulation, his followers picked up his experimental technique: the novelty and significance of Harvey's discovery focussed attention – it will be argued in this chapter – on his experiments.

As an old man, after he had written *De motu cordis*, witnessed the consequent European controversy, answered Riolan and written the introduction to the book on the generation of animals, his natural philosophy was expressed differently. It now existed in a different intellectual world, which contained also that of Descartes and a growing band of neoterics. He now felt the need to think about and to rationalise his method of procedure. He now found it appropriate to present an abstract discussion of the methods of gaining knowledge, a discussion in which he was more concerned than he had been in *De motu cordis* to give a theoretical justification for experimentally derived observational knowledge.

Was this a late rationalisation? Or was Harvey simply now making explicit a formulation of a theory of knowledge that he, like other Paduans, had addressed earlier in life? There are five main locations within his writings where Harvey discusses, or at least is explicit about his use of a method in natural philosophy. The first is in the anatomy lectures, where he uses a Platonic device, the Rule of Socrates, in collecting up instances of the thing under discussion and forming a composite image of it, which is then disarticulated into its natural parts. It is a mode of discovery, and in a perhaps limited sense is a procedure from observed particulars to a universal and back again; but Harvey does not use such terms. In teaching in the anatomy lectures Harvey uses the Galenic hierarchy structure-action-use-utility as a kind of Aristotelian demonstration from first principles.

One of the things he looked for in the body was the *utilitates propter quid* of the parts, their purposes or causes (including the final).[1] These were terms of the natural philosophy of his education, and terms he preferred not to use in the period when – secondly – he was defending *De motu cordis* and extolling the virtues of experiment, and when he made it a virtue of method that he had *not* considered the causes and purposes of the circulation.[2] That is, the discovery of the circulation changed Harvey's approach to *propter quid* knowledge. Harvey could not demonstrate the causes of circulation, particularly its final cause or 'utility'. He could not, then, give an apodictic demonstration, which the traditional philosophers agreed was alone true, causal, knowledge. He had to rely on *to oti* demonstrations, analytically reaching a description, *historia*. He necessarily relied on *autopsia* and experiment when presenting his case in *De motu cordis*.

<hr />

[1] G. Whitteridge, ed. and trans., *The Anatomical Lectures of William Harvey. Prelectiones Anatomie Universalis. De Musculis* (with Latin text), Edinburgh and London, 1974, pp. 8, 12.
[2] It has nevertheless been argued that Harvey was constantly looking for the purpose of circulation. See W. Pagel, 'William Harvey and the purpose of circulation', *Isis*, 42 (1951), 22–38.

Thirdly, in defending himself against Hofmann Harvey called himself an analytical philosopher, and an analyst who used an *analytica disciplina*.[3] The term clearly relates to the anatomical dissection of the body (in another context it could also signify the first stage of various kinds of logical procedure: we have to be clear that Harvey was not using it in that sense).[4] Harvey uses it in the anatomical sense and calls himself an *anatomicus analyticus*.[5] He said that the result of analysis was *historia*, that is, a simple description of what was found (we have seen the term was used for the 'empirical' observations of Hippocrates). What was found was in the simplest manner demonstrated to the senses. None of this was a rational process, and Harvey said that the production of *historiae* comes *before* looking for causes or resolving doubts: two of the traditional and highly rational ways of completing an enquiry.[6] For the process of revealing *historiae* analytically, Harvey also used the traditional Latin term *quod sit*,[7] simply, 'that it is', in comparison to which *propter quid* was the search for causes (expressed in Harvey's early anatomy as the *utilitates propter quid*). He also used the Greek term *to oti* for simple analytical demonstration in preference to *to dioti*, the equivalent of *propter quid*.[8] (It is probable, although Harvey is not explicit, that the *historiae* are the instances that were to be collected up in the Rule of

---

[3] For Harvey's letter to Hofmann, see also E. V. Ferrario, F. Poynter and K. Franklin, 'William Harvey's debate with Caspar Hofmann on the circulation of the blood. New documentary evidence', *Journal of the History of Medicine*, 15 (1960), 7–21. Care should be taken with the text of Hofmann's letter to Harvey, for neither Franklin's translation nor the earlier printed version (Richter) do justice to the original (published by Whitteridge; see note 8 below).

[4] A number of medieval and Renaissance writers from Gentile da Foligno to Leoniceno and beyond made formal distinctions between different types of procedure. The three disciplines or methods discussed by Galen at the beginning of the *Tegni* formed a basis for many commentaries of this sort. See Turrisianus, *Plusquam commentum in parvam Galeni Artem . . . Hali, qui Galeni Artem primus exposuit. Ioannitii ad eandem Introductio. Gentilis, qui primum eiusdem Artem librum partim explicando partim dubitando declaravit. Nicolai Leoniceni Quaestio de tribus doctrinis*, Venice, 1557; also P.-G. Ottosson, *Scholastic Medicine and Philosophy. A Study of Commentaries on Galen's Tegni (c. 1300–1450)*, Uppsala, 1982. 'Analysis' could also imply of course Aristotle's *Prior* and *Posterior Analytics*, important statutory parts of the arts course. Piccolomini also identified the physical business of dissection with the philosophical progression from universals to particulars. But for him both are *rational* processes reaching parts invisible to the senses. Archangelus Piccolomineus, *Anatomicae Praelectiones*, Rome, 1586, book 1, lecture 1, p. 3; book 2, lecture 1, p. 39.

[5] Ferrario, Poynter and Franklin, 'Harvey's debate'.

[6] Harvey may have regarded them as being 'synthetic' as opposed to analytical, and there is little evidence that he regarded them as proper parts of procedure.

[7] W. Harvey, *Exercitatio anatomica de circulatione sanguinis*, Cambridge, 1649, p. 76. The terminology does not survive Franklin's translation.

[8] The text of Hofmann's letter to Harvey is given as an appendix to G. Whitteridge, *William Harvey and the Circulation of the Blood*, London and New York, 1971, p. 238. Harvey's reply is also given (p. 248), in a text fuller than that of the seventeenth-century collection: G. Richter, *Epistolae selectiores III mantissae sex, IV spicilegium*, Nuremberg, 1642, p. 808. Thus Harvey's Greek phrase *to oti* is represented in the shorter text simply by *historia* (and his *to dioti* is given the meaning of 'giving causes').

Socrates to form a kind of composite universal.) Harvey sometimes used the Greek term *deiktikos* for the simple demonstration of *historiae*.[9]

Fourthly, and as we have seen, when Harvey replied to Riolan he raised 'limited explanation' as a principle of procedure. This was essentially *to oti* knowledge. Lastly, Harvey gave a considered account of the modes of reaching knowledge in the preface to his book on the generation of animals.

Because Harvey discussed means of reaching knowledge in general terms in the preface to *De generatione animalium* we may suppose he intended it to cover retrospectively also the knowledge that he had obtained about the motion of the heart and which he had tried to transmit in *De motu cordis*. As a *post hoc* rationalisation of the procedure of 'gaining knowledge' of the circulation – that is, its discovery – we might expect to see Harvey now attempting to justify, by more elaborate means, the validity of knowledge gained directly by the senses, including that revealed by experiment. This is what he does.[10] Because it was Harvey the discoverer of the circulation who was now writing about the philosophical acquisition of knowledge and doing so moreover in a book based on further experiments, we might guess that his discussion of experimental knowledge was not ignored by his contemporaries.

To understand Harvey's argument here, we must briefly look at what his readers' expectations were – what they thought knowledge was. As before, we can assume that Harvey thought carefully about how he was to address his readers and therefore what sort of argument he should choose. We can gain some idea of the expectations of an educated audience by glancing at the opinions of the Paduan philosophers Zabarella and Pace. Zabarella had died a few years before Harvey was in Padua, but was a very well-known and influential author by the time Harvey was addressing Hofmann, Riolan and the readership of the book on generation. Zabarella's discussion about the various ways of gaining knowledge resulted in a generalised statement about the school-technique known as the *regressus*. He conflated the Aristotelian distinction between *to oti* and *to dioti* knowledge with the Galenic analytic and synthetic, and with the medieval *quia* and *propter quid*. The result was a double method of obtaining new knowledge, beginning with the particulars of observation. This, says Zabarella, is a lightweight and undeveloped mode of treatment, producing mere *historiae* like the causeless narratives of those who write histories and like Aristotle's *Historia animalium*.[11] The second part

---

[9] Harvey's reply to Hofmann in Whitteridge, *William Harvey*, appendix.

[10] In a useful paper on Harvey's methods, A. Wear argues that the method of acquiring knowledge that Harvey sets out in *De generatione* was a method he had consistently held since writing *De motu cordis*. A. Wear, 'William Harvey and the "way of the anatomists"', *History of Science*, 21 (1983), 223–49.

[11] Jacopo Zabarella, *In Aristotelis libros physicorum, commentaria*, ed. Julius Zabarella, Basle, 1622, p. 3.

of the *regressus* was the discovery of causal first principles and the explanation of the particulars of observation in terms of them. This is *scientalis*, true knowledge, the discovery of the unknown from the known and the 'exquisite portrayal of causes' that is intended by the new term 'auscultation' with which the new look at Aristotle in Padua had replaced the vulgar old *octo Physicorum* of the medieval curriculum.

Harvey's connections with Pace were slightly less tenuous than with Zabarella, for as we have seen, there is evidence that Harvey was familiar with his work. But in putting different emphases on the matter Pace presents a natural philosophy from which Harvey in practice differed more than he did from Zabarella. Beginning his commentary on book 2 of the *Physics* (where it was agreed that Aristotle really got down to business) Pace at once describes the *regressus* of the schools. The first part of it is used, he says, when the principles of demonstration are unknown to us and a *to dioti* demonstration accordingly is not available.[12] This first part is *to oti*; but unlike that of both Zabarella and Harvey, its purpose it to proceed analytically from effects to *causes*. While this corresponds quite closely to Glisson's argument *a posteriori*, it is not at all like Harvey's analytic discovery of *historiae*. The second part of Pace's *regressus* is a 'negotiation' of the intellect by which we gain better knowledge of the causal principles; and its third and principal part is a true *to dioti* demonstration. Here his discussion of what is first in nature and what first in the senses is close enough to Zabarella. Like him too, Pace discusses the scholarship behind the change in names from the *octo Physicorum* to 'Auscultations' (the change implies that the scholars thought of themselves as 'listening' to Aristotle directly rather than through the old commentators). It is all part of the new Paduan Aristotelianism of the late sixteenth century. But it is not at all clear that Harvey had a Paduan philosophical justification for his views on analysis, *historia* and *to oti* knowledge. He may instead have developed these views later in life in an attempt to rationalise the importance that he had been obliged to give to experiment.

If Harvey did not owe a direct debt to Pace and Zabarella, he was certainly familiar with a related discussion in the anatomical textbook of André du Laurens, which he had used extensively in preparing the anatomy lectures at the College of Physicians. According to du Laurens, who called his book an 'anatomical history' of the human body, there are two parts of anatomy, *historia* and doctrine. *Historia* is gained by inspection, whether of vivisected animals, dissected men or pictures in books: it is analytical.[13] Because it is a

---

[12] G. Pacius, ed., *Aristotelis Stagiritae, Peripateticorum principis, Naturalis auscultationis libri VIII*, Frankfurt, 1596, p. 422.

[13] A. Laurentius (du Laurens), *Historia anatomica*, Frankfurt, 1602, chap. 9, p. 23.

sensory affair, *historia* is more certain. In contrast, doctrine is, to du Laurens, more noble: it is knowledge, *scientalis*, not mere observation. (*Historia* and *scientalis* are also the terms used by Zabarella.) As such it was concerned with 'causes, actions and uses'; as part of *scientia* it had universal *theoremata* and broad notions, from which are built the first, true, best-known and immediate demonstrations, said du Laurens.[14] This part of du Laurens' anatomy, then, was *demonstrative* in a way that Harvey's *historiae* could not be.

Harvey was aware of the philosophy of the schools, if not explicitly from Zabarella or Pace. It is important for us that he also knew that the philosophically and medically inclined of his readers would be likely to agree with the two Paduan philosophers and the French anatomist on what constituted true and new knowledge. How then could he show that the circulation was knowledge if his method stopped at what Zabarella called the lightweight narrative mode of *historia*? In the preface to the book on generation,[15] Harvey tries to overcome this problem by taking the method further. He argues that the principles by which Aristotle made apodictic demonstration were universals, first in nature, but not first in our senses. There is an apparent paradox here, for Aristotle was also widely taken to have said that there is nothing in the mind that was not first in the senses, that is, first to us. Harvey resolves the paradox by arguing that what is first to us, first in our senses, the particulars of observation, once seen, *form a kind of universal* when the senses are directed elsewhere. The sensation of 'yellow' is not only separate from its subject-matter when the eyes look elsewhere, but repeated experience builds up in the memory the abstracted, universal, memory of 'yellow'.

Harvey's universal, constructed in this way, takes on the active role of a Platonic idea or form. The portrait painter who examines the face of his sitter has that face as a Platonic *eidos* in his mind thereafter, able to produce a multitude of physical copies on canvas, all different, but all related in being derived from the original idea, just as Platonic ideas are represented in the physical world. Harvey's message here is the importance of repeated sensory observation in dissection and experiment; but the process is not one of induction, but of reinforcing the universal that can occur from simple observation. Harvey contrives to make Aristotle say something similar in a passage where Aristotle describes how even animals, possessed of sensory perception and memory, can learn to act with 'prudence' in relation to what is good and bad for them and so clearly have judgment about memories that are more than mere accidents of observation.

So Harvey claimed that a universal could be generated directly from sensory

---

[14] Ibid., pp. 27, 38, 39.
[15] W. Harvey, *Disputations Touching the Generation of Animals*, trans. G. Whitteridge, Oxford, 1981, Harvey's preface.

experience. He can then give some philosophical weight to the matter by announcing the particulars of observation in conjunction with the universal as if from first principles in an apodictic demonstration.[16] Thus while the formation of his universal is expressly a means of *discovery*, when he begins to *teach* – to transmit what he has discovered – he starts, in the book on generation, in the *propter quid* way, from first principles. Above all, the sensory experience from which Harvey claims his universals are built, in the plumbing of the body as in its generation, is *experimental*. There is a clear sense in which a repeatable experiment is universal: it will *always* happen that blood will spring from a living, punctured and contracting heart. This is the importance of repeated *autopsia* on the part of Harvey's audience, his 'jury'; and in the preface to *De generatione animalium* he indeed urges his readers to accept on his authority alone nothing he has written, but to use their own eyes.

To put the matter slightly differently, Harvey was claiming that observation itself was a type of knowledge.[17] Knowledge of both structure and *action* was to be gained by observation, as the anatomists had been arguing for some time. (They were resisted by Aristotelians like Cremonini.) However, knowledge of *use*, or 'utility' or 'purpose', the top of Harvey's hierarchy of structure-action-use and approximating to a final cause, was for the later Harvey a matter for theory,[18] not for observational knowledge by experiment; he does not seem to have thought so earlier while giving the anatomy lectures.

To summarise, while Harvey clearly saw in 1628 that there would be at least among his medical readers an appreciation of the value of experiment, twenty years later he felt the need to put additional emphasis on, and some extra theory behind, experiment as a means of overcoming the philosophical limits of an analytical presentation of *historia*. It is for this reason that in replying to Riolan he brings forwards experiments that he had not considered worth his while to include in *De motu cordis*. To the same end he also struggled to perform Galen's reed-in-artery experiment,[19] which at the earlier period he had thought impossible, contrived some new ones and added, in this reply to Riolan, some theoretical justifications of experiment which he now found it necessary to make.[20]

---

[16] W. T. Costello, *The Scholastic Curriculum at Early Seventeenth Century Cambridge*, Harvard University Press, 1958, p. 95.

[17] This argument is made strongly by A. Wear, for whom Harvey's use of observation-knowledge is 'perhaps *the* epistemological discovery of the seventeenth century'. See Wear, 'William Harvey', pp. 224, 236.

[18] Ibid., p. 229.

[19] W. Harvey, *Exercitatio anatomica de circulatione sanguinis. Ad Johannem Riolanum filium Parisiensem* . . . (at p. 43, cont. pagination is 'Exercitatio altera at Johannem Riolanum in qua multae conta circuitum sanguinis objectiones refelluntur'), Cambridge, 1649, p. 46.

[20] Harvey, *Exercitatio anatomica*, p. 81.

It seems likely that Harvey's rationalisation about the formation of universals by observation had little impact on his readers, at least in comparison with that of his experimental method. By the time the book on generation appeared the controversy about the circulation was well-nigh over, and had given the world not only the basis of a new medicine, but a huge recommendation for the experimental method. Yet many of those who experimented were arguing that experimental results had no need of a theoretical or philosophical justification of the kind that Harvey had now turned his mind towards. More than the final finding of universals, Harvey's earlier robust declaration of the primacy of *to oti* knowledge, his 'principle of limited explanation', were central to the concerns and procedures of Experimental Philosophy. While anatomists of the early part of the century, like du Laurens, were striving to make 'demonstration' in anatomy a causal, Aristotelian affair, as the middle of the century approached there was a growing agreement that 'demonstration' in such a context was sensory and autopsical. Gassendi, as we shall see, thought of medicine that'l'art tout entier est conjectural', that is, in not containing demonstrations in any formal sense. Likewise, by the time Nathaniel Highmore published his anatomy book (in 1651, the same year as Harvey's book on generation) he could confidently assert that true demonstration belonged only to mathematics (no longer to apodictic demonstration) and that medicine proceeded on the basis of probabilities, not certainties. Highmore was finally fulfilling a pledge he had made in 1642 to defend Harvey against Primrose (the Civil War had held him up) and, like Gassendi, he derides Primrose's demand that Harvey should show the arteries-to-veins transit through the flesh by traditional demonstration. Such things are simply not possible in medicine, said Highmore: we argue *probabiliter*, or by induction, that fluids pass through the mesenteric vessels, the liver or the kidneys. The art of medicine simply is not demonstrative, and it is enough for the doctor to reason from probabilities: 'Ars Medica non est demonstrationibus ornata . . . nobis sufficiat ex probabili ratiocinari'.[21] Highmore is perfectly plain that it is by anatomical and natural-philosophical experiments and by *autopsia* that modern medicine is so superior to the dialectical and dissectionless medicine of the past. It is Harvey the perceptive, *oculatissimus*,[22] who has crowned the practical tradition in the Republic of Anatomy.[23] In the language of Boyle, Highmore and the Harvey of *De motu cordis*, the experimental method produced 'matters of fact' that relied on observation, claimed no philosophical certainty but only 'probable' truth and

---

[21] N. Highmore, *Corporis human disquisitio in qua sanguinis circulationem in quavis corporis particula plurimis typis novis et aenygmatum medicorum succincta dilucidatione ornatam prosequutus est*, The Hague, 1651, p. 149.
[22] Highmore's address to Harvey, *Corporis humani disquisitio*.
[23] Highmore's address to the reader, *Corporis humani disquisitio*.

avoided connections with complete and contentious systems.[24] Not only did Highmore write this at (or at least near) Boyle's house at Sherbourn, he was, so to speak, using Boyle's notepaper.[25]

The significance of Harvey's experiments for the Experimental Philosophy of the century might seem capable of easy assimilation by the historian of science. It is his task, after all, to find science in the past. When he finds it, it is by the intuitive process by which we find anything, by recognising its identifying characteristics. One such characteristic of science is that it is experimental; and the historian of science has long considered the seventeenth century as central to his interests. But Harvey was not practising science. He called himself a philosopher and practised natural philosophy.[26] Natural philosophy was a subject that was not necessarily experimental. Up to Harvey's time it was not even practical. Nor was it concerned with discovery. In order to understand what happened to produce the Experimental Philosophy, we need to look at more of the circumstances that made experiment a good strategy for Harvey and others.

## The medical experiment

It will be useful to begin by thinking of the theory of medicine (let us say at the time of Harvey's anatomy lectures) as 'advanced natural philosophy'. The physician after all began where the philosopher finished,[27] and related

---

[24] On the experimental production of probabilistic knowledge, see the valuable study by S. Shapin and S. Schaffer, *Leviathan and the Air-Pump. Hobbes, Boyle and the Experimental Life*, Princeton University Press, 1985.

[25] When Highmore makes a merely passing remark at the beginning of book 1 about the beauty of the human body and directly asserts that what is of interest to the physician is rather the analysis of its parts he crowns an attitude that could scarcely be more different from someone on the other side of the philosophical and religious divide. For Parigiano – and we have glanced at his example – the beauty of the body was an almost inexpressible centre-point of a medical, philosophical and above all religious system, to which an experimental method could add nothing.

[26] The terms 'science' and 'natural philosophy' still cause problems to historians. The assumption has been made throughout the present book that it is pointless to talk about 'science' in the seventeenth century because the term has irreducible modern connotations and was not used at the time. It follows that the 'scientific revolution' did not occur. For the problems of the traditional historiography see D. C. Lindberg and R. S. Westman, *Reappraisals of the Scientific Revolution*, Cambridge University Press, 1990, esp. H. Cook, 'The new philosophy and medicine in seventeenth-century England', pp. 397–436.

[27] We can recall that Primrose, a model Galenist, as late as 1650 insisted that the theory of medicine was indeed natural philosophy and that the medical man began his own special business with semiotics. J. Primrose, *Encheiridium medicum. Sive brevissime medicinae systema*, Amsterdam, 1650, preface. See the discussion by C. Schmitt, 'Aristotle among the physicians', in A. Wear, R. K. French and I. Lonie, *The Medical Renaissance of the Sixteenth Century*, Cambridge University Press, 1985, pp. 1–15, esp p. 15 on the phrase 'ubi desinit philosophus'.

the physical principles of the world to the particulars of the patient's condition. The educated medical man was necessarily also a philosopher in having passed through an arts course. In beginning his medical studies he was entering a field of knowledge that was not only practical in its purposes, but which had a tradition of experiment going back through Colombo and Vesalius to Galen.[28] Whatever it was that made Harvey first settle a disputed question by puncturing an animal's cardiac ventricle, he would have been aware of Galen's similar experiments in Rome, as well as having Fabricius' practical Aristotelianism as a model.

We can illustrate the medical sources of experiment and glimpse at the importance of Harvey's experimental method by concluding the story of Glisson. We left him performing a series of experiments which owed a great deal to Harvey's earlier experiments: he was but one of the many who saw the persuasive power of Harvey's pre-1628 experimental technique. Glisson uses a terse, descriptive and unrhetorical language;[29] within it he employs the term *experimentum* in more or less its modern sense (it does not signify simple experience alone). It is equivalent to the term he uses in his more formal titles in these manuscripts, 'administration'. Glisson's phrase *administrationes anatomicae* would have been immediately recognisable to any educated medical man of the seventeenth century as the title of Galen's most practical book on dissection (known to us as the *Anatomica Procedures*).[30] Galen's other major anatomical work, *On the Use of the Parts*, was a philosophical and partly natural-theological account of the actions and uses of the parts of the human body. In contrast to this the *Administrationes anatomicae* was closer in nature to a dissection manual for the Barbary ape. In choosing the term *Administrationes* Glisson was stating what kind of anatomy he was going to engage in: direct, descriptive, observational, experimental and vivisectional. This is why Glisson uses the language of experiment, so different from his rhetoric, and part of the protocol which invested experiments with the power to convince.

We have seen too that anatomy was very generally regarded as part of

---

[28] See R. Colombo, *De re anatomica*, Venice, 1559, who at once tells the 'candid reader' that he has a particular method, *administratio*. It includes Galen's vivisectional experiment on the recurrent laryngeal nerves, reproduced on a dog (p. 259). Harvey grouped Colombo with Vesalius for their useful vivisections of the heart and pulmonary vessels: Harvey, trans. Whitteridge, *Anatomical Lectures*, p. 266.

[29] Sloane 3312, f. 12. Glisson's terse text has been given in the previous chapter. In Glisson's terms these 'administrations' are *a posteriori*.

[30] At the time only the first half of Galen's text on anatomical procedures was known, the second having been preserved only in Arabic. There exists an English translation from the Greek of the early books by C. Singer, *Galen on Anatomical Procedures*, Oxford University Press, 1956. See also *Galen on Anatomical Procedures. The Later Books*, trans. W. L. H. Duckworth, ed. M. C. Lyons and B. Towers, Cambridge University Press, 1962.

natural philosophy. It revealed the work of God, taught man to Know Himself and related microcosm to macrocosm. Its medical purposes came second. Bartholin even wanted anatomy to be the first stage of natural philosophy, preceding all else. When anatomy came to be conspicuously successful in its experiments – as Harvey's were – then a model of procedure was available for the rest of natural philosophy.

Anatomy then, was a link between medicine and natural philosophy. While in itself, in the Galenic mould, it included consideration of function and extended to experiment, it also offered to natural philosophy other practical, indeed empirical, aspects of medicine. Let us see how. For performing an 'experiment' in the modern sense, Bartholin,[31] Pecquet, Kyper and Sanctorius,[32] all practitioners of a medical natural philosophy, all use the phrase *facere periculum*, 'to put to the test'. So does Galileo, so celebrated by historians for his experiments; and it seems more likely that he derived it from a medical source than that he 'influenced' the medical writers.[33] Galileo studied medicine in his early years; Sanctorius was in the same Paduan circle. Sanctorius' experiments and quantitative methods were designed to refine Galenic theory. He had studied medicine in Padua and was first ordinary professor of theory of medicine there from 1611 to 1624.[34] So he certainly used *periculum* in a *medical*-experimental sense.[35] The connotations of the phrase are – to be more precise – Hippocratic. All medical students and many more

---

[31] 'Mecum testantur Harvejus, Walaeus, et quotquot periculum fecerunt.' T. Bartholin, *Anatomia, ex Caspari Bartholini parentis institutionibus, omniumque recentiorum et propriis observationibus tertium ad sanguinis circulationem reformata*, Leiden, 1651, p. 252. He is reporting on the experiment of puncturing the ventricles of the heart.

[32] Pecquet: 'Nec vero me putes in majoribus Arteriarum duntaxat, aut venarum canalibus sanguineae circulationis fecisse periculum.' 'Neither imagine thou that I have but once made Trial of the Circulation of the Blood in the greater Vessels of the Veins and Arteries.' J. Pecquet, *Experimenta nova anatomica . . . Dissertatio anatomica de circulatione sanguinis et chyli motui . . . De thoracis lacteis dissertatio*, Paris, 1654, p. 30; *New Anatomical Experiments of John Pecquet of Diep*, London, 1653, p. 52. Albert Kyper, *Institutiones medicae, ad hypothesis de circulari sanguinis motu compositae. Subjugitur ejusdem-transsumpta medica, quibus continentur medicinae fundamenta*, Amsterdam, 1654 (*Transsumpta*), p. 3. Sanctorius put his art, of which he had thirty years' experience (*experientia*) 'to the test' (*periculum feci*) and later referred back to his experiments. S. Sanctorius, *De statica medicina et de responsione ad Statomasticem, ars . . . aphorismorum sectionibis octo comprehensa*, Venice, 1660: the *ad lectorem*. See also Charles Schmitt, 'Experience and experiment: a comparison of Zabarella's view with Galileo's in *De Motu*', in his *Studies in Renaissance Philosophy and Science*, London, 1981: item viii, p. 120. Schmitt also notes the use of 'periculum . . . fecerit' in a medical context by Nicander Iossius in 1580 and supposes that it might be of frequent occurrence in the medical literature.

[33] Although Galileo is luminous in traditional history of science, and celebrated for his use of experiment, he is rarely mentioned by the medical men of the middle of the century, at least those who wrote about the circulation.

[34] See N. Siraisi, *Avicenna in Renaissance Italy. The Canon and Medical Teaching in Italian Universities after 1500*, Princeton University Press, 1987, p. 206.

[35] Schmitt, 'Experience and experiment', pp. 80–138; 117.

men besides would have been familiar with the first and most famous aphorism of the Father of Medicine: life is short, the art is long; opportunity fleeting, *experiment dangerous*, judgment difficult. In the differing translations of the aphorism, including the well-known ones by Cornarius and Leoniceno,[36] the one constant is the phrase *experimentum periculosum*. While *experimentum*, like *experientia*, can mean 'experience' as well as 'experiment', or 'trial', yet because *periculum* also signifies an attempt or trial, together with the attendant dangers the whole phrase *experimentum periculosum* can hardly mean passive experience. The point of qualifying the noun *experimentum* with an adjective derived from *periculum* in translating the Greek seems to have been to emphasise that what is meant is an active attempt with an uncertain outcome. Whatever had been intended by the Greek author, his Renaissance translators saw in his words a clinical or at least medical trial.

In this way there seems to have been a Hippocratic as well as a Galenic source for the medical experiment. 'Experience' in its more passive sense also made a contribution: even those with the most limited reading of medical texts would see a strong and authoritative connection in the first aphorism between the making of experiments and the life-long, patient, empirical and Hippocratic observation in the art, where shortage of time makes 'judgment difficult'. It was to make judgment more secure that Sanctorius broke from the usage of his predecessors, who had explained the theory of medicine by reasons and authority taken from Galen (says Sanctorius), and instead sought to confirm theory *from practice*. The 'curing, experiments, instruments and the static art',[37] although directed towards a Galenic theory, were derived from the difficulties of practice so tersely put in the first aphorism. Sanctorius formally defined the relationship between practice and theory in a manner consistent with a newly practical natural philosophy: the theory of medicine, he said, can *only* be recognised from practice, and by means of a posteriori reasons and demonstrations *quia*. Since his practice was 'curing, experiments, instruments and the static art' we see in his techniques a direct experimental road to theory; and theory in turn represented axiomatic or philosophically real knowledge,

[36] See *Hippocratis Coi liber aphorismorum, Iano Cornario medico physico interprete*, in Cornarius' *Hippocratis Coi medicorum omnium longe principis, opera quae ad nos extant omnia*, Basle, 1558, p. 600: *Vita brevis, ars longa, tempus praeceps, experimentum periculosum, iudicium difficile*; and *Aphorismorum Hippocratis liber primus, Nicolao Leoniceno interprete*, in *Hippocratis Coi Medicorum Omnium longe principis, opera*, Basle, 1526, p. 343: 'Vita brevis, ars vero longa, occasio autem praeceps, experimentum periculosum, iudicium difficile.' Compare an eighteenth-century edition: *Hippocratis Aphorismi*, ed. Janssonius ab Almeloveen, Paris, 1759: 'Vita brevis, ars longa, occasio celeris, experimentum periculosum, judicium difficile.'
[37] 'Sanatio, et experimenta, necnon etiam instrumenta, et statica ars . . . ' Quoted by Siraisi, *Avicenna*, p. 210.

because Sanctorius used it in turn to demonstrate a priori the intelligibility of practice with a proper *demonstratio propter quid*.[38]

In short, the *facere periculum* of our authors was 'to put to the test' in medical circumstances. It implied proof and had connotations of legal trial, and Sanctorius claimed philosophical validation for his proof. But he did not express it in this way, discursively, with reasons and causes, but chose to construct *aphorisms*.[39] Nothing could more clearly express the importance of the form for a medical man, the respect in which the Hippocratic aphorisms were held, and the interpretation put upon them in the seventeenth century: that is, Sanctorius implies that Hippocrates, 'our great Dictator', had expressed himself with great authority and economy, had chosen aphorisms to avoid 'systems', had used a vast experience and had philosophical validity for his conclusions, although never expressed.[40] Sanctorius' work generated an immediate reputation and because it was experimental must have contributed like Harvey's to a feeling that the medical experiment was a valuable technique.

But there is more to the first Hippocratic aphorism than that. What Harvey and Glisson had to say about the greater impact of the visual and tactile might be summarised by us with the word 'empirical'. But rational and learned medicine had the most pressing professional needs never to be involved with anything empirical. Only one model of anything remotely empirical was allowable, and that was again Hippocrates, now in the person of the apparently detached and minute observer, eschewing 'systems' and recording case histories, *historiae*. It was Hippocrates the author of the *Aphorisms* and *Epidemics* who justified experiment within the context of patient and impartial recording of empirical facts. He did so moreover in a style of expression that might well have contributed to what men like Glisson thought was appropriate language for the experimental part of philosophy: terse, descriptive, based on observation and without rhetoric or systems.

Thus the medical man as an experimenter, wanting to give proper weight to his *autopsia* of experimental results, had to employ strategies such as invoking Hippocrates the observer to overcome the dangers of being perceived as an empiric. We may see how these strategies appeared to the traditional doctor by

---

[38] Quoted by Siraisi, *Avicenna*, p. 210.

[39] 'Ego veri primus periculum feci, et (nisi me fallat genius) artem ratione et triginta annorum experientia ad perfectionem deduxi, quam consultius judicavi doctrina Aphoristica, quam Diexodica describere.' Sanctorius, *De statica medicina*, the *ad lectorem*.

[40] Sanctorius (in the same *Ad lectorem*) glories in following in Hippocrates' footsteps, and also felt compelled by necessity to express the *esperimenta* (*sic*) of so many years in aphoristic form. The point for Sanctorius was this: Aphorisms were linked in a certain order, which demonstrated their significance, like honey that bees extracted from many flowers and afterwards elaborated and set in order (in the combs). By implication, the philosophical validity that Hippocrates' aphorisms contain in an unexpressed form lay in their inter-connectedness.

taking an almost final look at James Primrose. We have already glanced at his late and systematic assertion of the traditional reliance of medicine upon natural philosophy: it was his final defence – in 1650 – of everything that seemed to him to be decent and *right* in the tradition of medical learning from Apollo to the Arabs. His criticisms of the sectarians is couched in terms of Galen's Rome,[41] with the dogmatists, empirics and methodists endangering the stability of the Art. But this is Primrose, the veteran of many skirmishes with the experimental neoterics of the seventeenth century, and when he discusses the empirics, he means those of his own time without proper medical learning: *his* medical learning. They are empirics because they do not look for causes, said Primrose, but depend simply on their own experience – *autopsia* – or on that of other people – *historia*. This pejorative conflation of experiment with empiricism and empirics is precisely what Harvey and the others sought to avoid, either by defending the validity of experimental knowledge, by limiting its philosophical liability (to 'matters of fact') or by contriving demonstration for it.[42]

Thus this part of the story of William Harvey's natural philosophy is that his use of experiment provided an enduring model in the development of the Experimental Philosophy. But it was not the only model. There are other authors who helped to promote the experimental method, important among them William Gilbert and Francis Bacon. Not only was what they had to say on experimentation widely known, and so perhaps indirectly of influence on the manner and extent of the taking up of Harvey's doctrines, but Harvey was acquainted with the work of both.

Let us look at Gilbert first. Harvey knew of Gilbert (who died in 1603) for he was the son-in-law of Gilbert's friend Lancelot Browne and is the source of the story about the vast sums that Gilbert spent on his experiments.[43] Moreover, Gilbert had been President of the College of Physicians and a predecessor of Harvey's as a royal physician. The 'magnetical philosophy' that Gilbert had begun was still alive in Harvey's time, for there were 'Gilbertinos' in Oxford,[44]

---

[41] Primrose, *Encheiridium medicum*, preface.

[42] The image of Hippocrates as the theory-free observer and author of terse medical wisdom survived the period when Galen and Aristotle were coming under successful attacks as too theoretical and scholastic. Aphorisms (those of Hippocrates survived longer than Galen's theory of medicine) could indeed be used as an anti-scholastic form. 'Experience' expressed aphoristically was used to great effect against ancient systems by Bacon, John Dee and Nicholas Hill. See E.-M. Schepers-Wilson, 'The natural philosophy of Nicholas Hill: an introduction to its biographical background and the Philosophia Epicurea, Democritiana, Theophrastica (1601)', MPhil thesis, University of Cambridge, 1990.

[43] Harvey estimated that Gilbert had spent £5,000 on his experiments, L. I. Abromitis, 'William Gilbert as scientist, the portrait of a Renaissance amateur', PhD dissertation, Brown University, 1977 (University Microfilms International), p. 84.

[44] Gilbert's work was the subject of disputations in Oxford in 1608. Abromitis, 'William Gilbert', p. 124.

and Harvey perhaps knew men who had been to Gilbert's monthly salon in his London house.[45] His experiments with lodestones and compasses drew upon an earlier series of experience and treatises reaching back to the Middle Ages.[46] This series was newly important in an age of commercial and political expansion that saw the defeat of the Armada and the circumnavigation of the globe. Just as (we shall see) Cardano's experiences with pumps reflected the industrial and commercial vigour of the Italian city states half a century before, so Gilbert, like Cardano, was able to use the experiences of craftsmen and the purposes of merchants to illustrate the working of new principles of nature.[47] Medical experience came into the same category of craft learning, and one of the new ways of philosophising in Gilbert's day was to accept the value of experiential knowledge, while using it in a philosophically elite way. Its practitioners addressed each other as the Hellenists had done in the previous century, as a cultural elite who looked down their noses at the vulgar crowd of common philosophers in the schools.

Gilbert was a generation before Harvey (he died in 1603) and was untouched by any feeling that experimental results had a validity outside that of any system they might be built up into. Gilbert relished his magnetic system and felt himself to be a member of a small elite company of 'true' philosophers.[48] His natural philosophy was couched in a language which stretched the capacities of the Latin language to express the rarity and height of his conception of the world.[49] (He also supplies a glossary of technical terms.) It is explicitly addressed to others who scorned the vulgar Aristotelianism of the schools and who would understand what was in his mind. Hariot and Galileo understood at least part of this, and thought highly of Gilbert as a result.[50] We do not know what Harvey thought.

[45]  See R. M. Hutchins, ed., *Gilbert, Galileo, Harvey*, Chicago, 1952.

[46]  See Duane H. D. Roller, *The De Magnete of William Gilbert*, Amsterdam, 1959; Abromitis, 'William Gilbert'. Gilbert himself gives an historical introduction to his work: W. Gilbert, *De magnete, magneticisque corporibus, et de magneto tellure; physiologia nova, plurimis et argumentis, et experimentis demonstrata*, London, 1600: chap. 1, 'Veterum et recentiorum scripta'.

[47]  It was among Gilbert's immediate predecessors that the traditional mathematical measuring instruments of the practical surveyor and navigator came to be used as instruments with the purpose of investigation within natural philosophy. This was of great importance in the rapid changes in natural philosophy in the seventeenth century. See J. A. Bennett, 'The challenge of practical mathematics', in *Science, Culture and Popular Belief*, ed. Stephen Pumfrey, Paolo Rossi and Maurice Slawinski, Manchester University Press, 1991, pp. 176–90, esp. p. 187.

[48]  Gilbert addresses, above the rabble of the semi-learned, the true philosophers, 'vobis tantum vere Philosophantis', who obtain their knowledge from things, not only from books. Gilbert, *De magnete*, preface to the reader.

[49]  W. Gilbert, *De mundo nostro sublunari philosophia nova*, Amsterdam, 1561, esp. p. 4.

[50]  Thomas Hariot wrote to Kepler in 1608 recommending him to read Gilbert's *De mundo*, which was circulating in manuscript. *De mundo* was collected together after William's death by his brother and circulated in manuscript, not appearing in print until 1651. Parts of it date back to

There is no evidence that Harvey drew any support from Gilbert's work.[51] Gilbert belonged to a line of scholarship from Cardano, Fracastoro, Scaliger and della Porta that sought for a new 'subtlety' and questioned the fundamentals of the Aristotelian world-picture in a way that was alien to Harvey's instincts.[52] Harvey tried not to depart further than necessary from his perception of Aristotelianism, while Gilbert expressly directed his new philosophy against Aristotle[53] and promoted a universe with only one Element, where the Qualities were replaced by material effluvia and where the planets moved in a Copernican way through a vacuum. Gilbert sought to provide a whole new philosophy based on magnetism, while Harvey stopped at a demonstration *quia*. Gilbert's experiments were on magnetic substances, polarity, dip and deviation of the compass: his subject-matter did not allow him to be analytical in the way that Harvey was with living organisms. Gilbert's experiments were of a kind that were well known – for example in Harvey's Cambridge – in astronomical and navigational circles, and were not at all like Harvey's experiments in the medical tradition. Gilbert's work on the magnet was a special case within his radically new philosophy of nature. Bacon indeed censured Gilbert for erecting a whole philosophy on the basis of magnetism: an exercise very different from Harvey's *demonstratio to oti*. We can only say that in general terms Gilbert provided encouragement for those who favoured experiential and experimental knowledge above school natural philosophy. Those who were thus encouraged might therefore have been more sympathetic to Harvey's and medical experimentation.

Something similar can be said about Bacon. His importance in the spread of the new philosophies of the seventeenth century is without doubt. He was widely read and quoted by English and Continental writers throughout the century and beyond. His promotion of a practically useful natural philosophy,

the 1570s. Gilbert's work was known by Paolo Sarpi and Galileo by 1602. Abromitis, 'William Gilbert', pp. 8, 125. Galileo is said to have first had his attention turned to magnetism by Gilbert, who he thought was 'great to a degree that is enviable': Hutchins, *Gilbert, Galileo, Harvey*.

[51] However, H. P. Bayon, 'William Harvey, physician and biologist: his precursors, opponents and successors', part 5, *Annals of Science* (1940), p. 368, argues that Harvey was 'influenced' by Gilbert's work.

[52] His words at the beginning of his address to the reader serve to identify his enterprise: 'Cum in arcanis inveniendis, et abditis rerum causis perquirendis, ab experimentis certioribus, et argumentis demonstratis, validiores existant rationes, quam a probabilibus coniecturis, et a vulgo Philosophantium placitis . . . ' That is, he is concerned with 'subtlety' and the hidden causes of things and thinks that experiments and demonstrative reasoning can provide a better rationality than the opinions commonly, *vulgo*, given by the philosophers. He even puts an asterisk by the most 'subtle' of his reasons.

[53] His very title page asserts that his is a *physiologica nova*. He tells the reader that he does not call upon the Greeks because neither 'little Greek arguments', *graecula argumenta*, nor Greek words, suffice to demonstrate or exemplify the truth. The *De mundo* is expressly *contra Aristotelem*, but it was put together and probably titled by Gilbert's brother.

antithetical to ancient authority and based on experiential and experimental knowledge was a direct stimulus to the formation of philosophical clubs, not least the Royal Society. But again, his place in this story is largely restricted to the indirect effect that his promotion of the value of experimental knowledge had on the reception of Harvey's experimental methods and results. He died two years before *De motu cordis* was published, and while it is possible that he heard about the circulation, he did not write about it or Harvey. He was anyway suspicious about the principles of traditional medicine and tended towards the empirics. As for Harvey, there are only a few fragments of evidence that he took notice of Bacon's programme. Bacon's *Advancement of Learning* was published in 1605 and its Latin development, *De augmentis scientiarum*, in 1620 and so were available had Harvey wished to read them before publishing *De motu cordis*. The same is true of the *Novum organum* of 1620, with which Bacon wanted to replace Aristotle's logical works. But there is good evidence that Harvey did not appreciate Bacon's strategy of reformulating natural philosophy, or share his dislike of Aristotle. It may be that it was in his capacity as Harvey's patient that Bacon impressed him with his wit and style, but it is well known that Harvey would not accept Bacon as a philosopher, remarking that Bacon wrote philosophy like a Lord Chancellor. No doubt he meant in attempting as a powerful legal man to call for a reform in a field not wholly his own and with a view to practical utility rather than to the traditional goal of intellectual understanding.

Of Bacon's works only the *Advancement of Learning* was available to Harvey before the date of the discovery of the circulation (rather than before *De motu cordis*) and there is no evidence to suggest that Harvey had read it or that it was important to him in making the discovery; nor is there evidence that Harvey made use of Bacon's works in writing *De motu cordis*. But there is a mention of Baconian method in Harvey's late rationalisation of the means of producing knowledge in the book on the generation of animals. In the twenty-fifth exercise of this he adopts Bacon's term and announces his passage to a 'second vintage', a *vindemiatio secunda*.[54] That is, up to this point he has been making exact observations, *historiae* (on the genitalia of the hen and the day-by-day growth of the developing egg). Now, he says, he wants to show what fruit, *fructum*, this will bear. So, citing the principle of Bacon's 'second vintage', he is about to collect propositions, *theoremata*, from the *historiae*.[55] (He expects some of these propositions will need further disputation and

---

[54] W. Harvey, *Exercitationes de generatione animalium*, London, 1651, p. 75. The title of exercise 25 is *Porismata quaedam ex praedicti Ovi historia desumpta.*
[55] 'theoremata itaque nonnulla, ex enarrata historia colliganda veniunt'. Harvey, *Exercitationes*, p. 75.

testing, as he had thought about the thesis, in the exercise to Riolan, about blood being the source of heat.)

The exercises immediately following are no longer *historiae*, but present quiddity, or knowledge structured by causes: mostly the material and efficient, but including 'use'. This is the procedure he refers to in the third part of the preface, 'setting out the knowledge of generation', that is, teaching or demonstrating it, where 'demonstration' is causal and equivalent to *to dioti* or *propter quid*. This does not make Harvey a Baconian, for he has simply noticed and used a similarity between Bacon's 'second vintage' and the progress from presentation of *historiae* to causal knowledge. It is all a kind of *regressus*, particularly that sort often used by anatomists, and Harvey goes on directly to say that his method is to begin with the whole animal, as that which has to be explained, and to proceed backwards in time to its ultimate beginnings, almost prime matter (just as the anatomist proceeded analytically to the similar parts). This means that he can then begin his teaching, his demonstration, with matter, efficient cause and nature's strategies as first principles (as in a *to dioti* explanation and the anatomists' synthetic mode of teaching). This connection with Bacon, and the way Harvey expresses himself in the preface, make clear a distinction otherwise perhaps obscure. *De motu cordis* had been the culmination of a research programme that Harvey found himself engaged on when explaining the identity of the heart's systole. It was a research report and told primarily of the ways in which Harvey finally found that the blood circulated. He added what else he could in support of his findings, but he was not in any systematic or clearly defined way *teaching* about the motion of the heart and blood. But now, in the book on the generation of animals and with half an eye on Bacon's programme, he has reached analytically certain of nature's first principles (he seems also to want to imply that he had done this also in *De motu cordis*) and is about to *teach* his doctrines of generation by working, like nature, from first principles to the complete and finished animal. This of course is close to causal demonstration of at traditional sort, but in making it a mode of teaching Harvey is at some distance from a philosophical proof in a research programme. It is in teaching, not research, that he contrives what his critics found missing in the book on the heart, a final cause.[56]

So as in the case of Gilbert, but to a greater extent, Bacon's part in the story of Harvey is mainly that he helped to promote experimental philosophy and so indirectly to add to the standing of Harvey's methods and result.[57] Indeed, it seemed to Boyle that Gilbert, Harvey and Bacon were engaged in the same

---

[56] 'finalis caussa': Harvey, *Exercitationes*, p. 299.

[57] Bacon's *Sylva sylvarum*, perhaps concerned more than Bacon's other works with experiment, appeared in 1627, the year before *De motu cordis*, but long after the discovery of the circulation.

programme and so their work was mutually supportive. For Boyle, it was a Baconian programme (no doubt because he thought that he was himself engaged on such an enterprise), providing system-free 'facts':

our great *Verulam* attempted with much skill and industry, (and not without some imagination) to restore the more modest and useful way practised by the antients, of enquiring into *particular bodies, without hastening to make systems*[58] . . . wherein the admirable industry of two of our *London* physicians, *Gilbert* and *Harvey*, has not a little assisted him.[59]

## Gassendi, scepticism and experiment

Another natural philosophy that we must glance at is that of Pierre Gassendi. It was again a philosophy that determined how its possessor reacted to Harvey's doctrine and one which adds to our story of experimental philosophy. We shall also see that Gassendi's reading of Bacon was important for the formation of his natural philosophy, or at least that part of it that he used in considering Harvey's doctrine. In fact Gassendi illustrates the argument suggested above, that Bacon's promotion of an experiential natural philosophy would have contributed to a consensus that the experimental method – including Harvey's – as a prime example – was valuable.

Like a number of other figures we have met, Gassendi did not like school Aristotelianism. But unlike many, he developed an alternative, which he taught at Aix-en-Provence.[60] He was first put off Aristotelianism, he said, by its ethics. These were not only pagan and so objectionable to one in Holy Orders like Gassendi, but did not produce that serenity of the soul that was the purpose of philosophy. Gassendi preferred the Stoic ethics of Cicero, which liberated the mind from the cares of competing claims upon its attention by suspending judgment upon them. But Gassendi's dislike of Aristotelianism extended to the physical works, that is, school natural philosophy. His alternative to this was the atomism of Epicurus, modified as necessary. The great advantage with atomism as a natural philosophy for Gassendi was that explanations of the natural world couched in terms of particles in motion rendered unnecessary forms, causes and other peripatetic apparatus. Not only that, but this was a philosophy which dealt with perception as the reception of effluvia coming away from the perceived object: what was directly perceived then, although real enough and even leading to direct sensory 'knowledge', was only the *superficial* aspect of things. There was no possibility of investigating the

---

[58] My italics.

[59] R. A. Hunter and I. Macalpine, 'William Harvey and Robert Boyle', *Notes and Records of the Royal Society*, 13 (1958), 115–27; 123.

[60] C. Schmitt, 'Towards a reassessment of renaissance Aristotelianism', *History of Science*, 11 (1973), 159–93; 163.

essences of things and no possibility of knowledge of them. Above all what was impossible was peripatetic causal demonstration of a thing, *to dioti* knowledge.

This Renaissance philosophical scepticism could also be used to neutralise competing rationalist claims about the nature of Reformed and Catholic religion.[61] It was part of the rhetoric of both sides and more clearly than ever distinguished revealed certainties from the problems of human rationality. Gassendi was convinced of the weakness of human intellect, both in religion and philosophy, and tried to establish its boundaries in his scepticism.

All this is reflected in Gassendi's reaction to the controversies over the motion of the chyle and of the blood. Like others, he treated of them as a pair of topics which could be linked to form a new doctrine of nutrition, that is, the generation and motion of blood in the body. His old interest in and indeed sympathy for Harvey's doctrine of the circulation seems to have been reawakened by a visit to Walaeus in Leiden in or shortly before 1648. Reviewing the still vigorous controversy, Gassendi wrote out a *Discours Sceptique* on it for a friend. He signed it with the mysterious initials 'S.S.' and modern historians have not been aware of it. It was known at the time, however, and Riolan ultimately found out who had written it, and attacked it,[62] as he attacked many of the participants in the controversy.

Why was Gassendi sceptical about the circulation? It was primarily because of the image that had stayed in his mind for over twenty years of the events of his student days in Aix, when he had assiduously visited the anatomy theatre.[63] There, as we have seen, the dissector negotiated a spatula through the septum and had concluded in favour of an 'insensible transpiration' of blood in the Galenic manner through the septum. But this too was a subject of controversy and in the end they had a formal disputation about it at Aix. It was in the course of this that one of the disputants, the surgeon Payen, offered to demonstrate a manifest passage: Gassendi repeats the story of the astonishment of the observers as Payen patiently explored the passage and finally demonstrated to their eyes not only the canal itself but the membrane which lined it. Here was a fact of observation that Gassendi, however sceptical a student, could neither gainsay nor forget. As a considered sceptic in his later years he said that it was this demonstration that caused him for ever afterwards to 'suspend his

---

[61] On scepticism, see R. H. Popkin, *The History of Scepticism from Erasmus to Descartes*, rev. edn, New York, 1968, and P. Dear, *Mersenne and the Learning of the Schools*, Cornell University Press, 1988.

[62] J. Riolan, *Notationes in tractum clarissimi D.D. Petri Gassendi . . . de circulatione sanguinis* (n.d.) in J. Riolan, *Tractatus de motu sanguinis euisque circulatione vera, ex doctrina Hippocratis*, Paris, 1652.

[63] 'S.S.' (Gassendi) *Discours Sceptique sur la passage du chyle & sur le mouvment du coeur*, Leiden, 1648, p. 82.

judgment' – the characteristic action of the sceptic – on the Harvey controversy.[64] It was not only that a Harveian account of the action of the heart destroyed the traditional concoction associated with the passage of blood through the septum but much more that Harvey's account of circulation was (to a sceptic) a *system* that tried to give confident knowledge about things hidden to the senses, particularly the invisible arteries-to-veins transit. No sceptic could accept such a thing, and in listing all the alternative views given by philosophers like Descartes and all the problems that the controversy had thrown up, Gassendi is employing the sceptical technique of showing how all attempted rationalist accounts differ and are therefore untrustworthy.[65]

After doing so indeed, Gassendi offers scepticism itself as the only certainty. It is grounded in the weakness of man's judgment and the misery of his condition;[66] it is certain that while God gave us the desire to know natural truths He has not given us in this life the ability to achieve such knowledge.[67] What passes for it in the natural philosophy of the schools, says Gassendi[68] (and he is referring to the 'vulgar philosophy'), comes from the barbarity of the masters who force the young to pass the flower of their youth in a bitter and unhappy education, by which the light of nature is suppressed and the pupils rendered unfit for reasoning for the rest of their lives.

But Gassendi's scepticism was not entirely debilitating to his natural philosophy. We have seen that he gave confident belief to simple sensory observations. If anything did, these represented knowledge. From them could be drawn possibilities or verisimilitudes; for example, the notion that a manifestly expanding and contracting organ might be doing so in order to fill and empty itself had *beaucoup de vraysemblence*.[69] He seems to have felt for Harvey's scheme an aesthetic appeal that we have noticed in others: he admired its ingenuity,[70] its neatness and *la belle oeconomie* that it invoked in the body.[71] In listing a large number of the arguments that we have now met for and against Harvey, Gassendi appears both as a man who would like to be convinced, and as a sceptic dwelling on the falsity of all rationalist arguments.[72] It has been

---

[64] Ibid., p. 83. He uses the same phrase in introducing the work, p. 4.

[65] Gassendi, ibid., p. 144, extends the sceptics' case by imagining the hundred thousand systems of philosophy that might be argued about by their proselytes in the centuries to come.

[66] Gassendi, *Discours Sceptique*, p. 144.

[67] Ibid., p. 149.

[68] Ibid., p. 147.

[69] Ibid., p. 67.

[70] Ibid., p. 139.

[71] Ibid., p. 56.

[72] 'Mais je voudrois bien que les sectateurs *d'Harvaeus* me donnassent la solution de celles que j'ay proposees, & qui m'empeschent d'embrasser une opinion vers laquelle je panche beaucoup, & laquelle je souhaitterois solidement establie.' Gassendi, *Discours Sceptique*, p. 139.

suggested indeed that Gassendi's scepticism was a device whose primary purpose was to attack Aristotelianism and which was not turned towards such systems as Copernicus' new astronomy. Here he says that the criterion of accepting Harvey's doctrine is that it should, like astronomy, satisfy all the phenomena and save all the appearances.

So in theory Gassendi could offer only scepticism and immediate sensory conviction as certain. Both were important in the areas we have been concerned with in this book, including experiments. Whether or not there was a 'sceptical crisis'[73] at this time, certainly a number of the authors we are concerned with gave attention to the rival claims to validity of rational and sensory knowledge. Gassendi himself had done so in the exercises against the peripatetics of 1624. He said that while all that man could know was the superficial effluvia (the atomic *species*) coming from things, yet some ratiocination was possible about them. Gassendi accepted that some things acted as 'signs', like smoke indicating a fire or beads of sweat indicating the existence of pores in the skin.[74] He also used an Epicurean notion of 'criterion', one of which was the senses, receiving the signs, and the other the intellect, which gives us the source of the signs. These seem to be the *criterium a quo* and the *criterium per quod*, which he refers to in the *Discours Sceptique*[75] and which appear to be the sceptical equivalent of *quia* and *propter quid* and their Greek equivalents. But as sceptical, they were more concerned than these were with sensory experience. Gassendi stressed the importance of the microscope and telescope as extensions of the senses.[76] It was their concern with the senses that made Gassendi and Peiresc develop the Epicurean doctrine of vision and dissect the eyes of animals in tracing the path of the *species*: they saw the retinal image.[77] It need not be emphasised that dissection of such a kind and the use of microscopes was an experimental technique. Gassendi consequently argued against Liceti that his own theory of vision was better than that of the peripatetics because experimental. In discussing Harvey's doctrine Gassendi gave as much attention to dissections and vivisectional experiments as did the practical medical men who were fighting for and against Harvey. While Gassendi's style does not have the urgent 'experimental' rhetoric that Glisson uses, there is no reason to doubt the importance of experiment to him. He seems to have used a fish – a pike[78] – that other experimenters had not chosen, and if he even did not

---

[73] On medical scepticism see J.-P. Pittion, 'Scepticism and medicine in the renaissance', in R. H. Popkin and C. B. Schmitt, *Scepticism from the Renaissance to the Enlightenment* (Wolfenbütteler Forschungen, Band 35), Wiesbaden, 1987, pp. 103–32.

[74] See B. Brundell, *Pierre Gassendi. From Aristotelianism to a New Natural Philosophy*, Dordrecht, 1987, p. 101.

[75] Gassendi, *Discours Sceptique*, p. 151.

[76] Brundell, *Pierre Gassendi*, p. 102.

[77] Ibid., p. 89.

[78] Gassendi, *Discours Sceptique*, p. 76.

perform Galen's reed-in-artery experiment, he reported it as performed by 'one of us' and was prepared to accept the significance of its result.[79] There seems little reason to doubt that he removed the hearts of a number of fish[80] and observed that having become cold and quiet they could be roused to action again by warmth.[81] He touched the exposed heart and arteries of an animal to discover their synchronous pulse,[82] and to identify systole.[83] He also ligated a vein of a living animal near the heart and measured the amount of blood in the heart of a human cadaver.[84] The attention he gives to Colombo's description of the pulmonary transit,[85] and to Harvey's quantitative experiments[86] (and perhaps also to the work of Fludd, which he dismisses)[87] all show his concern with experiments.

Despite his scepticism it thus seems that in practice Gassendi was prepared to see experimental results build up to some greater scheme. Indeed, many of his arguments are those used by others to preserve traditional theory of medicine. He did not want to abandon the function of the heartbeat in producing spirits and heat;[88] he maintained the difference between venous and arterial blood[89] and the separateness of the traditional humours;[90] and like others he was concerned that circulation would destroy traditional medical practice, from the taking of the pulse[91] to bloodletting and frictions.[92] Moreover, Gassendi, however sceptical, was even ready to put forward his own system, which centred on the noble role of the auricles in controlling the amount of flow of blood into the heart. Driven by Harvey's quantitative argument and by Descartes' notion of drops of blood entering the heart, Gassendi asserted that blood entered and left the heart in quantities – perhaps one eight-thousandth of an ounce at every beat – that sufficed only for nourishing the parts.[93]

The evidence of the senses was that *evidentia* which – said Gassendi – presents itself to the senses in such a way that it cannot be called into question. In doing so it generates immediate faith in itself and than which nothing could be more probable. What is derived from evidence and signs by the intellect was for Gassendi not truth, but probability, as it had been for the Epicureans.[94] This sceptical technique was *empirical*. There may well have been medical as well as natural-philosophical sources for it. Gassendi is said to have been impressed by the attack on Aristotle's theory of demonstration by the teacher of medicine

[79] Ibid., p. 74.
[80] Ibid., p. 68.
[81] Ibid., p. 71.
[82] Ibid., p. 73.
[83] Ibid., p. 75.
[84] Ibid., pp. 130, 128.
[85] Ibid., p. 86.
[86] Ibid., p. 88.
[87] Ibid., p. 80.
[88] Ibid., p. 58.
[89] Ibid., p. 97.
[90] Ibid., p. 137.
[91] Ibid., p. 60.
[92] Ibid., p. 137.
[93] Ibid., p. 89.
[94] Brundell, *Pierre Gassendi*, p. 140.

in Toulouse, Francesco Sanches, who had in its place urged the value of immediate intuitive apprehension.[95] Also well known by the end of the previous century were the scepticism of Sextus Empiricus and that of Celsus' medical proem, in which he dealt sympathetically with the Empirics' attack on the arguments of the rationalists. All in all, then, Gassendi's scepticism, empiricism and the value he put on sensory evidence encouraged him in the belief that the probable truth of experiments was preferable to the false certainty of systems, an opinion which also contributed to the growing consensus about experiments.

Now, the experiments of Galen had been essentially *rationalist* in seeking to link Galen's anatomy-based rationalism to the wider aspects of natural philosophy. The medical tradition followed him. It was in their anatomies that the university doctors sought to promote the rationality as well as the learning of their medicine and, as we have seen, to defend it against the empirics. But by the middle of the seventeenth century a new dignity had been given to experiments that were more *empirical*. Harvey claimed that observation (mostly experimental) was a kind of knowledge of its own; Gassendi the sceptic thought that knowledge through observation was the only possible kind; Sanctorius argued that theory could only be known through practice; and as Galen and his theoretical medicine declined in popularity in comparison to Hippocrates, the empirical observer implicit in the Hippocratic works also gave dignity to empirical observation. So did Celsus, the 'Latin Hippocrates'. Celsus dignified the ancient sect of Empiricists, and so made them superior to the unlicensed practitioners – empirics seen as quacks – of Gassendi's day. He also supplied additional material, not to be found in the Hippocratic works, for an attack on dogmatism, or rationalism.

In other words, if there was sympathy for a medical sceptical defence of empiricism, this may be a second reason why medical experiments ceased to serve systems, and in an additional way acted as a model for the Experimental Philosophy as a whole. If this is so, then it would explain why the experimenters often made the sceptical claim that experiments did not reveal truth, but only probabilities. When Gassendi met Walaeus, the latter asked him whether he thought Harvey had *demonstrated* the circulation. Gassendi replied that the whole of medicine was conjectural and that whether or not Harvey had made a demonstration, the rigour of this kind of argument had no place in medicine.[96] A sceptical influence in experimentation might help to explain why experimental knowledge was probabilistic, a 'matter of fact' that did not contradict the various rationalisms.

---

[95] See the chapter 'Theories of knowledge' by R. H. Popkin in C. Schmitt and Q. Skinner, eds., *The Cambridge History of Renaissance Philosophy*, Cambridge University Press, 1988, pp. 668–84.

[96] Gassendi, *Discours Sceptique*, p. 56.

### Life is short

We have seen then that Gassendi could not accept the truth of Harvey's claim about the motion of the heart and blood because it looked to him too much like a rationalist system, and because of the reality – to a sceptic – of the sensory image of the porous septum. His differences with Harvey were less about the details of the circulation than about the possibility of arriving at knowledge of this kind.

But Gassendi was not without optimism that some natural philosophy could be arrived at, in time, and he says that he has often sought a philosophy (other than that of the schools), neater and more reasonable.[97] But where to find it? Gassendi believed that it would be found in the well-springs of the philosophy of Democritus.[98] Here, since all parts of nature are linked, the discovery of certainty in one part would lead to the certainties of all. But this is just the privilege that Gassendi believed God will not extend to man until the next life.

But again, however sceptical, Gassendi did not despair of 'ceste science que nous cherchons'. He identified it with the *desiderata* of Bacon, that is, those aspects of man's knowledge and enquiry that Bacon thought had been neglected and which would be important in a new programme of work. *Ceste science* was therefore to be concerned with practicality and utility, not attempts to understand causes; with accumulating experience rather than with intellectual illumination drawn from a few first principles. This feature of it appealed to Gassendi the sceptic, as too did the collaborative nature of Bacon's programme: it was to be a method that would take time to bear fruit, but all the more certain for the time spent in constructing it. Time was, to rework an old phrase, of the essence in Bacon's programme, for a single philosopher could not hope to experience directly more than a fraction of experiential knowledge. Bacon's techniques therefore included ways of speeding the processes of experience and of sharing the results.

Gassendi found that Bacon declared each *desideratum* as he moved through the branches of knowledge in the *De augmentis scientiarum*. As a sceptic Gassendi would have agreed with Bacon's description of human knowledge as a pyramid, founded on the reality given by sensory observation and culminating in God's actions, unreachable by the human intellect.[99] Like Highmore, he agreed with Bacon that medicine was entirely conjectural.[100] He would have shared Bacon's criticism of extreme sceptics who denied

---

97  Ibid., p. 146.
98  It is not clear that Gassendi had in mind Democritus *physicus*, the traditional archetypal natural philosopher, or Democritus as atomist. Gassendi, *Discours Sceptique*, p. 148.
99  *The Works of Francis Bacon*, ed. J. Spedding, London, 1857–74, vol. I, p. 567.
100  Ibid., vol. I, pp. 587–8.

the validity of even sensory knowledge[101] and shared with him the notion that such knowledge contained signs, which pointed the way to further knowledge. As an anti-Aristotelian Gassendi would have relished Bacon's image of Aristotle killing off other philosophies so that his own could rule safely, just as the sultan of the Ottoman Turks killed his brothers upon his accession.[102]

Most of Bacon's *desiderata* that relate to Gassendi's limited scepticism are concerned with modes of handling observation of nature. Bacon held it to be useful in investigating nature's normal processes to look systematically at examples where they have gone wrong. He wanted also to formulate systematically the experience of the diverse human arts. All three taken together were 'natural history', *historia naturalis*[103] and an important *desideratum* was the inductive treatment of natural history which led to philosophy. The induction was to be performed on 'experiences' which Bacon always calls *experimenta*. *Desiderata* from written sources include systematic statements of old problems in the study of nature, both general and particular – a 'Calendar of Doubts' – and a consideration of philosophy derived from biblical prophecies and classical myths.[104] Bacon's overall aim was to produce a traditional *sapientia*, a knowledge of things human and divine,[105] a goal that Gassendi would perhaps have thought too ambitious. Perhaps too Gassendi would not have followed Bacon in the construction of axioms or of a new style of metaphysics. But Gassendi surely read with sympathy Bacon's account of the various kinds of experimental procedure. Bacon lists and gives examples of Variation, Production, Translation, Inversion, Compulsion, Application and Joining of Experiments, and of Chance Experiments.[106] Many of these are simply observations, which lead to new observations, or to axioms and thence to new 'experiments'. Others are more experimental in the modern sense, but all of them are 'empirical' in that they were not made, as medical experiments had previously been, to support a rationalist position.

In this way then the *desiderata*, the systematisation of experience, the categorisation of experiments, the calendar of doubts and the inductive discovery of axioms were all devices having the important function of condensing for greater utility experience that would otherwise be gathered only over a long period of time. As Bacon says this is a remedy for the difficulty expressed in the aphorism 'life is short and the art is long'.[107] The allusion is plain: like the men mentioned above, Bacon found that medical *experimentum* of the first of the *Aphorisms* had a Hippocratic venerability that helped to

[101] Ibid., vol. I, p. 621.
[102] Ibid., vol. I, p. 563.
[103] Ibid., vol. I, p. 496.
[104] Ibid., vol. I, pp. 515, 520.
[105] Ibid., vol. I, p. 540.
[106] Ibid., vol. I, p. 623.
[107] Ibid., vol. I, p. 567.

protect it from the censure of being medically empirical. We can see too that Bacon's espousal of the empirical experiment and techniques, appropriately expressed in a medical aphorism, was a potent example of Experimental Philosophy for the new philosophers.

### Conring, Bacon and demonstration

The value of experiments was seen not only by sceptics and Baconians, but also by those who wanted more than probabilistic knowledge. One of them was Hermann Conring, who as we saw came, experimentally, to agree with Harvey. His natural philosophy was radically different from those of Bacon and Gassendi but in its explicit attachment to Aristotle not very different from that of Harvey. His experiments as part of that philosophy also differed, although as important within his system as were experiments in a 'system-free' approach. We also saw that Conring was an influential teacher and our picture of seventeenth-century experimental philosophy will not be complete unless we include the place of experiments within as well as outside philosophical systems. After all Harvey himself would have claimed to have experimented within an Aristotelian methodology.

Unlike Bacon's and Gassendi's, Conring's experiments were essentially rationalist and related directly to his theory of knowledge. Where some were making claims about the validity or at least utility of sensory knowledge and others chose to express themselves in aphorisms so that experience could be expressed in a way free of systems, Conring adumbrated his natural philosophy in a series of theses, where chains of argument were of the essence.[108] This natural philosophy relied on experiential and experimental knowledge in a way uncommon before Harvey and represents an attempt to defend the rigours of Aristotelian procedure against the neoterics. It is because they are so distinct in Aristotle's treatment that Conring derides Bacon's classification of the natural part of philosophy as being made up of physics and metaphysics.[109] He energetically denies Bacon's claim that Aristotle burned the books of Democritus so that his own philosophy would reign supreme.[110] This was an act symbolically attributed to Aristotle, the same charge that Aristotle acted like the Turkish sultan in killing his brothers in order to reign in safety. It was symbolic for those who were opposed to Aristotle, for this is Democritus Physicus, representing an older and more plausible view of nature: we have seen that Gassendi wanted to draw his philosophy from

---

[108] H. Conring, *Introductio in naturalem philosophiam et naturalium institutionum liber I*, Helmstadt, 1638.
[109] Ibid., thesis III.
[110] Ibid., thesis VII.

Democritus' well-springs and that Severino wanted to replace Aristotle entirely with a Democritean programme. That Democritus' name was also linked to atomism undoubtedly made it more popular with the anti-Aristotelians.

Conring also has to defend Aristotle against the ancient sceptics who denied the possibility of knowledge of natural things because of their mutability. We may not be able to step into the same river twice (because the water flows on) but such mutability is of particulars, says Conring, while knowledge is of (Aristotelian) universals. Unlike Gassendi and the new sceptics, Conring is confident that certain knowledge of natural things is attainable by the human intellect.[111] This *scientia naturalis*, Conring tells his readers, is achieved by the use of two great Aristotelian instruments, induction and demonstration.[112] Among all the authors we are considering Conring is very unusual in giving a major role to induction. While Bacon also gave a major role to induction in the production of matter-of-fact useful knowledge, Conring's natural philosophy was a rationalist system, and he uniquely claimed that induction could lead to true philosophical demonstration. Traditionally induction could never lead to a universal because it was always incomplete: one can never see all the examples of a kind and cannot produce a perfect generalisation. But Bacon and the Baconians accepted the limitation of human intellect and asserted that induction could give probabilistic knowledge that in practice proved useful in handling the natural world. Conring's unique position was to argue that induction could reveal *true* first principles. For him induction was sensory experience and *experiment* (we have seen that Conring vivisected dogs in deciding whether the blood circulated). According to Conring induction reveals in the first place descriptions, *historiae*. But these are more complex than the simple Hippocratic case 'history' and the results of Harvey's analysis, which we have met. Conring says that there are two ways of composing a history, an enumeration of the particulars (as the natural historians did) and the digestion of them into species and genera[113] (as in Aristotle's *Historia animalium*). What the histories reveal, says Conring,[114] are the principles of natural science: either we come to know them, or we prove them, by induction. But they are not generated or constructed by induction, for as primary principles they are undemonstrable. The importance of sensory observation is that it is the only way of coming to know these first principles. The importance of the principles is that from them arises certain, apodictic[115] and *to dioti*[116]

[111] Ibid., thesis V.
[112] Ibid., thesis VI.
[113] Ibid., thesis XXXII.
[114] Ibid., thesis XXIII.
[115] Ibid., thesis XXII.
[116] Ibid., thesis XVII.

knowledge. This is as much an attack on scepticism as on Bacon's denial of demonstration.[117] Conring wants to show not only that certain knowledge is possible but that it can only arise from sensory observation that reveals first principles. There can be no *scientia* of things remote from the senses, he says.[118] But not all induction reveals first principles, and in that case the histories have to be used as starting points,[119] and the knowledge they produce is no more than probable.[120] If accepted, Conring saw, Bacon's denial of demonstration would have meant that Conring was wrong in claiming certain knowledge from induction;[121] and Conring vigorously upheld his own method against that of Bacon. In short, Conring was highly unusual in holding that experiments would produce demonstrated knowledge. As an influential teacher he must have encouraged a number of people who would otherwise have been sceptical over the limitations that empiricism seemed to impose on experimental methods and the knowledge that arose from them.

## Experimental evidence: juries

Observation of the results of an experiment, whether producing knowledge directly or indirectly in some of the ways we have now discussed, could only do so in the mind of an observer. In order to convince many people – and thus hope to establish a consensus – the experimenter could arrange for as many people as possible to see the result. He could also try to make his big audience as distinguished as possible so that he could employ a second device, that is, to persuade people who had not seen his experimental result by referring to the trustworthiness of those who had.

When Hofmann told Harvey what he thought Harvey's duties were as an anatomist, he like Harvey[122] used the Greek term *deiktikos* for the simple demonstration of the *historiae* of experiment: 'Your office is to deal with spectators in the ancient way, that is, *deiktikos* . . . ' and 'hoc est, videte; hoc ita sit, considerate'.[123] In other words Hofmann's advice to Harvey was to demonstrate to the 'jury' who witnessed the dissection just as Galen had demonstrated, saying to them, 'Here it is, see it; observe it to be thus.' As mentioned above, this was not a *rational* demonstration and Harvey appropriately said that what it generated in the observer was the most convincing

---

117  Ibid., thesis VI.
118  Ibid., thesis XXX.
119  Ibid., thesis XXV.
120  Ibid., thesis XXX.
121  Ibid., thesis VI.
122  Harvey's reply to Hofmann in Whitteridge, *William Harvey*, appendix.
123  Both Harvey and Hofmann use the term. Whitteridge, *William Harvey*, appendix.

kind of *faith* that a thing was 'thus'.[124] The same term is used by the sceptical Gassendi.[125] We have already seen that the advantage of a sensory 'faith' in things was that it dispensed with the 'reasoning' that was seen to be at the basis of the different 'systems' of thought, and that the disadvantage was that *to oti* demonstration could be seen as revealing only particulars and in a way that looked close to empiricism; now we can see that another way to give credibility to *to oti* demonstrations was to make them before a competent audience. Hofmann also made it clear that the credibility of the anatomist among the learned depended on the worth of the jury. Choose a jury of skilled anatomists, he urged Harvey, and look after your reputation: do not dissect in front of barbers, moneylenders or self-important politicians:[126] Hofmann is using the language of the elite, the 'true' philosophers.

The importance of having a jury of good quality was clear to the anatomists. Colombo had demonstrated a dying bitch licking the pups he had just cut from her uterus to three bishops, a cardinal, two knights and a crowd of lesser folk.[127] Colombo in fact usually named his jury. John Caius saw his dissection of the hymen. The pope's physician was shown the vocal organs. Philosophers were useful members of the jury and Antonio Mirandola, the 'prince of philosophers of our time' had the pleasure of inspecting a pair of abnormally large kidneys. In a similar way Harvey could gain credibility for his observations by recalling that he had demonstrated them to the President and Fellows of the College and even to the king.[128]

Part of the purpose of an experiment, then, was to convince others. While Harvey's first experiments were private, designed to satisfy himself about the movement of the blood, experiments were much more often used as devices to convince. The experimenter was in a difficult situation. Where there was a convention that only *to oti* demonstration was acceptable, there were great difficulties in arranging matters so that a large number of people could use their own eyes. Fabricius and others had given attention to the design of anatomy theatres to maximise the number of observers – the size of the jury – but for the experimental result to be broadcast, a consensus reached and a change made in

---

[124] Harvey, *Exercitatio anatomica*, p. 81. Slegel uses the same word, *fides*, for the knowledge arising from vivisection: P. Slegel, *De sanguinis motu Commentatio, in qua praecipue in Joh. Riolani VC Sententiam inquiritur*, Hamburg, 1650, p. 22; and compare Gassendi, *Discours sceptique*, above.

[125] Brundell, *Pierre Gassendi*, p. 102.

[126] Whitteridge, *William Harvey*, appendix.

[127] R. Colombo, *De re anatomica*, Venice, 1559, pp. 256ff.

[128] We have seen how contemporaries took Harvey's 1628 dedication to Argent as evidence that the college had, like a jury, decided in Harvey's favour. Harvey said that Charles I 'much delighted in this kind of curiosity [the dissection of the organs of generation of deer] and was pleased many times to be an eye-witness to my discoveries'. Harvey, *Generation of Animals*, p. 336.

natural philosophy, large numbers of people had to be reached. Where there was no convention about the validity of *to oti* knowledge, then experiments seemed only to produce – to use Aristotle's language – particulars or accidents. In either case, beyond the immediate jury, the propagation of experimental observations was a business of words; and even where the words included exhortations to the readers to repeat the experiments, the verbal formula in which it was expressed was as much a device of rhetoric as a hope for the proliferation of juries. Becoming a business of words made such experimental results open to dialectical attack.

Harvey's critics Primrose and Parigiano represent those who did not accept the convention of the validity of *to oti* knowledge. The same can be said of Edward Leichner, who quoted them both approvingly and proceeded to argue that it was not possible to reach sound conclusions from unnatural experiments.[129] What is more absurd, he asks, than to judge the quantity of a humour (he is dealing with Harvey's quantitative experiment) in the heart of a vivisected and dying animal by the eye alone?[130] Leichner's arguments are entirely dialectical and he thought that Harvey had *tried but failed* to find *to dioti*, cause-and-effect (says Leichner), knowledge of the pulse: without a final cause, Harvey's argument must fail. Like other teachers such as Liceti and Riolan, Leichner found it necessary to pronounce on the controversy, and he does so without mention of *autopsia*. Indeed he asserts that in abstruse things,[131] certainty comes from reason, not sense, for the most subtle things evade our senses: the soul conceives more certainly than the eye can see.[132] While Hofmann could use the Aristotelian notion and argue that Harvey's quantitative argument about the emitted blood was mathematical and so revealed no essence of things, Leichner could additionally argue that as arithmetical the method was not even logical.[133] Clearly, experimental evidence was not a category that Leichner recognised and the eyes of a jury were not important.

While the faith or conviction that came upon a perhaps blood-spattered experimenter as a result of his experiment had to be transmitted to most other people verbally and could be attacked verbally, it could also be strengthened in the same way. One verbal technique was Harvey's and Glisson's use of a rhetoric of experiment, leading the audience intellectually into the dissecting room. Another was to conjure authority by reference to ancient experiment: *administrationes*. The consensus that formed among Harvey's followers

---

[129] E. Leichner, *De motu sanguinis exercitatio anti-Harveiana*, Arnstadiae, 1646, unpaginated: sig. Ai.
[130] Ibid., sig. Fvii.
[131] Ibid., sig. Gii.
[132] Ibid., sig. Giii.
[133] Ibid., sig. Gvii: 'nedum syllogistica'.

included agreement that experimental knowledge was valid, and limited. If the body under experiment behaved not in a capricious way, but in a uniform way, then one experimental result could be repeated. As suggested above, upon such a principle of repeatability the particular of sensory observation, the experimental observation, could in a way become a universal, known to many men. This is the urgency behind the words of many anatomists in calling upon their readers or auditors to perform the experiment themselves.

## Harveian experimentation in England

Above all it was in the work of Harvey that medical tradition of experimentation was seen to be most successful. Recognising this gives us a rather different image of the seventeenth-century 'revolution' in natural philosophy, a revolution customarily seen by historians as centred on the physical and mathematical aspects of 'science'. Only recently has the importance of Harvey's work been recognised.[134] There were, in the first place, a very large number of doctors[135] – men with a special interest in Harvey's work and a potentially large consensus. Not only was it a profession in a commercial sense, but in England at least religious and political disturbances closed off other professions.[136] Secondly, although physicians tended towards conservatism in matters of natural philosophy and based their theory of medicine in intellectual and social terms on a Galenic–Aristotelian natural philosophy, yet, as we shall see, as they came under attack from other organisations they developed the experimental part of their tradition and a mechanistic view[137] of the body that could support both experiment and Harvey's conclusions. This was in contrast to the vast majority of arts-course teachers – philosophers – within the university, who held on to their Aristotle rather longer than the university medical men adhered to Galen. Because the teaching of medicine and the experimental investigation of 'novelty' was also a university business, we should perhaps

---

[134] A welcome sign of change is the attention given to the medical side of natural philosophy by two recent historians. See H. Cook, 'The new philosophy and medicine in seventeenth-century England', in D. C. Lindberg and R. S. Westman, *Reappraisals of the Scientific Revolution*, Cambridge University Press, 1990, pp. 397–436, esp. 399–405. See also C. Schmitt in the works detailed in note 138.

[135] C. Webster, *The Great Instauration. Science, Medicine and Reform 1626–1660*, London, 1975, esp. pp. 138ff.

[136] Walter Charleton thought that the Civil War 'almost wholly discouraged men from the study of Theologie, and brought Civil Law into contempt'. See W. Pagel, 'The reaction to Aristotle in seventeenth-century thought. Campanella, van Helmont, Glanvill, Charleton, Harvey, Glisson, Descartes', in *Science, Medicine and History*, Oxford University Press, 1953, vol. I, pp. 489–509, p. 497. Webster, *The Great Instauration*, p. 149, points to the growth of the medical faculties in the Civil War.

[137] See Theodore Brown, *The Mechanical Philosophy and the 'Animal Economy'*, New York, 1981, esp. chap. 3.

revise the rather negative idea we have of the role of the universities in the 'revolution' in natural philosophy.[138]

Even Primrose, who had so scornfully pointed to the fashion for 'novelties' and their experimental investigation in the universities, was ultimately driven to experiment. Tirelessly attacking Plemp nearly thirty years after Harvey's announcement of the circulation,[139] Primrose was still arguing against the rapid ejection of large quantities of blood from the heart. He could not see how, if the arteries were full of blood, any more could be pushed into them by the heart. He now argued that the arteries and heart changed shape in pulsation, but did not alter in their internal capacity, so that little or nothing was ejected in systole. His experiment was to introduce two ounces of milk into the beating heart and see how much emerged. During six beats of the heart nothing did, and Primrose considered that he had demonstrated his argument. The description of the experiment is brief to the point of obscurity and his account of the apparatus ambiguous; but if we rule out deliberate imposture, it is clear that the traditional[140] and dialectical Primrose who had framed a reply to Harvey in a fortnight and another to the Dutch disputations in a matter of hours, had been finally compelled to recognise the force of experiments in establishing one's case. That even Primrose saw this is good evidence that the medical experiment, so closely associated with Harvey's name, was by the

---

[138] For a revised view of medicine within the universities, see C. Schmitt, 'Science in the Italian universities in the sixteenth and early seventeenth centuries', in his *The Aristotelian Tradition and the Renaissance Universities*, London, 1984, pp. 35–56. See also C. B. Schmitt, 'Aristotelianism in the Veneto and the origins of modern science. Some considerations on the problem of continuity', in the same book, pp. 104–23. His argument is stronger in his *Studies in Renaissance Philosophy and Science*, London, 1982, esp. 'Towards a reassessment of renaissance Aristotelianism', *History of Science*, 11 (1973), 159–93; at 177 Harvey is 'pivotal'. Schmitt also thinks the habit of dividing history of philosophy from that of 'science' is unsatisfactory, because often philosophy was the same thing as *scientia*. From the point of view of this book, however, many such difficulties disappear if we see natural philosophy in place of 'science'. Schmitt also gives a salutary warning of the dangers of the modern habit of concentrating historical attention on the accessible vernacular texts at the expense of the great mass of important Latin writings. Frank also gives a fresh picture of the new philosophy at Oxford. See Schmitt, 'Renaissance Aristotelianism', and R. Frank, 'Science, medicine and the universities of early modern England: background and sources, part 2', *History of Science*, 11 (1973), 239–69.

[139] Primrose remained an energetic controversialist. Despite being attacked by 'circulators' and receiving 'emissaries' from Walaeus, Primrose never tired of airing his old arguments and finding new ones. His experiment is described in his attack on Plemp's textbook, the *Fundamenta medicinae* (discussed above): *Destructio Fundamentorum medicinae Vopisci Fortunati Plempii in Academia Lovaniensi Medicinae Professor*, Rotterdam, 1657 (the year of Harvey's death), pp. 86, 87. Replies were made to him by Plemp (*Munitio Fundamentorum medicinae V.F.P adversus Primirosium*, 1659) and by G. Blasius (*Impetus J. Primirosi in V.F.P retusus*, 1659).

[140] Primrose retained his view of the learned tradition and here reasserts the value of the old commentators, including Gentile da Foligno, Ugo Benzi, Jacobus de Partibus, Jacobus Forliviensis, Thomas de Garbo and Nicholas of Florence. Although the circumstances of his

end of his life widely acknowledged as a valuable procedure in natural philosophy.

Within medicine, then, there were a number of sources for what the anatomists and others saw as a tradition of inherited, experiential and experimental knowledge of which they were part. A considered use of empirical observation, experiment and the proper use of language in which to express both almost certainly informed the work of Harvey, Glisson and others. Some of these others, like Ent and Scarburgh, were members of the circle known to historians as the '1645 group'. The interest of the group was declared by Wallis, Glisson's pupil,[141] to be 'The New or Experimental Philosophy'. Wallis was one of the few to mention Galileo in connection with experiment, but there are a number of reasons to suppose that Harvey must have contributed greatly to their conception of experiment. Firstly, the group was English, set up to rival foreign groups, and so the more readily adopted Harvey's work. Secondly, indeed, Glisson, Ent, Scarburgh and Merrett were all 'protégés of Harvey'.[142] Thirdly, the interests of the group tended towards novelties and included anatomy (that is, form and action) and natural experiments. When they discussed the circulation of the blood and the apparent vacuum above the mercury in the Torricellian apparatus they were adding new physical experiments to Harvey's older vivisectional experiments, for the two came to be linked (as we shall see). Of course, they 'misunderstood' Harvey in a number of ways that have become clear to us in the course of this book. The most general was to force Harvey's doctrines into a particulate, often Cartesian framework. Ralph Bathurst, disputing about respiration for his Oxford MD in 1654, followed and accepted Ent's defence of Harvey against Parigiano, but wanted to explain the body *mechanice*, avoiding qualities and faculties, especially of attraction. His explanation for the absence of a vacuum is the Cartesian circular displacement of air.[143]

The 1645 group was formalised to the extent that members had to pay subscriptions to allow the performance of the experiments. They also paid fines for non-attendance. It was, in other words, a group in which a consensus on a topic like the circulation of the blood might be reached, and as such is part of the story of Harvey's doctrines. The network of communication along which such things were disseminated included the 'Invisible College', consisting

---

life would lead one to suppose that he was a Protestant, when arguing with Plemp about the entry and action of the soul in the body, Primrose quotes (p. 237) as his authority pope Sixtus IV, surely not a Protestant strategy.

141 Webster, *The Great Instauration*, p. 56.

142 Ibid., p. 55.

143 T. Warton, *The Life and Literary Remains of Ralph Bathurst, MD, Dean of Wells and President of Trinity College in Oxford*, London, 1721, pp. 127, 129, 147, 149. This disputation is otherwise known as the *Praelectiones tres de respiratione*.

largely in correspondence to and from Boyle in 1646 and 1647. Also to be included in the English network is the Oxford group of the 1650s, directly influenced by Harvey during his period in Oxford,[144] from 1642 to 1646. It was during this period in Trinity that Highmore, George and Ralph Bathurst, John Lydall and John Aubrey worked on anatomy, chemistry and practical mathematics. After the siege was lifted, of the circle around Harvey only Willis, Ralph Bathurst and Edward Greaves stayed on. But their number was supplemented by others, and after Harvey's period of tenure as Warden of Merton, the group there continued under Jonathan Goddard, and included Charles Scarburgh.[145] William Petty arrived in 1649. He had studied with Walaeus and with Hogelande and saw the circulation in a Cartesian way. He had also pursued anatomical work in London and Paris, and in Oxford he set to work to organise the Experimental Philosophy Club (it included Wallis, Willis and Bathurst, and was 'patronised' by Boyle and Wilkins).[146] Petty became Tomlins' Reader in anatomy and must have played a role analogous to that of Glisson in Cambridge, helping to create an Oxford consensus and a seminary of Harveians. Thus he began his public lecture at an Act of 1651 with a verse praising Harvey; a number of theses were defended on topics consistent with circulation, such as the location of sanguification.[147]

Harvey was also very influential in the College of Physicians, the main arena for his followers.[148] Walter Charleton in 1657 painted a glowing picture of the college as 'Solomon's house', where the Fellows were 'Sons of Democritus', that is, 'Democritus Physicus', the sylvan dissecter of animals who inspired Severino. The analogy was apt, for Boyle, impressed by Harvey's use of animals, had called Harvey the 'English Democritus', and the fellows appear equally appropriate as the allegorical sons of Harvey as of Democritus.[149] (Boyle perhaps either did not see Democritus as the symbolic equivalent of Aristotle, or see Harvey as an Aristotelian.) The result of their activity was a great development of comparative anatomy (on the Galenic, not Aristotelian model). Part of their plan was to 'confirm and advance' Harvey's discovery; they

---

[144] The story of these groups has been well told by Webster and need not be repeated here, particularly as they become important at the very end of the period under consideration.

[145] Frank, 'Science, medicine and the universities', pp. 251ff.

[146] See also J. Gascoigne, 'A reappraisal of the role of the universities in the scientific revolution', in D. C. Lindberg and R. S. Westman, eds., *Reappraisals of the Scientific Revolution*, Cambridge University Press, 1990, pp. 207–60; p. 241.

[147] See R. Frank, 'The image of Harvey in Commonwealth and Restoration England', in J. Bylebyl, ed., *William Harvey and his Age. The Professional and Social Context of the Discovery of the Circulation*, Johns Hopkins University Press, 1979, pp. 103–143.

[148] See also Robert G. Frank, *Harvey and the Oxford Physiologists. A Study of Scientific ideas*, University of California Press, 1980. His useful discussion of the followers of Harvey also takes us beyond the *terminus ad quem* of this book.

[149] Hunter and Macalpine, 'William Harvey', 118–19.

have already brought the Doctrine thereof to so high a degree of perfection that it is not only admitted and admired by all the Schools in *Europe*, but the advancers of it also are able to solve most of the difficult phenomena in Pathology, only by that Hypothesis.[150]

The College of Physicians was one of the groups that found the experimental method attractive. In the period up to the Civil War the college was facing stiff professional competition from the surgeons and apothecaries, and sought ways of maintaining an image (and the monopoly that depended on it) that was more attractive than classical Galenism. It admitted some forms of the popular chemical medicine and adopted the strategy – and here Harvey was instrumental – of emphasising the experimental nature of up-to-date medicine. Experimental results did not necessarily clash with institutional Galenism, and as we shall see, methods were evolved of reading the ancients selectively, so that ancient *experiential* authority could combine with modern scepticism about systems.[151] The reliance of the medical men on sensory observation – sometimes noted disparagingly by the philosophers[152] – ultimately made possible a dismissal of Galen.

Similar groups and correspondences existed elsewhere. The short-lived group at Gresham College was particularly interested in structural and functional anatomy.[153] On the Continent there were attempts to foster supranational Protestant and Catholic groups for purposes related to religious promotion, natural knowledge and economic gain. Such groups and networks existed alongside the universities, which continued to produce their own kind of knowledge. Harvey himself engaged in a degree of correspondence later in life, exchanging letters with J. Nardi of Florence, R. Morison in Paris and J. Horst of Hesse-Darmstadt. The pattern of these and other exchanges was the individual's contribution to a consensus: to write to the major actors in a controversy, asking their opinion, enclosing one's latest book for 'review' and requesting an opinion of a third party and *his* controversy. It was through all such channels that Harvey's work was taken as an important model in the 'revolution' in natural philosophy.

---

[150] Quoted by C. Webster, 'The College of Physicians: "Solomon's House" in Commonwealth England', *Bulletin of the History of Medicine*, 41 (1967), 393–412.

[151] For the 'crisis' in Jacobean medicine and the College's reaction see Webster, *The Great Instauration*, pp. 315ff. and 'William Harvey and the crisis of medicine in Jacobean England', in J. Bylebyl, ed., *William Harvey and his Age. The Professional and Social Context of the Circulation*, Johns Hopkins University Press, Baltimore, 1979, pp. 4ff.

[152] Fortunius Licetus (Liceti), *De tertio-quaesitis per epistolas clavorum virorum, arcana postulantium, Responsa Fortunii Liceti Genuensis*, Utini, 1646, p. 137.

[153] See T. M. Brown, 'Physiology and the mechanical philosophy in mid-seventeenth century England', *Bulletin of the History of Medicine*, 51 (1977), 25–54.

## Experiential knowledge: how to avoid systems

Ocular demonstration, Harvey's principle of limited explanation and *to oti* knowledge were all similar to experimental results in producing fragments of knowledge not directly related to 'systems'. Such knowledge could be useful or attractive, like religious or philosophical scepticism, when the systems of the world, whether religious or philosophical, seemed irreconcilable. To illustrate this, let us recall what the ordinary professor of medicine at Leiden, Albert Kyper, wrote in his *Institutes*. He was acutely aware of the clash between his own fledgling Protestant republic and the Catholic monarchy it had escaped from; he was equally aware of the clash between the Calvinist Aristotle and the mechanical Descartes that had disturbed the peace at Utrecht and had had repercussions in his own university.[154] It seemed to him that the time had come to build for the future with a stability that had been lacking in the past.

He chose to do this, in his own subject, by writing a systematic textbook. We have seen that his address to a group of prominent lawyers and syndics of the state invokes a parallel between classical political philosophy and the new Dutch state as a basis for stability in the period after Spanish rule. Now is the time, says Kyper, to build a firm structure of true religion and true learning. The medical part of this learning, the subject of Kyper's book, is to be constructed on the firm foundation of the circulation. It was now 1654, and we must assume that a consensus had been formed in Leiden at least in favour of Harvey's doctrine. But Kyper sought stability also in keeping where possible to traditional sources within his medicine; in other words for him Harvey's doctrine was no longer attached to Cartesian mechanism, as it had been for Regius. Kyper not only avoids the Cartesian system but gives a structural interpretation to many of the traditional terms he uses, thus avoiding traditional causal systems of antiquity. Nor does he give credence in his medicine to contemporary chemical theory, which could invoke another system.[155]

In the sea of uncertainty in medicine, caused by its close encounter with a Cartesian *physica*, Kyper offers a lifeboat. It is built of physical principles brought over from natural philosophy. Knowing that medicine traditionally rested on natural philosophy and that the philosophers were in disagreement, Kyper's lifeboat offers his students a set of inbuilt and independent physical principles with which to steer between Scylla and Charybdis.[156] The principles

---

[154] Kyper, *Transsumpta*.

[155] Kyper retains the traditional categories of vegetative, sentient and rational soul. Kyper, *Transsumpta*, p. 4.

[156] Most of the details of what follows are found in the separately titled and paginated *Transsumpta medica, ea ex physicis repetentia, quibus continentur Medicinae fundamenta*, Amsterdam, 1654.

are minimal, certainly, but not to have had them would have diminished rather than increased the stability he was seeking. They are Christian principles (for example, God as efficient cause created the elements *ex nihilo*),[157] and they attempt to reconcile peripatetic and more modern theories of matter.

The circulation and these physical principles are intended to be the natural philosophy on which his medicine rests; but in practice his overriding consideration is to show that medicine is an art, not a *scientia*. He can in this way establish its autonomy from the uncertainties, confusion and difficulties surrounding the new philosophy. In a way reminiscent of Paracelsus Kyper argues that medicine was created by God in a particular way, so that a special revelation of it was possible for men with God-given capacities for it.[158] This religious position also distances medicine from *scientia*, rational knowledge. The art of *methodus medendi*, the way to cure, he says, remains the same despite the controversies in theory, *scientia*. 'The learned doctor is a poor practitioner' is a proverb for him.[159] The basis of practice in light of this, Kyper says, is to avoid rational, *to dioti* explanations and to prefer those *to oti*. *To oti* for Kyper as for others is concerned with experience, *experientia*, and the particulars of observation therein. Since he founded his entire medicine on the circulation of the blood, we can assume that he was familiar with Harvey and his experiments; indeed, he could hardly have been in Leiden without seeing the significance of animal experimentation. His experiential *to oti* knowledge surely includes experimental results.

But for Kyper induction from these particulars can produce universals in the mind. He is at pains to point out that the induction need not be complete, as long as the experienced particulars are mutually consistent. On the basis of assuming that nature has also made the unseen particulars consistent Kyper can proceed fairly directly, as Harvey did in his then recent book on generation, from particular to universal. Kyper too seems to have felt the need for a philosophical strength in medicine. The importance of this in medical practice, for Kyper, was that practical medicine is always concerned with individuals and particulars of observation made by the doctor in relation to them.[160] Not far away from Kyper's words is the image of Hippocrates as the patient and empirical collector of the particulars of observation. But Kyper's universal is not *causal* in the Aristotelian sense and his argument from it is not demonstrative. It is not part of a system. What Kyper has elected to do, in order to be of use to the wise and practical doctor, is to handle the particulars so as to

---

[157] *Transsumpta*, p. 19.
[158] It is his tenth 'foundation', *Transsumpta*, p. 4.
[159] *Transsumpta*, address to the reader.
[160] Particulars of observation are of course close to experimentally observed 'matters of fact'. See p. 4 of the separately paginated *Transsumpta*. The discussion of *to oti* is also in the *Transsumpta*, address to the reader.

produce an *aphorism*. It is here that Kyper is concerned with the *experientia periculosa*,[161] which might very well be in the passage from particulars to universal, from observations to aphorism. Kyper clearly believed he had found a philosophically sound method of arriving at medically useful universals without recourse to the troubled area of medical theory, which he avoided as *to dioti* knowledge. As with Sanctorius, who also gave experimental and philosophical justification for his aphorisms, we again see the importance of the venerable and system-free figure of Hippocrates lending authority to an empirical art.

That to Kyper *to oti* methods produced reliable and useful facts is seen in his discussion on how to read the ancient authors. He says that we can read the ancients in two ways: either in the *to oti* manner, that is, for their experience, or (less satisfactorily) following *to dioti*, for the reasons by which those facts were supported or discovered.[162] By this device Kyper could adhere to much of ancient therapy as experiential knowledge, emphasising the value of traditional medicine while carefully accepting some novelty in the theory of medicine, like circulation. We have seen that Riolan the Younger said much the same, in order to 'save the authors' and his father had used a similar device.[163] Hofmann too argued that we should take the ancients' *to oti* observations without their *to dioti* reasons. Again, it is a very clear illustration that the value of experimental or experiential knowledge was that it did not bind its user to a particular system or involve him in the destructive battles between rival systems. In short, Kyper, an important teacher in a significant battleground for and against Harvey's doctrines, recognised both the power of experiments to convince and the validity of experimental knowledge.

### 'Attraction', valves and machines

The problem of attraction was central to the new philosophy. It was partly medical in origin and was important in the question of the motion of blood in the body. The problem was handled by experiments partly derived from the medical tradition. By glancing at it we shall learn more about changes in natural philosophy in the middle of the seventeenth century, particularly

---

161 Kyper, *Transsumpta*, p. 4.
162 Ibid., address to the reader.
163 The elder Riolan, in commenting on Fernel's *De abditis rerum causa* and the 'subtlety' of its physical principles, which Fernel championed as a neoteric improvement on ancient knowledge, claimed that the ancients had in fact much experiential knowledge of the 'subtleties' of poisons, but did not know the reasons, in a *to dioti* way, behind the actions of poison. J. Riolan the Elder, *Opera cum physica, tum medica*, Frankfurt, 1611: chap. 10 of his commentary on Fernel.

those brought about by experiments, including those derived from Harvey's experimentation.

We met the problem of attraction above, with George Ent, and saw that for the new philosophers there were a number of difficulties about 'attraction': within the body it was the action of a 'faculty', an explanation which was coming increasingly to be seen as a form of words that explained nothing; outside the body it looked like action at a distance or the operation of a 'form' (for example of a lodestone) neither of which was acceptable to the new philosophers. Where 'attraction' appeared to be exerted by a incipient or potential vacuum, the traditional explanation often offered a sort of local sentience and vigilance on the part of nature, who drew things into where a vacuum might form in order to prevent it forming. The new philosophy often preferred explanations to be couched in terms of action by contact, generally by way of particles. But how then could one explain the apparent attraction so manifest in sucking actions, like that of inspiration in the body or by the action of a suction pump (see fig. 24)? In answering this question the philosophers came to draw parallels that had not been there before between the body and machines. We shall follow them.

In seeing how the question of attraction was tackled we shall see also a conflation of arguments from the fields of medicine, the physical part of natural philosophy and technology.[164] Let us first look at the latter. When Harvey discovered that the blood circulated, few people would have seen any essential similarity between the body and a machine.[165] Anatomists like Varolius[166] and (as we have seen) Piccolomini in the previous century saw the body as the material expression of the faculties of the soul. All agreed that the body was animated and that most of its actions were derived from the faculties that were functions of the soul. Many argued that the body was embryologically generated and developed by the soul. We have seen that for authors like Parigiano, Cremonini and Piccolomini this was consistent with and so supported by the religious use of the doctrine of soul. Bauhin and du Laurens used lofty rhetoric in declaring the body to be the image of God (and hardly therefore a mere machine).[167]

In none of this is any parallel between the body and a machine made obvious. Machines after all, were not animated, had no faculties, were (unlike animal species) perishable and above all were *unnatural*. When Harvey first

---

[164] See also H. B. Burchell, 'Mechanical and hydraulic analogies in Harvey's discovery of the circulation', *Journal of the History of Medicine*, 36 (1981), 260–77.

[165] See C. Webster, 'William Harvey's conception of the heart as a pump', *Bulletin of the History of Medicine*, 39 (1965), 508–19.

[166] C. Varolius, *Anatomiae, sive de Resolutione de corporis humani*, Frankfurt, 1591, pp. 2–6.

[167] C. Bauhin, *Theatrum anatomicum*, Frankfurt, 1605, dedication; A. du Laurens, *Historia anatomica*, Frankfurt, 1599?, address to reader.

discovered the action of the heart, he gave no indication that it reminded him of a pump.

Yet there were other elements in contemporary thought that became increasingly clear as the period with which this book is concerned progressed. Harvey may not have seen the heart as a pump, but he talked about and experimented with the blood vessels as pipes. Harvey had a feel for the concrete, which reached from his principle of limited explanation – his readiness to forego final causes – to his account of the plumbing of the body. His experiments on the heart and vessels would have worked on a machine. It is significant that Primrose, Parigiano and other of his opponents did not see this: in declaring Harvey's experiments as worthless because *unnatural*, they were pointing to the essential difference between a living and a non-living system. The traditional doctor feeling the pulse had his fingers on the vital faculty itself, not an 'accident' resulting from the pump-like action of the heart.

Harvey's concern with valves is part of this story. They were, first of all, central to the discovery. The notion that the blood was ejected from the ventricles of the heart in quantities too large to be assimilated by the flesh depended absolutely on the effectiveness of the arterial valves preventing reflux into the heart. Secondly, it was the fact that the valves in the veins pointed to the heart that (it is argued here) triggered his recognition of the circulation.[168] (Later, he used the valves in the veins as the only illustration in

Fig. 24. Attraction in the body and in machines.
The new philosophy sought to discredit all examples of attraction, whether inside the body or not. Regius shows with this series of pictures that the action of sucking air in during respiration (made visible by the image of a tobacco-pipe) is the same as that of bellows (used as an analogy of the expanding heart since ancient times) and water pumps, *siphones suctorii*. As a Cartesian, Regius' purpose is to show that the expanding thorax of the smoker, the boards of the bellows and the pistons of the water pumps all displace air as they move in an outward direction, causing a circular thrust which in turn compels smoke, air or water into the hollow vessels.

[168] Harvey's moment of insight seems to have included a reinterpretation of the meaning of 'valve' when such a structure was in a vein. 'What is it to be a valve?', he might have asked himself in an Aristotelian way. We might equally ask of the period 'when is a valve not a valve?' When it is ajar, of course, and allows blood to flow in a Galenic direction. It was Boyle who asked Harvey how it was that he came to think of a circulation of blood and who received the answer about the valves: R. Boyle, *A Disquisition about the Final Causes of Natural Things: Wherein it is Inquir'd, whether, And (if at all) with what cautions, a Naturalist should admit them?*, London, 1688, p. 157. See also Boyle's *Some Considerations Touching the Usefulness of Experimental Naturall Philosophy*, 2nd edn, Oxford, 1664, p. 34: 'Thus the Circular motion of the Blood, and the Structure of the Valves of the Heart and Veins (The consideration

(i)

(ii)

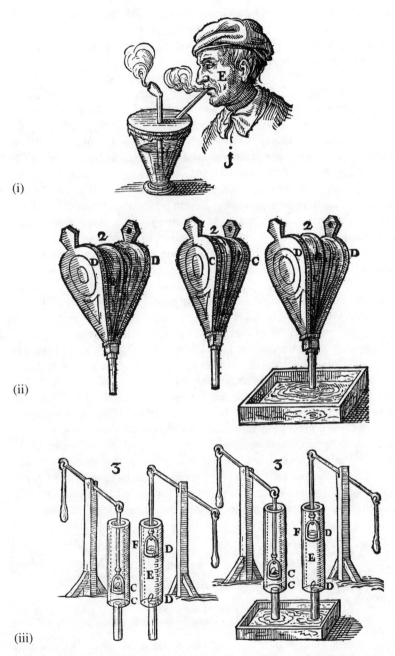

(iii)

Fig. 24

*De motu cordis.*)[169]. Valves are an image in which we can see the changes in natural philosophy as clearly as we see them in 'attraction'. Where 'attraction' or its new-philosophy replacements account for many kinds of micro- and macrocosmic motion, valves imposed direction on that motion. They had done so by nature's planning and skill since the Hippocratics and Galen, but now, to Cartesians like Hogelande, they were cardinal examples of natural actions in the body that *did not* have purpose and acted simply mechanically. Neither Descartes nor Hogelande would have denied that God had originally designed the body, but argued that the laws which it obeyed in its functioning were mechanical and did not need God's constant attention; the purpose or design they both denied was that the valve closed *in order* to impose a unidirectional flow. What they were denying was similar to what they denied in attraction by *fuga vacui*: a local, purposeful (and even sentient) action instituted by nature. Valves and attraction are symbols of the changes in natural-philosophical thinking; and because valves were also important to Harvey, we must spend a little time on the topic (see fig. 25). The importance of valves seems to us a natural part of Harvey's discovery. But this is because we are using our notion of 'valve', which was largely formed at about Harvey's time. Anatomists before him had neither the structure, action or name that we attribute to 'valve'. Firstly, what we call a 'valve' was for them a collection of structures, between two and four in number. What they called *valva* or some term that is generally translated as 'valve', we call the *flaps* of the valve. Thus it was commonly said[170] that the heart contains eleven 'valves'. Our 'valve' for them would have been *valva* together with *orificium*, or some similar term, indicating the orifice of the vessel where the flaps hinged. Secondly, it was a commonplace of anatomy that the flaps did not entirely close the orifice. In Galenic theory every concoction was a process of refinement and produced some waste material, which had to be ejected, if necessary by way of a valve. The action of the mitral valve in not closing completely and so allowing the emission of sooty wastes (which exasperated Harvey) was perhaps the most notable example. In short, where pre-Harveian anatomists used some term to mean 'door' in relation to these structures, as they often did, their notion of what they

---

whereof, as himself told me, first hinted the Circulation to our Famous *Harvey*) . . . ' See also J. J. Bylebyl, 'Boyle and Harvey on the valves in the veins', *Bulletin of the History of Medicine*, 65 (1982), 351–67, who plays down the importance of the valves in Harvey's discovery.

[169] It is plausibly argued by Don Bates (personal communication) that the reasons why Harvey selected this illustration was that it was so eminently *demonstrable* both pictorially and in the living body.

[170] For example, R. Colombo, *De re anatomica*, Venice, 1559, p. 179: 'Observandum est itaque orificio quatuor vasorum, quae sunt ad cordis basim, undecim membranas astarent quae trifulcae, vel tricuspides appellantur . . . '

were writing about did not coincide with ours in name, structure or function.[171]

Some shift from this meaning to the modern[172] was closely allied to Harvey's discovery of the circulation, and we should look at it a little more closely. It is partly the story of the use of mechanical analogy in anatomy. We can start with some of the authors whom we can be reasonably confident that Harvey read. Galen used the term *hymenes*, 'membranes', for the cardiac valves. He was referring, as anatomists continued to do, to the flaps of the valves. It was a word of wide application, and for example, Aristotle used it for the membranes of the brain.[173] But these flaps were *sui generis* for Galen, who did not know of any other such flaps in the body, and did not compare them to structures outside the body. The same is true of the 'Hippocratic' work *De corde*, for the author of which the cardiac valves were a unique instance of the skill of nature. Aristotle did not know of these flaps and their action (and *De corde* is normally dated after his time on that basis).

In *De corde* the flaps of the right ventricle are said not to close completely. Whether or not this was a source for Galen, he had other reasons to argue the same about *all* the cardiac flaps. These were concerned with the need to exchange impurities and other materials in the series of concoctions that progressively purified the nutriment.[174] So for Galen it was the *normal* mode of action for the flaps of the cardiac orifices to allow a two-way flow. They were not valves in our sense. Even when Galen compared the action of the heart to that of bellows, he was seeking to illustrate the powers of *attraction* of the

---

171  In particular we should beware of saying that these anatomists were mistaken in allowing the valves to be 'incompetent', a modern term indicating a pathological state.

172  The English term 'valve' does not seem to be older than 1615, when it appeared as a considered translation of Bauhin's *valvula* in Helkiah Crooke's *Microcosmographia* (published in London). Crooke also remarks 'Some men had rather call them *Ostiola* then *Valvulae*, which word we do not know better how to English then to call them *Floodgates* which stoppe and intercept the currents of waters.' (I have used the edn of 1631: p. 853.) This is close to Harvey's 'valvularum quibus cursus fluminum inhibentur in morem' (*De motu cordis*, p. 56), which suggests that Harvey used Crooke's text in the preparation of his lectures (the phrase is not in Crooke's source, Bauhin.)

173  Galen, *De usu partium*, book 6 and in particular chap. 14; Galen, *Claudii Galeni Opera Omnia*, ed. D. C. G. Kühn, Leipzig, 1821–33, vol. III, p. 477. Other uses of the term may be found in the dictionaries, for example, G. Liddell and R. Scott, *Greek–English Lexicon*, Oxford, 1883.

174  For *De corde* see for example the edition of E. Littre, *Oeuvres Completes d'Hippocrates*, Paris, 1861; facsimile reprint, Amsterdam, 1962: vol. IX, p. 86. The work has been translated by F. Hurlbutt, 'Per Kardies', *Bulletin of the History of Medicine*, 7 (1939), 1104–13. For Galen, *De usu partium*, book 6, chapter 16: see the translation by M. T. May, *Galen on the Usefulness of the Parts of the Body*, Cornell University Press, 1968, 2 vols.; vol. I, p. 319. See also C. R. S. Harris, *The Heart and the Vascular System in Ancient Greek Medicine*, Oxford, 1973, p. 394.

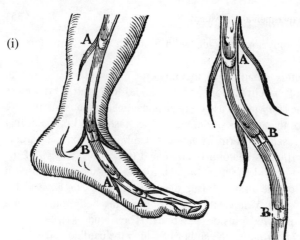

(i)

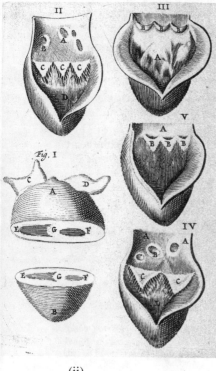

(ii)

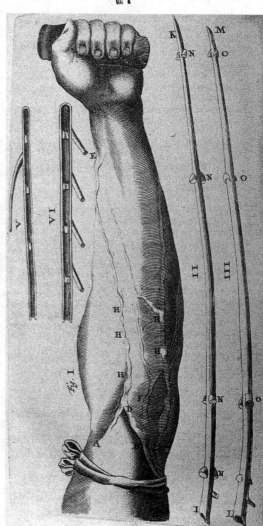

(iii)

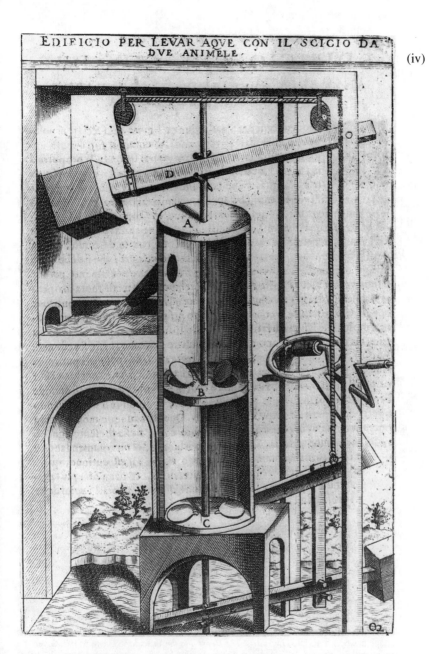

Fig. 25. Valves.

Where attraction was denied in the body and in machines, it was replaced by impulsion. While Cartesians like Regius relied on the notion of a circular thrust of displacement, others thought that the impulsion was derived from the spring and the weight of the air. What controlled the flow of impulsed motion in the body and machines were valves, highlighted by Harvey's doctrines and Renaissance technology. Here (i) Regius illustrates the valves in the veins; and (ii) Bartholin illustrates those of the heart and (iii) arm. They were seen as exactly analogous to valves (iv) in contemporary machines.

heart (like bellows being opened) not the action of the flaps. Indeed, the bellows Galen had in mind were simple bag-and-pipe affairs in which the air was drawn in and expelled through the same orifice: they did not have valves.[175] He seems originally to have drawn the analogy between the heart and bellows from *De corde*; what made them so appropriate an analogy was that the bellows, like the auricles of the heart, were paired (so that a constant movement of air could be maintained by their alternate expansion and contraction). *De corde* also said that the auricles served (like bellows) to serve the innate heat of the heart.

In other words Galen had no idea of a 'valve' in our sense as a device that imposes unidirectional flow. Instead he saw flaps that controlled the flow of a large amount of fluid in one direction and a small amount of a different fluid in another. He made no comparison with, and presumably saw no similarity to mechanical contrivances such as the rigid and unidirectional valves of hydraulic devices described before Galen's time by Ctesibus, Vitruvius and Hero of Alexandria.[176]

Like Galen, the anatomists of the Renaissance, many of whom Harvey read, discussed how the flaps controlled a two-way flow. For the flaps many of them used words which mean 'little doors', probably from Mondino's use of *ostiola*[177] (which 'hinged' in the *orificium* of the vessel). The Galenic two-way flow could be conflated with Aristotle's ignorance of the valves and allowed a number of anatomists to elaborate schemes of bloodflow around the heart that were non-Galenic and which often sought some symmetry between the right and left sides of the heart. Massa, Ulmus, Varolius and others produced schemes that departed radically from Galen and which form the background of the pulmonary transit controversy; but there is no space here to discuss them,

---

[175] Galen (1968), vol. I, p. 316, explains that the bellows is the best analogy with which to explain the attractive powers exerted by the heart. He returns to this topic in *De Hippocratis et Platonis Placitis*, book 8: I have used the *Opera omnia* in the edition of Junta, Venice, 1625: Prima Classis, p. 278r; Kühn, *Galeni Opera Omnia*, vol. V, p. 708. He also refers to it in *De Differentiis Febrium*, book 1, chap. 1: Kühn, *Galeni Opera Omnia*, vol. VII, p. 277. See also Harris, *The Heart*, p. 318.

[176] See A. G. Drachmann, *The Mechanical Technology of Greek and Roman Antiquity*, Oxford, 1973, p. 394; B. Woodcroft, trans., *The Pneumatics of Hero of Alexandria*, reprinted London, 1971, pp. 37, 105. Don Bates has reminded me that Galen's conception of 'valve' included what he had read about the cardiac valves in Erasistratus, where the flaps act partly at least by the mechanical action of the enclosed material and do not allow any return flow. The relevant passage has been translated by Harris, *The Heart and the Vascular System*, p. 197. Given the particular constraints of Galen's system that made some backflow necessary, I do not think that Galen's knowledge of Erasistratus' account of the flaps widens very much Galen's narrow view of 'valves'.

[177] Mondino argued that blood entered and left the heart across the 'valve' at the orifice of the vena cava. See Jacopo Berengario de Carpi, *Commentaria cum amplissimis additionibus super Anatomia Mundini* (with the text), Bologna, 1521, f. cccxxxii r–v.

especially as it cannot be shown directly that Harvey read the relevant parts of these authors' writings.[178]

With the development of Renaissance technology, the anatomists began to see parallels between structures in the body and in engineering. One of the first to do so in relation to the flaps of the heart was Alessandro Benedetti. As a dedicated Hellenist, Benedetti gave as much attention as did Galen and the author of *De corde* to the structure and action of the cardiac flaps as wonderful examples of the skill of nature. He called them *valvulae*, apparently a non-classical derivation from *valva*, a door (or leaf of a folding door), so that our tricuspid valve was *trivalvium*, a device with three doors. The function of the *valvulae* was to allow a two-way flow in the case of both the vena cava and aorta. But now the anatomist saw parallels in the outside world, and to illuminate his meaning Benedetti says the flaps of the heart are 'like some mobile doors', 'quasi claustra quaedam mobilia'.[179] This looks like a comparison with floodgates or sluices, which are moved to control flow of water, generally to hold *back* the mass, while allowing a small quantity to flow on, much as the cardiac flaps acted. Fernel, the widely read modern, used the term *valva* (rather than its diminutive) in terms which suggest that it was a newly applied name.[180]

Then the anatomists discovered flaps in the veins which reminded them of those in the heart and which provided a third image to use in discussing the *valvulae*. In the heart, where three flaps occluded an orifice, the flow of the smaller quantity of fluid was distinct but small, and where only two flaps were in operation (in the orifice of the arterial vein) it was greater. When Harvey's teacher Fabricius found single flaps at places in the veins, it was natural for him to conclude that the amount of blood that passed in what we would want to call the 'wrong' direction across the 'valve', was larger still. It was still, however, small in comparison to the mass that was held up, and Fabricius saw the function of his 'little doors' as controlling the flow of blood in the Galenic, centrifugal direction to the limbs. It is important for us not to call these structures 'valves' because if we do we have to think of Fabricius as fudging the issue, inventing an 'incompetence' or flow in the 'wrong' direction in order to meet the demands of Galenic theory (that blood moves centrifugally). What

---

[178] The texts in question are Niccolo Massa, *Anatomiae liber introductorius*, Venice, 1559, chap. 28, pp. 53ff., the text of which is the same as the first edn of 1536: see L. R. Lind, *Studies in Pre-Vesalian Anatomy*, Philadelphia, 1975, p. 169; Varolius, *Anatomiae libri IIII*, pp. 54, 71; T. Knobloch, *Disputationes Anatomicae et Physiologicae*, n.p., 1612 (a 'controversy' collection, published by P. Helvigius).

[179] A. Benedictus, *Anatomice, sive de Hystoria corporis humani libri quinque*, Strasburg, 1528 (dedication dated 1503), p. 44v.

[180] 'Caeterum mirificum hic naturae arcanum contemplemur in appellatis valvis positum.' J. Fernel, *De partium corporis humani descriptione*, book 1, chap. 8: I have used the text in the *Universa medicina*, Geneva, 1643, p. 42.

was in Fabricius' mind when writing the tract of 1603 was that little doors open as well as close: here their function to give the blood controlled *access* to the parts, ensuring that it did not accumulate in excessive quantities by its weight in the lower limbs.[181]

Fabricius explicitly drew strength for his interpretation from hydraulic devices. He said that nature does in the veins what art does in directing water through channels and watergates, *ostiola*. Italian engineers, continued Fabricius, use the vernacular *clausas* and *rostas* for devices they use to dam up water for mills and other machines. These are equivalent to the Latin term *claustra*, used by Fabricius and Benedetti, and again we can see that what was intended was a sluice, which holds up the bulk of the water, allowing only a portion across.

Harvey was familiar with his teacher's account of the flaps in the veins. So was Bauhin, whose work was one of Harvey's major sources for the anatomy lectures. It may have been that Fabricius' example prompted Bauhin to look for other such structures in the body; at all events in 1579 he discovered the colonic 'valve'. With this extra example of the kind, Bauhin set up a generalised account of 'valves'. He read widely and distinguished the literary tradition in which the flaps were called 'membranes' (*hymenes, pelliculae, membranarum epiphyses*) from that in which they were 'doors'; he used Galen's bellows analogy and Fabricius' reference to hydraulic engineering. The result was that he could give a 'common' use of all valves and a 'proper' use in each case.[182] The common use was that valves acted largely to impose a unidirectional flow, and the proper use was to determine the relative direction of flow in each case. But the generalisation was not perfect. Bauhin did not depart far from Galenic theory, and had to retain a two-directional flow in the case of the valves of the veins and the mitral valve (a term that he claims to have invented).

Thus when Harvey began his anatomy lectures, it had not been long since the category and name 'valve' had first been put together from the 'little doors', 'membranes' and so on of the body, and from the various water-controlling devices of Renaissance engineering. In his pre-circulatory anatomy lectures Harvey includes a number of other things in the category, and they are mostly unidirectional devices. The full bladder compresses a flap over the orifice of the ureters and prevents reflux, even of experimentally introduced air. The embryonic foramen ovale is a *valvula* that prevents reflux. The colonic valve resisted the reflux of air introduced as an anatomical demonstration (but which sometimes allowed water through). There are two or three *valvulae* (flaps) in

---

[181] H. Fabricius, *De venarum ostiolis*, in his *Opera omnia anatomica et physiologica*, Leipzig, 1687, pp. 150–60.
[182] Bauhin, *Theatrum anatomicum*, p. 425.

the bile duct.[183] But more important than Harvey's enlargement of the category 'valve' is his argument for the forceful systole and the true nature of the pulse. This depended absolutely on the non-reflux action of the valves at the orifice of the aorta. We should remember that during the course of the lectures he extended his notion of the forceful systole to the lungs, asserting from his vivisections that there was a pulse in the arterial vein. We have seen how this allowed Harvey to accept that the blood crossed the lungs and not the septum of the heart. But if the venous artery had a pulse like that of the aorta, its valve too must be one-way; and the blood thus sent across the lungs could have no natural motion back into the lungs from the left ventricle: the mitral valve must also be a one-way affair. Here Harvey necessarily differed from Bauhin (who did not accept the pulmonary transit).

In other words while believing in a forceful systole and a pulmonary transit, but yet before recognising the circulation, Harvey was obliged to see the valves of the heart as entirely unidirectional. Within his own enlarged category of valve, the *only obvious exception* to the rule of the unidirectional common function of valves were the valves in the veins. A major part of Harvey's answer to the problems of the quantity of blood was that the flaps in the veins really were valves like all others. They allowed the blood to flow back to the heart and did not allow reflux to the limbs.

While Harvey did not see the heart as a pump when he made his discovery, he was thinking in terms of 'water bellows' and their clack-valves at about the time of *De motu cordis*,[184] and by 1649, when he replied to Riolan, the analogy of the pump was a natural one.[185] So was it to many others, such as Glisson,[186] who said that the blood spurted more vigorously from a wounded artery at the moment when the pulse was felt, just as water emerged with force from a pump when the piston was depressed. Sometimes analogy proceeded to identity: the heart was a vital pump, a *vitalis Antlia* (reported Pecquet).[187] There were by now, after all, many similarities between machines and the body. Machines were built for a purpose and had been put together with that part of divine reason which was man's estate, just as God had constructed the body. The

---

[183] See Whitteridge's edn of the *Praelectiones*, pp. 201, 262, 108 and 156 for these examples in the order given.

[184] Harvey wrote in the notes for the anatomy lectures that blood crosses the heart 'as by two clackes of water bellows to rays water' in about 1627, according to Whitteridge (p. 272 of her edn). See also Webster, 'The heart as a pump'.

[185] Harvey, *Exercitatio anatomica*, uses the analogy of the *sypho* on pp. 13, 51, 72 and 108.

[186] Sloane 3312 (the third unmarked folio after 357): the pump is a *sipho*, the piston a *manubrium*.

[187] J. Pecquet, *Experimenta nova antomica, quibus incognitum hactenus chyli recaptaculum et ab eo per thoracem in ramos usque subclavius vasa lactea deteguntur. Ejusdem Dissertatio anatomica de circulatione sanguinis, et chyli moti*, Paris, 1652; I have used the edn of Paris, 1654: pp. 62, 63; Pecquet, *Experimento nova anatomica* (1653 edn), p. 113: Pecquet is referring to those who argued in favour of attraction by means of forceful diastole of the heart.

structure–action–use hierarchy that many still saw in the body had its counter-part in machines, in which the attributes of the hard, flexible and liquid parts were utilised in the overall purpose of the whole. Moreover, although bodies were animated, their matter consisted of related mixtures of the same four elements as did that of machines. And although machines were unnatural in being artificial, the art used in making them imitated nature. As we have seen, some people even claimed that machines like clocks had an internal principle in motion, a real 'nature' of their own.[188]

The image of the clock again provides us with a clue to the intellectual shift in the seventeenth century. Regius the Cartesian,[189] seeking to remove from natural philosophy the peripatetic notion of form, pointed out that the motion, size, position and shape of the parts of a clock are 'accidental' to the steel, the matter of the clock (but 'essential' to the clock as a whole). So 'form' is a congeries of accidents, and not something tied up with natural motions and their destinations. All motion is local motion, said Regius. It was precisely in this sense that Hogelande and Descartes saw the action of the valves as purely *mechanical*, a local motion forced on the valves by the pressure of blood, without any participation in purpose. Although having a different metaphysics, Glisson expressed much the same idea in his chain of local necessity. It is seen too in the refusal to admit local sentience and judgment in nature's putative attempt to prevent a vacuum, to which Pecquet preferred the expression *aequipondi necessitate*,[190] 'by necessity of pressure'.

So machines could be used as analogies in rhetoric, and increasingly as images that explained how the body worked. They also came to be used in experiment. In order to explain attraction medical men used the simple cupping-glass, which on cooling 'attracted' blood through scarified skin (see fig. 16 on p. 000). They used the medical syringe, a piston and cylinder device that was used to inject liquids into bodily orifices. Berigard explains how the syringe, a medical *sipho* with a piston, was the model for devices sometimes used (before 1643) in attempts to demonstrate a vacuum by pulling the piston away from the closed nozzle[191] (see figs. 22 and 26). The doctors also explained the motion of the blood in terms of the simple inverted U-tube siphon. The varying terminology and the difficulty[192] the writers had in

---

[188] C. Webster, 'William Harvey and the crisis of medicine in Jacobean England', in J. Bylebyl, ed., *William Harvey and his Age. The Professional and Social Context of the Discovery of the Circulation*, Johns Hopkins University Press, Baltimore, 1979, p. 20, gives a number of examples of the importance of technology and practical chemistry in the Platonic and alchemical traditions of the early seventeenth century.

[189] H. Regius, *Fundamenta Physices*, Amsterdam, 1654, p. 6.

[190] Pecquet, *Experimenta nova anatomica* (1654 edn), p. 62.

[191] Claudius Berigardus (Berigard), *Circulus Pisanus . . . de veteri et peripatetica philosophia in priores libros Phys. Arist.*, Utini, 1643, p. 57.

[192] Pecquet's chap. 6: *Experimenta nova anatomica* (1654 edn), p. 43; (1653 edn), p. 77.

explaining the simple actions of these machines reflect the novelty of using technology as an explanation of what was going on in the body. Sometimes *sipho* was our 'siphon' and sometimes a pump, for which however the more usual term was *antlia*. In such a machine the piston was a *manubrium*,[193] a name occasionally given to the pump's clack-valves. Sometimes the piston was an *embolus*[194] (mistranslated as 'clack' in the English version of Pecquet's text).[195]

The pump in its various guises was central to the question of attraction. The force required to draw *manubrium* of a medical syringe away from the nozzle, blocked to deny access to the air, was felt as a tangible effort to overcome nature's attempt to prevent the occurrence of the vacuum that was apparently being created. Some felt it as the attraction exerted by nature's *horror vacui*. Whatever was trying to 'attract' the piston back to its former place was generally identified with the force that made air enter a bellows as the two sides were drawn apart. The medical side of things was never very distant. All 'attraction' could be seen as a species of sucking, as with the mouth. Respiration itself looked like sucking and could be explained in a number of ways. It might be traditional *fuga vacui*, nature avoiding the formation of a vacuum as the thorax distended. It might be, as Descartes claimed, that the expanding thorax displaced particles of air which transmitted their motion to others that ultimately entered the lungs. Or it might be the weight and the 'spring' of the air that forced it into a place where resistance was small.

### Experimental apparatus

Technological devices, used successively as images in rhetoric and as explanatory models, could also be used physically as devices with which to carry out experiments, many of them concerned with attraction. The inability of suction pumps to raise water more than about thirty-two feet[196] generated an interest in those with enough education to be familiar with the principles of nature and enough contact with the practices of the world of industry. In wondering about its cause, Galileo thought he was dealing with the strengths of materials (the column of water) and talked about the attraction of the vacuum.[197] Others, like Kenelm Digby, thought it was to do with the limits of

---

[193] Sloane 3312, f. 359.

[194] Pecquet, *Experimenta nova anatomica* (1654 edn), p. 63.

[195] Pecquet, *Experimenta nova anatomica* (1654 edn), p. 62; (1653 edn), p. 114.

[196] 'Which height, Galileo telleth us from the workmen in the Arsenall of Venice, is neere 40 foote': Sir Kenelm Digby, *Two Treatises. In the one of which the Nature of Bodies; in the other the Nature of Man's soule; is looked into: in the way of discovery of the immortality of reasonable soules*, Paris, 1644, p. 160.

[197] See R. S. Westfall, *The Construction of Modern Science*, Cambridge University Press, 1971, p. 43.

materials in the pump's manufacture (at great heights, he said, the 'sucker' of the pump admits air).[198] The availability of very long glass tubes to Pascal, who lived in a glass-manufacturing town, made possible experiments which demonstrated the limited height of water in a tube sealed at one end. The essence of Torricelli's experiment was to formulate a portable version of this apparatus using mercury instead of water. Torricelli walked up the mountain and demonstrated the weight of the air in his apparatus in 1644, but the issues were well known before that. Regius, arguing with Primrose in the same year, claimed that all right-thinking philosophers denied *horror vacui*; Primrose stoutly defended it.[199] Regius' explanation of the piston-activated suction pump, his *sipho suctorius*,[200] is the Cartesian circular thrust of displaced particles rather than the Torricellian weight of the air. He likewise has a Cartesian explanation for the thermometer (see fig. 27). The same range of experimental devices were used by those who believed in Cartesian displacement of air and those who held that the air had weight. A thermometer-like 'weather glass' modelled on the one made by Robert Fludd was commercially available. While Regius' thermometer depended on the expansion of air to move a column of water, others depended on the expansion of water itself.[201] The device illustrated by Regius in which a smoker puffs through two pipes and water in a container was also illustrated by George Ent in a similar discussion about the motion of blood.[202] Bellows were used routinely. Not

Fig. 26. Experimental anatomy.
The title-page of Hemsterhuis' 'Golden Harvest, containing the newest and most useful Anatomical Experiments'. This picture shows a number of things. At the centre of the picture is the great anatomist Riolan and on his right is Vesling. The whole is a display of anatomy as the public statement of the rational and learned physician and their kind of medicine. Part of the display is the cabinet of anatomical instruments (as we saw in fig. 2, of the earlier Leiden anatomy theatre). Directly above Riolan's head is the medical syringe, used in the practice of medicine, in anatomy and in Experimental Philosophy for experiments about vacua. The rational medicine of the educated physician was now Experimental, an image fostered by the physicians for professional reasons. The book contains marketable tracts on anatomical controversies, expressly experimental and now investigated principally in northern Europe.

[198] Digby, *Two Treatises*, p. 160.
[199] James Primrose, *Antidotum adversus Henrici Regii Ultraiectensis medicinae professoris venenatum Spongiam*, Leiden, p. 45.
[200] Regius, *Fundamenta physices*, pp. 36, 38, 88.
[201] Pecquet, *Experimenta nova anatomica* (1652 edn), p. 28.
[202] G. Ent, *Apologia pro circulatione sanguinis: qua respondetur Aemilio Parisano Medico Veneto*, London, 1641, p. 153.

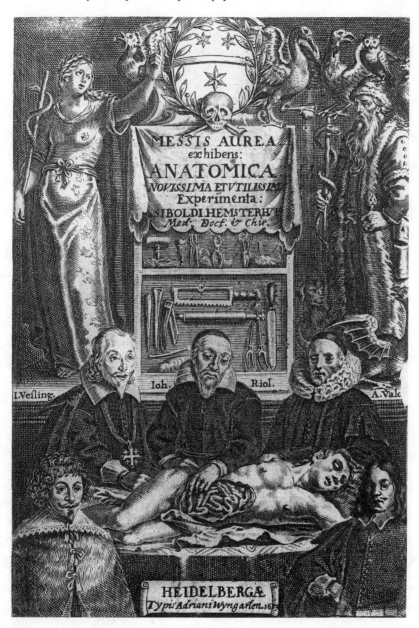

Fig. 26

uncommon were the cupping-glass and the aeolipile (which had been discussed by Descartes and Hogelande.) Simple devices based on piston and cylinder pumps to imitate and demonstrate the effect of the weight of air were part of the mathematical philosopher's stock in trade.[203] Even those who defended attraction used experimental machines.[204]

Jean Pecquet was an important author who used machines as experimental apparatus to destroy the notion of attraction. Unlike Regius the Cartesian, Pecquet used the weight and the spring of the air to show that there was not natural *horror vacui*. His concern was firstly to demonstrate his discovery, the lacteals and their connections, and then to fit their function in with the circulation of the blood. The second of these exercises – he calls it a *Dissertatio anatomica* – is the bigger, and includes a section devoted to *Experimenta physico-mathematica de vacuo*. His overall purpose remains medical, however, and is largely to show how the blood moves into the heart at diastole. He is arguing against those who claimed that the active phase of the heart's motion was diastole and that the expanding heart *attracted* the blood to itself. Pecquet professed to be embarrassed by the very term 'attraction'[205] and his energetic refutation of it was drawn from the *Machinorum mysteria*,[206] the world of technology. By now (1652) there was a variety of pneumatic machines that Pecquet could draw on to explain the weight and the *elater*, the spring of the air, and he saw nothing inappropriate in calling the heart a vital pump; indeed, he was making a point about the machine-like nature of the body by using such a term.[207] The existence of an English translation helps us with the terminology. It is the weight of the air on the terraqueous globe that forces water into the *antliae tubum*: 'That the water followeth the Clack in a Pump-pipe.' *Elater* is glossed 'that is, by its spontaneous dilatation'.[208] The aeolipile is a 'Wind-gun' in which air is compressed. Here the English translator may have been out of his depth, for 'aeolipile' – recorded in English from 1611 – meant Hero's device for showing the force of air rushing from a heated vessel,

---

203 They are described and illustrated by Pecquet, *Experimenta nova anatomica* (1652 edn) and come mostly from French sources.

204 Pecquet's use of machines is partly designed to counter such defenders of attraction: 'It pleaseth me to fight with the same Engins, that being vanquish'd by their own Arms, at last they may confess those examples they bring, of the Air in the Bellows; of the water in the Aeolipilaes, or Pump, or Reed; And to conclude, of the Flesh in cupping Glasses, succeeds by no allurement of succing, but onely by the violence of *External Impulsion*.' Pecquet, *Experimenta nova anatomica* (1654 edn), p. 87.

205 '... how superfluous it is to appoint an *Attractive*, or rather if you will, a *sucking* vertue, which in the business of fluid things I ever tolerated with tingling ears'. Pecquet, *Experimenta nova anatomica* (1654 edn), p. 87.

206 Pecquet, *Experimenta nova anatomica* (1652 edn), p. 26.

207 'Putant enim actum de nostra sententia, nihilque fore quod objici queat, cum, insigni nomenclatura, vitalis Antliae titulum cordi contulere.' Ibid., p. 62.

208 Pecquet, *Experimenta nova anatomica* (1654 edn), p. 26; (1653 edn), p. 44.

Fig. 27. Regius' thermometer.

Although there was a priority dispute about the invention of the 'thermo-scope' between Sanctorius and Galileo, the addition of a scale (not shown in Regius' illustration) to the instrument for the sake of precision is safely attributed to Sanctorius. His purposes included refining traditional medical theory, in which heat played such a major part, by means of instruments. Such medical instruments clearly had a role to play in the new Experimental Philosophy.

which corresponds to the experimental device used or perhaps simply described by Descartes and Hogelande. The translator omits the Latin passage in which Pecquet defines *elater* and in which too he describes the pneumatic device known as the *sclopus*, in which air was compressed in order to project a piece of lead with great force: a true airgun. Pecquet later calls it a pneumatic *catapulta*, known in the French of his native Dieppe as *une harquebuse* or *canne a vent*. Pecquet argued that the difference in weight between an airgun full of compressed air and another with air at the usual pressure demonstrated that air had weight.

The link between technology and theory is nicely illustrated by Pecquet when he says that the mechanics who designed the pumps, their *inventores*, believed that the rising water followed the moving piston, *embolus*, by nature's fear of a vacuum. They do not (he says) know the real cause (which was available, that is, only to the theoretical philosopher of the Torricellian sort).[209] While the mechanic seemed to be seeing by direct and simple observation that the moving piston sucks up the water, Pecquet is aware of the pitfalls of reliance on the senses: recalling Roberval's experiment, Pecquet remarks on his own astonishment at the swelling of the carp's bladder as the mercury descended. His eyes seemed to be in error, he said (because they told him the opposite of what he thought would happen) and he could only believe them when his 'mind cured the errors of the eyes', 'nisi mens oculorum erroribus mederetur'. So even apparently simple and direct observational experimental results had to be interpreted by means of reason.[210] Indeed, it

Fig. 28. All of Pecquet's *experimenta physico-mathematica* were designed to disprove the notion of attraction in the body, especially that of the heart in diastole. His explanation of blood moving to the heart is that it is impelled, ultimately by the weight and spring of the air. This relies on the general principle that vacua do exist and that the effort of air or a piston to enter it is simply the weight of air surrounding the earth. The experiment he found the most striking was that of Roberval, in which a carp's air bladder, C, is submerged in a flask containing mercury and sealed at one end, A. When the flask is inverted into an open dish of mercury, the level of mercury falls to a level E corresponding to the weight of the external air. Meanwhile in the vacuum above the mercury the residuum of air in the bladder swells, being no longer compressed by the weight of air. Those who did not believe in vacua argued that the experiment demonstrated that air penetrated the glass and bladder.

[209] Pecquet, ibid. (1654 edn), p. 63; (1653 edn), p. 114.
[210] Pecquet, ibid. (1654 edn), p. 53.

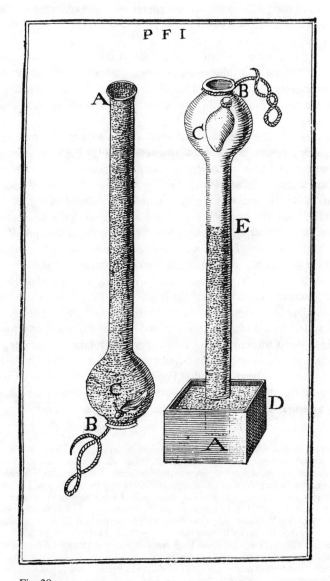

Fig. 28

is clear from Pecquet's accounts of contemporary experiments that the same experiment could be used both to excuse and to deny a vacuum[211] (see fig. 28).

Pecquet's work marks something of a watershed in the circulation controversy. It symbolises two things: the beginning of a general acceptance of Harvey's doctrines in one form or another, and the spread of a mechanical vision of the body. Signs of this are seen in two authors we have not yet considered.

A few days after the publication of Pecquet's 'mathematical' treatment of the circulation, a copy of the book reached Nicholas Papin in Alençon, a medical practitioner with a taste for philosophical controversy.[212] He clearly had a good intelligence service to the capital, where Pecquet's book was published. Papin felt obliged to reply to it and had a pamphlet printed by the local printer, who was bookseller to 'the College', no doubt of Herault, whose Gymnasiarch Papin addressed the pamphlet. Papin had just finished writing a critical review of Descartes' book on the passions of the soul; to do this properly he had had to investigate Harvey's doctrine of the circulation which as we have seen was often associated with Cartesian natural philosophy. Papin was prepared to accept that the blood circulated,[213] but like so many others, including Descartes, he could not accept the forceful systole described by Harvey. He disarticulated Harvey's doctrine at this point and found it preferable to reconstruct an ancient view of the forceful *diastole*, arguing even that Hippocrates had known of the circulation.[214] But it was the circulation as presented by Pecquet that prompted Papin to defend the traditional theory. He did so in a traditional way, dismissing the vivisections of the neoterics not only as cruel (as Riolan and Leichner thought) but as misleading (like

---

[211] A simple experiment that could be interpreted in a number of ways was Fludd's placing a bell-jar over a candle burning in a dish of water. See A. Debus, *The English Paracelsians*, London, 1965. Another experimental device used to extend the powers of observation, although hardly a machine, was the lens. With its not entirely satisfactory help Pecquet claimed that the blood crossed from arteries to veins by small anastomoses and synanastomes, by which he meant openings to the flesh like Harvey's 'pores' rather than continuous vessels like the capillaries later described. See Y. Elkana and J. Goodfield, 'Harvey and the problem of the "capillaries"', in I. B. Cohen, ed., *Studies on William Harvey*, New York, 1981 and *Isis*, 59 (1967), 61–73. Pecquet called the lens a *microscopium*, Englished as 'Spectacles'; Pecquet, *Experimenta nova anatomica* (1653 edn), p. 68; (1954 edn), p. 38.

[212] He wrote on problems of tidal action (1647) and in 1651 on 'sympathetic powder', part of the mid-century dispute on 'sympathies' as occult actions. He died after 1653 and was the uncle of the better-known Denis Papin (b. 1647) who constructed a 'digester' or pressure-cooker. *Nouvelle Biographie Générale*, Paris, 1862.

[213] N. Papin, *Cordis diastole, adversus Harveianam innovationem defensa*, Alençon, 1653.

[214] Papin, *Cordis diastole*, p. 2. Papin also wanted to write an account of 'Platonic respiration' (p. 6). He was, that is, employing the not uncommon strategy of legitimating a new discovery by arguing that the ancients had in some ways been aware of it without discussing it as a theoretical issue.

Primrose and Parigiano). Papin was no Experimental Philosopher, but a medical man of conservative instincts. No vivisection that lethally wounded the animal and filled it with pain and fear could ever show the natural economy of the heart; as others had argued, experiments are *unnatural*, said Papin.[215] What offended Papin most was Pecquet's denial of attraction in the expanding and filling heart. For Papin the heart acted in the traditional way, moved by the soul and attracting blood in diastole by a faculty of attraction.[216] He was using precisely the kind of argument that Pecquet was denying.

But Papin's treatment of Pecquet and the circulation was not just an insistence on the Galenic alternative. Not only did he accept the circulation, but he saw the force of Pecquet's experiments and machines and accepted them as mathematical.[217] Indeed, he took Pecquet's arguments and used them against him, claiming that the heart is indeed like the bellows, in which force must be used to pull the sides apart and draw in air: by analogy the diastole of the heart was forceful. The language of, and the arguments from machines were potent for Papin: they are blind, he said, who cannot see that the forceful systole is the primary cause of blood entering the heart; it is like the violent motion of the piston (*epistomium*) of a pump being the cause of the water rising. In saying that the walls of the heart act as the moving parts of a pump and that the heart's faculty is a *Facultas Haustoris* exercising the function of an *epistomium Motoris*, Papin has adopted a language of machines that in fact distances him from the traditional Galenic faculty.[218] Although he recognised that Pecquet's array of machines had been introduced simply to deny the attractive faculty of the heart yet the terms of the discussion have been changed. By now – 1653, when Brady and Barwell were defending Glisson's theses in Cambridge – some analogy with machines and some language of mechanism was inevitable. As Papin said, it was a new question whether the air enters the bellows and the blood enters the heart by *fuga vacui*, (Cartesian) circular displacement or (Torricellian) spring and weight of the air (see fig. 29). According to Papin, the resolution of such questions is not the affair of the medical man.[219]

Another philosopher to see the power of mathematical demonstration in the natural world, including animals, was Adrien Auzout (Latinised as Auzotius). He is known to historians as the designer of an instrument to measure the

---

[215] Papin, *Cordis diastole*, pp. 3, 13.
[216] Papin, *Cordis diastole*, p. 3.
[217] Papin is one of the few medical men to refer to Galileo as an authority; but it is the motion of the sea, not experiments, that is under discussion. Papin, *Cordis diastole*, p. 15.
[218] Ibid., p. 7.
[219] Ibid., p. 10 (but he gains strength for his own view of the motion of the heart by calling the spring of the air 'diastaltic').

apparent diameter of heavenly bodies,[220] and like Roberval and Pascal the younger he had made experiments on vacua with tubes and mercury. Pecquet used one of them in his denial of attraction, and this may have prompted Auzout to think about such questions in relation to the body. At all events he addressed Pecquet in a publisher's collection of marketable novelties, described as both anatomical and 'experimental' to add to their attraction to the reading public. This collection included Pecquet's text and those of Bartholin and Rudbeck on the lymphatics, but nothing on the motion of blood. So, by 1654 these topics had eclipsed the circulation as an exciting novelty. For Auzout the circulation was now history, 'that other great anatomical discovery of our century, now old, and as clear as light itself'.[221] Moreover, Auzout was satisfied that circulation depended on mechanical principles and that everything that related to it would be explained on such principles:[222] the measurements and proportions of the veins and arteries, the size of their parts and the speed of the blood in the vessels.

Fig. 29. Tubes, valves and pressure.
Bartholin's illustrations show some of the frequent experiments by which the action of the heart was demonstrated. His first figure represents a living heart in systole. The aorta has been ligated at B, and is swollen under pressure of blood from the heart. An incision has been made at C, and blood is shown spurting out. The arterial vein (pulmonary artery) has also been ligated and it too is swollen under the pressure of blood. The lungs, AA, have been drawn back to show the vessels. FF is the front face of the heart, hardened in contraction.

The second figure shows the heart at diastole. Here the two branches, aa, of the venous artery (pulmonary vein) have been ligated and are full of blood which cannot return from the lungs to the left auricle, b. The vena cava, C, has also been ligated and consequently swells outside the ligature and is flat and empty towards the right auricle, d.

The third and fourth figures show the inside surface of the auricles, with the orifices of the vessels and the fibrous attachments of the valves.

There is a clear parallel here with the new philosophers who were discussing the 'weight and spring' (we would say 'pressure') of the air and who were experimenting with heights of liquids in tubes, with suction and force pumps and with valves. While Pecquet was denying attraction in the heart by means of 'mathematical' demonstrations with machines, here Bartholin is being equally geometrical with the living body.

---

[220] He communicated with Hooke, Oldenburg and Petty and others in the Royal Society, and was one of the first members of the Académie des Sciences. See *Nouvelle Biographie Universelle*, Paris, 1852.

[221] Auzout's text is included in S. Hemsterhuis, ed., *Messis Aurea Triennialis, exhibens; Anatomica: novissima et utilissima Experimenta*, Leiden, 1654, p. 337.

[222] *ex Principiis Mechanicis*, Auzout (1654), p. 343.

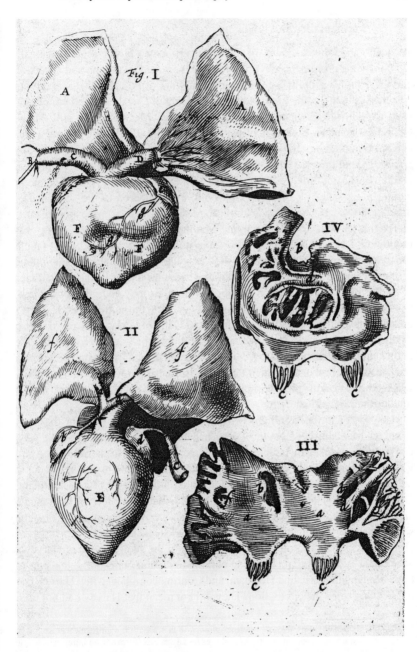

Fig. 29

## Mathematics and medicine

Pecquet called his account of these experiments 'physico-mathematical'. Obviously the prominence he gives to the experiments on vacua and attraction derives from his proximity to the important work of Pascal and Roberval, but his purpose in including them in his new account of the lacteals and circulation is to explain the *medical* problem of attraction. Medicine was still, at the theoretical level, an extension of natural philosophy. By Pecquet's time it was becoming more common to call the non-medical parts of natural philosophy *physica*,[223] but the old relationship between art-course natural philosophy and medicine was not broken. Medical men writing out 'institutes' of medicine or natural philosophy, or often enough both, even adhered to the sequence of topics followed by Aristotle dealing, for example, with the question of time directly after that of the vacuum. Mathematics on the other hand was traditionally part of the liberal arts – the quadrivium– and had been taught separately from natural philosophy. It is easy enough to see that by the middle of the seventeenth century the universities were no longer the sole guardians of these subjects and that as a result natural philosophy could become mathematical. The historical literature is instinct with the notion that Harvey's quantitative method is somehow parallel to Galileo's or at least represents a significant introduction of mathematics. Probably this view derives from the knowledge that modern science is mathematical and from the belief that science started in the seventeenth century. But what did men at the time think was mathematical or 'physico-mathematical'? And what did they think was its relationship to medicine?

Harvey's quantitative argument (that more blood emerges from the heart than can be assimilated by the body) had great force and as we have seen convinced a number of people, but its force did not lie in the relevance and vigour of its arithmetic. Many still held with Aristotle that mathematics could not reveal essences or causes. Hofmann called it the device of an accountant, *logista*. Certainly accountants use arithmetic, but the force of Hofmann's argument is that Harvey was using a tradesman's trick of calculation, when he should have been using his eyes, like an anatomist and philosopher. It is part of Hofmann's flow of rhetoric about a vulgarity, of the audience and of Harvey's accountant's clothes, that could add nothing to natural philosophy. It seems to have been in this sense that Hofmann and Conring complained that Harvey had not *demonstrated* the circulation. They did not mean that Harvey had not used

---

[223] Regius, *Fundamenta physices*, p. 1 defines *physica* in this way. It is significant that Regius in so doing limits its subject-matter to those things having matter, form and an internal principle of motion: God and the angels, lacking matter, are not included in the subject-matter of *physica*. The same is true of Conring, but because he is following Aristotle's distinction between physics and metaphysics.

logical demonstration in the absolute Aristotelian sense (which was clearly impossible in the circumstances and which was anyway becoming unfashionable) but that he was using reason – logic – where ocular demonstration was required.

Secondly, 'mathematics' in these contexts meant primarily geometry. For Charleton,[224] 'demonstrations Mathematical' which were used in anatomy related to the geometry that God had used in building the microcosm. Pecquet's physico-mathematical experiments are not in the least mathematically *quantitative* in the arithmetical sense.[225] To the modern mind they are indeed only faintly geometrical; but Pecquet thought it worthwhile to give them the title he did. While part of the traditional charm of geometry (for example to Descartes) was the certainty with which the conclusion was deductively reached from the axiom, what seems to have been important here was that geometry was also a *visual* business. At a time when many voices were crying for autopsy – seeing for oneself – there was a strong sense in which a geometrical proof was indissolubly linked to the diagram. The old tag that even a slave could be made to understand a geometrical proof showed too that proof did not depend on a whole tradition of learning or systems but could be generated by visual means and natural reason. For Harvey too, geometry was important to his argument in favour of sense observation: it was for him a *demonstratio* about sensibles, taken from sensibles; given his context (his discussion about procedure in his reply to Riolan) he meant *to oti*, or *quia*.[226]

In this way diagrams, designed for the visual imagination of the reader, carried some of the force of geometrical argument. The diagram 'worked' for the reader; it was part of the argument. When Glisson drew his diagram of angels moving with putative infinite speed between heaven and earth, he labelled it as one would a geometrical diagram, with the letters a, b and c denoting the lines. The same technique was used by Pecquet and Regius for their diagrams of apparatus. Regius applied it as readily to the woodcut of a hand pulling up a stone with a leather sucker on the end of a piece of string as to a formally geometrical analysis of motion.

Using diagrams or drawings, as we have seen, was well known in the medical tradition from Berengario da Carpi onwards.[227] Berengario uses woodcuts to give an account where the shape of a part is too complex to be described in words. With Vesalius the woodcuts were designed to demonstrate the parts by a kind of vicarious *autopsia*, to those without access to dissections.

---

[224] Webster, 'Solomon's House', p. 400.
[225] Pecquet, *Experimenta nova anatomica* (1654 edn), p. 51: 'Experimenta Physico-Mathematica de Vacuo.'
[226] Harvey, *Exercitatio anatomica*, p. 98. Note that the Latin does not support Franklin's translation.
[227] See chap. 2 above.

Vesalius saw that not only can illustrations give a more precise idea of shape than can words, but that his woodcuts acted in a *geometrical* way.[228] It could be argued that the advantage of a diagram, whether anatomical in this way, or a geometry of motions, or a piece of labelled apparatus or machinery, was that although present to the reader as a single particular – in Vesalius' case a *historia* – it in some way represented a universal. Regius' woodcut of the clack-and-piston water pump somehow represents the essence of *all* clack-and-piston water pumps, just as the right-angled triangle in the square-on-the-hypotenuse theorem is a universal.

The same can be said of another source of the seventeenth-century practice of using diagrams geometrically. Jerome Cardano had in the previous century been seeking an alternative to Aristotelian physical principles.[229] He denied that fire was an element, and in place of Aristotle's complex system of causality he believed that matter moved by sympathy, contact-impulsion and rarefaction. To illustrate the last two principles he liberally used diagrams of pumps: single and double-section, suction and pressure pumps. Most of them are piston and clack-valve pumps. A number were described by ancient writers like Ctesibus, Frontinus, Vitruvius and Hero, but Cardano knew and named the engineers and blacksmiths of his own city – he probably meant Milan or Pavia – who were making such machines for use in the commercial and industrial life of the city. His picture of Bartholomew Bramble's bilgepump has the same geometrical-argument and 'universal' function as anything reconstructed from the ancients (see fig. 30). Likewise his treatment of the balance – so basic to the economic life of the Italian city states – has the same function and characteristically gave rise to an entirely abstract geometrical diagram which 'worked' for the reader in explaining the principles of the balance. His questioning of Aristotle became well known and provided material for later commentators like Berigard.[230]

We should remember that in the seventeenth century 'mathematical' was also a term used for astronomy and astrology, surveying, cartography and navigation. Measuring instruments and diagrams were of the essence in these

---

[228] A. Vesalius, *De fabrica corporis humani*, Basle, 1543, p. 4, of the address to Charles V. In the letter to the publisher Oparinus that follows (unpaginated) Vesalius was anxious that his woodcuts should not appear 'vulgar and scholastic': he too saw himself as part of an elite, above and apart from the schools.

[229] H. Cardanus, *De subtilitate libri XXI*, Basle, 1553; *De rerum varietate*, Basle, 1557.

[230] Berigard, *Circulus Pisanus*, p. 57 explains that the avoidance of a vacuum lies behind the phenomena noted by Cardano. Cardano's physical principles are illustrated by a large number of examples, often of strange occurrences. Harvey quotes two of them in the anatomy lectures: see the edition by Whitteridge, pp. 13, 221. Cardano became well known partly as a result of an attack on him by J. C. Scaliger. W. Pagel, 'Harvey and Glisson on irritability with a note on van Helmont', *Bulletin of the History of Medicine*, 41 (1987), 497–514, pp. 501, 503, 504, argues that a refutation of Scaliger's notion of a separate spirit was important in Harvey's and Glisson's monism.

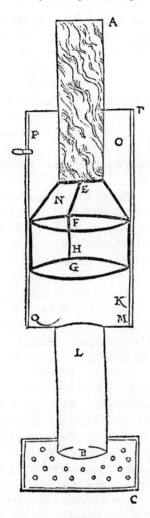

Fig. 30. Cardano and Bartholomew Bramble's bilgepump.
Cardano had seen the machine of Bartholomaeus Brambilla in Milan, and was proud that it was as good as anything from antiquity. Cardano was one of the first, in explaining the 'subtleties' of the physical world with the help of mathematics, regularly to use geometrical diagrams to set out the *essence* of a machine. His explanation was geometrical and complex, but the reader who could follow it would find that the diagram was an essential part of the argument and worked for him in a geometrical and physical way.

businesses, and 'geometrical' explanations applied equally to instrumentation, machinery, the trajectory of projectiles, the design of the gun and the mathematical explanations Pecquet offered of attraction within the body. In expressing both the living body and the machine as geometry, complete with indication letters, much of the old structure of knowledge was lost. Traditional faculties, like attraction, could not be drawn; and while motion might be indicated by 'a', 'b' and so on as changes of *place*, the old distinction between action, use and utility could not be represented. Above all the *purpose* of a part, its Aristotelian final cause, without which the school philosophers maintained that true knowledge was unobtainable because demonstration was impossible, could have no place in a diagram or drawing.

After Cardano we can find a number of authors publishing on machines. Their works are generously illustrated and probably were intended partly as advertising to the military, civil and private engineering markets of Renaissance society. They called their art 'mechanics' and sought to justify it not only in terms of its civil and military usefulness but also intellectually as a branch of *mathematics*. This could be justified by reference to Aristotle's *Physics*, where he lists mechanics among the physical branches of mathematics.[231] Thus Ramelli presents a series of machines from pumps to pontoon bridges with elegant woodcuts that would be intelligible and attractive to a potential patron, prefaced by an account of how, in essence, mathematics is the *theory of mechanics*. Thus mathematics is presented in a way that would appeal to potential patrons: arithmetic is important in commerce, geometry in surveying land and estates and in understanding how machines work. (We should note that music and astronomy/astrology, the other traditional mathematical *scientiae*, are not invoked, because inappropriate to Renaissance commercial expansion.) Mathematics thus not only dignified commercial, civil and military necessities, but was itself dignified by its practitioners seeking a *prisca scientia* status for it from hermetic and biblical sources.[232] The point of this for us is that mathematics – geometry – as the 'theory of mechanics' naturally led to the mechanical diagram's deriving some explanatory force from geometry and offering some form of understanding of the physical world. This is why Pecquet as well as Ramelli thought he was partaking in mathematical demonstrations.

---

[231] But 'mechanics' largely in the sense of what is needed for drawing and understanding machines. See W. Charlton, trans. and ed., *Aristotle's Physics Books I and II*, p. 26 (194a): 'those branches of mathematics which come nearest to the study of nature, like optics, harmonics and astronomy'. The pseudo-Aristotelian text's 'mechanical problems' was also influential.

[232] There is a convenient facsimile reprint of A. Ramelli, *Le Diverse et Artificiose Machine*, Paris, 1588: *The Various and Ingenious Machines of Agostino Ramelli (1588)*, ed. Martha Teach Gnudi and Eugene S. Ferguson, Johns Hopkins University Press/The Scolar Press, 1976.

Apart from pumps, the archetypal machine of the Renaissance was the clock. We have already seen how the Aristotelians found it an uneasy image and how the neoterics relished it. Elaborate clockwork automata, even travelling peepshows,[233] were well known by the seventeenth century, and the technology involved was a source of Renaissance pride in that in this field at least the ancients had been left behind. The first holder of the chair of mathematics established by Ramus cited automata in making such a claim. The clock was seen as solid geometry and those who designed them were geometers. Besson the engineer called his book 'Mathematical and Mechanical Instruments'[234] and his machines were geometrical diagrams in action. Clearly neoterics who favoured 'mechanism' within and outside the body could claim for it some of the mathematical order and precision that was evident in clockwork and could make much of the argument for the superiority of moderns over ancients. They could even claim some of the power of demonstration that geometry had. When Descartes was being particularly confident of his own account of the action of the heart, he said it was mathematical. In fact Descartes' words nicely illustrate the relationship between mechanical structure and mathematical–geometrical demonstrations:

Aureste affin que ceux qui ne connoissent pas les force de demonstrations Mathematiques, et ne sont pas accoutumez a distinguer les vrayes raisons des vray-semblables, ne hasardent pas de nier cecy sans l'examiner, Je les veux avertir que ce mouvement que je vien d'expliquer, sui aussy necessairement de la seule disposition des organes qu'on peut voir a l'oeil dans le coeur, et de la chaleur qu'on y peut sentir avec les doigts, et de la nature du sang qu'on peut connoistre par experience, Que fait celuy d'un horologe, de la force, de la situation, et de la figure de ses contrepois et de ses rouës.[235]

With this emphasis on things visual, we can see that the vivisectional as well as the physical experiment was in many ways the equivalent of an *argument*.

---

[233] See Alex Keller, 'Mathematical techniques and the growth of the idea of technical progress in the sixteenth century', in *Science, Medicine and Society in the Renaissance. Essays to honour Walter Pagel*, ed. Allen G. Debus, 2 vols., London, 1972; vol. I, pp. 11–27.

[234] *Livre des Instruments Mathematiques et Mechaniques (1571–2)*. See Keller, 'Mathematical techniques'.

[235] R. Descartes, *Discours de la Methode pour bien conduire sa Raison, et chercher la Verité dans les Science plus La Dioptrique Le Meteores et La Geometrie qui sont des essais de cette Methode*, Tours, 1987, p. 46: 'For the rest (so that those who do not know the force of mathematical demonstrations and are not in the habit of distinguishing true reasons from apparent reasons should not venture to deny this without examining it), I want them to put on notice that this movement that I am going to explain follows just as naturally from the mere disposition of the organs that can be seen in the heart by the unaided eye and from the heat that can be felt with the fingers, and from the nature of blood that can be known through experience, as do the motions of a clock from the force, placement and shape of its counterweights and its wheels.' Translation by Donald A. Cress: R. Descartes, *Discourse on the Method of Rightly Conducting One's Reason and of Seeking Truth in the Sciences*, Indianapolis, 1980, pp. 26–7.

Before beginning the vivisection, the experimenter set out the issues at stake, as if they were unknown to his audience: he was positing a disputed question or putting up an axiom (as one might in geometry). He then went through a series of physical and visible procedures (tying or releasing a ligature, puncturing a vessel, injecting fluids and so on) each of which was related to its predecessor and designed to produce a final outcome, the presence of which was a demonstration of the question or axiom. This point is illustrated by Henry Power's report (1652) on the controversy surrounding Harvey.[236] As we have seen, he dismissed most of the arguments of Harvey's opponents as 'paper-skirmishes', that is, merely verbal battles, and saw Harvey's principal feature as a use of 'Sense and Autopsy': for Power even anatomical *experiments* were like mathematical – geometrical – 'Postula or Principles'. Power, taken by Harvey's anatomical experiments and observations, including those on small animals, reported with satisfaction the very visible results of Glisson's experiment in which water and milk were pumped from a clyster bag through the liver and lungs, and made a number of similar experiments himself.[237]

## Consensus

It may be useful here to summarise the various ways, many of which have been touched on earlier in this book, in which agreement was finally reached that the blood circulated. This was, after all, an outstandingly important agreement, and the mechanisms that produced it may well be useful in understanding how such changes in natural philosophy took place.

It is clear that consensus took place in stages. The first stage was the individual. He might be convinced by his teachers, by his reading, by hearing, taking part in, or being called upon to settle a disputation, or by his experiments. The ultimate condition for his accepting the doctrine was that it could be made acceptable to what was in his mind already, his religious–physical world-picture.

The second stage was the group. We have seen how professional colleges, university faculties, clubs and schools, and similar formal structures (even hospitals)[238] were groups whose members shared some belief. Often enough

---

[236] F. J. Cole, 'Henry Power and the circulation', *Journal of the History of Medicine*, 12 (1957), 291–324; 294.

[237] See J. Gascoigne, 'A reappraisal of the role of the universities in the scientific revolution', in Lindberg and Westman, *Reappraisals*, pp. 207–60; 208. As a student of Glisson, an admirer of Harvey and of geometry, Power thought that the chief feature of the New Philosophy was indeed experiment: he addresses his later *Experimental Philosophy* (1664) to his fellow 'generous virtuosi and Lovers of Experimental Philosophy'.

[238] St Bartholomew's (Harvey's hospital) had a circle of doctors concerned with the circulation. See J. D. Alsop, 'A footnote on the circulation of the blood. Joseph Colston and Harvey's discovery in 1642', *Journal of the History of Medicine*, 36 (1981), 331–4.

such a belief was the criterion for entering the group, and often enough the shared belief contributed largely to the public image of the group. It might be that it was 'professional' to be a Galenist; or it was necessary to have faith in experiment in order to belong to this or that club; or to be learned to claim monopoly of practice. Larger groups were the professions, like the physicians, surgeons and professional teaching philosophers. These too had a social role to play, an image to project and interests to preserve. All such groups tended towards self-preservation, which was favoured by stability of organisation and constancy of professional knowledge. All could come under pressure at the national level on matters that related to their knowledge. Different nations and different religions were major groups that had interests that may or may not have made possible the adoption of new knowledge. In other words, irrespective of the truth of Harvey's doctrine, there were social pressures that encouraged or discouraged its adoption. Most of them discouraged it. Stability within groups was consciously sought and protected at the social and therefore also intellectual level. Most individuals remained constrained by the pressures for conformity within their group and the number of people who straight-forwardly changed their minds and adopted Harvey's doctrine wholesale was small. In the twenty-five or so years covered by this book one of the factors contributing to consensus was simply the rise of a new generation with different group affiliations.

The formation of clubs like the 1645 group, the Oxford group and the Italian *Corus Anatomicus*[239] implies not only a common interest, but a degree of formalism that enabled the members to control entry to the club and which imposed a group 'ethics' upon them. Group 'ethics' are deeper-than-rational rules of behaviour which bind the group together. These rules, governing the expressed beliefs and behaviour of the individual members, control the group's efficiency in its common business and its relationship with other groups. Groups with 'ethics' that do not do this may disappear, and with them the accepted knowledge, the consensus, of the group. Successful groups offer their consensus to the learned world.[240]

---

[239] This was a group formed in Bologna in 1650 by nine anatomists meeting in the house of B. Massari for the purpose of investigating anatomical novelties. See Bayon, part 2, 1938, p. 97.

[240] That is not to say that all members of a group with a professional 'belief' either hold it by individual conviction or seek for that reason to convince others. But a group ethical-belief may nevertheless convince outsiders by the very power it gives to the group. In our period doctors were quite explicit about aiming the technical content of their discourse slightly over their patients' heads, to produce belief. The doctors' professional interests were served by the belief they could generate among their patients. See my chapters in A. Wear, S. Geyer-Kordesch and R. French, *Doctors and Ethics: The Earlier History of Professional Ethics*, London, 1993. In the Harvey affair too the authority of a group could contribute towards a wider consensus.

Because of the tendency towards conservatism within groups, a condition of Harvey's doctrine being accepted was that it was readily available when other conditions permitted its adoption. We have looked at different means of communication which operated here: disputations; networks of correspondents, the sending of letters, books, opinions on disputations and controversies; publishers issuing collected controversies; letter-writers publishing collections of their letters and replies;[241] patronage; travel; the disputation–textbook–review copy sequence. Textbooks by famous teachers at important centres were important. Vesling's *Syntagma* of 1645 was wielded at Montpellier by the travelling Bartholin, and was used in at least one Oxford college.[242] We have seen too that such communication had its boundaries, and at all levels it was open to distortion by a variety of non-intellectual agents, whether political, religious, or economic.

An important group was the university.[243] The medical and the university component of the new philosophy of the seventeenth century has been consistently undervalued by historians. It has been a modern conception of science that has directed attention to the physical and mathematical aspects of natural philosophy. Yet we have seen that Descartes, although outside the universities, chose a medical topic, the motion of the heart and blood as a prime example of his natural philosophy and chose a medical context in which to attempt to insert his philosophy into the universities.

There are some examples that we have not yet met which illustrate some of these points. The correspondence of Harvey himself at the time on the subject of the Riolan affair and other matters shows some of the pattern of the mid-seventeenth-century network. As noted above, in a major controversy like that of the circulation, a doctor with some learning or ambition might write to the major figures involved, asking their opinion, perhaps also of some other controversy, like that of the lacteals (so often bracketed with the circulation) and enclosing a book. Harvey replied in 1651 to such a letter from J. Nardi of Venice, and sent a copy of *De generatione animalium* with his

---

[241] We have not yet met Bartholin as a correspondent of Anton Deusing, to whom he wrote of Sylvius' experiments in Leiden; Deusing defended the circulation as *praeses* in disputations in Groningen in 1648. See G. A. Lindeboom, 'The reception in Holland of Harvey's theory of the circulation of the blood', *Janus*, 46 (1957), 183–200; p. 193 and J. Schouten, 'Johannes Walaeus (1604–1649) and his experiments on the circulation of the blood', *Journal of the History of Medicine*, 29 (1974), 259–79; 275. By 1650 Bartholin and his correspondents found the new work on the lymphatics more interesting than circulation: the controversy was virtually over. T. Bartholin, *Epistolarum medicinalium a doctis vel ad doctis scriptarum centuria* [I–IV], The Hague, 1740, vol. II from, for example, p. 444.

[242] See Frank, 'The image of Harvey', pp. 49, 50, 103. J. Vesling, *Syntagma anatomicum*, Padua, 1647, pp. 117–21.

[243] See C. Schmitt, 'Science in the Italian universities in the sixteenth and early seventeenth centuries', in his *The Aristotelian Tradition and Renaissance Universities*, pp. 35–56.

reply.[244] Robert Morison, in Paris, wanted to know Harvey's opinion of the lacteals, as did Johan Daniel Horst of Hesse-Darmstadt, who also wanted Harvey's opinion on the Riolan affair.[245]

Another example is the disputation staged in 1652 by Olaus Stenius in Uppsala, which helped to confirm a pro-circulation consensus in northern Europe.[246] It was defended by Olaus Rudbeck, who had been born in the year in which Harvey published *De motu cordis*, 1628. Rudbeck was of the new generation and had little difficulty in accepting the circulation. In any case the circulation controversy was by now nearly over, and indeed Rudbeck himself contributed to its demise by shifting interest away from it to the lymphatics, the discovery of which he announced in the following year.[247]

The dispute took place while Descartes was at the court of Queen Kristina, and it has been supposed that Stenius, whose teaching these twenty-six theses must represent, was a Cartesian.[248] No doubt the presence of Descartes drew attention to the circulation of the blood, which was such a central topic in his mechanical philosophy, and certainly his translation from Holland to Sweden is part of our story about the importance of travel in prompting discussion. But these theses of Stenius and Rudbeck are not Cartesian. Dedicated to Kristina in terms similar to those of Harvey's dedication to his monarch, they are closer to Harvey than to Descartes. Thus for Rudbeck it is the Harveian forceful systole of the heart that moves the blood (not a forceful diastolic expansion of the blood); the contraction of the heart is muscular in nature and does not depend on the impulsion of spirits; and his description of the heart's rising up and knocking on the chest wall in systole is very close to Harvey's.[249] These theses report some experiments that are not found elsewhere, and we may suppose that the Harveian experimental method was pursued in Sweden with vigour, and even led Rudbeck on the path to the discovery of the lymphatics. Rudbeck reports that the forceful systole of the heart may be felt directly by a finger inserted into a hole made in the ventricle of a living heart; he counted the total number of pulses made by the detached hearts of cats, eels, crabs and fish; he discusses an experiment in which blood was squeezed in either direction from a vein opened for phlebotomy (it confirmed a venous flow towards the heart).[250] In describing in a rather teleological way the *use* of circulation,

---

[244] W. Harvey, *The Works of William Harvey*, trans. Robert Willis, London, 847, reprinted, New York and London, 1965 and 1989, p. 603.

[245] Harvey, *Works* (1847/1989), pp. 610, 612.

[246] Olaus Rudbeck, *Disputatio de circulatione sanguinis*, (*Praeses* O. Stenius), Västerås, 1652 (22 May); facsimile reprint, *Suecica Rediviva*, no. 71, Stockholm, 1977.

[247] See S. Lindroth, 'Harvey, Descartes and the young Olaus Rudbeck', *Journal of the History of Medicine*, 12 (1957), 209–19.

[248] Ibid., p. 217.

[249] The *Disputatio* is unpaginated. These topics are covered in theses V, XIII, XII.

[250] Theses XII, XIII, XVIII.

Rudbeck is alien to the spirit of Cartesian mechanism (according to Rudbeck, the purposes of circulation are to enable nutrition and the removal of wastes to occur, and to allow externally applied medicines to be distributed over the whole body).[251] Altogether it seems clear that Kristina's court agreed with the university of Uppsala that the blood circulated, and there was thus a consensus of sorts.

Like Stenius and Hofmann, Conring also found that a series of disputations based on the results of interpretations of natural or medical questions was a convenient basis for a subsequent book. For him, as for the authors in the Low Countries whom we have already looked at, a series of experiments was the first stage in the chain leading to disputation and its proof-by-overcoming-objections, and thence to the book and correspondence. Conring used the same technique again a little later, having his pupil Sebastian Scheffer defend a series of theses which built up into a general introduction to medicine. It records the general acceptance of Harvey's doctrines that we see increasingly by the middle of the century.[252]

Much the same may be said of Anton Deusing, who in 1648 arranged for a student, Johannes Sicman, to defend the circulation in a disputation in Groningen.[253] By 1651 he had defended Harvey and summed up the whole of the Dutch debate (with Hogelande, Descartes, Walaeus, Beverwyck and others) in a series of disputations which he published as a *De motu cordis* in 1655. It was published together with some anonymous notes that criticise Deusing's retention of the notions of faculty and soul; such things are *unintelligible*, said the annotator in terms like those of the Cartesian Regius.[254]

Medical controversies like the lacteals, circulation and lymphatics presented opportunities for publishers. Often related or opposed treatises would be published together. *De motu cordis* was published in Leiden in 1639 together with the refutations of Primrose and Parigiano,[255] and it first appeared in

---

[251] Thesis XXVI.

[252] H. Conring, *Introductio in universam artem medicam singulasque ejus partes quam ex publicis praecipue dissertationibus . . . concinnatam . . . publice examinandam proponit Sebastianus Schefferus*, Helmstadt, 1654, p. 111: 'passim per eruditam orbis magis magisque Harvejana sententia assensum inveniat'.

[253] Schouten, 'Johannes Walaeus', p. 275.

[254] A. Deusing, *De motu cordis et sanguinis. Itemque de lacte et nutrimento foetus in utero*, Groningen, 1655. The disputations were at Groningen and *Omlandiae* (not identified in the *Orbis Latinus*: see J. G. Th. Graesse, *Orbis Latinus oder Verzeichniss der lateinischen Benennungen der bekanntesten Städte*, Dresden, 1861) and the prefatory material for those on the heart is dated 1651. By the date of Harvey's death the controversy was over and was not a live issue in books published in Holland, perhaps the biggest theatre of dispute. See for example B. Bausner, *De consensu partium humani corporis*, Amsterdam, 1656, p. 135.

[255] W. Harvey, *De motu cordis et sanguinis in animalibus, anatomica exercitatio. Cum refutationibus Aemylii Parisani Romani, philosophi, ac medici Veneti et Jacobi Primirosii in Londinensi Collegio doctoris*, Leiden, 1639.

Italy with Parigiano.[256] A larger and later collection, containing not only the pamphlets on the Dutch theses but also the controversy over the lacteals, was the *Disceptationes* of 1649, the year of Harvey's reply to Riolan. (It was a publishing opportunity like Martet's, which also deals – in the vernacular – with the lacteals.)[257] In 1647 the sixth Leiden edition of *De motu cordis* appeared, and the following year saw its first edition in Rotterdam. The publisher was Arnout Leers, who specialised in English medical works and who (as we have seen) fleshed out the slender *De motu cordis* with Sylvius' introduction and De Back's *Dissertatio de corde* (both were friends and co-citizens).[258] There was an edition of Harvey's and Walaeus' books in Padua in 1643.[259] By 1650 Walaeus had reached his eleventh edition.[260]

## Conclusion

So what *was* William Harvey's natural philosophy? We have seen that it had its roots in the new Paduan Aristotelianism of the early seventeenth century, where Fabricius was looking at the animal books in a medical context. We have also seen that Harvey's medical context enabled him to see similarities between some procedures of Aristotelian *research* – a new conception – and a Platonic–Socratic method of generating knowledge. Above all, Harvey's natural philosophy was experimental. It was so partly because he had examples to draw on within medicine and because his first discovery, the forceful systole, had been discovered experimentally and had to be defended experimentally. Perhaps at first Harvey thought that he was going to discover, among his animals, significant correlations of the Aristotelian–Fabrician kind; but he found, because he was studying a direct, tangible, visible *action* (the forceful systole) and not a generalised *function* (such as 'nutrition') that a series of vivisectional experiments in individual animals was a better mode of persuading others of his truth. Indeed, they were perhaps the only way, for

---

[256] See C. B. Schmitt and C. Webster, 'Harvey and M. A. Severino. A neglected medical relationship', *Bulletin of the History of Medicine*, 45 (1971), 49–75, 57.

[257] Martet's book was *Abbrege des Nouvelles Experiences Anatomiques*, Toulouse, 1652, and Paris, 1655 and 1664. See W. R. Lefanu, 'Jean Martet a French follower of Harvey', in *Science, Medicine and History. Essays on the Evolution of Scientific Thought and Medical Practice written in Honour of Charles Singer*, ed. E. Ashworth Underwood, 2 vols., Oxford University Press, 1953, vol. II, pp. 33–40.

[258] See M. J. van Lieburg, 'Zacharias Sylvius (1608–1664), author of the *Praefatio* to the first Rotterdam edition (1648) of Harvey's *De Motu Cordis*', *Janus*, 65 (1978), 241–57; 245.

[259] W. Pagel, *William Harvey's Biological Ideas. Selected Aspects and Historical Background*, New York, 1967, p. 31. For the publishing history of Harvey's works during the Harveian controversy, see also Sir Geoffrey Keynes, *A Bibliography of the Writings of Dr William Harvey 1587–1657*, Cambridge University Press, 1953.

[260] Lindeboom, 'Reception in Holland', p. 197.

vivisectional experiments could not claim demonstrative proof. Aristotelian–Fabrician correlations on the other hand could do so, for they linked the presence or absence of organs, and their differences, to the mode of life and the habitat of the animal, thus displaying causal relationships. Harvey tried to gain similar credibility with his early, Platonic 'Rule of Socrates' and with his late rationalisation about the formation of universals from sensory experience, but for the presentation of the circulation in *De motu cordis* and the subsequent battle for its acceptance, Harvey relied on the force of direct experimental demonstration. This agreed with and surely helped to form a consensus that experimental results stood apart from both rationalist systems and philosophical demonstrative truth.

There is a direct sense in which a complete philosophical system of the world was also a religious system, for natural philosophy dealt with a created world. Since its invention in the thirteenth century natural philosophy had had the role – although not necessarily the explicit purpose – of explaining the world in terms of man's relationship to his Maker and of cementing both understanding and the stability of society. The religious troubles of the sixteenth and the first half of the seventeenth century were troubles between religious systems of the world and we have seen that natural philosophy, whether new or old, was sometimes welcome and sometimes not, depending on whether it was congruent with, and therefore supported, rival religious systems. By the middle of the century there was a broad intellectual change. Many began to see that the different churches had many things in common – they were all after all Christian – and that trouble could be avoided by emphasising their similarities. One important thing they had in common was the belief that nature was creation, and that a study of nature was a way to develop theology. Others had seen similar problems with the great moral and legal systems of the different nation states, and sought a non-contentious pragmatic set of rules that drew on what was common to the different systems and upon natural reason. The parallel change in philosophy was to seek and agree upon something that was not related to contentious systems and did not claim a truth through systems; was drawn from or appealed to what was common to people exposed to systems; was pragmatic; appealed to natural reason and dealt with a Created world. Experiments and their results did these things. The Harvey of *De motu cordis* was largely judged, whether he like it or not, according to how his doctrines met these criteria.

That the practice of natural philosophy had useful social effects was often clear to those who practised it. It was clear to those who invented it, and we have seen a number of examples of how a stable philosophy was seen as a prerequisite for a stable society. It was clear too to Harvey. Writing some notes in his own copy of his book on generation he observed that vulgar natural philosophy (that is that of the schools) was allowed to exist because it 'strengthens the character of the vulgar'.[261] Here Harvey makes reference also to Bacon, who also saw that the natural philosophy of the schools was useful in civil life, making for stability.[262] Bacon's own natural philosophy was, not surprisingly, one that would lend support to society as he wished to see it.[263]

Harvey is here using the language of a philosophical elite, as we have seen others do. He saw the vulgar philosophy of the schools (*scolasticorum*) as that which could be manipulated in disputation to prove anything. He saw, that is, that the philosophy of the great religious systems was ever contentious. True philosophy, he thought, had been mutilated by passing through the hands of 'presbyters and theologians' who had involved it in questions about angelic spirits, demons, the immortality of the soul and the generation of the world. We have seen that during Harvey's lifetime many people did indeed extend natural philosophy to cover some of these topics, and they had been part of school natural philosophy from the beginning. But Harvey in rejecting them is not making a break between religion and natural philosophy, for his form of natural philosophy still had the divinely-created physical world as its subject-matter. The wisdom, foresight and divinity of nature was part of his metaphysics, appearing more naturally in the work on generation, where Harvey took an expressly Christian view of the Creator as the ultimate cause. Although Harvey saw God as present in the structure of all natural things,[264] he does not take a sectarian view of God and man. He more easily uses the term 'nature' than God, and does not share the Counter-Reformation views of Piccolomini or Parigiano, or the metaphysics and spirits of Glisson. His view of the Created world was a 'matter of fact' in the same way that experimental results were, that is, it could be accepted by any Christian without the danger of producing a clash of different 'systems'.

Little attention has been paid in this book to the thesis that Harvey's doctrines on the motion of the heart and blood were accepted because they were true. The fact of their being true had of itself no power. Some other active thing was needed to persuade people of Harvey's truth. People were persuaded of Harvey's truth by mechanisms which the historian can recognise. They were the same mechanisms that have persuaded other people of other authors' falsities. The result – belief – was the same in both cases. Historically, 'truth' was what was believed. If truth were an active factor then we should not see so

---

[261] The sophists who teach it are 'ad firmandos vulgi mores utiliores'. See Harvey, trans. Whitteridge, *Disputations*, p. 457.

[262] It was for this reason that Bacon did not want to demolish the old philosophy in establishing his own, but to allow the latter to grow up alongside. See J. Devey, ed., *The Physical and Metaphysical Works of Lord Bacon*, London, 1853, pp. 382, 436.

[263] See also Julian Martin, 'Natural philosophy and its public concerns', in *Science, Culture and Popular Belief in Renaissance Europe*, ed. Stephen Pumphrey, Paolo Rossi and Maurice Slawinski, Manchester University Press, 1991, pp. 100–18.

[264] Harvey, trans. Whitteridge, *Disputations*, esp. p. 269.

many authors – on whom this book reports perhaps to the point of tedium – modify and misunderstand Harvey, often in extreme ways and often too in similar ways. When a first consensus was reached it was because the misunderstandings and modifications had added up only to agreement that the venous blood returned to the heart. This commonly defined Harvey's topic as 'the circulation'; and after agreement was reached on this it was natural to go back to the author of the doctrine for the details – a post-controversy consensus.

It is arguable that the truth of Harvey's doctrines was clear because other people could do what he did and see what he saw. But the agent here was not an active truth – Harvey's – but someone else's enquiring mind seeking to satisfy itself in a controversy. We could argue that Harvey's system, because it was true, could make better predictions about what would happen in such cases, but the proof of our argument (i.e. to show that this actually happened) would still be a historical examination of the mechanisms of persuasion – experiments, groups, the nature of knowledge and so on, none of which have any unique relationship with truth and all of which have acted also in the past to produce consensuses of falsity. But the argument about repeatability and predictability is a natural one to make, and it seems too that it was made in the seventeenth century. That is to say, the important event in the Harvey business was not that the light of Harvey's truth could no longer be resisted, but that it came to be thought that truth, or the best possible approximation to it, could be discerned by experiment.

# Index